E.C. Merger Control

AUSTRALIA
LBC Information Services
Sydney

CANADA AND USA
Carswell
Toronto

NEW ZEALAND
Brooker's
Auckland

SINGAPORE AND MALAYSIA
Sweet & Maxwell Asia
Singapore and Kuala Lumpur

E.C. Merger Control

Third Editon

C.J. Cook
M.A., Solicitor

and

C.S. Kerse
LL.B., Ph.D., Solicitor

London
Sweet & Maxwell
2000

First Edition   1991   *EEC Merger Control*
Regulation 4064/89
Second Edition   1996   *E.C. Merger Control*

Published in 2000
by Sweet & Maxwell Limited of
100 Avenue Road, Swiss Cottage, London NW3 3PF
www.sweetandmaxwell.co.uk
Typeset by Wyvern 21 Ltd, Bristol
Printed by Athenæum Press Ltd, Gateshead, Tyne Wear
Reprinted 2001

No natural forests were destroyed to
make this product; only farmed timber was used and replanted.

**A CIP catalogue record for this book is available
from the British Library**

ISBN 0 421 660 805

© C.J. Cook and Dr. C.S. Kerse
2000

Preface

Since the second edition of this book in 1996, E.C. merger control has, without doubt, come of age. The Commission has shown itself able to handle an ever increasing workload as Monetary Union supersedes the single market as a driving force for consolidation in the European Union. Last year the Merger Task Force considered over 200 notifications, a record year, and has now passed the thousandth decision mark.

The burgeoning workload has been accompanied by significant changes to the Merger Regulation and developments in the jurisprudence since the last edition. In March 1998 a new set of turnover thresholds, extending the Commission's jurisdiction, was introduced, to supplement the original thresholds and protect the one-stop shop concept, which has suffered serious erosion as a result of a proliferation of national merger control regimes in Europe. The taking of undertakings in stage one inquiries was also legitimised, and through changes to the definition of "concentration", the Regulation was extended to structural joint ventures notwithstanding the fact that their creation might have an impact on competition between undertakings which remained independent. These changes have led to the issue of fresh notices and guidance. But perhaps of ultimately more significance than the legislative changes were two judgments of the European courts. In *Kali und Salz* the European Court of Justice confirmed that the Regulation extended to situations where positions of collective dominance were created or enhanced and was not limited to risks of single firm dominance, while the Court of First Instance, in *Gencor v. Commission*, held that, in establishing collective dominance, it was sufficient to find a relationship of economic interdependence between the undertakings concerned but not essential to discover legal or structural links: this judgment brought the concept of collective dominance into line with the economic thinking. These judgments encouraged the Commission to abandon its circumspect approach to oligopolistic mergers, as evidenced in its Article 8 decision in *Price Waterhouse/Coopers & Lybrand*, and in *Airtours/First Choice* it issued its first decision of incompatibility in a case where three major competitors would remain following the notified transaction.

In this new edition, notwithstanding the plethora of new developments, we have maintained the structure adopted in the second edition but have discarded much of the historical background of earlier editions. Chapter 5 has been re-written and much extended, particularly in view of developments in the concepts of collective dominance and in the sophistication of the Commission's economic analysis in the increasing number of Article 8 decisions.

We have endeavoured to state the law as at October 1, 1999 and to deal with all decisions published, or the results of which had been made public, at that date. We have also considered the three new draft notices, published in the summer of 1999 (on commitments, ancillary restraints and accelerated procedures) which may indeed have been adopted by the time this edition is published.

Last but not least, we would like to acknowledge our debt and express our thanks to those friends and colleagues who found the time to comment on the text, in particular Martin Howe and John Temple Lang. Thanks must also go to Jane Beardon, who managed the task of typing the manuscript. The views expressed, as well as all errors and omissions, remain our own.

C.J. Cook
C.S. Kerse
November 1, 1999

Contents

STUDY
EACH
CHAPTER
× 4

Preface		v
Table of Cases		xv
Table of Legislation		xviii
Alphabetical Table of Merger Decisions		xxiii
1	**Introduction**	1
	1.1 Community Merger Control—A Reality	1
	1.2 Background to E.C. Merger Control	1
	1.2.1 Use of Articles 81 and 82	2
	1.3 The Merger Regulation—Adoption and Review	3
	1.4 The Main Features of the E.C. Regime	4
	1.4.1 Compulsory Notification	4
	1.4.2 Concentrations	4
	1.4.3 Community Dimension	5
	1.4.4 Joint Ventures	5
	1.4.5 Assessment of Competitive Effect by Commission	6
	1.4.6 The Merger Regulation—Supporting Instruments	6
	1.5 Outline of Procedure	8
	1.5.1 Merger Task Force	8
	1.5.2 Procedural Steps	9
	1.5.3 Contact Number	9
	1.6 Reciprocity	10
	1.7 Territorial Scope of Regulation	11
	1.8 E.C.–U.S. Co-operation Agreement	14
	1.9 Relationship of the Regulation with Articles 81 and 82	16
	1.9.1 The One-Stop Shop	16
	1.9.2 Disapplication of Regulation 17	16
	1.9.3 National Courts	17
	1.9.4 Articles 84 and 85	18
	1.10 Relationship with ECSC Treaty	20
	1.11 EEA	20
2	**Concentrations**	23
	2.1 Introduction	23
	2.2 The Meaning of "Concentration"	23
	2.2.1 The Definition in Article 3(1)	23
	2.2.2 Two or More Undertakings	24
	2.2.3 Acquisition of Part of an Undertaking	25
	2.2.4 Undertakings Previously Independent	25
	2.2.4.1 Control by the State	26

2.3   Merger (Article 3(1)(a))   27
2.4   Acquisition of Control (Article 3(1)(b))   29
        2.4.1   Meaning of Control   29
        2.4.2   The Exercise of Decisive Influence   29
                 2.4.2.1   Decisive Influence   30
                 2.4.2.2   The Possibility of Influence   30
                 2.4.2.3   Balance of Power   31
                 2.4.2.4   The Nature of Control   31
                 2.4.2.5   Control by a Public Authority   32
                 2.4.2.6   Future Rights   32
                 2.4.2.7   Inadvertent Changes of Control   33
                 2.4.2.8   Direct or Indirect Control   34
        2.4.3   Means of Control   35
                 2.4.3.1   Shareholding Levels   37
                 2.4.3.2   Qualified Minority Shareholding   37
                 2.4.3.3   *De Facto* Sole Control   37
                 2.4.3.4   Levels of Shareholding Conferring
                           Control   38
                 2.4.3.5   Management Agreements   39
                 2.4.3.6   Shareholder Agreements   40
                 2.4.3.7   Special Rights   41
                 2.4.3.8   *Renault/Volvo*   41
2.5   Changes in Nature of Control   43
2.6   Joint Control   44
        2.6.1   The Existence of Joint Control   44
        2.6.2   Common Interests   45
2.7   Concentration or Co-operation?   48
        2.7.1   Redefinition of "concentration"   48
        2.7.2   Full Function Joint Ventures   49
                 2.7.2.1   Autonomous Economic Entity   50
                 2.7.2.2   Lasting Basis   52
        2.7.3   Consortium Bids   52
2.8   Special Exceptions (Article 3(5))   53
        2.8.1   Financial Institutions   53
        2.8.2   Liquidators and Receivers   54
        2.8.3   Financial Holding Companies   55

3   Community Dimension   56
3.1   Introduction   56
        3.1.1   Jurisdiction   57
        3.1.2   The Original Turnover Thresholds   57
        3.1.3   The Additional Turnover Thresholds   58
        3.1.4   Relationship with Original Thresholds   58
        3.1.5   Concentrations Below the Thresholds   59
3.2   Application of Turnover Criteria   59
        3.2.1   Worldwide and Community Turnover   59
        3.2.2   Member State Turnover Criteria   60
        3.2.3   The Two-Thirds Rule   60

	3.2.4	The Turnover Test in Operation	61
3.3		Calculation of Turnover	64
	3.3.1	The Basic Rule (Article 5(1))	64
	3.3.2	Meaning of "Turnover"	65
	3.3.3	Relevant Financial Year	66
	3.3.4	Conversion of Turnover into Ecus and Euros	67
	3.3.5	Disregard of Intra-Group Transactions	67
	3.3.6	Geographical Allocation of Turnover	68
3.4		"Undertakings Concerned"	70
	3.4.1	Identifying the "Undertakings Concerned"	71
	3.4.2	Calculating the Turnover of Each Undertaking Concerned (Article 5(4))	73
3.5		Particular Types of Transaction	76
	3.5.1	"Mergers"	76
	3.5.2	Acquisition of Sole Control Over an Entire Undertaking	77
	3.5.3	Acquisition of Sole Control Over Part of an Undertaking	77
	3.5.4	Acquisition in Stages of Sole Control Over Parts of an Undertaking	78
	3.5.5	Acquisition of Sole Control where Previously there was Joint Control	79
	3.5.6	Acquisition of Joint Control: Newly-Established Companies	79
	3.5.7	Acquisition of Joint Control: Existing Company	80
	3.5.8	Acquisition by Jointly Controlled Company/ Joint Venture	80
	3.5.9	Changes in Shareholdings in a Pre-Existing Joint Venture	82
	3.5.10	Where the "Undertakings Concerned" are already Shareholders in an Existing Joint Venture (Article 5(5))	83
	3.5.11	Asset Swaps	83
	3.5.12	Management Buy-Outs	83
	3.5.13	Acquisitions of Control by Individuals	84
	3.5.14	Acquisitions of Control by State Companies	84
3.6		Special Rules for Credit and Other Financial Institutions, and Insurance Undertakings	85
	3.6.1	Credit and Other Financial Institutions (Article 5(3(a))	85
	3.6.2	Insurance Undertakings (Article 5(3(b))	86
	3.6.3	Financial Conglomerates	87
3.7		Some Practical Considerations	88
4		**Notification and Investigation**	**90**
4.1		General Observations	90
4.2		Merger Task Force	91
4.3		Notification	91
	4.3.1	Principle of Prior Control	91

	4.3.2	Form CO	92
	4.3.3	Who Must Notify	95
	4.3.4	When Notification Must be Made	95
	4.3.5	What Must be Notified	97
	4.3.6	Short-form Notification	100
	4.3.7	Copies, Supporting Documents, Languages	101
	4.3.8	Completeness, Effective Date and Timetable	102
	4.3.9	Confidentiality	103
	4.3.10	Material Changes	104
	4.3.11	Conversion of Notifications	105
	4.3.12	Fines in Relation to Notification	106
4.4	Suspension	106
	4.4.1	Background	106
	4.4.2	The Rule	107
	4.4.3	Exception	107
	4.4.4	Exemption	107
	4.4.5	Breach of Article 7	108
		4.4.5.1 Fines	108
		4.4.5.2 Nature and Extent of Invalidity	108
		4.4.5.3 Effect Under English Law	109
	4.4.6	Relationship Between Article 7 and Article 4	110
4.5	The Initial Examination Period	111
	4.5.1	Stage One Proceedings	111
	4.5.2	Third Parties	112
	4.5.3	Member State Competition Authorities	113
	4.5.4	Types of Initial Decision (Article 6)	114
4.6	Fact-Finding Powers	114
	4.6.1	Requests for Information	114
	4.6.2	Investigations	115
	4.6.3	Comparison with Regulation 17	116
	4.6.4	Failure to Co-operate	116
4.7	Detailed Assessment	117
	4.7.1	Stage Two Proceedings—Timetable	117
	4.7.2	Article 6(1)(c) Decision	118
	4.7.3	Statement of Objections	118
	4.7.4	Access to the File	119
	4.7.5	The Parties' Response	120
	4.7.6	Oral Hearings	120
	4.7.7	Third Parties—Right to be Heard	121
	4.7.8	Consultation of the Advisory Committee	122
4.8	Final Decisions	123
4.9	Transmission of Documents	123
5	**Appraisal of Concentrations**	**124**
5.1	Introduction	125
	5.1.1	The Appraisal Process: The Basic Objective	125
	5.1.2	Competition or Industrial Policy?	126
5.2	Compatibility with the Common Market	127

	5.2.1	The Elements of the Compatibility Test	
		(Article 2(3))	128
	5.2.2.	Creating or Strengthening Dominance	129
	5.2.3	Dominance	130
	5.2.4	Dominance and Competitive Structure	130
	5.2.5	Dominance in the Common Market or a	
		Substantial Part of it	131
	5.2.6	Single Firm or Collective Dominance	131
5.3	The Appraisal Process—Market Definition		132
	5.3.1	The Notice on Market Definition	134
	5.3.2	Relevant Product Market	135
	5.3.3	Geographic Market Definition	139
		5.3.3.1 Trade Patterns	141
		5.3.3.2 Prices	141
		5.3.3.3 Location and Identity of Suppliers	
		and Purchasers	142
		5.3.3.4 Supply Conditions	143
		5.3.3.5 Customer Preferences	144
		5.3.3.6 Transport Costs	144
		5.3.3.7 Public Procurement	145
		5.3.3.8 Other Regulatory Factors	145
		5.3.3.9 World Markets	147
5.4	The Appraisal Decision		147
	5.4.1	General Background to the Appraisal Decision	148
	5.4.2	The General Nature of the Appraisal	149
	5.4.3	Judging Dominance	149
		5.4.3.1 Single Firm or Collective Dominance	150
		5.4.3.2 Horizontal and Vertical Impact	151
		5.4.3.3 "Significantly Impeding Effective	
		Competition"	151
		5.4.3.4 Market Shares	152
		5.4.3.5 Competitors	156
		5.4.3.6 Barriers to Entry	158
		5.4.3.7 Buyer Power	160
		5.4.3.8 Economic and Financial Power	161
		5.4.3.9 Portfolio Power	162
		5.4.3.10 Access to Supplies or Markets	163
5.5	Compatibility—Co-ordination Effects		163
5.6	Compatibility—Vertical Issues		165
5.7	Collective Dominance		168
	5.7.1	*Kali und Salz*	169
	5.7.2	The Current Position	170
	5.7.3	Establishing Collective Dominance	171
	5.7.4	*Gencor/Lonrho*—Duopolistic Markets	171
	5.7.5	*Price Waterhouse/Coopers & Lybrand*—	
		Oligopolistic Markets	172
	5.7.6	*Airtours/First Choice*	173
	5.7.7	Collective Dominance—Conclusions	174
5.8	Countervailing Benefits		175

5.8.1	Technical and Economic Progress	176
5.8.2	Efficiency	178
5.8.3	Failing Firm	178
5.8.4	Social Considerations—The *Perrier* Judgment	180
5.9	Case Study—*Guinness/Grand Metropolitan*	180
5.9.1	Product Markets	181
5.9.2	Geographic Markets	182
5.9.3	Dominance	182
5.9.3.1	Greece	183
5.9.3.2	Spain	183
5.9.3.3	Ireland	183
5.9.3.4	Belgium/Luxembourg	183
5.9.4	Remedies	184

6 Ancillary Restraints — **185**

6.1	Background	185
6.2	The Approach under Article 81	186
6.3	Restrictions	187
6.3.1	Directly Related	187
6.3.2	Necessary to the Implementation of the Concentration	188
6.4	General Principles of Evaluation	188
6.5	Non-Competition Clauses	189
6.6	Licences of Intellectual Property and Know-how	193
6.7	Trademarks, Business Names, Logos, etc.	194
6.8	Restrictions on the Disclosure and Use of Confidential Information	195
6.9	Purchase and Supply Obligations	196
6.10	Consortium Bids	198

7 Decisions, Undertakings and Appeals — **199**

7.1	Introduction	199
7.2	Initial Decisions (Article 6)	199
7.2.1	Types of Decision	199
7.2.2	Format of Decisions	200
7.3	Final Decisions—Article 8	201
7.3.1	Declaration of Compatibility	201
7.3.2	Declaration of Incompatibility	202
7.3.3	Divestment, etc. Orders—Restoring Competition	202
7.3.4	Revocation of Decision of Compatibility	203
7.4	Modifications, Undertakings, Commitments	203
7.4.1	Introduction	203
7.4.2	Structural and Behavioural Remedies	204
7.4.3	Divestments, etc.	205
7.4.4	Behavioural Commitments	207
7.4.5	Transparency and Timing	209
7.4.6	Monitoring of Commitments	211
7.4.7	Amendment of Decisions	212
7.4.8	Informal Assurances	212

7.5	General Points on Decisions	213
	7.5.1 Reasons	213
	7.5.2 Sanctions	213
	7.5.3 Notification of Decisions	214
	7.5.4 Habilitation	214
	7.5.5 Publicity	215
7.6	Appeals to the Court	216
	7.6.1 General	216
	7.6.2 Acts which can be Challenged	216
	7.6.3 Who can Bring an Action	218
	7.6.3.1 Shareholders	219
	7.6.3.2 Competitors	220
	7.6.3.3 Employees	221
	7.6.3.4 Other Third Parties	222
	7.6.4 Grounds of Appeal	222
	7.6.5 Interim Relief	223
7.7	Reopening the Commission's Proceedings	224

8 National Authorities and National Law **227**

8.1	Liaison with National Competition Authorities	227
	8.1.1 Pre-notification	227
	8.1.2 Notification	228
	8.1.3 Examination	230
	8.1.4 Advisory Committee	230
8.2	The Place of National Law	232
8.3	Article 9—Distinct Markets	233
	8.3.1 Background	233
	8.3.2 Criterion of Distinct Market	234
	8.3.3 Procedure	235
	8.3.4 Practice	236
8.4	Protection of Member States' Legitimate Interests	238
	8.4.1 Background	238
	8.4.2 The Three Identified Interests	238
	8.4.2.1 Public Security	238
	8.4.2.2 Plurality of the Media	239
	8.4.2.3 Prudential Rules	240
	8.4.3 Other Cases	240
	8.4.3.1 Defence	240
	8.4.3.2 Any Other Public Interest	241
	8.4.3.3 Recognition Procedure	242
	8.4.3.4 Member States' Action	243
8.5	EEA	243
8.6	Concentrations without a Community Dimension	245
	8.6.1 Member States' Request	245
	8.6.2 Applicable Provisions	246

Appendix 1 Council Regulation (EEC) 4064/89 of 21 December 1989 on the control of concentrations between undertakings (1990 O.J. L257/14) — 250

Appendix 2   Commission Regulation (EC) No 447/98 of 1 March 1998 on the notifications, time limits and hearings provided for in Council Regulation (EEC) No 4064/89 on the control of concentrations between undertakings (OJ 1998 L61/1)   270

Appendix 3   Draft Commission Notice on restrictions directly related and necessary to concentrations   302

Appendix 4   Commission Notice on the concept of full-function joint ventures under Council Regulation (EEC) No 4064/89 on the control of concentrations between undertakings (OJ 1998 C66/01)   309

Appendix 5   Commission Notice on the concept of concentration under Council Regulation (EEC) No 4064/89 on the control of concentrations between undertakings (OJ 1998 C66/02)   313

Appendix 6   Commission Notice on the concept of undertakings concerned under Council Regulation (EEC) No 4064.89 on the control of concentrations between undertakings (OJ 1998 C66/03)   322

Appendix 7   Commission Notice on the concept of undertakings concerned under Council Regulation (EEC) No 4064/89 on the control of concentrations between undertakings (OJ 1998 C66/04)   333

Appendix 8   Commission Notice on the definition of relevant market for the purpose of Community competition law (OJ 1997 C372/03) √   346

Appendix 9   Merger Procedures   356

Index   361

Table of Cases

Bold type indicates textual references as opposed to footnote references.

AKZO Chemie and AKZO Chemie U.K. Ltd v. Commission (Case 5/85) [1986] E.C.R.
2585; [1987] 3 C.M.L.R. 716 .... **4.6.3**, 7.5.4
A.M. & S. Europe Ltd v. Commission (Case 155/79) [1982] E.C.R. 1575; [1982] 2
C.M.L.R. 264 .... 4.6.1
Ahlström Oy and Others v. Commission (Woodpulp) (Joined Cases 89, 104, 114, 116–
117 and 125–129/85) [1993] E.C.R. I–99; [1993] 4 C.M.L.R. 407; [1988] E.C.R.
5193; [1988] 4 C.M.L.R. 901 .... **1.7**
*Ahmed Saeed Flugreisen and Another v. Zentrale zur Betäemfung, Unlauteren Wettbew-
erbs e.V.* (Case 66/86) [1989] E.C.R. 803; [1990] 4 C.M.L.R. 102 .... **1.9.3**
Amministrazione delle Finanze dello Stato v. Simmenthal (Case 106/77) [1978] E.C.R.
629; [1978] 3 C.M.L.R. 263 .... **1.9.3**
Atlanta Fruchthandelsgesellschaft mbH v. Bundesamt fur Ernahrung und Forstwirtschaft
(Joined Cases C–466/93 and 465/93) [1995] E.C.R. I–3761, 3799 .... 8.1.2
BASF AG v. Commission (Joined Cases T–78, 84–86, 71–92, 94, 96, 98, 102 and 104/
89) [1992] E.C.R. II–315; [1992] 4 C.M.L.R. 357 .... 7.6.2
BAT and Reynolds v. Commission (Philip Morris) (Joined Cases 142 and 156/84) [1987]
E.C.R. 4487; [1988] 4 C.M.L.R. 24; [1986] E.C.R. 1899; [1987] 2 C.M.L.R.
551 .... **1.2.1**, 4.7.7
BPB Industries and British Gypsum v. Commission (Case C–310/93P) [1995] E.C.R. I–
865; [1997] 4 C.M.L.R. 238 .... 4.7.4
BRT v. SABAM (Case 127/73) [1974] E.C.R. 51; [1974] 2 C.M.L.R. 251 .... **1.9.2, 1.9.4**
Brasserie de Haecht v. Wilkins-Janssen (No. 2) (Case 48/72) [1973] E.C.R. 77; [1973]
C.M.L.R. 287 .... **1.9.3**
Campus Oil Ltd v. Minister of Industry and Energy (Case 72/83) [1984] E.C.R. 2727;
[1984] 3 C.M.L.R. 544 .... **8.4.2.1**
Coca-Cola Company v. Commission (Case T–125/97) **7.6.3**
Comité Central d'Entreprise de la Société Anonyme Vittel v. Commission (Case T–12/
93) [1995] E.C.R. II–1247; [1993] E.C.R. II–785 .... **5.8.4**, 7.6.3.3, 7.6.5
*Comité Central d'Entreprise de la Société Générale des Grandes Sources v. Commission
(Perrier Case)* (Case T–96/92) [1995] E.C.R. II–1213   4.5.2, 4.7.6, 4.7.7, **5.1.2**, 7.6.3.3, 7.6.5
Commission v. Council (Case 22/70) [1971] E.C.R. 263; [1971] C.M.L.R. 335 .... 7.6.2
Commission v. France (Case C–265/95) [1997] E.C.R. I–6959 .... 8.4.2.1
Commission v. Lisrestal and Others (Case C–32/95P) [1996] E.C.R. I–5373; [1997] 2
C.M.L.R. 1 .... 4.7.7
Consolidated Gold Fields Plc v. Minorco SA 871 F. 2d 252; 890 F. 2d 569 (2nd Cir.) .   1.7
Delimitis v. Henninger Bräu AG (Case C–234/89) [1991] E.C.R. I–935; [1992] 5
C.M.L.R. 210 .... 4.4.5.3
Endemol Entertainment Holdings BV v. Commission (Case T–221/95) [1999] 5 C.M.L.R
611 .... 4.6.1, 4.7.4, 7.6.4, 8.6.2
Europemballage Corporation and Continental Can Co. Inc. v. Commission (Case 6/72)
[1973] E.C.R. 215; [1973] C.M.L.R. 199 .... **1.2.1**
Foster v. British Gas plc (Case C–188/89) [1990] E.C.R. I–3313; [1990] 2 C.M.L.R.
833 .... **2.4.2.5**
French Republic v. Commission (Case C–327/91) [1994] E.C.R. I–3641; [1994] 5
C.M.L.R. 517 .... **1.8**

French Republic v. Commission (Kali und Salz) (Joined Cases C–68/94 and 30/95)
[1998] E.C.R. I–1375 .... **1.4.5, 4.3.4**, 4.7.7, 5.1.2, 5.2.1, 5.2.2, **5.2.6, 5.3,**
5.4.3.1, 5.4.3.4, 5.7, 5.7.1, 5.7.2, 5.7.5, 5.7.7, **5.8.3, 5.8.4,**
5.9.4, 7.4.6, 7.4.8, 7.6.1, 7.6.3 7.6.3.4, 7.6.5, 7.7, 8.1.3
Gencor v. Commission (Case T–102/96) [1999] 4 C.M.L.R. 971 .... **1.4.5,** 1.7, 2.4.2, 5.2.2,
5.4.3.1, 5.7, 7.4.2, 7.6.3
Gøttrüp-Klim v. Dansk Landbrugs Grovvareslskab Amba (Case C–250/92) [1994] E.C.R.
I–5641; [1996] 4 C.M.L.R. 191 .... **5.2.3,** 6.2
Granaria BV v. Hoofdproduktschap voor Akkerbouprodukten (Case 101/78) [1979]
E.C.R. 623; [1979] 3 C.M.L.R. 124 .... 8.1.2
Griffin v South West Water Services Ltd (unreported) 2.4.2.5
Hilti v. Commission (Case T–30/89) [1991] E.C.R. II–1439; [1990] E.C.R. II–163; [1992]
4 C.M.L.R. 16 .... 5.2.3
Hoechst v. Commission (Joined Cases 46/87 and 227/87) [1989] E.C.R. 2859; [1991] 4
C.M.L.R. 410 .... 4.6.2
Hoffmann-La Roche & Co A.G. v. Commission (Case 85/76) [1979] E.C.R. 461; [1979]
3 C.M.L.R. 211 .... **4.7.4,** 5.3.1
Hydrotherm v. Andreoli (Case 170/83) [1984] E.C.R. 2999; [1985] 3 C.M.L.R. 224 .... 3.4.1
IBM v. Commission (Case 60/81) [1981] E.C.R. 1857; [1981] 3 C.M.L.R. 635 .... **7.6.2**
ICI and Others v. Commission (Dyestuffs) (Cases 48, 49 and 51/69) [1972] E.C.R. 619;
[1972] C.M.L.R. 557 .... **1.7**
Iberian U.K. Ltd v. BPB Industries plc and Another [1996] 2 C.M.L.R. 601 .... **1.9.3**
Johnston v. Chief Constable of the Royal Ulster Constabulary (Case 222/84) [1986]
E.C.R. 1651; [1986] 3 C.M.L.R. 240 .... 8.4.2.1
Kaysersberg SA v. Commission (Case T–290/94) [1995] E.C.R. II–2247; [1997] E.C.R.
II–2137; [1998] 4 C.M.L.R. 336 .... 4.3.10, 4.5.2,
4.7.7, 7.5.1, 7.6.4, 8.1.4
*Kledingverkoopbedrijf de Geus en Uitdenborgerd v. Robert Bosch GmbH and NV Maats-
chappij tot voortzetting van de zaken der Firma Willem van Rijn (Bosch)* (Case 13/
61) [1962] E.C.R. 45; [1962] C.M.L.R. 1 .... **1.9.3**
Ministère Public v. Lucas Asjes and Others (Nouvelles Frontières) (Air Tariffs Case)
(Joined Cases 209–213/84) [1986] E.C.R. 1425; [1986] 3 C.M.L.R. 173 .... **1.9.3**
Musique Diffusion Française v. Commission (Pioneer) (Joined Cases 100–103/80) [1983]
E.C.R. 1825; [1983] 3 C.M.L.R. 221 .... 8.1.4
Nefarma v. Commission (Case T–113/89) [1990] E.C.R. II–797 .... 7.6.2
Orkem v. Commission (Case 374/87) [1989] E.C.R. 3283; [1991] 4 C.M.L.R. 502 .... 4.6.1
Otto BV v. Postbank NV (Case C–60/92) [1993] E.C.R. I–5683 .... 4.6.1
Participation Ouvrière Compaigne Nationale Air France v. Commission (TAT) (Case T–
2/93) [1994] E.C.R. II–323; [1995] E.C.R. II–533 .... 7.5.1,
7.6.3.2, 7.6.4
Plaumann & Co v. Commission (Case 25/62) [1963] E.C.R. 95; [1964] C.M.L.R. 29 ... 7.6.3
Pouchet v. AGF and *Pistre v. Cancova* (Joined Cases 159 and 160/91) [1993] E.C.R. I–
637 .... 3.4.1
Pronuptia de Paris GmbH v. Pronuptia de Paris Irmgard Schillgallis (Case 161/84)
[1986] E.C.R. 353; [1986] 1 C.M.L.R. 414 .... 6.2
*R. v. Secretary of State for Trade and Industry and another, ex p. Airlines of Britain
Holdings PLC and Others, The Times,* December 10, 1992, CA 1.9.2
Remia BV and Others v. Commission (Case 42/84) [1985] E.C.R. 2545; [1987] 1
C.M.L.R. 1 .... 6.2
Società Italiano Vetro SpA v. Commission ("Italian Flat Glass") (Case T-68/69) [1992]
II E.C.R. 1403; [1992] 5 C.M.L.R. 302 .... 5.4.3.1
Société Anonyme à Participation Ouvrière Com. Air France v. Commission (Dan Air)
(Case T–3/93) [1994] E.C.R. II–121 .... **1.9.2, 1.9.4, 3.5.3,**
4.1, **7.6.2,** 7.6.3.2, **7.6.4**
Société Co-operative des Asphalteurs Belges (Belasco) v. Commission (Case 246/86)
[1989] E.C.R. 2117; [1991] 4 C.M.L.R. 96 .... 3.2.3
*Société Commerciale des Potasses et de l'Azote (SPCA) and Enterprise Minière et
Chemique (EMC) v. Commission* (Case C–30/95) joined with Case C-68/94, *French
Republic v. Commission*) [1998] E.C.R. I-1375 .... 5.7

Sogecable SA v. Commission (Case T–52/96R) (Spanish Cable TV) [1996] E.C.R. II–797; [1996] 5 C.M.L.R. 570 .... **7.6.2, 7.6.5**

Stichting Sigarettenindustrie (SSI) v. Commission (Joined Cases 240–242, 261, 268 and 269/82) [1985] E.C.R. 3831; [1987] 3 C.M.L.R. 661 .... 7.5.1

The Scottish Football Association v. Commission (Case T–46/92) [1994] E.C.R. II–1039 .... 4.6.1, 7.6.3.3

Union Carbide Corporation v. Commission (Case T–322/94R) [1994] E.C.R. II–1159 . **7.6.5**

United Brands v. Commission (Case 27/76) [1978] E.C.R. 207; [1978] 1 C.M.L.R. 429 .... 5.2.3, 5.3, 5.3.3, 8.3.2

Viho Europe BV v. Commission (Case T–102/92) [1995] E.C.R. II–17; [1997] 4 C.M.L.R. 469 .... 2.2.4, 3.4.1

Zuckerfabrik Suederdithmarschen AG v. Hauptzollamt Itzehoe (Joined Cases 143/88 and C–92/89) [1991] E.C.R. I–415; [1993] 3 C.M.L.R. 1 .... 8.1.2

Zunis Holding v. Commission (Case T–83/92) [1963] E.C.R. II–1169; [1994] 5 C.M.L.R. 154 .... **7.6.3.1, 7.7**

Table of Legislation

Bold type indicates textual references as opposed to footnote references.

Community Treaties

1951 ECSC Treaty **1.4.6,**
   1.10, 2.8.2,
   3.3.1, 4.7.4
1951 Treaty of Paris **1.2**
   Art. 66 .... **1.2**
1957 Treaty of Rome **1.2**
1986 Single European Act **1.6**
1991 Canada Agreement [1991]
   O.J. L175/49 .... **1.8**
   E.C.–U.S. Co-operation
   Agreement **1.8,** 1.9.3
   Art. 2 .... **1.8**
      (3)(b) **1.8**
   Arts 3, 4, 5 .... **1.8**
   Art. 6 .... **1.8**
      (1)(c) **1.8**
   Art. 7 .... **1.8**
1992 E.C. Treaty **1.4.6,**
   1.5.1, 1.10, 1.11,
   2.4.2.5, 3.1, **5.2.6**
   Art. 2 .... **5.1.2, 5.8.4, 8.5**
   Art. 3(g) **5.1.2**
   Art. 4 .... **7.6.2**
   Art. 5 .... 3.1, **7.5.2**
   Art. 7 .... **7.5.2, 7.6.2**
      (1) **7.5.2**
   Art. 8(3), (4) **7.5.2**
   Art. 12 .... **8.4.3.2**
   Art. 21 .... 8.4.2.1, **8.4.3.3**
      (3) **8.4.2.1,**
      8.4.3.2, 8.4.3.3,
      8.4.3.4, 8.5
   Art. 22 .... **1.9.4,**
      8.6.1, 8.6.2
      (3) **8.6.1, 8.6.2**
      (4) **8.6.1, 8.6.2**
      (5) **8.6.2**
   Art. 28 .... **8.4.1**
   Art. 30 .... **8.4.1, 8.4.2.1**
   Art. 36 .... **1.9.2**
   Arts 46, 54 .... **8.4.2.1**
   Art. 57(2)(a) **8.5**
   Arts 65, 66 .... **1.10**

1992 E.C. Treaty—*cont.*
   Art. 81 (ex Art. 85) .. **1.1, 1.2,**
      1.2.1, 1.4.4, 1.5.1,
      1.7, 1.8, **1.9–1.9.4,**
      1.11, 2.1, 2.2.1,
      2.2.2, **2.2.4, 2.4.3.8,**
      2.7.1, 2.7.3, 3.1,
      3.2.3, 3.3.3, 4.1,
      4.3.3, 4.3.4, 4.3.5,
      4.3.11, 4.3.12, 4.6,
      4.6.2, 4.6.4, 4.7.4,
      5.1, 5.2, 5.2.1,
      5.2.6, 5.3.1, 5.3.2,
      5.4.2, 5.4.3, 5.4.3.4,
      5.5, 5.6, 5.7.1,
      5.7.7, 6.1, 6.2,
      6.3, 6.4, 6.5,
      6.6, 7.4.2, 8.1
      (1) **1.9.3, 2.7.1,**
      4.3.5,
      5.1.1, **6.2**
      (2) **5.2**
      (3) **1.9.4, 2.7.1,**
      4.3.5, 4.3.11,
      5.1.1, 5.8.1,
      5.8.2, 7.4.2
   Art. 82 (ex Art. 86) .. **1.1, 1.2,**
      1.2.1, 1.4.4, 1.5.1,
      1.7, 1.8, **1.9–1.9.4,**
      1.11, 2.1, 2.2.2,
      3.1, 4.1, 4.3.12,
      4.6, 4.6.2, 4.6.4,
      4.7.4, 5.1.1, **5.2.1,**
      5.2.2, 5.2.3, 5.2.4,
      5.2.6, 5.3.1, 5.3.2,
      5.3.3, 5.4.3, 5.4.3.4,
      5.7, **5.7.7, 6.1,**
      6.3, 6.4, 6.5,
      7.4.2, 7.6.3.4,
      8.1, **8.3.2**
      (2) **1.9.3**
   Art. 83 .... **1.7, 1.9.2,**
      4.1, 4.3.11
   Art. 84 .... **1.9.3, 1.9.4,**
      3.2.3

1992   **E.C. Treaty**—*cont.*
    Art. 85 .... **1.9.3, 1.9.4,**
        3.1.1, 4.1,
        4.7.4, **8.6.2**
     (1) **2.7.1,** 5.1
    Art. 85(3) **2.7.1,**
        5.1, **5.8.2**
    Art. 86 .... **1.2.1, 1.9.3,**
        3.1.1, 4.7.4, 5.3.2
    Art. 87 .... **1.9.2**
    Art. 104(2) **7.6.5**
    Art. 130 .... 5.1.2
    Art. 173 .... **7.6.2,**
        7.6.3.3, 7.7
    Art. 229 .... **7.6.1**
    Art. 230 .... 4.7.7, **7.6.1,**
        7.6.2, 7.6.3,
        7.6.3.1, 7.6.4, 7.6.5
    Art. 232 .... **7.6.1**
    Art. 235 .... **1.9.2,** 1.9.4
    Arts 242, 243 .... **7.6.5**
    Art. 253 .... **7.5.1, 7.6.4**
    Art. 254 .... **7.5.3**
    Art. 287 .... **4.3.9**
    Art. 296 .... **5.1.2, 8.4.1,**
        8.4.2.1, 8.4.3.1
    Art. 297 .... **8.4.2.1**
    Art. 298 .... **8.2, 8.4.3.1**
     (1)(b)...................... **8.2**
    Art. 305 .... **1.10, 3.3.1**
    Art. 308 .... **1.9.2, 1.10,**
        4.7.4
    Protocol 21—
     57(2) **1.11**
    Protocol 24 .... **1.11, 8.5**
     Art. 6 .... 1.11, **8.5**
     Art. 7 .... **8.5**
    Protocol 25 .... **1.11**
    Maastricht Treaty 3.1,
        5.1.2
    European Economic Area
    Agreement (EEA) **1.11**
     Annex IV **1.11**
     Annex XIV **1.11**
     Arts 53, 54 .... **1.11**
     Art. 57 .... **1.11, 4.3.7**
      (1), (2) **1.11**
     Art. 58 .... **8.5**
     Arts 59, 105, 106 .... **1.11**
    European Economic Area
    Agreement Protocol 24—
     Art. 3(1) 8.1.2
1998   E.C.–U.S. Operation of the
    Positive Comity Principle
    Agreement 1991
    E.C.–U.S. Co-operation
    Agreement **1.8**
    Vienna Convention **1.8**

Decisions

Decision 24/54—
  Art. 3(2) 2.8.2

Directives

Directive 73/212/EEC 5.7.1
Directive 77/80/EEC [1997] O.J. L322/12
  .... **3.6.1**
Directive 77/187/EEC **5.8.4,**
    7.6.3.3
Directive 78/815/EEC [1978] O.J.
  L259/36 .... 2.2.4.1
Directive 78/660/EEC [1978] O.J.
  L222/11 .... **2.8.3, 3.3.2, 3.4.2**
  Arts 22–26 .... 3.3.2
  Art. 28 .... **3.3.2**
  Art. 43 .... 3.3.6
Directive 79/267/EEC [1990] O.J.
  L330/50 .... 1.6
Directive 84/349/EEC [1983] O.J.
  L193/1 .... 3.4.2
Directive 84/569/EEC [1984] O.J.
  L314/28 .... **2.8.3, 3.4.2**
Directive 86/635/EEC [1986] O.J.
  L372/1 .... **3.6.1**
Directive 89/646/EEC [1989] O.J.
  L386/1 .... 1.6, **3.6.1**
Directive 90/434/EEC [1990] O.J.
  L225/1 .... 2.2.4.1
Directive 90/618/EEC [1990] O.J.
  L330/44 .... 1.6
Directive 91/156 .... **5.3.3.8**
Directive 94/45 .... **4.7.7**

Regulations

Reg. 17/62 .... **1.4.4, 1.7, 1.9.2–1.9.4,**
    2.1, 2.2.2, **2.7.1,**
    4.1, **4.2,** 4.3.2,
    4.3.4, 4.3.5, 4.3.11,
    4.6, 4.6.1, 4.6.3,
    4.6.4, 5.5, 6.1,
    7.3.1, 7.4.6, **7.4.8,**
    7.5.1, 7.5.2
  Art. 9(1), (3) 1.9.4
  Arts 10–21 .... **4.1**
  Art. 14 .... **8.1.3**
Reg. 1017/68: [1968] O.J. L175/1 ..... 4.1
Reg. 2779/72: [1972] O.J. L292/23—
  Art. 4 .... 3.4.2
Reg. 1984/83—
  Art. 4(2) 3.4.2
Reg. 1983/84: [1983] O.J. L3173/1 3.4.2
Reg. 417/85: [1985] O.J. L53/1—
  Art. 10(14) 3.4.2
Reg. 418/85: [1985] O.J. L53/5—
  Art. 7(1) 3.4.2

Reg. 4056/86: [1986] O.J. L378/4 ..... 4.1
Reg. 3975/87: [1987] E.C.R. 374/1 ... 4.1
Reg. 4064/89: 1989] O.J. L395/1;
   [1990] O.J. L257/14: [1997] O.J.
   L180/1: [1998] O.J. L450/17 .... **1.1,**
              1.3, 1.4.1–1.4.6, 1.5.1,
              1.5.2, 1.6–1.9, 1.9.2,
              1.9.3, **1.10, 1.11,**
              2.1, 2.2.3, 2.3,
              2.4.1, 2.4.2.1–2.4.2.5,
              2.4.2.7, 2.4.3, 2.4.3.2,
              2.4.3.8, 2.6, 2.7.1,
              3.1, 3.4.1, **3.5,**
              3.7, 4.1, 4.3.2,
              4.3.11, 4.5.2, 4.6,
              4.7.4, **4.7.7, 4.9,**
              5.1.1, 5.1.2, 5.2.2,
              5.2.6, 5.3.2, 5.4.2,
              5.4.3.10, 5.5, 5.8.3,
              6.4, 6.9, 6.10, **APP 1**
Recitals 1–4 .... 5.1.2
Recital 4 .... **5.1.2, 5.8.1**
Recital 7 .... **1.9.2,** 8.2
Recital 8 .... **1.9.2, 8.1.1**
Recital 12 .... **2.2.2, 2.2.4.1,**
              2.4.2.5, 3.5.14
Recital 13 .... **5.1.2, 5.8.1, 5.8.4**
Recital 15 .... **5.1.2, 5.4.3.4,** 5.7
Recital 17 .... **4.3.1, 4.4.5.2**
Recital 20 .... 8.1
Recital 23 .... **2.2.1**
Recital 24 .... 6.10
Recital 25 .... 2.6.2, **6.1**
Recital 27 .... 8.2
Recital 28 .... 8.2, **8.4.3.1**
Recital 31 .... 4.7.7
Art. 1 .... 1.4.1, 1.7, 3.1,
           3.4.2, 7.6.3, 7.6.4
  (2) **3.1.2, 3.1.3, 3.1.4,**
           3.2.1, 3.2.3, 3.2.4,
           3.3.1, 3.3.3, 3.3.6,
           3.5.4, 3.6.2
    (a) **1.3, 3.2.1, 3.2.4**
    (b) **3.2.1, 3.2.4,**
           3.3.6, 3.4, 3.6.2
  (3) **1.4.3, 1.8, 3.1.3,**
           3.2.1, 3.2.3, 3.2.4,
           3.3.6, 3.5.4, 3.5.8,
           3.6.2
    (a) **3.2.1**
    (b) **3.1.4, 3.2.4**
    (c) **3.2.4**
    (d) **3.2.1, 3.2.4**
Art. 2 .... **1.9.3, 4.3.1, 4.3.5,**
           5.1, 5.2.1, 5.2.5,
           5.2.6, 5.3, 5.3.1,
           5.4.3, 5.4.3.4, 5.4.3.5,
           5.6, 5.7, 5.7.1,
           8.3.1, 8.4.3.2

  (1) **5.1, 5.2.1, 5.4.3,**
           5.4.3.4, 5.4.3.10,
           5.8.3, 8.6.2
    (a) **5.1, 5.2,**
           5.4.3, 5.4.3.5, 8.6.2
    (b) **4.3.5, 5.1,**
           5.2, 5.3.2, 5.4.3,
           5.8.1, 8.6.2
  (2) **1.11, 2.7.1, 5.1,**
           5.2, 5.4.3.8,
           5.8.3, 8.6.2
  (3) **2.7.1, 5.1, 5.2,**
           5.2.1, 8.6.2
  (4) **2.7.1, 2.7.3, 5.1,**
           5.2, 5.2.1, 5.2.4,
           5.5, 7.4.1
Art. 3 .... **1.9.2–1.9.4, 2.2.1,**
           2.2.3, 2.4.3, **2.7.1,**
           4.4.5.3, 4.4.6, 5.1,
           6.4, 6.5, 7.2.1, 7.6.4
  (1) **2.2.1, 2.2.3,**
           2.4.2.8, 2.4.3,
           4.3.2, 8.5
    (a) **2.2.4, 2.3, 2.8.3**
    (b) 2.2.2, **2.2.3,**
           2.2.4, 2.3, 2.4, 2.4.1,
           2.4.3, **2.5,** 2.6,
           2.8.3, 4.4.6, 7.5.2
  (1)(b)–(4) 2.3
  (2) **2.7.1, 2.7.2,**
           5.4.2, 5.5
  (3) **2.4.1, 2.5,**
           2.6, 3.4.2, 3.5.2
  (5)(a) **2.8.1, 4.4.6**
    (b) **2.8.2**
    (c) **2.8.3, 4.4.6**
Art. 4 .... 2.4.2.7, 4.3.1, 4.3.4,
           4.4.3, 4.4.6, 7.4.5,
           8.5, 8.6.2
  (1) 3.3.3, **4.3.1,**
           4.3.4, 4.3.12, 4.4.6
  (2) **2.3, 4.3.3, 7.5.4**
  (3) **4.3.8, 4.5.1, 4.5.2**
Art. 5 .... 1.7, **3.3.1, 3.5.10,**
           3.7, 7.6.4, 8.5,
           8.6.2
  (1) **1.7, 3.3.1, 3.3.2,**
           3.3.5, 3.3.6,
           3.4.2, 3.5.3,
           3.6.1
  (2) **3.5.3, 3.5.4**
  (3) 3.2.3, **3.6, 3.6.2**
    (a) 3.1.3, **3.6.1**
    (b) **3.6.2**
  (4) **1.7, 3.3.5, 3.3.6,**
           3.4, 3.4.2, 3.5.8,
           3.5.13, 3.6.3
    (a) 3.4.2
    (b)–(e) **3.5.10**

(b) **3.4.2, 3.5.10**
(c) **3.4.2, 3.5.8**
(d) **3.4.2**
(e) 3.4.2, 3.5.8
(5) **3.5.8, 3.5.10**
(a) **3.3.5**
(b) 3.5.10
Art. 6 .... 2.4.3.8, 4.1, **4.2,**
4.4.5.3, 4.5.1, **4.5.4,**
7.1, 7.2.1, 7.2.2,
7.2.2, 7.3.4, 7.4.1,
7.4.3, 7.4.4, 7.4.6,
7.5.1, 7.5.4, 7.5.5,
7.6.2, 7.7, 7.7,
8.1.2, 8.1.4, 8.3.2,
8.5, 8.6.2
(1) **4.5.1, 6.1, 6.2,**
7.5.3
(a) 2.5, 2.6.2,
2.6.3, 3.4.1, 4.3.8,
4.5.4, 5.5, 7.2.1,
7.6.2, 7.6.3.1, 7.7,
8.1.2
(b) 2.5, 2.6.1,
3.5.13, **4.3.4, 4.3.8,**
4.3.12, 4.4.2, 4.5.4,
5.3, 5.3.2, **5.4,**
5.4.3.4, **5.5, 5.7.1,**
5.7.7, **7.1, 7.2.1,**
7.2.2, 7.3.4, 7.4.5,
7.7, 8.1.2
(c) **2.7.1, 3.5.12,**
4.5.4, 4.7.2, 4.8,
5.1, **7.2.1, 7.3,**
7.4.5, 8.1.2
(2) **7.4.1,** 7.4.3
(3) **7.4.6**
(b) **7.3.4**
Art. 7 .... **1.9.3, 2.4.2.7, 4.3.1,**
4.4.1, 4.4.4, 4.4.5,
4.4.5.2, 4.4.5.3, 4.4.6,
7.1, 8.6.2
(1) **4.4.2, 4.4.5.1,**
4.4.5.2, 4.4.6, 4.5.1
(2) 4.4.5.1
(3) **4.4.3,** 5.4.3.5
(4) **4.4.3, 4.4.4,**
4.4.5.3, 5.3, 7.5.2
(5) **4.4.5.2, 8.1.2**
Art. 8 .... 2.4.2.1, 2.4.3, **2.4.3.4,**
4.1, **4.2, 4.3.4,**
4.3.9, 4.4.5.3, 5.1.2,
5.3.2, 5.3.3.8, 5.3.3.9,
5.4.3.2, 5.4.3.4, 5.4.3.7,
5.4.3.9, **5.5,** 5.6,
5.7, 5.7.1, 5.7.3,
5.7.5, 5.8, 5.8.3,
5.9, 7.1, 7.3.4,
7.4.1, 7.4.3, 7.4.6,

7.4.8, 7.5.1, 7.5.4,
7.5.5, 7.6.2, 7.6.3,
7.7, 8.1.3, **8.1.4,**
8.2, 8.3.1, **8.3.2,**
8.5, 8.6.1, 8.6.2
(2)–(5) **4.8, 7.3, 7.5.5**
(2) **1.4.6, 4.4.2, 6.1,**
6.2, 7.3.1, 7.4.1,
7.4.3, 7.4.5, 7.5.2,
7.5.3, 7.6.4, 7.7,
8.6.2
(3) 7.3.3, **7.3.4, 7.5.3,**
7.6.3, 8.6.2
(4) 4.7.8, **7.3.3,**
7.5.2, 8.6.2
(5) 4.7.8, **7.3.1,**
7.4.6, 7.7
(a) **7.7**
(b) **7.3.4**
(9) 5.3.2
(16) 5.3.3.6
(23) **5.3.2**
(48), (49) 5.3.3.8
Art. 9 .... **1.3, 1.5.2, 1.9.4,**
4.5.3, 5.2.5, 5.3.3,
7.1, 7.2.2, **7.6.2,**
8.1.1, 8.1.2, 8.2,
8.3.1, 8.3.4, 8.4.3.4,
8.5, 8.6.2
(1)(c) **4.6.2**
(2) 3.4.2, **4.5.3, 8.3.3**
(a) **8.3.1, 8.3.3**
(b) 5.2.5, **8.3.1, 8.3.3**
(3) **1.3, 8.3.3**
(4), (5) **8.3.3**
(6) 8.1
(7) **4.3.5, 8.3.2**
(8) 1.7, **8.3.3**
Arts. 10–20 .... **8.6.2**
Art. 10 .... 4.1
(1) **4.3.4, 4.3.8,**
4.5.1, 7.4.1, 7.5.3,
8.3.4
(3) **4.7.1, 7.5.3**
(4) **4.6.2, 4.7.1**
(5) **7.6.1, 7.7**
(6) **4.4.2, 4.5.4, 7.1, 7.2.1,**
7.2.2, 7.5.1, 8.1.2, 8.3.4
Arts. 11–20 .... 4.1
Art. 11 .... **4.5.1, 4.5.2, 4.6.1,**
4.6.4, 4.7.1, 7.6.2
(5) **4.6.1, 4.6.4**
Art. 13 .... **4.5.1, 4.6.2, 4.6.3,**
4.7.1, 7.6.2
(1) **4.6.2**
(b) **4.6.3**
(3) **4.6.2**
Art. 14 .... **4.6.3, 8.6.2**
(1) 7.5.2

(a) **4.3.4, 4.3.12**
(b) **4.3.12, 7.3.4, 7.7**
(c) **7.3.4, 7.7**
(2) 7.5.2
(a) **4.4.4, 7.3.1,
7.3.4, 7.4.6,
7.5.2, 7.7**
(b) **4.4.4,
4.4.5.1, 7.5.2**
(c) **7.3.2, 7.3.3,
7.5.2**
(4) 7.5.2
Art. 15 .... **4.6.4**
(2) 7.5.2
(a) **4.4.4, 7.4.6**
(b) **7.3.1, 7.3.3**
Art. 16 .... 7.6.2
Art. 17 .... **4.3.9**
(2) **4.3.9**
Art. 18 .... **7.3.3, 7.6.3.3**
(1) 4.5.1, **4.7.3, 8.3.3**
(3) **4.7.3, 4.7.4,
4.7.5, 7.5.1**
(4) **4.7.7, 7.6.3.3**
Art. 19(1) **4.3.8, 8.1.2, 8.1.3**
(2) **4.5.3,** 8.1,
8.1.3, 8.3.3
(3) **4.7.8**
(4), (5), (6), (7) **8.1.4**
Art. 20(1), (2) 7.5.5
Art. 21 .... **8.2, 8.5, 8.6.2**
(2) **1.7, 2.1, 8.2, 8.3.3**
(3) **4.5.3, 5.1.2,
7.6.2, 8.2**
Art. 22 .... **1.3, 2.4.3, 3.1.5,
3.2.3, 7.3.3**
(2) **1.9.2**
(3)–(6) **1.9.4**
(3) **1.9.4,** 3.1.5,
7.6.2, 8.2, 8.6.2
(5) 1.7
Art. 24 .... **1.6, 1.7**
Art. 28 .... 3.3.6
Annex 8 .... **7.5.4**
Reg. 2367/90: [1990] O.J. L219/5 . 1.4.6,
4.3.11
Reg. 3666/93: [1993] O.J. L336/1 .. 1.4.6
Reg. 3384/94: [1994] O.J. L377/1 . 1.4.6,
4.3.2
Art. 2(1) 4.3.2
Art. 4(3) 2.4.2.3
Reg. 3385/94: [1994] O.J. L337/28 ... 4.1
Pt. D **4.3.11**
Reg. 1475/95: [1995] O.J. L145/25—
Art. 4(2) 3.4.2

Reg. 240/96—
Art. 10(8) 3.4.2
Reg. 1310/97: 30 June 1997 .... **5.1,
5.2.5**
Art. 1(4) 3.6.1
Reg. 447/98: [1998] O.J. L61/1 ..... **1.4.6,
1.11, 4.1, 4.3.2, 4.3.8,
4.3.10, 4.9, 8.1.1, APP 2**
Recital 5 .... 4.3.2
Recital 8 .... **4.7.6**
Recital 10 .... 4.1, **4.3.2**
Art. 1(1), (3) **4.3.3**
Art. 2(1) **4.3.2, 4.3.3**
(2), (3), (4), (5) **4.3.7**
Art. 3 .... 4.3.2
(1)(a), (b) **4.3.3**
(2) **4.3.2, 4.3.6**
Art. 4 .... 4.3.2
(1) **4.3.8**
(2) **4.3.6**
(3) **4.3.10**
(4) **4.3.8**
Art. 5 .... **4.3.11**
(1), (2) **4.3.11**
Art. 6(1)(b) **4.3.8**
(4) **4.3.8**
(5) **4.7.1**
Art. 7(4) **4.3.8**
(6) **4.7.1**
(8) **4.3.8, 4.7.1**
Art. 8 .... **4.3.8, 4.7.1**
Art. 9 .... **4.3.8,** 4.6.2, **4.7.1,** 4.7.4
(1)(d) **4.3.10**
(3) **4.3.10**
Art. 10(1) **4.3.2, 7.5.3**
Art. 13(2) **4.7.3**
(3) **4.7.4**
(b) **4.7.4**
(4) **4.7.5**
Art. 14 .... **4.7.6**
(1) **4.7.5**
Art. 15 .... **4.7.6**
(1), (2), (4), (5) **4.7.6**
Art. 16 .... **4.7.6**
(1), (2) **4.7.7**
Art. 17 .... **4.7.4**
Art. 18(1), (2) **7.4.5**
Art. 20 .... 4.7.3
(1), (2), (3) **4.9**
Art. 21(1) **4.3.8**
Art. 22 .... **4.3.4**
(3) **4.3.4**
Art. 23 .... **4.3.4**
Annex 1 .... **4.3.2**

Alphabetical Table of Merger Decisions

Bold type indicates textual references as opposed to footnote references.

ABB/BREL 2.5, **5.4.3.4**
ABB/Daimler-Benz [1997] O.J. L11/29; [1995] 5 C.M.L.R. 577 .... 4.7.7, 7.4.3, 8.3.4
ABB/Renault Automation [1994] 4 C.M.L.R. 605 .... 2.5, 7.2.1
AG/Amev [1991] 4 C.M.L.R. 847 .... 3.6.2, 5.3
AGF/La Union y el Fenix 6.5
AGF/Royal [1998] 4 C.M.L.R. 821 .... 5.3
AGFA-Gevaert/DuPont [1998] O.J. L211/22; [1998] 4 C.M.L.R. 486 .... **7.4.4**
AKZO Nobel/Monsanto [1995] 4 C.M.L.R. 315 .... 6.6
AMB/Rodutch [1996] 5 C.M.L.R. 255 .... 5.3
AT&T/NCR [1992] 4 C.M.L.R. M41 .... 5.4.3.8, 5.4.3.10
AXA/UAP [1997] 4 C.M.L.R. 200 .... 5.3
AXA/GRE [1999] 4 C.M.L.R. 807 .... 5.3
AXA-UAP/Royale Belge [1998] 5 C.M.L.R. 152 .... 5.3
Abeille Vie/Viagère/Sinafer [1997] 5 C.M.L.R. 142 .... 5.3
Accor/Wagons-Lits [1992] O.J. L204/1; [1993] 5 C.M.L.R. M13 .... 5.3.2
Aegon/Scottish Equitable [1993] 5 C.M.L.R. 117 .... 5.3
Aegon/Transamerica [1999] O.J. C130/9 .... 4.5.1
Aérospatiale/MBB [1992] 4 C.M.L.R. M70 .... 5.4.3.5
Aérospatiale-Alenia/de Havilland [1991] O.J. L334/42; [1992] 4 C.M.L.R. M2 .... **5.3.3.9,**
                                                                                  5.8, 5.8.3, 7.3.2
Ahold/Jeronimo Martins/Inovacao [1993] 5 C.M.L.R. 16 .... 4.3.11, 5.3.3
Air France/Sabena [1994] 5 C.M.L.R. Ml **2.2.2, 3.3.6,** 4.3.4, 4.3.11, 5.4, 7.4.4, 8.1.3
Airtours/First Choice [1999] 5 C.M.L.R. 25 .... **4.3.9, 5.2.2,** 5.4.3.10, 5.7.5, **5.7.6,**
                                                                   7.3.4, **7.4.4, 7.5.5, 8.1.4,** 8.3.4
Albacom [1995] 5 C.M.L.R. 388 .... **2.4.3.6,** 7.2.1
Albacom/BT/ENI/Mediaset [1998] 4 C.M.L.R. 14 .... 6.9
Alcan/Inespal/Palco [1993] 5 C.M.L.R. 16 .... 5.4.3.4
Alcatel/AEG Kabel **5.3.3.7,** 8.3.4
Alcatel/STC [1993] 5 C.M.L.R. 311 .... **3.3.6,** 7.2.1
Alcatel/Telettra [1991] O.J. L122/48; [1991] 4 C.M.L.R. 778 .... **2.4.2.5,**
                                                                           5.4.3.7, 5.4.3.10, 7.4.4
Alcoa/Inespal [1997] 5 C.M.L.R. 763 .... 6.5
Alfred C. Toepfer/Champagne Céréales 2.4.3.3
Alliance Unichem/Unifarma [1998] 5 C.M.L.R. 306 .... 8.3.4
Allianz/AGF [1998] 5 C.M.L.R. 22 .... 5.3
Allianz/Deutsche Krankenversicherung **3.6.2,** 5.3
Allianz/Elvia/Lloyd Adriatico [1995] 4 C.M.L.R. 611 .... 5.3
Allianz/Vereinte [1996] 5 C.M.L.R. 663 .... 5.3
Allied Lyons/HWE-Pedro Domecq **2.2.2, 5.4.3.7,** 6.7
Allied Products Corp/Vernon Industrial Group [1989] 9 E.C. Bull 25 .... 6.2
American Cyanamid/Shell [1994] 4 C.M.L.R. 23 .... **5.4.3.4,** 6.8
American Home Products (AHP)/American Cyanamid 1.7, 5.3.3.8
American Home Products/Monsanto [1998] 5 C.M.L.R. 664 .... 2.3, 6.5, **7.4.4**
Ameritech/Tele Danmark [1998] 4 C.M.L.R. 206 .... 6.3.2
Anglo American/Lonrho [1998] O.J. L149/21; [1997] 4 C.M.L.R. 377 .... **2.4.2.8, 2.4.3,**
                                                        2.4.3.2, 2.4.3.4, 3.4.2, 5.3.3.9, 7.4.3, 7.4.5, 8.1.4

Apollinaris/Schweppes [1992] 4 C.M.L.R. M78 .... 4.3.11
Arjomari-Prioux/Wiggins Teape Appleton [1991] 4 C.M.L.R. 854 .... **2.4.3.3,**
                                                                          3.4.2, 7.2.1
Asko/Jacobs/Adia [1993] 4 C.M.L.R. M14 .... **2.2.2,** 3.5.8, 3.5.13
Auchan/Pao de Acucar [1996] 5 C.M.L.R. 374 .... 5.2.5
Avesta/British Steel/NCC [1992] O.J. C258 .... 3.3.1
Avesta II **2.4.2.7, 3.5.9, 4.4.6**
Avesta III [1994] 5 C.M.L.R. 503 .... 2.4.3.3, 2.5

BAI/Banca Popolare di Lecco [1994] 4 C.M.L.R. 405 .... 5.3.3
BASF/Shell II [1998] 4 C.M.L.R. 215 .... 6.9
BAT/Rothmans [1999] 4 C.M.L.R. 800 .... **6.5**
BAT/Zurich [1998] 4 C.M.L.R. 488 .... 2.3, 6.5
BBL/American Express 6.7
BD/CIGI 6.7
BHF/CCF/Charterhouse [1993] 5 C.M.L.R. 207 .... 5.3.3
BMW/Rover 4.3.11
BP/Amoco [1999] 4 C.M.L.R. 176 .... **2.3, 7.4.3**
BP Amoco/Atlantic Richfield **5.7.6**
BS/BT [1994] 4 C.M.L.R. 607 .... 7.2.1
BSCH/Champalimaud [1999] 5 C.M.L.R. 607 .... 8.4.2.3, 8.4.3.4
BT/AT&T **5.4.2, 7.3.1**
BT/ESB [1998] 5 C.M.L.R. 18 .... **6.3,** 6.3.2, 6.5
BT/Tele DK/SBB/Migros/UBS [1997] 4 C.M.L.R. 978 .... 6.5
BTR/Pirelli 5.4.3.7
Banco Santander/Banesto 2.8.2
Banco Santander/British Telecom [1994] 4 C.M.L.R. 607 .... **2.4.2.6**
Bank Austria/Creditanstalt [1997] 4 C.M.L.R. 651 .... 5.3
Baxter/Nestlé/Salvia [1992] 5 C.M.L.R. M33 .... 7.2.1
Bayerische Vereinsbank/FGH Bank [1998] 4 C.M.L.R. 492 .... 6.5
Bayernwerk/Isarwerke [1997] 4 C.M.L.R. 23 .... 8.3.4
Behringwerke AG/Armour [1995] 4 C.M.L.R. 609 .... 5.3.3.8
Bertelsmann/Kirch/Premiere [1999] O.J. L53/1; [1999] 4 C.M.L.R. 700 .... 7.3.2, 7.4.4,
                                                                           8.1.4, 8.3.4
Bertelsmann/Wissenschaftsverlag-Springer [1999] O.J. C46/29; [1999] 4 C.M.L.R. 389 .. 4.3.10
Birmingham International Airport [1997] 4 C.M.L.R. 831 .... 6.5
Blokker/Toys 'R' Us [1998] O.J. L316/1; [1997] 5 C.M.L.R. 148 .... **2.4.3, 5.8.3,** 7.3.2,
                                                                           7.3.3, 8.6.1, 8.6.2
Boeing/McDonnell Douglas [1997] O.J. L336/16; [1997] 5 C.M.L.R. 270 .... **1.8, 5.4.3.4,**
                                                                           5.4.3.5, 7.4.4, 8.1.4
Borealis/IPIC/OMV/PCD [1998] 5 C.M.L.R. 299 .... 6.9
British Aerospace/Lagardere [1996] 5 C.M.L.R. 523 .... 8.4.3.1
British Aerospace/VSEL 8.4.3.1
British Airways/Dan Air [1993] 5 C.M.L.R. M61 .... **3.4.2,** 3.5.3, **8.6.1, 8.6.2**
British Airways/TAT [1993] 4 C.M.L.R. 10 .... 2.4.2.6, **2.7.2.2, 3.3.6,** 6.5
British Gas/Group 4 [1996] 5 C.M.L.R. 526 .... 2.7.2.1
British Steel/Svensk Stal/NSD [1994] 5 C.M.L.R. 505 .... 3.3.1
British Steel/UES [1995] 4 C.M.L.R. 605 .... 2.5
British Telecom/MCI [1995] 5 C.M.L.R. 285 .... **1.8,** 2.3, 2.4.3.7, **2.7.2.1,**
                                                                           4.3.11, **5.5,** 7.2.1, **7.4.4**

CAMPSA 2.5, 5.3.3
CCIE/GTE **2.4.3.2,** 2.4.3.5, **6.9**
CEA Industrie/France Télécom/Finmeccanica/SGS-Thomson 2.2.4.1, **3.5.14,** 5.3.3.9
CGP/GEC Alsthom/KPR/Kone Corporation **6.5**
CLT/Disney/Super RTL [1995] 4 C.M.L.R. 711 .... 6.6
CSME/MDPA/SCPA [1999] 5 C.M.L.R. 301 .... **8.3.4**
CTC/GE/Bank America **2.4.2.3**

CU Italia/Banca delle Marche 5.3
CVC/WMO/Wavin [1999] 4 C.M.L.R. 604 .... 6.9
CVC Capital Partners/Dynoplast [1999] 4 C.M.L.R. 609 .... 3.5.12
CWB/Goldman Sachs/Tarkett [1994] 4 C.M.L.R. 533 .... **3.5.12, 5.4.1**
Cable & Wireless/Maersk Data-Nautec [1997] 5 C.M.L.R. 146 .... 4.3.8, 6.9
Cable & Wireless/Schlumberger [1995] 4 C.M.L.R. 161 .... 5.3.3.9, **6.3**, 6.3.2
Cable & Wireless/VEBA [1995] 5 C.M.L.R. 263 .... 6.5
Cable I Televisio de Catalunya [1998] 4 C.M.L.R. 411 .... 2.4.2.3
Cableuropa/Spainco/CTC [1998] 4 C.M.L.R. 411 .... 2.4.2.3
Cardo/Thyssen [1997] 4 C.M.L.R. 20 .... 4.3.8
Cargill/Continental Grain [1999] O.J. C52/8; [1999] 4 C.M.L.R. 382 .... 6.5
Carrier Corporation/Toshiba [1999] 4 C.M.L.R. 801 .... 6.7
Cereol/Continentale Italiana [1992] 4 C.M.L.R. 346 .... 3.5.3, 7.2.1
Chrysler/Distributors (Benelux and Germany) [1998] 4 C.M.L.R. 208 .... 6.5
Ciba-Geigy/Sandoz [1997] O.J. L201/1; [1996] 5 C.M.L.R. 257 ..... **5.4.3.4, 7.4.4, 7.4.6**, 8.1.4
Coca-Cola/Amalgamated Beverages [1997] O.J. L218/15; [1997] 4 C.M.L.R. 368 ..... 5.4.3.7, 5.4.3.9, **5.6, 7.6.3**
Coca-Cola Company/Carlsberg [1998] O.J. L145/41; [1997] 5 C.M.L.R. 564 .. 4.7.1, **5.4.3.7**, 5.4.3.9, 5.6, **7.4.4**
Codan/Hafnia [1993] 5 C.M.L.R. 17 .... 5.3, **5.4.3.4**
Commercial Union/Berlinische [1998] 5 C.M.L.R. 158 .... 5.3
Commercial Union/General Accident [1998] 5 C.M.L.R. 824 .... 5.3
Commercial Union/Groupe Victoire 5.3
Compagnie Industrielle Maritime/Elf/Compagnie Nationale de Navigation **8.3.4**
Conagra/Idea [1992] 5 C.M.L.R. M19 .... 6.5
Costa Crociere/Chargeurs/Accor [1993] 5 C.M.L.R. 206 .... 5.3.2
Courtaulds/SNIA 2.7.2.1
Crédit Lyonnais/BFG Bank **2.4.3.1**
Crown Cork & Seal/Carnaud Metalbox [1995] O.J. L75/23; [1996] 4 C.M.L.R. 9 ..... **5.3.2, 7.4.3**

DASA/Fokker 5.3.3.9
DBV/Gothaer/GPM [1997] 4 C.M.L.R. 374 .... 5.3
DENSO/Magneti Marelli [1999] 4 C.M.L.R. 1182 .... 6.5
DHL/Deutsche Post [1998] 5 C.M.L.R. 156 .... 6.5
Dalgety/Quaker Oats Company [1995] 4 C.M.L.R. 604 .... **6.7**, 6.8, 8.5
Delhaize/PG 5.3.3
Delta/PanAm [1992] 5 C.M.L.R. M56 .... **3.3.6**, 3.5.3
Deutsche Bank/Banco de Madrid 5.3.3
Deutsche Post/Securicor [1999] O.J. C15/2; [1999] 4 C.M.L.R. 600 .... 4.5.1
Deutsche Post/Trans-o-flex [1999] O.J. C130/9; [1999] 4 C.M.L.R. 1198 .... 4.5.1
Deutsche Telekom/Beta Research [1999] O.J. L53/1; [1999] 4 C.M.L.R. 700 .... 7.3.2, 7.4.4, 8.1.4, 8.3.4
Digital/Philips [1994] 4 C.M.L.R. M4 .... 6.9
Direct Line/Bankinter [1995] 4 C.M.L.R. 318 .... 5.3, 6.7
Dow/Buna [1995] 5 C.M.L.R. 131 .... 6.3.2
Dow Jones/NBC–CNBC Europe [1998] 4 C.M.L.R. 410 .... 6.5, 6.9
DuPont/ICI [1993] O.J. L7/13; [1993] 5 C.M.L.R. M41; [1995] 4 C.M.L.R. 323 .... 3.5.11, **5.3.2, 5.3.3.3**, 5.3.3.6, **5.3.3.8**, 5.4.3.5, **5.8.2**
DuPont/ICI [1997] 5 C.M.L.R. 758 .... 6.5, 6.6, 6.9

EDF/Edison-ISE [1995] 5 C.M.L.R. 23 .... 5.3.3
EDF/London Electricity [1999] 4 C.M.L.R. 374 .... **8.3.3**, 8.3.4, **8.4.3.2**
ENEL/France Telecom/Deutsche Telekom [1998] 5 C.M.L.R. 152 .... **5.5**, 6.3, 6.5, 6.9
ENW/Eastern **2.7.2.1**
ERC/NRG Victory [1994] 5 C.M.L.R. 24 .... 5.3
Eastman Kodak/Sun Chemical [1998] 4 C.M.L.R. 40 .... 6.9
Elf Atochem/Rohm and Haas **2.7.2.1**, 6.6
Elf Atochem/Rütgers **2.4.2.6**
Elf/BC/CEPSA 2.6.1

Elf/Enterprise [1992] 5 C.M.L.R. M66 .... 4.3.11, 6.5
Elopak/Metal Box-Odin [1990] O.J. L209/15................................. **5.5, 6.2**
Employers Reinsurance Corporation/Aachener [1995] 5 C.M.L.R. 133 ...... 5.3, 6.7
Employers Reinsurance/Frankona [1995] 5 C.M.L.R. 133 .... 5.3
Enso/Stora [1999] 4 C.M.L.R. 21 .... **7.4.8**
Ericsson/Hewlett Packard [1993] 5 C.M.L.R. 403 .... 5.3.3.9, 5.4.3.4
Ericsson/Nokia/Psion (Symbian I) [1998] 5 C.M.L.R. 464 .... **2.6.2**
Ericsson/Nokia/Psion/Motorola (Symbian II) [1999] 4 C.M.L.R. 378 .... **2.6.2**, 7.2.1
Eridania/ISI 2.4.3.7, 2.5, **3.4.2**
Eucom/Digital 3.5.8
Eureko [1992] 4 C.M.L.R. 543 .... **2.6.2**, 6.5
Eurocard/Eurocheque-Europay 7.2.1
Eurocom/RSCG 2.3, **3.4.2**
Exxon/Mobil [1999] 5 C.M.L.R. 296 .... **5.7.6**, 8.3.4
Exxon/Shell [1998] 5 C.M.L.R. 160 .... 7.4.3

Ferruzzi Finanziaria/Fondiaria [1995] 5 C.M.L.R. 24 .... 2.5, 5.3
Fiat Geotech/Ford New Holland [1991] 4 C.M.L.R. 330 .... 6.7, **7.4.4**
Fletcher Challenge/Methanex 2.6.2
Ford/Hertz 2.4.2.2, **2.4.2.6**, 3.5.9, 7.2.1
Ford/Volkswagen [1993] O.J. L20/14; [1993] 4 C.M.L.R. 232 .... **5.5**
Fortis/CGER [1993] 5 C.M.L.R. 534 .... 2.2.4.1, **5.3.3.4**
Fortis/La Caixa 5.3
Fyffes/Capespan 6.9

GE/Bayer [1998] 5 C.M.L.R. 151 .... 6.9
GE/CIGI 5.3, 5.4.3.4, 6.5, 6.7
GE/ENI/Nuovo Pignone [1994] 5 C.M.L.R. 22 .... 2.4.2.6, **2.4.3.6**
GE Capital/Sea Containers [1998] 4 C.M.L.R. 822 .... 6.5
GEC/Siemens-Plessey [1990] O.J. C239/2 .... **5.5**
GEC/Thomson [1996] 5 C.M.L.R. 13 .... 8.4.3.1
GEC/VSEL 8.4.3.1
GEHE/Lloyds Chemists **8.3.4**
GEHE/OCP [1993] 5 C.M.L.R. 15 .... 5.3, 5.3.3
GRE/PPP [1998] 4 C.M.L.R. 487 .... 6.5
Gencor/Lonrho [1997] O.J. L11/30; [1999] 4 C.M.L.R. 1076 .... 1.7, **2.4.2**, 5.3.3.9, 5.5,
                                                             5.7.3, 5.7.4, 7.3.2, 7.4.2, 7.6.3
Gencor/Shell 5.3.3.9
General Re/Kölnische Re [1994] 5 C.M.L.R. 503 .... 5.3, 6.5
Generali/Central Hispano-Generali 5.3
Generali/Comit/R. Flemings 5.3
Generali/France Vie [1995] 5 C.M.L.R. 265 .... 5.3
Generali/Unicredito 5.3
Glaxo/Wellcome [1995] 4 C.M.L.R. 321 .... 5.3.3.8
Grand Metropolitan/Cinzano [1992] 4 C.M.L.R. 349 .... 5.3.3.5, 6.7
Guinness/Grand Metropolitan [1997] 5 C.M.L.R. 760 .... **1.8, 5.4.3.6, 5.4.3.7, 5.4.3.9,
                                                             5.4.3.10, 5.6, 5.9, 7.4.4**

Hagemeyer/ABB Asea Skandia [1997] 5 C.M.L.R. 759 .... 6.7
Halliburton/Dresser [1998] 5 C.M.L.R. 165 .... 2.3
Harrisons & Crosfield/AKZO [1993] 4 C.M.L.R. 114 .... 6.5, 6.6
Havas/Bertelsmann/Doyma [1998] 5 C.M.L.R. 470 .... 6.5
Hercules/Betzdearborn [1998] 5 C.M.L.R. 661 .... 6.5
Hermes/Sampo/FGB-FCIC [1998] 5 C.M.L.R. 19 .... 4.3.8, 5.3
Hicks, Muse, Tate & Furst/Hillsdown Holdings [1999] 5 C.M.L.R. 599 ...... 3.6.12
Hochtief/Aer Rianta/Dusseldorf Airport [1998] 4 C.M.L.R. 210 .... 6.3.1
Hoechst/Marion Merrell Dow [1995] 5 C.M.L.R. 134 .... 5.3.3.8

Hoffmann-La Roche/Boehringer Mannheim [1998] O.J. L234/14; [1998] 4 C.M.L.R. 412 **5.4.3.6**
Holdercim/Cedest 5.3.3.6, **8.3.4**
Holdercim/Origny-Desvroise **2.4.3.4**
Home Benelux B.V. [1998] 5 C.M.L.R. 661 .... 5.5
Hong Kong & Shanghai Bank/Midland **3.6.1, 3.6.3**

IBM France/CGI **8.4.2.1**
ICI/Tioxide [1991] 4 C.M.L.R. 792 .... **2.5, 3.4.1,** 5.4.3.10
ICI/Williams [1998] 4 C.M.L.R. 824 .... 6.8, 6.9
IFINT/EXOR 3.4.2
IMI/Heilmann **2.2.4,** 2.3
ING/BBL [1998] 4 C.M.L.R. 411 .... 5.3
ING/BHF [1999] 4 C.M.L.R. 18 .... 5.3
ING/Barings [1995] 4 C.M.L.R. 615 .... **2.8.2, 4.4.4,** 5.3.3
Imetal/English China Clays [1999] O.J. C70/7; [1999] 4 C.M.L.R. 1194 .... 4.3.8
Inchcape/IEP [1994] 4 C.M.L.R. Ml1 .... **6.8**
Ingersoll-Rand/Clark [1995] 5 C.M.L.R. 27 .... 7.2.1
Ingersoll-Rand/MAN 2.4.2.6, 2.5, 7.2.1
Irish Distilleries/Cooley Distillery 5.9.3.3
Italian Flat Glass [1981] O.J. L236/32; [1982] 3 C.M.L.R. 366 .... **5.4.3.1**

Jefferson Smurfit Group/Munksjo [1995] 5 C.M.L.R. 261 .... **5.4.1**

KLM/Martinair [1999] 5 C.M.L.R. 302 .... 4.5.1
KNP/Bührmann-Tetterode/VRG [1993] O.J. L217/35; [1993] 5 C.M.L.R. 116 .... **5.3.3.4**
KNP BT/Bunzl/Wilhelm Seiler [1997] 4 C.M.L.R. 373 .... 6.5
Kali und Salz/MdK/Treuhand [1994] O.J. L186/38; [1994] 4 C.M.L.R. 526; [1998] 5
    C.M.L.R. 292 .... **2.2.4.1, 3.5.14, 4.3.4,** 4.7.1, **5.3.3.5, 5.4.3.1, 5.4.3.3, 5.4.3.6,** 6.5
Kelt/American Express 2.6.1, 2.8.1, 4.4.4, **5.4.1**
Kesko/Tuko [1997] O.J. L110/53; [1997] 4 C.M.L.R. 24 ..... **5.4.3.6,** 7.3.2, 7.3.3, 8.6.1, 8.6.2
Kimberley Clark/Scott Paper [1996] O.J. L183/53; [1996] 4 C.M.L.R. 461 .... 7.3.4
Kingfisher/Darty [1993] 4 C.M.L.R. 403 .... **5.3.3**
Kingfisher/Grosslabor [1999] 4 C.M.L.R. 1174 .... 6.5, 6.7
Kingfisher/Wegert/Promarkt 6.7
Kirch/Richemont/Multichoice/Telepiù **6.5**
Kirch/Richemont/Telepiù 2.6.2
Kodak/Imation [1998] 5 C.M.L.R. 878 .... **6.3.1,** 6.5, 6.9
Koipe-Tabacalera/Elosua 4.3.11
Krauss-Maffei/Wegmann [1998] 5 C.M.L.R. 167 .... 8.3.4
Kuoni/First Choice [1999] 4 C.M.L.R. 1190 .... 5.7.5
Kyowa/Saitama Banks [1992] 4 C.M.L.R. M105 .... 1.7, **2.3**

LGV/BTR 6.6
La Redoute/Empire [1992] 5 C.M.L.R. M39 .... **2.4.3.2,** 3.4.2
La Rinascente/Cedis Migliarini [1995] 4 C.M.L.R. 606 .... 2.4.3.3
La Roche/Syntex [1994] 5 C.M.L.R. 27 .... 5.3.3.8
Lear/United Technologies [1999] 4 C.M.L.R. 1186 .... 1.7
Linde/Fiat **3.5.3, 3.5.6**
Lucent Technologies/Ascend Communications [1999] 4 C.M.L.R. 807 .... **3.2.4**
Lufthansa/Menzies/Sigma at Manchester [1999] 4 C.M.L.R. 372 .... 6.5
Lyonnaise des Eaux/Northumbrian Water [1996] 4 C.M.L.R. 145 .... 8.4.3.2, **8.4.3.3**

MAN/Sulzer 5.2.2
MSG/Media Service [1994] O.J. L364/1; [1994] 5 C.M.L.R. 499 .... **2.4.2.1,** 5.1.2, **5.8.1,**
                                                                                                7.3.2, 7.4.2, 8.3.4
McCormick/CPC/Rabobank/Ostmann [1993] 5 C.M.L.R. 535 .... **2.4.2.2,** 7.1, 8.1.2, **8.3.4**
McDermott/ETPM [1998] 5 C.M.L.R. 148 .... 3.5.10
Maersk Air/LFV Holdings [1998] 5 C.M.L.R. 159 .... 6.5, 6.9

Magneti Marelli/CEAc [1991] O.J. L222/38; [1992] 4 C.M.L.R. M61 .... **3.5.3, 5.3.3.3**
Mannesmann/Hoesch [1993] O.J. C128/4; [1993] O.J. L114/34 .... **5.2.1, 5.3.3.6, 5.3.3.7,**
                                                          5.4.3.4, 5.4.3.7, 8.3.4
Mannesmann/Olivetti/Infostrada [1998] 4 C.M.L.R. 407 .... 6.5
Mannesmann/Vallourec/Ilva [1994] O.J. L102/15; [1994] 4 C.M.L.R. 529 ...... **5.1.2, 5.3.3.1,**
                                   5.3.3.2, 5.3.3.8, 5.4.3.5, 5.4.3.6, 5.8, 8.1.3
Marconi/Finmeccanica 2.2.4.1, 3.5.13, 6.3.2
Matra/Aérospatiale 8.4.3.1
Matra/CAP Gemini Sogeti 5.4.3.7
Matra BAE/Dynamics/DASA/LFF **6.3**
Matra Marconi Space/British Aerospace Space Systems 3.5.6,
                                                          5.3.3.9, 6.5, 6.6
Matra Marconi Space/Satcomms **2.8.2, 4.4.4,** 6.8
Matsushita/MCA [1992] 4 C.M.L.R. M36 .... 1.7, 5.4.3.8
Medeol/Elosua [1994] 5 C.M.L.R. 150 .... **2.4.2.8**
Mederic/Urrpimmec/CRI/Munich Re 6.5, 6.9
Mediobanca/Generali [1994] 4 C.M.L.R. Ml 2.4.2.7, 2.4.3.4,
                                                     7.2.1, **7.6.3.1, 7.7**
Mercedes-Benz/Kässbohrer [1995] O.J. L211/1; [1995] 4 C.M.L.R. 600 .... **5.4.3.6, 8.1.4**
Merck/Rhône-Poulenc-Merial 6.9
Metallgesellschaft/Feldmühle 3.5.3
Metallgesellschaft/Safic Alcan [1997] 4 C.M.L.R. 19 .... 5.3.3.9
Michelin [1981] O.J. L353/33; [1982] 1 C.M.L.R. 643 .... 5.3.2
Möller, A. P. [1999] 4 C.M.L.R. 392 .... **4.3.12**
Mondi/Frantschach 5.3.3.9

Neste/IVO 7.4.3
Neste/Statoil [1994] 4 C.M.L.R. 532 .... **8.5**
Nestlé/Perrier [1992] O.J. L365/1; [1993] 4 C.M.L.R. M17 .... **4.7.7, 5.1.2,**
            5.3.2, 5.3.3.2, **5.3.3.6, 5.4.3.5, 5.4.3.7,** 5.8.4, **7.4.4, 7.6.3.3, 7.6.5**
Newspaper Publishing 8.4.2.2
Nokia Corporation/SP Tyres U.K. [1995] 4 C.M.L.R. 605 .... 2.6.1, **2.6.2**
Nordic Capital/Mölnlycke Clinical/Kolmi [1998] 4 C.M.L.R. 409 .... 6.3
Nordic Capital/Transpool [1995] 5 C.M.L.R. 237 .... 6.5
Nordic Satellite Distribution [1996] O.J. C63/3; [1996] O.J. L53/20; [1995] 5 C.M.L.R.
     258 .... 5.8.1,
                                   5.8.2, 7.3.2, 7.4.2, 7.4.5, **7.4.6,** 8.5
Nortel/Norwell [1998] 4 C.M.L.R. 652 .... 6.5
Northern Telecom/Matra Communication 3.5.7
Novartis/Maïsadour [1999] 5 C.M.L.R. 291 .... 6.6
Nutricia [1983] O.J. L376/22; [1984] 2 C.M.L.R. 165 .... **6.2**

Omnitel [1995] 4 C.M.L.R. 613; [1999] 5 C.M.L.R. 15 .... 4.3.11, **4.4.4**
Orkla/Volvo [1996] O.J. L66/4; [1995] 5 C.M.L.R. 388 .... **1.11, 5.3.3.8**
Owens Illinois/BTR Packaging [1998] 4 C.M.L.R. 820 .... 7.4.3

Paribas/CDC/Beaufour [1999] 4 C.M.L.R. 182 .... **2.6.2**
Paribas/MTH/MBH 3.3.6
Paribas Belgique/Paribas Nederland 6.5
Paribas/Ecureuil-Vie/ICD [1998] 5 C.M.L.R. 472 .... 5.3
Pasteur Mérieux/Merck [1994] O.J. L309/1; [1993] 5 C.M.L.R. 206 .... **4.3.11**
Pepsico/General Mills 1.7, **2.4.3.6**
Pepsico/KAS [1993] 4 C.M.L.R. 236 .... 5.3.3.5, **5.4.3.4, 5.4.3.7**
Philips/Grundig 2.6.2
Philips/Hewlett Packard [1997] 4 C.M.L.R. 373 .... 6.5
Philips/Hoechst [1994] 4 C.M.L.R. 606 .... 5.3.3.9
Philips/Lucent Technologies [1999] 4 C.M.L.R. 371 .... 6.1, 6.9

Philips/Thomson/SAGEM 2.7.2.1, 4.3.11
Pilkington-Techint/SIV [1994] O.J. L158/24; [1994] 4 C.M.L.R. 405 .... **5.3.3.3, 5.3.3.6,**
                                                                                                                        5.4.3.7
PowerGen/NRG 4.7.1
Preussag/Hapag Lloyd/Touristik Union International [1998] 4 C.M.L.R. 21 .... 8.3.4
Price Waterhouse/Coopers & Lybrand [1999] O.J. L50/27; [1999] 4 C.M.L.R. 665 .... **3.4.1,**
                                                                                                           5.4.3.4, 5.4.3.7, **5.7.5**
Procordia/Erbamont [1993] 5 C.M.L.R. 115 .... 5.3.3.8
Proctor & Gamble/VP Schickedanz II [1994] O.J. L354/32; [1994] 5 C.M.L.R. 146 .... 4.7.6,
                                                    5.3.2, 5.3.3.1, 5.3.3.2, **5.4.3.4, 5.4.3.6,** 7.4.5
Promodes/BRMC 5.3.3
Promodes/Casino [1997] 5 C.M.L.R. 766 .... **8.3.4**
Promodes/S21/Gruppo GS [1998] 4 C.M.L.R. 656 .... **8.3.4**

Quantel International Continuum/Quantel SA [1992] O.J. L235/9; [1993] 5 C.M.L.R.
   497 .... 6.2, 6.5

RTL/Veronica/Endemol [1996] O.J. L134/21; [1996] O.J. L294/14 .... 6.3.2, **7.3.2,** 7.3.2,
                                                                                                     7.4.4, 8.1.4, 8.6.1
RWE/Thyssengas [1997] 4 C.M.L.R. 23 .... 8.3.4
RWE-DEA/Enichem Augusta [1995] 5 C.M.L.R. 261 .... 3.5.14, 6.9
Recticel/Greiner [1997] 4 C.M.L.R. 830 .... 6.3, 6.6
Redland/Lafarge [1998] 4 C.M.L.R. 218 .... **8.3.4**
Renault/Volvo [1991] 4 C.M.L.R. 297 .... 2.3, **2.4.3.8, 5.4.3.5,** 7.2.1
Reuter/BASF [1976] O.J. L254/40; [1976] 2 C.M.L.R. D44 .... **6.2**
Rheinelektra/Cofira/Dekra 4.3.11
Rhône-Poulenc/Cooper 5.3.3, 5.3.3.8
Rhône-Poulenc Rorer/Fisons [1995] 5 C.M.L.R. 389 .... **3.4.2,** 3.5.3
Rhône-Poulenc/SNIA II 5.4.3.4
Rhône-Poulenc/SITA **5.3.3.8**
Rohm and Haas/Morton [1999] 4 C.M.L.R. 1195 .... 1.7, 7.2.2, 7.4.3
Royal & Sun Alliance/Trygg-Hansa 5.3
Royal Bank of Canada/Bank of Montreal **2.3**
Royal Bank of Scotland/Bank of Ireland 7.2.1

SBG/Rentenanstalt 7.2.1
SEHB/VIAG/PE-Bewag [1997] 5 C.M.L.R. 285 .... 8.3.4
Saint Gobain/Wacher-Chemie/NOM [1996] O.J. L247/1; [1997] 4 C.M.L.R. 25 .... 4.3.3,
                                                               5.4.3.6, 5.4.3.9, 5.8.3, 7.3.2, **7.4.4**
Samsung [1998] 4 C.M.L.R. 494 .... **4.3.12**
Sanofi/Synthélabo [1999] 4 C.M.L.R. 1178; [1999] 5 C.M.L.R. 13 .... **4.3.8, 5.3,** 7.3.4
Sanofi/Sterling Drug [1993] 5 C.M.L.R. Ml **3.5.6,** 5.3.3.8
Sanofi/Yves Saint Laurent 2.3
Sappi/DLJMB/UBS/Warren [1995] 4 C.M.L.R. 35 .... 1.7, 6.8
Sara Lee/BP Food Division [1993] 4 C.M.L.R. 402 .... **2.4.3.1, 5.3,** 6.5
Saudi Aramco/MOH [1995] 5 C.M.L.R. 23 .... 6.9
Schweizer Re/M & G [1996] 5 C.M.L.R. 661 .... 5.3
Schweizer Rück/NCM [1998] 5 C.M.L.R. 157 .... 5.3
Schweizer Rück/Elvia [1992] 4 C.M.L.R. 348 .... 1.7, 5.3
Securicor/Datatrack [1995] 4 C.M.L.R. 607 .... **5.4.3.4,** 6.3.2, 6.9
Sedame/Precilec 6.2
Sextant/BGT-VDO [1993] 4 C.M.L.R. 237 .... 5.3.3.9
Shell Chemie/Elf Atochem [1995] 4 C.M.L.R. 314 .... **2.7.2.1**
Shell/Montecatini [1994] O.J. L332/48; [1996] 4 C.M.L.R. 469 .... **5.3.3.8, 5.3.3.9,**
                                                                                          5.4.3.6, 5.8.2, 7.4.7
Shell/Montedison [1996] 4 C.M.L.R. 741 .... 2.5
Shell UK/Gulf Oil (Great Britain) [1998] 4 C.M.L.R. 18 .... 6.7
Sidmar/Klöckner Stahl [1994] 5 C.M.L.R. 25 .... 4.7.1

Siebe/BRT [1999] 4 C.M.L.R. 371 .... 2.3
Siemens/Elektrowatt [1999] O.J. L88/1; [1998] 4 C.M.L.R. 15 .... 7.4.3, 7.5.5
Siemens/Philips 8.3.4
Singapore Airlines/Rolls-Royce [1999] 4 C.M.L.R. 1193 .... 6.8
Skanska/Scancem [1999] O.J. L183/1; [1999] 4 C.M.L.R. 16 .... **2.5**, 4.3.8, 4.6.2, **5.4.3.6, 5.6,**
　　　　　　　　　　　　　　　　　　　　　　　　　　　　7.3.3, 7.4.3, 7.4.5, 8.1.4
Société Générale de Belgique/Générale de Banque 2.4.3.4
Solvay/BASF [1999] 5 C.M.L.R. 22 .... 6.9
Solvay-Laporte/Interox [1992] 5 C.M.L.R. 116 .... 2.4.3.3, 2.5, **3.5.5,** 6.9, 7.2.1
Spar/Dansk Supermarked [1992] 4 C.M.L.R. 343 .... 2.7.2.1, 5.3.3
Steetley/Tarmac [1992] 4 C.M.L.R. 343 .... **3.5.6, 5.3.3.6, 8.3.4**
Sun Alliance/Royal Insurance [1996] 5 C.M.L.R. 136 .... 5.3, **8.4.2.3**
Swiss Bank Corporation/S.G. Warburg [1995] 5 C.M.L.R. 132 .... 6.3.1
Swiss Life/INCA [1995] 5 C.M.L.R. 582 .... 5.3
Swiss Life/Lloyd Continental [1999] 4 C.M.L.R. 1176 .... 3.3.4, 5.3, 6.5
Synthomer/Yule Catto [1993] 5 C.M.L.R. 533 .... 3.5.9

TNT/GD Net [1996] 5 C.M.L.R. 260 .... **2.4.2.8,** 6.9
TPG/Technologistica 4.5.2
Telia/Ericsson [1997] 4 C.M.L.R. 648 .... 6.5
Telia/Sonera/Lithuanian Telecommunications [1998] 5 C.M.L.R. 467 .... **5.5**
Telia/Telenor/Schibsted [1999] 4 C.M.L.R. 216 .... 2.7.1
Telia Sonera/Motorola/UAB Omnitel [1998] 5 C.M.L.R. 467 .... 6.9
Terra Industries/ICI [1998] 4 C.M.L.R. 206 .... 6.9
Tesco/Catteau [1993] C.M.L.R. 402 .... **5.3.3, 6.5**
Tetra Pak/Alfa-Laval [1991] O.J. L290/35; [1992] 4 CMLR M81 .... **5.4.3.4, 5.4.3.6**
Texaco/Chevron [1998] 5 C.M.L.R. 881 .... 6.7, 6.9
Texaco/Norsk Hydro [1995] 4 C.M.L.R. 313 .... **2.2.4.1**
Thomas Cook/LTU/West LB **2.4.3.6,** 3.5.7
Thomson/Pilkington 6.5, 6.6
Thomson/Fritidsresor [1998] 4 C.M.L.R. 414 .... 6.5
Thomson CSF/Deutsche Aerospace [1995] 4 C.M.L.R. 160 .... 5.4.3.7, **6.3.2,** 6.5, 6.9
Toyota Motor Corp/Walter Frey Holding/Toyota France [1993] 5 C.M.L.R. 205 ... 2.7.2.1, 5.3.3
Tractebel/Distrigaz 2.4.2.5
Tractebel/Synatom 2.4.2.5
Tyler/Linde 6.2

UAP/Provincial [1994] 5 C.M.L.R. 504 .... 6.5, 6.7
UAP/Transatlantic/Sun Life [1995] 5 C.M.L.R. 264 .... 5.3
UAP/Vinci 5.3, 6.7
UBS/Mister Minit [1997] 5 C.M.L.R. 147 .... **2.4.3, 3.4.1,** 7.2.1
UAP/Sun Life 5.3
UPM-Kymmene/April [1998] 5 C.M.L.R. 151 .... 4.3.8, 6.3, 6.9
UPM-Kymmene/Finnpap [1997] 4 C.M.L.R. 649 .... 6.9
Unichem/Alliance Sante [1998] 4 C.M.L.R. 211 .... 6.3.1
Union Carbide/Enichem [1995] 4 C.M.L.R. 602 .... 6.9
Unisource/Telefónica [1997] 4 C.M.L.R. 913 .... 7.2.1
Upjohn/Pharmacia [1995] 5 C.M.L.R. 390 .... 5.3.3.8
Usinor/Cockerill [1999] 4 C.M.L.R. 383 .... 7.4.3

VEBA/Degussa [1998] O.J. L20/102; [1998] 4 C.M.L.R. 19 .... 4.3.8
VIAG/Bayernwerk [1994] 5 C.M.L.R. 22 .... 5.3.3
VIAG/Orange UK 6.9
VTC/BPT 4.3.11
Vacuum Interrupters [1997] O.J. L48/32; [1977] 1 C.M.L.R. D67 .... 5.5
Vaessen/Morris [1979] O.J. L19/32 .... 2.2.2
Valinox/Timet 6.9
Varta/Bosch [1991] O.J. L320/26; [1992] 5 C.M.L.R. Ml **5.3.2, 5.3.3.3,**

5.4.3.5, 5.4.3.8, 8.3.4
Vendex/Bijenkorf **8.3.4**
Vesuvius/Wulfrath 2.4.3.6, 5.4.3.4
Volkswagen/VAG (UK) [1993] 4 C.M.L.R. 402 .... **2.4.3.5**, 6.5
Volvo/Atlas [1992] 4 C.M.L.R. 345 .... **3.5.6**
Volvo/Lex **3.5.4**
Volvo/VME 2.5
Volvo Aero/ABB/Turbogen [1999] 4 C.M.L.R. 18 .... 6.5

Wacker/Air Products [1998] 5 C.M.L.R. 301 .... 6.6
Waste Management/SAE **5.3.3.8**
Westdeutsche Landesbank/Carlson/Thomas Cook [1999] 4 C.M.L.R. 608 .... **5.6,** 5.7.5, 6.5
William Hill/Cinven/CVC [1999] 4 C.M.L.R. 804 .... 3.5.12, 7.2.2
Winterthur/DBV [1994] 5 C.M.L.R. 24 .... 5.3
Winterthur/Schweizer Rück [1995] 4 C.M.L.R. 605 .... 5.3
WorldCom/MCI [1991] O.J. L116/1; [1999] 5 C.M.L.R. 876 .... **1.8,** 2.3, 7.4.3

Zurich/MMI [1993] 5 C.M.L.R. 14 .... 2.2.3, 5.3
Zurigo/Banco di Napoli **2.7.2.1**

1   Introduction

1.1   COMMUNITY MERGER CONTROL—A REALITY

The Community's regime, established by Council Regulation 4064/89[1] ("the Regulation"), for regulating major cross-border merger activity has been in operation for nine years. In that time the Commission's Merger Task Force, into whose hands the day-to-day operation of the regime is entrusted, has shown itself able to deal with well over one thousand cases within a restricted timetable. In large part the desire of businessmen in a Single/Community market to operate under one clear system of merger regulation at the E.C. level has prevailed over the concerns of Member States' governments to retain (sometimes well-tried) national regimes. Brussels has gained necessary experience and respect. The Commission's procedures and practice have developed, some being incorporated into the formal legislative framework when, in 1998, the Regulation was reviewed. But, as will be seen, Member States, all of whom now have domestic merger controls, have remained reluctant to increase the Commission's remit, save where the case for lessening the regulatory burdens of industry consequential on the operation of overlapping national laws has been compelling. E.C. merger control can, nevertheless, be said to have come of age. Over the last four years there has been a steady and substantial increase in the number of mergers examined each year. In 1998 the Commission received 235 notifications and made 238 "final" decisions.[2]

In this introductory chapter we shall endeavour to explain the historical background, philosophy and essential features of Community merger control. In the chapters which follow, the detail of the Regulation's rules and procedures will be examined, as well as the scope for intervention of national laws and for action under Articles 81 and 82 (ex Articles 85 and 86) E.C.

1.2   BACKGROUND TO E.C. MERGER CONTROL

Unlike the Treaty of Paris, which contains specific merger controls in Article 66, the Treaty of Rome, agreed six years later in 1957, contained no equivalent. That difference is unlikely to have been inadvertent. In 1966, the Commission published a memorandum on concentrations, which considered the prospects of controlling those which affected competition at Community level

---

[1] [1989] O.J. L395/1, corrigendum O.J. L257/14. Last amended by Regulation 1310/97 [1997] O.J. L180/1, corrigendum [1998] O.J. L40/17. See Appendix 1.
[2] Twenty-Eighth Report on Competition, para. 136.

through the use of Articles 81 and 82.[3] At that time the Commission considered Article 81 unsuitable as a means of control[4]: a prohibition, resulting in the nullity of infringing transactions, with a limited exempting power exercisable only on the satisfaction of very specific criteria, was considered inappropriate for concentrations. Article 81 is directed at agreements or concerted practices between undertakings which remain economically independent. Provisions to control concentrations are concerned primarily with lasting changes in market structure—a distinction emphasised in the final text of the Regulation and in its application by the Commission. The 1966 memorandum did not, however, exclude the application of Article 82 to mergers. The Commission had regarded Article 82 as capable of infringement where one undertaking, already enjoying a dominant position in the Community or a substantial part of it, acquired a competitor, even if the ability to make the acquisition was not attributable to, or dependent on, that existing dominance.

1.2.1   Use of Articles 81 and 82

While the Commission's views on the use of Article 81 were to change its approach to the use of Article 82 to regulate concentrations remained fairly consistent, the Article was used on a number of occasions to exercise a significant measure of control, albeit often informal, over Community takeover activity. The European Court of Justice bolstered the Commission's view when, in 1973, in *Continental Can*,[5] it found that the acquisition of a competitor could constitute an abuse of a dominant position falling within Article 82. It confirmed that Article 82 could apply to the acquisition of a competitor by a firm enjoying a dominant position:

> "Abuse may . . . occur if an undertaking in a dominant position strengthens such a position in such a way that the degree of dominance reached substantially fetters competition, *i.e.* that only undertakings remain in the market whose behaviour depends on the dominant one."[6]

The test for intervention under Article 82 is therefore a strict one. The Court suggested that an acquisition has to result in the virtual elimination of competition in that product market before the Article could be infringed.[7] But *Continental Can* provoked the Commission soon after to propose a form of prior

---

[3] Commission's Memorandum on the Problem of Concentration in the Common Market, Brussels 1966.

[4] The Committee of Experts advising the Commission in relation to the 1966 Memorandum had taken a contrary view. Bernini, *Jurisdictional Issues: E.E.C. Merger Regulation, Member State Laws, and Articles 85 and 86* (1990).

[5] Case 6/72, *Europemballage Corporation and Continental Can Co. Inc. v. Commission*: [1973] E.C.R. 215; [1973] C.M.L.R. 199. The Commission had decided that Continental Can, a U.S. manufacturer of metal containers, had infringed Art. 86 by acquiring Thomassen, a Dutch can manufacturer and a potential competitor in the German market. The Court in the event annulled the Commission's decision for inadequate consideration of supply-side substitutability.

[6] *ibid.*, para. 26.

[7] It did, however, comment at para. 29 that "such a narrow precondition as the elimination of all competition need not exist in all cases". The concept of collective dominance developed under Article 82 and the Regulation (see Chapter 5) implies that Article 82, absent the Regulation, could now be a more subtle weapon against increased concentration in oligopolistic markets.

control over concentrations and, significantly, the Commission took the opportunity to consider, albeit informally, a number of mergers under Article 82. It publicised its approach in its Tenth Report on Competition Policy. This achieved the results the Commission was looking for and prudent advisers tended increasingly to assess market concentration levels at Community and national level and, if the magic figure of 40 per cent was breached, to consider carefully at least informal approaches to the Competition Directorate (as DGIV is now known). The latter part of the 1980s saw much greater use of such techniques as consortium bidding and financial leveraging to support a number of hostile acquisitions. The intervention of the Commission in a consortium bid for Irish Distillers showed the way for using the E.C. competition rules as a spoiling tactic.

But it was the Court of Justice which was to be the catalyst for change. The comforting position that Article 81 had no application to mergers was upset in *Philip Morris*.[8] The judgment did nothing, however, to resolve the precise ambit of the application of Article 81 to mergers and acquisitions. Ambiguities in the judgment were fully exploited by the Commission and the resulting uncertainty was used skilfully, particularly by the then Competition Commissioner, Mr Peter Sutherland, to persuade Member States to return to the negotiating table on a new draft of the Regulation first proposed by the Commission in 1973. The process was skilfully completed under his successor, Sir Leon Brittan.

1.3 THE MERGER REGULATION—ADOPTION AND REVIEW

Against this background, on December 21, 1989, after several months of intense negotiations, the Council of Ministers finally adopted Council Regulation 4064/89. The Regulation came into force on September 21, 1990. The Commission is empowered, under a Community instrument designed specifically for the purpose, to assess on competition grounds concentrations with a Community dimension. The fundamental principle, and from industry's view the great advantage of the Regulation, is the "one-stop shop" rule. A single authority, the Commission, examines and assesses mergers having a Community dimension uniformly within a strict and short-timetable and has exclusive Community-wide competence.

But how many and which mergers should be scrutinised by the Commission was controversial. In particular, the levels of the thresholds which help define the scope of the Regulation had engendered much debate among Members States. The turnover thresholds in Article 1(2)(a) (worldwide) and (b) (E.C.-wide) were ultimately agreed at 5,000 million ECU and 250 million ECU respectively. The Commission had pressed for significantly lower levels, but a number of Member States, including the United Kingdom and Germany, had insisted on higher thresholds, particularly to ensure a "trial" period during which the Commission would have time to gain experience in its new role. To secure the compromise the Regulation provided for a review of the thresh-

---

[8] Joined Cases 142 & 156/84, *F 'T and Reynolds v. Commission* [1987] E.C.R 4487; [1988] 4 C.M.L.R. 24.

olds before the end of 1993. The Commission gave notice at the time of the adoption of the Regulation that it would be seeking reductions in the thresholds to 5,000 million and 100 million ECU[9] respectively.

In the event, when 1993 came, no political agreement could be reached and the Commission concluded that it was "premature" to propose a reduction in the thresholds. Many factors, meticulously recorded by the Commission in its (1993) Twenty-Third Report on Competition, pointed in favour of a reduction in thresholds. The only fly in the ointment appeared to be "national competition authorities", among whom there was "considerable hesitancy not only as regards threshold reduction but also as regards any legislative change to the Regulation at the present time". The Commission therefore recommended that further experience should be gained before any formal changes to the Regulation be put on the table. It suggested that the Council should look again at the possibility of thresholds reduction, the referrals procedures (*i.e.* Article 9(3)) and other revisions at the latest by the end of 1996.

When the review process reopened in 1996, a number of Member States remained reluctant to increase what they saw as the Commission's already considerable power over mergers. The Commission's bid to have the threshold figures reduced was again rejected. Member States were, however, prepared to accept certain additional thresholds to deal with mergers which if not examined by the Commission would be subject to multiple filings under Member States' merger control laws. It was also agreed that all full function joint ventures (described below) should be brought within the scope of the Regulation, thus accelerating the procedures applicable to these operations. The opportunity was taken to update the rules for the calculation of turnover for credit and financial institutions. Alterations were also made to Articles 9 and 22 of the Regulation concerning the position of the Member States.

1.4 THE MAIN FEATURES OF THE E.C. REGIME

1.4.1 Compulsory Notification

The Regulation introduces a compulsory system of prior notification for substantial cross-border mergers and acquisitions, or "concentrations" (the term used in the Regulation and which will be used hereafter) with a Community dimension, as defined in Article 1. Companies risk fines and the legal validity of their transaction if they fail to notify.

1.4.2 Concentrations

The Regulation applies not simply to mergers, in the technical sense, but to all concentrations, whether through the acquisition of shares or assets, including situations where an undertaking acquires control (defined as the possibility of exercising decisive influence) on its own, or jointly with other undertakings,

---

[9] With the commencement of the third stage of Monetary Union, the Euro replaced the ECU. References hereafter are therefore to Euros.

over another undertaking, such that they can no longer be considered independent. This influence may derive from substantial minority shareholdings, but may also arise from a number of other factors, individually or in combination, such as management agreements or close commercial links between the undertakings concerned.

With the exception of public bids, and other cases where individual dispensations have been granted by the Commission, the Regulation forbids the implementation of a concentration with a *Community dimension* prior to notification and until it has been declared by the Commission to be compatible with the Common Market.

1.4.3 Community Dimension

Only mergers having a "Community dimension" have to be pre-notified to the Commission. Whether an operation has a Community dimension depends on the worldwide and E.C.-wide turnovers of the parties involved. The 1989 Regulation fixed the levels at 5 billion Euro (combined world-wide turnover) and 250 million Euro (individual E.C.-wide turnover). As already mentioned, when these figures were reviewed in 1997 the Member States rejected any general threshold reduction, but they accepted that the notion of Community dimension should be amended in response to the proliferation of national merger control laws which merging firms faced. Every Member State has its own merger control arrangements which, while in many instances are broadly similar to the E.C. Regulation, have different rules, procedures and appraisal times. While the Commission originally put forward a proposal cast in terms of multiple filings, the new rules give the Commission added jurisdiction where the merger involves firms in at least three Member States. These rules are drawn by reference to levels of turnover in the Member States rather than by reference to the need to file a notification under local rules. This approach should discourage "forum shopping". Under the new rules (Article 1(3)) a merger has to be notified to the Commission if it involves firms doing business in three or more Member States; those firms have a combined annual worldwide turnover of at least 2.5 billion Euro; in at least three Member States the firms have a confirmed business turnover of at least 100 million Euro; and, in each of those three Member States, two of the firms involved each have turnover of at least 25 million Euro.

1.4.4 Joint Ventures

Consistently over the past years joint ventures have made up half of the concentrations notified. But the 1989 Regulation only applied to "concentrative" and not "co-operative" joint ventures. A risk of co-ordination, via the joint venture, of the activities of the parents took the operation outside the Regulation and required it to be assessed under the competition rules in Articles 81 and 82, with different substantive tests, procedures and deadlines. The 1997 changes bring all "full function" joint ventures, whether concentrative or co-operative, under the Regulation. The key definitional issue has shifted to

whether or not the joint venture is "full function", *i.e.* whether it has the
financial resources, staff and assets necessary to operate a business on a lasting   NB
basis. It must be able to perform all the functions of an autonomous economic
entity. The rationale for the change is that full function joint ventures have a
structural impact similar to fully-fledged mergers, regardless of whether or not
the parents remain in the same or related market. The largest such ventures so
far have been in telecommunications and civil aviation markets, but they have
spread into many other areas including traditional manufacturing industries.
Though full-function joint ventures must be notified and will be processed
under the Regulation, any co-operative aspects will be dealt with under Article
81 E.C. but under the procedural regime of the Regulation and not Regulation
17/62.

1.4.5 Assessment of Competitive Effect by Commission

The Regulation gives the Commission exclusive competence to assess concentrations with a Community dimension subject to a few exceptions. Assessment
is, procedurally, a two-stage process, and is concerned predominantly with the
effect of the concentration on effective competition in the Common Market
through the creation or strengthening of dominance. There is no presumption
that a concentration with Community dimension is incompatible with the
Common Market, whatever levels of market share result, or whatever the size
of the undertakings concerned.

The test of compatibility is based firmly on competition criteria: a concentration is incompatible with the Common Market only if it creates or   N ∜
strengthens a dominant position as a result of which effective competition is
significantly impeded. In contrast with earlier versions of the proposal, if a
concentration is found to be incompatible, the Commission is not empowered
to authorise or exempt on the ground that benefits of the concentration out-
weigh the adverse effect on competition in the Community.

Most notifications under the Regulation raise only the issue of whether the
concentration will lead to the creation or strengthening of a single entity dominant in one or more markets. From the outset there was doubt (and dispute)
as to whether the Regulation applied to so-called "collective dominance".
This was resolved in the Court of Justice in its decision in the *Kali und Salz*
case.[10] Within a year the Court of First Instance confirmed in its judgment in
Gencor v. Commission[11] that it was not necessary to establish structural links
between firms before a finding of collective dominance could be made provided that a relationship of economic interdependence could be demonstrated
between them. The general issue of oligopoly is discussed further in Chapter 5.

1.4.6 The Merger Regulation—Supporting Instruments

While the Regulation, as amended, lays down the main substantive provisions
for the new regime of Community merger control, to obtain a working under-

[10] Joined Cases C-68/94 & 30/95 *French Republic v. Commission* [1998] E.C.R 1-1375.
[11] Case T-102/96 [1999] 4 C.M.L.R. 971.

standing of the regime one must read the Regulation in the light of a number of other instruments. Most importantly, Commission Regulation 447/98 of March 1, 1998[12] ("the Implementing Regulation") sets out certain important procedural aspects of the operation of the merger control regime, including the mechanics and content of notifications, the calculation of time limits, and their suspension in certain cases, and provisions for hearings and representation by the parties, and third parties. Changes made in 1998 take account of the amendments made to the principal Regulation as well as experience in operating the earlier Implementing Regulations. An Annex to the Implementing Regulation contains a Form CO,[13] which indicates the information which must be given if a proper notification is to be made to the Commission.

It is also necessary to have regard to a number of Notices issued by the Commission. These give guidance as to its views on key provisions of and concepts used in the Regulation and also on certain procedural matters. While such Notices are strictly speaking of no legal effect in relation to particular cases, they indicate how the Commission has and can be expected to apply the Regulation.[14] They do not bind the Court.[15]

Immediately following the adoption of the Regulation in 1989 the Commission published two Notices, one on the distinction between concentrative and co-operative joint ventures and the other on ancillary restraints. As the legislative text of the Regulation has changed and the Commission's practice has developed so have the Notices. Only one of the original Notices published in 1990 remains and even this is in the process of being revised. This is the Notice[16] providing guidance on the subject of "ancillary restrictions". As will be explained in more detail in Chapter 6, Article 8(2) of the Regulation provides that clearance of a concentration also operates as a clearance of any ancillary restrictions (such as non-competition clauses) which are necessary to allow the concentration to take place.

At the end of 1994 the Commission, with the benefit of four years experience in operating the Regulation, revised Form CO and adopted four new Notices. The first, on the distinction between concentrative and co-operative joint ventures,[17] replaced and elaborated upon the earlier 1990 Notice on the same subject. The second dealt in particular with the concept of acquisition of control.[18] The third dealt with the notion of undertakings concerned[19] and identified the undertakings concerned in different types of concentration. Finally, there came a fourth—the Notice on the calculation of turnover. In 1998 the position changed again. With the introduction of substantial changes to the Regulation and its procedures, the Commission replaced a number of the

---

[12] [1998] O.J. L61/1, replacing Reg. 3384/94 (which had replaced Reg. 2367/90, as amended by Reg. 3666/93).

[13] It has been thought necessary to revise Form CO twice in the light of practical experience. The current Form CO is analysed in Chap. 4.

[14] Reliance on a Notice may be a mitigating factor in the imposition of fines. As to the effect of Notices generally, see Kerse, *EC Antitrust Procedure* (4th ed., 1998) paras 1.03 and 7.35.

[15] This is expressly recognised in at least two of the Notices.

[16] Commission Notice (90/C203/05) regarding restrictions ancillary to concentrations: [1990] O.J. C203/5.

[17] Commission Notice on the distinction between concentrative and co-operative joint ventures: [1994] O.J. C385/1.

[18] Commission Notice on the notion of a concentration: [1994] O.J. C385/5.

[19] Commission Notice on the notion of undertakings concerned: [1994] O.J. C385/12.

existing Notices with new versions, and introduced new Notices. Most importantly an entirely new Notice on Market Definition was also produced, published very shortly before those changes came into force.

The first Notice,[20] published in 1990, had contained guidance from the Commission on the distinction between concentrative and co-operative arrangements. (The Regulation initially drew a critically important distinction between
concentrations and co-operative activity between independent firms, the latter
falling outside the Regulation.) In 1997 the Regulation was extended so that,
in addition to concentrations, it now applies to full function joint ventures (a
term explained and analysed in Chapter 2). The Notice on the distinction
between concentrative and co-operative joint ventures no longer has such relevance and has consequently been replaced by a Notice on the concept of full
function joint ventures.

Two new Notices have replaced the 1994 Notice on the notion of concentration. There is now a Notice on the concept of a concentration[21] and a Notice
on the concept of undertakings concerned.[22] Further, as regards those Notices
dealing with the basic scope of application of the Regulation, a new Notice
on calculation of turnover.[23] Finally, as regards the changes made in 1998,
mention should be made of the Notice concerning alignment of procedures for
processing mergers under the ECSC and E.C. Treaties.[24] By so doing the
Commission has sought *inter alia* to meet the expectations of companies
involved in merger operations covered by both sets of rules.[25]

Before leaving the subject of Commission Notices, it should be noted that
the Competition DG has recently published draft texts of three new Notices.
The first would replace the 1989 Notice on ancillary restraints. The Notice is
updated to reflect the Commission's current practice in the field—it is considered further in Chapter 6. The other two draft Notices deal with the assessment,
acceptance and implementation of commitments (described further in Chapter
7) and the provision of a simplified procedure for certain merger cases (see
Chapter 4).

1.5   OUTLINE OF PROCEDURE

1.5.1   Merger Task Force

The application and enforcement of the competition rules of the Treaty are
principally the responsibility of Directorate-General for Competition of the
Commission ("Competition DG"—formerly known as DGIV). The Regulation, which fills in certain gaps in those rules and which is a logical extension
of Articles 81 and 82, is applied by the Merger Task Force, a separate director-

---

[20] [1990] O.J. C203/10. Commission Notice regarding the concentrative and co-operative operations under
Council Regulation 4064/89 of December 21, 1989.
[21] [1998] O.J. C66/5.
[22] [1998] O.J. C66/14.
[23] [1998] O.J. C66/25.
[24] [1998] O.J. C66/36. And see para. 1.10, below.
[25] Twenty-Seventh Report on Competition Policy (1997), para. 160. The Commission says that it should
be possible for E.C.S.C. companies to familiarise themselves with the E.C.M.R. procedures with a view
to the forthcoming expiry of the E.C.S.C. Treaty. See para. 1.11, below.

ate within the Competition DG. The Merger Task Force is described further in Chapter 4.[26] MTF

1.5.2 Procedural Steps

Details of concentrations must be notified to the Commission according to the requirements of Form CO. Concentrations generally must not be put into effect before such notification and until it has been declared compatible with the Common Market by Commission decision. The validity of any transaction carried out in breach of that embargo rests on the Commission's final decision. The Commission must carry out an initial examination within one month of notification to ascertain whether the merger falls within the scope of the Regulation and if so whether serious doubts are raised as to its compatibility with the Common Market. The one month is extendable to six weeks where after notification the undertakings offer commitments to remove any incompatibility or where a Member State seeks to have the merger referred back to national jurisdiction.[27] If serious doubts remain a further examination (up to four months in length) is set in motion to determine whether the concentration creates or strengthens a dominant position as a result of which competition would be significantly impeded. Where the Commission finds that a concentration significantly impedes competition, it must declare it incompatible with the Common Market. To assist it in the performance of that task the Commission has certain coercive powers of inquiry (discussed below in Chapter 4). Before, however, any decision on the concentration is reached the parties must be told of the case against them and given the opportunity to respond. The Commission may order remedial action to be taken if it considers such action necessary.[28] The Commission has powers to impose fines and penalties to back up its powers of inquiry and powers to take suspensive and remedial action. During the procedure the Commission may be assisted by the competent authorities of the Member States. The procedures under the Regulation must be carried out in close and constant liaison with the competent authorities of the Member States. Decisions of the Commission are subject to judicial review. Appeals go to the Court of First Instance and from there, on points of law, to the Court of Justice.

1.5.3 Contact Number

The special helpline established in 1990 no longer exists, but general inquiries may be addressed to the head of the Merger Task Force on (00322) 295 8681.

---

[26] Except where a distinction is specifically being drawn between the Merger Task Force of DGIV and the Commissioners themselves reference is made to the European Commission to cover both decisions made under the *habilitation* procedure and those reserved for the Commissioners. See para. 4.2, below.

[27] Under the Art. 9 procedure. See para. 8.3, below.

[28] Note that such a decision need not be taken within the four months period within which a decision on compatibility must be taken.

1.6　RECIPROCITY

The emergence of uniform technical, regulatory, and prudential standards applicable throughout the Community, particularly since the Single European Act of 1986 and the impetus generated by the single market programme, has increased its attractiveness as a place to do business, but, at the same time, has given Member States greater bargaining power to secure for European firms non-discriminatory access to third-country markets. As with proposals for E.C. regulation of investment, insurance and banking services,[29] the negotiations leading to the adoption of the Regulation led certain Member States to call for a mechanism to be built into the Regulation enabling the Commission to retaliate against third countries which discriminated against European firms in the application of their own merger and other controls. Others, led by the United Kingdom, strongly resisted the use of the Regulation as a way of discriminating in favour of E.C. companies or of retaliating against third countries who used their regulatory controls to protect their own champions.

Article 24 of the Regulation reflects the final compromise adopted between the opposing factions on this issue. It requires Member States to inform the Commission of any "general difficulties" undertakings encounter in seeking to make acquisitions outside the Community. The Commission is charged with reporting,[30] periodically, on the results of its examination of how Community undertakings are treated in non-Member countries. Where the Commission believes that a particular third country does not treat Community undertakings as it does undertakings established in that third country, the Commission may submit proposals to the Council that the Commission should negotiate with the third country concerned in order to ensure non-discriminatory treatment. Unanimity in the Council is necessary for measures under Article 24. Any action taken must comply with the international obligations of the Community and its Member States.

Article 24 is a defensive mechanism and certainly not a bulwark of "Fortress Europe". The existence of a formal mechanism which may ultimately lead to the opening of negotiations may well offer positive benefits to international companies based in the Community in that it enables them to bring into play the negotiating strength of the Community as a whole if they are treated in a discriminatory fashion, or if there are prospects that they will be so treated. Although the mechanism generated much debate when the Regulation was being negotiated there has been no resort to it as yet.

1.7　TERRITORIAL SCOPE OF REGULATION

The Regulation defines the situation where the Community, as opposed to the Member States, will have jurisdiction over a merger. Article 1 defines a concentration with a Community dimension (described briefly above and dis-

---

[29] See Council Directive 79/267 on direct life insurance ([1990] O.J. L330/50); Council Directive 90/618 on motor insurance services ([1990] O.J. L330/44); and Second Council Directive 89/646 on banking services ([1989] O.J. L386/1).

[30] The reports are to be made to the Council, and may contain recommendations for appropriate remedial action.

cussed further in Chapter 2). Article 21(2) grants the Commission exclusive jurisdiction over them. Quite separate is the question when it will be legitimate for the Community to take jurisdiction over a "foreign" concentration, that is where one or both parties are outside the Community.[31] The Commission has already had to deal with a substantial number of such cases.[32] A variety of situations may arise. For example, there may be a concentration between an undertaking in a Member State and an undertaking in a third state, or there may be a concentration between undertakings in the same or different third states, with or without the presence of branches or subsidiaries in the Community. It is well-known that the assumption of jurisdiction, particularly where it gives rise to the extra-territorial application of law, may create conflicts. This is no less true in relation to merger control.[33]

In a number of cases the Commission has accepted jurisdiction over mergers which have had effects in markets outside, but little, if any, inside, the Community. In these cases the question of jurisdiction has not been contested. The parties have notified voluntarily, perhaps using the short Form CO, and received a clearance decision within a month without having to change their commercial plans. Though they may have had to bear the expense of notification their interests have not been prejudiced. And the Court of First Instance has made clear that notification of an operation and suspension of its implementation does not imply voluntary submission to the Commission's jurisdiction and stop the parties from later challenging the jurisdiction.[34]

In the meantime, the Commission has been developing its viewpoint on large global mergers. The Commission has claimed "competence" over such cases on the basis of "the impact of the operation on conditions of competition in the common market".[35] Where mergers take place on global markets involving large companies active worldwide, the application of the Regulation, as the Commission has acknowledged, may involve extraterritorial elements. This is likely to be the case where companies are based outside the Community and the operation has also taken place outside the Community. The Commission's approach comes close to the so-called "effects doctrine", which when applied vigorously by U.S. authorities has proved to be highly contentious, on occasion triggering retaliatory action from other countries.

An examination of the history of the negotiation of the Regulation shows that, at the same time as the Council Working Group was heavily engaged in the detail of the discussion of the individual articles of the Regulation the Court was seised of the jurisdiction questions relating to Articles 81 and 82 raised by the *Woodpulp* case.[36] For this and other reasons the Working Group

---

[31] The writing on jurisdiction is extensive. For a general introduction see Brownlie, *Principles of Public International Law* (4th ed., 1990), pp. 298–321.

[32] See *e.g. Matsushita/MCA; Kyowa/Saitama Banks; Pepsico/General Mills; Schweizer Rück/Elvia; American Home Products (AHD)/American Cyanamid; Sappi/DLJMB/UBS/Warren; Lear/United Technologies;* and *Rohm and Haas/Morton.*

[33] See *Consolidated Gold Fields Plc v. Minorco SA* 871 F. 2d 252; 890 F. 2d 569 (2nd Cir.). A U.S. court blocked the merger cleared by the U.K. MMC.

[34] Case T-102/96 *Gencor Ltd v. Commission* [1999] 4 C.M.L.R. 971, para. 76.

[35] See Twenty-Seventh Report on Competition Policy (1997), para. 168. See also *Gencor/Lonrho* [1997] O.J. L11/30, paras 14–18A.

[36] Joined Cases 89, 104, 114, 116-117 & 125-129/85 *Ahlström Oy and Others v. Commission* [1988] E.C.R. 5193; [1988] 4 C.M.L.R. 901. The jurisdiction of the Community under the competition rules in Articles 81 and 82 in the Treaty is itself a somewhat controversial one, at least in the sense that it is not settled

was reluctant to enter into the issue. A study of the history of the Regulation shows the deletion from the final text of references to such concepts as effects. Although the issues of jurisdiction, both substantive and enforcement, were raised in the discussions, no Article addresses them expressly. This is not, however, to say that the Regulation leaves the issue totally uncertain.

The definition of a concentration with a Community dimension, and in particular the criterion of turnover within the Community to be applied in the light of the definition in Article 5 (especially Article 5(1) second paragraph), will frequently lead to the result in practice that the Regulation gives jurisdiction over a particular concentration on a sound and substantial territorial basis. In many if not the vast majority of cases the requirement for turnover in the Community will necessitate activity, albeit without establishment, within the Community sufficient to justify the assumption of jurisdiction although that will not necessary involve any threat to the competitive structure of E.C. markets. Even so, it would be wrong to draw the conclusion that Article 1 of the Regulation addresses the issue of jurisdiction in the sense presently under consideration.

It is, however, ultimately for the Court of Justice, in the absence of express rules in the Regulation, to determine the jurisdiction of the Commission under the Regulation as regards "foreign" concentrations. It would be surprising if the approach taken in relation to Articles 81 and 82 in *Dyestuffs* and *Woodpulp* were not followed. The Regulation is consistent with the territorial approach adopted by the Court in those cases. This is evidenced by the final clause of Recital 11 which provides:

> "whereas that is also the case where the concentrations are effected by undertakings which do not have their principal fields of activity in the Community but which have substantial operations there".

The Court of First Instance, in *Gencor*, rejected the argument that the term "substantial operations" (or Article 24, discussed above) required the location of production facilities within the Community. The Court said:

> "Far from supporting the applicant's view, that criterion [*i.e.* the reference in *Woodpulp* to the implementation of an agreement] for assessing the link between an agreement and Community territory in fact precludes it. According to *Woodpulp*, the criterion as to the implementation of an agreement is satisfied by mere sale within the Community, irrespective of the location of the sources of supply and the production plant. It is not disputed that Gencor and Lonrho carried out sales in the Community before the concentration and would have continued to do so thereafter".[37]

and there are differences of view as to its extent. The matter has been before the Court of Justice on at least two occasions, in the *Dyestuffs* (Joined Cases 48, 49 & 51-69 *ICI and others v. Commission* [1972] E.C.R. 619; [1972] C.M.L.R. 557) and *Woodpulp* cases. In both instances the Court has, contrary to the views of its Advocates General, chosen not to adopt the so-called effects doctrine but to insist upon some territorial link as the basis for jurisdiction. Admittedly in its application of the concept of territoriality the Court has taken some apparently novel steps.

[37] *Gencor* (above), para. 87.

It is noteworthy that in assessing the position under Community law the Court of First Instance did not adopt any notion such as "the impact of the operation on conditions of competition in the common market", as had been used by the Commission. Nor did the Court openly apply the "effects" doctrine. However, in dealing with the question of the compatibility of the Commission's decision in *Gencor/Lonrho* with international law, the Court adopted a test reminiscent of the limitations adopted by U.S. law in relation to the doctrine of effects.[38] The Court said: "Application of the Regulation is justified under public international law when it is foreseeable that a proposed concentration will have an immediate and substantial effect in the Community".[39] The Court offered no authority or discussion as to the history or legitimacy of such a rule in international law, customary or otherwise.[40]

In order to determine if the Commission has jurisdiction it may, it is submitted, be necessary, to the extent that the application of the criterion of turnover in the Community does not already do so in a particular case, to examine what activities are carried out by the undertakings concerned in the Community. A wider notion of "undertaking" may be relevant here. The rules relating to the calculation of aggregate turnover in Article 5(4) appear to exclude[41] the wider definition of undertaking (that is of independent economic entity irrespective of legal form) adopted by the Court of Justice in such cases as *Dyestuffs* when it comes to determining what are the undertakings concerned for the purposes of the Regulation.[42] But the fact that the Regulation adopts a particular definition for one purpose would not exclude the possibility of applying the wider definition for the jurisdictional purposes of the Regulation discussed in these paragraphs.

Finally, a word should be said about enforcement jurisdiction. As is the case for Regulation 17 and the other implementing regulations under Article 83 E.C., neither the Regulation nor the Implementing Regulation deals with the matter. The Regulation does, however, appear to recognise the principle that one state should not take enforcement action in respect of the territory of another.[43] In relation to the enforcement of Articles 81 and 82 the Court of Justice itself has not always paid the closest regard to this principle and it seems not to be the practice of the Commission to respect it. Two decisions, it is said, have put the question whether the Commission asserts extraterritorial enforcement jurisdiction under the Regulation beyond doubt.[44] In *Gencor/Lonrho* the Commission would apparently have prohibited the merger of the South African platinum interests of a British company and a South African company because it would have created collective dominance in the platinum and rhodium markets. Secondly, the Commission did not hesitate to exercise jurisdiction over the *Boeing/McDonnell Douglas* merger. Clearance was made conditional on Boeing abandoning for at least 10 years certain long-term

---

[38] See the Opinion of A.G. Darmon in *Woodpulp* (above), paras 40 and 54.

[39] *Gencor* (above), para. 90.

[40] Indeed, in this context it is interesting to note the conclusions of A.G. Darmon in *Woodpulp* above. At para. 57 of his Opinion he said: "there is no rule of international law which is *capable of being relied upon against* the criterion of the direct, substantial and foreseeable effect". Emphasis added.

[41] See para. 3.5.2, below.

[42] See para. 3.5, below.

[43] Arts. 9(8) and 22(5) of the Regulation.

[44] Griffin, *Extraterritoriality in US and EC Antitrust Enforcement* (1999) 67 Antitrust Law Journal 157 at 178.

exclusive supply contracts. The exercise of enforcement jurisdiction extraterritorially may be particularly problematic, both potentially and practically. In practice disputes with other countries involved may be avoided by consultation and co-operation, whether in the context of traditional comity or under the auspices of a specific co-operation agreement.

1.8   E.C.–U.S. CO-OPERATION AGREEMENT

In September 1991 the Commission purported to conclude an Agreement with the U.S. Government for co-operation and co-ordination of their respective competition laws, defined to include merger control under the Regulation. The Agreement's legality was challenged by the French.[45] The Court of Justice held that while the Agreement was binding as a matter of international law (under the Vienna Convention) the Commission did not have the power to bind the Community as a matter of (internal) E.C. law. The Council has now in effect ratified the Commission's action by its decision of April 10, 1995.[46]

Under the Agreement there are five principal obligations on the parties (in the case of the Community to be performed by the Commission):

(i)   to notify the other where its enforcement activities may affect the activities of the other (Article 2);

(ii)   to exchange information (Article 3);

(iii)   to render assistance (Article 4);

(iv)   to co-operate in the enforcement of the other's competition laws (so-called "positive comity") (Article 5); and

(v)   to have regard to the important interests of the other (traditional comity) (Article 6).

Confidentiality of information rules must be respected (Article 7). In several respects the Agreement formalised what was the practice between the respective competition authorities in the U.S. and the E.C. although the "positive comity" obligation is a substantial development in the arrangements for co-operation and co-ordination. The Agreement was strengthened in 1998 by the conclusion of a further Agreement on the operation of the positive comity principle. That Agreement does not apply to mergers because of the mandatory and time-limited obligations placed on the Commission under the Regulation.

As regards mergers, the 1991 Agreement expressly provides, in relation to the co-operation obligation, that notifications would ordinarily be appropriate in relation to "a merger or acquisition in which one or more of the parties to the transaction, or a company controlling one or more of the parties to the transaction, is a company incorporated or organised under the laws of the other

---

[45] Case C-327/91 *French Republic v. Commission* [1994] E.C.R. I-3641; [1994] 5 C.M.L.R. 517.
[46] [1995] O.J. L95/45.

party or one of its States or Member States''.[47] As to when notification should be made, Article 2(3)(b) of the Agreement provides that where the Commission is seised under the Regulation notification shall be made:

(i) when notice of the transaction is published in the O.J. pursuant to Article 4(3) of the Regulation;

(ii) when the Commission decides to initiate proceedings pursuant to Article 6(1)(c) (*i.e.* when it moves to a second stage investigation); and

(iii) in advance of the adoption of a final decision in the case.

In the last instance the Agreement provides that notification shall be far enough in advance to enable the other party's views to be taken into account.

In practice the majority of notifications made between the U.S. and E.C. authorities under the Agreement have been merger cases. Some of them have been of high profile, such as *Boeing/McDonnell Douglas, BT/MCI, Guinness/Grand Metropolitan* and *WorldCom/MCI*. In addition to traditional comity, co-operation has involved discussions between case handlers on the relevant product and geographical markets, the potential anti-competitive effects of the operation, ascertaining law and fact in the other jurisdiction, and, not least, avoiding conflicting remedies. The last was of particular concern in *Boeing/McDonnell Douglas*.[48] In several cases the U.S. authorities have been able to participate, as observers, in the Commission's hearings. However, as already mentioned, confidentiality rules must be respected and unless the parties waive their rights[49] such rules may curtail the transfer of sensitive information under the Agreement. In practice parties have been willing to facilitate discussions on the proposed remedies. This was particularly important in *WorldCom/MCI*, where the Commission had to tailor the divestment remedy to meet the different practice and procedure of the U.S DOJ.[50]

The Community has recently concluded a co-operation Agreement with

---

[47] The use of the place of incorporation as the relevant connecting factor (as opposed *e.g.*, to some behavioural or structural impact on the territory of the other party) has been explained on pragmatic grounds. There was no better or more easily applied criterion and the place of incorporation test would catch most cases in which the other party was likely to be interested. See Griffin, *EC/US Antitrust Co-operation Agreement: Impact on Transnational Business* (1993) 24 Law and Policy in International Business 1051 at 1057.

[48] The Commission described the *Boeing* case as "particularly sensitive because of the important interests involved, both in civil and military terms and because of its economic repercussions on competition". See Twenty-Seventh Report on Competition, paras 169–171. There were numerous contacts and consultations, between the U.S. and E.C. authorities within the framework of the bilateral agreement. The merger was cleared in the U.S. and the U.S. Government informed the Commission of its concerns that if the Commission prohibited the merger U.S. defence interests would be undermined. The Commission cleared the merger subject to certain commitments by Boeing concerning the cessation of exclusive supply deals. The Commission has said that it took the U.S. Government's concerns into consideration "to the extent consistent with EC law' and limited the scope of its action to the civil side of the operation. One commentator has said that the case demonstrates the limits of co-operation under the Agreement. For successful co-operation to take place the parties must stay within the boundaries of antitrust analysis and rules. Issues of trade policy should not be allowed to become entwined with the competition issues. See Griffin, *Extraterritoriality in US and EC Antitrust Enforcement* [1999] 67 Antitrust Law Journal 159 at 186.

[49] As was done to enable the settlement in the *Microsoft* case (an Art. 81/82 case).

[50] See *e.g.*, *WorldCom/MCI* [1999] O.J. L116/1.

Canada.[51] As in the case of the E.C.–U.S. Agreement the Canadian Agreement
is intended to build on and strengthen existing co-operation. The terms of the
Agreement are similar to those of the first E.C.–U.S. Agreement, providing
for reciprocal notification of cases under investigation and for exchange of
non-confidential information. It also provides for both traditional and positive
comity.

1.9   RELATIONSHIP OF THE REGULATION WITH ARTICLES 81 AND 82

1.9.1   The One-Stop Shop

As already mentioned, one of the main objectives in the negotiation of the
Regulation was to create the so called "one-stop shop". This meant that so
far as practicable concentrations with a Community dimension should be dealt
with exclusively by the Commission and that others should remain with the
Member States; the relationship between Community law and national law
should be clear.[52] That remained an important consideration in the negotiation
of the changes made in 1997, in particular the Commission's response to
development of national merger controls leading to multiple notifications in a
substantial number of cases. However, an equally important facet of the notion
of the "one stop shop" has been the position under Community law itself.
Anyone shopping in the Community should know precisely which Community
shop to enter. Concentrations with a Community dimension should therefore
be dealt with exclusively under the Regulation and not be liable to challenge
under Articles 81 and 82.

1.9.2   Disapplication of Regulation 17

The Regulation does not purport to apply or disapply Articles 81 and 82,
except in so far as the test of compatibility for full function joint ventures
incorporates the criteria of Article 81 in so far as the joint venture has co-
ordination effects. It hardly needs saying that since those provisions are Treaty
Articles they cannot be applied or disapplied without express authority in the
Treaty (such as Article 36 confers in relation to agriculture) or Treaty amendment. Moreover Articles 81 and 82 are directly applicable and the Court has
held that they create direct rights which can be asserted in the national courts
and which the national courts are bound to uphold.[53] Set against the objective
that there be a "one stop shop" (or, in the words of Recital 7, the Regulation
should be "the only instrument applicable to . . . concentrations") the Regulation provides the best solution available procedurally to deal with the interac-
tion of the new scheme of control provided by the Regulation and the existing
rules in Articles 81 and 82.

---

[51] The text of the Agreement and supporting documents is now published: [1999] O.J. L175/49.
[52] Discussed in Chap. 7.
[53] Case 127/73 *BRT v. SABAM* [1974] E.C.R. 313; [1974] 2 C.M.L.R. 238, para. 16.

The Regulation is made under both Articles 87 and 235 of the Treaty (now Articles 83 and 308 respectively) . As, however, Recital 8 indicates, it is based "principally" on Article 308, and only to the extent that the Regulation gov- erns situations which may be within the scope of Articles 81 and 82 is reliance placed on what is now Article 83. The Court of Justice has recognised that the Regulation is more extensive than Articles 81 and 82 on its application to concentrations likely to produce a detrimental effect on competition.[54] It is Article 308 which provides the basis for both the substantive rules governing, for example, the scope of application and the assessment criteria, and the procedural rules of the new regime, including notification, investigation, and enforcement. With the establishment of the new regime under Article 308, Article 83 enables the Council to disapply the existing implementing Regula- tions made earlier under that Article. The power to disapply is exercised in Article 22(2) of the Regulation, which provides that Regulation 17, and the other implementing Regulations in respect of particular sectors, "shall not apply to concentrations as defined in Article 3". As explained below, this has a number of legal consequences in relation to proceedings before national courts and action by national authorities and the Commission.[55]

1.9.3 National Courts

Although Articles 81 and 82 remain directly applicable, the effect of disapply- ing Regulation 17 is to suspend the rule in Article 81(2) (providing for the automatic nullity of agreements contrary to Article 81(1)) and to preclude national courts from holding that a concentration within the meaning of Article 3 of the Regulation is incompatible with Article 81(1). This appears to be the consequence of the Court of Justice's judgments in *Bosch*,[56] *Brasserie de Haecht*,[57] and the *Air Tariffs* cases.[58] The position is different for Article 82. In *Ahmed Saeed*[59] the Court held that Article 82 was fully applicable to the air transport sector even in the absence of implementing Regulations. The sole justification, the Court said, for denying full effect to Article 81 pending such Regulations was the possibility that an exemption might be granted by national

---

[54] Joined Cases C-68/94 & C-30/95 *French Republic and Others v. Commission* [1998] E.C.R I-1375, para. 170.
[55] Other views may, however, be taken as to the respective purposes of Arts 83 and 308. In the *Dan Air* case, *R. v. Secretary of State for Trade and Industry and another, ex p. Airlines of Britain Holdings PLC and others*, *The Times*, December 10, 1992, the English Court of Appeal (*per* Lord Justice Neill) took a more expansive view of the effect of Article 83: "It seems to me to be quite clear that Regulation 4064 has been adopted as an 'appropriate regulation' to give effect to the principles set out in Article 86 . . . the effect of the Regulation is to require the Commission to deal with all questions arising under Articles 85 and 86 and to leave it to the national courts to apply their own domestic competition legislation to concentrations within their purview". The issue in point was the applicability of Art. 84 (discussed below). But experience in relation to the conclusion of the E.C.–U.S. Co-operation Agreement (described above) supports the authors' view on the legal significance of Art. 308 of the Treaty. The addition of that Article to the legal base of the Decision of the Council and the Commission adopting the Agreement was considered necessary by the Council and, on reflection, the Commission. See 1 Competition Policy Newsletter 4 at 54.
[56] Case 13/61 [1962] E.C.R. 45; [1962] C.M.L.R. 1.
[57] Case 48/72 [1973] E.C.R. 77; [1973] C.M.L.R. 287.
[58] Cases 209-213/84 [1986] E.C.R. 1425; [1986] 3 C.M.L.R. 173 (also known as *Nouvelles Frontières*).
[59] Case 66/86 [1989] E.C.R. 803; [1990] 4 C.M.L.R. 102.

authorities or the Commission under the transitional rules in Articles 84 and
85 respectively. Since Article 82 contains no provisions for exemption there
is no similar possibility. There is, therefore, nothing to prevent a national court
applying the prohibition in Article 82. The situation is less straightforward
where Article 81 is concerned.[60]

Whilst in theory a challenge before a national court to stop a bid, or other
concentration, on the basis of Article 82 is possible, in practice it is unlikely
to be successful or effective. Where the concentration has a Community
dimension, the Regulation will apply, and, given the relationship between the
assessment criteria in Article 2 of the Regulation and Article 82, it is not only,
in any factual situation, most unlikely, but also, it is submitted, legally unten-
able for the Commission to find that a concentration which contravenes Article
82 is compatible with Article 2. A national court should stay any application
under Article 82 and pay appropriate regard to the findings of the Commission
under the Regulation.[61] The effect of Article 7, providing for the suspension
of concentrations, may in some cases render it unnecessary for a national court
to have to intervene to grant interlocutory relief. Moreover there is, in any
event, considerable doubt whether national courts will grant interim injunctions to restrain alleged breaches of Article 82 in such circumstances.[62] Where
a concentration falls within the Regulation and has been duly notified a
national court is likely to regard an application on the basis of Article 82 as
frivolous, though it should, of course, entertain applications in aid of the provision in Article 7 suspending the implementation of concentrations with Community dimension.[63] The Regulation does not, however, preclude the application of Articles 81 and 82 to conduct of the merged enterprise after completion
of the merger operation.

1.9.4 Articles 84 and 85

As regards the authorities of Member States[64] the key question is whether the
effect of Article 22 of the Regulation is to revive their capacity under Article
84 (ex 88) of the Treaty to apply the competition rules in Articles 81 and 82.
As long as Regulation 17 could apply to concentrations, national authorities
could apply those rules only as long as the Commission had not initiated a

---

[60] See n. 8 and discussion at para. 1.2, above.
[61] See Laddie J. in *Iberian UK Ltd v. BPB Industries plc and Another* [1996] 2 C.M.L.R. 601.
[62] In the GEC/Siemens bid for Plessey, the High Court, though initially granting *ex parte* an injunction to
Plessey, later, when it had heard both sides, refused to grant interim injunctions to restrain GEC/Siemens
making an offer for Plessey's shares (judgment of Morritt J. December 1989, unreported). The High
Court, in looking at the balance of convenience, had regard to the fact that an interim injunction would
have the effect, especially in the light of the timetable under the City Code, of preventing the bid
completely. Whereas if the *ex parte* injunctions were lifted, the joint bid, even if successful, was expressly
conditional upon the Commission not raising objection to the proposals for restructuring the former
Plessey business, and had been notified to the Commission under Reg. 17.
[63] Case 106/77 *Amministrazione delle Finanze dello Stato v. Simmenthal* [1978] E.C.R. 629; [1978] 3
C.M.L.R. 263, paras 21 and 24.
[64] The phrase "authorities of Member States" excludes the ordinary courts: Case 127/73 *BRT v. SABAM*
[1974] E.C.R. 51; [1974] 2 C.M.L.R. 238.

procedure, and could not, in any event, grant exemptions under Article 81(3).[65]

As regards concentrations within the scope of the Regulation (*i.e.* those with a Community dimension or referred to the Commission under Article 22(3)), the Regulation itself provides an adequate procedural framework within which the Commission can act. Moreover any complainant or other third party can take part in the Commission's procedure under the Regulation. Both the Member States and the Commission have acknowledged that the Regulation should be the exclusive means of Community control (see the joint statement by the Council and Commission).[66] The English Court of Appeal has accepted the argument that the Regulation creates a seamless system for dealing with concentrations within the Community.[67] Concentrations with a Community dimension are handled by the Commission unless and to the extent remitted (under Article 9) to a Member State. A concentration which falls short of having a Community dimension is dealt with by a Member State applying its own national competition law, though a Member State is able to refer the matter to the Commission under Article 22(3). Action under Articles 84 and 85 may in practice be discounted.

As regards cases without a Community dimension there remains the possibility for the Commission and the authorities in Member States to enforce the competition rules. The Commission has expressly reserved its position under Article 85 but indicated that "it does not intend to take action in respect of concentrations with a worldwide turnover of less than ECU 2,000 million or below a minimum Community turnover level of ECU 100 million on the grounds that below such levels a concentration would not normally significantly affect trade between Member States".[68] The Member States have (with very few exceptions[69]) not shown any great enthusiasm to act under Article 84. But if they were to take action against a merger Member States would more likely use domestic powers[70] or instigate the procedures under paragraphs 3 to 6 of Article 22.[71] It remains possible, however, for a complainant to try to trigger action by a Member State or by the Commission under Articles 84 and 85 of the Treaty and the involvement of national courts at the instigation of a beleaguered target company cannot be ruled out entirely.

---

[65] This is the effect of Art. 9(1) and (3) of Reg. 17.

[66] ad Art. 22

"(b) Joint statement by the Council and the Commission

> The Council and the Commission note that the Treaty establishing the European Economic Community contains no provisions making specific reference to the prior control of concentrations.
> Acting on a proposal from the Commission, the Council has therefore decided, in accordance with Article 235 of the Treaty, to set up a new mechanism for the control of concentrations.
> The Council and the Commission consider, for pressing reasons of legal security, that this new Regulation shall apply solely and exclusively to concentrations as defined in Article 3."

[67] See the *Dan Air* case, described in n. 55, above.

[68] Minute Statement by the Commission ad Art. 22. See App. 7 of the first edition.

[69] The U.K. authorities took powers to act in the *BA/American Airlines* alliance.

[70] Even though action by Member States' authorities under Art. 84 has recently been encouraged by the Commission's Notice on co-operation between national competition authorities and the Commission: [1997] O.J. C313/1.

[71] See para. 8.6, below.

1.10 RELATIONSHIP WITH ECSC TREATY

The Regulation is made under the provisions, principally Article 308 (ex Article 235), of the E.C. Treaty and, in accordance with Article 305 of the Treaty, has no effect on the provisions of the ECSC Treaty governing the Common Market in coal and steel. The ECSC Treaty is, however, due to expire in the year 2002, and considerable discussion has already taken place as to the future. The E.C. Commission has expressed a preference for an alignment of administrative practices, to the maximum extent possible, between the E.C. and ECSC Treaties so that by 2003 any special regulation still considered necessary for coal and steel can be effected under the E.C. Treaty, with the minimum of Treaty amendment.[72] Already the Merger Task Force has been seeking to bring the approach taken under Articles 65 and 66 into line with that under the Regulation. Commission officials dealing with ECSC concentrations have been brought within the Merger Task Force.

In 1998 the Commission published a Notice "concerning alignment of procedures for processing mergers under the ECSC and EC Treaties".[73] Certain procedural changes have been made to the handling of mergers under the ECSC Treaty, providing in particular for the publication in the Official Journal of the fact of notification of the merger to the Commission, for the issuance of a statement of objections where the Commission plans to subject the authorisation of the merger to conditions or to prohibit it, for access to the file and the possibility of an oral hearing, and for publication in the Official Journal of final decisions. Provided the parties use Form CO (and provide five copies) the Commission will abide by time limits broadly similar (though not identical) to those under the Merger Regulation.

1.11 EEA

The Agreement on the European Economic Area (EEA) entered into force on January 1, 1994. Made between the Community, its Member States and certain EFTA States it provides for the free movement, among Contracting Parties, of goods, persons, services and capital (*i.e.* the four freedoms which are the cornerstones of the Common Market). It also provides common rules on competition and state aids as well as for co-operation in fields such as research and development and social policy. With their accession to the Community, Austria, Finland and Sweden moved, on January 1, 1995, from the EFTA side of the EEA Agreement to that of the Community.[74] The EEA, therefore, presently comprises, on the Community side, the fifteen Member States and for EFTA States, Norway, Iceland and Liechtenstein ("EFTA/EEA" States).

Competition rules were from the outset recognised as an essential ingredient

---

[72] See, in particular the Commission's communication to the Council and European Parliament, *Future of the ECSC Treaty:* SEC (91) 407 final.

[73] [1998] O.J. C66/36.

[74] Somewhat unique transitional arrangements were made by a Transitional Arrangement Agreement: for history and detail see Tichy and Dedichen, *Securing a smooth shift between the two EEA pillars: prolonged existence of EFTA institutions with respect to former EFTA States after their accession to the European Union* (1995) 32 C.M.L. Rev. 131.

of any package creating a homogenous EEA and it was quickly realised that in the interests of uniformity those rules would have to mirror those in the E.C. Treaty. The principal competition rules of the EEA Agreement are set out in Articles 53 and 54 (restrictive practices and dominant positions, mirroring Articles 81 and 82 E.C. respectively), Article 57 (mergers) and Article 59 (public undertakings). Rules for coal and steel are set out in Protocol 25. The mirror image extends beyond the primary rules to the secondary legislation. With certain necessary adaptations the E.C. secondary legislation on competition (*i.e.* block exemptions and procedural rules) are adopted by the EEA Agreement (see Annex IV to the Agreement). As regards the enforcement of the EEA competition regime the EEA Agreement provides what is generally described as ''a two pillars approach'' which is, at the same time, a ''one stop shop''. Both the Commission and, for the EFTA States, the EFTA Surveillance Authority, have enforcement responsibilities. The EEA Agreement provides rules for the division of cases between them (described below) and for co-ordination and co-operation (described in Chapter 8).

In the case of mergers Article 57 of the EEA Agreement does two things: it provides a substantive rule for the control of mergers and allocates jurisdiction between the Commission and the EFTA Surveillance Authority for the exercise of that control. The substantive rule in Article 57(1) is based on that in Article 2(2) of the Regulation and provides that concentrations which create or strengthen a dominant position as a result of which effective competition would be significantly impeded within the EEA or a substantial part of it, shall be declared incompatible with the EEA. The detail, procedural and substantive, is added by the incorporation with appropriate amendment of the Regulation and the Implementing Regulation.[75]

As regards the division of enforcement responsibilities, Article 57(2) provides that, for cases falling under Article 57(1) (note the Commission's ability to apply the Regulation in other cases is in no way prejudiced by the EEA Agreement),

(a) the Commission will handle cases falling under the Regulation (*i.e.* where the necessary turnover criteria, etc., are met) in accordance with the Regulation but also taking account of the effects on competition in EFTA/EEA countries when assessing such cases (this is the practical effect of the reference in Article 57(2) to Protocols 21 and 24 and Annex XIV);

(b) the EFTA Surveillance Authority will deal with cases not falling within (a) where the relevant (*i.e.* those except ''worldwide turnover'') thresholds are fulfilled in EFTA/EEA countries.

The practical effect of these rules may be that Commission examines a merger in relation to which the main or sole competition concerns relate to an EFTA/EEA country, such as Norway.[76] It is to be noted that Article 57 does not introduce any concept of EEA dimension but keeps separate the Community

[75] The 1997 E.C. changes were taken on board by Decision of the EEA Joint Committee No. 27/98 of March 27, 1998: [1998] O.J. L310/9.
[76] See *e.g.*, *Orkla/Volvo* [1996] O.J. L66/17.

and EFTA dimensions. As has been pointed out this may result in a loss of control by either authority of concentrations which possess neither a Community dimension nor an EFTA dimension but which may still have an EEA dimension.[77]

Where the Commission has jurisdiction it has sole competence. The Member States cannot, as in cases falling under the Regulation *simpliciter*, apply their own domestic competition laws except in very limited circumstances. Nor can the EFTA States apply their own laws.[78] But this position does not apply to mergers caught by Article 57(1) but falling to be dealt with by the EFTA Surveillance Authority. Whilst the "one stop shop" principle applies between the Surveillance Authority and the EFTA/EEA countries, it does not apply to E.C. Member States who remain competent to apply their national laws to such concentrations.

As already mentioned the EEA rules, substantive and procedural, mirror those of the Community. Uniformity in application is supplied by Articles 105 and 106 (the keeping under review of the case law of the European Court of Justice and the EFTA Court, and action in case of difference). This reinforces the practical scheme of co-operation between the Commission and the EFTA Surveillance Authority laid down in Protocol 24. Against this background of the mirror image of the EEA rules on mergers to those of the Regulation this book does not consider them separately although attention will be drawn, where relevant, to points of difference in approach or treatment.

---

[77] Broberg, *The Delimination of Jurisdiction with regard to Concentrative Control* [1995] 1 E.C.L.R. 30.
[78] Except, again, in the very limited (analogous) circumstances. See Art. 6 of Protocol 24.

2 Concentrations

2.1 INTRODUCTION

Mature anti-trust regimes typically employ a combination of controls covering structural changes brought about through mergers and acquisitions, anti-competitive agreements, and abuse of market power. The purpose of the Regulation was to give the Commission, for the first time, a power to examine and, where necessary, prohibit transactions involving lasting changes to the structure of competition in the Common Market and to add to the original controls in Articles 81 and 82 over anti-competitive agreements and abuses of dominant position.

The essential purpose of the Regulation is, therefore, to cover situations where structural change occurs because previously independent undertakings lose their independence through merger (in the legal sense, discussed below) or by coming under common control. The Regulation terms such situations "concentrations" and Article 21(2) gives the Commission exclusive competence, subject to limited exceptions, over concentrations which have a Community dimension. The test of Community dimension is discussed in Chapter 3. This chapter is concerned with the meaning of the term "concentration", and the circumstances in which a concentration will be treated as occurring.

The main change since the last edition has been an important one: the boundary between concentrations (dealt with under the Regulation) and co-operative joint ventures (previously all dealt with under Regulation 17/62) has been moved. In relation to concentrations taking place from March 1, 1998, the fact that a joint venture may have an impact on the competitive behaviour of undertakings which remain independent (usually the shareholders in the joint venture) no longer rules out a notification under the Regulation and a decision according to the procedures and timetable laid down under it. The change is discussed in more detail below.[1]

2.2 THE MEANING OF "CONCENTRATION"

2.2.1 The Definition in Article 3(1)

Recital 23 of the Regulation describes concentrations as operations "bringing about a lasting change in the structure of the undertakings concerned". Article

---

[1] Para. 2.7.

3(1) defines more precisely the nature of the changes which will bring about a concentration within the meaning of the Regulation, and provides that:

"A concentration shall be deemed to arise where:

(a) two or more previously independent undertakings merge, or
(b) one or more persons already controlling at least one undertaking, or
—one or more undertakings

acquire, whether by purchase of securities or assets, by contract or by any other means, direct or indirect control of the whole or parts of one or more other undertakings."

A concentration may therefore arise either as a result of a merger between independent undertakings or as a result of a change of control. Many concentrations will involve one undertaking acquiring control of another, but the notion of concentration also covers situations where a change in the nature or quality of control occurs, as where one shareholder in a joint venture sells out to another shareholder or to a third party. Concentrations may even occur inadvertently.

The Commission has supplemented the definition in Article 3 with guidance in the form of a notice, explaining how it interprets and applies the concept of "concentration". The original notice,[2] issued in 1994, was replaced by a new notice[3] in 1998, necessitated particularly by the change extending the Regulation to all structural full-function joint ventures, even where they have co-operative elements requiring analysis under Article 81 of the E.C. Treaty. For convenience, this notice is referred to as "the Concentration Notice".

2.2.2 Two or More Undertakings

A concentration will occur only when it takes place between undertakings, that is, normally, commercial profit-making businesses.[4] Acquisition of an undertaking by an individual or group of individuals,[5] or by a legal entity which does not carry on economic activities and so does not constitute an undertaking under Community law, will involve a concentration within the meaning of the Regulation only if the individuals or the entity[6] concerned already control at least one or more other undertakings.[7] Thus, in *Asko/Jacobs/Adia*, Asko, a German holding company, and Mr Jacobs, a private Swiss investor, acquired joint control of Adia, a Swiss company. Jacobs was consid-

[2] [1994] O.J. C385/5.
[3] [1998] O.J. C66/2.
[4] But note that an acquisition of assets *simpliciter* may be sufficient to give one undertaking control over another, and that a group of assets may constitute an undertaking in itself, *e.g.* the sale of a brand, the goodwill and customer lists.
[5] Note, however, that individuals may be "undertakings" for the purposes of Arts. 81 and 82 (*e.g.* a self-employed inventor exploiting his patents by licensing: *Vaessen/Morris* [1979] O.J. L19/32). But for present purposes, as the Regulation implies, the ownership of assets or the act of acquisition in itself does not constitute the individual an undertaking.
[6] Art. 3(1)(b) uses the term "persons".
[7] As noted in Chap. 4 the powers of the Commission to obtain information (but not to investigate) have been extended to individuals, in contrast with the similar powers in Reg. 17.

ered to be an "undertaking concerned" because of the commercial interests he held in other businesses, notably industrial chocolate, sugar confectionery and coffee.[8] The holding of shares by an investment company, is also considered to be an economic activity. The Concentration Notice (at paragraph 8) confirms what may be inferred from Recital 12 to the Regulation, that the term "persons" in Article 3(1)(b) must also be taken to include public bodies, including the state itself[9] and other administrative bodies such as the Treuhand, the organisation which was established to oversee the privatisation of the state industries of the former East Germany.

2.2.3 Acquisition of Part of an Undertaking

It is clear from Article 3(1) that a concentration may occur where one or more undertakings acquire the ability to control not the whole of an undertaking but a part or parts of it. However, the part over which control is acquired must be capable of functioning as an undertaking in its own right. Difficulties may therefore arise in distinguishing a simple purchase of assets from a situation where the assets for sale are sufficient to constitute an undertaking or enterprise (even if not organised as such at the time) and thus where a concentration may result within the meaning of the Regulation. This may be the case, for example, with the sale of particular brands or intellectual property licences, but the Commission considers that the assets in question must be capable of constituting a business to which market turnover can be readily attributed.[10]

References to the acquisition of parts of one or more undertakings in Article 3(1)(b) of the Regulation also covers the situation where undertakings amalgamate certain existing businesses, or parts of existing business, into a new joint venture company. The criteria for determining whether such an arrangement constitutes a concentration within Article 3 is discussed below.

2.2.4 Undertakings Previously Independent

Article 3(1)(a) refers to two or more "previously independent" undertakings. These words seem otiose but appear to have been inserted for the avoidance of doubt, to exclude the situation where undertakings formally merge (in the sense described below) but are in substance already "concentrated" in an economic sense. Such situations are likely to be rare in practice, but such an economic merger between undertakings which remained legally distinct is illustrated in an Article 81 context by *IMI/Heilmann*.[11]

---

[8] See also *Allied Lyons/HWE-Pedro Domecq*, where the acquired company was previously jointly controlled by Allied and Mr Mora Figueroa.

[9] In *Air France/Sabena*, para. 11, the Commission, having concluded that Sabena was to be treated as a joint venture of Air France and the Belgian State commented that "this conclusion cannot be called into question by the fact that the Belgian state, is not an 'undertaking': Art. 3(1)(b) of Regulation 4064/89 provides explicitly that the parties exercising joint control may be 'persons'."

[10] See Concentration Notice, para. 11, and *Zurich/MMI*.

[11] The facts are set out in detail at p. 16 of the first edition: see also the Seventh Report on Competition Policy (1977), points 29 to 32. In *IMI/Heilmann* the Commission rejected a complaint that arrangements between IMI and Heilman, U.K. and Swiss zip manufacturers respectively, infringed Art. 81. The Com-

The requirement of previous independence applies also in relation to an acquisition of control within the meaning of Article 3(1)(b). Since a concentration is limited to changes in control it follows that internal restructuring within a group cannot constitute a concentration within the meaning of the Regulation.[12]

2.2.4.1   Control by the State

The mere fact that two companies are both state-owned does not necessarily mean that they cannot be treated as independent undertakings. This issue is relevant both to questions of competitive overlap and to the calculation of turnover. Recital 12, directed at the latter question, enunciates a principle of non-discrimination between the public and the private sectors, declaring that:

> "in the public sector, calculation of turnover of an undertaking concerned in a concentration needs, therefore, to take account of undertakings making up an economic unit with an independent power of decision, irrespective of the way in which their capital is held or of the rules of administrative supervision applicable to them."

Thus where two public companies were formerly part of different economic units having an independent power of decision the operation will be deemed to constitute a concentration and not merely an internal restructuring.[13]

The principal objective behind Recital 12 is clear, to avoid situations where, in a case involving a major state-owned industrial group such as IRI in Italy, the turnover of all undertakings under state control would have to be brought into the calculation of Community dimension. The underlying principle holds good when competitive overlaps between state-owned undertakings are being assessed. In *Texaco/Norsk Hydro*, for example, the Commission had to consider whether Norsk Hydro, owned as to 51 per cent by the Norwegian State, operated independently of the government. The State also owned 100 per cent of Statoil, a major player on the market on which the notified joint venture was to operate. The Commission accepted that the State did not take part in decisions regarding Norsk Hydro's commercial activities and that there were no formal or informal relationships between Norsk Hydro and Statoil at any level attributable to the fact that the State was the majority shareholder of both. There was thus no co-ordination of their commercial activities through the intervention of their common shareholder and Hydro's market position,

---

mission found that, although there had been no formal merger between the companies, nor acquisition of one by the other, a series of arrangements which grew up over a period of years which created a single management committee and an identity of financial and commercial interests meant that the two companies could no longer be treated as independent economic units for the purposes of Art. 81.

[12] In the light of the judgment of the Court of First Instance in Case T-102/92 *Viho v. Commission* one cannot rule out entirely the possibility that a group which operates in a highly decentralised way may constitute separate economic units capable of being treated as independent undertakings.

[13] See, *e.g.*, *CEA Industrie/France Télécom/Finmeccanica/SGS-Thomson*, where Thomson-CSF, France Telecom and CEA-Industries were considered independent undertakings although all were owned by the French State.

and that of the notified joint venture, was evaluated without regard to Statoil's position.[14]

Difficulty remains, however, in justifying and applying the distinction. The Commission's view is that the necessary independence does not normally exist where the undertakings are within the same holding company[15] and that public companies are part of the same industrial holding when they are subject to a co-ordinated strategy. But the attempt to give effect to Recital 12 of the Regulation can lead to some artificial conclusions. In *Kali und Salz/MdK/Treuhand*, for example, the Commission treated former state enterprises in East Germany as part of one economic unit only where they were supervised by the same administrative division within the Treuhandan.[16]

2.3 MERGER (ARTICLE 3(1)(a))

A concentration is deemed to arise where "two or more previously independent undertakings merge". There is no definition or explanation in the Regulation of what is meant by the term "merge". "Merger" in the Regulation (for example in Article 4(2)) is used merely to refer to the type of concentration falling within Article 3(1)(a). The absence of definition here is in stark contrast to the case of concentration by the acquisition of control, dealt with in Article 3(1)(b), where three paragraphs are spent clarifying the concept. A wide economically-orientated definition of "merger" would render Article 3(1)(b) to (4) largely, if not completely, redundant. It would appear, therefore, that "merger" in Article 3(1)(a) is to be given a narrow meaning, the primary intention being to refer to a merger in the technical sense of "*fusion*". This is the sense in which the term "merger" is used in the Third Directive on Company Law. A merger will occur where all the rights and liabilities of one or more companies are transferred to another company (which may be formed for the purpose). The members of the acquired company or companies receive shares in the acquiring company with or without an additional cash payment. Following the transfer of the assets and liabilities, the acquired company or companies as a general rule cease to exist.[17] An early example is *Kyowa/*

---

[14] See also *Marconi/Finmeccanica* where the Commission held that although the Italian State-holding company IRI owned some 82 per cent of Finmeccanica, it operated as a fully independent company and was to be considered as "an economic unit with an independent power of decision" as described in Recital 12 of the Regulation (point 5 of the decision). IRI's function was limited to that of a holding company on behalf of the Italian State. The same approach was taken in Siemens/Italtel where STET, owned by IRI, was also considered to operate as a fully independent company. In particular in this case the Commission, in assessing the risk of co-ordination arising from the notified operation, had to consider the role of Marconi (jointly owned by GEC and the Italian State-owned company Finmeccanica) as a competitor of Italtel (the notified joint venture between Siemens and STET) in the relevant markets. The Commission took the view that although IRI was the ultimate holding company of both Finmeccanica and STET, there was no link between them: both operated as separate economic units conducting their business independently of each other. See also *Fortis/CGER* where, in concluding that there was no risk of co-ordination of competitive behaviour, the Commission concluded that the "Office Central de Crédit Hypothécaire", although owned by the state, was pending its sale managed by the "Credit Communal" a banking institution which was dependent on the municipalities and provinces.

[15] Point 8, para. 4, of the Concentration Notice.

[16] Directive 78/815: [1978] O.J. L295/36.

[17] See also the definition of "merger" in Directive 90/434 removing tax disincentives on cross-border mergers: [1990] O.J. L225/1.

Saitama Banks where the notified transaction was a merger having the features just described carried out in accordance with the relevant provisions of the Commercial Code of Japan. More recent illustrations are provided by *Royal Bank of Canada/Bank of Montreal, BP/Amoco* and *Newell/Rubbermaid.*[18]

Such mergers are rare animals in some Member States, including the United Kingdom,[19] though merger by legal fusion is somewhat more common in civil law and other jurisdictions (including some common law jurisdictions such as Delaware).[20] *Siebe/BRT* provided an example of a merger through a scheme of arrangement under the Companies Acts. In the Commission's own proposal for a European Company one of the means of formation is the merger (*fusion*) of two companies governed by the laws of different Member States. A narrow approach to the term ''merger'' is reflected in the Commission's implementation and application of the Regulation.[21] In the notification form, Form CO (s. 2, para. 2.1(a)) reference is made to a ''full legal merger''. It is unclear whether ''merger'' covers anything less, such as a partial acquisition of assets or some form of economic concentration. Although a concentration will, of course, usually be effected by legal changes in the ownership of shares or assets of the undertaking over which control is acquired, this is not invariably so and the term ''economic merger'' is often used to describe a concentration which comes about between two undertakings without the establishing of a parent and subsidiary relationship or either undertaking ceasing to exist as a legal entity. These situations will generally fall within Article 3(1)(b) of the Regulation, which provides that acquisition of control by contract or other means can be sufficient to give rise to a concentration within the Regulation.

Nonetheless, the Commission's Concentration Notice states that a merger within the meaning of Article 3(1)(a) may occur where, in the absence of a legal merger, the combining of previously independent undertakings results in the creation of a single economic unit.[22] The existence of a permanent single economic management is a pre-requisite for this, although other factors such as internal profit and loss compensation between the parties and their joint external liability are also relevant. Such an amalgamation may in practice be reinforced by cross-shareholdings. As the Notice points out the critical factor of common economic management will be established contractually. The amalgamation might, for example, take the form of a *Gleichordnungskonzern* in German law, certain *groupements d'interéts economiques* in French law, and certain partnerships.

It must be recognised, however, that the practical effect of the distinction

---

[18] See also *Halliburton/Dresser, BAT/Zurich* and *American Home Products/Monsanto.*

[19] In the U.K. these mergers are effected by means of compromises or schemes of arrangement under ss. 425-427 of the Companies Act 1985. For mergers involving public limited companies (*i.e.* those subject to the Third Directive) those sections take effect subject to the provisions of a new s. 427A and of a new Schedule 15A introduced by the Companies (Mergers and Divisions) Regulations 1987. And see generally Scott and Lewis, ''Schemes of arrangement. Using them in a recommended takeover'' [1992] Jan/Feb. Practical Law for Companies 17.

[20] See *e.g. British Telecom/MCI (II)* and *WorldCom/MCI* [1991] O.J L116/1.

[21] Support for the view that Art. 3(1)(a) is concerned solely with ''legal'' mergers in the narrow sense described above can be seen in the approach of the Commission in its decision in *Renault/Volvo*, but as a possible example of an economic merger, discussed at para. 2.2.3, above—see *IMI/Heilmann*, Report on Competition Policy 1977, points 29–32.

[22] [1998] O.J. C66/5, para. 7.

between mergers within Article 3(1)(a) and other concentrations is minimal.[23] Moreover, in a number of cases, although the operation under review has involved a merger (fusion) between companies, the Commission has found the concentration to fall within Article 3(1)(b).[24]

2.4   ACQUISITION OF CONTROL (ARTICLE 3(1)(b))

2.4.1   Meaning of Control

Article 3(1)(b) provides that a concentration occurs in the case of an acquisition of control. Article 3(3) of the Regulation defines "control":

"For the purposes of this Regulation, control shall be constituted by rights, contracts or any other means which, either separately or in combination and having regard to the considerations of fact or law involved, confer the possibility of exercising decisive influence on an undertaking, in particular by:

(a) ownership or the right to use all or part of the assets of an undertaking;
(b) rights or contracts which confer decisive influence on the composition, voting or decisions of the organs of an undertaking."

It is clear that "control" here means something less than legal control, in the sense of a controlling interest. Indeed, this is to be expected since the Regulation is aimed at transactions which have the effect of creating a concentration between formerly independent entities even if the concentration does not result in them formally becoming parent and subsidiary.

2.4.2   The Exercise of Decisive Influence

The key issue is whether the rights which one undertaking acquires in another are sufficient to confer on it "the *possibility* of exercising *decisive* influence" [emphasis added] over that other. A concentration occurs when that point is reached. A new concentration, requiring notification, will take place whenever there is a change in the nature of control, for example where an undertaking previously subject to the joint control of undertakings A and B comes under A's sole control on its purchasing B's interest in the joint venture. This is discussed further below. But the Regulation recognises only step changes in the nature of control and not situations generally which may reinforce an undertaking's ability to control another. This is understandable since it is difficult to accommodate such situations within a concept of decisive influence: influence is either decisive or it is not. The issue may, however, have important regulatory consequences, as *Gencor/Lonrho* illustrates. Prior to the notified operation, which was prohibited, Gencor already had effectively a 27 per cent

---

[23] But note that a concentration consisting of a merger within Art. 3(1)(a) must be notified jointly (Art. 4(2)). This provision supports the interpretation of "merger" suggested by the authors.
[24] See, *e.g. Sanofi/Yves Saint Laurent*, where the Commission's decision considered the acquisition by Elf of the merger of Sanofi and Yves Saint Laurent, itself "un projet de fusion absorption", and *Eurocom/RSCG*.

shareholding in Lonrho's platinum mining company, LPD. Nonetheless the notifying parties maintained, both in the notification and in the response to the Commission's statement of objections, that LPD was run entirely independently of Gencor. Later, however, when challenging the Commission's decision of incompatibility before the Court of First Instance[25] the parties sought to argue the opposite—but without success.[26] Had the transaction not resulted in a change of control, there would have been no notifiable concentration and no ground for intervention by the Commission.

2.4.2.1   Decisive Influence

The use of the adjective "decisive" in the definition of control is important. This differentiates control in the sense used in the Regulation from lesser degrees of influence. Management, and major shareholders of a company may well find it prudent to consult the company's bankers, or significant minority shareholders, such as an investment trust or pension fund, over major decisions of strategy. This does not give the consultees control within the meaning the Regulation unless, at least, they enjoy some formal veto right relating to commercial strategy. This does not mean, however, that lower degrees of influence can be ignored when assessing the competitive impact of a concentration. For example, in *Media Service Group*[27] (MSG), the Commission took into account Deutsche Telecom's 16.6 per cent shareholding (together with board representation) in SES, the main European satellite operator, when assessing the competitive advantages MSG would enjoy in the markets concerned.

2.4.2.2   The Possibility of Influence

The possibility of exercising decisive influence is sufficient to constitute control within the meaning of the Regulation. An undertaking can be treated as controlling another even if it chooses not to exercise its power to do so, or does not need to. For example, in *McCormick/CPC/Rabobank/Ostmann* voting procedures ensured that the approval of all three shareholders was necessary for decisions regarding the management and commercial policy of a newly-established joint venture, giving each the possibility of exercising decisive influence. Though Rabobank, which had an investment interest only, said it would not participate in major business decisions the Commission commented that "Rabobank's low capital share and the agreement on fixed return cannot rebut the fact that Rabobank has the legal right to exert a decisive influence on the joint venture". The Concentration Notice confirms this. It is not neces-

---

[25] Case T-102/96, judgment of March 25, 1999.
[26] See paras 167 to 194 of the judgment.
[27] Art. 8 decision of November 9, 1994, [1994] O.J L364/1.

sary for the Commission to demonstrate that influence has in fact been exercised.[28]

2.4.2.3 Balance of Power

Situations may exist where a minority shareholder holds sufficient votes to tip the balance between two major shareholders who are unable to agree on policy. This kind of deadlock between major shareholders may give special influence to a small shareholder beyond that which it would normally expect to gain from its shareholding. It is, however, most unlikely that the fact that a small shareholder holds the balance of power in such a way would lead to the conclusion that it had control over the company concerned, even jointly with one of the two major shareholders. Such fluctuating alliances are unlikely to create the kind of enduring relationship which would be necessary to trigger a lasting structural change as contemplated by the Regulation. In fact, such situations indicate that joint control does not exist between any particular group of shareholders.[29] Changing relationships between shareholders, even in the absence of changes in their shares or the voting rates attaching, may trigger the notification obligation. The impact under the Regulation of changing shareholder relationships is seen in *CTC/GE/Bank America*. In November 1997, the European shareholders in CTC pooled their rights with the result that they together acquired joint control over CTC, a cable operator which had won a concession to build and operate a cable network in Catalonia. This led the two U.S. investors in CTC, BankAmerica and General Electric, to respond by entering into a voting agreement, so creating a block of votes sufficient to veto strategic commercial decisions of CTC, and re-establishing joint control with the European shareholders block.[30]

2.4.2.4 The Nature of Control

The Commission has made it clear that, when it makes judgments about control, it is not concerned with rights which have the limited purpose of protecting the financial interests of minority shareholders, for example, in the event of a winding up or major disposal. Rather, the Regulation is concerned with influence over the business strategy of an undertaking. This is nowhere made explicit in the text but it follows from the fact that the Regulation is concerned with lasting changes which affect business activities and competition between undertakings. Only if common control over the commercial strat-

---

[28] See para. 9 of the Notice, and also *Ford/Hertz*, where Ford, though a minority shareholder, had the legal right under a shareholders agreement to secure at any time, forthwith and at no further cost, a majority on the Hertz board. The Commission had no difficulty in finding that this right in itself gave Ford *de facto* sole control of Hertz.

[29] See para. 2.6, below, and generally the Concentration Notice—App. 5.

[30] Note that the Commission suspended the proceedings in *Cable 1 Televisio de Catalunya* by virtue of Art. 4(3) of Commission Regulation 3384/94 on the final day for its stage one decision on the basis that the voting agreement between the U.S. shareholders, which was subsequently notified some days later (*Cableuropa/Spainco/CTC*), constituted a material change of facts in the original notification. The Commission then took simultaneous decisions on the two notifications on January 28, 1998.

egy and activities of two undertakings is achieved on a lasting basis are they to be treated as one economic unit and thus "concentrated" within the meaning of the Regulation. If, therefore, minority protection rights for investors stop short of conferring a veto over business decisions they will be ignored in determining control for the purposes of the Regulation. It is the possibility of control over commercial strategy which counts. If, however, more extensive rights are given to a shareholder the Commission will not disregard them simply because the shareholder is purely a financial investor who would not normally expect or intend to be involved in business decisions.

2.4.2.5   Control by a Public Authority

There is one exception where the Commission is prepared to take into account the purpose for which rights of control are conferred. Prerogatives exercised by a Member State *qua* public authority, and not *qua* shareholder, do not, in the Commission's view, confer control within the meaning of the Regulation since they do not have as their object or effect the exercise of decisive influence on the business activity of the undertaking, but the protection of the public interest. This situation arises not uncommonly in relation to undertakings operating in regulated sectors.[31] The Commission is thus prepared to "look behind" a major state holding, or veto rights conferred, for example, by a "golden" share and decide for what purpose the power is actually held. Nor, if there is no control in a commercial sense, will the surrendering of such rights result in a change of control under the Regulation. This approach may be politically convenient but it seems to put a gloss on the principle of non-discrimination between state and other undertakings enunciated in Recital 12 of the Regulation. Though perhaps justified to some extent by Article 295 of the E.C. Treaty, the approach is somewhat questionable, particularly where there is evidence that such powers are actually exercised to influence business decisions, for example, to ensure that major contracts go to national suppliers, as appeared to be the case, for example, in *Alcatel/Telettra*.

2.4.2.6   Future Rights

A difficult question which has arisen in several cases is the relevance of options and similar rights in determining whether one undertaking has decisive influence over another. On the one hand, Article 3 requires only the possibility of decisive influence for control to exist. On the other, the influence must actually be held at the time the assessment is being made and not merely occur on some future event. It must also be more than a transitory phenomenon. In *Ford/Hertz* the Commission decided that no change in control had taken place as a result of the acquisition by Ford of the 50 per cent of Hertz shares it did

---

[31] See, in the energy sector in Belgium, *Tractebel/Synatom* and *Tractebel/Distrigaz*. Contrast the approach in cases on direct effect where control, *e.g.* through a licensing regime, has been used to justify treating a private sector undertaking as a public authority. See Case C-188/89 *Foster v. British Gas plc* [1990] E.C.R. I-3313, applied in *Griffin v. South West Water Services Ltd* (unreported).

not already own: Ford's unconditional right to obtain at any time a majority on the Hertz board already gave Ford *de facto* sole control over Hertz. The impact of the so-called "shadow effect" of rights exercisable at some future time may, as *Ford/Hertz* demonstrates, be important in assessing the nature of existing relationships. Indeed, the Commission was really concerned in that case with the present impact of rights which Ford already had but had simply chosen not to exercise. But the exact nature of future rights, and the events which trigger their exercise must be considered carefully in each case. It would be wrong to assume that they will always be relevant to consideration of whether a concentration exists. The converse may also be true: present rights may be disregarded if they are temporary, or the beneficiary is liable to be divested of them at the whim of another party. For example, in *Banco Santander/British Telecom* the Commission took the view that the rights which BS retained for only three years combined with the influence BT could exert by threatening to exercise its put option were insufficient to make BS a joint controller with BT. There was no lasting element to the rights BS had, and the Commission's judgment on where control lay was, rightly, it is suggested, proleptic. By contrast, in *Elf Atochem/Rütgers* the Commission did not regard the put option granted to Elf Atochem as affecting in any way the issue of control: it was simply a mechanism to terminate the joint venture.[32] These mechanisms are becoming common in major joint ventures, their purpose being not to change control but to avoid deadlocks as to how the venture should develop and operate.

The Commission's normal practice is to pay little, if any, regard to the hypothetical future exercise of such options but, where appropriate, to treat any exercise of that option as a further transaction which may itself constitute a notifiable concentration.[33] It should be recalled that the purpose of the Regulation is to enable lasting structural changes to be supervised at Community level. It would be inappropriate to apply a concept of control which caught situations where one undertaking lacks any enduring ability to control the commercial behaviour of another.

2.4.2.7 Inadvertent Changes of Control

Sometimes control may be acquired inadvertently as a result of the actions of third parties. For example, in *Avesta II* the disposal by one of the four parties to a joint venture of its minority shareholding of only 7.5 per cent (to be placed with Swedish investors) gave rise to a change in the ownership of the joint venture which constituted a concentration and hence triggered a require-

---

[32] Likewise, in *Ingersoll-Rand/MAN* the agreements between the parties included a call option which would allow IR to buy out MAN's share of the joint venture. Again the Commission took the view that this was in reality a mechanism to terminate the joint venture should the parents so decide, and did not affect the day-to-day joint control arrangements between the parties while the joint venture remained in being. Contrast *GE/ENI/Nuovo Pignone*.

[33] See *British Airways/TAT* where BA was granted an option to purchase the outstanding shares at any time up to April 1, 1997 and TAT was granted an option to require BA to do so on April 1, 1997. The Commission decided that, since it was not certain whether these options would be exercised, the possible second transaction would not be taken into account for the assessment of the operation that was currently taking place.

ment to notify by the remaining three parties under the Regulation.[34] Such a
situation may also occur in the event of a rights issue, where control may
change because one major shareholder takes up its rights, while another does
not, with the result that the balance of shareholding changes sufficiently to
result in a concentration.[35] Such situations will not, however, be common. But
it is safe to assume situations like this have occurred and gone unnotified.
While the Commission would no doubt treat leniently any failure to notify in
accordance with the Regulation, the automatic suspension provided for in Article 7 could pose more intractable problems. This may be a case where Article
4 of the Regulation takes precedence over Article 7. The relationship between
these Articles is discussed at paragraph 4.4.7.

2.4.2.8   *Direct or Indirect Control*

The reference in Article 3(1) to the possibility that control may be acquired
indirectly is of considerable practical importance. The undertaking actually
purchasing shares or assets may itself be controlled by one or more other
undertakings and in certain circumstances they will thereby acquire indirect
control over the target undertaking. This happens, for example, where a consortium launches a bid through a joint bid vehicle or where a company is
established to hold shares (or the voting rights attached) simply as a mechanism to express the common interests of the ultimate owners or exercise their
votes in unison. Thus, in *TNT/GD Net*, five national postal administrations
holding together 50 per cent of an international courier operation in which
TNT held the remaining shares, established GD Net BV as their joint corporate
instrument to balance their commercial interests against those of TNT and to
ensure they were not outvoted on management and strategy issues. In *Medeol/
Elosua*, Medeol acquired indirect control over Elosua through its acquisition
of Bessoll which in turn owned another company which held 20 per cent of
the shares in Elosua. This holding, taken together with a further 37 per cent
already held indirectly by Medeol, gave it sole control. A more recent example
is *Anglo American/Lonrho* where the Commission analysed in detail the relationships between Anglo American and associated companies and attributed
their shareholdings in Lonrho to Anglo American finding that it enjoyed
decisive influence with around 27 per cent of the voting capital of Lonrho.[36]
The Commission also recognises that there may be exceptional situations

---

[34] The case involved a joint venture in the steel sector *Avesta Sheffield* formed in 1992 and cleared under
the Regulation. Avesta was jointly controlled, by virtue of a shareholders' agreement between British
Steel (with 40 per cent of the shares), NCC (25 per cent), Axel Johnson (7.5 per cent) and AGA (7.3
per cent). The agreement provided that major decisions governing the joint venture required the consent
of British Steel, NCC and one of either Axel Johnson or AGA. The notified transaction involved the
disposition by Axel Johnson of its shareholding. The existing shareholders' agreement would continue
to operate following the exit of Axel Johnson, with the result that the agreement of all of British Steel,
NCC and AGA would now be required for major decisions. The Commission considered that AGA's
position in the joint venture was significantly changed by the exit of Axel Johnson, since AGA gained
the ability to exercise a negative veto right.

[35] See *Mediobanca/Generali*. It is a nice question whether there is a concentration where a significant
minority shareholder sells down his holding to several different purchasers leaving another significant
shareholder in a pre-eminent position and capable of exercising decisive influence.

[36] The case is discussed further at para. 2.4.3.4 below.

where the formal holder of a controlling interest differs from the undertaking which has the real power to exercise the rights deriving from that interest.

2.4.3 Means of Control

The means by which control is acquired is largely irrelevant in determining whether a concentration has occurred, provided that control extends to commercial policy. Article 3(1)(b) makes clear that a concentration may occur through the purchase of shares, or assets, or by contract or by any other means. Control may thus be conferred by a combination of legal and other factors. Since the concept of a concentration is also predominantly an economic one, it is not surprising that the Regulation focuses on the substance of the transaction concerned and its likely effect on the behaviour of undertakings, and not its form. Usually, however, control will be achieved through an acquisition of shares, or the key assets of the acquired undertaking, and it will be exceptional for *de facto* control to arise from other circumstances. But economic dependence may result from, for example, long-term supply agreements or credits provided by suppliers or customers and such relationships, coupled with structural links, may confer decisive influence.[37] It will be rare, though, that contractual and similar relationships will, taken alone, confer decisive influence, and there are no examples in cases decided so far under the Regulation. In *UBS/Mister Minit* the Commission held that the Regulation did not apply: although the owner of the Mister Minit franchise owned and leased to franchisees the key equipment necessary for their businesses, it did not thereby control those businesses, which remained independent undertakings. The relevance of franchise arrangements to the issue of control was also raised in *Blokker/Toys'R'Us*.[38] Blokker, the leading toy retailer in the Netherlands, acquired the rights to the Toys'R'Us operation in that Member State in a complex transaction, the core element of which Blokker alleged was a franchise agreement and not a concentration within the Regulation. The Commission, to which the transaction was referred by the Dutch government pursuant to Article 22 of the Regulation, rejected this contention, commenting[39]:

> "The mere fact that a franchise agreement is a part of the operation cannot exclude the whole operation from the application of the Merger Regulation. The decisive question is whether the whole set of agreements concluded between Toys'R'Us and Blokker will give Blokker control of the Toys 'R'Us business which remains on the Dutch market . . . In this operation Blokker takes over all the assets (leases, fixtures and inventory, personnel, use of brand name) which make up the business of Toys'R'Us in the Netherlands. To this business, a turnover can clearly be attributed. The operation leads to a lasting change in the structure of the undertakings con-

---

[37] See the Concentration Notice, para. 9. Normally, however, contractual links will not be so long-lasting as to create the enduring relationship which would be regarded as a concentration within Art. 3 of the Regulation.

[38] Art. 8 decision of July 26, 1997 [1998] O.J. L316/1.

[39] Para. 14.

cerned since the agreements underlying the operation are of a long-lasting nature.''

The Commission also noted that Toys'R'Us had indicated it was ceasing to operate in the Dutch market and could not be viewed as retaining control of its Dutch business. It concluded that Blokker acquired control of parts of the Toys'R'Us undertaking within the meaning of Article 3(1) of the Regulation.

As mentioned above, and as the Concentration Notice indicates, it is likely only to be a significant acquisition of shares or assets which justifies a conclusion that a new concentration has occurred. It will be necessary to examine in each case the voting and other rights which a particular level of shareholding carries with it, and the influence which the shareholding gives according to the constitution and regulations of the company in which it is held. As will be seen when considering the issue of veto powers and joint control, if a special majority of shareholders' votes is required for certain strategic business decisions a minority shareholder whose votes alone confer a blocking minority may well be considered to have decisive influence. But if a special majority is required only for proposals which might affect the position of minority owners the ability to exercise a veto over proposals of that kind will be irrelevant as far as control within the meaning of the Regulation is concerned. For example, a special majority is often required to change a company's articles of association, or to increase its share capital substantially. But these are not issues which usually have any direct effect on commercial strategy.[40]

In analysing whether a concentration occurs by virtue of a combination of reciprocal shareholdings and directorships, and possibly contractual and management links, it must also be remembered that the legal and commercial effect of those ''rights, contracts, or other means' will depend upon the applicable national law. This can give rise to some interesting legal questions. A significant minority shareholder might, by virtue of its holding, acquire more extensive rights in some Member States than in others. For example, under Belgian company law, all the parties to certain kinds of joint venture have equal rights, and rights of veto, even though only one may hold sufficient shares to have what would normally be considered as a legally controlling interest. National legislation may also confer a degree of control upon persons other than the shareholders (for instance to bodies representing the employees). Even in these situations, however, the Commission will apply the concept of control as defined under the Regulation which is related ''only to the means of influence normally enjoyed by the owners of an undertaking''.[41] In *Anglo American/Lonrho*[42] the Commission supported its conclusion on control by pointing out that Anglo American's representative on the Lonrho board was the only non-executive board member with relevant industrial and mining experience and that he could therefore be expected to wield a disproportionate influence, beyond his single vote, on commercial decisions.[43]

---

[40] See para. 2.4.2.4, above. Note, however, para. 27 of the Notice on the notion of a concentration which suggests that a veto right over investments may affect business strategy depending upon the level at which approval is required and the extent to which investment is necessary to a successful business strategy.

[41] Concentration Notice, para. 17.

[42] Art. 8 decision of April 23, 1997 [1998] O.J L149/21.

[43] Para. 38.

2.4.3.1 Shareholding Levels

Sole control most often results from the acquisition by an undertaking of a majority of the capital and voting rights in another undertaking. Where an undertaking holds an absolute majority of the shares of the target undertaking there will generally be no doubt as to where decisive influence lies. If there are no other elements of fact or of law, it matters not whether the acquired shareholding is 50 per cent of the share capital plus one share, as in *Crédit Lyonnais/BFG Bank*, or 100 per cent of the share capital, as in *Sara Lee/BP Food Division*.

2.4.3.2 Qualified Minority Shareholding

Where there is no shareholder with an absolute majority the situation is less predictable. In this situation sole control may be acquired by a "qualified minority shareholder" either on a legal or *de facto* basis. On a legal basis sole control may occur where specific rights are attached to the minority shares or accorded by agreement to the minority shareholder: for example, where preferential shares confer a majority of the voting rights or other rights which enable a minority shareholder to determine the strategic commercial behaviour of the target company, such as power to appoint more than half of the members of the supervisory board or the administrative board or the company's senior management.[44] In *CCIE/GTE* CCIE obtained only 19 per cent of the voting rights in EDIL, but in addition it had a permanent seat on the board and power to appoint the chairman and chief executive officer. The director appointed by CCIE also had a veto over all significant decisions of EDIL. In *La Redoute/ Empire*, a concentration occurred only when La Redoute purchased a further 12 per cent of the issued shares of GUS, increasing its holding from 25 per cent to 38 per cent. As the Commission noted,[45] this level of shareholding meant that La Redoute was obliged to make a full bid for Empire under the rules of the UK Takeover Code—the Code recognising the reality that a 30 per cent shareholding may well confer *de facto* control. In *Anglo American/ Lonrho*, however, the Commission refused to accept that it followed that control within the meaning of the Regulation could not exist at a level of shareholding below 30 per cent.

2.4.3.3 De Facto *Sole Control*

A minority shareholder may also be deemed to have sole control on a *de facto* basis. For instance, where there is a large number of shareholders, and particularly if shares are widely dispersed among the public, a minority share-holder may in fact be able to achieve a lasting majority in the shareholders' meeting. In such a situation it is most unlikely that all the smaller shareholders will be present or represented at the shareholders' meeting. The first case in

[44] See para. 14 of the Concentration Notice.
[45] Para. 3 of the decision.

which these issues were critical was *Arjomari/Wiggins Teape Appleton*. The Commission concluded that a shareholding of 39 per cent held by Arjomari in WTA gave it the ability to exercise decisive influence. It noted that no other shareholders in WTA had more than four per cent of the equity, and only three minority shareholders had as much as three per cent each. The Commission sought evidence of past voting patterns at general meetings, and predicted that a holding of 39 per cent would in practice guarantee Arjomari control of WTA.[46]

2.4.3.4 Levels of Shareholding Conferring Control

The Commission regularly has found sole control to exist on a *de facto* basis at shareholding levels between 35 per cent and 50 per cent. But in several cases it has gone further. In *Société Générale de Belgique/Générale de Banque*, where shares were widely held among small investors and the public, and history showed that shareholders meetings were not well attended, the Commission found that an increase from 20.94 per cent to 25.96 per cent in Société Générale's stake in Générale de Banque gave it sole control. The Commission carried out a projection of attendance at future shareholders' meetings of Générale de Banque, assuming the participation of all shareholders holding more than 0.06 per cent of its capital, and concluded that the increased shareholding held by Société Générale was sufficient to give it enduring *de facto* control.[47] The Commission confirmed this approach in its Article 8 decision of incompatibility in *Anglo American/Lonrho*[48] where it found that Anglo American had sole control of Lonrho with a direct and indirect shareholding of 27.47 per cent which, on an analysis of polls held at Lonrho shareholder meetings in the period 1993 to 1996, showed that such a holding would have accounted for more than 50 per cent of the votes cast.[49] The Commission reinforced its conclusion by reference to three other factors.[50] First, the next largest shareholder to Anglo American in Lonrho, SA Mutual, with only three per cent of voting capital, also had significant shareholdings

[46] Similarly, in *Avesta III* the Commission considered that British Steel would enjoy sole control over ASAB in view of its 49.9 per cent shareholding and taking into account the dispersion of the remaining shareholders in ASAB. In *La Rinascente/Cedis Migliarini* a shareholding of 35.81 per cent by IFIL was held sufficient to give sole control over La Rinascente and in *Alfred C. Toepfer/Champagne Céréales* the Commission assumed that a 36 per cent stake had the same effect given the wide dispersion of small shareholdings. This contrasts with the decision in *Solvay/Laporte* where the Commission held that Solvay's 24.96 per cent shareholding in Laporte was not sufficient to enable Solvay to exercise decisive influence over Laporte, even though the next largest shareholder in Laporte had only six per cent of the equity.
[47] Contrast *Mediobanca/Generali* where the Commission decided that the increase of Mediobanca's stake in Assicurazioni Generali from 5.98 per cent to 12.84 per cent would not enable Mediobanca to exercise, solely or jointly, decisive influence over Generali. Once again, in reaching this conclusion the Commission looked at the traditional levels of shareholder attendance over the preceding five years and found that the percentage of shareholders present and voting varied between 26.4 per cent and 34.4 per cent. It added to these figures the extra 6.84 per cent acquired by Mediobanca to give a presumed attendance of between 33.24 and 41.24 per cent of all shareholders. Accordingly the 12.84 per cent held by Mediobanca would not be enough to guarantee Mediobanca the ability to control Generali in general meetings.
[48] Art. 8 decision dated April 23, 1997 [1998] O.J. L149/21.
[49] The analysis is set out as Annex I to the decision.
[50] The full analysis of the Commission in paras 1 to 45 of its decision is noteworthy.

in Anglo American and subsidiary and associate companies. This commonality of commercial and financial interest meant SA Mutual would vote together with Anglo American. Secondly, Anglo American was the only industrial or mining company with a significant interest in Lonrho and nominated a mining expert to Lonrho's board. Finally the Lonrho directors could be expected to support the Lonrho board, which was controlled by Anglo American. The Commission held that the fact that Anglo American's holding had not reached the 30 per cent threshold at which a bid for all Lonrho's shares would have been obligatory under the United Kingdom Takeover Code was not material since the assessment of control under the Regulation involved a different test. As, however, *Holdercim/Origny-Desvroise* illustrates, the investigation of past voting patterns may show the opposite—that a very significant shareholding may not confer *de facto* control. Although Holdercim held a 42 per cent stake in Origny-Desvroises it had previously failed to achieve a majority at the three most recent annual general meetings and its shareholding gave it power to appoint only a minority of board members.

Although the level of shares, and, more importantly, the attendant voting and other rights, interpreted in the light of the constitution of the undertaking in which the shares are held, is often decisive on the question of control, examples abound where, as a result of special rights or agreements between shareholders and third parties, control is shared with or even ceded to minority parties, and sometimes even to parties without any shareholding at all. Some common situations are discussed below. It is critically important to recognise these situations lest a notified transaction occurs and the need to notify is not recognised.

2.4.3.5 *Management Agreements*

Management agreements often stipulate how business decisions will be taken. In an exceptional case, such as *Volkswagen/VAG*,[51] a shareholder with 100 per cent of the shares in a company may surrender management control to another undertaking which has no shares at all. Less unusually, a management committee may be established to run an undertaking which may include parties who are not shareholders but have expertise to offer in the undertaking's field of activity. Agreements which simply confer day-to-day management responsibility on an undertaking will not, however, confer decisive influence or, rather, will not deprive other undertakings who enjoy veto rights over commercial strategy of a share of decisive influence. It is control over the business policy, rather than day-to-day operation, which is important.

---

[51] In *Volkswagen/VAG* the Commission took the view that Volkswagen, although it did not have any shareholding in VAG, shared joint control of VAG with Lonrho (owner of all the share capital of VAG) through a Co-ordination Committee which took the decisions on major issues of commercial policy. By contrast, in *CCIE/GTE* the Commission took the view that, although the financing provided to EDIL by Siemens to support the buy-out of EDIL and various commercial agreements (concerning intellectual property rights, R&D and supply) between Siemens and EDIL, might afford Siemens some limited influence over EDIL, this influence was not considered to be permanent and long-lasting or decisive. Therefore, it was decided that Siemens would not control EDIL.

2.4.3.6   Shareholder Agreements

It is very common, particularly in the case of newly-established joint ventures, for issues of strategic control to be dealt with explicitly in a shareholders agreement. This will often simply reflect the parties' respective individual interests in the joint venture. It may, however, change the position radically from that attributable to shareholding interests alone. This is one of the main reasons why shareholders' agreements are put in place. In *Thomas Cook/LTU/West LB* the two shareholders, LTU and West LB, had respectively 90 per cent and 10 per cent of the shares of Thomas Cook, but they entered into a shareholders' agreement under which the consent of both parties was required for important strategic decisions including the adoption of annual and five-year plans. The Commission concluded that the two shareholders exercised joint control.[52] In the absence of such an agreement, a significant minority shareholder may have no say at all. In *Pepsico/General Mills*, a shareholding of 40.5 per cent was held not to confer joint control, when weighed against the 59.5 per cent shareholding of Pepsico. Nor will a shareholders' agreement alter the situation attributable to shareholding levels if the rights which it confers are only designed to protect the financial investment of participants.[53] Conversely, in exceptional cases, a shareholders' agreement may confer rights which go beyond those normally attaching to a minority shareholding without, in the Commission's view, conferring decisive influence. For example, in *GE/ENI/Nuovo Pignone*, the fact that ENI, the vendor of Nuovo Pignone, had to approve changes to the initial business plan did not give it joint control with GE because ENI's right lapsed after three years. Likewise, in *Albacom*, the Commission concluded that veto rights lasting only for three years were too transient, judged in the context of a long-term investment in the telecoms sector in Italy, to make the holder of those rights a joint controller, even temporarily. These are further examples of the principle already discussed, namely that the assessment of where control lies must look to rights which are enduring ones.

As might be expected from the need for rights to extend to business matters if decisive influence is to be established, a shareholders' agreement will not create control if it deals only with ownership aspects. It is not uncommon for significant minority shareholders to seek to protect their investments by agreeing mutual rights of pre-emption, or a stand-still (*i.e.* a mutual moratorium on the acquisition of further shares). Nor will mechanisms, such as put and call options, designed to allow a joint venture arrangement to be terminated fairly and efficiently, be treated as conferring joint control. They govern the dissolution of the joint venture rather than its commercial strategy as a going concern, although such mechanisms may be relevant to the question of control if they

---

[52] Similarly, in *Vesuvius/Wulfrath*, a shareholding split of 75/25 per cent was accompanied by a shareholders' agreement providing for joint control (unanimous instructions of both parents were necessary for all major decisions, including approval of annual financial statements, investment plans, any change of product lines and the conclusion of licence agreements).

[53] Such rights are typically confined to winding up, sale of the business or major assets, the issue of new shares (particularly in ways which might dilute the existing shareholders' interests) and major investments and borrowings outside the ordinary course of business.

are designed to resolve commercial deadlock in such a way that in practice they create an inevitable atmosphere of consensus.

2.4.3.7 Special Rights

Where a minority shareholder is given any form of protection beyond that normally attributable to its shareholding and capable of affecting commercial matters, the Commission tends to conclude that it enjoys joint decisive influence with other major or minor shareholders. This is particularly likely the more influence is conferred over the commercial strategy of the undertaking concerned, even if the minority shareholder does not enjoy board representation. In addition, the Commission has referred to a number of other relevant factors. The most important are: the right to approve the appointment of senior executives and their terms; the right to veto strategic commercial decisions, even indirectly by way of approval of budgets and business plans; and the right to approve dividend and investment policy, particularly where that is likely to affect strategic commercial decisions such as the introduction of new products. All these rights go beyond the usual protection afforded to a minority shareholder for the protection of its financial investment.[54]

2.4.3.8 Renault/Volvo

The very first notification ever made to the Commission under the Regulation illustrates the complex nature of these problems and the need to assess legal, economic and other factors in combination when making a judgment on the issue of control. The Commission was notified of a proposed collaboration between the French vehicle manufacturer, Renault, and its Swedish counterpart, Volvo. Under the arrangements notified Renault and Volvo agreed to take shareholdings of 25 per cent in each other's motor car businesses, and 45 per cent in each other's truck and bus divisions. They also agreed to establish three joint committees, a General Policy Committee, a Joint Car Committee, and a Joint Truck and Bus Committee, to determine overall policy. The Commission concluded that the cross-shareholdings in relation to the car businesses did not constitute a concentration, but that the larger cross-shareholdings in the truck and bus businesses did. The Commission explained its conclusion that the cross-shareholding, and related arrangements, for the bus and truck businesses amounted to a concentration on the following basis:

---

[54] See also *Eridania/ISI* where the Commission found that veto rights over the merger of the undertaking concerned with another company, its liquidation, modifications in its capital structure or a change of its registered seat was not sufficient to give the minority shareholder decisive influence over the commercial behaviour of the undertaking concerned. Similarly, in *British Telecom/MCI* the Commission decided that a veto over certain decisions including substantial acquisitions or disposals were normal minority protection rights and did not give British Telecom joint control over MCI. The fact that a minority shareholder has veto rights in respect of a limited range of decisions does not deprive the majority shareholder of sole control of the company. Nor does the fact that for certain decisions at the board level the majority shareholder's representatives will need support of other directors deprive it of decisive influence over the affairs of the company.

"These share acquisitions are substantial interests resulting in an almost equal sharing of losses and profits. The economic interests involved create a strong situation of common interest which, together with the other factors mentioned hereafter, lead to a *de facto* permanent common control situation and thus establish a single economic entity between the two parties."[55]

A number of other elements of the proposals were emphasised by the Commission in its clearance decision. The Joint Truck and Bus Committee, set up under a technical and industrial co-operation agreement, had the power to take decisions binding on both companies. Moreover, the parties had already entered into legally binding obligations to integrate their truck and bus businesses at all stages up to marketing and distribution. Common purchasing policies and specialisation in research and development would, the Commission suggested, lead to such a position of inter-dependence between the Renault and Volvo groups that the integration could be reversed only if one of the parties was prepared to risk a two to three year setback in its competitive position. The change was therefore likely to be a lasting one, and to lead the respective businesses to operate as a single economic unit.[56] The Commission came to a different conclusion, however, in relation to the co-operation between the car businesses of the two groups. It did not accept that cross-shareholdings of between 20 to 25 per cent predicated common control over the respective car businesses. It remained possible, in the Commission's opinion, for Renault and Volvo to act independently, and a "stand-still" agreement under which neither party would take its shareholding in the other above 25 per cent "secured the majority position of each party in its own [car] business". Reciprocal directorships simply reflected the shareholding levels and did not confer greater influence than would have been expected to flow naturally from that level of holdings. Furthermore, the technical and industrial co-operation agreement was, at the time of the notification, less developed than the corresponding agreement in relation to the trucks and bus businesses. It remained commercially feasible for each of the parties to continue along its own chosen path in relation to its car business, notwithstanding co-operation with the other.

The Commission contrasted the different degrees of integration in cars, and in trucks and buses. It analysed the two situations separately, and did not find that the significant cross-shareholdings in trucks and buses, together with the other supporting links, spilled over into the car business such that the whole vehicle businesses of Renault and Volvo became in practice concentrated as one economic unit. There was, however, no reference in the decision to the way the respective businesses were organised to justify such separate treatment. The result was that the co-operation in relation to the car businesses fell to be considered under Article 81 and the decision under the Regulation cleared only the concentration in trucks and buses.[57]

---

[55] Point 5.

[56] In fact, as it turned out, the engagement was terminated four years later.

[57] The decision under the Regulation was a decision in terms only of Art. 6 of the Regulation and did not give a view on the application of Art. 81, although the Commission's press release, announcing the first clearance under the Regulation, stated that the Commission was "informing the parties that there are no grounds for concern under general E.C. competition law".

2.5 CHANGES IN NATURE OF CONTROL

The Regulation applies not simply to the acquisition of control of one under-taking by another or a merger (*fusion*) but to any transaction which results in a change in the nature of control of an undertaking. In *ICI/Tioxide* the Com-mission referred to the "change in quality of decisive influence"[58] as capable of giving rise to a concentration within the meaning of the Regulation. Such a change triggers the requirement to notify. The Concentration Notice clarifies the circumstances in which a change of control may occur.

It is, for example, now well established that a concentration may occur where an undertaking previously having sole control over another undertaking introduces a partner as a joint controller. The reverse is equally true: where one joint venture partner buys out the other a concentration will usually occur as a result of the change from joint to sole control. In *ICI/Tioxide* the Commis-sion considered a proposal under which ICI would acquire from Cookson the 50 per cent of Tioxide which it did not already own. The Commission took the opportunity to emphasise the distinction between sole and joint decisive influence. Having found that Tioxide was currently owned and controlled jointly by ICI and Cookson the Commission went on to point out:

> "Article 3(3) refers to control by whatever means, conferring the possibility of exercising decisive influence on an undertaking. Decisive influence exer-cised *singly* is substantially different to the decisive influence exercised *jointly*, since the latter has to take into account the potentially different interest of the other party or parties concerned.
>
> By changing the quality of decisive influence exercised by ICI on Tiox-ide, the transaction will bring about a durable change of the structure of the concerned parties. Tioxide will become a wholly owned subsidiary of ICI; and by acquiring the ownership of all assets of Tioxide as well as the uncon-tested influence on the composition and decisions, etc. of Tioxide, ICI will obtain full control of Tioxide within the meaning of Art.3(1)(b) in connec-tion with Art.3(3) of the Regulation." [emphasis added]

This approach has been followed in other cases.[59] The most notable is *Skanska/ Scancem*, where, after a struggle for control of Scancem with the Norwegian group, Aker, Skanska found itself in a position of sole control with just under half the voting rights. Upon becoming aware of the share purchases and their impact the Commission required Skanska to submit a notification and Skanska was ultimately required to divest itself of its shareholding in Scancem.

Where separate businesses of the joint venture are divided up between the shareholders more than one concentration may be involved and the Commis-sion may issue more than one decision.[60] The Commission maintains its view

---

[58] Point 4 of its decision.

[59] See for instance *ABB/BREL*; *British Steel/UES*; *Volvo/VME*; *AVESTA III*; *Shell/Montedison*, and *Ferruzzi Finanziaria/Fondiaria*. At para. 10 of the latter case the Commission confirmed the general principle stating ". . . Ferruzzi will have passed from joint control to sole control, a change which constitutes a concentration under the Merger Regulation."

[60] Of particular interest is *Solvay-Laporte/Interox*. Each parent took over a distinct part of the jointly con-trolled business, thereby acquiring sole control of it. The Commission took the view that the economic and legal result of the operation was that two independent undertakings each moved from a position of

that a change in ownership of a joint venture constitutes a new concentration even if one of the shareholders was a "sleeping partner".[61]

2.6   JOINT CONTROL

Article 3(1)(b) refers to a concentration brought about where "one or more" undertakings acquire direct or indirect control of another undertaking, recognising that an undertaking may be under the joint control of two or more other undertakings. Article 3(3) identifies a number of factors giving rise to control, but the Regulation itself is silent as to the circumstances in which two or more undertakings will be treated as exercising control jointly. Reflecting the experience gained by the Commission the Concentration Notice deals extensively with situations of joint control. The Notice on the meaning of "undertaking concerned" also deals with the acquisition of joint control, providing guidance on identifying the undertakings concerned in the concentration for the purpose of carrying out the calculation of turnover.

For the purposes of the Regulation, an undertaking which is under the control of more than one other undertaking is treated as a joint venture. Joint ventures may be concentrative, that is, to be equated with mergers or straightforward acquisitions as far as their effects on competition are concerned, or they may be co-operative, if the joint venture lacks full functionality.[62]

2.6.1   The Existence of Joint Control

To establish whether joint control exists is often far from simple. The discussion above of the various factors which may confer control has illustrated many common situations giving rise to joint control but establishing *de facto* joint control and identifying when informal understandings or common interests between shareholders exist can prove problematical.

Straightforward instances of joint control arise where undertakings enjoy "the absolute mutual veto over strategic policy issues which the Commission normally considers an essential element of joint control of an undertaking".[63] The typical situation of joint control occurs in 50:50 joint ventures where there will be deadlock unless a shareholders agreement provides a mechanism, such

---

joint to sole control over two different sets of specific assets and products. The same approach is taken when an operation consists of different transactions and the nature of the control exercised by the undertakings concerned is different for each transaction. In both *ABB/Renault Automation* and *Ingersoll-Rand/MAN* the Commission considered the transactions notified to comprise two separate concentrations because of differences in the nature of control exercised. In each case, two decisions were issued, one under Art. 6(1)(b) and another under Art. 6(1)(a). But compare *Campsa* where the Commission decided that the division of certain company assets between its main shareholders by acquisition of sole control over part of those assets by the various shareholders constituted a one single concentration.

[61] For instance, in *Eridania/ISI* the Commission took the view that although Eridania already played the major role in the running of ISI it nevertheless did not have sole control of ISI because it had to seek the approval of its fellow shareholder, Finbieticola, on the more fundamental issues going beyond day-to-day management.

[62] See para. 2.7, below.

[63] *Nokia Corporation/SP Tyres UK*, para. 6 of the Commission's Art. 6(1)(b) decision. See generally paras. 18 to 20 of the Concentration Notice.

as appeal to the parent companies' chief executives, to resolve disagreements.[64] Where, for example, business decisions require a 75 per cent majority of shareholder votes, any undertaking holding more than 25 per cent of the votes will, as a matter of law, enjoy a veto power, and, if two or more undertakings hold such blocking minorities, it is inevitable that they must reach agreement on major business decisions.[65]

Joint control may also be found where individual shareholders have some pre-existing relationship or common commercial interest. That relationship or common interest may be expressed in legal form. For example, a syndicate of banks financing a management buy-out may pool the voting rights conferred by their separate financial interests through a voting agreement or establish a joint venture among themselves to exercise collectively their rights in the buy-out vehicle.[66]

2.6.2 Common Interests

Joint control shared among several shareholders is not, however, confined to situations where the legal mechanism of a joint voting company or pooling agreement is adopted.[67] The Commission's view is that a common commercial or financial interest among a number of shareholders can justify the inference that they are acting together to exercise control jointly. The Commission recognises that such cases will be rare.[68] Indeed, where a company has a number of minority shareholders, the possibility of fluctuating alliances between them depending upon the particular business decision at issue and their own individual reactions to or interests in it will make it less rather than more likely that a controlling group with a stable majority will emerge on a lasting basis. While it is clear that in the case of a company with only two shareholders, each owning half the shares, joint control can readily be presumed, it is suggested that, without further evidence, no such presumption follows either where there are more than two shareholders or where there are two main shareholders but neither is in a position to block strategic commercial

---

[64] If the mechanism gives one shareholder the right to override the other then this would usually negative joint control but the giving of day-to-day management responsibility to one shareholder is not inconsistent with joint control since it does not imply that the other has relinquished its rights in relation to strategic matters.

[65] See, *e.g. Elf/BC/CEPSA* where Elf and BC each held approximately 34 per cent of the votes in CEPSA, in which a 75 per cent majority was needed for matters of major business strategy. At para. 4 of its Art. 6(1)(b) decision the Commission commented that "BC et ELF devront coopérer d'une manière permanente afin d'éviter un bloquage réciproque lors des votes sur les décisions concernant les activités essentielles de CEPSA/ERTOIL."

[66] See *Kelt/American Express* and the CTC notifications referred to above, para. 2.4.2.3 and footnote 30, above.

[67] In *Kirch/Richemont/Telepiù* Richemont became the holder of 25 per cent of the shares of Telepiù. The other principal shareholders were Kirch (34.72 per cent), Fin.Tel. Srl (23.39 per cent) and Reti Televisive Italiane (10 per cent). Kirch and Richemont entered into a shareholders agreement under which they agreed to co-ordinate their voting in shareholders' meetings and in the board of directors of Telepiù.

[68] Para. 32 of the Concentration Notice. This is despite it having pressed, in the early days of the Regulation, for notifications to be made in certain cases where a new undertaking was established with a small number of shareholders which the Commission presumed to be joint controllers. One such case, where ultimately the parties succeeded in resisting the Commission and no notification was made, was the establishing of the B/Sky/B satellite TV company.

decisions. Indeed, in recent cases the Commission has been more circumspect. In *Eureko*, a joint venture was established among five E.C. insurance companies. Although each partner had similar interests and rights, the Commission concluded that Eureko was not controlled by any of its shareholders. The Commission also refused to accept that a common interest existed sufficient to infer common control in *Nokia/SP Tyres*. A flotation of Nokia Tyres meant that the former parent, Nokia, would hold between 25 and 40 per cent of its shares. SP Tyres, a Japanese tyre manufacturer, held 20 per cent and the public and investment institutions the rest. Despite the fact that co-operation arrangements had existed between Nokia and SP Tyres for more than a decade and that the two had executed a shareholders' agreement providing that their board representatives would use their best endeavours to achieve a consensus on important strategic decisions, the Commission rejected the parties' contention that they jointly controlled Nokia Tyres and found that the transaction was not a concentrative joint venture and was therefore outside the Regulation.[69] In *Ericsson/Nokia/Psion* the Symbian joint venture created by Ericsson, Nokia and Psion to develop and market an operating system for mobile digital data systems was notified and cleared by the Commission under the Regulation. When, however, Motorola subsequently joined Symbian the Commission refused to accept that Symbian continued to be under the joint control of its shareholders. *Ericsson/Nokia/Psion/Motorola* is an excellent illustration of the concept of joint control under the Regulation. The table below shows the shareholdings on the creation of Symbian (Symbian I) and on the participation of Motorola (Symbian II).

	Symbian I	Symbian II
Ericsson	30	23.08
Nokia	30	23.08
Psion	40	30.77
Motorola	–	23.08

Strategic decisions on senior appointments, business plans and budgets required a 67 per cent majority vote according to the Symbian I Shareholders' Agreement. This meant that each of the three original shareholders individually had veto rights. The admission of Motorola meant that this was not the case: none of the shareholders retained a unilateral veto right and there was no amendment of the shareholders' agreement which would have created a situation of *de facto* joint control. The Commission rejected the parties' view that a situation of *de facto* joint control existed, concluding that (i) Psion's interest was different from the other shareholders since they would produce products incorporating Psion's system; and (ii) no sufficient common interest was established between the other three given that they would be competitors downstream in a new market in which their interests and strategies might well diverge. On this basis shifting alliances between the shareholders was to be

[69] The Commission emphasised that Nokia had withdrawn from tyre markets and markets upstream and downstream and its continued interest in Nokia Tyres, though significant, was essentially financial. It could not, therefore, be assumed always to approach issues from the same perspective as SP Tyres.

expected and the Commission referred to the statement in paragraph 35 of the Concentration Notice that "the possibility of changing coalitions between minority shareholders will normally exclude the assumption of joint control".[70]

The inference will be different where the common commercial interest is strong,[71] or common interests are reinforced by a shareholders agreement.[72] Common interests sufficient to warrant a finding of joint control may also exist among undertakings which participate already in the joint control of another venture, particularly if that existing venture operates in related markets, or where undertakings have acted in concert to acquire control over another undertaking.[73] According to the Concentration Notice (paragraph 34), where a new joint venture is created there is a higher probability that the undertakings involved in its establishment will be carrying out a common policy, particularly where they have each made contributions vital to the joint venture's future operations. It is suggested, however, that the contribution of a vital resource to a newly-created joint venture is not in itself sufficient to make the contributor a joint controller. For example, a contributor of essential intellectual property rights may rely on the terms of the grant of those rights to the joint venture to protect any interest it may wish to preserve in that intellectual property without the necessity of acquiring influence over the joint venture's future commercial strategy. In this area generalisations need to be treated with extreme caution and the basic principles underlying the concept of control must never be lost sight of. *Ericsson/Nokia/Psion/Motorola* shows that the Commission will require cogent evidence of commonality of interest before concluding that joint control exist. Joint control will rarely arise *de facto*, as the Concentration Notice emphasises.[74]

In the absence of the indications discussed above the mere fact that an undertaking has a small number of major shareholders does not mean that they exercise *joint* control. If each is free to vote as it wishes and there is nothing to compel collective voting there is every likelihood that they will vote differently on different issues as they arise over time. This is inconsistent with the existence of *de jure* or *de facto* joint control on a lasting basis which alone is sufficient to create an enduring structural change.

---

[70] Para. 17 of the Art. 6(1)(a) decision of December 22, 1998. See also *Paribas/CDC/Beaufour*. Contrast the attitude of the Merger Task Force to the creation of the Scancem cement undertaking where it took the view that the low prospect of shifting alliances and the alleged common commercial interests of Skanska and Aker, the two main shareholders, each of whom had some 33 per cent of the voting rights in Scancem indicated *de facto* joint control. No steps were taken, however, to compel notification of the establishment of Scancem, which was cleared by the merger control authorities in Sweden and Norway.

[71] See *Philips/Grundig* where the joint controllers were all financing banks which had identical interests in the transaction.

[72] As in *Fletcher Challenge/Methanex*.

[73] See generally paras 30 to 35 of the Concentration Notice. The inference of joint control will not, however, be appropriate where the undertakings co-operated in a consortium bid but then propose to divide up the target's businesses between them in such a way as to create a situation envisaged by Recital 25 of the Regulation.

[74] Para. 35. The Commission has not always been consistent in its approach. In the early years of the Regulation it is understood to have been more ready to infer that joint control existed and to have sought notifications, not always with success—see note 68 above.

2.7 CONCENTRATION OR CO-OPERATION?

2.7.1 **Redefinition of "concentration"**

One of the most significant changes made by the 1997 amendments to the Regulation was a redrawing of the boundary line between those joint ventures which fell within the assessment procedures and timetable established under the Regulation and those falling to be dealt with under the appraisal criteria in Article 81(1) and (3) and the procedures established by Regulation 17/62.

Prior to March 1, 1998, even if a transaction created a full-function joint venture of lasting and structural effect within the Common Market, it would not meet the definition of concentration in Article 3 of the Regulation if it had the object or effect of co-ordinating the competitive behaviour of independent undertakings—the so-called "negative condition" for establishing the existence of a concentration.[75] Transactions having a co-ordinating effect were dealt with entirely under Article 81 though some procedural short cuts were available: the Form CO notification could serve as a Form A/B notification and a "fast-track" assessment procedure was introduced for structural, but co-operative, joint ventures. Even so, cases commonly still took several months to resolve, rather than the four weeks available usually under the Regulation, and by the less legally secure means of comfort letters rather than formal decisions.

After much discussion, the solution adopted was to delete the negative condition from the definition of concentration in Article 3[76] and to introduce a new provision, Article 2(4), incorporating on Article 81 analysis into the assessment of compatibility in the case of structural joint ventures having co-ordination effects. The new Article 2(4) reads:

> "To the extent that the creation of a joint venture constituting a concentration pursuant to Article 3 has as its object or effect the co-ordination of the competitive behaviour of undertakings that remain independent, such co-ordination shall be appraised in accordance with the criteria of Article 8[1](1) and (3) of the Treaty, with a view to establishing whether or not the operation is compatible with the common market.
>
> In making this appraisal, the Commission shall take into account in particular:
>
> —whether two or more parent companies retain to a significant extent activities in the same market as the joint venture or in a market which is downstream or upstream from that of the joint venture or in a neighbouring market closely related to this market;
>
> —whether the co-ordination which is the direct consequence of the creation of the joint venture affords the undertakings concerned the possibility of eliminating competition in respect of a substantial part of the products or services in question".

For full-function, structural joint ventures which have the object or effect of co-ordinating the behaviour of competing undertakings the test of compatibil-

---

[75] See earlier editions of this book for a more detailed explanation of the distinction between concentrative and co-operative joint ventures.

[76] By deleting the first paragraph of Art. 3(2) entirely and the reference to co-ordination in the second paragraph thereof.

ity is now bi-partite. A dominance test applies to the creation of the joint venture but Article 81 applies to the extent that there are co-ordination effects. In the context of the Regulation the Commission, in applying Article 81, is directed to take particular account of the matters set out in the two indents in the second paragraph of the new Article 2(4). Where the Commission has no serious doubts on a dominance basis but does have serious doubts on the Article 81 criteria it may open a second-stage examination under Article 6(1)(c) to deal solely with those concerns. Although the Article 3 definition of concentration has been extended the Commission has chosen to differentiate Article 2(4) cases from the normal run of cases subject only to the dominance test by designating the former "JV" cases.[77]

The change is to be welcomed. It avoids the acute difficulty of trying to apply the "negative condition" in the old Article 3(2) at the jurisdiction stage, *i.e.* in determining whether a concentration, and therefore an obligation to notify, exists. Moreover it subjects all structural joint ventures to the same stage one and stage two timetables applicable to other transactions which have the character of concentrations. Article 2(4) incorporates into the Regulation a means of applying Article 81 in cases where a joint venture may have an appreciable effect on competition between undertakings which remain independent. This results in some anomalies. For example, whereas an efficiency defence is no answer to a charge of dominance it may constitute economic progress within Article 81(3) and be capable of being taken into account as a benefit outweighing any anti-competitive effects of a joint venture. But the change has not altered the law applicable except that a decision of compatibility under the Regulation is not time-limited, whereas an exemption under Article 81(3) in the context of Regulation 17 must be. The co-operative elements of a structural joint venture always fell to be assessed under Article 81: that remains the position and Article 2(4) requires all the criteria in Article 81 to be applied, notwithstanding the special emphasis placed on market overlaps and the elimination of competition in the two indents to Article 2(4). It is simply that the Regulation's procedures have been modified where some structural joint ventures are concerned. Chapter 5 considers the principles applicable to the assessment required to be carried out under Article 2(4) and the case law thus far.

2.7.2 Full Function Joint Ventures

Notwithstanding the recent amendments to the Regulation it remains the case that, in accordance with Article 3(2), a joint venture must perform all the functions of an autonomous economic entity if it is to be treated as concentrative. The change to the definition of concentration required a new Notice on the concept of full-function joint ventures (hereinafter the "Full-Function Notice").[78] To qualify as a full-function joint venture the key factor is that the joint venture has a long term (*i.e.* lasting) presence on a market independently of its parents. It must have a market profile and be able "to stand on its own two feet". These essential characteristics are examined further below.

---

[77] At the time of writing there have been 24 such notifications.
[78] [1998] O.J. C66/1. The Notice is reproduced in Appendix 4.

2.7.2.1   Autonomous Economic Entity

The autonomous full-function character of an undertaking depends on it (i) having a presence and carrying out a recognised activity on a market; (ii) being self-sufficient or largely self-sufficient in terms of resources; and (iii) having sufficient commercial independence and identity of its own that it is not simply operating as an auxiliary or service company for its shareholders. These factors are inter-related, for example, a joint venture's operations may be confined to manufacturing a single raw material. If there is a market for that raw material, through traders, resellers or end-users who are not vertically-integrated upstream, and other companies are similarly active in producing and selling that material, element (i) is likely to be satisfied.[79] However, if the joint venture manufactures only for its shareholders and is not free to produce for others, then element (iii) will be missing and the joint venture will be considered as ancillary to its parents' businesses and not as an independent market entity. Indeed production for captive consumption within a vertically-integrated is not usually taken into account when assessing the players on the market and their market shares. But the fact that a joint venture initially serves only one or more of its shareholders is not fatal to full-functionality if it is intended to supply third parties. In *British Gas/Group 4* the parties established a meter reading joint venture to perform such services for British Gas and, as the market developed, other suppliers of gas and other utility services. The market was still in its infancy and the joint venture's exclusive supply arrangement with British Gas was essential to the market's development as well as to the viability of the joint venture itself.

To qualify as a full-function undertaking the joint venture must have the necessary resources, including finance, staff and assets (tangible and intangible) and intellectual property rights necessary to carry on its business activity.[80] In *Elf Atochem/Rohm and Haas* the Commission concluded that the joint venture constituted an autonomous economic entity for the following reasons: the physical and human resources necessary for the production and sale of the product were transferred to it and the construction of a new production facility in the ownership of the joint venture was to start soon thereafter; the parent companies granted it exclusive irrevocable intellectual property licences needed for manufacturing; and it was to have its own research and development facilities and distribution network. This gave it the necessary ability to act as an independent supplier and buyer on the market. This analysis is reflected in a number of other decisions under the Regulation. It does not matter if the joint venture derives its resources from its shareholders provided that they are securely within its control. This was found not to be the case in *ENW/Eastern* where the telecommunications joint venture established by the

---

[79] In the Full Function Notice, para.15, the Commission defines a trade market as a market "characterised by the existence of companies which specialize in the selling and distribution of products without being vertically integrated in addition to those which may be integrated, and where different sources of supply are available for the products in question". It is not, therefore, fatal that the joint venture does not operate at all levels of a market if, *e.g.*, packaging or sub-contract manufacturing are recognised in a particular sector or industry as independent commercial functions.

[80] Full Function Notice, para. 13.

parties was found not to have sufficiently secure rights over ENW's infrastructure to qualify as a full-function joint venture.

The Commission will examine the relationship between a joint venture and its parent shareholders in order to judge whether the joint venture has a real commercial existence independent of their needs: a joint venture established to supply products and services exclusively to its parents or which is wholly dependent on its parents for supplies will not be concentrative. In *British Telecom/MCI* the Commission had serious doubts as to the genuine autonomy of the joint venture established by BT and MCI, because, despite the assets, financial and personnel resources made available to it, all its services were committed to its parents.[81] But this is not necessarily fatal if this will only be so during the start-up phase of the joint venture provided the objective is to establish a fully-fledged entity on a lasting basis.

Similarly, when a joint venture purchases from its parent companies, the Commission will examine the commercial arrangements closely, in particular where little added value is attributable to the contribution made by the joint venture itself.[82] In *Shell Chimie/Elf Atochem* the parents undertook to guarantee substantially all the joint venture's raw material requirements. The Commission found that the joint venture was more than just a captive outlet carrying out some common sales function for its parents; it would have a genuine industrial processing activity, judged by reference to the value-added by the production/processing activity of the joint venture performed on the raw material supplied by Shell and Elf. Nor will commercial relationships between a joint venture and its parents, even if initially exclusive, endanger its full-function status provided that it is free, in the longer term, to accept competitive offers from third parties. It is also often the case that a joint venture requires extensive support services from its parents until it is properly established. These "outsourcing" arrangements are consistent with full functionality and rarely impinge on a joint venture's external profile on the market.

Furthermore, the fact that a joint venture makes use of the retail outlet or dealer network of one or more of its shareholders will not normally disqualify it as a "full-function" joint venture as long as the parents are acting only as its agents, *i.e.* it is present on the market in its own right. In *Zurigo/Banco di Napoli*, for example, the Commission considered that the new joint venture was an autonomous economic entity despite the fact that it would use the retail banking network of one of its parents to distribute its insurance products.[83] Such an arrangement was typical in Italy in that sector.

---

[81] This approach was also followed in *Philips/Thomson/SAGEM* where the parties had set up a joint venture for the manufacture of liquid crystal displays mainly to meet their own supply requirements. In contrast, it appears from *Courtaulds/SNIA* that where one of the shareholders supplies raw material to the joint venture that supply arrangement is not inconsistent with the joint venture being regarded as concentrative provided that the supply agreement is non-exclusive and the joint venture is purchasing the raw material on the open market. See also *Spar/Dansk Supermarked* and *Toyota Motor Corp./Walter Frey Holding/ Toyota France* where the joint venture company was able to obtain supplies from third parties.

[82] The Commission considers that in such situations the joint venture may be closer to a joint sales agency. See the Full Function Notice, para. 15.

[83] The Commission noted that (i) the parent would be acting only as agent of the joint venture and (ii) this was the normal way to operate in the market concerned, *i.e.* other insurance companies operating on the same market distribute their products through agency contracts with independent distributors, normally banks.

2.7.2.2   Lasting Basis

A concentrative joint venture must also have some permanence. A transient
impact will not create structual change in the market place. A joint venture
must be established and intended to operate on a "lasting basis". This is likely
to be the case where the parents invest substantial financial resources in the
joint venture or transfer significant technical or commercial know-how to it.
It is not essential that the duration of the joint venture should evidence an
intention to establish it as a permanent feature of the market concerned. In
British Airways/TAT the Commission recognised that a period of six and a
half years was long enough to create a lasting structural change "in particular
in a sector such as air transport which faces at present rapid and important
legal and economic changes".[84] The key factor is whether the joint venture
operates as an enduring independent existence on a market and is intended so
to do by its shareholders. Normally, a five to 10 year time horizon should be
sufficient, although much will depend on the nature of the markets in which
the joint venture operates.

2.7.3   Consortium Bids

The deletion of the negative condition and the introduction of Article 2(4) has
much simplified the application of the Regulation to consortium bids. The
co-ordination effects of such a bid are no longer fatal to it constituting a
notifiable concentration under the Regulation. Moreover, Article 2(4) will have
no application to a consortium bid if it is a break-up bid where the target
company's business will be sold to different members of the consortium, or
to third parties, and where there is no joint control over any of the target's
commercial operations except in the very short term.[85] Equally, a joint acquisition by parties who are not competitors among themselves, or of the acquired
company, is unlikely to raise issues under Article 81.

An interesting example of a consortium bid where Article 2(4) could still
be relevant was the proposed joint bid by General Utilities, a subsidiary of the
French group Vivendi, and SAUR, owned by the Bouygues group, for the
English water company, Mid Kent. The bid announcement proposed that Mid
Kent's operations should be split between the joint bidders, who already controlled neighbouring water companies on the eastern and western boundaries
of Mid Kent's water supply area, and the Commission concluded that the
proposal could not be treated as a consortium bid within the Regulation. First,
the splitting up of Mid Kent's operations could not be effected immediately
after the acquisition. Secondly, the proposal involved the creation of a bulk
supply water company which would own certain key water resources of Mid
Kent and which would supply long-term only to the joint bidders. It was

---

[84] Normally, however, one would expect a joint venture to be established for 10 years or more, if not on
an open-ended basis. Mechanisms for dissolution are recognised as necessary to protect shareholders and
will not negative the enduring character of the joint venture. See the Full Function Notice, para. 16.
[85] It is doubtful whether the original consortium bid for Irish Distillers Ltd—discussed in para. 8.2 of the
first edition—would now fall within the Regulation since the parties proposed to operate the target
company's spirits distillery on a joint basis.

therefore dealt with, and prohibited, under the special provisions in the Water Act 1991 applicable to mergers in the United Kingdom between water undertakings. This would not necessarily be the case today, since the co-operative aspects of the case could be dealt with under the Regulation provided that the target company continued to be operated as a full-function joint venture of lasting duration.

Even before a consortium is finalised, it is common for its members at the highest levels of management to agree, at least informally, that they will not make independent bids or join with or form any other consortium. Such restrictions are to be treated as ancillary to the concentration consisting of (i) the acquisition of joint control, and (ii) the division of the target undertaking between consortium members and third parties. Consortium bids will still need to be looked at carefully. But it is clear that the joint bid itself, and the obligations by the consortium members not to bid independently, are to be treated as restrictions integral to the joint acquisition, and not as a separate matter to be dealt with under Article 81.[86] The essential (and welcome) result is that a consortium bid for an undertaking will be subject to the same principles which apply to all concentrations and Recital 24 of the Regulation will lose any relevance it had.

2.8 SPECIAL EXCEPTIONS (ARTICLE 3(5))

Article 3(5) sets out three quite separate cases which are not to be treated as concentrations for the purposes of the Regulation. Although only the third of the three cases is expressly limited by reference to Article 3(1)(b), concentration arising by acquisition of control, it is doubtful if the first or second is capable of applying in the case of a merger within the meaning of Article 3(1)(a). Since these cases are exceptions to the general obligation to notify they are construed, and applied, narrowly by the Commission.

2.8.1 Financial Institutions

The first exception (Article 3(5)(a)) covers certain situations where banks and other financial institutions hold shares on a temporary basis. The intention was, *inter alia*, to ensure that underwriters left with a large holding sufficient to give them control are not caught by the Regulation. The exception is also of benefit in situations common in Germany where private companies are often sold through banks. The key features of the exception are that: (i) the financial institution's normal activities must include securities transactions for their own account or the account of others; (ii) the securities acquired must be held on a temporary basis and with a view to resale; (iii) voting rights must not be exercised in order to determine the undertaking's competitive behaviour or, if exercised, must only be with a view to disposal of the whole or part of the

---

[86] See Part IV of the Commission Notice on Ancillary Restraints, which takes a benevolent approach to the restrictions which are necessary to establish and implement a consortium bid.

undertaking or its assets[87] or the securities; and (iv) the disposal of the acquired undertaking or securities must take place within a year of acquisition. The last condition may, on application, be varied by the Commission where the financial institution can show that disposal was not reasonably possible "within the period set" (these last words suggest the extension may be renewed). What is "reasonably possible" should take account of the market price for the securities. The Commission is therefore able to extend the term where there is, for example, a sudden unexpected fall in the market and where, therefore, it would be unreasonable to expect the institution to dispose of the securities.

An interesting situation occurs in the event of a "rescue operation". This situation typically involves the conversion of existing debt into a new company through which a syndicate of banks may acquire joint control of the rescued company. Although the primary intention of the rescuing banks is to restructure the financing of the undertaking concerned for its subsequent resale, the Commission takes the view that this type of operation may normally be considered to be a concentration as the restructuring programme usually requires the controlling banks to exercise their joint control by determining the strategic commercial behaviour of the rescued undertaking. Therefore, the exception set out in Article 3(5)(a) is normally not applicable.[88]

2.8.2   Liquidators and Receivers

The second exception (Article 3(5)(b)) is intended to exclude from the Regulation the situation where a liquidator or administrator acquires control, by virtue of his office, of undertakings which happen to be competitors.[89] The purpose of the appointment of office-holders in insolvency proceedings is to safeguard the creditors' interests and generally such situations are subject to stringent legal checks and controls designed to do so. It would be potentially detrimental to the creditors concerned if the appointment of the liquidator and the safeguarding of the assets were dependent upon prior notification to and approval (on competition grounds) by the Commission. The reference to control being acquired "by an office-holder" makes it clear, however, that the sale of the undertaking by the office-holder to a third party will be subject to the Regulation where applicable. For instance, in *Matra Marconi Space/Satcomms*, Matra notified to the Commission its acquisition of certain assets of Ferranti, which was in administrative receivership. Similarly, in *ING/Barings*, the acquisition by ING of substantially all the assets of Barings from its administrators was considered a concentration. It is also to be noted that the exception covers situations where control is acquired "according to the law of a Member State". The phrase would appear wide enough to cover situations not only where office-holders are appointed by court order or other operation of law

---

[87] This contemplates the situation in Germany where a GmbH is to be acquired. N.B. The exception does not cover cases where banks hold shares on a long-term basis.

[88] See the Concentration Notice, para. 45. This was the approach the Commission took in *Kelt/American Express.*

[89] There is a similar, but not identical, exemption from ECSC Rules governing concentrations—see Art. 3(2) of Decision 24/54.

but also under contracts, security instruments or by meetings of creditors or shareholders.[90]

2.8.3 Financial Holding Companies

Finally, Article 3(5)(c) excludes from the Regulation operations otherwise falling within the scope of Article 3(1)(b) (*i.e.* concentrations by the acquisition of control) when carried out by a financial holding company as defined in the Fourth and Seventh Company Law Directives.[91] As in the case of those Directives, this was a matter of concern for one Member State in particular, Luxembourg. A financial holding company is essentially a company whose sole object is to acquire holdings in undertakings, and to manage such holdings and turn them to profit, without involving themselves directly or indirectly in the management of those undertakings. The scope of the exemption is limited.[92] There is a restriction on the exercise of voting rights: they may only be exercised to maintain the full value of the holding, but not to determine directly or indirectly the competitive conduct of the undertaking. The exemption only covers concentrations which arise by virtue of the financial holding company acquiring control. It therefore would not exclude from the Regulation a concentration arising, for example, where the undertaking whose shares are held by the financial holding company acquires control of another undertaking. Moreover, the exemption does not appear to cover the takeover of a financial holding company by another undertaking or the disposal by a financial holding company of one undertaking to another. Finally, as mentioned above, the exemption only relates to operations referred to in Article 3(1)(b). Mergers within the meaning of Article 3(1)(a) between financial holding companies are not outside the Regulation.

---

[90] It is interesting to note that in *Banco Santander/Banesto* the rescue of Banesto by the Banco de Espana, through the subscription by the Fondo de Garantia de Depositos of the increased share capital of Banesto, does not appear to have been considered as giving rise to a concentration. Instead, the acquisition by Banco Santander of the Banesto's shares held by Fondo de garantia de Depositos, was notified to the Commission and considered a concentration.

[91] Council Directive 78/660 on the annual accounts of certain types of companies ([1978] O.J. L222/11) and Council Directive 84/569 on consolidated accounts ([1984] O.J. L314/28).

[92] But arguably not as limited as some would suggest. Sorensen and Kennedy, "Hollow Ring to Merger Control Regulation Exception" [1995] 5 E.C.L.R. 267.

3 Community Dimension

3.1 INTRODUCTION

Article 1 states that the Regulation shall apply to all concentrations "with a Community dimension". The concept of "Community dimension" expresses policy objectives fundamental both to the European Community generally and to the specific requirements of E.C. merger control, in particular that it should be clear whether the Commission or Member States has jurisdiction over a merger and that there should be, so far as possible, a "one-stop shop" within the European Union. Concentrations with a "Community dimension" (broadly speaking, multi-national mergers and joint ventures) should be subject to scrutiny by the Commission under the Regulation, but not by national competition authorities under Member State merger control regimes. Nor, indeed, should they be subject to Commission scrutiny under Articles 81 and 82 E.C. On the other hand, concentrations which have no Community dimension, and are therefore more "national" in character, should be subject only to national controls. Recognition of the political concept of "subsidiarity",[1] dictating that objectives should, where appropriate, be achieved by action at the level of national authorities, has reinforced the view that the Commission should deal only with those concentrations which, by reason of their scale and likely effects, have genuine cross-border characteristics and that, in other cases, merger control should be left to individual Member States. As outlined in Chapter 1, in the face of proliferating national merger controls, the need to preserve the "one-stop shop" objective led to the extension of the concept of Community dimension by the introduction of an additional set of turnover criteria which create, as it were, a second level of jurisdiction. The new criteria will go some way to avoiding multiple national merger filings.

This chapter is devoted to the application of the turnover criteria and the calculation of turnover, having regard to both the updated Turnover Notice (reproduced in Appendix 7), decisions under the Regulation, and the changes taking effect on March 1, 1998 which introduced the additional thresholds and

---

[1] This principle is now formally recognised in the E.C. Treaty (by virtue of the 1992 Maastricht Treaty). Art. 5 of the E.C. Treaty provides that, in areas which do not fall within the Community's exclusive competence (and competition policy has long been recognised as an area of mixed competence between the Community and Member States):

> "the Community shall take action, in accordance with the principle of subsidiarity, only if and in so far as the objectives of the proposed action cannot be sufficiently achieved by the Member States and can therefore, by reason of the scale or effects of the proposed action, be better achieved by the Community. Any action by the Community shall not go beyond what is necessary to achieve the objectives of this Treaty".

modified the definition of turnover in certain special cases. The Regulation has now been in force for nearly a decade and the principles for applying the turnover thresholds have become well-established and exemplified in decisions of the Commission under the Regulation. Novel points are now rare, though not completely unheard of, and the 1998 Turnover Notice, which replaced the original of 1994, was necessary only because of the new set of turnover thresholds (discussed below) and not because the earlier Notice had become unreliable.

3.1.1 Jurisdiction

In the case of Articles 81 and 82 E.C. one limit on the Commission's jurisdiction is the requirement that the behaviour complained of must have an actual or potential effect on trade between Member States. This criterion has come to be interpreted so broadly that the difficulty has been to identify cases which clearly do not, or could not, fall within the Commission's remit. Once the need for merger control at the supra-national level had been accepted, it was universally recognised, however, that the jurisdiction rules for mergers had to be much more clear-cut. Since notifications were to be made mandatory under the Community regime, with fines for failure to notify, business needed to be able to identify transactions requiring clearance in Brussels. A threshold based on turnover was adopted as the most satisfactory method. The limitation had the advantage not only of meeting the political desire of Member States to retain a degree of national control over mergers but also of solving a practical problem of resources for the Competition Directorate.

3.1.2 The Original Turnover Thresholds

The objective of a one-stop shop requires the respective jurisdictions of the Community and Member States to be clearly defined. Article 1(2), which established the original concept of "Community dimension", seeks to meet this requirement:

"For the purposes of this Regulation, a concentration has a Community dimension where:

(a) the combined aggregate worldwide turnover of all the undertakings concerned is more than 5,000 million euro; and

(b) the aggregate Community-wide turnover of each of at least two of the undertakings concerned is more than 250 million euro,

unless each of the undertakings concerned achieves more than two-thirds of its aggregate Community-wide turnover within one and the same Member State."

A turnover test provides a relatively straightforward practical means whereby undertakings can be reasonably certain whether a planned acquisition falls within the Commission's competence under the Regulation, or falls within domestic controls.[2] It also has the merit of identifying those concentrations where the parties involved carry on significant commercial activity in more than one Member State of the European Union. A test based on asset values, such as that adopted under section 64(1)(a) of the United Kingdom's Fair Trading Act, would not have guaranteed that result.[3] Another possibility, a test based on market share, would have introduced all the problems associated with defining product and geographic markets at the initial jurisdictional stage when it is particularly important to minimise uncertainty and conflicts of jurisdiction.

3.1.3   The Additional Turnover Thresholds

Chapter 1 describes the background to and rationale for the additional turnover thresholds.[4] Along with other changes to the Regulation, the new thresholds came into effect on March 1, 1998 in relation to concentrations occurring on or after that date. As from that date, even if a new concentration fails to meet the original turnover thresholds in Article 1(2), it will fall within the Commission's jurisdiction if the following alternative criteria set out in a new Article 1(3) of the Regulation are met:

(a) the combined aggregate worldwide turnover of all the undertakings concerned is more than 2,500 million euro;

(b) in each of at least three Member States, the combined aggregate turnover of all the undertakings concerned is more than 100 million euro;

(c) in each of at least three Member States included for the purpose of point (b), the aggregate turnover of each of at least two of the undertakings concerned is more than 25 million euro; and

(d) the aggregate Community-wide turnover of each of at least two of the undertakings concerned is more than 100 million euro;

unless each of the undertakings concerned achieves more than two-thirds of its aggregate Community-wide turnover within one and the same Member State.

3.1.4   Relationship with Original Thresholds

Since March 1, 1998 determining whether a concentration now falls within E.C. merger control has in practice become a two-stage process. The original Article 1(2) criteria are applied first. If they are not met, the additional thresholds come

---

[2] The role of national authorities in the operation of the Regulation is discussed in Chap. 8.
[3] It is noteworthy, however, that under Art. 5(3)(a) in its original form an assets test replaced worldwide turnover in the special case of credit and other financial institutions and a complex ratio (based on loans and advances to Community residents) had to be substituted for Community-wide turnover. See para. 3.7.1, below.
[4] Para. 1.3.

into play. The same principles relating to the definition and calculation of turn-over and the identification of undertakings concerned govern the application of the additional thresholds as they do the original thresholds. What is new is that the additional thresholds do not merely involve a lowering of the aggregate worldwide and Community aggregate levels familiar in Article 1(2) but intro-duce two novel criteria. The first is the requirement in Article 1(3)(b) of a min-imum combined aggregate turnover threshold of 100 million euro which must be achieved in at least three Member States for all the undertakings concerned. The second is that in at least three Member States where that threshold is exceeded, at least two of the undertakings concerned must each earn turnover of more than 25 million. There must be a combined presence of some "cross-border" signi-ficance before the extended jurisdiction of Brussels comes into play. This goes some way to address the practical problem of multiple filings. Even so, the "two-thirds" rule, explained below, is preserved. Experience of the first calendar year of the additional thresholds shows, however, that only fourteen extra cases have been caught, 6 per cent of the total in 1998.

While, in practice, the application of turnover thresholds may have proved somewhat more complex than predicted when the Regulation was adopted, Commission decisions and notices have eradicated most of the difficulties. It remains the case, however, that many international companies do not record turnover internally in ways which facilitate application of the turnover criteria in the Regulation.

3.1.5 Concentrations Below the Thresholds

The basic rule delineating the responsibilities of the Commission and the Member States leaves concentrations which lack Community dimension to be dealt with by Member State authorities. It must be remembered, however, that Article 22 (discussed in Chapter 8) provides a procedure whereby the Commission can, at the request of a Member State, examine a concentration even though it lacks Community dimension where a concentration creates or strengthens a dominant position as a result of which competition will be significantly impeded within the territory of "the Member State concerned".[5]

3.2 APPLICATION OF TURNOVER CRITERIA

3.2.1 Worldwide and Community Turnover

The original and the additional thresholds share two criteria in common; the first is based on the aggregate worldwide turnover of all the "undertakings concerned" in the concentration; the second, formulated somewhat differently, relates to Community-wide turnover.

The criterion in Article 1(2)(a) (the original thresholds) is satisfied if the

---

[5] The process is likely to fall into disuse now that all Member States have their own merger controls. Even the Dutch, who in 1989 were such strong proponents of the Article 22(3) procedure that it became known as "the Dutch clause", have now introduced domestic mergers controls.

aggregate worldwide turnover of all the undertakings concerned exceeds 5,000 million euro. The corresponding figure in Article 1(3)(a) (the additional thresholds) is 2,500 million euro.

The criterion in Article 1(2)(b) and Article 1(3)(d) (its equivalent in the additional thresholds) requires that, in calculating Community turnover, the aggregate of each of at least two of the undertakings concerned must be more than 250 million euro or more than 100 million euro respectively. It does not say that *all* the undertakings concerned must achieve those levels of Community turnover. It is thus not possible to avoid the application of the Regulation by including in the concentration one or more undertakings with little or no Community turnover if there are at least two with significant turnover in the Community. Moreover, it is not necessary that one of those undertakings is in the acquiring group and the other in the target group, although this will normally be the case. This has important implications for consortium bids and joint ventures. For example, if company A and company B make a bid for joint control of company C, the size and turnover of company C may well be completely irrelevant to the question whether the Regulation applies if A and B by themselves fulfil the criteria for Community dimension in Article 1(2) or 1(3).

3.2.2 Member State Turnover Criteria

Under the new thresholds the Commission has jurisdiction if the combined turnover of all the undertakings concerned exceeds 100 million euro in at least three Member States if at least two of the undertakings whose turnover goes to make up that combined 100 million threshold achieve at least 25 million euro of sales in the same three Member States where the combined 100 million aggregate is achieved. The application of these criteria are illustrated in the examples given below.

3.2.3 The Two-Thirds Rule

Even if the turnover criteria in Article 1(2) and 1(3) are met, a concentration will not have Community dimension if each of the undertakings concerned which carries on business in the Community achieves more than two-thirds of its aggregate Community-wide turnover within one and the same Member State. This proviso ensures that where significant Community turnover is involved but is earned in one and the same Member State the concentration remains within the jurisdiction of the competition authorities of that Member State. Subject, as already mentioned, to the special case provided for in Article 22 of the Regulation and the theoretical possibility of action under Article 84 of the E.C. Treaty, the Commission has no jurisdiction in such cases, even when a concentration between two undertakings within the same Member State may have significant implications for trade between Member States.[6]

The two-thirds rule can be critical in determining whether a merger comes under the Regulation or under national merger control. A striking example occurred in the United Kingdom in 1992, when rival bids to take over Midland Bank were launched by the Hongkong & Shanghai Banking Corporation (HSBC) and by Lloyds Bank. Both proposed concentrations—HSBC/Midland and Lloyds/Midland—would have satisfied the 5,000 million euro worldwide turnover test, and each of the banks concerned had a Community-wide "turnover" of more than 250 million euro.[7] But while Midland achieved more than two-thirds of its Community-wide "turnover" in the United Kingdom, HSBC did not, and so the HSBC bid for Midland was subject to scrutiny under the Regulation. By contrast, Lloyds achieved more than two-thirds of its Community-wide turnover in the United Kingdom and, because Midland did as well, this took the proposed Lloyds/Midland merger outside the Regulation, and made it subject to United Kingdom merger control. The Lloyds/Midland merger was referred to the United Kingdom Monopolies and Mergers Commission; no such reference could be made in respect of the rival HSBC bid. This gave the HSBC bid a significant advantage in the battle for control of Midland, and in the event Midland accepted the HSBC bid.

3.2.4 The Turnover Test in Operation

Examples 1 and 2 below demonstrate the basic operation of the original turnover test in Article 1(2).

Example 1

Undertaking A acquires a controlling interest in undertaking B. Their turnover is as follows:

Turnover (in million euro)	Undertaking A	Undertaking B
Worldwide	3,500	2,000
Community-wide	1,500	200
Two-thirds earned within one Member State	No	No

---

[6] *cf.* the application of Art. 81 in such circumstances: *e.g.* Case 246/86 *Société Co-operative des Asphalteurs Belges (Belasco) and others v. Commission* [1989] E.C.R. 2117, at 2181, [1991] 4 C.M.L.R. 96 at paras 33–38. The Commission's Statement in relation to Art. 22 that concentrations with a worldwide turnover below 200 million euro or Community turnover below 100 million euro are unlikely to have a significant effect on trade between Member States looks questionable when one compares the case law in relation to Art. 81.

[7] The concept of turnover for credit and other financial institutions is subject to special rules in Art. 5(3) of the Regulation: see para. 3.7, below.

The acquisition does not have a Community dimension under Article 1(2). Article 1(2)(a) is satisfied: the combined aggregate worldwide turnover of A and B is 5,500 million euro, 500 million euro above the threshold. Article 1(2)(b), however, is not satisfied: although undertaking A has very significant Community-wide turnover, undertaking B's turnover in the Community is only 200 million euro, below the 250 million threshold which must be met by each of at least two of the participants. No other undertakings are concerned in the concentration.

If, however, in the same example a third undertaking, C, with a Community-wide turnover of 300 million euro, was concerned in the concentration, Article 1(2)(b) would be satisfied and the concentration would have a Community dimension by virtue of the original thresholds: both A and C have a Community-wide turnover in excess of 250 million euro. Since we have already assumed that A and B each do not earn more than two-thirds of their aggregate turnover within one and the same Member State the tailpiece of Article 1(2) does not take the acquisition outside the Regulation, and this remains the case irrespective of where C's Community turnover is earned. Even if all C's turnover was earned, for example, in the United Kingdom it would not affect the result since the tailpiece requires that each of the undertakings concerned—that is, A, B and C—earns more than two-thirds of its aggregate Community turnover within one and the same Member State if the acquisition is to remain a matter for national merger control.

Example 2

Undertaking A acquires a controlling interest in undertaking B. Turnover is as follows:

Turnover (in million euro)	Undertaking A	Undertaking B
Worldwide	3,500	2,000
Community	1,500	300
United Kingdom	1,100	250
Rest of Community	400	50

In this example, although both Article 1(2)(a) and 1(2)(b) are satisfied, each of the two undertakings concerned in the concentration achieves more than two-thirds of its aggregate Community turnover in the United Kingdom, that is, within one and the same Member State. Thus, the concentration lacks Community dimension under the original threshold for E.C. jurisdiction in Article 1(2) of the Regulation.

Example 3

Example 3 builds on the first example above and illustrates the operation of the additional thresholds in Article 1(3) of the Regulation.

Turnover (in million euro)	Undertaking A	Undertaking B
Worldwide	3,500	2,000
Community-wide	1,500	200
Germany	75	100
France	110	15
Italy	100	30
United Kingdom	1,200	30
Netherlands	15	25
Two-thirds earned within one Member State	Yes-U.K.	No

The acquisition of undertaking B by undertaking A (the two undertakings concerned) would not fall within the original jurisdiction of the Commission because B does not earn 250 million euro turnover in the Community. The acquisition would, however, be caught by the additional thresholds since:

(a) A and B each earns more than 100 million euro from sales in the Community (Article 1(3)(d) is satisfied);

(b) the combined aggregate turnover of A and B exceeds 100 million euro in four Member States (France, Germany, Italy and the United Kingdom) (Article 1(3)(b) is satisfied);

(c) the aggregate turnover of each of A and B is more than 25 million euro in Germany, Italy, and the United Kingdom (Article 1(3)(c) is satisfied); and

(d) the two-thirds proviso does not apply since B does not earn more than two-thirds of the Community turnover in the United Kingdom (or, indeed, any Member State) even though the acquirer A does.

Thus, the transaction falls within the jurisdiction of Brussels.

The turnover assumptions can be varied to illustrate other aspects of the new Article 1(3) thresholds. For example, if undertaking B earned no turnover in Italy, Article 1(3)(c) would not be satisfied because in only two Member States (Germany and the United Kingdom) would A and B each earn more than 25 million euro. On the same assumption, however, Article 1(3)(b) would still be met in France, Germany and the United Kingdom. But note that Article 1(3)(c) must be satisfied for the same three Member States in relation to which Article 1(3)(b) (the 100 million euro aggregate per Member State) is satisfied. The following example, involving a multilateral joint venture, illustrates this point:

Example 4

Turnover (in million euro)	Undertaking A	Undertaking B	Undertaking C	Undertaking D
Worldwide (2635)	900	85	150	1500
Community-wide	135	85	125	140
Denmark (105)	25	20	60	—
Finland (90)	60	—	—	30
Germany (180)	30	50	40	60
Sweden (110)	20	15	25	50
Two-thirds earned within one Member State	No	No	No	No

In this case the Commission would not have jurisdiction over the joint venture and individual filings might well need to be made to national merger control authorities. This is because Article 1(3)(b) is satisfied in Denmark, Germany and Sweden but Article 1(3)(c) is not satisfied in respect of the same three countries, but in respect of Germany, Sweden and Finland. In Denmark, which must be brought into account if Article 1(3)(b) is to be satisfied, only undertaking C earns turnover of more than 25 million euro. Criteria (b) and (c) are thus not satisfied in respect of the same (at least three) Member States. *Lucent Technologies/Ascend Communications* provides a recent example of a concentration which fell within the Regulation by virtue of the Article 1(3) thresholds.[8]

In order to apply the additional thresholds correctly, and timeously, it is even more important since March 1, 1998 that companies record turnover by Member State in accordance with the principles relating to the definition and treatment of turnover in the Regulation.

3.3 CALCULATION OF TURNOVER

3.3.1 The Basic Rule (Article 5(1))

Article 5 deals in detail with the definition of turnover, and its calculation, and makes provision for a number of special cases. Article 5(1) (first sub-paragraph) provides:

> "Aggregate turnover within the meaning of Article 1(2) shall comprise the amounts derived by the undertakings concerned in the preceding financial year from the sale of products and the provision of services falling within the undertakings' ordinary activities after deduction of sales rebates and of value added tax and other taxes directly related to turnover. The aggregate turnover of an undertaking concerned shall not include the sale of products

---

[8] Case No IV/M.1440, para. 5.

or the provision of services between any of the undertakings referred to in paragraph 4''.

It should be noted that turnover in ECSC products should be included in any calculation for the purposes of the Regulation where a notified concentration involves a coal or steel undertaking. There is no express exclusion for such turnover in the Regulation, nor would exclusion be required by Article 305 of the E.C. Treaty. This is implicitly confirmed in the calculations of turnover in cases notified under both the Regulation and the ECSC Treaty.[9]

3.3.2 Meaning of "Turnover"

Article 5(1) defines the aggregate turnover of an undertaking as comprising amounts derived "from the sale of products and the provision of services falling within the undertaking's ordinary activities" after the deduction of sales rebates, VAT[10] and other turnover taxes. This definition follows closely that of "net turnover" in Article 28 of the Fourth Company Law Directive.[11] One would not therefore expect to include in the calculation income from participating interests, other investments and loans forming part of the fixed assets, other interest and similar income, and extraordinary income (such as profit from sales of items where they are assets employed in the business but not products of that business).[12] All the profit and loss formats provided by the Fourth Directive require the statement of net turnover.[13] Companies, however, may not maintain their accounts or accounting records in a form which immediately suits the turnover criteria in the Regulation, and the practical difficulties of ascertaining accurate turnover figures in the time within which a notification is required should not be under-estimated.

In the Turnover Notice, the Commission recognises the difficulty of ascertaining turnover in the case of certain service sectors, such as tourism and advertising, where the service is sold through the intermediary of other suppliers. The Commission acknowledges that the turnover of a service undertaking which acts as an intermediary may consist solely of the amount of commissions which it receives.[14]

As we have said, Article 5(1) requires the deduction "of sales rebates and of value added tax and other taxes directly related to turnover". The Notice makes clear that "sales rebates" should be taken to mean all rebates or discounts which are granted by the undertakings during their business negotiations with their customers and which have a direct influence on the amounts

---

[9] *e.g. Avesta/British Steel/NCC* and *British Steel/Svensk Stal/NSD*.

[10] SSAP 5 (Accounting for value added tax) provides that the profit and loss account should exclude VAT on taxable outputs. If it is wanted to show gross turnover, the VAT relevant to that turnover should be shown as a deduction in arriving at the turnover exclusive of VAT.

[11] Fourth Council Directive on the annual accounts of certain types of companies: 78/660 [1978] O.J. L222/11.

[12] For the position in U.K. law, see para. 55 of Sched. 4 to the Companies Act 1985.

[13] See Arts. 22–26 of the Fourth Directive.

[14] Turnover Notice, paras 12 and 13.

of sales.[15] "Other taxes directly related to turnover" means other forms of indirect taxation such as taxes on alcoholic beverages.[16]

3.3.3   Relevant Financial Year

Aggregate turnover is calculated on the basis of turnover in the preceding financial year; that is, the completed financial year immediately preceding the year in which the concentration is notified. If a concentration takes place in September 1999 between two undertakings, A and B, and A's financial year ends at the end of March, and B's at the end of October, the turnover figures would be those for the financial years April 1, 1998 to March 31, 1999 and November 1, 1997 to October 31, 1998 respectively.

In practice the most recent audited accounts are treated by the Commission as definitive in assessing turnover, even if they may not be fully representative of the undertaking's true financial position. Thus, for example, where there has been a temporary change in the undertaking's financial position as a result of a decrease in orders or a slow-down in production in the period prior to the transaction, such factors will be ignored for the purposes of calculating turnover. No adjustment to the definitive accounts will be made to incorporate them.[17] Likewise, in contrast with certain block exemptions in the case of Article 81 E.C., there is no provision under which, where the turnover figures in the more recent audited accounts are only marginally in excess of a particular threshold in Article 1(2), account could be taken of earlier years.

Problems can arise where notification of a concentration takes place shortly after the end of the financial year and audited figures are unavailable for that financial year. The Commission is generally reluctant to rely on unaudited, provisional or management accounts.[18] However, in exceptional cases, where there is a major divergence between the audited accounts of an earlier year and the unaudited accounts of the immediately preceding financial year, and final draft figures are available for the immediately preceding year, the Commission should, it is submitted, take those final draft figures into account, if it is to comply strictly with the terms of the Regulation.[19]

According to the Turnover Notice, where there has been an acquisition (for example of a subsidiary or a factory) in the period between the date of the audited accounts and the event triggering the notification obligation under the Regulation,[20] the turnover generated by the company or assets acquired must be added to the undertaking's turnover as set out in its most recent audited accounts. By the same token, where the undertaking disposes of a subsidiary or closes a factory in that period, the turnover generated by that subsidiary or factory must be subtracted from the most recent audited accounts.[21] Presum-•

---

[15] *ibid.*, para. 20.
[16] *ibid.*, para. 21.
[17] *ibid.*, para. 28.
[18] *ibid.*, para. 26.
[19] *ibid.*, para. 26.
[20] That is the conclusion of the agreement to form the concentration, or the announcement of the public bid, or the acquisition of a controlling interest (Art. 4(1) of the Regulation).
[21] Turnover Notice, para. 27.

ably the same applies where an undertaking has been recently formed and has earned turnover, but has not completed a financial year, in the period prior to notification of the concentration—although there is no formal Commission guidance on the point. These statements of practice appear, however, to be glosses, albeit sensible ones, on the Regulation itself and it will be interesting to see what approach the Community courts take if a challenge to the Commission's jurisdiction turned on one of these points. It is worth recalling that the Turnover Notice does not bind the Court.

3.3.4 Conversion of Turnover into Ecus and Euros

The turnover thresholds in the Regulation are expressed in euros. In converting the figures in an undertaking's accounts from Member State currencies, where this is still necessary, the exchange rate adopted should be the overall average rate for the twelve-month period concerned—a figure which can be obtained from the Commission; it should not be a sum of component quarterly, monthly or weekly sales figures converted individually at the corresponding average quarterly, monthly or weekly rates.[22] Where an undertaking has sales in a range of currencies, the conversion into euros should be from the currency as given in the consolidated audited accounts. Local currency sales as recorded outside the consolidated audited accounts should not be converted directly into Euros.[23]

These principles apply equally to the calculation of turnover in ecus following the introduction of the euro on January 1, 1999. The Commission's practice in cases where a financial year bridges that date is to convert the turnover in ecus earned before January 1, 1999 into euros on a one-to-one basis.[24]

3.3.5 Disregard of Intra-group Transactions

Article 5(4) provides that the turnover of an undertaking concerned in a concentration is to be calculated by aggregating the turnover of all members of the group, as defined in that Article (although it is to be noted that the word "group" is never used). The impact of this provision is discussed below. However, Article 5(1) (second sentence) ensures that the supply of products or the provision of services by one group company to another is excluded in making the calculation, thus avoiding any element of double-counting. Turnover is that achieved on supplies to parties outside the "group".[25] Under Article 5(5)(a) supply between the parties to the concentration and jointly controlled undertakings is also excluded. Standard accounting practice may not always reflect these provisions. The objective, however, is to ensure that the calculation of turnover is carried out in such a way as genuinely to reflect the economic strength of each undertaking concerned in the concentration.

[22] *ibid.*, para. 49.
[23] *ibid.*, para. 50.
[24] *Swiss Life/Lloyd Continental*, para. 6 and footnote 1.
[25] See also Turnover Notice, paras 22 and 23.

3.3.6   Geographical Allocation of Turnover

In order to ascertain whether there is a "Community dimension", it is necessary to know where the turnover of the undertakings concerned has been
"achieved": in particular, how much has been achieved within the Community, and how much has been achieved in a particular Member State of the
Community, since (as we have seen) these are among the criteria laid down
in Article 1(2). Allocation to Member States is even more important to the
correct application of the second set of thresholds in Article 1(3). Article
5(1) (second paragraph) attempts to clarify how turnover is to be allocated
geographically:

> "Turnover, in the Community or in a Member State, shall comprise prod-
> ucts sold and services provided to undertakings or consumers, in the Com-
> munity or in that Member State as the case may be."

This simply begs the question: is the place where the turnover is achieved the
place where the products are sold and the services provided, or the place where
the undertakings are located? They are not always identical. For example, a
motor car might be sold in Berlin to a customer who is resident in Paris. It is
not always easy for parties to obtain figures on the geographical breakdown
of their turnover. The notes to company accounts may give some geographical
breakdown but commonly they are insufficient for the purposes of applying
the thresholds in the Regulation.[26] The Turnover Notice states that, in the
absence of figures in the audited accounts, the Commission "will rely on the
best figures available provided by the companies in accordance with the rule
laid down in Article 5(1)".[27] This is a necessary exception to the Commission's general reluctance to admit material from unaudited management or
provisional accounts such as those prepared to effect a disposal of a business.[28]

    The Turnover Notice implies that the crucial question is where the transac-
tion takes place, even when the customer may not be located there. However,
the Notice points out that "in most circumstances" the place where the deal
was made, the turnover for the supplier in question was generated and competition with alternative suppliers took place, is the place where the customer
is located. Where this is so, turnover should be attributed to the place where
the customer is located (and if the place where the billing was subsequently
made is different from this, turnover should nonetheless be allocated to the
place where the customer was located).[29]

    Special difficulties have arisen in the geographical allocation of airlines'
turnover. In *Delta/PanAm* the Commission noted that there were three possible

---

[26] Art. 43 of the Fourth Company Law Directive requires the following information: "8, the net turnover
within the meaning of Art. 28, broken down by categories of activity and into geographical markets in
so far as, taking account of the manner in which the sale of products and the provision of services falling
within the company's ordinary activities are organised, these categories and markets differ substantially
from one another".

[27] Para. 29.

[28] Turnover Notice, para. 26.

[29] Turnover Notice, para. 46.

methods of assessing where the turnover of an airline is achieved. The revenues from a flight could be attributed:

(i)   to the final destination point outside the home country of the airline; or

(ii) on a 50/50 basis between the country of origin and the country of final destination; or

(iii) to the country where the ticket sale occurred.

In that case, however, the Commission refused to decide which of these methods should be adopted: it was unnecessary to do so since the particular concentration had a Community dimension whichever of the above methods was chosen. In *Air France/Sabena* and *British Airways/TAT*, the Commission followed its approach in *Delta/PanAm*, both in identifying the three possible methods and in declining to express a preference between them because whichever method was applied, the concentrations in question had a Community dimension. The only (slight) indication of the Commission's preference came in *Air France/Sabena*, where the decision notes that "the second criterion seems to be the one closest to the spirit of Article 5(1) as it is directed towards the two places between which the air transport service was in effect supplied, thus having regard to its cross-border character".

The transcontinental provision of services also caused difficulties of calculation in *Alcatel/STC*. The parties included all turnover earned from any submarine telecommunications system which had at least one landfall in the Community, *i.e.* a direct physical link. But the Commission rejected this approach in favour of apportioning turnover based on the place of establishment of the undertaking owning an individual share of a submarine cable and the extent of its interest. The market for which turnover had to be judged was not the service of conveying messages *via* undersea cables but the supply of capacity on such cables by the owners and operators. Care needs to be taken in applying the turnover thresholds in any case where an international dimension is involved and the prudent course is to raise the issue in pre-notification discussions with the Merger Task Force.

The issues which arise in allocating "turnover" in the case of credit and financial institutions and insurance undertakings has also given rise to problems. These are considered in paragraph 3.7 below.

A further complication in connection with assessing "Community-wide turnover" has arisen as a result of the expansion of the European Community. At the time of the last enlargement, in 1995, the territories of Austria, Sweden and Finland were added to the Community. Other countries have already applied to join. The question which arises is whether turnover from a new Member State should count as part of "Community-wide turnover" where the concentration has occurred shortly after that Member State has joined the Community, but during the period represented by the relevant accounts (*i.e* the "preceding financial year") the Member State had not yet joined. This question arose in 1991, shortly after the territory of the former East Germany was incorporated into the Federal Republic and thus became part of the Community. The French company Paribas and the German company München Trust Holding acquired joint control of the former East German enterprise

MBH, which had achieved much of its turnover in the former East Germany. By the time of the concentration, the former East Germany was part of the Community, but for part of the preceding financial year it had not been. Nevertheless, the Commission took the view that the turnover from the former East Germany throughout the preceding financial year should be regarded as Community turnover.[30] The Commission said:

> "MBH achieved most of its turnover in a territory that for part of 1990 did not belong to the European Community. As to the question of determining the size of the Community-wide activities of an undertaking for which, according to Article 1(2)(b) of the Merger Control Regulation, the turnover is the decisive criterion, one has to look at the time when the concentration was carried out, not the financial year preceding the concentration. Article 5(1) of the [Regulation] determines only the reference period for the calculation of the turnover. This provision does not contain any stipulation as to which territorial part of the European Community should be taken into account when considering the Community-wide activities of undertakings. With respect to this question, the general rules, regarding the assessment of the legal/technical characteristics of the undertakings participating in the concentration, such as whether or not they belong to the same group (Art. 5(4)), apply. According to this provision, one should look at the situation at the time of the concentration."

This is consistent with the overall objective of measuring the economic strength of an undertaking concerned in a concentration at the time it occurred. This interpretation also has significance when turnover is being considered which has been earned in a new Member State.

3.4   "UNDERTAKINGS CONCERNED"

It will have become apparent that the concept of "undertakings concerned" is central to the application of the turnover test. There are two stages here. First, for the purposes of applying both sets of turnover thresholds it is necessary to identify which are the "undertakings concerned" in the transaction.[31] Secondly, Article 5(4) requires that, in calculating the turnover of each undertaking concerned, it is necessary to aggregate that particular undertaking's turnover with the turnover of the rest of the group of which it forms a part—or, more precisely, with the turnover of every subsidiary, parent and collateral undertaking, and of every other undertaking in which any of the above undertakings together have "control rights" of the type listed in Article 5(4) (described below).[32]

    It is tempting to conflate these two stages, by identifying each undertaking concerned as the group of which it forms a part. But to do so would be misleading and could, in practice, lead to mistaken conclusions in applying the Regulation. Take, for example, a transaction under which undertaking AB, a joint venture of undertaking A and undertaking B, acquires control of under-

---

[30] *Paribas/MTH/MBH.*
[31] See para. 3.1.3, above.
[32] Para. 3.5.2.

taking C. Undertakings A and B are major industrial concerns with significant turnover earned in operations throughout the Community. The turnover figures are as follows:

Undertaking	Worldwide turnover	Community-wide turnover
A	2,500 m euro	325 m euro
B	3,000 m euro	300 m euro
AB	60 m euro	60 m euro
C	50 m euro	40 m euro

If undertakings A and B are themselves identified as "undertakings concerned", the acquisition will have a Community dimension; under Article 1(2)(b), each of at least two of the undertakings concerned has a Community-wide turnover of more than 250 million euro. But if AB is the undertaking concerned, and the turnover of undertakings A and B is brought into account only by virtue of the operation of Article 5(4), there will not be a Community dimension; only one undertaking, AB, has (by virtue of aggregation under Article 5(4)) a Community-wide turnover of more than 250 million euro.

It is therefore crucial in applying the Regulation both to identify the undertakings concerned and, having done so, then to calculate their turnovers by the aggregation required under Article 5(4).

3.4.1 Identifying the "Undertakings Concerned"

Guidance on identifying the "undertakings concerned" in a concentration is given both by cases decided under the Regulation and by a Notice on the notion of undertakings concerned (hereafter "the Undertakings Notice") (reproduced in Appendix 6).[33]

The concept of an undertaking is a familiar one in E.C. jurisprudence, and has been considered by the Court of Justice on several occasions.[34] Broadly speaking, it means an autonomous economic entity, regard being given to the functional substance of that entity rather than to its legal form. Thus an undertaking might be a single company, a group of companies, a joint venture, a partnership or an individual, depending, in each case, on whether the entity has economic autonomy.

The concept still throws up occasional difficulties in the context of the Regulation. In *Price Waterhouse/Coopers & Lybrand*, the Commission satisfied itself that Price Waterhouse operated a sufficiently centralised organisation

---

[33] The current notice [1998] O.J. C66/14 replaces the original 1994 version on the notion of undertakings concerned under the Regulation.

[34] See, *e.g.* Case 170/83 *Hydrotherm v. Andreoli* [1984] E.C.R. 2999; [1985] 3 C.M.L.R. 224; Joined Cases 159/91 & 160/91 *Poucet v. AGF* and *Pistre v. Cancova* [1993] E.C.R. I-637; Joined Cases 159/91 & 160/91; see also the judgment of the Court of First Instance in Case T-102/92, *Viho v. Commission* [1995] E.C.R. 11–17. The latter case, in particular, which considered whether the Parker Pen group in the E.C. constituted one or more economic units capable of operating intra-group arrangements falling within Art. 81 has important implications generally for international groups.

and strategy to justify the conclusion that its national constituent accountancy partnerships together constituted a single economic entity for the purposes of calculating turnover.[35] It left open the question whether Coopers & Lybrand was similarly one undertaking. Since the relevant Community threshold could be satisfied by taking the turnover of the Dutch, German or United Kingdom operations of Coopers & Lybrand, jurisdiction could be established even on the basis of treating the national partnerships as distinct economic units.

The question of which are the undertakings concerned in a concentration is more complex, and the jurisprudence yet to be developed. The Undertakings Notice states, in paragraph 3, that the undertakings concerned "are, broadly speaking, the actors in the transaction in so far as they are the merging, or acquiring, and acquired parties" and, in paragraph 5, that they are "the *direct participants* in a merger or acquisition of control" [emphasis added]. In *UBS/ Mister Minit* the acquirer sought to qualify its acquisition of the Mister Minit franchise operation as a concentration with Community dimension by aggregating the turnover of all the franchisees with that of the franchisor. It was argued that the degree of control exercised by the franchisor, which also owned the essential machinery and equipment leased to each franchisee, meant the franchisees did not constitute undertakings economically independent of the franchisor. Not surprisingly, this ingenious attempt at forum shopping was rejected by the Commission in an Article 6(1)(a) decision.

It follows from this that, in an acquisition of sole control, the vendor is not an "undertaking concerned" in the concentration. The vendor is not a direct participant in the concentration; on the contrary, by virtue of the acquisition, the vendor has left the stage. As the Commission says in the Undertakings Notice (paragraph 8):

> "Although it is clear that the operation cannot proceed without [the vendor's] consent, his role ends when the transaction is completed since, by definition, from the moment the seller has relinquished all control over the company [being acquired], his links with it disappear."

This explains *ICI/Tioxide*. ICI and Cookson each had 50 per cent of the shares in Tioxide. Under the transaction, ICI acquired from Cookson the 50 per cent which it did not already own. The Commission identified the undertakings concerned as ICI (as acquirer) and Tioxide as a whole (as acquired), but not the vendor Cookson. The Undertakings Notice explains that "in [such a] situation, the undertakings concerned are the remaining (acquiring) shareholder and the joint venture. As is the case for any other seller, the 'exiting' shareholder is not an undertaking concerned".[36]

The position is more difficult in cases where joint control is being acquired, established or exercised. For instance, in the hypothetical example discussed above, where AB (jointly controlled by A and B) acquires control of C, which are the undertakings concerned? The complexities involved here are discussed in more detail below[37] but, as a general rule, the jointly-controlled AB will

---

[35] [1999] O.J. L50/27, paras 7 to 17; point 18.
[36] Para. 31 of the Notice.
[37] See paras 3.6.7, 3.6.8.

count as an ''undertaking concerned'' if it is a full-function joint venture with sufficient financial and other resources to operate a business activity on a lasting basis, but will not be an ''undertaking concerned'' if it is merely a shell or a vehicle for the acquisition of the target company.[38]

3.4.2 Calculating the Turnover of Each Undertaking Concerned (Article 5(4))

Once the identity of the undertakings concerned in the concentration has been established for the purposes of Article 1, the turnover of each such undertaking is calculated by aggregating its own turnover with the turnover of other undertakings which are related to the undertaking concerned in any of the ways described in paragraphs (b) to (e) of Article 5(4). To the turnover of the undertaking concerned itself must be added the turnover of:

(i) undertakings in which the undertaking concerned, directly or indirectly:

— owns more than half the capital or business assets, or
— has the power to exercise more than half the voting rights, or
— has the power to appoint more than half the members of the supervisory board, the administrative board or bodies legally representing the undertakings, or
— has the right to manage the undertakings' affairs; (Article 5(4)(b))

(ii) undertakings having the rights or powers listed in (i) above, in the undertaking concerned; (Article 5(4)(c))

(iii) undertakings in which a ''parent'' undertaking within (ii) above has the rights or powers listed in (i) above; (Article 5(4)(d)) and

(iv) undertakings in which two or more other undertakings, being the undertaking concerned itself, or any undertakings within (i) to (iii) above jointly have the rights or powers of ownership or control mentioned in (i) above. (Article 5(4)(e)).

While the definition of turnover in Article 5(1) mirrors that in the Fourth Directive on Company Accounts, the definitions in Article 5(4) owe nothing to the Seventh Company Law Directive on Consolidated (or group) Accounts.[39] Article 5(4) follows, with the exception of sub-paragraph (e) (which deals with the particular phenomenon of jointly-owned entities), the formula which has been used in other Community competition law measures.[40]

---

[38] Undertakings Notice, paras 26 to 28.

[39] Directive 83/349 [1983] O.J. L193/1. The Directive contains six separate definitions of parent and subsidiary, of which only three or four (depending on the Member State concerned) are mandatory. The Directive does not provide a sufficiently harmonised result to be acceptable in the context of the Regulation.

[40] The formula has been used for nearly 20 years: see, *e.g.* Art. 4 of Regulation 2779/72 (block exemption for specialisation agreements). It is used in a variety of contexts to define ''group'', ''participating undertakings'' or ''connected undertakings'': see Form A/B, Introduction, Part K; Regulation 1983/84, block exemption for exclusive distribution agreements, Art. 4(2); Regulation 1984/83, block exemption for exclusive purchasing agreements, Art. 4(2); Regulation 1475/95, block exemption for motor vehicle

The indents to Article 5(4) set out different circumstances where one under-taking has to be treated as being connected with another. The indents are not mutually exclusive. A person who owns more than half the capital of a com-pany will usually have the power to exercise more than half the voting rights. On the other hand it is possible for a person to exercise more than half the voting rights without having more than half the capital,[41] because, for example, of the system of allocation of voting rights under the company's constitution or because it has the benefit of a voting agreement. It is also conceivable that more than one undertaking can have the rights referred to in Article 5(4)(b): for example, one company may have more than 50 per cent of the issued share capital but another more than 50 per cent of the voting rights.

The power to appoint members of the board may exist as a consequence of a majority shareholding or by virtue of the constitutional provisions of the company or some other legal arrangement. The question also arises whether a *de facto* ability to appoint the majority of the board, by being able to secure the passing of a resolution at the relevant meeting of the undertaking in ques-tion, gives rise to the relationship in the third indent of Article 5(4)(b). In *Arjomari-Prioux SA/Wiggins Teape Appleton plc*, the Commission proposed that, in the third indent of Article 5(4)(b), the power to appoint the majority of the board, should be interpreted not simply in absolute legal terms but by reference to the *de facto* ability to secure the passing of a resolution at the relevant meeting of the undertaking in question:

> "[the power to appoint] may also exist where an undertaking, although not having an absolute majority of the voting rights in an undertaking, holds the largest share and the remaining voting rights are dispersed. When it can be proved that the undertaking holding such a share has actually been able to make these appointments by controlling more than 50 per cent of the voting rights in the general meeting due to the absence of other rights, it is reasonable to assume that the power referred to under Article 5(4)(b) third indent exists."

The same principle was followed in *Eurocom/RSCG* and *Eridania/ISI*. In the latter case Article 5(4) was held to allow the entire Ferruzzi Group's turnover to count in the calculation of Eridania's turnover, since Eridania was controlled by Montedison, and the Ferruzzi Group had a 43.69 per cent shareholding in Montedison. The 43.69 per cent shareholding conferred Article 5(4) control rights on Ferruzzi because of "the extremely diverse nature of the remaining shareholders" (the next largest held just 11.4 per cent of the share capital) and the fact that all the board members were appointed directly or indirectly by Ferruzzi.[42]

This interpretation has been criticised as leading to legal uncertainty and considerable difficulty of application. Strictly speaking, the statement in

---

distribution, Art. 10(8); Regulation 240/96, block exemption for technology transfer of agreements, Art. 10(14); Regulation 417/85, block exemption for specialisation agreements, Art. 7(1); Regulation 418/85, block exemption for R&D agreements, Art. 9(2); and the Notice on Minor Agreements, Part II, para. 9.

[41] This appears to have been the position of MNG in *La Redoute/Empire*.

[42] See also *IFINT/EXOR* where the Commission noted that IFINT was described as "belonging to the AGNELLI group" in a public bid notice prepared for the French Stock Exchange and all the members of its board were in fact proposed and appointed by IFI, a subsidiary of the holding company, AGNELLI et Cie.

Arjomari is *obiter* since the Commission, even with this interpretation of Article 5(4), lacked jurisdiction. The practice in marginal cases, however, seems to be to examine how votes have been cast at recent AGMs or EGMs of the undertaking whose turnover is being considered for aggregation in accordance with Article 5(4). In its Turnover Notice[43] the Commission suggests that the "management" test in Article 5(4) is "somewhat different" from the "control" test in Article 3(3) of the Regulation but this appears questionable. Admittedly the "control" test is critical to the issue of whether a concentration has occurred[44] but the "management" test may be equally critical in determining whether a transaction has Community dimension such as to require an obligatory notification in accordance with Form CO.

The diagram below illustrates the operation of Article 5(4) in the context of an acquisition by undertaking A, a member of a major industrial group, of the widgets business of undertaking B. Only the calculation of A's turnover is covered in the diagram. The turnover of each of the undertakings shown in the diagram must be included in the turnover of A, the undertaking concerned, for the reasons indicated alongside each undertaking in the group. As already noted, intra-group transfers are excluded in aggregating the turnovers of the related undertakings, by virtue of Article 5(1) (second sentence).

Illustration of Article 5(4) in operation

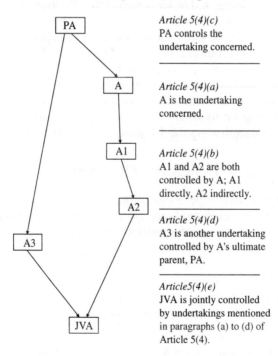

PA

Article 5(4)(c)
PA controls the
undertaking concerned.

A

Article 5(4)(a)
A is the undertaking
concerned.

A1

Article 5(4)(b)
A1 and A2 are both
controlled by A; A1
directly, A2 indirectly.

A2

Article 5(4)(d)
A3 is another undertaking
controlled by A's ultimate
parent, PA.

A3

Article5(4)(e)
JVA is jointly controlled
by undertakings mentioned
in paragraphs (a) to (d) of
Article 5(4).

JVA

---

[43] Para. 42.

[44] See now *Anglo American/Lonrho*—a striking recent illustration the Commission's approach on the "control" issue, where it found that Anglo American was in sole control of Lonrho through its influence over a shareholding of 27.47 per cent of the voting capital. The Commission justified this conclusion by reference to the following factors: Lonrho's shares were widely dispersed; in recent shareholder meetings a shareholding of 27 per cent would have been sufficient consistently to command more than 50 per cent of the votes

Difficult issues can also arise where an undertaking has terminated or disposed of its activities in a particular sector. In *BA/Dan Air* it was a condition of the acquisition of the Dan Air business by BA that Dan Air closed its loss-making charter business. The effect of omitting the turnover of that business from the calculation of Community dimension meant that the acquisition fell under United Kingdom and Belgian merger control but not under the Regulation. Competitors of BA failed in their attempts to persuade the Commission and the Court of First Instance that the acquisition was governed by the Regulation. However, *BA/Dan Air* was distinguished in *Rhône Poulenc Rorer/Fisons* where the issue was whether the turnover of certain business which had already been sold by Fisons conditionally upon regulatory and shareholder approval should be taken into account in calculating whether the acquisition of Fisons by Rhône Poulenc Rorer had a Community dimension and so fell within the Regulation. The Commission noted that both at the time of the notification and at the time of its first stage clearance decision the business disposals by Fisons still remained conditional and therefore concluded that the turnover attributable to those businesses had to be taken into account. The Commission's approach is described in the Turnover Notice.[45] Conversely, where a business has been acquired since the accounts for the preceding financial year have been prepared the turnover attributable to that business must be added in performing the turnover calculation required under the Regulation. It is suggested in such a case that the turnover to be taken into account will be that attributable to the acquired business as shown in the accounts of the vendor company for its financial year preceding that in which the concentration being notified occurred. Often, however, no distinct figure may be shown. For example, the acquisition may have been of particular assets to which turnover was not separately attributed in the accounts of the vendor undertaking. In such a case the disposal accounts and financial due diligence may contain information to satisfy the notification requirements if, indeed, the issue is critical to establishing the Commission's jurisdiction.

3.5   PARTICULAR TYPES OF TRANSACTION

The cases decided under the Regulation, together with the Turnover and Undertakings Notices, give guidance on the application of the general principles described above to specific types of transaction.

3.5.1   "Mergers"

Whereas in the United Kingdom concentrations usually occur as a result of acquisitions by one firm over another (typically called "mergers") or the

---

cast; the next largest shareholder in Lonrho, SA Mutual, held only 3 per cent of the voting shares but also held approaching 10 per cent of the shares in both Anglo American and De Beers thus creating a commonality of interest with the major shareholder in Lonrho; Anglo American was the only industrial/mining company among Lonrho's shareholders and the only such company represented on its board. Having analysed voting patterns during the period 1993 to 1996. The Commission also found that the decisive influence wielded by Anglo American was sufficiently stable and enduring to bring about a lasting structural change of the kind capable of constituting a concentration within the meaning of the Regulation.
[45] Para. 27.

formation of joint ventures in which the parties pool parts of their respective businesses, in many other legal systems it is not uncommon to see true "mergers" (*fusions*)[46] in which the parties pool the whole of their business together to form a single new company or business entity without either party having acquired control over the other. The treatment of such mergers for the purpose of calculating turnover is relatively straightforward. The "undertakings concerned" are the (two or more) previously independent entities, but not the new merged entity.[47]

3.5.2 Acquisition of Sole Control Over an Entire Undertaking

Where sole control is acquired over an entire undertaking, there are two "undertakings concerned": the acquiring undertaking and the acquired undertaking or target.[48] This is the case even where sole control (within the meaning of Article 3(3)) is conferred by virtue of the acquisition of a minority shareholding.[49]

3.5.3 Acquisition of Sole Control Over Part of an Undertaking

By way of exception to the basic rule, where the concentration consists in the acquisition of parts of one or more undertakings, only the turnover achieved by the acquiring undertaking and the parts acquired is taken into account in calculating turnover; the vendor's residual turnover is not counted.[50] This is an example of the principle, discussed above,[51] that the vendor "has left the stage" by virtue of the acquisition, and is no longer an "actor", so that the vendor should not be counted as one of the "undertakings concerned". Article 5(2) (first paragraph) provides:

> "By way of derogation from paragraph 1 [*i.e.* Article 5(1)], where the concentration consists in the acquisition of parts, whether or not constituted as legal entities, of one or more undertakings, only the turnover relating to the parts which are the subject of the transaction shall be taken into account with regard to the seller or sellers."

Although this provision refers to the acquisition of "parts" in the plural, the Undertakings Notice makes clear that it includes the singular.[52] The part or parts may be one or more separate legal entities (such as subsidiaries), or divisions without legal personality, or specific assets which in themselves constitute a business to which a turnover can clearly be attributed. Such assets

---

[46] See the discussion of true mergers at para. 2.3, above.
[47] Undertakings Notice, para. 12.
[48] *ibid.*, para. 13.
[49] See also the Commission's Notice on the notion of a concentration under the Regulation, [1998] O.J. C66/02, paras 13 to 17. The Notice is reproduced in App. 5.
[50] See, *e.g. Cereol/Continentale* and *Metallgesellschaft/Feldmühle*.
[51] See para. 3.4.1, above.
[52] Para. 14.

could include brands or licences or, in the case of airlines, specific routes.[53] Where it is a condition precedent of an acquisition that the acquired business will cease a particular activity, the activities which continue to be carried on will be treated as the "parts" acquired for the purposes of Article 5(2), whereas the activities ceased will be disregarded.[54]

Article 5(2) will apply wherever "sole control" is acquired over part of an undertaking, even though the vendor retains a minority stake. This was the case in *Magneti Marelli/CEAc*,[55] where Fiat acquired 50.1 per cent of a part of Alcatel Alsthom, its subsidiary CEAc, with the vendor (Alcatel Alsthom) retaining 48.3 per cent. Because the acquisition gave Fiat sole control over this part of Alcatel Alsthom, the Commission—applying Article 5(2)—had regard to the turnover of Fiat and of the part acquired by Fiat (CEAc). This case is to be contrasted with *Linde/Fiat*, in which Linde acquired 51 per cent of a part of Iveco, its subsidiary Carrelli, with the vendor (Iveco) retaining 49 per cent. It was held that, notwithstanding its 51 per cent shareholding, Linde had not acquired sole control over Carrelli, since Iveco's 49 per cent was accompanied by veto rights over business plans, budgets, etc., giving Linde and Iveco joint control. As a result, the turnover thresholds were calculated having regard not only to Linde and Carrelli, but also to Iveco.

3.5.4 Acquisition in Stages of Sole Control Over Parts of an Undertaking

The provision in Article 5(2) requiring that only the turnover of parts be taken into account does not allow avoidance of the Regulation through the piecemeal acquisition of parts of an undertaking in stages over a period of time. Article 5(2) (second paragraph) contains an anti-avoidance provision whereby if, within a two-year period, two or more acquisitions of parts of an undertaking take place in transactions between the same persons or undertakings, those acquisitions are to be treated together as one and the same concentration, and that concentration is deemed to have taken place on the date of the last acquisition.

An example of such a "staggered operation" is *Volvo/Lex*. Within the space of four months, Volvo first acquired the assets of a Lex subsidiary in the United Kingdom, and subsequently acquired the shares of a Lex subsidiary in the Republic of Ireland. In the second transaction, the Community-wide turnover of the part acquired was just 20 million euro (*i.e.* below the threshold). However, the second transaction was nevertheless deemed to be a concentration with a Community dimension, because the 20 million euro turnover was aggregated with the 784 million Euro Community-wide turnover of the part acquired in the first transaction. It should be noted, however, that acquisition of a shareholding in stages over a two-year period is not covered by this anti-avoidance provision.[56] A "staggered" operation, the constituent parts of

---

[53] *Delta/PanAm.*
[54] *British Airways/Dan Air*; upheld by the Court of First Instance in Case T-3/93 *Air France v. Commission* [1994] E.C.R. II-121. Distinguished in *Rhône-Poulenc Rorer/Fisons*, see para. 3.5.2, above.
[55] [1991] O.J. L222/38.
[56] This contrasts with the position in the U.K. under s. 66A of the Fair Trading Act 1973.

which bridge March 1, 1998, the date when the additional turnover thresholds began to apply, will fall to be considered under Article 1(3), as well as Article 1(2), as a result of deeming the concentration to occur on the date of the acquisition of the final part of the undertaking, provided always that that occurs within the two-year period.

3.5.5 Acquisition of Sole Control where Previously there was Joint Control

Generally transactions in which an undertaking acquires sole control where previously there was joint control fall into two types. The first and more common situation will be where one shareholder in a joint venture acquires the stake previously held by the other shareholder or shareholders (or at least a sufficiently large stake to constitute sole control). The second is where there is a "demerger" by which a joint venture's assets are broken up such that each parent acquires sole control of some of them. In the first case, the principle discussed in paragraph 3.5.1 applies.[57] An example of the second type of transaction is *Solvay-Laporte/Interox*. Interox was a joint venture in which Solvay and Laporte each had a 50 per cent shareholding. The parents agreed to break up Interox, with Solvay acquiring sole control (100 per cent) over one of Interox's businesses, and Laporte acquiring sole control (100 per cent) over the other. The transaction was regarded as comprising two concentrations; in one the relevant turnovers were those of Solvay and the part of Interox which it acquired, and in the other the relevant turnovers were those of Laporte and the part of Interox which it acquired.

3.5.6 Acquisition of Joint Control: Newly-Established Companies

The Undertakings Notice (paragraph 21) takes the view that, if a joint venture is a newly-established company, it could never have had a turnover of its own, so that the relevant "undertakings concerned" are only the companies acquiring joint control. An example of this is *Steetley/Tarmac* where the proposed joint venture was to be a new company to which the parents were transferring parts of their businesses: the relevant "undertakings concerned" were the whole of each of the two parent companies.

It should be noted, however, that there has been some inconsistency in the extent to which the Commission will have regard to the entire group turnover of the parent companies. In *Volvo/Atlas*, as in *Steetley/Tarmac*, the Commission took into account the entire group turnover of the undertakings participating in the joint venture. However, in *Sanofi/Sterling Drug*, the Commission had regard to the turnover of the immediate "parents" of the joint venture, Sanofi and Sterling Drug, but not to the corporate groups to which they belonged—Elf Aquitaine and Eastman Kodak respectively. Similarly, in the *Linde/Fiat*[58] case, it is surprising that the Commission had regard to the turn-

---

[57] Undertakings Notice, para. 31.
[58] Discussed in para. 3.5.3, above.

over of Iveco, which remained one of the "parents" with joint control over Carrelli, but not the entire group turnover of Fiat, of which Iveco was a subsidiary.[59] Because of these inconsistencies, it is sensible for the parties to have informal pre-notification discussions with the Merger Task Force where this issue would be material to determining whether there is a Community dimension. The issue is also relevant in ensuring that their notification is complete. The inconsistency in the Commission's approach is probably explained by the fact that once it has established to its satisfaction that the notified concentration has a Community dimension these issues become academic. Nevertheless, with the Commission now taking a stricter line on the completeness of notifications, it is prudent not to leave such issues unresolved.

3.5.7 Acquisition of Joint Control: Existing Company

Where joint control is acquired over an existing company or business, the Commission regards the relevant "undertakings concerned" as being each of the companies acquiring joint control, and also the existing acquired company.[60] Where joint control arises as a result of a parent which previously had sole control over an existing subsidiary company selling a shareholding in that subsidiary to another party (and thereby creating joint control over the company), the relevant "undertakings concerned" are each of the new parents and the target company (the former subsidiary, which is now jointly controlled).[61]

3.5.8 Acquisition by Jointly Controlled Company/Joint Venture

Acquisitions by jointly-controlled companies give rise to particular complexities. The determination of whether there is a "Community dimension" depends on whether the jointly-controlled company has been specifically formed for the purposes of the acquisition, or was a previously-established full-function joint venture.[62] Either way, the turnover of the parent companies and their groups is taken into account, by virtue of Article 5(4). However, the crucial difference lies in which parties are treated as the "undertakings concerned". As explained above,[63] the criterion that each of at least two "undertakings concerned" must have a certain level of Community-wide turnover (and, in the case of Article 1(3), Member State turnover) means that identifying the "undertakings concerned" can be decisive in assessing whether there is a Community dimension.

Where the acquisition is by a joint venture which is no more than a "vehicle" used by its parent companies for the acquisition—as in a consortium bid—the "undertakings concerned" will be each of the parent company and the target company, but not the joint venture itself. The Undertakings

---

[59] See also the questionable approach taken by the Commission in *Matra Marconi Space/British Aerospace.*
[60] Undertakings Notice, para. 22. See, *e.g. Thomas Cook/LTU/West LB.*
[61] *ibid.*, para. 23. See also *Northern Telecom/Matra Communication.*
[62] See para. 2.7.3.2, above.
[63] See para. 3.5, above.

Notice (paragraph 28) gives a list of examples of joint ventures as "vehicles". These include where the joint venture has not yet started to operate, or has no legal personality, or is not a full-function joint venture,[64] or is an association of undertakings, or is acquiring a target operating on a different product market, or otherwise appears not to be the "real player" in the acquisition (for instance, because the parent companies are significantly involved in the initiative, organisation and financing of the acquisition).[65]

In calculating the turnover of each "undertaking concerned" Article 5(4) requires that the turnover for each parent company is to be aggregated with the turnover of the rest of its group. As the parent companies are both "undertakings concerned" the calculation of turnover also needs to take into account the provisions of Article 5(5).[66]

The position is to be contrasted with acquisitions made by full-function joint ventures which are already operating on the market. Here, the "undertakings concerned" will be the joint venture itself and the target company but not the parent companies of the joint venture.[67] This does not mean that the turnover of the parent companies is ignored but merely that the parent companies do not count as separate "undertakings concerned". The Commission takes the view that Article 5(4) requires that the turnover of the joint venture must be aggregated with the turnover of both its parent companies and their groups. The reasoning behind this view lies in an interpretation of Article 5(4)(c), which provides that the turnover of an "undertaking concerned" includes the turnovers of:

"those undertakings which have in the undertaking concerned the rights or powers listed in (b) [*i.e.* owning more than half the capital or business assets, exercising more than half the voting rights, having the power to appoint more than half the board, or having the right to manage the undertaking's affairs]."

Although it is obviously not the case that each parent in a jointly-controlled company owns "more than half" the capital business assets of the joint venture, or has the power to exercise "more than half" the voting rights or to appoint "more than half" of the board, nevertheless it is arguable that both undertakings (jointly) have the right to manage the undertaking's affairs. The Commission takes the view that, because Article 5(4)(c) refers to "those undertakings", *i.e.* in the plural, having the relevant rights in the "undertaking concerned", it is proper to have regard to both undertakings which jointly control a joint venture. This interpretation can be criticised. The use of the plural "those undertakings" in Article 5(4)(c) appears to be merely a matter of drafting style rather than an indication that it applies to joint control.[68]

[64] As defined in the Commission's Notice on the distinction between concentrative and co-operative joint ventures under the Regulation, paras 13–16.
[65] See, for examples of this reasoning, *Asko/Jacobs/Adia* and *Eucom/Digital*.
[66] See para. 3.6.10, below.
[67] Undertakings Notice, para. 57.
[68] This view is supported by the fact that Art. 5(4)(e), which does relate to joint control (in circumstances where normal companies within the same Group jointly have rights or powers of control over an undertaking), expressly uses the term "jointly", whereas Art. 5(4)(c) does not.

Nevertheless, the Turnover Notice states that Article 5(4)(c) is intended to apply to parent companies of a jointly-controlled "undertaking concerned".[69]

3.5.9 Changes in Shareholdings in a Pre-Existing Joint Venture

There are various types of transaction which may lead to a change in the composition of the shareholdings in a joint venture or jointly-controlled company. The most important of these are considered below.

Where one or more existing shareholders leave the joint venture, the effect may be to give one of the remaining shareholders sole control where previously there was joint control. In such circumstances, the principles described in the first case in paragraph 3.5.5 above apply: the "undertakings concerned" are, first, the shareholder which has acquired sole control and, secondly, the company over which it exercises such sole control (previously the jointly-controlled company). Other shareholders in the company which do not exercise (sole or joint) control are not counted as "undertakings concerned".[70]

Another situation is where there is a departure of shareholders from the joint venture, but it does not lead to the acquisition of sole control by any of the remaining shareholders. There are two possibilities. First, the departure of the existing shareholder(s) may lead to "joint control" being exercised by more of the remaining shareholders than before. This was the case in *Avesta II*. Before the transaction there had been a joint venture between four main shareholders; two of these, British Steel and NCC, had exercised full veto rights, while the other two, Axel Johnson and AGA, each had only limited veto rights. Under the transaction, Axel Johnson sold its shares and left the joint venture, with the result that AGA's position was enhanced as it now exercised full veto rights. The Commission held that this meant that AGA's position in the joint venture would have "changed significantly" as a result of the transaction, and a change in the quality of control had occurred.[71] The relevant "undertakings concerned" in such a situation are each of the remaining shareholders exercising joint control and also the joint venture.[72] Secondly, if there is merely a reduction in the number of parties exercising joint control, without a change in the quality of control, the transaction is not a new concentration at all.[73]

Finally, there is the situation where a new shareholder "enters" the joint venture, whether or not one of the existing shareholders also "exits". The relevant "undertakings concerned" are each of the parent companies exercising joint control following the transaction (both existing shareholders and new shareholders), and the joint venture itself, but not the joint company which has exited.[74]

---

[69] Para. 38(3), maintaining in the 1998 Turnover Notice the same view expressed in its 1994 Notice.
[70] Undertakings Notice, paras 35–37.
[71] Contrast *Ford/Hertz* where Ford's move from *de facto* to legal control was not treated as a qualitative change.
[72] Undertakings Notice, para. 39.
[73] *ibid.*, para. 38.
[74] *ibid.*, paras 40–45; and *Synthomer/Yule Catto*.

3.5.10 Where the "Undertakings Concerned" are already Shareholders in an Existing Joint Venture (Article 5(5))

Where the "undertakings concerned" in a concentration already jointly have the "control rights" listed in Article 5(4)(b)[75] over another undertaking, Article 5(5) makes special provision to deal with the aggregation of turnover of that jointly-controlled entity. First, no account is taken of turnover resulting from goods or services passing between the joint venture and each of the "undertakings concerned" or, with any other undertaking the turnover of which falls to be aggregated with any undertaking concerned in accordance with Article 5(4)(b) to (e). Secondly, turnover achieved by the joint venture's sales to third parties is aggregated with the turnover of the undertakings concerned, by apportioning that turnover equally between the parent companies, irrespective of the actual ratio of their interests in the joint venture. Thus, if undertaking A and undertaking B are 50:50 shareholders in a joint venture company, the turnover of the joint venture is to be apportioned equally between them, and the apportioned figures aggregated with other turnover in accordance with Article 5. However, a 50:50 split of turnover will also be made if the joint venture is owned 60:40. The Commission also applies the same 50:50 split in cases where three parties, A, B and C, operate a joint venture, but only A and B are "undertakings concerned" in the concentration, provided that the interests of A and B in the joint venture are sufficient to give them joint control.[76]

3.5.11 Asset Swaps

Where two companies exchange assets (regardless of whether the assets constitute legal entities or not), the acquisitions of control by each over the other's assets are regarded as separate concentrations. In each case, the "undertakings concerned" are the acquiring company and the assets acquired.[77] One side of the swap may be a concentration with Community dimension while the other is not, even though the two halves of the transaction are inter-dependent and each conditional upon the other.[78]

3.5.12 Management Buy-Outs

Management buy-outs (MBOs) and similar operations raise a number of difficult issues in identifying the "undertakings concerned". The crucial question is: who will enjoy control of the undertaking after the buy-out—the individual managers, a vehicle company or outside investors? Where the managers acquire the target through a MBO company, the "undertaking concerned" will only be the MBO company if it is a full-function joint venture, rather

---

[75] See para. 3.5.2, above.
[76] Turnover Notice, para. 40. For an example of the application of Art. 5.5(b), see *McDermott/ETPM*.
[77] Undertakings Notice, paras 49 and 50.
[78] For an actual example which led to a second stage examination, see *Dupont/ICI*.

than a mere vehicle such that the individual managers and/or outside investors are the "real players".[79] If control is to be exercised by outside investors (rather than by the individual managers), and the acquisition company is merely a "vehicle", it is the outside investors which will be regarded as the "undertakings concerned". In *CWB/Goldman Sachs/Tarkett*, for example, two investor groups each held 44 per cent of the voting shares in a newly corporated company to carry out the MBO. One of the investor groups was itself jointly controlled and no more than a vehicle. The "undertakings concerned" were, therefore, the two parent companies of the jointly-controlled investor group, and also the other investor group. There are numerous Article 6(1)(c) decisions of this kind where no substantive competition issues arise.[80]

Where the control is actually held by the individual managers, they will only be regarded as "undertakings concerned" if they are actually "undertakings".[81]

3.5.13 Acquisitions of Control by Individuals

The Commission will regard an individual as an "undertaking" if he carries on outside economic activities of his own.[82] The "turnover" of the individual as "undertaking concerned" is to be calculated by aggregating the turnovers of the undertakings which he controls under Article 5(4).[83]

3.5.14 Acquisitions of Control by State Companies

Recital 12 to the Regulation makes clear that the control of concentrations will "respect the principle of non-discrimination between the public and the private sectors", implying that a state company may be an "undertaking concerned". The turnover of a state enterprise will comprise the turnover of all undertakings "making up an economic unit with an independent power of decision, irrespective of the way in which their capital is held or of the rules of administrative supervision applicable to them" (Recital 12). This principle was applied in *CEA Industrie/France Télécom/Finmeccanica/SGS-Thomson*.[84] Its application can give rise to some artificial results. In *Kali und Salz/MdK/ Treuhand* the Commission took the view that in calculating the turnover of MdK, the former East German potash producer, the turnover of all the undertakings supervised by the same departmental division of the Treuhandanstalt should be taken into account. It is not clear, however, why administrative units within an agency or government department should serve as a surrogate for the true economic entities which may make up a group in the private sector.

---

[79] Undertakings Notice, para. 53, read with paras 27 and 28.
[80] Recent examples include *CVC Capital Partners/Dynoplast, William Hill/Cinven/CVC* and *Hicks, Muse, Tate & Furst/Hillsdown Holdings*.
[81] *ibid.*, para. 53.
[82] *ibid.*, paras 51 and 52. See para. 2.2.2, above.
[83] The Undertakings Notice cites *Asko/Jacobs/Adia*, in support of this proposition, although the application of the principle is not apparent from the text of the published decision (an Art. 6(1)(b) decision).
[84] Where the French State's atomic energy company and its telephone company were regarded as separate "undertakings concerned", in spite of both being owned by the same Government.

Treatment of the Italian State-owned industries has also been somewhat anomalous.[85] The principle of non-discrimination seems to have been taken too far.

3.6   SPECIAL RULES FOR CREDIT AND OTHER FINANCIAL INSTITUTIONS AND INSURANCE UNDERTAKINGS

For credit and other financial institutions, and for insurance undertakings, special rules were considered necessary for the calculation of Community dimension. These rules are set out in Article 5(3) of the Regulation, which was substantially modified in the March 1998 changes as regards the calculation of banking turnover.

3.6.1   Credit and Other Financial Institutions (Article 5(3)(a))

Originally, for credit and other financial institutions, a calculation based on the worldwide assets of the institutions concerned applied by virtue of Article 5(3)(a) instead of turnover as defined generally in Article 5(1) of the Regulation.[86] Following *HKSB/Midland* the Merger Task Force began a review of the provisions regarding the calculation of banking turnover. As a result of this review Article 1(4) of the amending Regulation replaces Article 5(3)(a) with rules for calculating the turnover of financial undertakings which closely reflect the general turnover rules but identify respectively the following items of income: interest and similar income; income from securities; commissions receivable; net profit on financial operations; and other operating income.

The new Article 5(3)(a), which, like the other changes, applies to concentrations occurring on or after March 1, 1998, also seeks to tackle a second problem arising from the original provisions, namely, the geographical allocation of turnover. A new final paragraph to Article 5(3)(a) now provides that the heads of income listed above are to be regarded as the turnover of a credit or financial institution in the Community or a particular Member State where they are received by a branch or division of that institution in the Community, or in the Member State in question. This clarification is welcome, particularly for applying the additional turnover thresholds where it is even more important to attribute turnover correctly between Member States.

These changes not only eradicate the most serious problems of using the original ''assets'' test but also have the merit of being based on specific heads of income recognised in the Bank Accounts Directive.[87] This alone facilitates the collection of the data necessary to apply the turnover thresholds in the case of a concentration involving one or more financial institutions and to determine whether a notification in Brussels is necessary in respect of it.

---

[85] See *CEA Industrie/France Telecom/Finmeccanica/SGS-Thomson, Marconi/Finmeccanica, RWE-DEA/ Enichem Augusta.*

[86] The practical difficulties posed by the ''assets'' measure were considered in earlier editions, as were the Commission's attempts to introduce some flexibility into its application. Second edition, paragraph 3.7.1.

[87] Directive 86/635 concerning the accounts of banks and other financial institutions: [1986] O.J. L372/1.

The Turnover Notice (paragraphs 51 and 52) defines "credit institution" by reference to the First Banking Directive[88]:

> "an undertaking whose business is to receive deposits or other repayable funds from the public and to grant credits for its own account."

The Notice defines "financial institution" by reference to the Second Banking Directive[89]:

> "an undertaking other than a credit institution, the principal activity of which is to acquire holdings or to carry on one or more of the activities listed in points 2 to 12 in the Annex."[90]

3.6.2 Insurance Undertakings (Article 5(3)(b))

Article 5(3) also makes special provision for insurance undertakings. The provision remains as originally enacted in 1989, save for an amendment consequent on the introduction of the additional thresholds in Article 1(3).

In the case of insurance undertakings, premium income replaces "turnover". Article 5(3)(b) treats premium income as the value of gross premiums written, comprising

> "all amounts received and receivable in respect of insurance contracts issued by or on behalf of the insurance undertaking concerned, including also outgoing reinsurance premiums, and after deduction of taxes and parafiscal contributions or levies charged by reference to the amount of individual premiums or the total volume of premiums".

Gross premiums received from Community residents and Member State residents respectively replace Community and Member State turnover for the purposes of Article 1(2)(b) and the proviso in the final part of Article 1(2). "Insurance undertakings" for these purposes comprise all businesses carrying on underwriting activity, including reinsurance, life assurance and pensions. Non-underwriting insurance businesses (such as insurance brokers or insurance consultants) are classified as "other financial institutions" and are to be treated in accordance with the rules set out above.[91]

In calculating the level of premiums in the preceding financial year, regard

---

[88] Directive 77/780 [1977] O.J. L322/12.
[89] Directive 89/646 [1989] O.J. L386/1.
[90] These activities include: lending (*inter alia*, consumer credit, mortgage credit, factoring and financing of commercial transactions (including forfaiting)); financial leasing; money transmission services; issuing and managing instruments of payment (credit cards, travellers' cheques and bankers' drafts); guarantees and commitments; trading on own account or on account of customers in money market instruments, foreign exchange, financial futures and options, exchange and interest rate instruments, and transferable securities; participation in share issues and the provision of services related to such issues; advice to undertakings on capital structure, industrial strategy and related questions and advice and services relating to mergers and the purchase of undertakings; money broking; portfolio management and advice; and safekeeping and administration of securities.
[91] Para. 3.7.1, above.

must be had not only to new insurance contracts made during that year, but also to all premiums related to contracts made in previous years which remain in force during the period taken into consideration.[92] Where (as is normal) an insurance undertaking holds investments, a distinction is made between those investments which give it a controlling interest over the undertaking in which it has invested—in which case the turnover of that undertaking is aggregated with the gross premiums written of the insurance undertaking itself—and those which are pure financial investments such that the insurance undertaking is not involved in the management of the undertaking—in which case the turnover is disregarded.[93] In *Allianz/DKV* the Commission also left out of account premiums from the reserves for reimbursements in life insurance which under German insurance law Allianz was entitled to record as premium income, despite being of a different character. Disregarding these amounts meant that the acquisition of DKV fell within the Regulation rather than under German merger control.

With regard to the geographical allocation of premiums, the basic rule is that they are allocated according to the place of residence of the customers who pay insurance premiums. Where those customers are banks or (in the case of reinsurance) other insurance undertakings, branches, divisions and other undertakings operating on a lasting basis but not having a legal personality are considered as resident in the countries in which they have been established.[94]

3.6.3 Financial Conglomerates

Further complications arise where an "undertaking concerned" in a concentration carries on the business of more than one "category" of institution. This is a common problem. Thus, in *HKSB/Midland*, the Midland Group comprised businesses which were: credit institutions; other financial institutions (such as stockbrokers); insurance undertakings; and ordinary commercial undertakings (Midland's then subsidiary Thomas Cook, the travel agent). The Regulation is silent on how to deal with such situations. The Turnover Notice (paragraph 64) suggests a method of calculation in such circumstances, but states pragmatically that detailed calculation need only be undertaken where it seems that the turnover of the financial conglomerate is likely to be close to the thresholds. The Commission recognises that the method it suggests "may in practice prove onerous".

Its suggestion is to calculate the "turnover" of each category of business in the conglomerate, according to the method appropriate to that category, and then to aggregate them as appropriate in order to obtain worldwide, Community-wide and Member State turnover. However, to calculate the "credit and financial institution" category, a special method is recommended:

(a) The "worldwide" figure should be one-tenth of "assets", calculated

---

[92] Turnover Notice, para. 59.
[93] *ibid.*, paras 60 and 61. See, as an example of the turnover of subsidiary undertakings being counted, *AG/ Amev*.
[94] Turnover Notice, paras 65 and 67.

for these purposes by having regard to the assets on the non-consolidated balance sheet of the financial holding company, and counting (i) bonds and other interest-bearing securities plus (ii) shares which the holding company has in undertakings in which it does not have Article 5(4) control rights.

(b) The "Community-wide" figure is calculated by multiplying one-tenth of the figure in (a) by the ratio between "loans and advances to Community residents" and "loans and advances worldwide".

(c) The "Member State" figure is calculated by multiplying the figure in (a) by the ratio between "loans and advances to residents in the Member State" and "loans and advances worldwide".

(d) For the purposes of (b) and (c), bonds and other interest-bearing securities are to be considered as loans and advances.

3.7 SOME PRACTICAL CONSIDERATIONS

The turnover thresholds in the Regulation are simply a jurisdictional tool, albeit an important one, for distinguishing concentrations subject to an obligatory filing under the Community regime from others. Their application rarely gives rise to practical problems, at least as far as the Commission is concerned, except in borderline cases, such as the bid for Midland Bank by HKSB in 1991. For companies, however, it is often difficult, without enormous work, to provide definitive figures calculated as required by the Regulation. This is particularly so for investment companies, and companies whose turnover is derived from a range of activities, particularly where they require different treatment in terms of calculating turnover. It need not, however, delay notification.

If it is abundantly clear that it has jurisdiction the Commission will not demand definitive figures as a condition of treating a notification as complete. Equally it may not need to explore precisely which undertakings are to be treated as comprising the groups to which the undertakings concerned belong if it is already satisfied that it has jurisdiction beyond doubt. In this way difficult questions of control arising under Article 5 of the Regulation need not always be determined conclusively.

Published merger decisions of the Commission recite, somewhat laconically, the bare turnover essentials in order to confirm that the Commission has jurisdiction. Indeed, in some cases, actual or approximate turnover figures are omitted as being confidential, where these are not otherwise publicly available. This may assuage fears of publicity, for example, where wealthy individuals are the ultimate controllers of undertakings concerned in a merger and would not otherwise be required to disclose the turnover of companies they own.

Perhaps the greatest practical difficulties companies face in relation to applying the turnover rules occurs not when they are actually in the process of notifying a transaction to the Commission but when they are still at the strategic planning stage, perhaps considering internally various proposals for acquisitions or joint ventures. There may be procedural and substantive advantages in falling within the Regulation. Procedurally, the one-stop shop becomes available. In the 10 years since merger control was introduced at the E.U. level, many Member States have introduced national merger controls. While ostensibly these follow the model established in the Regulation, in practice, consistency of treatment cannot be taken for granted. A second advantage is that the Commission must make its initial decision within the relatively short one month timetable. Substantively, as explained in Chapter 5 below, the Commission has a considerable hurdle to overcome before it can intervene to prohibit or impose conditions on a merger. In some Member States, concentrations can be examined and prohibited on competition grounds without establishing dominance, or the grounds for intervention are broader and less well-defined. Decisions of the Commission are also subject to appeal, whereas review in Member States is often very much more limited. Against this, in some Member States at least, notification is voluntary and, furthermore, there may be no embargo on the implementation of a transaction pending clearance. Overall, however, meeting the thresholds in the Regulation confers more advantages than disadvantages and it is as well for companies and their advisers to know as well in advance as possible to which jurisdictions their acquisition strategies will take them and by what tests their proposals will be scrutinised. This may even give them critical advantages over rival acquirers, as HKSB found in beating off the rival bid by Lloyds Bank for Midland.

4 Notification and Investigation

4.1 GENERAL OBSERVATIONS

The procedural rules governing the notification and appraisal of concentrations are set out in the Regulation and the Implementing Regulation. The basic pattern follows that of the implementing regulations (made under Article 83 (ex 87) of the E.C. Treaty) relating to the application and enforcement of the competition rules in Articles 81 and 82 of the Treaty.[1] The reader will note the similarity between Articles 11 to 20 of the Regulation and Articles 10 to 21 of Regulation 17. There are, necessarily and otherwise, differences in the detail. The more significant differences, which have over the last few years effected a cultural change in the Commission's handling of cases generally, are dictated by the rules in the Regulation which provide, in the interest of legal certainty, that all procedures are to be concluded by decision,[2] actual or deemed (Articles 6 and 8), and which lay down rigorous time restraints (Article 10). These rules have to date left no room for comfort letters ("closing the file") and other forms of informal settlement. Having said this, because of the complexity of the procedure and the time restraints, the need to have informal contact with the Commission, both before and during the procedure, is in practice paramount and is rightly encouraged by the Commission.[3] Pre-notification meetings are a key feature in the Commission's "Best Practice Guidelines", published on the Competition Directorate's website on the Internet.[4]

As indicated in Chapter 1, the Commission has recently published three draft Notices. Two of them directly affect procedures under the Regulation. The draft Notice on commitments is dealt with in Chapter 7 below. The Notice "on a simplified procedure for processing certain concentrations" should be mentioned here. The essence of the proposal is that the Commission will refrain from adopting a formal clearance decision in certain cases, with the consequence that the mergers in question will be approved automatically upon expiry of the phase I deadline (R. Article 10(6)). There are implications for the earlier stages in the procedure. In particular, practitioners will have to pay

---

[1] Council Regulation 17 of 6.2.62; Council Regulation 1017/68 (inland rail, road, and waterways transport); Council Regulation 4056/86 (maritime transport); and Council Regulation 3975/87 (air transport).
[2] And see the "decision" in the *Dan Air* case: Case T-3/93 *Air France v. Commission* [1994] E.C.R. II-121 discussed at para. 7.6.2, below.
[3] Form CO and Recital 10 to the Implementing Regulation specifically refer to this process. Similar words have now been added to Reg. 3385/94 dealing with notifications (in accordance with Form A/B) for Art. 85 cases under Reg. 17.
[4] Under "Mergers —Other documents"—http://europa.eu.int/comm/dg04/

special attention to the definition of "affected markets" in the completion of Form CO. The draft Notice again emphasises the importance of pre-notification meetings and discussions with the Merger Task Force.

4.2 MERGER TASK FORCE

The Commission's Competition Directorate is made up of a number of directorates, each with a designated sectoral or other functional responsibility. The Merger Task Force, itself now Directorate B, comprises some 50 to 60 staff led by a director (A2). Below the director there are four teams (Operating Units i-iv)—each with a team leader—containing approximately eight or nine examining officers and clerical and secretarial support staff. The case team, however, does not work in a vacuum. It can draw on the sectoral knowledge of the appropriate operational directorate in the Competition Directorate. It will also keep in touch with Directorate A (responsible *inter alia* for overall policy and co-ordination). The Task Force is also able to call on outside experts and specialists as necessary. Other Directorates of the Commission may need to be consulted depending on the subject-matter of the case. The Legal Service will in practice also be involved and its opinion will be sought at key stages, for example before issuing a statement of objections or before a decision is made under Article 6 or 8 of the Regulation. Ultimately, however, decisions are taken not by officials but by the Commission itself, either by all the Commissioners together (the college) or by an individual Commissioner under delegated authority (*habilitation*). The Regulation contemplates something in the order of 30 different types of decision in the context of a notification and, following the practice in other competition cases under Regulation 17, a considerable number of these decisions have been delegated to the Commissioner having the responsibility for competition. In some cases there may be further delegation to the Director-General, and the director of the Merger Task Force.

4.3 NOTIFICATION

4.3.1 Principle of Prior Control

Although the Regulation contains no rule of prohibition or presumption against concentrations with a Community dimension (Article 2 provides a regime which starts from a neutral position), such a concentration cannot, as a general rule, be put into effect until it has been first notified to the Commission and the Commission has had an opportunity to examine it. Recital 17 lays down the principle that "to ensure effective control" undertakings should be obliged to give prior notification of concentrations with a Community dimension. The obligation itself is contained in Article 4(1). This requires a concentration to be notified to the Commission not more than one week after (i) the conclusion of the agreement, (ii) the announcement of the public bid, or (iii) the acquisition of a controlling interest. In some transactions more than one of these elements may be involved in the process of concentration. Article 4(1) recognises this by providing that the period within which notification must be made begins to run from when the first of those events occurs. For example, prior to a public bid, the offeror may purchase shares of the target undertaking in the market, or may gain irrevocable undertakings to accept the forthcoming public offer from one or more significant shareholders in the target, tactics which may conceivably give rise to a concentration at a time when no bid has been announced.[5] Article 7 provides for an automatic period of suspension during which a concentration must not be ''put into effect''. (Suspension is discussed in detail below.) In this fundamental respect the procedural approach of the Regulation is quite different, for example, from United Kingdom domestic controls, which include a procedure for voluntary pre-notification but do not make notification mandatory[6] or impose automatic suspension of a proposal.[7] In this respect the Community regime follows more closely the German model and now that adopted in a number of other Member States.

4.3.2 Form CO

Annex 1 to the Implementing Regulation is entitled ''Form CO relating to the notification of a concentration pursuant to Council Regulation (EEC) No. 4064/89''. A closer examination, however, reveals that Form CO is not a form as such: rather it sets out what information must be supplied in order to constitute a ''notification'' for the purposes of the Regulation and provides the format in which that information should be provided.[8] Article 3(1) requires notifications to contain all the information, including documents, requested by the form. Form CO was last updated in 1997 to take account of the substantive changes made to the Regulation and effective from March 1, 1998.

The form requires a comprehensive, if not exhaustive, statement of the facts, circumstances and potential consequences and effects of the concentration. The time and effort necessary to complete a notification must not be underestimated. It will be prudent to begin preparation as early as possible. Indeed for major companies whose business strategies may include acquisitions, it is prudent to maintain up to date information about the company, its turnover, its products and services, and the markets in which they are sold. For U.S. listed companies SEC filings are a useful source of such data. If the need to prepare is not recognised by all concerned the timetable for closing a deal may be severely disrupted. There is substantial volume of documents and other data to collect and organise. It is wise to check for prior notifications/filings

---

[5] This is but one example of the practical difficulties which are likely to arise in distinguishing steps toward concentration from the point at which the concentration is treated as taking place. The difficulties are accentuated by the apparent inconsistency between Arts. 4 and 7.

[6] Under ss. 75A to 75F of the Fair Trading Act 1973, a voluntary pre-notification system exists for proposals which have been made public. If a proposal is carried into effect prior to clearance, the benefit of the pre-notification procedure, essentially a guarantee of a decision on reference to the Competition Commission within a maximum of 35 working days, is lost.

[7] But see s.75(4A) of the Fair Trading Act 1973 imposing temporary restrictions on share dealings once a merger reference to the Competition Commission is made.

[8] IR.Art. 2(1) thus provides that information must be submitted ''in the manner prescribed'' by Form CO. This is also the approach of the equivalent procedural rules for Reg. 17 cases: see Art. 2(1) of Reg. 3385/94.

by the parties with the Commission as well as with national competition authorities including, where relevant, those outside the E.U. with whom the Commission has a special relationship (for example, the United States). The preparatory work should also include, at an early stage, a thorough analysis of the legal and economic issues. An assessment should also be made of the anti-trust and other regulatory risks. These may need to be taken into account in the negotiation of the transactional documents, in determining how these risks, in terms of costs and time, are being borne between the parties. Provision may be needed for divestment options/obligations, re-negotiation of price, etc.

The Implementing Regulation says that it is for the notifying parties to make "full and honest disclosure" of all facts and circumstances relevant for taking a decision on the concentration.[9] While it is difficult to set or to achieve an absolute standard of completeness against which a notification can be matched, the Commission has increasingly adopted the practice of declaring notifications incomplete. The Commission has recognised that it is potentially burdensome to parties but a certain amount of information is required at the outset of the procedure if the rigorous timetable in the Regulation, in particular the initial one month examination period, is to be met. At the same time the burdens on the Commission do not give it the luxury of flexibility with regard to the information requirements of Form CO. Clearly a balance has to be struck. The Commission's procedures provide for the possibility of a short-form version of notification though this is currently restricted to joint ventures.[10] The Regulation itself, however, requires the notification to be complete if time is to start running against the Commission for its initial assessment of the merger (Article 10(1)).[11]

Two other provisions may serve to lessen the burden on parties. Both are mentioned in paragraph B of Form CO. First, where a party is unable, because information is unavailable, to provide a response to a question or can only respond to a limited extent, it should indicate this and give reasons. If possible, the Commission should also be given an indication as to where the information might be had. Clearly this concession will be important in, for example, a contested bid situation, where the bidder may well not have, or have access to the information requested in relation to the target company. Secondly, Article 3(2) of the Implementing Regulation enables the Commission to dispense with the obligation to provide any particular information requested by Form CO where it considers such information is not necessary for the examination of the case. The Implementing Regulation does not itself say when this power can be exercised, in particular whether it can be exercised before a notification is made. However, Recital 10 specifically contemplates that, at the request of the parties concerned, the Commission will provide an opportunity "before notification to discuss the intended concentration informally and in strict confidence". The Commission quickly put this procedure into effect, despite doubts expressed as to the *vires* of the Commission exercising what is in effect

---

[9] IR. Recital 5.

[10] See para. C of Form CO, discussed at para. 4.3.6, below.

[11] It was felt that a general two-stage notification procedure along the U.S. lines of a Hart Scott Rodino preliminary filing and second request would not have been possible given the terms in which the Regulation was drafted.

a dispensing power prior to the making of an actual notification.[12] For example, it is prepared to discuss on a "without prejudice" basis the nature and detail of the information required in any particular case, and may be prepared to indicate its view on the basis of a draft notification which can then be amplified as necessary, within the terms of the Regulation and Implementing Regulation.[13] In practice such preliminary discussions often result in reducing significantly the amount of information to be supplied and in identifying where there are omissions which the Commission wishes to see made good.[14] Even though the opinion of officials given in such circumstances may not estop the Commission from later refusing to exercise the dispensing power, in practice changes of tack are unlikely.

Legal advisers may find their clients reluctant to enter into such prior discussions with the Commission. In the past, particularly in the context of public bids, offerors were unwilling to approach the Commission prior to announcement because of concerns about confidentiality. The Commission, however, responded to these concerns, especially in the security procedures which have been adopted in the Merger Task Force. In particular, where necessary, preliminary discussions and information will be confined to two, or at most three, individuals in the Merger Task Force, the case officer concerned, and his head of division, or the director himself.

It is important to recognise the benefits of early discussion with the Commission. Problems of interpretation of the Regulation may be cleared up, and, if a concentration gives rise to no significant concerns on compatibility, waivers may be obtained in relation to the content of the notification which will very significantly relieve the burden of the obligation to notify.[15] But to be beneficial the parties must be adequately represented (i.e. by persons who know the markets) and be prepared to disclose information and to be candid with the Commission. The first meeting should be at least one or two weeks before notification Is due and in some cases may need to be much earlier. The Commission usually expects a briefing memorandum at least three working days before that meeting. Following that meeting a draft Form CO is frequently submitted. The Commission likes a week to review it before any further meeting or telephone conference on the adequacy of the draft. Parties and their advisers should approach the exercise with a preparedness to modify proposals. It is not unusual for pre-notification discussions to extend over a month. But the time may be well spent if it avoids a notification being declared incomplete (this is discussed below). The exercise will also be important where a significant competitive overlap is identified which could readily be remedied by undertakings given in the first stage. In order to allow these to be considered by Member States and be subjected to "market testing" with competitors and

[12] In the authors' view there is, however, no doubt once the obligation to notify has arisen. It may be significant that in the changes made in 1994 by Reg. 3384/94 the dispensing power was moved from Art. 4 (Effective date of notification) to Art. 3 (Information and documents to be provided).

[13] This may place the competent authorities of the Member States at a disadvantage. They will not be privy to the discussions of the case prior to notification. The notification may then not give them all the information available to the Task Force. This makes assessment by the Member States even more difficult.

[14] This is expressly acknowledged in para. A of Form CO.

[15] This may be particularly relevant to Section 7 of Form CO, where the Commission recognises that there are likely to be few, if any, "compatibility" problems.

customers, the sooner they are discussed and tabled the better. Some discussions do not have to await formal notification.

4.3.3 Who Must Notify

The basic rule is that the notification must be made by the acquirer, *i.e.* the person or undertaking acquiring control for the purposes of Article 3(1)(b) (R.Article 4(2), and IR.Article 1(1)). Where, however, there is a merger within the meaning of Article 3(1)(a) or there is the acquisition of joint control for the purposes of Article 3(1)(b) then the notification must be made by the parties to the merger or those acquiring joint control, as the case may be (R.Article 4(2)). Where a situation of *de facto* joint control arises from the acquisition of a significant minority shareholding in another undertaking by a new investor, a joint notification is required. This may give rise to difficulties in practice, but the question of who is actually obliged to notify may pale into insignificance compared to some of the other problems thrown up by these exceptional situations. Article 2(1) of the Implementing Regulation requires the joint notification to be submitted "on a single form". This rules out the possibility of there being more than one notification. However, this does not prevent the Commission from seeking further information separately from one or more of the joint bidders or controllers. For example, the Commission may, in the circumstances of a joint bid, wish to explore in confidence with each party the particular commercial rationale behind the acquisition. Joint notification should, but need not, be submitted by a joint representative authorised to transmit and receive documents on behalf of all the notifying parties (IR.Article 1(3)). Although a joint notification will be one document (or bundle of documents!) care must be taken to make sure that business secrets of one notifying party are not disclosed to the other by virtue of there having to be one joint notification.[16] If market information were to be exchanged in the process of preparing a notification Article 81 could be infringed. Correct identification of business secrets and the preparation even of non-confidential versions also facilitates access to the file if second-stage proceedings are opened.

4.3.4 When Must Notification be Made

Article 4 of the Regulation provides that notifications must be made not more than one week "after the conclusion of the agreement, or the announcement of the public bid, or the acquisition of a controlling interest", the week beginning when the first of those events occurs. The Commission has no power to grant extensions of the period.[17] The Implementing Regulation may, however, give some marginal relief. It appears to specify more precisely when this one week period ends. Where the last day of the period of the week is not a working day or is a public holiday in the country of despatch, the week is

---

[16] See para. 4.3.9, below, on Confidentiality.
[17] The Commission may, however, find it necessary to respond to the burdens on notifying parties by accepting very short periods of grace, provided that it has been kept fully informed by the parties.

deemed to end with the expiry of the following working day (IR.Article 22(3)).[18] It is to be noted that whilst the Regulation fixes a time by which notification must be made, it does not preclude notification before the happening of the events specified in Article 4 of the Regulation provided always that the other requirements of notification and Form CO can be satisfied. The end of the one week period may still arrive too soon having regard to the amount of information which may have to be supplied, particularly since senior executives, whose input to the notification will be critical, may be heavily committed to the commercial and other aspects of the transaction.

What happens if the deadline cannot be or is not met? The parties are liable to a fine under Article 14(1)(a) of the Regulation.[19] The Commission cannot waive the one week period but in practice would be prevented from imposing a fine where they had acquiesced in an extension of time or had been informed in advance of the transaction. To date the Commission has only imposed fines in two cases,[20] though it has made threatening noises in a number of other cases. A late notification does not mean that the notification is for that reason an invalid one or that the procedures of the Regulation do not apply. The time periods which commence by virtue of the delivery of a complete notification remain applicable. It is thus more important for a notification to be complete than timeous. The Regulation expressly contemplates a notification being made in accordance with the time limit in Article 4(1) but not being complete in certain respects (R.Article 10(1)). Where a concentration has been put into effect before notification, there is also the risk of divestiture in the event of an adverse finding by the Commission. Fines may also be imposed where a concentration is put into effect prior to notification or in disregard of the rules requiring suspension of concentrations.[21] Having said this, the Commission can be flexible and has permitted various modifications of notifications, withdrawals, and renotifications.[22] An exceptional situation occurred in *Kali und Salz* where the Commission's original Article 8 decision was quashed by the Court of Justice. The transaction appears not to have been renotified. The Commission, however, considered the original notification incomplete and the parties provided information to update the position. On receipt of the complete notification the Commission carried out a new examination which led to an Article 6(1)(b) clearance decision under the original case number.

---

[18] Working days are defined (IR.Art. 23) to mean all days other than Saturdays, Sundays, public holidays and other holidays as determined by the Commission. They are publicised in the O.J. The 1999 dates were given in [1999] O.J. C102/03. The definition of working day (by excluding holidays) in Art. 22 would appear to make the reference, in IR.Art. 22(3), to a public holiday in the country of despatch redundant. Is this just careless drafting? Or is it intended to cover the situation where the country of despatch is outside the Community (or the EEA) and the public holiday is not therefore necessarily one listed by the Commission?

[19] There is no automatic fine. The Commission did not fine in, *e.g. Air France/Sabena*, which involved a notification under the Regulation and a (part) notification under Reg. 17. The Commission considered that the transaction was complex and noted that the framework agreement for the deal, the "*protocol d'accord*" had been furnished to the Commission for consideration under Art. 81 and decided not to impose fines.

[20] See para. 4.3.12, below.

[21] In *Torres/Sarrio*, where, in breach of Art. 7(1), the concentration was put into effect some considerable time before notification, the Commission justified its decision not to impose fines (which it described as exceptional) on the basis of the complexities posed in calculating the turnover of the undertakings concerned in the concentration.

[22] Withdrawals will be published in the O.J.. See, *e.g. KLM/Martinair* [1998] O.J. C298/8.

Delivery by hand or courier service should be made during normal working hours at the Merger Task Force's premises at 150 Avenue de Cortenberg, Brussels B-1049.

4.3.5 **What Must be Notified**

Form CO is divided into 12 sections, the final section being simply a declaration to be signed by or on behalf of all the notifying parties. The first four sections of the form require formal details of the parties to the concentration (section 1), the concentration itself (section 2), ownership and control within the group to which each party belongs (section 3), and links between undertakings in the groups concerned and other undertakings (section 4). It will not, therefore, be sufficient to list only undertakings whose results are consolidated into group accounts. Even so, much of this information can be prepared in advance of any proposed acquisition, and it could well be a wise precaution for major international companies planning acquisitions in the Community to prepare a schedule of the information required to complete this part of the form. The information in sections 1 to 4 should allow the Commission to assess whether the notified proposals involve a concentration and, more importantly, whether that concentration has a Community dimension. The complexity which can be involved in this calculation has been considered fully in Chapter 3. If this information is prepared in advance, it may also alert the undertakings concerned to opportunities to structure the transaction so as to fall within or outside the Regulation, whichever is to their best advantage. Furthermore, when the parties first approach the Commission fully prepared on the information which should be within their knowledge, they will be in a better position to convince the Commission that there is no reason why concessions should not be made in respect of information required in later sections of the form.

Section 5 sets out requirements for the delivery of supporting documentation: copies of documents bringing about the concentration (in a public bid the offer document), copies of the most recent annual reports and accounts, etc. Paragraph 5.4 may not be without its difficulties. It requires "copies of analyses, reports, studies and surveys submitted to or prepared for any member(s) of the board of directors, the supervisory board or the shareholders' meeting, for the purpose of assessing or analysing the concentration with respect to competitive conditions, competitors (actual and potential), and market conditions". Documents prepared to impress or "sell" a proposal to one such audience may not have been prepared with Form CO in mind and may need some explaining! The Commission is not slow to point out inconsistencies between such internal documents and information and argument prepared with a regulatory audience in mind.[23]

Sections 6 and 7 require the information which the Commission needs to carry out an assessment of the effects of the concentration on Community markets. Section 6 is particularly important; the parties must identify the relevant product and geographical markets and the markets affected by the notified

---

[23] See, for example, *St. Gobain/Wacker Chemie/NOM*.

concentration. Identification of relevant product and geographic markets is a necessary prerequisite to identifying the markets affected by the concentration, which is the key to every assessment under the Regulation.[24] General guidance may be had from the Commission's Notice on the definition of the relevant market.[25] Though the Commission's approach to markets does not remain static, the Notice merits careful reading. In practice discussion of potentially affected markets is one of the main objects and benefits of pre-notification meetings with the Merger Task Force. If there are no affected markets the burden of Form CO is reduced very significantly (and, if the Commission's current proposals are adopted, the concentration may benefit from the new simplified procedure). Section 6 defines the relevant geographic market in similar terms to Article 9(7) of the Regulation.[26] In relation to product markets, Form CO is intended to ensure that the Commission receives information from the notifying parties on the narrowest possible definition. In practice it may be helpful to look at previous decisions of the Commission. It is common for the Commission to refer to such precedents as it has and then to distinguish them as may be necessary having regard to the time factor and any other relevant considerations. Form CO does not assume that classifications made by the undertakings concerned for marketing purposes are *prima facie* evidence of the true product market.

A market is affected for the purposes of a notification only if a market share of 15 per cent or more is created or enhanced by the concentration (a horizontal relationship) or where any party has a 25 per cent or greater market share in any market which is linked, downstream or upstream, with any other market in which another party to the concentration is active (a vertical relationship). If such a 15 or 25 per cent relationship is present, the parties must provide data on the market for the products in the EEA, the Community, the territory of the EFTA States, any Member State or any EFTA State and describe the relevant product and geographic markets. In addition to information on affected markets the parties must also describe markets closely related to the affected market where any of the parties are active. If there are no affected markets the parties must still identify and describe the product and geographic scope of the markets on which the notified operation would have an impact. Again, in many cases, much of the statistical market information will be capable of being collected in readiness for a notification from an undertaking's own market intelligence. Clearly, some of the information is best presented in tabular form. Other information, such as that concerning product markets, is more descriptive in character. Where there are differences of view over market definitions, it is advisable to produce market shares on one or more alternative bases.

Section 7 requires quite detailed information on markets affected for each of the last three financial years. Further information is required here by section 8 but it is of a more general kind to enable the Commission to assess general conditions in the relevant markets. This will be particularly important in cases of possible oligopolistic dominance, where the Merger Task Force will pay

[24] See generally Chap. 5.
[25] [1997] O.J. C372/5.
[26] See para. 5.3.2, below.

special attention to a market's underlying characteristics. Any prognosis of the effect of a concentration is inevitably a matter of judgment, and often a difficult one, but historical data on certain key indicators can give considerable insight into how the market actually operates, and how undertakings in it are likely to behave in future. Information required in section 8 includes the following: details of market entry; the structure of supply and demand; the importance of research and development; the available systems of distribution and servicing; details of major suppliers and customers; the relevance of co-operation agreements; the trade associations active in the market; and the worldwide context in which the concentration is taking place. As one would expect, most of these information requirements can be readily associated with aspects of the test of compatibility set out in Article 2 of the Regulation.

Section 9 is entitled "General market information". It requires information on any conglomerate aspects of the proposed concentration, that is where any party holds a market share of 25 per cent or more in any product market in which there is no horizontal or vertical relationship (as described above in the context of section 6). While it is possible for the notifying party or parties to make the case for the concentration wherever appears appropriate in the notification (the notification does not have to be submitted on Form CO), section 9 invites the parties to give an overview of the markets. In particular it requires the parties to "describe how the proposed concentration is likely to affect the interests of intermediate and ultimate consumers, and the development of technical progress". This echoes Article 2.1(b) of the Regulation which directs the Commission to take such matters into account when making its compatibility assessment.

Section 10 was introduced in 1998 to accommodate the changes made to the Regulation extending its ambit to all full-function joint ventures. Entitled "Co-operative effects of a joint venture", section 10 requires the parties to identify whether or not the parents to the joint venture retain to a significant extent activities in the same market as the joint venture, or upstream, downstream or in a neighbouring market. Details relating to such markets must be supplied, together with any arguments that the creation of the joint venture will not lead to co-ordination contrary to Article 81(1). The parties are also required to explain how the criteria for exemption in Article 81(3) might apply, as they would on an application for exemption in accordance with Form A/B.

Section 11, which has now taken over the title "General matters", requires the parties to identify and justify any ancillary restraints. This is also important. If ancillary restraints are not identified and justified they will not be dealt with by the Commission in its decision. They may have to be dealt with later under Article 81.[27] If restraints, the ancillary nature of which is questionable, are identified as such the parties may find themselves in Article 81 discussions with the Commission. This may be a needless nuisance if the restrictions have no appreciable impact on competition or trade between Member States. Finally, section 11 deals with the transfer of notifications from the Merger Regulation to Regulation 17 or one of the other implementing regulations for the purpose of obtaining an exemption under Article 81(3) of the Treaty, for example, in the event that the agreement is considered to fall entirely outside

---

[27] See, *e.g. Recticel/Greiner.*

the scope of the Regulation and within the scope of Article 81 where a joint venture is considered not to be "full function".[28]

Even a brief indication of the matters covered by Form CO, such as that given above, indicates that, in practice, there is considerable leeway in completing a notification even before a party needs to pray in aid the formal provisions permitting a waiver to be granted by the Commission, or excusing the notifier from furnishing information which it cannot obtain even after using all its best efforts. Experience of the operation of the Regulation by the Merger Task Force bears out statements by Commission officials and others that, wherever possible, the Task Force will do its utmost to alleviate the burdens of the notification process.

4.3.6   Short-form Notification

The possibility of a short-form notification was first introduced in 1994. The scope of such notification is described in paragraph C of Form CO. It is limited to joint ventures which have no, or very little, actual or foreseen activities within the territory of the EEA. The notion of joint venture in this context is wide enough to cover a variety of circumstances including the joint acquisition of a larger company, the creation of a joint venture to which the parent companies contribute their activities and the case of entry of a new controlling party into an existing joint venture. The Implementing Regulation sets down two thresholds which the joint venture must not exceed. First, the turnover of the joint venture and/or the turnover of the contributed activities must be less than 100 million ECU in the EEA territory. Secondly, the total value of assets transferred to all joint ventures must be less than 100 million ECU in the EEA territory. Where the assets transferred generate turnover, then either the value of the assets or that of the turnover may exceed 100 million ECU. Paragraph C(c) of Form CO sets out by reference to the sections of the Form what information has to be and, more importantly, need not be supplied. The main benefits are that the parties are spared from supplying the detailed information on affected markets required by sections 7, 8 and 9. They do, however, have to supply information, by reference to the EEA territory, the Community as a whole, each Member State and each EFTA State, of sales and volume, as well as market shares, and the five largest customers and the five largest competitors in the affected markets.

Delivery of a short-form notification does not preclude the Commission from asking for further information for its purposes. Moreover, the Commission can request a full, or partial, notification where the short-form thresholds are not met or where it appears necessary for an adequate investigation of the possible competition problems on affected markets. The Commission takes the view that in such cases the short-form notification may be considered incomplete in a material respect pursuant to Article 4(2) of the Implementing Regulation. The parties will be informed without delay and in writing and a deadline for submission of a full, or partial, notification fixed. The notification, Form CO says, only becomes effective on the date on which all information required

---

[28] On conversion of notifications, see para. 4.3.11, below.

is received. Given the inevitable need to discuss the proposed concentration in advance with the Commission it may be debatable whether in a particular case the short-form notification has anything to offer which cannot be gained from a ''full'' notification in relation to which the Commission has exercised its power (under Article 3(2) of the Implementing Regulation) to dispense with the obligation to provide information.

4.3.7 Copies, Supporting Documents, Languages

Twenty-four copies (including the original) of the notification and of the supporting documents must be supplied (IR.Article 2(2)). Supporting documents must be originals or copies; if the latter, the notifying party must confirm that they are true and complete (IR.Article 2(3)). One copy of the bundle goes to the competent authority of each of the Member States and the EFTA Surveillance Authority, the other copies being required for the Commission services. (This potential readership is an important factor to remember when preparing documents). Clearly with what may be voluminous documentation and short time scales (especially for distribution to the Member States and initial examination) it is unreasonable to expect the Commission to be delayed while copies are taken. It is also in the parties' interest to begin the Article 9 clock running against Member States by virtue of their receipt of copies of the notification. ''Supporting documents'' includes copies of the final or most recent versions of all documents bringing about the concentration. If reports or analyses have been prepared by the parties or their advisers in order that management can consider the proposals bringing about the notified concentration, and at least one affected market is identified, copies of those documents must also be furnished in support of the notification.[29] However, the Commission has power to require documents in the list, and any other information it feels is necessary for a proper assessment and Commission officials may be less impressed than investors or senior management by bullish predictions of the market-dominating benefits of a proposed acquisition!

The notification must be made in one of the official languages of the Community (IR.Article 2(4)). This language then becomes the language of the proceeding for all the notifying parties. Other parties, for example, the company being acquired or a third party such as a competitor, may use another official language, if they wish. Supporting documents must, however, be submitted in their original language (IR.Article 2(4)). Only where this language is not one of the official languages[30] is it necessary to attach a translation which must, in this event, be in the language of the proceeding. Notifications made pursuant to Article 57 of the EEA Agreement are subject to different language rules.[31] There may be advantages in using one of the more common E.U. languages in order to avoid delays of translation or of appreciation.

[29] Section 5 of Form CO.
[30] The official languages are Danish, Dutch, English, French, German, Greek, Italian, Portuguese, Spanish, Finnish and Swedish.
[31] See IR.Art. 2(5).

4.3.8 Completeness, Effective Date and Timetable

The effective date of notification is the day when the notification is received
by the Commission (IR.Article 4(1)). But the notification must be "complete".
If information is incorrect or misleading the notification will not be complete
(IR. Article 4/(4)), nor if there are material changes.[32] Article 4(3) of the
Regulation requires the Commission, where it finds that a notified concentration may fall within the Regulation, to publish the fact of notification, and
identify the names of the parties, the nature of the concentration and the economic sectors involved.[33] Such a notice does not, however, provide any con-
firmation that the notification is complete. The Commission always reserves
its position. But where a notification is incomplete *in a material respect* the
Commission must without delay inform the parties and fix a time period for
the information to be supplied (IR.Article 4(2)).[34] It does this by what it calls
a declaration of incompleteness. Though restricted to "exceptional" cases, the
numbers have increased and in practice just under 10 per cent of notifications
are now declared incomplete.

The incompleteness may not be discovered until the Commission is one or
two weeks into its investigation.[35] A notification may be judged incomplete
for various reasons: failure to identify all the relevant parties or relationships[36];
inadequate or unclear information regarding the affected markets and the parties' shares; failure to identify the affected markets. For example, Norsk Hydro
had to renotify its proposed takeover of a rival Norwegian oil and gas explora-
tion firm, Saga Petroleum, when the Commission discussed that Norsk Hydro's
offer was shared with Statoil. The Commission took the view that the operation
should be considered as a joint venture. Prior contact with the Commission
may assist in avoiding having a notification found to be incomplete, and the
Commission's Best Practice Guidelines strongly urge this. What is needed,
and how long it takes, to make "complete" an incomplete notification will
depend on the circumstances.[37] When it is made complete the Commission
will publish notice of completion or renotification in the Official Journal.[38]
The notification becomes effective on the day the requested information is
received by the Commission. It is critical to know the precise date of an
effective notification because commencement of certain time periods are
dependent upon it; in Article 10(1), for the one month (or possibly six weeks)
period for the initial decision on applicability of the Regulation, and whether

---

[32] See para. 4.3.10, below.
[33] Ultimately it may be decided that the concentration falls outside the scope of the Regulation and an Art.
6(1)(a) decision issued.
[34] In fixing the period the Commission must have regard to the time necessary to respond, the urgency of
the case and public holidays: IR.Art. 21(1).
[35] See, *e.g. Cardo/Thyssen*, where after two weeks the Commission discussed that the product market
definitions proposed by the parties were not technically sound. The necessary information was supplied
a week later.
[36] *e.g. VEBA/Degussa* [1998] O.J. L20/102, where there was a failure to disclose that a subsidiary of the
parties was doing business through a joint venture on one of the relevant markets.
[37] In *Cable & Wireless/Maersk Data-Nautec*, the problem was rectified in six days. By contrast, it took
over a month in *UPM-Kymmene/April* and over two months in *Skanska/Scancem* [1999] O.J. L183/1.
And it needed two attempts in *Hermes/Sampo/FGB-FCIC*.
[38] See, *e.g. Imetal/English China Clays* [1999] O.J. C70/7. Third parties will be given a further 10 days to
submit observations.

or not there are serious doubts on competition grounds; and Article 19(1), for the three working days for transmission of the notification to the Member States. In *Sanofi/Synthélabo* the incompleteness did not come to light until after the Commission had issued an Article 6(1)(b) clearance decision. This was then revoked and disposal undertakings negotiated before a new decision was taken.

Detailed rules relating to the calculation of the one month period are set out in the Implementing Regulation. For the purposes of Article 10(1) the one month period starts on the first working day following the effective date of the notification (IR.Article 6(4)). The period ends with the expiry of the day in the following month which falls on the same date as the day on which the period started (IR.Article 7(4)). If there is no such day (because notification was on, *e.g.* 31 May) in that month then the period ends with the last day of that month. If the last day of the one month period, having applied these rules, is not a working day then the period ends with the expiry of the next working day (IR.Article 7(8)). Where the one month period includes a public holiday or other holiday of the Commission, the one month period is extended by the corresponding number of days (IR.Article 8). Similar rules apply for the calculation of the six weeks where the initial period is so extended by action of a Member State under Article 9 (distinct market)[39] or of the undertakings submitting commitments intended to form the basis of a clearance decision under Article 6(1)(b) (the procedure relating to commitments is described in Chapter 7).

4.3.9 Confidentiality

Both the Treaty (Article 287) and the Regulation (Article 17) require the Commission to protect business secrets. But the principal burden of ensuring confidentiality both as between notifying parties (whether between acquirer and acquired, or between joint acquirers) is on the owner of the business secret. A notifying party should therefore identify such material by marking appropriate pages with the words "Business Secrets". Where it is necessary to keep information from another party to the notification (for example in the case of mergers and joint acquisitions) then the material should be placed in a separate clearly marked annex. In all cases where confidentiality is claimed for information the claimant must give reasons why the information must not be divulged or published[40] and be prepared to supply non-confidential versions where needed. It is for the Commission, subject to review by the Court of Justice, to decide whether information provided by an undertaking can properly be said to be a business secret. Even if it agrees with an undertaking's assertion of business secrecy, Article 17(2) makes it clear that it is for the Commission to consider whether the rights of defence, and the obligation on the Commission to publish notice of notification and final decisions under Article 8, override the need for business secrecy. Following the necessary procedures for protecting business secrets creates particular burdens in the context of handling

---

[39] For distinct market, see para. 8.3, below.
[40] Form CO. Section F, Confidentiality.

merger cases but access to the file will only apply in second-stage proceedings. Even then the Commission's view seems to be that only the parties and not third parties, such as complainants are entitled to access to the file.[41] It is understood, for example, that in the second-stage proceedings in *Airtours/First Choice* other travel companies named as being among those who might enjoy a position of collective dominance were not granted access to the file.

4.3.10 Material Changes

Article 4(3) of the Implementing Regulation provides that material changes in the facts specified in the notification, which the notifying parties know or ought to have known, must be communicated to the Commission voluntarily and without delay. In short this requires the parties to update their notification as regards material changes. It is difficult to see how a party can notify something which it does not know but "ought to have known". It is not clear to what extent this limb of the obligation will go beyond the need to add to or correct earlier material supplied as and when a party learns of the error or omission. Article 4(3) suggests that an undertaking must keep its notification under review in order to identify any changes in material facts. The provision is clearly intended to impress upon a notifying party that its obligations in this regard do not cease when the notification has been delivered to the Commission. A proposed commitment offered by the parties is not necessarily "material". Something is only material if it is "inherent" to the notified concentration.[42] Further, the Regulation treats commitments separately from material changes.

What is the effect of failing to notify a material change? The Implementing Regulation provides two sanctions. The first is in Article 4(3). When material changes could have a significant effect on the appraisal of the concentration, the notification may be considered by the Commission as only becoming effective on the date on which the material change is received by the Commission. The Commission is obliged to inform the parties of this in writing and without delay. A notice of renotification may be published in the Official Journal.[43] The second sanction is the suspension of the relevant time period for the first or second examination stage as the case may be, but this is dependent upon a decision of the Commission requesting the further information. Article 9(1)(d) of the Implementing Regulation provides that the examination stage may be suspended where the Commission by decision requires information of the material change to be supplied. The relevant period is extended by a period calculated from the day after the occurrence of the change of facts and the day following that on which the (correct) information is supplied. If that day is not a working day then the next working day ends the period of suspension (IR.Article 9(3)). Save as described above, the procedure appears to be unaffected. This obligation will need to be borne in mind, for example,

---

[41] See para 4.7.6, below.
[42] Case T-290/94 *Kaysersberg SA v. Commission* [1997] E.C.R. II-2137, para. 137.
[43] See, *e.g. Bertelsmann/Wissenschaftsverlag Springer* [1999] O.J. C16/9.

when the parties to a consortium bid modify their proposals for the target company during the course of the bid.

4.3.11 Conversion of Notifications

There may be cases where it is not possible or easy to say at the outset whether a transaction is a concentration or an agreement to which the general competition rules apply. Article 5 of the Implementing Regulation provides for the conversion of the notification from one under Regulations 4064/89 and 2367/90 to one under Regulation 17 or other implementing regulations made under Article 83 of the Treaty.[44] Article 5(1) enables the Commission, where conversion has been requested by the notifying parties, to treat the notification as an application and/or notification under one of the other implementing regulations. In this event some further information may be required to supplement that given in the notification. The Commission must fix a time for its delivery and provided the information is supplied within that time the application or notification is deemed to fulfil the requirements of the appropriate implementing Regulation as from the date of the original notification for the purposes of the Regulation (IR.Article 5(2)). Thus an individual exemption under Article 81(3) could be back-dated to that date.

Prior to the extension of the Regulation to all full-function joint ventures, there were numerous examples of conversions of notifications.[45] Typically they involved joint ventures which the Commission found to be co-operative rather than concentrative. An interesting example (which is still relevant) is *Pasteur Mérieux/Merck* where the Commission proceeded to a formal decision under Regulation 17 having earlier found that the joint venture would not perform on a lasting basis all functions of an autonomous economic entity and therefore was not a concentration.[46] It is to be noted that conversion only operates one way, *i.e.* from the Regulation to one under the other implementing regulations. Secondly, the possibility of conversion under Article 5 of the Implementing Regulation only deals with the case where the transaction has been bona fide but mistakenly notified under the Regulation. It may still be possible for the parties to achieve a fast track consideration under Article 81 where the transaction concerns a structural partial-function joint venture.[47] Such transactions will normally continue to be dealt with by the relevant sectoral division within the Competition Directorate and not by the Merger Task Force. Finally, where ancillary restraints or other restrictions cannot be dealt with under the Regulation, a separate notification on Form A/B will be necessary under Regulation 17.[48] Article 5 does not excuse the parties from making such an additional notification.

[44] Note the recitals in the Implementing Regulation relating to *vires*, and in particular the second to fifth "Having regard to" clauses.
[45] Examples include *Apollinaris/Schweppes*; *Elf/Enterprise*; *Philips/Thomson/SAGEM*; *Omnitel*; *Rheinelektra/Cofira/Dekra*; *British Telecom/MCI*; *Pasteur Mérieux/Merck*; *Koipe-Tabacalera/Elosua* and *VTC/BPT*.
[46] [1994] O.J. L309/1.
[47] The Commission has introduced a fast track procedure for such joint ventures under Reg.17—see the new Form A/B and the information which must be given in such cases (Part D) Reg. 3385/94.
[48] Examples of notifications under both the Regulation and Reg. 17 can be seen in *Air France/Sabena*; *Ahold/Jeronimo Martins/Inovacao*; and *BMW/Rover*.

4.3.12   Fines in Relation to Notification

The Commission is empowered by Article 14(1)(a) and (b) to impose fines of from ECU 1000 to ECU 50,000 on a person who, intentionally or negligently, fails to notify a concentration in accordance with Article 4(1), or furnishes incorrect or misleading information in a notification. As mentioned above, the Commission has to date only imposed fines in two cases, *Samsung* and *A.P. Möller*, though there have been a number of cases where the lateness of notification has been criticised and the decision (under Article 6(1)(b)) has made reference to the fact that the Commission was considering the question of a fine. What is clear from the two decisions is that the Commission, not surprisingly, is following the same approach as it does in cases of infringement of Articles 81 and 82 and their procedural rules. In *Samsung* (1998) the Commission imposed a fine of Euro 33,000 for the Korean company's failure to notify its acquisition of the American company AST Research Inc. The Commission described the fine as being "relatively small". It gave credit for the fact that the merger had no damaging effect on competition, the breach appeared not to have been intentional, and Samsung had recognised the breach and co-operated with Commission. On the other hand there had been a significant period of time between implementation of the merger and its notification. In the second case, *A.P. Möller* (1999), a somewhat higher, though still not large fine, Euro 219,000, was imposed. The infringement covered three cases where concentrations (ultimately cleared by the Commission) had been notified late. Credit was given for recognition of the breach of the rules, voluntary notification and the fact that the mergers in question did not damage competition. Allowance was also made for the fact that the Commission had not at the time of the infringement adopted its (first fining) decision in *Samsung*.

4.4   SUSPENSION

4.4.1   Background

The imposition of automatic suspension was a controversial subject, particularly towards the end of the negotiations. Its reintroduction in the E.C. regime was a condition of German acceptance of the Regulation.[49] Automatic suspension is not, however, a feature of all Member States laws governing concentrations. In the United Kingdom there is an automatic temporary prohibition on the acquisition of shares once a reference to the Competition Commission has been made, and other suspensory measures may be imposed by order or undertaking on the acquirer.[50] Article 7 of the Regulation originally provided that a concentration should not be put into effect before its notification or within its first three weeks following its notification. Thereafter any suspension was dependent on a decision by the Commission in the particular case. The changes made in 1997 extend the scope of suspension by removing the three-

---

[49] Janicki, *E.C. Regulation on the Control of Concentrations between Undertakings in the Process of Implementation* ([1990] March Wirtschaft und Wettberwerb), p. 195.
[50] Fair Trading Act 1973, s. 75(4A).

week limitation period, which was always somewhat odd in not being coterminous with the stage one decision. The changes were made "to ensure effective control".[51]

4.4.2 **The Rule**

Following the changes in 1997, Article 7(1) provides that a concentration must not be put into effect either before its notification or until it has been declared compatible with the Common Market pursuant to a decision by the Commission under Article 6(1)(b) or Article 8(2) (*i.e.* at the end of the first or second stage, as the case may be) or on the basis of a presumption of compatibility pursuant to Article 10(6). Accordingly it is no longer necessary for the Commission to expend resources on considering the question of continuation of suspension. The questions of exception and exemption remain relevant.

4.4.3 **Exception**

To the general rule of suspension there is one exception and also the possibility of exemption. The exception, in Article 7(3) of the Regulation, protects public bids and allows them to be implemented provided they are notified in the one week period laid down in Article 4. The exception is dependent on the acquirer not exercising voting rights in the shares in question or doing so with the permission of the Commission (granted under Article 7(4)) only to maintain the full value of the investment. One might doubt whether a party would proceed to buy shares if they could not be voted. But buying them may stop others buying them. The shares may be resold in which event the voting rights may be reactivated.

4.4.4 **Exemption**

Article 7(4) provides that the Commission can, upon reasoned request, exempt a transaction from the rule relating to suspension. The Commission is required to "take into account *inter alia* the effects of the suspension on one or more undertakings concerned by a concentration or on a third party and the threat to competition posed by the concentration".[52] For example, in *Matra Marconi Space/Satcomms* a derogation was granted to enable the parties to complete the acquisition of a division of a company in administrative receivership. Similarly, in *Omnitel* a derogation was granted to enable the newly-created joint venture, OPI, to meet the deadlines imposed in the GSM licence awarded by the Italian Ministry of Post and Telecommunications. OPI would then be able to start competing against Telecom Italia which already had its network in place and had established a strong presence in mobile telephony in Italy.

---

[51] Twenty-Seventh Report on Competition 1997, para. 157.
[52] Changes were made to Art. 7(4) in 1997 to give the Commission greater flexibility in responding to requests in light of the suspension. There were five cases in 1998.

Recognition of the commercial urgency of introducing a new competitor is, however, unusual and most derogations have been in the context of rescue operations such as *ING/Barings*.[53] Other cases have involved the need to meet requirements of national laws on public bids. If it is necessary to put the concentration into effect speedily the parties should make contact with the Task Force at an early opportunity to identify the potential problem. It is to be noted that such an exemption can be sought and given at any time, "even before notification or after the transaction". It can therefore be retrospective in effect. This may be particularly important where third parties', including employees', rights may be prejudiced by the inadvertent or other putting into effect of the concentration in contravention of Article 7. Finally, it should be noted that in granting an exemption under Article 7(4) it is possible for the Commission to impose conditions and obligations to ensure conditions of effective competition. Breach of a condition means that the exemption does not apply and may render a party liable to a fine under Article 14(2)(b). Failure to comply with an obligation renders a party liable to a fine under Article 14(2)(a). A periodical penalty payment may be imposed under Article 15(2)(a) to enforce compliance with an obligation (attached to an exemption) imposed by decision under Article 7(4). That said, the Commission is very reluctant to grant derogations and a strong case needs to be made out.

4.4.5   Breach of Article 7

4.4.5.1   Fines

Putting a concentration into effect in breach of the ruling, Article 7(1) (automatic suspension) renders a party liable to a fine under Article 14(2)(b).[54] It may also affect the validity of transactions.

4.4.5.2   Nature and Extent of Invalidity

Article 7(5) is concerned with the validity of transactions carried out in contravention of the rule in paragraph (1). It was recognised that there was a potential problem because of the direct applicability of the rules relating to suspension. What is the effect on the validity of a transaction, in particular sales and acquisitions of shares in the market place, of a breach of the suspension rule? In the absence of any provision in the Regulation, the relevant national law would apply to determine what the effect would be on transactions effected contrary to Article 7. Were that to have the effect of rendering a transaction null and void, then this could have serious adverse consequences for innocent third parties. Recital 17 provides that "in the interests of legal certainty the validity of transactions must nevertheless be protected as much as necessary".

---

[53] Where it was clearly critical to complete the notified operation as soon as possible. See also, *e.g. Kelt/American Express.*

[54] Art. 14(2)(b) also refers to the possibility of a fine 'in disregard of a decision taken pursuant to Article 7(2)''. But as Art. 7(2) has been deleted, no such case, except for decisions before March 1, 1999, can arise.

The Regulation gives certain measures of protection but it does not answer all questions relating to the civil law consequences of breach of Article 7.

First, there is an express exception for securities traded on a stock market. Article 7(5) provides that the validity of the transaction is in no way affected unless both buyer and seller knew or ought to have known the transaction was carried out in contravention of Article 7(1). In the United Kingdom context, where there are few if any matched transactions, the exception should render secure Stock Exchange transactions; but off-market transactions may be more vulnerable.

The second way in which the Regulation protects the validity of the transaction is to provide that that validity is dependent on the decision of the Commission of clearance or prohibition. The effect is to achieve under the Regulation a position similar to that under German law,[55] namely that an ultimate finding of compatibility will legitimate retroactively a transaction carried out in breach of the automatic prohibition in Article 7(1). In the meantime the agreement is unenforceable.[56] The agreement itself is not, however, invalid and void. Article 7(1) does not operate to prohibit the making of agreements or public bids but only their performance to the extent that this amounts to putting the concentration into effect. A national court should not therefore order or otherwise compel one party to do anything that is prohibited (for example to complete).

4.4.5.3 *Effect Under English Law*

Where a transaction is effected contrary to Article 7 then, under common law, it is likely to be treated as illegal and void. Parties may therefore be unable to recover moneys paid under contracts (except perhaps by action for money had and received) or to enforce other contracts (for example for a loan) if to do so requires reference to the illegality. Similarly where property (for example, a lease or shares) has been transferred their recovery may be prevented. But the court should look closely at the purpose of the prohibition and in that light consider the usefulness in applying the general rule of non-recovery.[57] The rule in Article 7 is hardly well served if it results in one party retaining the benefit of contracts or assets and thereby exercising "control" for the purposes of Article 3, perhaps in some cases at the expense of innocent third parties. It is suggested that courts should be willing, and may indeed be obliged, to find more appropriate national remedies to give effect to Article 7.[58] In such a situation much would depend on the ultimate finding of the Commission and the scope of remedial orders it may make. The Commission's powers under the Regulation are likely to prove more flexible in unscrambling a transaction

---

[55] Transactions in violation of the prohibition in s. 24(a)(4) of the German law (above) are ineffective. According to Mattfield, "legal acts and measures taken are in principle in suspense and without effect, although this can be cured": *Merger control in the EEC* (1988) at 68.

[56] The prohibition in Art. 7 does not, it is submitted, stop all action by the parties, *e.g.* regulatory and shareholder approvals can be sought, finance arrangements made, inventories checked and valued, and the completion documents prepared in readiness.

[57] See generally Treitel, *The Law of Contract* (9th ed. 1995), Chap.11, Section 3.

[58] *e.g.* the temporary restriction on the exercise of voting rights.

than the traditional remedies of English common law dealing with illegality.[59] Given the fact that ultimately validity or invalidity is dependent on the Commission's decision (under Article 6 or 8) it is likely that a national court would stay any enforcement or recovery proceedings pending the final outcome before the Commission.[60]

In practice, however, parties are likely to make transactions conditional upon clearance by the Commission, and the difficulties discussed above will arise only where concentrations take place in ignorance of the obligations in Article 7 of the Regulation.

Finally, as already mentioned, it is possible for the Commission to grant a derogation under Article 7(4) at any time, including retrospectively.

4.4.6   Relationship Between Article 7 and Article 4

Article 7(1) expressly provides that a concentration shall not be put into effect before its notification. On the other hand Article 4(1) provides that concentrations must be notified to the Commission not more than one week after conclusion of the agreement, or the announcement of the public bid, *or the acquisition of a controlling interest* (emphasis added). It is the acquisition of a controlling interest which may result, in accordance with Article 3(1)(b), in a concentration arising for the purposes of the Regulation. Article 4 therefore contemplates the situation where it is quite lawful for a party to complete the transaction in advance of notification. The apparent inconsistency between Article 4 and Article 7 is understandable when one appreciates the different types of case with which Article 4(1) is intended to deal. The acquisition of a controlling interest is a residuary category. There may well be cases where there is no agreement and no public bid. A party may, for example, take up a rights issue in a situation where other parties do not and the consequence is that its shareholding increases to such an extent that it has control within the meaning of Article 3. Such a situation is clearly not a public bid and it would be artificial to treat it as "an agreement" for the purposes of Article 4(1). Consider also the case where circumstances change and the conditions governing the application of the exemptions in Article 3(5)(a) or (c) cease to apply with the consequence that a concentration is deemed to arise. Such situations may be rare but not unknown. Thus in *Avesta II* the Commission found that the sale, through the market for cash, of one shareholder's shareholding had the effect of changing the nature of the control exercised by the remaining shareholders. A timeous notification may be difficult in these cases. Similarly it is both impractical and potentially grossly unfair to apply Article 7, automatic suspension, in such situations. It is, therefore, submitted that Article 4(1) takes precedence over Article 7(1) in the case where the obligation to notify under Article 4 arises by virtue of the acquisition of a controlling interest

---

[59] In accordance with the general principle of the supremacy of Community law measures taken by the Commission would have to be capable of enforcement as between the parties by appropriate measures in national courts.

[60] See generally Case C-234/89 *Delimitis v. Henninger Brau AG* [1991] 1 E.C.R. 935; [1992] 5 C.M.L.R. 210, and the Commission's Notice on co-operation between national courts and the Commission [1993] O.J. C39/6.

otherwise than pursuant to an agreement or public bid within the meaning of that provision.

4.5 THE INITIAL EXAMINATION PERIOD

4.5.1 Stage One Proceedings

The Regulation charges the Commission with examining the notification "as soon as it is received" (R.Article 6(1)). Where it finds that a notified concentration falls within the scope of the Regulation, the Commission must publish the fact of the notification as well as the names of the parties, the nature of the concentration and economic sectors involved (R.Article 4(3)). This is done in the Official Journal (C series) and, in so far as knowledge of the proposed concentration is not already in the public domain, provides the opportunity for third parties to react.[61] Typically, interested parties will be asked to respond, by fax or by post, within 10 days. This is a very short timescale indeed, particularly when one considers that the Official Journal notice may appear some days after the actual notification. At the end of the initial examination of the notified concentration, the Commission must take a decision on the applicability of the Regulation and on whether the concentration raises serious doubts as to its compatibility with the Common Market. During the initial examination period (and beyond, into the second stage if there is one) the parties are obliged, by virtue of Article 7(1) of the Regulation, not to put the concentration into effect. As mentioned above, the prohibition in Article 7(1) may be waived.

There are few formal rules governing the procedure at this stage in the proceedings. The Commission will examine the notification to ascertain if it is complete. As indicated in the recitals to the Regulation, during this period there will be close contact with the parties so that, wherever possible, practical and legal problems can be resolved. If necessary the Commission can obtain more information, whether from the parties themselves, or third parties, by means of requests under Article 11 or inspections under Article 13 of the Regulation, although given the time restraints the latter may not be a practical proposition.[62] Information may also be obtained from, or volunteered by, Member State authorities. Before reaching its decision on the applicability of the Regulation and the initiation of proceedings, there is no requirement for the Commission to put objections to the parties.[63] Although the time period is short, there is nothing to preclude negotiation and discussion with the parties. Whilst it is mainly done prior to notification so that the notified concentration is already in acceptable form, Recital 10 to the Implementing Regulation expressly recognises the possibility of removing practical or legal problems by mutual agreement. Following the changes made in 1997 the Regulation itself now expressly provides for undertakings to modify the notified concen-

---

[61] For an example see *Aegon/Transamerica* [1999] O.J. C130/9. Where a concentration has to be renotified, a new publication will be made in the O.J., again asking interested parties to respond. See, *e.g. Deutsche Post/Securicor* [1999] O.J. C15/2.

[62] There may be more scope when, *e.g.* an initial notification is not complete. Experience has shown that information may be obtainable from third parties in such circumstances.

[63] Note that Art. 18(1) of the Regulation does not apply to decisions under Art. 6.

tration and to offer commitments to the Commission. Where commitments are submitted the initial examination period is increased from four to six weeks (R.Article10(1)). In practice there is substantial scope for negotiations during the first stage but the timetable is extremely tight. The Commission's practice of accepting commitments from the notifying parties is described in Chapter 7.

Where a notification is withdrawn because, for example, the parties abandon the planned merger, it is the Commission's practice to publish a notice of "Withdrawal of notification of a concentration" in the Official Journal.[64] The same is true if withdrawal occurs in second stage proceedings.[65]

4.5.2 Third Parties

As already mentioned, concentrations are not as such prohibited under the Regulation. They must be notified to and then examined by the Commission to determine their compatibility with the Common Market. It is not surprising therefore that the Regulation does not contemplate complaints. This said, both the Regulation and the Implementing Regulation acknowledge the existence of third parties and the potentially significant role they can play. What competitors and customers say about the operation is very important.[66] They will understand the industry and markets concerned better than the Commission can hope to do in the time available, at least in stage one proceedings. Third parties can approach the Commission at any time and are, by virtue of the publication requirements in Article 4(3) of the Regulation, promptly alerted to the existence of a concentration and can therefore comment on the proposal and intervene, as necessary, in the proceedings. Typically the notice gives 10 days for comments. This reflects the tight timetable facing the Commission. Experience shows that notifications may elicit comments from third parties. For example, in the case of Airtours proposed acquisition of First Choice Holidays the Commission is reported to have been swamped by the reactions of an unusually high number of customers and competitors.[67] Formal complaints are, however, rare. A recent example can be seen in the Hutchison Port Holding and Rotterdam Port-Authority proposed acquisition of the Rotterdam container terminal operator European Combined Terminals. P&O Nedlloyd submitted a formal complaint to the Commission against the proposed merger.[68] Complainants should have a credible and verifiable case to present and be prepared to describe the adverse effects of the merger on competition, and not just on themselves as competitors, customers or end users. Although the first stage proceeding time is short the Merger Task Force tries to seek out third parties' views, especially on specific issues. The Commission will commonly seek information from competitors and customers on such matters as market definition and share, and, importantly, on commitments offered by the notifying parties. On occasion it has exercised its power under Article 11

---

[64] See, *e.g. Deutsche Post/Trans-o-flex* [1999] O.J. C130/9.
[65] See, *e.g. KLM/Martinair.*
[66] See, *e.g. TPG/Technologistica*, para. 28.
[67] *European Report*, June 5, 1999. The Commission has opened second-stage proceedings in the case.
[68] *European Report*, April 17, 1999.

of the Regulation to seek information from third parties who have not volunteered it.[69]

The legal position of third parties is, however, substantially inferior to that
of the parties to the merger.[70] This is particularly the case as regards such
matters as the receipt of information (where a third party may only receive
edited versions, often prepared by the notifying parties), as to the time in
which comments may be advanced and in relation to access to the file. Third
parties only have the right to be heard provided they have so requested and
have shown that they have a sufficient interest to be heard.[71] A competitor has
a right to be heard, if it so requests, in order to make its views known on the
harmful effects of the notified concentration. But, the Court of First Instance
has said, that right must be reconciled with the observance of the rights of
defence and the primary aim of the Regulation "which is to ensure effectiveness of control as well as legal certainty for the undertakings to which the
Regulation applies".[72]

The Commission commonly seeks the views of third parties on commitments proposed by the parties to the merger. The changes introduced with
effect from 1998, extending the first stage from four to six weeks where such
commitments are offered after notification, may serve to improve the position
of third parties in this respect. But it seems that a third party cannot complain
that it has had very little time in which to respond.[73] The Regulation specifies
no minimum period and the need to consult must be adapted to the need for
speed which characterises the general scheme of the Regulation and requires
the Commission to take decisions within strict time limits. The third party
must have sufficient information, for example on commitments offered, to
comment, though the Commission is not obliged to provide the final texts of
commitments.[74] It does, however, attach importance to "market testing" such
commitments.

4.5.3 Member State Competition Authorities

During the initial period the competition authorities of the Member States will
also be looking at the notification. If a distinct market problem is identified
the Member State must notify the Commission within three weeks of receiving
its copy of the notification (R.Article 9(2)—see Chapter 7). This causes the
initial period to be extended automatically to six weeks. The Commission may
well in this event want additional information from the Member State concerned. Article 19(2) of the Regulation contemplates this possibility as well
as a formal dialogue with the Member State on the question whether the case
should be referred to the Member State pursuant to Article 9. Apart from any

---

[69] The fact-finding powers of the Commission are discussed generally at para. 4.6, below.
[70] This is because "they are merely liable to suffer the incidental effects of the decision". *Per* the CFI in
Case T-290/94 *Kaysersberg SA v. Commission* [1997] E.C.R. II-2137, para. 105.
[71] Case T-96/92 *CCE de la Société Generale des Grandes Sources and Others v. Commission* [1995] E.C.R.
II-1213, para. 6.
[72] *Kaysersberg* (above), para. 109.
[73] *Kaysersberg* (above), para. 113 (two days).
[74] *Kaysersberg* (above), paras 119–120.

question of a distinct market or legitimate interests (R.Article 21(3)), the Member States may also offer comments on the case at this stage and seek from, or supply information to, the Commission. The involvement of the national authorities is dealt with more fully in Chapter 8.

4.5.4 Types of Initial Decision (Article 6)

Before the end of the initial period, the Commission must take one of three decisions; a decision of inapplicability (Article 6(1)(a)), of compatibility (Article 6(1)(b)); or of initiation of (second stage) proceedings (Article 6(1)(c)). These are described in more detail in Chapter 7. Where the Commission fails to make, or deliberately abstains from taking, a decision (the latter is a key feature of the Commission's proposal for a simplified procedure for processing certain concentrations) the concentration is deemed to have been approved and declared compatible with the Common Market (R. Article 10(6)).

4.6 FACT-FINDING POWERS

The Regulation confers certain fact-finding powers on the Commission to assist it in carrying out its tasks under the Regulation. As one would expect, these powers are modelled very closely on the tried and tested provisions which appear in Regulation 17 and enable the Commission to investigate alleged infringements of the competition rules in Articles 81 and 82 of the Treaty. Their use is not limited to stage one or stage two proceedings, although in practice, because of the time restraints, their use at stage one is less likely.

4.6.1 Requests for Information

Article 11 of the Regulation empowers the Commission to "obtain all necessary information" from Member State governments and competent authorities as well as from undertakings, associations of undertakings, and persons other than undertakings (including individuals). This contrasts with requests for information under the corresponding power in Regulation 17, which cannot be addressed to persons other than undertakings. In practice the Commission will use its formal powers under Article 11 frequently as the timetable will rarely permit preliminary or informal requests for information. In cases of real urgency or importance the Commission will contact third parties and invite them to a meeting with the case team. Parties are under a duty to co-operate and the confidentiality or secrecy of documents is no excuse for their non-delivery to the Commission.[75] Legal professional privilege exists,[76] but the privilege against self-incrimination is quite limited in Commission competition

---

[75] Case 374/87 *Orkem v. Commission* [1989] E.C.R. 3283; [1991] 4 C.M.L.R. 502, para. 27. On the obligation to co-operate, see also Case T-46/92 *The Scottish Football Association v. Commission* [1994] E.C.R. II-1039.
[76] Case 155/79 *A.M. & S. Europe Limited v. Commission* [1982] E.C.R. 1575; [1982] 2 C.M.L.R. 264.

procedures.[77] There is no obligation for parties to reply in writing and in view of the timescale the Commission is justified in following up unanswered Article 11 requests and in gathering evidence over the telephone rather than proceeding to take formal decisions under Article 11(5).[78] Indeed it might be disproportionate to resort to Article 11(5) particularly where small undertakings are concerned.

4.6.2 Investigations

Article 13 of the Regulation gives the Commission power to carry out investigations at the premises of undertakings. This power, however, cannot be exercised against individuals.[79]

A detailed examination of the nature and application of the powers themselves is outside the scope of this book.[80] Certain points, however, should be noted. As under Regulation 17, the Commission, when exercising its investigatory powers, may proceed by way of formal decision or by a simple mandate or authorisation. The approach adopted does not affect the extent of the powers available (*i.e.* to inspect books or records, etc.) but an undertaking or association of undertakings is obliged to submit to an investigation only if it has been ordered by decision (R.Article 13(3)). No doubt the Commission's policy on the use of these powers will evolve pragmatically as circumstances demand. In examining possible infringements of Articles 81 and 82 the Commission has increasingly relied on investigations ordered by decision, without prior notice to the undertaking concerned, but the Regulation is concerned with concentrations not cartels. Article 13 of the Regulation has been used very rarely by the Commission.[81]

Enforcement policy under the Regulation may also be affected by the provisions dealing with the suspension of the consideration periods allowed to the Commission: Article 10(4) of the Regulation provides that both ''first'' and ''second'' stages within which the Commission must make a decision on compatibility may be suspended where, *inter alia*, it has had to order an investigation by decision pursuant to Article 13. Suspension may be triggered only in so far as the Commission considers that it is not in possession of all information necessary in order to adopt its decision. Moreover the suspension operates only where one of the notifying parties or another involved party is responsible for the circumstances leading to the Article 13 decision. It is doubtful, therefore, whether a decision to order an investigation as a precautionary measure in the absence of a prior refusal or other evidence of a failure to co-operate can bring a suspension into play. This interpretation is supported by Article 9(1)(c) of the Implementing Regulation which treats an undertaking as

---

[77] *Orkem* (n. 75 above), paras 34 and 35, and Case C-60/92 *Otto BV v. Postbank NV* [1993] E.C.R. I-5683.
[78] Case T-221/95 *Endemol Entertainment Holdings BV v. Commission* [1999] E.C.R. II-000, para. 84.
[79] The inviolability of an individual's home (but not the premises of undertakings) was accepted as a common principle of human rights in the laws of Member States in Joined Cases 46/87 & 227/88 *Hoechst v. Commission* [1989] E.C.R. 2859; [1991] 4 C.M.L.R. 410, para. 19, and, wisely, it was not seen as necessary to tackle this sensitive issue in the context of E.C. merger control.
[80] See generally, Kerse, *EC Antitrust Procedure* (4th ed. 1998), Chap. 3.
[81] See *e.g. Skanska/Scancem* [1999] O.J. L183/1, d-para. 11.

responsible, *inter alia*, where it "has refused to submit to an investigation deemed necessary . . . on the basis of Article 13(1) of [the Regulation] or to co-operate in the carrying out of such an investigation".[82]

4.6.3 Comparison with Regulation 17

There are certain differences, most of them very minor, between the powers of the Commission in Article 13 of the Regulation and its equivalent powers under Regulation 17. Article 13(1)(b) expressly recognises the right of the Commission to demand copies of extracts from the books and other business records of an undertaking.

The Commission must also operate under somewhat stricter rules than hitherto in its liaison with the competent authorities of the Member States in which an investigation is to take place. If it proposes to launch an investigation the Commission must inform the relevant competent authority in writing,[83] but it is not required to notify the competent authorities of other Member States where other undertakings concerned in the concentration are established. Where the Commission proposes to take a decision ordering an investigation it is, furthermore, required to hear the competent authority concerned before making its decision. In similar circumstances, Regulation 17 simply requires consultation, and the different provisions clearly reflect the determination of at least some Member States to bring a somewhat more formal process into play.

4.6.4 Failure to Co-operate

The sanctions applicable in relation to requests for information and investigations are provided for in Articles 14 (fines) and 15 (periodic penalty payments) of the Regulation. Where books or other business records are produced in incomplete form or an undertaking fails to submit to an investigation ordered by decision, fines of from 1,000 to 50,000 ECU may be imposed where the failure is intentional or negligent. Similar levels of fine apply where incorrect information is furnished in response to an Article 11 request or there is a failure to supply information within the time fixed by an Article 11(5) decision. The maximum fines are a 10-fold increase on those available under the corresponding provisions of Regulation 17. It is therefore no surprise that in its recent White Paper on modernisation of the rules implementing Articles 81 and 82 that the Commission proposes updating and increasing the levels of fine under Regulation 17.

Where an undertaking refuses to submit to an investigation ordered by decision, or fails to supply complete and correct information following an Article 11(5) decision, the Commission may by decision impose periodic pen-

---

[82] Although Art. 9 of the Implementing Regulation clearly indicates the specific instances in which an undertaking will generally be held responsible for delay, the Implementing Regulation cannot, of course, amend the Council Regulation, or limit the generality of the wording in Art. 10(4).

[83] Case 5/85 *AKZO Chemie BV and AKZO Chemie UK Ltd v. Commission* [1986] E.C.R. 2585; [1987] 3 C.M.L.R. 716.

alty payments of up to ECU 25,000 for each day during which the Commission is prevented from carrying out its investigation.

The circumstances in which the Commission will need to resort to its power to make investigations at premises are likely to be very rare.[84] Undertakings concerned in concentrations falling within the Regulation have every incentive to co-operate in order not to delay the timetable for a decision, and to ensure that they are able to put their concentration fully into effect as quickly as possible. This is also true in relation to the powers in Article 11. Since sanctions exist in relation to the content of notifications themselves, there is less need for the Commission to exercise its Article 11 powers simply to ensure the completeness and accuracy of information. So far the Commission has used only its Article 11 powers, and predominantly against third parties, to seek information verifying or amplifying that in the notification. As is the case under the Regulation, the Commission's powers of inquiry extend to third parties.

4.7   DETAILED ASSESSMENT

4.7.1   Stage Two Proceedings—Timetable

Where the Commission initiates proceedings it must take a final decision on the compatibility of the proposed concentration with the Common Market within four months of the date the proceedings are initiated (R.Article 10(3)). In practice, the Commission will publish a notice of initiation of proceedings in the Official Journal. Third parties will be invited to submit observations on the proposed concentration.[85] As will be seen, because of the number of procedural steps which must be completed in this period, it will in practice put both the parties and the Commission under considerable pressure. This may be compounded where inquiry is also being made under other aspects of Community competition law.[86] The Commission's tasks include, where necessary, negotiation with the parties to secure modifications to the notified arrangements, or agree conditions subject to which they might be allowed to proceed as being compatible with the Common Market.[87] The diagram, Merger Procedure—Phase II, set out in Appendix 9, shows the procedures at this stage.

Detailed rules relating to the calculation of the four month period are set out in the Implementing Regulation. The starting date is the first working day after the day on which the proceedings are initiated (IR.Article 6(5)). The period ends with the expiry of the day in the fourth month thereafter which falls on the same date as the day on which the period started (IR.Article 7(6)). If there is no such day (for example the 31st) in the fourth month then the

[84] Indeed during the negotiation of the Regulation some Member States felt that powers to launch "dawn-raids" were unnecessary in the context of the Regulation.

[85] See, *e.g. The Coca-Cola Company/Carlsberg A/S* [1997] O.J. C148/14. Typically, third parties will be given 15 days to submit their observations.

[86] *e.g.* state aids, as in *Kali und Salz/MdK/Treuhand*; *Sidmar/Klockner Stahl*; and *PowerGen/NRG*.

[87] By contrast, *e.g.* the U.K. Competition Commission is a purely investigatory body. It does not engage in negotiation with the parties in merger references. This role is reserved for the Secretary of State for Trade and Industry, with the assistance of the Director General of Fair Trading.

period ends with the last day of that month. If the last day of the four month period, having applied these two rules, is not a working day then the period ends with the expiry of the next working day (IR.Article 7(8)). There are two more rules which in practice may operate to further extend the period. The first concerns holidays. If the four month period includes a public holiday or other holiday of the Commission, the four month period is extended by the corresponding number of days (IR.Article 8). Secondly, as Article 10(4) of the Regulation contemplates, the four month period may be suspended whilst the Commission awaits the response from one or more of the undertakings involved in the concentration to requests for information taken by decision under Article 11 or investigations ordered by decision under Article 13 or when the notifying parties have failed to inform the Commission of any material changes. Article 9 of the Implementing Regulation sets out detailed rules for the calculation of the period of suspension.

4.7.2   Article 6(1)(c) Decision

As well as issuing a brief press release indicating that it has opened second stage proceedings, sometimes supplemented by oral briefing at Commission press conferences, the Commission will issue a section Article 6(1)(c) decision to the parties indicating the basis for its decision and why, in its view, serious doubts exist about the compatibility of the concentration with the Common Market. These decisions are not published and vary considerably in length and detail. They are not the Commission's statement of the case against the transaction, which follows some weeks later (see below).

4.7.3   Statement of Objections

Article 18(1) of the Regulation provides that the undertakings concerned must be given the opportunity to make known their views on the objections against them. This right exists "at every stage of the procedure up to the consultation of the Advisory Committee". In practice the right will crystallise when the Commission proposes to take a particular decision affecting them, especially a final decision on the compatibility of the proposed concentration with the Common Market. Article 13(2) of the Implementing Regulation requires the Commission to inform the notifying parties concerned, in writing, of its objections. That document must fix a time limit for the parties' response.[88] The Commission generally aims to serve its statement of objections on the parties and, in some cases, interested third parties, within approximately six weeks of the opening of second stage proceedings. In some cases interested third parties have instead received summaries, sometimes quite brief, of the Commission's objections. In others a complete but non-confidential version has been supplied. Under Article 18(3) of the Regulation the Commission can base its decision only on objections on which the parties have been able to submit

---

[88] The time set has to take account of the time needed for preparing a defence, the urgency of the case and public holidays—Art. 20 of the Implementing Regulation.

their observations. Other involved parties must be informed of the objections and a time limit fixed for them to give their written views (IR. Article 13(2)).

4.7.4 Access to the File

Whilst the law and practice on this subject developed somewhat slowly in proceedings based on Articles 81 and 82, the right of the parties to have access to the file in order to prepare their response to the Commission's objections is expressly recognised in Article 18(3) of the Regulation. The detail is spelt out in Article 13(3) of the Implementing Regulation and in the Commission's Notice on access to the file.[89] Once the notifying parties have received the Commission's objections they can request access to the file. They should, so far as is possible, identify the documents or types of documents sought although the Commission is not thereby discharged from itself identifying and listing documents. Other involved parties, such as the vendor or target company, may similarly on request be given access to the file but only "in so far as this is necessary for the purposes of preparing their observations" (Article 13(3)(b)). The Commission is reluctant to grant such requests, particularly because of its resource and time implications. The access to the file procedure is subject to the supervision of the Hearing Officer. He will rule on any difference between the Commission and the parties as to whether access to particular documents should be given.

The Community courts have held that disclosure of certain types of document may be refused by the Commission; in particular documents or parts of documents containing other undertakings' business secrets, internal Commission documents and information enabling complainants to remain anonymous where so desired.[90] The special position of business secrets is recognised in Article 17 of the Implementing Regulation.[91] It should be noted that claims that all or part of documents are business secrets may have to be justified. Parties should also be prepared to supply non-confidential versions. Any disagreement with the Commission over whether a document is a business secret will be determined by decision of the Hearing Officer.

The question arises as to what extent the Commission is entitled to use information as a basis of, or support for, its observations against a party where that party cannot see it. Article 18(3) of the Regulation expressly provides that the rights of defence must be fully respected and that the Commission's decision shall be based only on objections on which the parties have been able to submit their observations. In *Hoffmann-La Roche* the Court said[92]:

---

[89] Commission Notice on the internal rules of procedure for processing requests for access to the file in cases pursuant to Arts 85 and 86 of the E.C. Treaty; Articles 65 and 66 of the ECSC Treaty; and Council Regulation 4064/89 [1997] O.J. C23/3.

[90] Case C-310/93P *BPB Industries and British Gypsum v. Commission* [1995] E.C.R. I-865, paras 26 and 27. Followed recently by the CFI in Case T-221/95 *Endemol Entertainment Holdings BV v. Commission* [1999] 5 C.M.L.R. 611.

[91] Art. 17 also refers to the need to protect "the internal documents of the authorities". It is noteworthy that the word "authorities", not "Commission", is used. Parties would appear therefore not to have any access to documents submitted by the Member States (*e.g.* pursuant to Art. 9) provided such documents remain "internal".

[92] Case 87/76 *Hoffmann-La Roche & Co. A.G. v. Commission* [1979] E.C.R. 461; [1979] 3 C.M.L.R 211, para. 11.

"the undertakings concerned must have been afforded the opportunity during the administrative procedure to make known their views on the truth and relevance of the facts and circumstances alleged and on the documents used by the Commission to support its claim that there has been an infringement of Article [82] of the Treaty."

The question in each case is whether non-disclosure of the document or the provision of an edited version would prejudice the right of defence. It must be established that non-disclosure might have influenced the course of the procedure and the content of the decision to the detriment of the applicant.[93] The regime of prior control goes beyond Article 82 (hence the need for Article 235 (now 308) E.C. as an enabling power) and does not presuppose any fault or wrongdoing which may justify a fine. The Commission is under strict time limits. In such circumstances the Court of First Instance may need some persuading that non-confidential summaries are not sufficient or that the anonymity of the parties should not be protected.

4.7.5 The Parties' Response

The Regulation refers to the parties' right "to submit their observations" on the Commission's objections (R.Article 18(3)). This right of reply (or defence) is, as in other competition procedures before the Commission, primarily exercised in writing. The original and 29 copies of the response must be supplied to the Commission (IR.Article 13(4)). The Implementing Regulation makes clear that in their written response the parties can set out all matters relevant to the case and may attach any relevant documents in proof of the facts set out. They may also propose that the Commission hear persons who may corroborate those facts (IR.Article 13(4)). The parties concerned are therefore free to advance what legal, economic or other arguments they wish and can challenge not only the factual but the legal and economic basis of the Commission's observations. Where a party wishes, in addition to its written response, to put forward arguments orally, this must be requested in that response (IR.Article 14(1)). The Commission may also allow the parties to present their case orally, without need of prior written submission.

4.7.6 Oral Hearings

Articles 14, 15 and 16 of the Implementing Regulation provide for oral hearings to supplement the written procedure. A written request to be heard orally is necessary and parties have to show "a sufficient interest". A person has a sufficient interest if he is to be the addressee of the decision. Further, the Commission *must* afford any party on whom it proposes to impose a fine or periodic penalty payment the opportunity to put forward their arguments orally in a formal hearing. Third parties may have "a sufficient interest". In addition they can, at the discretion of the Commission, be invited to attend.

---

[93] See *Endemol*, above, paras 65–91.

The Commission fixes the date for the hearing and summons the persons to be heard to attend. The hearing date is likely to be shortly (for example one week) after the date fixed for the delivery of the written reply. Individuals may appear in person or by a legal or other authorised representative (IR.Article 15(2)). Undertakings are represented by duly authorised agents. Such agents must be someone on their permanent staff.[94] Independent lawyers and other qualified persons may assist the parties being heard. Exceptionally there may need to be two oral hearings.[95]

The hearing is conducted by the Hearing Officer (IR.Article 15(1)). Hearings are not public and the Implementing Regulation provides for parties to be heard separately or together (IR.Article 15(4)). Arrangements are flexible but business secrets must be protected and therefore a party should advise the Hearing Officer in advance if and when business secrets and other confidential information, such as the commercial objectives of each party in a consortium bid, is to be presented, so that suitable arrangements can be made for the party to be heard separately for the whole or part of the hearing as may be appropriate in the circumstances. Representatives of the competent authorities of the Member States have the right to attend the oral hearing. They can and do ask questions. Finally, the Implementing Regulation provides that the statements made by each party must be recorded (IR.Article 15(5)). There is no need for the Commission to produce minutes of the whole hearing to be read and approved by the parties concerned.

4.7.7 Third Parties—Right to be Heard

The observance of the right to be heard is, in all proceedings liable to culminate in a measure adversely affecting a particular person, a fundamental principle of Community law.[96] It is clear that a third party may be affected by a finding that a concentration is, or is not, compatible with the Common Market.

So far as the right to be heard is concerned the Regulation provides that third parties may be heard if the Commission or the competent authorities of the Member States consider it necessary (R.Article 18(4)). This is a general and wide power and in practice the Commission will hear anyone who is bona fide and has something relevant to contribute to the facts and issues of the proceedings. The Regulation, however, requires the Commission to hear all natural or legal persons showing a sufficient interest (for example, a competitor—especially one with whom the Commission considers an undertaking concerned to share a collective dominant position[97]). Members of the administrative or management bodies of the undertakings concerned and the reco-

---

[94] Recital 8 to the Implementing Regulation specifm of the possibility of being assisted by a lawyer: Case T-96/92 *Comité Central d'Entreprise de la Société Generale des Grandes Sources v. Commission* [1995] E.C.R. II-1213, para. 63.

[95] As in *Procter & Gamble/VP Schickedanz II* [1994] O.J. L354/32.

[96] Case C-32/95 P *Commission v. Lisrestal and Others* [1996] E.C.R. I-5373, para. 21.

[97] Joined Cases C-68/94 & C-30/95 *French Republic and Others v. Commission* [1998] E.C.R. I-1375, para. 174.

gnised representatives of the employees[98] are automatically treated as having such an interest. This recognises the special concerns of both the management and employees in concentration cases. The question of whether a particular works council or trade union organisation is a recognised representative of the employees of the undertakings concerned is for national law to determine. As the Court of First Instance held, in the *Perrier* cases, it is for the Member States to define which organisations are competent to represent the collective interests of employees and to determine their rights and prerogatives, subject to the adoption of harmonisation measures (such as the Works Council Directive 94/45).[99] But the Commission has taken the view that the Merger Regulation cannot be used to obtain information which employees may be entitled to receive under that Directive.[1]

It is important to note that third parties entitled to be heard are not automatically entitled to see the objections sent to the parties concerned or otherwise learn of the Commission's intentions regarding the proposed concentration (this information is potentially price sensitive and therefore commercially confidential).[2] Article 16(1) of the Implementing Regulation provides that the Commission must inform third parties (who have made written application to be heard) in writing "of the nature and subject matter of the procedure". The Commission will fix a time within which a third party must make known its views in writing or orally. The Implementing Regulation contemplates that there may only be time for oral comments but allows such statements to be confirmed in writing (IR.Article 16(2)). Third parties do not have any automatic right of access to the file,[3] nor, as in stage one proceedings, to see final texts of any commitments offered by the notifying parties.[4]

4.7.8 Consultation of the Advisory Committee

Before taking a final decision,[5] or one imposing a fine or penalty, the Commission must consult the Advisory Committee on Concentrations, made up of representatives of the authorities of Member States (R.Article 19(3)). The need to consult the Advisory Committee has therefore to be taken into account in the Commission's timetable. The procedure of the Committee is described in Chapter 7.

---

[98] The position of employees was a matter of particular concern for the European Parliament. See also Recital 31 of the Regulation.

[99] See Case T-96/92 *Comité Central d'Entreprise de la Société Générale des Grandes Sources and Others v. Commission* [1992] E.C.R. II-2579, para. 34. See also para. 7.6.3.3, below, on the question whether the express reference to recognised representatives of employees in Art. 18(4) accords automatic *locus standi* for the purpose of bringing appeals under Art. 230 of the Treaty.

[1] See *ABB/Daimler-Benz* [1997] O.J. L11/1, para. 149.

[2] The Court of Justice has indicated that the procedural rights of complainants are not as far-reaching as the right to a fair hearing of the parties and, in any event, the limits of the rights are reached where they begin to interfere with the parties' right to a fair hearing: Joined Cases 142 & 156/84 *BAT and Reynolds v. Commission* [1987] E.C.R. 4487, para. 20.

[3] Case T-96/92 *Perrier* (above), para. 64.

[4] Case T-290 *Kaysersberg SA v. Commission* [1997] E.C.R. II-2137, paras 119–120.

[5] The Committee must also be consulted on decisions ordering divestment, etc. (when a separate decision under Art. 8(4)) or revoking a clearance under Art. 8(5).

4.8 FINAL DECISIONS

When proceedings have been initiated under Article 6(1)(c) (*i.e.* because there are serious doubts as to compatibility with the Common Market) they must be closed by one of the decisions provided for in Article 8 paragraphs (2)–(5). These are described in Chapter 7.

4.9 TRANSMISSION OF DOCUMENTS

Time limits under the Regulation are generally short and hence the Implementing Regulation makes special provision for the transmission of documents, enabling use to be made of modern technology. The Commission has the choice of five ways to send documents: (a) delivery by hand against receipt; (b) registered letter with acknowledgement of receipt; (c) telefax with a request for acknowledgement of receipt; (d) telex; (e) electronic mail with a request for acknowledgement of receipt (IR Article 20(1)). The same five ways are generally available for the parties and third parties to send documents to the Commission, but there are exceptions (IR Article 20(2)). Notification (Form CO) must, for example, be delivered or sent by registered letter. Article 20(3) of the Implementing Regulation provides that where a document is sent by telex, fax or e-mail it is deemed to have been received on the day on which it was sent.

5 Appraisal of Concentrations

5.1 INTRODUCTION

Chapters 2 and 3 have discussed the two elements of the jurisdictional test adopted in the Regulation, the concepts of "concentration" and "Community dimension". This Chapter deals with the nature of the substantive appraisal which the Commission is required to carry out when a transaction falls within its jurisdiction.

Article 2 of the Regulation is headed "Appraisal of Concentrations" and Article 2(1) requires the Commission to assess concentrations notified to it to establish "whether or not they are compatible with the common market". Article 2(2) elaborates upon the concept of compatibility with the Common Market, and provides that:

> "A concentration which does not create or strengthen a dominant position as a result of which effective competition would be significantly impeded in the Common Market or in a substantial part of it shall be declared compatible with the Common Market."

Conversely, if the concentration does create or strengthen a dominant position, the Commission must declare it incompatible with the Common Market (Article 2(3)). In determining compatibility Article 2(1)(a) and (b) directs the Commission to take into account a number of general factors (discussed further below), most of which are familiar from the jurisprudence under Article 81 of the E.C. Treaty.

There have been two significant developments in this area since the last edition, one judicial and substantive, the other legislative and procedural. First, the European Court has confirmed that the Regulation does apply to so-called collective dominance or oligopoly. Secondly, the Article 81 appraisal of the co-ordination effects of structural joint ventures has been brought within the Regulation by an amendment to the compatibility test in Article 2. Following the changes made by Council Regulation 1310/97, in the case of co-operative structural joint ventures, an additional and subordinate limb has been introduced into the test, carried out under the Regulation: the "co-ordination effects" of such a joint venture must be assessed according to the criteria in Article 81 of the E.C. Treaty.[1] In such cases compatibility becomes an amal-

---

[1] Art. 2(4) of the amended Regulation requires that

"To the extent that the creation of a joint venture constituting a concentration pursuant to Article 3

gam of the dominance element in Article 2 as originally enacted and an Article 81 element.[2]

As already outlined in Chapter 1, the appraisal which the Commission makes of a notified concentration may take place in two stages. Nonetheless, in both stages, the Commission is applying precisely the same test of compatibility.[3]

5.1.1 The Appraisal Process: The Basic Objective

Certain preliminary comments need to be made about the compatibility test, particularly in the light of the history of the proposal, and the importance of the precise formulation of the test in the ultimate acceptance of an E.C. merger control regime. For a number of Member States, including the two with the then most developed systems of merger control, the United Kingdom and Germany, a substantive test based squarely on competition issues was a prerequisite for any form of control at E.C. level.

It is clear from the Regulation that the object of E.C. merger control is to preserve and promote an effective competitive structure within the Common Market to the benefit of customers and consumers. Concentrations which, through creating or enhancing a dominant position within the Common Market or a substantial part of it, have a significant adverse impact on competition must be prohibited. Significantly, there is no mechanism for exemption or authorisation of concentrations found incompatible with the Common Market.[4] Equally, there is little scope for any form of balancing exercise within the appraisal process itself which would admit factors unrelated to competition.[5] However, the co-ordination effects of certain joint ventures falling to be dealt with under the Regulation since March 1998 are capable of being exempted under Article 81(3) even if they have an appreciable effect on competition.

---

has as its object or effect the co-ordination of the competitive behaviour of undertakings that remain independent, such co-ordination shall be appraised in accordance with the criteria of Article 85(1) and (3) of the Treaty, with a view to establishing whether or not the operation is compatible with the Common Market. In making this appraisal, the Commission shall take into account in particular:

— whether two or more parent companies retain to a significant extent activities in the same market as the joint venture or in a market which is downstream or upstream from that of the joint venture or in a neighbouring market closely related to this market;

— whether the co-ordination which is the direct consequence of the creation of the joint venture affords the undertakings concerned the possibility of eliminating competition in respect of a substantial part of the products or services in question". See Chap. 2, para. 2.7.1.

[2] See para. 5.5, below.

[3] This is reflected in the fact that the Commission does not publish any formal decision at the end of the first stage when it proposes to open proceedings in accordance with Art. 6(1)(c) of the Regulation.

[4] Contrast Art. 81 of the E.C. Treaty. Under Art. 82, however, there is no possibility of exemption or approval to excuse the abuse of a dominant position.

[5] In the course of the various draft proposals a two-stage substantive process (with an assessment of competitive effect followed by a possibility of exemption or authorisation) was abandoned and the concept of "dominance" was introduced, so bringing the test in the Regulation much nearer the principle of Art. 82, which the Commission had been using, prior to the adoption of the Regulation, as a means of supervising mergers with major Community implications.

5.1.2　Competition or Industrial Policy?

Considerable debate took place between Member States as to the precise nature of the criteria by which the Commission should assess concentrations notified to it. The draft proposals published in 1988[6] and 1989[7] gave the Commission power to authorise concentrations which were found to be significantly anti-competitive, but gave little indication of the grounds for such an authorisation. Several Member States objected to such a power of authorisation or exemption[8] and, largely due to German and United Kingdom insistence, the criteria for assessment finally emerged firmly based on factors relating to competition in the Common Market. However, as will be seen, those factors do not totally exclude other considerations, in particular technical and economic progress.[9]

Allowance also has to be made for the fact that the final decision lies with the college of Commissioners in cases which go to a full investigation. That body is political, even though its decisions must be taken in accordance with the Regulation and are subject to judicial review. The outcome of its deliberations is not always predictable.[10] Moreover, the Regulation recognises that national policy considerations unrelated to competition cannot be totally excluded.[11] Article 21(3) specifies certain legitimate interests which Member States may protect, including public security, the plurality of the media, and supervision over financial and investment institutions, notwithstanding the Commission's monopoly of assessing concentrations with a Community dimension.[12]

The Regulation also recognises that a balance must be struck between promoting the basic objective in Article 3(g) of the Treaty of ensuring "that competition in the common market is not distorted", and allowing scope for businessmen to make appropriate commercial reactions through joint ventures and concentrations to the emerging single European market and to Monetary

---

[6] [1988] O.J. C130/4.
[7] [1989] O.J. C22/14.
[8] See Hawk, B.E., "The EEC Merger Regulation: The First Step Toward One-Stop Merger Control" (1990) 59 Antitrust L.J. 195.
[9] Discussed in para. 5.8, below. Note that, though the Maastricht Treaty added a new Art. 130 (Industry) to the E.C. Treaty, the emphasis on competition was preserved by the final sentence: "it shall not provide a basis for the introduction by the Commission of any measures which could lead to a distortion of competition". The emphasis on competition was maintained in the Commission's 1994 report, prepared by DGIII, entitled "An Industrial Competitiveness Policy for the European Union". In its diagnosis of the performance of E.C. industry the Commission said:

> "It is also important to remember that industrial competitiveness is based essentially on the existence within the industrial fabric, of the largest possible number of companies in a position to expand and make profits on all markets on which they are active. The more exacting the demand and the stronger the competition, the more a company's positive performance is indicative of competitiveness. These conditions exist in the European Union, and the positive results achieved by a very large number of companies demonstrate that they have been able to adjust to this competitive environment."

[10] It is understood that in *Mannesmann/Vallourec/Ilva* the Commissioners were deadlocked and that the draft decision of the Merger Task Force prohibiting the deal had to be rewritten as a conditional clearance to avoid the embarrassment of a deemed outright clearance by default as a result of the Commission's failure to deliver a formal decision within the time allowed.
[11] As does Art. 296 of the E.C. Treaty itself in relation to defence matters.
[12] For further discussion, see Chap. 8, below.

Union.[13] Recital 4, in particular, recognises that developments are to be welcomed which increase the competitiveness of European industry, enable it to grow, and raise living standards in the Community. Recital 13 requires the Commission to make its assessment of a concentration "within the general framework of the achievement of the fundamental objectives" of Article 2 of the Treaty "including that of strengthening the Community's economic and social cohesion". But, against this background, the Regulation takes a clear stand: the processes of reorganisation within the Community must not result in lasting damage to competition in the Community as a consequence of the structural changes brought about by major concentrations. While Recitals are used by the Court as aids to the interpretation of Community legislation they cannot override the legal effect of unambiguous dispositive provisions. This overriding emphasis on the preservation of competition is reflected in the approach taken by the Merger Task Force. In several cases it has made a point of emphasising that economic progress does not justify detriment to competitive market structures.[14] The Court of First Instance, however, has been a little more ambivalent: in its judgment in *Perrier*[15] it appears to have placed more emphasis on employment and social considerations and the impact of Recital 13 than might have been expected. The European Court of Justice, however, was clear in *France v. Commission*[16] that little persuasive weight could be attached to a recital which is not developed or reflected in the operative part of the Regulation.

5.2 COMPATIBILITY WITH THE COMMON MARKET

Each concentration has to be appraised from a neutral starting point in accordance with the factors listed in paragraphs (a) and (b) of Article 2(1) in order to arrive at a decision of compatibility or incompatibility. The absence of any presumption against a notified concentration means that there is no automatic prohibition as in Article 81(2). Everything hinges on the ultimate decision of the Commission and Article 2(3) obliges it to declare a concentration incompatible with the Common Market where it "*creates or strengthens a dominant position* as a result of which *effective competition would be significantly impeded* in the common market or in a substantial part of it" (emphasis added). The onus is on the Commission to justify its decisions on the basis of realistic predictions and judgments derived from information available to it. A concentration which does not have such an effect must be declared compatible, and allowed to proceed. No other outcomes are possible. It is a competition test. Compatibility and incompatibility, Article 2(2) and (3), are opposite sides of the same coin. But one qualification must be made to this analysis where

---

[13] Note Recitals 1 to 4 and 13.

[14] See, *e.g.* the Art. 8 decision in *MSG Media Service*, paras 100 and 101, discussed in para. 5.5.1, below.

[15] Case T-96/92 *Comité Central d'Entreprise de la Société Générale des Grandes Sources and others v. Commission* [1992] E.C.R. II-2579. Discussed further at para. 5.8.4, below.

[16] Joined Cases, C-68/94 & C-30/95 (referred to hereafter in this chapter as *Kali und Salz*). Judgment of March 31, 1998, at points 176 and 177, where the court rejected the argument of the French Government, based on Recital 15 of the Regulation, that it was not intended to apply to the creation or strengthening of collective dominant positions. Discussed further at 5.7, below.

Article 2(4) applies: it is, since March 1998, possible that a joint venture could be declared incompatible under the Regulation as a result of failing the Article 81 criteria because of its effects on competition between undertakings which remain independent notwithstanding the creation of the joint venture.

5.2.1   The Elements of the Compatibility Test (Article 2(3))

The discussion in this section concerns the dominance appraisal to which all concentrations notified under the Regulation are subject. The Article 81 appraisal which now forms part of the compatibility test under Article 2(4) of the Regulation and which applies only to certain kinds of joint ventures which, prior to March 1998, fell wholly outside the Regulation, is discussed in section 5.5, below.

The test of compatibility involves two elements:

  (i)   the creation or strengthening of a dominant position;
  (ii) as a result of which effective competition would be significantly impeded in the Common Market or in a substantial part of it.

This test places more emphasis on market structure than the early drafts of the Regulation[17] and it was only in the April 1989 draft that the requirement of a "dominant position" was introduced. Nonetheless a separate appraisal test has been created and not a mere reproduction of the concept of dominance from Article 82.

As regards the relationship between the two limbs of the test of compatibility in Article 2(1) the Commission has not adopted a mechanistic approach in applying the Regulation. The requirement that the dominant position must significantly impede competition in practice is a two-part composite test, and is a formulation broadly consistent with existing case law under Article 82. At the same time the Commission has the flexibility and discretion it clearly needs when making assessments under Article 2. It is doubtful, moreover, whether it is helpful to think in terms of the shifting of the burden of proof, or the creation of a presumption against the notifying party once the criterion of dominance is established. For example, an undertaking with a 40 per cent share of a product market in the Community may acquire a competitor with a 2 per cent share of the same market. Clearly, there is some aggregation of market share but such a concentration would be unlikely of itself to result in competitive detriment because the reality is that no significant competition has been eliminated as a result of the concentration. This approach has been made more apparent in Commission decisions under the Regulation in recent years. Its correctness has now been confirmed by the European Court in *Kali und Salz*. The Court interpreted the second limb of the compatibility test as emphasising the need for a causal link between the creation or strengthening

---

[17] See the drafts of 1973, 1981 and 1984 published respectively in [1973] O.J. C92/1; [1982] O.J. C36/3; and [1984] O.J. C51/8.

of a dominant position and a significant detrimental impact on effective competition, observing[18]:

> "The introduction of that criterion is intended to ensure that the existence of a causal link between the concentration and the deterioration of the competitive structure of the market can be excluded only if the competitive structure resulting from the concentration would deteriorate in similar fashion even if the concentration did not proceed."

The apparent flexibility of the second limb of the compatibility test can also be seen in the practice of the Commission. In *Mannesmann/Hoesch*, for example, the Commission concluded that the merged entity would occupy a dominant position on the German market for certain types of gas pipeline but found that the dominance would be short-lived because of the imminent introduction of mandatory competitive tendering by the companies' traditional customers. The strengthening of the existing dominant position would not, therefore, hinder effective competition. Interestingly the issue of the enduring nature of the joint venture's dominance, which might well have been subsumed within the analysis of the dynamics of the markets concerned, or of dominance itself, appears to have been dealt with under the second rather than the first limb of the compatibility test. It is questionable, however, whether the result would have been different if the Commission had not been able to rely on the second limb of the test. It could equally well have based its conclusion on a prediction as to how the relevant market would evolve in the near future, and this approach has been preferred in other cases.

5.2.2 Creating or Strengthening Dominance

One of the shortcomings in applying Article 82 to concentrations was that the acquirer had already to enjoy a dominant position if the acquisition was to be established as an abuse. An acquisition which created a dominant position fell outside the ambit of Article 82. The better view was also that the acquisition of a competitor with an existing dominant position by a non-dominant rival could not be challenged under Article 82.[19] In this regard the Regulation gives the Commission a more extensive and more flexible power of control. A concentration may be attacked if it creates a dominant position in the Common Market, or a substantial part of it, and not only where an existing position of dominance is reinforced. In practice the Commission has considerable leeway, but it faces a more difficult task in assessing whether a position of dominance is created and predicting and substantiating its future effects than it does in a case involving a clear reinforcement of pre-existing dominance. A striking recent example is the Commission's Article 8 prohibition decision in *Airtours/First Choice* (not yet published) where it found that a position of collective

---

[18] Points 110 and 115: see generally 106 to 116 of the judgment.

[19] Contrary views have been expressed including by officials of the Competition Directorate speaking in a personal capacity. The writers are not aware that Art. 82 has ever been used in such a way in any formal decision. Note, however, the apparent application of Art. 82 to the creation of a monopoly through the merger of two non-dominant duopolists in *MAN/Sulzer*.

dominance in the U.K. travel trade would be created notwithstanding the continued existence of three major vertically-integrated travel groups in the U.K. A finding of incompatibility is justiciable. The Court of First Instance has recognised, however, that, in reviewing such a finding "the Community judicature must take account of the discretionary margin implicit in the provisions of an economic nature which form part of the rules on concentrations".[20]

5.2.3 Dominance

Dominance is essentially an economic concept, indicating the ability of an undertaking to act without regard to its competitors, actual and potential, or its customers, and, in particular, to set prices as it chooses. The behaviour of a dominant firm cannot be constrained effectively by the reactions of competitors (actual or potential), suppliers or customers. Under Article 82 the Court of Justice has tended to express the concept of dominance in such terms. In *Gottrup-Klim* the Court said:

> "The concept of a dominant position is defined in settled case-law as a position of economic strength enjoyed by an undertaking which enables it to prevent effective competition being maintained on the relevant market by giving it the power to behave to an appreciable extent independently of its competitors, its customers and ultimately of the consumers".[21]

But while the concept may be easy to formulate, determining dominance in practice is rather less straightforward. Dominance is not a black and white concept. It occurs not only where the competitive restraints on an undertaking are absent but also where they are too weak in practice to affect its behaviour. The picture is blurred further by the recognition of degrees of market power or influence short of dominance.[22] Moreover, under the Regulation, appraisal of a proposed concentration necessarily involves predictions about how the market will generally operate, and the players in it respond and behave, if the concentration takes place. It is not confined to assessing simply the potential for the undertakings concerned in the concentration to engage in abusive conduct. For instance a concentration may endanger effective competition within the Common Market, or a substantial part of it, simply through the deterrent effect on new entry or investment in new capacity which could be caused by the presence of the enlarged undertaking.

5.2.4 Dominance and Competitive Structure

The central objective of merger control is to preserve the competitive structure of markets, while cartel prohibitions seek to preserve independent commercial

---

[20] Judgment of March 25, 1999 in Case T-102/96 *Gencor Ltd v. Commission*, para. 165, echoing the European Court of Justice in *Kali und Salz*, paras 223 and 224.
[21] Case C-250/96 *Gottrüp-Klim v. Dansk Landbrugs Grovvareselskab Amba* [1994] E.C.R. I-5641, para. 47. See also Case 27/76 *United Brands v. Commission* [1978] E.C.R. 207, paras. 65 and 66, and Case T-30/89 *Hilti v. Commission* [1991] E.C.R. II-1439, para. 90.
[22] Under Art. 81 or in the regulation of public telecommunications operators.

behaviour among competitors. Indeed, earlier versions of the compatibility test spoke only of the preservation of "effective competition" without reference to "dominance". Conflicting political and legal objectives led, however, to the wording being modified: Article 2(3) prohibits any "concentration which creates or strengthens a dominant position as a result of which effective competition would be significantly impeded in the common market or in a substantial part of it". This formulation was preferred, in part for political reasons—a wish to limit the new discretion conferred on the Commission—and in part for legal reasons—the disapplication of Article 82 had to be legally sustainable.[23] The introduction of the concept of dominance inevitably pointed in the direction of the jurisprudence of the Court in Article 82 cases, even though that jurisprudence centres on abusive commercial behaviour by dominant firms rather than the preservation of competitive market structures.

5.2.5 Dominance in the Common Market or a Substantial Part of it

A finding of compatibility or incompatibility depends on whether dominance is created or strengthened in the Common Market or a substantial part thereof. There is little authority at the E.U. level as to what constitutes a substantial part of the Common Market, or what considerations are relevant to make such a judgment. If, however, the threat of dominance exists only in a regional or local market in a Member State not constituting a substantial part of the Common Market, it is suggested that the Commission would have no grounds for a finding of incompatibility under Article 2 of the Regulation. This seems necessarily to follow from the way Article 2 formulates the test of incompatibility. Indeed in some cases the Commission has examined the effects of a concentration on competition in areas which arguably do not constitute substantial parts of the Common Market.[24] This would be legitimate if, by reason of chains of substitution, or impact on purchasing power at a national level, those areas formed part of a wider geographic market or competitive effects were more widespread but not all cases can be explained on such grounds.

This problem seems to have been recognised in the changes made in the Article 9 procedure by Regulation 1310/97. This Commission is now obliged to refer a case (or part of a case) back to a Member State where a request is made for it to do so on the basis that a notified concentration "affects competition on a distinct market within that Member State which does not constitute a substantial part of the Common Market".[25]

5.2.6 Single Firm or Collective Dominance

The great majority of notifications under the Regulation raise only the issue of whether the acquisition or joint venture concerned will lead to the creation

---

[23] But the new millennium may see a reconsideration of the test on the grounds that it poses too high a threshold for the Commission, particulary as regards preventing the emergence of oligopolistic markets.

[24] *e.g. Auchan/Pao de Acucar.*

[25] Art. 9(2)(b) of the Regulatio the referral back procedure is discussed fully in Chap. 8.

of a single entity dominant in one or more markets. It is well recognised, however, that markets characterised by the presence of only a small number of firms with significant market shares may operate as uncompetitively as a market dominated by a single undertaking. However, neither the original rules on competition in the E.C. Treaty, nor the Regulation itself, are expressed so clearly as to put it beyond doubt that behavioural or structural controls could be used to prevent or police collective dominance in oligopolistic markets. This issue has been the most contentious and interesting feature of the first decade of E.C. merger control. Only in March 1998, with the judgment of the European Court of Justice in *Kali und Salz*, were the doubts laid to rest. The Court held[26] that:

"... the Regulation, unlike Articles [81] and [82] of the Treaty, is intended to apply to all concentrations with a Community dimension in so far as they are likely, because of their effect on the structure of competition within the Community, to prove incompatible with the system of undistorted competition envisaged by the Treaty ...

A concentration which creates or strengthens a dominant position on the part of the parties concerned with an entity not involved in the concentration is liable to prove incompatible with the system of undistorted competition which the Treaty seeks to secure. Consequently, if it were accepted that only concentrations creating or strengthening a dominant position on the part of the parties to the concentration were covered by the Regulation, its purpose as indicated in particular by the abovementioned recitals would be partially frustrated. The Regulation would thus be deprived of a not insignificant aspect of its effectiveness, without that being necessary from the perspective of the general structure of the Community system of control of concentrations ... It follows ... that collective dominant positions do not fall outside the scope of the Regulation."

The application of the Regulation to positions of collective dominance and the assessment of oligopolies under Article 2 raises a number of questions and complexities beyond those which arise in the hitherto more typical case where a notified concentration risks creating a single dominant firm. For these reasons collective dominance is discussed separately in Section 5.7 below.

5.3   THE APPRAISAL PROCESS—MARKET DEFINITION

To assess whether an undertaking is dominant it is clearly necessary first to identify the market or markets in which dominance may exist. As the European Court of Justice noted in *Kali und Salz*, "a proper definition of the relevant market is a necessary precondition for any assessment of the effect of a concentration on competition".[27] This involves determination of both the product

---

[26] Paras 165 to 178.

[27] At para. 143 of the judgment: the Court approved the definition given in Case 27/76 *United Brands v. Commission*, of the relevant geographical market as "a defined geographical area in which the product concerned is marketed and where the conditions of competition are sufficiently homogeneous for all economic operators, so that the effect on competition of the concentration notified can be evaluated rationally" (paras 11 and 44).

markets (goods or services) and the geographical markets within which that undertaking competes.[28]

The Commission has been criticised for defining markets narrowly. This criticism is, we suggest, misplaced. It is the role, and, indeed, the legal duty of the Commission to protect competitive market structures by identifying any risk that a notified concentration will create or strengthen a dominant position. It must, therefore, seek to identify all markets affected, however small the turnover in them or however specialist or niche they may be. Moreover, if there are different but equally plausible views as to whether the market includes product A and product B or only product A, it is appropriate for the Commission to play safe and adopt the narrower alternative in view of its obligation under Article 2 of the Regulation, particularly in the stage one procedure when it has little time, and perhaps too little information, on which to make a definitive analysis. Companies and their advisers must recognise the context in which the Commission operates in preparing notifications. As *Sanofi/Synthélabo* shows, it is highly risky to overlook niche markets, however easy they are to enter or insignificant the turnover for which they account. In that case the original notification of January 18, 1999 was declared incomplete and renotified so as to be effective on February 15, 1999. The merger was cleared by an Article 6(1)(b) decision on March 15, 1999. But this was revoked on April 21, 1999—the first time the Commission has taken this step—because the parties had failed to describe in their notification their overlapping activities in stupefying active substances. The Commission nonetheless allowed the merger to take effect, granting an exemption under Article 7(4) of the Regulation from the normal embargo on implementation, the parties having committed themselves to dispose of Synthélabo's overlapping activities (which generated turnover of only some 3 million Euro).

The Commission is careful not to commit itself to particular market definitions where it is not necessary to do so. The majority of notifications raise no threat of dominance whatsoever, and the Commission often contents itself with a statement such as that made in *Sara Lee/BP Food*:

> "In view of the generally small market shares of CFBG [the food division of BP which was being acquired by Sara Lee] under the narrowest possible market definition (individual product groups such as ham, frankfurter sausages, etc. at national level) and the absence of any significant overlap between Sara Lee and CFBG in the Community, exact market definitions may be left open, since no dominant position is created or reinforced."

Even so, assessing whether a notified concentration is compatible with the Common Market does involve some determination, however tentative, both of the product markets and the geographic markets affected by the concentration. Moreover, as decisions now illustrate in many sectors, even tentative conclusions on market definition in first stage examinations, if applied repeatedly

---

[28] Market definition is also essential for a second purpose under the Regulation. In order to judge co-ordination effects of a concentration the Commission must determine in which markets the undertakings concerned operate in order to assess whether the notified transaction carries a risk of co-ordination between undertakings which remain independent.

and reflecting consistent information and opinion provided in notifications by companies active in the sector, can build up to a body of precedent from which the Commission is unlikely to depart.[29]

5.3.1   The Notice on Market Definition

In 1997 the Commission published a notice for guidance on "the definition of relevant market for the purposes of community competition law" ("the Market Definition Notice").[30] As the title makes clear the notice applies not merely to the Regulation but to all the competition rules, including state aid cases. The Notice is a valuable and concise summary of the Commission's working approach or "orientation", as the Notice puts it, to market definition within the context of the definitions of the concepts of product and geographic market given by the Court of Justice.[31] The Notice, for instance, confirms the priority which the Commission gives to demand-side substitutability at the stage of market definition. It relegates supply-side substitutability and potential competition to the stage which follows, namely, the analysis of competition in the markets defined by reference to demand-side factors, unless there is a ready ability to switch existing production such that the impact is so effective and immediate that it can be treated as equivalent to the demand substitution effect.[32] For the first time, the Commission has emphasised the importance of a test of demand-side substitutability, espoused for some time by U.S. anti-trust authorities, that is, to examine how customers would react to a hypothetical small but not insignificant (between five and 10 per cent of current prevailing prices) permanent price rise in the product under analysis. This is known among economists as the "SNIP test"[33] or the "hypothetical monopolist test". To establish whether product A constitutes a distinct economic market, assume that firm X has a monopoly in the supply of that product. If, in response to X raising its prices by a significant amount, customers switched to product B supplied by undertaking Y in such numbers as to make the price increase unprofitable products A and B must logically be in the same market. The test is repeated until all the true substitutes for product A, and all the actual and potential competitors of undertaking X, have been identified.

---

[29] See, *e.g.* in the insurance sector *AG/Amev; UAP/Transatlantic/Sun Life; Schweizer Rück/Elvia; Allianz/ Deutsche Krankenversicherung; Fortis/La Caixa; Zurich/MMI; Codan/Hafnia; Aegon/Scottish Equitable; UAP/Vinci; Generali/Central Hispano-Generali; ERC/NRG Victory; Winterthur/DBV; GE/CIGI; Commercial Union/Groupe Victoire; General Re/Kölnische Re; Direct Line/Bankinter; Winterthur/Schweizer Rück; Allianz/Elvia/Lloyd Adriatico; Generali/Comit/ Flemings; Ferruzzi Finanziaria/ Fondiaria; Employers Reinsurance/Frankona; Employers Reinsurance/Aachener; Generali/France Vie; UAP/Sun Life; Swiss Life/INCA; Generali/Unicredito; Sun Alliance/Royal Insurance; AMB/Rodutch; Schweizer Re/ M & G; Allianz/Vereinte; AXA/UAP; DBV/Gothaer/GPM; Bank Austria/Creditanstalt; Abeille Vie/Viagère/ Sinafer; ING/BBL; GRE/PPP; Hermes/Sampo/FGB-FCIC; Commercial Union/General Accident; AGF/ Royal; Allianz/AGF; AXA-UAP/Royale Belge; Schweizer Rück/NCM; Commercial Union/Berlinische; Paribas/Ecureuil-Vie/ICD; ING/BHF; AXA/GRE; Swiss Life/Lloyd Continental; Royal & Sun Alliance/ Trygg-Hansa;* and *CU Italia/Banca delle Marche.* None of these notifications went beyond stage one.
[30] The Notice is published in O.J. C372, 9.12.97, p. 5. It is reproduced in Appendix 8.
[31] In its judgment of February 13, 1979 in Case 85/76 *Hoffmann-La Roche,* followed in subsequent judgments both by the Court and the CFI.
[32] Para. 20 of the Notice.
[33] The acronym standing for Significant Non-transitory Increase in Price.

The Notice also sets out a working hierarchy[34] of factors considered by the Commission particularly relevant to market definition and explains how it seeks to gather and use empirical data to inform and support its analysis. Individual factors are discussed further below.

Another point to note from the Market Definition Notice is the distinction which the Commission draws between cases under the Regulation and cases under Articles 81 and 82 of the E.C. Treaty. The analysis of the effects of a concentration essentially involves making a prognosis about future behaviour, not simply of the merged firm but of its competitors, customers and suppliers. This prospective approach is different from that adopted where the issues concern past behaviour, which may, in itself, be relevant to market definition as well as the assessment of dominance. The Regulation is concerned with protecting against structural changes of lasting duration which will significantly damage effective competition. If, within a short time horizon, customers could protect themselves, for example, by self-supply or introducing new buying techniques, this would be relevant to the appraisal of compatibility in Article 2 of the Regulation.

5.3.2 Relevant Product Market

The Commission's approach to product market definition has followed the traditional line taken in applying Articles 81 and 82, with the emphasis on demand-side substitutability, *i.e.* the ability of the customer to switch to alternatives in response to a significant price increase or a shortage of supplies. Not only is this approach consistent with established practice but it is reinforced by the terms of the Regulation itself. Among the factors identified in Article 2(1)(b) are "the alternatives available to suppliers and users". Form CO also invites parties to provide information on relevant product markets on the presumption that the relevant market is the narrowest which can be identified, *i.e.* that used by an undertaking for its own marketing purposes.[35] This ensures that all credible product markets are identified to see whether the notified concentration will create or enhance unacceptable levels of market power. One product will be regarded as in the same product market as another if there is sufficient substitutability between the two to guarantee effective competition.[36] Often, however, particularly in Article 6(1)(b) decisions, the Commission's determination of the relevant product market is based largely, if not exclusively, on an examination of the physical characteristics and functionality of the products concerned. These two criteria, indicating suitability for a customer's purposes, tend in practice to merge into one critical question: whether a product's characteristics render it capable of fulfilling the needs of potential buyers. Physical characteristics may include speed of operation, level of performance, diversity of application, and any other factors which buyers would regard as important parameters of the functionality they seek.

---

[34] The Commission emphasises that such a hierarchy cannot be applied rigidly—see para. 25 of the Notice.

[35] Note, in particular, the final sentence of Section 5 of the Form CO entitled "Product Markets". Note, however, the recognition in para. 3 of the Market Definition Notice that the concept of "relevant market" in competition terms may be different from its use in other contexts, such as in marketing.

[36] See the 1991 Competition Policy Report, para. 110.

The fact, however, that products are capable of performing the same functions does not necessarily mean that they form part of the same product market. A test based on pure functionality would often produce the wrong result. The question is not simply whether, if one product were not available, alternatives would be found which could serve the same purpose. Those alternatives might not be equally suitable for all groups of customers and might well not be such close substitutes as to exercise a real constraint on market power. They would not provide *effective* competition. The Commission requires closer substitutability. For example, in *Nestlé/Perrier*, the Commission, not surprisingly, rejected a product market definition based on simple functionality—the quenching of a consumer's thirst—commenting "a limited substitutability in terms of functionality alone is not sufficient to establish substitutability in competition terms".[37] The empirical evidence showed also that companies supplying bottled source water were able to act largely independently, particularly as to price, of companies selling soft drinks, and that the consumer attraction of bottled water was its apparent purity and freedom from artificial additives—not a characteristic always associated with soft drinks! Moreover, as already mentioned, the Market Definition Notice now places the emphases not on practical functionality as the key to substitutability but on the reaction of customers to an assumed small but significant (in the five to 10 per cent range) non-transitory price increase in the product concerned.

Usually, however, data on prices and sales volumes is simply not available in sufficient detail or over a sufficient period to provide empirical support for the SNIP analysis. The lack of adequate data perhaps explains why, notwithstanding the emphasis on the SNIP test in the Market Definition Notice, such analysis rarely figures significantly in the Commission's approach to market definition even in Article 8 cases. Instead, the Merger Task Force commonly surveys customers to gauge their reaction to a hypothetical price increase in the product concerned. The statements of customers in such circumstances must, however, be treated with caution. Such surveys are unscientific and no substitute for proper price correlation analysis. The hypothetical monopolist or SNIP test sets the correct framework for product market definition but it cannot confer scientific legitimacy on the results of such surveys. It is suggested that a careful examination of a product's uses, functionality and physical characteristics is more reliable than customer surveys which are not able to be supported by empirical evidence of customers' behaviour when faced with price changes or supply shortages.

Understandably, it is in the Article 8 cases where the most difficult issues of product market definition arise. Empirical evidence of consumer behaviour and, in particular, analysis of price data is important. Ultimately it is the relationship between the price of two products, or an increase in demand for one product where the other increases in price, that provides best evidence of substitutability. When using price data and making price comparisons in product market definition the Commission will often seek to judge whether switching from one product to another would occur if the merged entity was to introduce a small but significant price increase in the five to 10 per cent range. Indeed, in stage two investigations the Commission will often survey cus-

---

[37] At para. 9 of the Art. 8 decision: [1992] O.J. L356/1.

tomers on this question, as it did in *Crown Cork & Seal/Carnaud Metalbox*. Customer reaction may, however, be able to be predicted more scientifically through price correlation and econometric analysis. If two products are genuinely substitutable and in the same market, movement in the price of one will lead to a corresponding shift in the price of the other. This analysis is, however, dependent on the availability of price information and, crucially, the ability to filter out extraneous factors. The latter may have a common effect on the price behaviour of two products and make it appear at first sight as if their price evolution is related when in fact prices are influenced by some external factor, such as increases in the level of duty on alcoholic spirits. Econometric analysis, which can factor volume-related data into the equation, can be more telling in its message, but not always to the notifying parties' advantage. A good illustration of the use of price data by the Commission occurred in *Proctor & Gamble/VP Schickedanz*. In its conditional clearance of Proctor & Gamble's acquisition of the German firm, VP Schickedanz, the Commission used consumer survey results and market and price data to show that, contrary to the arguments of the notifying party, sanitary towels and tampons were separate product markets. Although the products performed the same function they did not share the same characteristics and significant price changes in the one product relative to the other were not sufficient to induce most consumers to switch. In *DuPont/ICI* the Commission confirmed the critical relevance of price comparisons in determining the ambit of the product market: "For two products to be regarded as substitutable, the direct customer must consider it a realistic and rational possibility to react to, for example, a significant increase in the price of one product by switching to the other in a relatively short period of time." [38] It has not, however, always espoused price data so enthusiastically. [39] It may well not give conclusive results and the Commission will always consider a wide range of factors in addition to price analysis. As already noted, the Commission does not focus as strongly on the SNIP test or price analysis generally, as one might have expected from reading the Market Definition Notice.

In some circumstances the structure of supply and demand may lead to the identification of separate product markets where an approach based on physical characteristics and functionality, and even price, may have suggested the opposite. A good illustration is *Varta/Bosch* where the Commission concluded that separate product markets existed for the supply of car batteries to vehicle manufacturers in the original equipment market and the supply of batteries to the replacement market. [40] The Commission justified its conclusion by stating:

"In general terms the distinction between the two product markets (*viz* the

---

[38] At para. 23 of the Art. 8 decision: [1993] O.J. L7/13. See also *Crown Cork/Carnaud Metalbox*.

[39] In 1993 Competition Policy Report, point 277, the Commission commented: "Price factors are also considered in some decisions. An attempt to investigate price elasticities was made in *Costa Crociere/Chargeurs/Accor* where a widespread enquiry among customers, tour operators and travel agencies revealed that a 10 per cent increase in the price of cruises would depress demand from about half of consumers, but would not affect the other half."

[40] See also the Art. 8 decision in *Accor/Wagons-Lits*, where motorway restaurant services were considered a distinct service market because of the different conditions under which motorway restaurants are regulated and operated, and the distinction drawn between new tyres and retreads in the Art. 86 decision in *Michelin*.

original equipment and the replacement markets) is not mainly based on the difference in the product itself or on the function of the product. It resides mainly in the fact that conditions of competition differ significantly on the two markets as a consequence of which the producers have to adapt their commercial and entrepreneurial policies to the different requirements of the two sales markets.''

In most cases, however, particularly at stage one, a comparison of physical characteristics and functionality is sufficient to achieve a workable product market definition. More sophisticated evidence and complex economic analysis, even if available, may not be capable of being used effectively within the timetable constraints imposed on the Commission. Nonetheless it is always advisable to attempt to survey empirical and other data thoroughly before presenting product market arguments to the Commission but changes in approach during an investigation can often damage credibility irretrievably.[41]

The phrase ''supply-side substitutability'', as opposed to demand-side substitutability, describes the ability of undertakings to switch production or other resources to enter a market in which they have previously not been active.[42] If they can do so relatively quickly and easily—without appreciable investment—their potential entry will exercise a significant and effective constraint on the ability of a company which is apparently dominant in that market to increase prices. But the Commission is reluctant to entertain arguments based on supply-side considerations at the stage of product market definition. In its 1993 Competition Policy Report it said:

"Supply-side substitutability is normally considered by the Commission under its assessment of possible dominance (that is, as potential competition). However, it is sometimes mentioned under product market definition, but it is not generally a sufficient condition for extending the definition of the relevant market.''[43]

The Market Definition Notice confirms that stance. Even so, parties should not be discouraged from making rational arguments based on supply-side substitutability and demonstrating that any market power apparently gained as a result of the notified concentration is constrained by the ability of other undertakings to switch resources towards the products manufactured by the merged undertakings. Cogent evidence of such potential competition is accepted by the Commission as relevant in determining whether a concentration gives an undertaking the ability to act independently of its competitors. Equally, the

---

[41] It is also wise to survey general market studies and the parties' own internal marketing strategies and surveys to see whether they are consistent with the way the notified concentration is presented to the Merger Task Force.

[42] There is considerable debate among economists as to where supply-side substitutability begins and ends. At one extreme a manufacturer of white paint could readily switch to produce blue paint if demand rose for the colour blue. At the other, the changes which a potential competitor might need to make to adapt production plant to manufacture a newly-developed product might be so costly or technically so difficult as to give it no advantage over a ''greenfield'' entrant. In such a case the analysis focuses rightly, it is suggested, on entry barriers rather than supply-side substitutability.

[43] At para. 276.

absence of such material may reinforce a narrow product market definition and a finding of dominance.

5.3.3 Geographic Market Definition

In the context of ascertaining the relevant geographic market for Article 82 purposes the Court of Justice has said: "this is an area where the objective conditions of competition applying to the product in question must be the same for all traders".[44] Article 9 of the Regulation (providing for referral of cases back to Member States) echoes this approach and provides a workable definition of the geographical market for the purposes of the Regulation:

> "the area in which the undertakings concerned are involved in the supply and demand of products or services, in which the conditions of competition are sufficiently homogenous and which can be distinguished from neighbouring areas because, in particular, conditions of competition are appreciably different in those areas."

In order to determine whether conditions of competition are sufficiently homogenous, so that different areas can be treated as constituting a single geographic market, the Commission commonly refers to a number of basic factors including the identity and market shares of suppliers, the nature of their relationships with customers, the channels of distribution to end users and market characteristics such as demand trends and prices.

While, for the reasons already explained, the Commission's predisposition to adopt the narrowest justifiable market definition also holds good for geographic market analysis, much will depend on the nature of the goods and services under consideration and the conditions under which they are supplied. For some products markets are, if not worldwide, self-evidently E.C.-wide. Market dynamics are also important: the benefits of the single market programme, the E.C. public procurement regime and Monetary Union are already beginning to change the character of traditionally national markets, in some sectors significantly and rapidly. Manufacturing processes and new technology are increasing the minimum efficient scale of operation of plants which may no longer be confined to supplying the local vicinity or the territory of just one Member State. Emerging capitalist economies in Eastern Europe are naturally directing their products to adjacent readily accessible markets in wealthier Western Europe. Such considerations are all reflected in the Commission's approach to geographic market analysis.

Depending upon the product or service concerned a wide range of factors may be relevant in determining the geographic market. The basic test, to which reference is most often made, particularly in stage two cases, is a comparison of prices across different national and geographic boundaries. Often, however, particularly at stage one, such price information is simply not available, or not in a sufficiently reliable form to enable a useful comparison to be made. The Commission therefore typically pays as much attention to other, non-price,

---

[44] Case 27/76 *United Brands Co. v. Commission* [1978] E.C.R. 207; [1978] 1 C.M.L.R. 429, para. 44.

considerations such as actual trade flows, barriers to trade, and transport costs (relative to the value or selling price of the product concerned).[45] The Commission's conclusion on the geographic market is invariably based on a combination of factors. The more important of these appear to be: comparative prices; trade patterns, and the extent of interpenetration between different Member States; a comparison of the active manufacturers, suppliers and customers and the distribution of their market shares; transport costs; consumer preferences and national demand characteristics; entry barriers; the nature of the products and services concerned; and, insofar as they are not already covered by the above specific factors, comparative supply and demand conditions. Differences and imminent changes in the regulatory or technical environment are also relevant.

In contrast with product market definition, it will be seen also that both demand and supply-side considerations are taken into account by the Commission in determining the relevant geographic market. Nevertheless, the Commission exercises considerable discretion in deciding the factors which are influential in any particular case, and rarely highlights any single characteristic as determining the relevant geographic market. It is therefore unsafe to assume that because, for example, a particular level of trade was taken to indicate a Community-wide market in one case, a similar level of established trade could lead to the same conclusion in another. With this caution against considering particular factors in isolation, for the purposes of explaining the Commission's approach as demonstrated by decided cases, a number of the most important factors are considered individually below.

Clear trends in the geographic market definition are now established in a number of sectors. In retailing, for example, the Commission tends to regard markets as regional or even local.[46] In *Tesco/Catteau*, it noted that "supermarkets draw customers from a local catchment area". While in *Kingfisher/Darty*, where the United Kingdom retailing group, Kingfisher, acquired the French electrical retailer, Darty, the Commission concluded that, since Kingfisher operated only in the United Kingdom and Darty only in France, there could be no question of the creation or enhancement of a dominant position in the same market. In the food, retailing and distribution sectors generally the tendency is to define markets as national or regional.[47] This may be reinforced further by national branding, consumer tastes and the need to have distribution networks capable of offering a just-in-time service.[48] As a consequence, of course, there is little consideration of potential cross-border competition and assessments may rest upon historic market conditions and traditional national boundaries.[49]

[45] *BHF/CCF/Charterhouse*, BHF/CCF II.
[46] See also the insurance cases listed, n. 29, above.
[47] For other "national market" cases in retailing, see *Ahold/Jeronimo Inovacao*; *BAI/Banca Popolare di Lecco*; *CAMPSA*; *SPAR/Dansk Supermarked*; *Promodes/BRMC*; *Deutsche Bank/Banco de Madrid*; *Delhaize/PG*; *ING/Barings*.
[48] *e.g. Toyota Motor Corp./Walter Frey/Toyota France* (vehicles); *Rhône-Poulenc/Cooper* (pharmaceuticals); *GEHE/OCP* (pharmaceuticals); *VIAG/Bayernwerk* (gas and electricity); *EDF/Edison-ISE* (electricity).
[49] The predisposition to assume that markets are national is, however, weakening, and for some products and services does not exist at all.

5.3.3.1   Trade Patterns

A two-way pattern of trade between one region and another at an appreciable level is treated by the Commission as good evidence, though not conclusive, that those regions form part of the same geographic market. In *Mannesmann/ Vallourec/Ilva* the Commission described penetration levels of between 30 and 60 per cent within Western Europe as "high" and strong evidence that the market was at least European wide. But the Commission has rejected the Elzinga-Hogarty test, commonly used by U.S. anti-trust authorities, to determine the geographic market. According to that test where exports or imports exceed 10 per cent of production or consumption respectively within a particular territory, that area is to be considered as belonging to a wider geographic market. The Commission's scepticism about the Elzinga-Hogarty test arose because it fails to measure mutual interpenetration between the territories concerned: the Commission made it clear that two-way trade was as important as the absolute level of imports or exports.

Trade patterns have been particularly influential, as one might expect, in judging whether the Community or Western Europe is part of a wider market including, for example, Eastern Europe, Asia or the U.S. In such cases, other factors, such as tariff barriers (considered below), will also be relevant. Conversely an absence of trade, or limited trade, is often used by the Commission to support a conclusion that separate geographic markets exist. In *Proctor & Gamble/Schickedanz*, where there were no obvious barriers to trade between Member States, such as high transport costs, the Commission emphasised the low level of intra-E.C. trade as a main reason for treating Germany and Spain as separate markets. The Commission will also be concerned to look at historical patterns and the evolution of trade flows. An upsurge in trade, for example, because of short-term currency imbalances will not be taken as an indication of a single geographic market.

Even if low levels of international trade lead the Commission to conclude that separate geographic markets exist it may, nonetheless, find that the potential for imports from markets outside that in which a merged undertaking enjoys high market shares may act as a constraint on its market power. For example, in *Mannesmann/Vallourec/Ilva* the Commission concluded that the relevant market did not include Asia but that, if the merged company raised its prices in Europe significantly, this would almost certainly attract imports from Japanese steel producers which, having established a pattern of trade and commercial relationships with European customers, would be difficult to displace. The threat of entry by Japanese producers, coupled with the commercial consequences for indigenous producers if such entry occurred, was a sufficient deterrent against monopolistic pricing.

5.3.3.2   Prices

Although detailed evidence of prices may frequently not be available or capable of verification, particularly during stage one examinations, the Commission will invariably regard significant price differences between one country and another as a strong indication that they constitute separate markets. For example, in *Mannesmann/Vallourec/Ilva* the Commission regarded price differences of 35 per cent between Japan and Western Europe as conclusive that the two regions were separate markets. It came to the same conclusion in relation to the U.S., where prices were only five per cent higher and there existed a 10 per cent import duty which would not be phased out completely until 2005. Price differences may be explained by short-lived currency fluctuations and similar transitory factors. The Commission will, therefore, be interested in looking at trends in prices and identifying uniformity in the evolution of prices between one country or region and another. If the data is available, the Commission prefers to base its analysis on a comparison of net realised prices. In many consumer markets market survey companies operating throughout the Community can provide volume and point of sale price data which is highly relevant for the purposes of market definition.

Price differences between different countries may be attributable to such a range of complex factors (such as exchange rates) or more simple factors (such as transport costs) that the Commission is understandably cautious about placing too much emphasis on even such a key indicator as price and appears to make less use of price information to determine the geographic market than it does to determine the product market. It has, however, explained its use of price correlation techniques as follows:

"Price correlations measure the extent to which price movements are similar from one geographical region to the other. The correlations are measured in coefficients ranging from zero, which indicates absence of correlation, to one, which indicates perfectly correlated price movements. If prices in different markets move independently from each other, one can reasonably conclude that the markets are separate and that the suppliers are able to discriminate with regard to prices. Consequently, a weak price correlation coefficient would tend to indicate separate geographic markets. However, the opposite is not necessarily true. A certain degree of price correlation cannot indicate the existence of a homogenous geographic market in the absence of other factors such as mutual interpenetration or similar structures of supply and demand in the different regions."[50]

Price correlation data has been provided by notifying parties in a number of cases but appears not to have been a decisive influence on the Commission's ultimate conclusions on the geographic market.[51]

5.3.3.3 *Location and Identity of Suppliers and Purchasers*

As the Commission has repeatedly stressed, the homogeneity of competitive conditions within a number of Member States or regions may indicate that they constitute a single geographic market. Such homogeneity may involve a number of different characteristics. One to which the Commission pays par-

[50] Twenty Third Competition Policy Report, para. 291.
[51] See in particular *Nestlé/Perrier* and *Proctor & Gamble/Schickedanz*.

ticular attention is the identity of the producers and suppliers who are active on the market, and their market shares in different parts of the E.C. If major producers are represented in most Member States and enjoy broadly equivalent market shares an E.C.-wide market is indicated. If there are wide disparities in market shares in different Member States, particularly when they are neighbouring countries, or, *a fortiori*, if some undertakings are active only in some Member States and not others, that may indicate separate markets. For example, in *Magneti Marelli/CEAc*, one of the two factors to which the Commission drew attention in concluding that the relevant geographic market was France was the disparity in market shares of the competing manufacturers: CEAc had 42 per cent of the French market but only five per cent in Germany. This factor, coupled with differences in prices, also led the Commission to identify Germany and Spain as distinct national markets for car batteries in *Varta/Bosch*.

The location of main manufacturing plants may also demonstrate that the relevant market is the E.C. For example, in *DuPont/ICI*, nylon carpet fibre producers and carpet manufacturers operated throughout the E.C. from their main centres in northern Europe and northern Italy. A survey of supplier/purchaser relationships showed that fibre producers sold to all the main carpet companies irrespective of whether the latter were located nearer to one particular centre of production than another. Likewise, in *Pilkington-Techint/SIV*, the evidence showed that prices for float glass throughout the main areas of demand in the E.C. all fell within a narrow band and moved up and down relative to one another.

5.3.3.4 Supply Conditions

Where a product or service is produced or made available from a particular region in Europe to consumers throughout the Community, supply conditions point to an E.C.-wide market. Where supply is regional or local in character, the reverse is true. In a number of cases the Commission has decided in favour of a national or local market on the basis that distribution channels are organised along Member State lines, or deliveries take place over regional or local areas. The same is true where ''just in time'' servicing and the supply of spare parts are required, for example, to guarantee continuous production. In *KNP/Bührmann-Tetterode/VRG* the Commission found that these characteristics existed for the maintenance and repair of printing machines and that markets were national, if not narrower. In the banking and insurance sectors, the Commission has tended to adopt the same approach, notwithstanding a number of Directives in the insurance field which are breaking down traditional national markets. The Commission has emphasised in *Fortis/CGER* that the retailing methods for financial services in France differ from those in some other Member States. Differences in channels and methods of distribution between one Member State and another may also be reinforced by customer familiarity with long-established names.

5.3.3.5   Customer Preferences

National consumer preferences and attitudes also figure strongly in the Commission's geographic market analysis, understandably, given the emphasis on
demand-side factors. In food and drinks markets, national tastes, often reinforced by national brands, militate in favour of national markets. But the
reverse may be true in cases involving international brands, such as Campari
or Pepsi.[52] In *Kali und Salz* the Commission noted the preference of German
farmers for potash fertilisers containing magnesium—a preference not shared
by other farmers in the E.C.—and concluded that two separate markets existed,
Germany and the Community excluding Germany. The Commission did not,
however, examine whether it would have been possible for potash producers
outside Germany to add magnesium to satisfy national tastes in Germany and
its conclusion was, unsurprisingly, subject to criticism before the Court of
Justice. Language and cultural factors are also important, particular in the
media, in some consumer sectors and in investment and financial services
where consumers have tended to remain loyal to established national names.

5.3.3.6   Transport Costs

In certain markets, such as the constructions material sector, transport factors
will have an important influence in delineating the relevant geographic market.
Usually this is because transport costs are high relative to unit value and it
soon becomes uneconomic and uncompetitive to transport products to distant
customers. Such factors have played an important part in several of the cases
referred back to Member States. In *Steetley/Tarmac*, which concerned bricks
and clay rooftiles, the Commission concluded that the affected markets in
bricks were predominantly regional within Great Britain. However, in the case
of clay rooftiles, where the transport costs were similar, the geographic market
included the whole of Great Britain. The best quality clay for making frost-
resistant rooftiles, Etruria marl clay, was found only in the West Midlands and
production plants adjacent to clay quarries supplied customers throughout the
country.[53] In other cases, factors such as the difficulty in handling a product
(float glass), a propensity to deteriorate or become unusable (keg beer, ready-
mixed concrete) or environmental factors (chemical waste) may militate in
favour of local or regional markets. For example, in *Pilkington-Techint/SIV*
the Commission paid particular attention to transport costs, noting that

> "the natural geographical area of supply from a given float-glass production
> plant can be represented by concentric circles with a length of radius deter-
> mined by the relative transport cost. Based on the information given by the
> parties 80 to 90 per cent of a plant's production is sold within a radius of
> 500 kilometres."[54]

---

[52] See *Grand Metropolitan/Cinzano* and *Pepsico/Kas*.
[53] One of the affected markets in *Holdercim/Cedest* was ready-mixed concrete, perhaps the perfect example
of a product capable of delivery only within a local radius of the place of production.
[54] Para. 46 of the Art. 8 decision: [1994] O.J. L158/24.

However, because natural supply areas overlapped significantly and there was evidence that prices moved within the same narrow band throughout the Community the Commission rejected a transport-cost based market definition.

There are no hard and fast rules for determining at what point transport costs relative to selling price become an influential factor. It is necessary to consider them in combination with other factors such as import duties. However, where the transport costs are less than five per cent of the value to the end consumer they are unlikely to play an influential part in determining the relevant geographic market. In *Mannesmann/Hoesch* the Commission did not regard even 10 per cent as decisive for most customers. But in *Nestlé/Perrier*, where there was strong evidence of differing national customer preferences, the Commission referred to transport costs estimated at 10 per cent of the final selling price over a delivery distance of 300 kilometres, rising to 20 per cent where glass bottles were used, to be a factor in its determination that the relevant market was France. Even high transport costs will have little impact on the Commission's analysis if all producers are located in the same part of the E.C. and therefore, broadly speaking, are equally affected by transport costs in competing for customers.[55]

5.3.3.7 *Public Procurement*

National buying habits and preferences have been referred to in a number of cases. Since the introduction of E.C. merger control a panoply of rules to open up public procurement has been adopted in the single market programme, including in the utilities sector. This is beginning to affect the Commission's approach in merger cases and the procurement rules have been identified as an important factor in several. In *Alcatel/AEG Kabel*, the Commission seemed reluctant to place too much emphasis on national buying preferences where the purchaser was a national monopoly or oligopoly capable of self-help simply by modifying its procurement policies in line with the objectives of the E.C. public procurement regime. There may have been a policy reason also underlying this approach, the Commission wishing to encourage nationalistic utilities to anticipate their obligations to operate Community-wide procurement. In *Mannesmann/Hoesch* the Commission took account of the procurement rules not so much to conclude in favour of a Community-wide market but rather to find that any apparent position of dominance gained by the new company would not endure, and therefore not capable of impeding effective competition to a significant degree.

5.3.3.8 *Other Regulatory Factors*

Regulatory factors may be internal to a particular Member State, for example, concerning the way a particular product must be manufactured or a service marketed to customers, or they may relate to external factors, such as trade barriers. The latter are now of little relevance within the EEA but are still influential in

---

[55] As in the supply of nylon carpet fibres in *DuPont/ICI*.

the Commission's determination of whether the geographic market is confined to the Community or EEA or extends further to include Eastern Europe, the USA or Asia and the Pacific. With investment taking place in the economies of the former Communist countries, the ability of producers in Eastern Europe to gain access for their products to neighbouring parts of Europe has also played a significant role in a number of decisions. For example, in *Shell/Montecatini,* the EEA was shielded by import duties of 12.5 per cent from outside producers and the fact that those duties would reduce to 6.5 per cent over a five year period did not justify treating the geographic market as wider than Western Europe. Similarly, in *DuPont/ICI* the Commission noted that producers of nylon carpet fibres from outside the E.C. faced a nine per cent import duty. On the other hand, in *Mannesmann/Vallourec/Ilva* the Commission seemed to suggest that the fact that a 10 per cent import duty for producers outside the EEA would be eliminated only over a 10 year period was not a significant factor in defining the relevant market. In most of these cases, however, the tariff barriers have been reinforced by price differences, different competitors and negligible trade flows, all of which indicate that the relevant geographic market is no wider than the EEA or Western Europe.

The position is more complicated when dealing with "internal" regulatory barriers. Many such barriers are now being broken down by the Commission's single market programme. Others remain and in a number of cases the Commission has drawn attention to national regulations as a factor justifying a conclusion that the relevant geographic market is still the Member State. Waste treatment services, apparently a growth sector for cross-border activities, provides an interesting illustration. In *Rhône-Poulenc/SITA* the Commission took into account E.C. Directive 91/156, which introduced the "proximity principle", *i.e.* that waste should be treated as near as possible to the location of the process creating the waste, to justify a preference for national or even regional markets. This conclusion was reinforced, in the Commission's view, by the fact that waste disposal sites tend to be regulated locally, and liability to third parties governed by national law. In *Waste Management/SAE*, however, the Commission distinguished the treatment of solid industrial waste from that of hazardous industrial waste. The latter service, the Commission intimated, was a Community-wide market in view of the cost, sophisticated technology and know-how required for waste treatment facilities. The Commission may place too much emphasis on matters of national regulation where the rules do not in themselves create conditions which are significantly different from one Member State to another. However, this could not be said of its Article 8 decision in *Orkla/Volvo*. There the partitioning effect of the state retail monopoly in beer, discriminatory alcohol taxes and a national scheme for recycling glass bottles all conspired to make Norway a separate market and the merged undertaking's position on it impregnable.

The pharmaceutical sector is another in which national regulations and purchasing policies mean that markets remain national, notwithstanding the fact, on the supply-side, that there has been major consolidation to create a limited number of worldwide pharmaceutical companies. For example, in 1996, in its Article 8 decision on the merger of Ciba-Geigy and Sandoz to form Novartis, the Commission reiterated its view that markets for pharmaceutical products remained national despite efforts at European standardisation.[56] The Commission pointed out that[57]:

> "At present, medicines can be registered in different Member States for different indications. The sale of medicines is influenced by the administrative procedures or purchasing policies which the national health authorities have introduced in the Member States. Some countries exercise a direct or indirect influence on prices, and there are different levels of reimbursement by the social security system for different categories of medicines."

The Commission reinforced this conclusion by reference to "far-reaching differences" in brand and pack-size strategies and in distribution systems for pharmaceutical products in the different Member States.

5.3.3.9 World Markets

In relation to products or services of high capital cost or technical sophistication the Commission shows itself ready to conclude that the geographic market is worldwide, particularly where there are a small number of suppliers. For example, in *Shell/Montecatini* the Commission concluded that the market for the licensing of the technology to manufacture polypropylene was worldwide: there were three rival technologies which would always be in competition for any new chemical production plant wherever located. Interestingly, however, in *Aérospatiale-Alenia/de Havilland* the market (regional turbo-prop aircraft) was treated as excluding China and Eastern Europe. There was little market interpenetration between those two areas and the rest of the world, western-built aircraft being too expensive for airline purchasers in China or Eastern Europe, and domestically manufactured aircraft in those two regions falling short of international safety and technical requirements and therefore being unsaleable in the rest of the world. However, in its Article 8 decision in July 1997 into the acquisition of McDonnell Douglas by Boeing, the Commission pointed to demand for commercial aircraft from China and the Eastern Bloc as a significant factor in recent market growth. Overall, however, there are relatively few cases where the Commission has ultimately decided in favour of a worldwide market.[58]

5.4 THE APPRAISAL DECISION

The remainder of this chapter is concerned first with the substantive application of the compatibility test by the Commission and, secondly, with the lim-

---

[56] See also the following merger decisions: *Sanofi/Sterling Drug* (1991); *Procordia/Erbamont* (1993); *La Roche/Syntex* (1993); *Rhône-Poulenc/Cooper* (1994); *AHP/Cyanamid* (1994); *Glaxo/Wellcome* (1995); *Behringwerke AG/Armour* (1995); *Hoechst/Marion Merrell Dow* (1995) and *Upjohn/Pharmacia* (1995).

[57] Paras 48 and 49 of the Art. 8 decision—[1997] O.J. L201/1.

[58] See *Mondi/Frantschach* (pulp); *Sextant/BGT-VDO* (aircraft instrumentation); *Ericsson/Hewlett-Packard* (support systems for telecoms networks); *DASA/Fokker* (aircraft); *Philips/Hoechst* (rewritable plastic magnetic optical storage media); *Metallgesellschaft/SAFIC Alcan* (rubber); *CEA Industrie/France Telecom/Finmeccanica/SGS-Thomson* (semi-conductors); *Gencor/Shell, Anglo American/Lonrho* and *Gencor/Lonrho* (metals and minerals); *Matra Marconi Space/British Aerospace* (space systems); and *Cable & Wireless/Schlumberger* (advanced telecoms services for international groups).

ited scope within the appraisal process to take account of balancing factors relating, for example, to the achievement through the notified operation of efficiency and cost-saving or of industrial and economic development within the European Union. A complete picture of the approach taken and principles applied would not be conveyed by considering only Article 8 decisions.[59]

Although the Commission is, not unnaturally, reluctant to commit itself to definitive conclusions in Article 6(1)(b) decisions where they are not strictly necessary, nonetheless these decisions remain highly relevant to the Commission's overall approach to the question of dominance.

5.4.1   General Background to the Appraisal Decision

As explained in Chapter 3, the obligation to notify a concentration to the Commission depends entirely on whether the turnover criteria are met. At this jurisdictional stage the impact of the concentration on competition is irrelevant. Indeed the majority of notifications raise no competition issues of any significance. This does not excuse notification. But it may enable the notifying parties to adopt a short form notification or to avoid the need to respond to those sections of Form CO which are required only where there are "affected markets".[60]

The Commission has considered but rejected the suggestion that *de minimis* transactions should be excluded from the scope of the Regulation, largely on the ground that it would be difficult to define satisfactorily those which have no significant effects on the structure of competition in the Community without losing jurisdictional certainty. It therefore felt that, with the availability of a short-form notification under Form CO and the possibility of further waivers on a case-by-case basis from the notification burden, little more could be offered other than to take short-form decisions before the end of the four week deadline applicable in first-stage examinations. There is nothing to prevent the Commission doing so and, where it is possible, it would surely be welcomed by companies and their advisers.

At the lowest scale of concern come those cases where the parties to the concentration have little or no turnover at all in the European Union or any E.U. turnover which they do have is attributable to businesses unconnected with the notified operation. Next come those cases where there is no horizontal overlap or vertical relationship between the notifying parties in markets in the European Union. Some types of transaction are by their very nature likely to come into this category. Financing or investment-motivated transactions are examples. In *Kelt/American Express* the shareholder rights conferred by a conversion of debt to equity on the members of the financing syndicate led to the lending banks being considered joint controllers of the company being rescued. Each bank thus became an undertaking concerned whose turnover had to be taken into account, thereby giving the transaction a Community dimension, but raising no competition issues. Institutional backing for management buy-outs may have similar consequences. *CWB/Goldman Sachs/Tarkett* involved a

---

[59] See para. 7.4.5, below, discussing the *Air France/Sabena* decision.
[60] See para. 4.3.5, above, for an explanation of the term "affected market".

management buy-out of the floor coverings and industrial foil businesses of the Swedish group, Stora. The case was readily cleared once the Commission had established that the backers did not have investments which gave them influence in any competing businesses. Even in these sort of cases the Merger Task Force is obliged by the Regulation to examine the compatibility of the transaction with the Common Market and to issue a formal decision.

Another commonly-occurring category of concentration which is invariably benign from a competition standpoint is where the notified transaction involves no "affected markets" as defined in Form CO. As confirmed by the Commission in *Jefferson Smurfit Group/Munksjo*, where there are no markets affected by a notified concentration, there can be no question of the creation or strengthening of a dominant position.

5.4.2 The General Nature of the Appraisal

In practice nearly all notifications requiring more than a cursory examination involve horizontal overlaps between actual or potential competitors at the same market level. Few cases have involved serious consideration of the vertical aspects of the transaction notified, although in recent years the Commission appears to take a more systematic approach to identifying and analysing such aspects than it did in the early years of the Regulation, as its experience and methodology has developed. Issues of conglomeracy have also received very little attention. Nonetheless we consider in more detail below the relevance of financial resources and the size and scope of an undertaking's business to the assessment of compatibility.[61]

As explained in Chapter 2, since March 1998 full function joint ventures which, prior to that date, failed the negative condition in Article 3(2) (first paragraph) and were assessed under Article 81 entirely outside the Regulation now qualify as concentrations. The assessment of their effects on the behaviour of undertakings which remain independent now takes place as part of the appraisal under the Regulation but in accordance with Article 81. Such cases are uncommon. Only one, *BT/AT&T*, (decision not yet published) has gone to a stage two investigation. For that reason, and because a detailed examination of the application of Article 81 is outside the scope of this book, this subordinate aspect of the compatibility appraisal is considered only briefly in section 5.5, below.

5.4.3 Judging Dominance

The following paragraphs consider the more significant factors which have influenced the Commission's judgment as to whether a particular transaction does in fact create or strengthen a dominant position capable of damaging effective competition. Not surprisingly certain factors recur in the Commis-

---

[61] Para. 5.4.3.8, below.

sion's analysis. They include a comparison of the merged undertaking with its actual and potential competitors (expressed in market share figures, and by reference to such attributes as financial resources and market reputation), market entry conditions, buyer power and the dynamics in general of the market in which high market shares exist. In addition, if the high market share exists in an already concentrated industry, the Commission may seek to analyse past behaviour, assessing the vigorousness of competition and auditing links through joint ventures and trade associations which may exist between the main players. This kind of analysis is particularly relevant if collective dominance is alleged.[62]

The approach which has emerged does not always correspond precisely with the considerations which are set out in Article 2(1) of the Regulation. When the Regulation was adopted there were concerns that the Commission had little experience of merger analysis. Member States wished to point the new Merger Task Force in the right direction by reminding it of factors which had already been well established as relevant in cases under Articles 81 and 82 cases, or appeared from Member States' own experience of domestic merger control to be key indicators of potential dominance. This resulted in Article 2(1)(a) and (b) presenting a list of factors considered relevant to the appraisal of compatibility. It is a melange of objectives and relevant considerations: the maintenance and development of effective competition within the Common Market in view of the structure of all the markets concerned, and the actual or potential from undertakings located inside and outside the E.C.; the market position of the undertakings concerned, and their economic and financial power; alternative sources for suppliers and users; access to supplies or markets; entry barriers (legal or otherwise); supply and demand trends; the interests of intermediate and ultimate consumers; and the development of technical and economic progress, provided it is to the consumer's advantage and creates no obstacle to competition.

While the Commission is certainly obliged to take into account the listed considerations, they do not constitute an exhaustive list. Nor is there any ranking of the factors listed. Rather, Article 2(1)(a) singles out certain basic principles which flow from the compatibility test itself, while Article 2(1)(b) lists the main factors relevant to the question of dominance. The Commission is free not only to take into account all factors it considers relevant in its examination of compatibility in each particular case, but also to judge where the balance and emphasis should lie in any particular case and an examination of its casework shows this discretion at work. Article 2 is therefore in no sense definitive and the Commission has felt little need to refer explicitly to it in its decisions.

5.4.3.1   *Single Firm or Collective Dominance*

In most cases where the Commission has had doubts about the compatibility of a notified transaction with the Common Market, it is because of the risk that a single firm would emerge as dominant or strengthen an existing domin-

---

[62] See para. 5.4.3.1, below, and section 5.7.

ant position. In assessing the risk of single firm dominance, the factors to be considered are somewhat different from when the possibility of collective dominance is being examined. The Commission's approach in cases of single firm dominance is now relatively well-developed after nearly a decade of experience, but the analysis in cases of possible collective dominance is still in its infancy. Only in 1998 did the Court of Justice confirm, in its judgment in *Kali und Salz*, that the Regulation applied to cases of collective or oligopolistic dominance. Subsequently, in *Gencor v. Commission*,[63] the Court of First Instance also acknowledged that the relationships necessary between oligopolists to establish collective dominance were not limited to the kind of formal structural links considered in *Italian Flat Glass*.[64] They also included the economic interdependence commonly referred to somewhat confusingly (at least to lawyers) as tacit collusion. This reflects economic thinking on which the concept of oligopoly or collective dominance is founded. In view of this the special issues arising in cases of suspected collective dominance are considered separately from the general consideration of single firm dominance.

5.4.3.2 Horizontal and Vertical Impact

The adoption of a "dominance" criterion for the assessment of compatibility with the Common Market inevitably puts the emphasis on the horizontal impact of a concentration as evidenced in particular by the accretions in market share which result from it. This is reflected too in the definition of "affected markets" for notification purposes. A market is "affected" by a concentration where the horizontal overlap between the parties is 15 per cent or above, but in the case of vertical relationships between the parties, a market is considered to be affected only where at least one party has a 25 per cent market share. Serious vertical issues have not commonly arisen. But the Commission now appears to pay more systematic attention to the vertical impact of a notified concentration than it did in the early days of the Regulation. Indeed there are several, more recent, Article 8 cases where vertical issues have led to prohibition decisions or the imposition of conditions. These are discussed in more detail in section 5.6 below.

5.4.3.3 "Significantly Impeding Effective Competition"

The relationship between this qualitative element of the test and the requirement that the concentration must create or enhance a dominant position has already been discussed. Perfect competition rarely exists outside economists' models, and this is recognised in setting the Commission's objective as protecting effective competition. The phrase "effective competition" describes the ability of imperfect markets to deliver products efficiently and at reasonable cost. Conversely, it gives the Commission the justification to reject rather theoretical or fanciful propositions advanced by notifying parties to counter

---

[63] Case T-102/96, judgment of March 25, 1999.
[64] *Società Italiano Vetro v. Commission* [1991] II E.C.R. 485.

allegations of dominance. The loss of a competitor through acquisition will make a market less perfect but will not necessarily involve significant detriment to those who supply to or buy in that market. The fact that a significant impediment must also be shown has the effect of raising somewhat the level at which the Commission will intervene to prohibit a concentration, or attach conditions to its implementation. At the same time it may give the Commission a peg on which to hang the remedial measures acceptable as a condition of clearance. Too much forensic weight should not, however, be attached to the requirement. It has been pointed out[65] that a finding of dominance necessarily implies adverse consequences for effective competition. But the test as a whole contributes to giving the Commission the flexibility necessary to marry theory with the way markets operate in practice and acts as a reminder that the notified concentration must have as its consequence a tangible worsening of the competitive structure in the markets affected. In *Kali und Salz* the Court of Justice explained this second limb of the compatibility test as serving to emphasise the need for a causal link between the dominance created or enhanced by a merger and the detriment to competition.

5.4.3.4   Market Shares

Market shares are meaningless unless they flow from a proper definition of the geographic and product market or market concerned. That said, the Commission has recognised that in defining dominance for Article 82 purposes market share figures are a useful starting point for analysis but need to be used with caution. In its tenth competition policy report it commented:

> "A dominant position can generally be said to exist once a market share in the order of 40 to 45 per cent is reached. Although this share does not in itself automatically give control of the market, if there are large gaps between the position of the firm concerned and those of its closest competitors and also other factors likely to place it at an advantage as regards competition, a dominant position may well exist. Strengthening by means of a merger is likely to constitute an abuse if any distortion of the resulting market structure interferes with the maintenance of remaining competition (which has already been weakened by the very existence of this dominant position) or its development. Such an effect depends, in particular, on the change in the relative market strength of the participants after the merger, *i.e.* the position of the new unit in relation to remaining competitors."[66]

In short the key factors are less the market shares of the merging parties than the position of remaining competitors and entry conditions in the market under scrutiny. On these factors depend the real market power of an undertaking with a high market share. The Commission has also suggested that a dominant position cannot be ruled out even if an undertaking has a market share of only between 20 to 40 per cent. However, Recital 15 of the Regulation itself seems

---

[65] Langeheine, *Substantive review under the EEC Merger Regulation* (1990).
[66] Para. 150.

to call into question the possibility of dominance where the company concerned has a market share at the lower end of that range.[67]

Recital 15 leads one to question whether there might be a reverse indication or presumption, that where the market share of the undertakings concerned exceeds 25 per cent then dominance will be assumed. However, the cases dealt with under the Regulation show no evidence of this approach. There is no *a contrario* presumption. The Commission must prove dominance in all cases. Indeed, in *Codan/Hafnia*, the Commission said of the merging undertakings, "the new entity will have 33 per cent market share, which in itself is not indicative of market dominance". Moreover, as the Court of Justice pointed out in *Kali and Salz*, Recital 15 is not reflected in the operative provisions of the Regulation. The Court also rejected any suggestion that the presence of that Recital called into question the application of the Regulation to collective dominance where the individual market shares of the main players may well be in the 20 to 30 range.

Even where the market shares resulting from a concentration are above the once magic 40 per cent (sometimes seen as a practical cut-off point for Article 82), the Commission is careful to point out the limitations of market share figures alone.[68] They are only as reliable as the product and geographic market definition on which they are based. Moreover, in several cases the Commission has emphasised the importance of assessing market shares in the context of a market's characteristics and the nature of the competition on it. Thus in a heterogeneous market showing growth, innovation and rapid technological change, high market shares may provide no indication of market power, particularly if entry barriers are low. For example, in *American Cyanamid/Shell* the Commission was unconcerned by market shares in the 25 to 35 per cent range, partly because Cyanamid's products were based on an ageing and relatively unsophisticated technology compared to those of some of its competitors and partly because "an analysis focusing on market shares alone is not particularly probative in a dynamic and R&D-intensive industry". As this suggests the Commission pays particular attention to market dynamics as indicated by entry and exit. Fluctuations in market share are very important, as is the pace of technological change and product innovation—aspects which are encompassed within the phrase "the structure of all markets concerned" in Article 2(1). Decisions under the Regulation necessarily involve predictions about how markets will develop if a concentration is to be permitted and, for many reasons, the past may be an unreliable guide to the future. This is well illustrated by the Commission's decision clearing the merger of the parties' steel tube businesses in *Mannesmann/Hoesch*. The Commission took into account the imminent introduction of the utilities procurement rules. This meant that in the German market, where in certain product sectors the merged entity would have over half the market, more than 50 per cent of contracts for gasline

---

[67] "Whereas concentrations which, by reason of the limited market share of the undertakings concerned, are not liable to impede effective competition may be presumed to be compatible with the Common Market; whereas, without prejudice to Articles [81] and [82] of the Treaty, an indication to this effect exists, in particular, where the market share of the undertakings concerned does not exceed 25 per cent either in the Common Market or in a substantial part of it."

[68] A number of concentrations giving rise to aggregate market share exceeding 40 per cent of the relevant market have been cleared at stage one. See *Rhône Poulenc/SNIA II*; *Vesuvius/Wulfrath*; and *GE/CIGI*.

pipes would have to be advertised and let competitively. The Commission said:

"Market shares characterise the current market position of an undertaking. High market shares represent an important factor as evidence of a dominant position *provided they not only reflect current conditions but are also a reliable indicator of future conditions*. If no other structural factors are identifiable which are liable in due course to change the existing conditions of competition, market shares have to be viewed as a reliable indicator of future conditions." [emphasis added][69]

In some markets, step changes may occur in competitive conditions. For example, in *Ciba-Geigy/Sandoz*, the Commission drew attention to the impact the introduction of a generic drug could very quickly have on traditionally high market shares when patent rights came to an end. This was reinforced by the ease with which pharmaceutical companies could extend production capacity[70]—another highly relevant consideration in examining the contestability of a market. In fact, the Commission's decision in that case provides a good illustration of the kind of factors which have to be taken into account in assessing whether high market shares really do indicate dominance. In a number of product areas the Commission found "very high market shares" not to be indicative of dominance in the light of significant market share fluctuations, the number and strength of competitors with significant R&D capability, the pace and impact of new product launches and the disciplining effect on price of generic alternatives. Indeed the Commission emphasised the need to make a dynamic assessment of market power by dealing explicitly with what it termed "future markets" in its decision.[71] This approach is particularly necessary in the pharmaceutical sector but it is by no means unique to it.

It is important, however, that predicted future changes in market conditions are reasonably certain to occur and to do so in a relatively short timescale. Moreover, if the Commission is to be persuaded to accept arguments based on the prospect of market change, cogent evidence will need to be submitted. Several cases mention two years as an acceptable period but there is no hard and fast rule as in the U.S. merger guidelines, where new entry has to be possible within such a period before it can be taken into account in assessing the future effect of an acquisition.

The higher the market share aggregate the more scrutiny a concentration will receive, and the more evidence will have to be offered to allay the Commission's concerns. In *Tetra Pak/Alfa Laval*, where markets shares above 90 per cent resulted from the notified operation, the Commission said:

"A market share as high as 90 per cent is, in itself, a very strong indicator of the existence of a dominant position. However, in certain rare circumstances even such a high market share may not necessarily result in dominance. In particular if sufficient active competitors are present on the market,

---

[69] At para. 91 of the Art. 8 decision.
[70] Para 61 of the Art. 8 decision: [1997] O.J. L201/1.
[71] See, *e.g.* paras 42 to 46 headed "(c) Future markets'.

the company with the large market share may be prevented from acting to an appreciable extent independently of the pressures typical of a competitive market.''

This comment, however, needs to be treated with caution: with market shares at such levels, it will be the ease of entry which constrains monopoly pricing and not the presence of inevitably small competitors. Apparent stability of market shares and lack of fluidity may also mask the reality of the competitive forces at work. For example, in *Price Waterhouse/Coopers & Lybrand*,[72] the Commission took into account the extent to which companies over the longer term switched auditors and the techniques they used to achieve competitive prices and quality in relation to auditing services, even though one might have expected these factors to show themselves in greater market share fluctuations.

In some markets, however, market shares are either unavailable or completely unreliable. In *Securicor/Datatrack* no appraisal could be made of the notified joint venture because its purpose was to introduce a vehicle tracking service to the Dutch market where no similar service was available.[73] Moreover, in *ABB/BREL* the Commission recognised that in relation to railway locomotives and rolling stock, market shares fluctuated wildly year to year because a few high value contracts were let in any one year among a small number of manufacturers. The Commission cleared the operation commenting: ''Of greater consequence than simple market shares, however, is the degree of competition likely to exist for future contracts, and there could not appear to be cause for concern given the competitive capability of the large European manufacturers such as AEG, Siemens, GEC Alsthom and others''.[74]

The extent to which market shares increase as a result of a concentration is also important. In *Pepsico/KAS* the Commission dismissed the possibility that a one per cent increase in Pepsico's existing 68 per cent in the Spanish market could possibly lead to the creation or enhancement of dominance. This approach was confirmed as a general principle in *Proctor & Gamble/Schikedanz*.[75] In other cases, however, where market shares have increased only by several percentage points, the Commission has expressed concern that because of the wide disparity in market shares between the merged undertaking and other competitors, the level of aggregation was significant and could not be ignored, even though it was in single figures. That said, there are many decisions where the Commission has dismissed concerns where the market share added to that already held by the acquiring undertaking is five per cent or below, and this generally remains so even when the acquirer has a high market share. This seems correct in principle, given the formulation of the compatibility test in Article 2 of the Regulation. As the Court of Justice emphasised in *Kali und Salz* there must be a causal link between the concentration and the creation or strengthening of a dominant position. The Commission's readiness to dismiss the risk of strengthened dominance as a result of Kali and Salz acquiring its former East German competitor should, however,

---

[72] Paras 82 to 94 of the Art. 8 clearance decision: [1999] O.J. C56/12.
[73] See also *Ericsson/Hewlett-Packard*.
[74] Para. 18 of the Art. 6(1)(b) decision of May 26, 1992.
[75] At para. 153. See also *Alcan/Inespal/Palco*.

be contrasted with its refusal to do so in relation to Boeing's acquisition of MDC (discussed above).

Different methods may be employed to calculate market shares. Since, from the Commission perspective, market shares are a proxy for market power, it will favour the method of calculation which, in a particular case, gives the best indication of market power or market dominance. For example, in heterogeneous product markets or markets where there is a broad price spectrum the Commission will prefer market share calculations based on value rather than volume since they will indicate, for instance, whether the notifying parties are able to achieve a premium on their sales. *Boeing/McDonnell Douglas*[76] provides an interesting illustration of some of the different approaches. The Commission calculated shares by value to reflect different prices and sizes of the various types of aircraft in the narrow and wide-bodied segments of the market for large commercial jet aircraft: the price of a Boeing 737 was around 40 million U.S. dollars whereas a 747 cost over 150 million U.S. dollars. On this basis the market shares of Boeing and McDonnell Douglas (MDC) in terms of backlog value[77] at the end of 1996 were 64 and 6 per cent respectively. On the alternative basis, however, of fleet in service, MDC had a share of 24 per cent, compared with 14 per cent for Airbus, the only other competitor in the worldwide market for large commercial jet aircraft. The Commission used this alternative to support its conclusion that Boeing's acquisition of MDC did strengthen Boeing's existing position of dominance even though it conceded that MDC was a spent force in the future in the production of civil aircraft.

Market share figures may deliver a very different message in cases which potentially involve collective dominance. In oligopolistic markets it is the symmetry of market shares which causes concern rather than wide disparity between them. It is unsafe in such situations to rely on the rule of thumb thresholds familiar from cases under Article 82 or of single firm dominance. The appraisal process will also differ radically where doubts about compatibility stem from the oligopolistic nature of a market rather than from the pre-eminent position of one particular firm.

5.4.3.5 Competitors

As already indicated, it is rare for serious doubts about compatibility with the Common Market to arise from the aggregate market shares of the merged entity alone: more illuminating is the relative market share. Can the structure of the market still provide effective competition? Invariably the Commission examines whether other companies could exercise a restraint on an apparently dominant firm. A small number of competitors with broadly equivalent positions in the market may be sufficient to maintain effective competition, provided that the Commission does not think that together they form an uncompetitive oligopoly. Where, however, there is considerable disparity between the shares of merging enterprises and competitors, the Commission may regard

---

[76] Art. 8 decision: [1997] O.J. L336/16.
[77] For an explanation of backlog value, see para. 28 of the decision.

the competitors' continuing presence on the market as insufficient to counter-act the dominance of the new enterprise for a variety of reasons.

The Commission's analysis here goes well beyond a simple market share comparison. It will judge the resources and reputation of the competitors. In *Varta/Bosch*, for example, the Commission emphasised the ability of Fiat, which had recently acquired the German battery manufacturer, Sonnenschein, to provide strong competition because of its reputation and resources even though Sonnenschein had only some five to 10 per cent of the German market against an aggregate share of 44 per cent held by the merged entity. Similarly, in *Renault/Volvo*, the Commission regarded Mercedes as able to exercise sufficient competitive restraint on Renault in the French bus market for it not to be concerned about the latter's 54 per cent share as compared with Mercedes' much smaller 18 per cent share. Even more strikingly, in *Boeing/McDonnell Douglas*, the Commission regarded the presence of Airbus, with 30 per cent of the large civil jet aircraft market as an ineffective constraint on Boeing, were it permitted to acquire MDC. A competitor's position may thus be less significant than its market share might suggest because of inferior technology or research and development capability[78] or its rival's success in erecting barriers to its potential to grow and compete.[79] These cases illustrate the margin of discretion involved in making these judgments.

The Commission will look at the propensity of other companies to provide effective competition as well as their ability to do so. In *Nestlé/Perrier*, BSN had traditionally not competed vigorously with Perrier on the French market for source waters even though it had a comparable market share. The Commission also drew attention to the fact that BSN was operating its main brands at full capacity. It was unable to produce more to increase market share even if it wished to.

The emergence of potential competition in a reasonable timescale is also considered by the Commission. Companies may be able to react by increasing output or by refocusing production. The price levels at which under-utilised or moth-balled plant could profitably be put into full production is an important consideration. So too are the profiles of production costs faced by competitors. The real scope, however, for potential competition depends critically upon entry barriers, and in appropriate cases competition from outside the E.C. may be relevant. The market for many sophisticated products, where transport costs are a small fraction of total costs, is worldwide. One would naturally expect that feature to be highly relevant in assessing the dominance of Community undertakings. Indeed Article 2(1)(a) directs the Commission to take competition from outside the Community into account in assessing the effect of a concentration.[80]

---

[78] In *DuPont/ICI*, the two groups were considered pre-eminent as a result, among other things, of their strength in and commitment to research and development.

[79] For example, Boeing's exclusivity deals with several major U.S. airlines which the Commission required it to terminate, and not re-establish for 10 years, as a condition of declaring its acquisition of MDC compatible with the Common Market.

[80] It is noteworthy that Art. 7(3) of the November 1988 draft proposal included "international competition" as a factor to be considered when authorising an anti-competitive concentration. Those who wished to see a place for E.C. industrial policy, and not just competition policy, under the Regulation will no doubt rely on the fact that the objective of maintaining and developing effective competition within the market is to be pursued "in view of, among other things, . . . the actual or potential competition from undertak-

Though the Regulation requires a dynamic appraisal of competitive structures in the Community, the Commission's approach confirms that there must
be some real prospect of competition from suppliers outside the E.C. and an
absence of significant legal or other barriers to their entry to Community markets, if this particular factor is to play a part in the analysis of compatibility.
There are few examples. *Aérospatiale/MBB* concerned the market for helicopters. The Commission concluded that the civil helicopter market (which it
distinguished as a separate product market from military helicopters) was a
world market. It was therefore necessary to consider the competitive pressures
from outside the Community and in particular the strength of U.S. manufacturers, when looking at Community and national markets. A clearance resulted
though combined market shares in the E.C. approached 70 per cent of the total
value of the market.[81]

Usually the Commission's conclusion on the geographic market will itself
determine the relevance of competition from outside the E.C. However, in
Mannesmann/Vallourec/Ilva, having limited the geographic market definition
to Western Europe the Commission accepted that potential imports from the
Far East could exercise a restraint upon the dominance of the merging undertakings.[82] There may be cases where comparative prices, existing import
duties, low trade flows and similar factors could justify confining the geographic market to Western Europe but where monopoly pricing by dominant
E.C. firms would quickly alter that balance and result in a significant level of
imports.

5.4.3.6   Barriers to Entry

High market shares do not necessarily imply dominance or even significant
market power. The assessment of entry conditions will always be a crucial
part of the consideration of whether a firm is dominant, or a group of firms is
collectively dominant. This involves an assessment both of entry barriers and
of the period of time likely to be needed for a potential entrant to overcome
any barriers and establish a viable presence in the market. It is not sufficient
for there to be a mere possibility of entry if the market power of a dominant
incumbent is to be constrained. Competition authorities will look for cogent
evidence that entry is a realistic prospect within a relatively short time period
before concluding that an apparently dominant position evidenced by a high
market share would prove to be shortlived should the firm seek to raise its
prices. And while it may be high prices and profits that make entry an attract-
ive proposition, a key factor in determining the likelihood of successful entry
will be the prices and profits that will rule thereafter. Therefore the impact of
entry upon the behaviour of the incumbent(s) in the market (upon which eco-

---

ings located ... outwith the Community". This might be taken as implying that if world markets are
competitive, the pursuit of a competitive structure for the Community should not necessarily take precedence over other considerations. But the Commission has made clear that creation of so-called Euro-
champions is not compatible with Art. 2.

[81] A comparative indication of manufacturers worldwide is given in the note to para. 7 of the decision.
[82] The result has been explained on the basis of political intervention at the Commissioner level and
criticised for having no respectable economic analysis to support it.

nomists have done much analytical work in recent years) will need to be taken into account—by both the potential entrant in its decision making and the Commission in its appraisal.

The Commission has identified a variety of entry barriers. These include the costs of advertising (*Procter & Gamble/Schickedanz*), the strength of established brands (*Guinness/Grand Metropolitan*), economies of sale (*Saint Gobain/Wacker-Chemie/NOM*), tariffs (*Mannesmann/Vallourec/Ilva*), national regulations (*Hoffmann-La Roche/Boehringer Mannheim*) and buying preferences (*Kali und Salz*), patents (*Tetra Pak/Alfa-Laval*) and other intellectual property rights (*Shell/Montecatini*) and the need to establish handling facilities (*Skanska/Scancem*) or distribution or servicing networks (*Kesko/Tuko* and *Mercedes-Benz/Kässbohrer*). Yet while entry barriers may take a number of different forms, they can be classified into three main, if sometimes overlapping types:

- absolute advantages enjoyed by incumbent over a potential entrant;
- strategic advantages of an incumbent;
- exclusionary practices of incumbents.

Absolute advantages arise where an incumbent owns, or has access to, resources that are not available to potential entrants. Examples include legal restrictions on entry, ownership of assets access to which is essential if an entrant is to compete and which it would be impossible or hopelessly uneconomic for the entrant to duplicate, and intellectual property rights which give the holder exclusive use of some technology or facility. Clearly, barriers of this type may make entry impossible, or at least delay it considerably.

Strategic advantages are those that derive from the fact that the incumbent is already established in the market (they are sometimes referred to as first-mover advantages). Examples of strategic entry barriers include the capital requirements of entry, economies of scale and scope, goodwill and brand loyalty, often built up by heavy advertising, and an established distribution system.

To illustrate by reference to economies of scale, a potential entrant will know that if it enters on a smaller scale than necessary for efficient production, it will operate at a cost disadvantage to the established firm(s), whereas if it enters on the scale necessary to reap all the economies, it is likely that prices and profits will fall by virtue of the expansion of total output. Another consideration will be the response of the incumbent. It might react aggressively to the entrant, for example by cutting its price or increasing its advertising expenditure or it might accommodate the entrant, if necessary by reducing its own output. The uncertainties will reduce the attractiveness of entry. This risk associated with the decision whether or not to enter will be compounded where the market is oligopolistic.

Entry in an industry characterised by economies of scale is very likely to involve the entrant in considerable sunk costs. It is where entry involves sunk costs that entry barriers arise. Sunk costs are those that cannot be recovered if entry fails. If the costs of entry are reversible and recoverable, the market is said to be contestable. While economists' analysis of contestibility has added considerably to the understanding of the role of potential competition in constraining the apparent market power of dominant firms, it has to be said that in practice few markets can be characterised as genuinely contestable. And even where the cost conditions in a market appear to make it contestable, the strategic responses of the incumbents can make entry a risky proposition. A reputation for aggressive responses to new entry can itself come to be an effective entry barrier.

The third type of entry barrier is exclusionary conduct by incumbents—which will often also be an example of strategic conduct. Incumbents' distribution policies, whatever else may be their purpose, may foreclose competitors from the market, or incumbents may refuse to supply some input or other resource to a less vertically integrated potential competitor. Another clear example of conduct that is both exclusionary and strategic is predatory pricing. Economists have traditionally thought that predatory conduct will rarely be encountered in practice because there seems no rational reason why a firm that is already in a dominant position should sacrifice some of its present profits for the uncertain prospect of higher profits at some uncertain time in the future. But the attraction of predatory pricing can be its strategic possibilities. An incumbent's reputation for responding aggressively to entry, even by predatory conduct, may come to constitute an effective entry barrier.

One factor that will invariably have a bearing on the likelihood of entry is the growth, or rather the prospective growth, of a market. Entry will be more likely, other things being equal, in a growing than in a static or declining market if only because it will be easier for an entrant to attract custom without causing a precipitous collapse of prices and profits.

It is no easy matter to assess the significance of entry barriers in a particular market or the time that may elapse before successful (that is, profitable) entry may occur. The Commission will be heavily reliant on information provided by the parties supplemented by the views of competitors and customers. As Form CO makes clear, if evidence of successful recent entry can be demonstrated, or if a market can be shown to be dynamic with a record of recent entry and exit, this is likely to go a long way to convincing the Commission that entry is likely, should a dominant firm attempt to exploit its position in the market. Hard evidence from the recent past will be more persuasive than theoretical analysis.

5.4.3.7   *Buyer Power*

The countervailing power exercised by customers of a dominant firm is a factor regularly considered by the Commission although it has been a major influence in relatively few cases. Retailer buying power exercised, for example, by the supermarket groups against food manufacturers was mentioned to support a clearance decision in *Allied Lyons/HWE-Pedro Domecq*, but the strength of brands may nullify the apparently countervailing strength of the retail buyer, as recognised in *Nestlé/Perrier*, *Pepsico/KAS*, the *Coca-Cola* cases and *Guinness/GrandMet*. A brand may be so important that a retailer must display it on its shelves, referred to as a "must stock" brand.[83]

---

[83] See paras 137 to 141 of the Art 8 decision in *Coca-Cola/Amalgamated Beverages*.

The Commission summed up the relevance of buyer power in *Coca-Cola/Carlsberg* when it said:

"... in an assessment of dominance the question is whether there is sufficient countervailing buyer power to neutralise the market power of the parties."[84]

As this comment implies the key factor is the relative degree of dependence of one party on the business of the other. One sector in which buyer power has been recognised as a prominent factor capable of counteracting high market shares is the motor car industry, where the Commission has been somewhat relaxed about mergers between automotive component suppliers because of the power wielded by the major European car manufacturers.[85]

A similar approach has been taken in relation to military products where the customer is a monopsony national defence ministry.[86] But if there is no credible alternative to a dominant supplier the financial or political muscle of its customers will be to no avail. Moreover buyer power may translate into seller power in markets downstream: countervailing power is no guarantee, therefore, of consumer welfare.

Excess capacity is also significant: the desire to improve utilisation levels can be exploited by buyers. Indeed, buying tactics in general are important and the Commission has taken into account in several cases a tradition of competitive tendering or multiple sourcing as behaviour by buyers which can impose credible restraints upon a pre-eminent manufacturer or supplier.[87] In some situations the buyer may even be instrumental in introducing a new competitor, or may have the resources to integrate vertically as protection against an apparently dominant firm. Moreover, the Commission also appears ready to take into account buyer power where there is little evidence that it has yet been exercised provided that the possibility exists. This is demonstrated especially in cases involving state monopoly or utility purchasers which could introduce more competition simply by abandoning national favourites and adopting the procurement practices obligatory pursuant to the E.C. public procurement rules. The Commission appears reluctant to prohibit concentrations where the customer could exercise self-help. This policy perhaps explains in part the reason why the Commission did not make a declaration of incompatibility in *Alcatel/Telettra* and *Mannesmann/Hoechst*.

5.4.3.8 *Economic and Financial Power*

Economic and financial power is an item which owes its appearance in the "checklist" of Article 2(2) to German merger control practice, where

---

[84] Para. 81 of the Art. 8 decision.

[85] See, *e.g. BTR/Pirelli* and *Pilkington-Techint/SIV*.

[86] See, *e.g. Matra/CAP Gemini Sogeti* and *Thomson CSF/Deutsche Aerospace*. In military procurement the Commission is pre-disposed to view markets as national, particularly since the impact of procurement rules may be blunted by Art. 296 of the E.C. Treaty.

[87] Note, for example, the emphasis placed by the Commission in *Price Waterhouse/Coopers & Lybrand* on the use of competitive tendering in the purchase of audit and accounting services.

emphasis had long been placed on the financial power of the undertakings concerned in addition to their market shares. Where market share data does not *prima facie* cause concern, the resources of a particular competitor may give it considerable immunity from the actions of its apparent competitors. For example, the capacity of a powerful firm to increase production may have a significant effect in deterring potential competition or actual firms in a market which is atomistic. The financial power of an undertaking may be assessed against a number of different parameters, including turnover, profitability and access to finance. This is one of the factors where there is some correlation between the test for jurisdiction and the substantive test of compatibility. In practice, however, the Commission has not placed great emphasis on this factor. A number of decisions[88] have made little more than passing reference to the relative strengths and resources of the undertakings concerned in notified concentrations. Paradoxically, however, there are more examples where the Commission has referred specifically to the resources and profile of competitors or potential competitors to support a clearance and the emphasis on conglomeracy in the revised Form CO has been downgraded as a result. Economic and financial power is merely one relevant factor among many in assessing both the strength of the undertaking created by the notified concentration and the strength of its competitors.[89]

5.4.3.9   *Portfolio Power*

While some economists are sceptical that "portfolio power" can be a distinct item in the scales of dominance, the Commission has identified in a number of merger decisions[90] the risk that the breadth and depth of an undertaking's product range and, specifically, a portfolio of strong brands may in itself create or strengthen a dominant position. The issue was discussed at length in *Guinness/Grand Metropolitan*.[91] The Commission did not treat the combination of spirits' products and brands in that case simply as a facet of the horizontal overlaps between the merging groups or a barrier to entry—though portfolio power could well operate as such. It attributed the following commercial and economic advantages to the portfolio effect: increased supplier power; greater pricing flexibility; tying potential and economies of scale and scope in marketing and distribution. The Commission recognised, however, that the potential effect of portfolio power on market structure depended on the strength of the particular brand, their portfolio spread across different product markets and the market shares they conferred compared with competitors' positions. The emphasis on portfolio power can be partly explained by the threat of tie-in and full-line forcing and partly by conglomeracy-type concerns.

While the two Coca-Cola decisions and that relating merger of Guinness and GrandMet to create Diageo all involved classic consumer brands in the

[88] But see *Varta/Bosch* where the financial backing of its new owner, Fiat, of the German undertaking, Sonnenschein, led the Commission to treat it as a credible constraint on the market power of *Varta/Bosch*.
[89] See, *e.g. AT&T/NCR*, para. 23; and *Matsushita/MCA*, para. 6.
[90] *Coca-Cola/Amalgamated Beverages* [1997] O.J. L218/15 and *Coca-Cola/Carlsberg* [1998] O.J. L145/41.
[91] Art. 8 decision of October 15, 1997 [1998] O.J. L288/24. See paras 38 to 42 entitled "Portfolio effects".

drinks industry considerations of portfolio effect have played a part in cases outside the consumer sector. For example, in *Saint Gobain/Wacher-Chemie/ NOM*,[92] one of the very few outright prohibitions under the Regulation, the Commission noted that the two merging firms, ESK and Saint-Gobain were the only two full-range suppliers of silicon carbide in the EEA and the main source of competition for abrasive silicon carbide was that arising between them.[93] It is suggested, therefore, that whether or not an undertaking's strength is dignified with the term ''portfolio power'', the appeal and range of its products will always be a relevant factor in determining whether dominance exists, particularly since it increases the opportunities for strategic anti-competitive conduct by the dominant firm.

5.4.3.10 *Access to Supplies or Markets*

A firm which has access to captive or well-established sources of supply or markets for its products, may have a cushion against adverse market trends affecting its competitors, whose links are less secure, and the scope to exploit any resulting market power. Article 2(1) recognises this, and Form CO requires details to be supplied to enable the Commission to assess the vertical effects of a notified concentration on the same basis as for horizontal effects. Where any member of one merging group has at least 25 per cent of a down-stream or upstream market in which any member of another merging group operates, detailed market information must be given.[94] Competitive structure can be effected by increased vertical integration, and in the strengthening of vertical relationships through a concentration with suppliers or customers formerly linked only by contract. Again, decisions under the Regulation show that the Commission will examine the vertical consequences of a concentration as a matter of course to identify any risk of market foreclosure.[95] The foreclosing effect of vertical integration may operate to entrench a dominant position by making it more difficult for non-integrated firms to compete, and by raising barriers to entry for potential competitors which, for example, may have to enter more than one market in order to have a credible presence.

In a number of consumer markets the Commission has also placed increased emphasis on the importance of distribution systems and access to outlets where strong incumbents may have economies of scale and scope, and the potential to develop new channels to the end user may be limited both by cost and regulatory factors.[96]

5.5   COMPATIBILITY—CO-ORDINATION EFFECTS

As already mentioned, when the Regulation was adopted, if the notified operation had, as its object or effect, the co-ordination of competition among firms

[92] Art. 8 decision of December 4, 1996 [1997] O.J. L247/1.
[93] Para. 179.
[94] Form CO, Section 5 ''Affected Markets''.
[95] See particularly *AT&T/NCR*; *ICI/Tioxide*; and *Alcatel/Telettra*.
[96] *e.g. Guinness/Grand Metropolitan* and *Airtours/First Choice*.

which remained independent—typically the parent companies of a newly-created joint venture—the transaction was disqualified from being treated as a concentration under the Regulation. Inappropriate notifications in accordance with Form CO could be accepted as Form A/B notifications under Regulation 17/62 and the transaction assessed under what is now Article 81.

In fact between September 1990, when the Regulation came into effect, and March 1998, when the new Article 2(4) came into effect, very few notifications were subject to Article 6(1)(a) inapplicability decisions because of their co-ordination effects. Moreover, the negative condition was widely criticised as difficult to apply and indeed inconsistent with the basic principle that all lasting structural changes should be subject to the Regulation.[97]

In a hybrid case, involving dominance and Article 81 appraisals, the practice of the Commission is to divide the appraisal section of its decision, entitled "Competitive Assessment" into two sub sections, "dominance" and "co-ordination of competitive behaviour". The assessment of dominance has already been dealt with.

In making the assessment of the co-ordination effects of the joint venture precedent and practice in applying Article 81 is clearly relevant, particularly in relation to the judgment of appreciability.[98] It must be remembered, however, that the Commission's approach to Article 81 has become more flexible in recent years, not least indeed because of its experience under the Regulation.[99] Earlier cases should be used with caution: decisions under the Regulation as originally enacted discussing the negative condition will be relevant, as will joint venture cases dealt with under the amended Regulation and applying Article 2(4).

Essentially Article 2(4) addresses what were traditionally referred to as "spillover" effects[1] in the analysis of co-operative joint ventures notified under Regulation 17/62. Even, however, in the case of Form A/B notifications of joint ventures the Commission's approach to "spillover" effects has developed somewhat, if one compares cases such as *Vacuum Interrupters*[2] and *GEC/Siemens-Plessey*[3] with *Elopak/Metal Box-Odin*[4] and *Ford/Volkswagen*.[5] The new appoach the Commission takes to vertical restraints will also contribute in practice to more flexibility in the application of Article 2(4) even though that provision primarily concerns horizontal issues.

In applying Article 2(4) the Commission first identifies in what markets the shareholders in the joint venture are actual or potential competitors and how those markets are related to those in which the notified joint venture operates. If only one parent of the joint venture is active on a market, that market will

---

[97] Art. 3(2) (first paragraph) of Regulation 4064/89, as originally adopted. The application of the negative condition was considered in detail in the second edition of this book, and subject to what is said below, inapplicability decisions prior to the March 1998 change are still relevant in determining the circumstances when co-ordination effects may be identified by the Commission.

[98] Note particularly the Notice on Joint Venture and the Notice on Agreements of Minor Importance.

[99] See, generally, Bellamy & Child, *Common Market Law of Competition* (4th ed. Sweet & Maxwell), Chap. 5.

[1] Bellamy & Child, *op. cit.* para. 5-041.

[2] [1977] O.J. L48/32.

[3] [1990] O.J. C239/2.

[4] [1990] O.J. L209/15.

[5] [1995] O.J. L20/14.

not be considered as a "candidate market for co-ordination".[6] Usually the assessments concentrate on existing activities rather than potential competition, although some consideration was given to potential competition in *ENEL/ France Télécom/Deutsche Telekom* and in other more recent cases. It would be wrong in principle to discount potential competition, albeit that co-ordination will be more difficult to prove to a satisfactory standard where the parents are not yet active on the same markets. The Commission will also not have regard to possible co-ordination effects in markets over which it lacks legal competence. Thus in *Telia/Sonera/Lithuanian Telecommunications*, it took no account of the Lithuanian market and examined the impact only in Finland and Sweden.

The Commission has emphasised that co-ordination effects must be both likely and appreciable: there must be real indications that co-ordination is the "likely" result. Co-ordination must then be more than a probability: it must be a high probability. The necessary causal link must also be established. The co-ordination must be a result of creating the joint venture and not, for example, of existing links between the parents of the joint venture. In *ENEL/ France Télécom/Deutsche Telekom* the Commission concluded that the absence of France Telecom and Deutsche Telecom from each other's home markets was not a result of their proposed joint venture in Italy.

In establishing a likely and appreciable effect, the Commission examines particularly the relative size of the "candidate" markets and the markets on which the joint venture is active. The approach to Article 2(4) is developing but it has so far been applied in detail only in one Article 8 case, BT/AT&T (decision not yet published).

5.6   COMPATIBILITY—VERTICAL ISSUES

As already noted, the vertical impact of a concentration is likely to be of less direct relevance to the issue of dominance than horizontal overlaps between competitors. This is recognised in the fact that a market is not defined as vertically "affected" in Form CO unless, regardless of any existing vertical relationship, at least one party, or the parties together, hold a share of at least 25 per cent in that market.[7]

Until recently cases were rare where the Commission had identified concerns about dominance as a result of the vertical effects of a concentration. A number of cases have, however, led to a development in the Commission's approach, which, incidentally, is also reflected in the radical new approach to Article 81 and the introduction of a general block exemption for vertical agreements.

A legitimate commercial motive for an acquisition or merger is the pursuit of vertical integration. Few, if any, economists would regard vertical integration, the common ownership of businesses at different levels in the product and supply chain, as anti-competitive in itself. Indeed vertical integration may achieve efficiency and technological gains which are pro-competitive. For

---

[6] Para. 28 of the Art. 6(1)(b) decision in *Home Benelux B.V.*
[7] Form CO, Section 6, III, "Affected Markets".

example, the avoidance of double-marginalisation (*i.e.* the need to provide satisfactory returns to each independent operator in the supply chain) or trans-action cost savings may enable prices to be lower to end users in vertically-integrated industries or groups. Another benefit of vertical integration is the encouragement of appropriate investment, particularly in capital intensive industries, where financing decisions which can be justified only over the longer term may turn on factors such as security of customers and outlets which long term contractual relationships with third parties may not guarantee to the same extent as vertical integration.

In assessing the advantages and disadvantages of vertical integration much depends not only on the characteristics of the industry concerned but also upon the extent of concentration in that industry and the commercial policies pur-sued within vertically-integrated groups. Vertical integration may have anti-competitive effects. It inevitably raises entry barriers, if it is seen as an essen-tial structure within an industry, because entry has to be made at more than one level, for example, at the manufacturing and the distribution level. In *Guinness/GrandMet* the Commission was concerned primarily with horizontal issues, but it also took account of vertical links between the production and distribution of spirits, commenting:

"vertical integration into distribution is advantageous in product markets where branding is important, because it allows the brand-owner to retain full control of product development, promotion and marketing."[8]

The Commission's view[9] was that the main function of the vertically-integrated distribution operations was to protect the parties' brand rather than to operate sell-standing distribution businesses.

But the main concern about vertical relationships in an industry is foreclos-ure, together with the possibility they facilitate collusion. As to foreclosure, if manufacturer A acquires company B, its supplier of raw materials, the Com-mission will wish to check that alternative sources of supply of that raw mat-erial remain available to A's competitors should A require B to deal exclus-ively with itself. While such behaviour might reduce B's profits in the short term, the policy could be strategically advantageous in the longer term. Whether foreclosure is feasible will depend upon such factors as B's share of the raw material market, the number of competitors at each level of the market, and the ease with which customers can switch to other suppliers. Foreclosure can also arise, of course, in relation to downstream acquisitions. As to facilitat-ing collusion, manufacturers may be more able to organise and police a cartel if they have control over downstream activities.

One sector which exhibits a degree of vertical integration, but varying con-siderably in extent between different Member States,[10] is the foreign package holiday industry.[11] The Commission has examined a number of mergers in the

---

[8] Para. 36.
[9] Para. 20.
[10] Compare, *e.g.* Ireland and Denmark.
[11] An examination of the impact of vertical integration was the main reason for the monopoly references to the Monopolies and Mergers Commission, as it then was, in 1996 by the U.K. Director General of Fair Trading. The MMC's clean bill of health stimulated a rapid increase in consolidation and integration.

travel sector. In *Westdeutsche Landesbank/Carlson/Thomas Cook*, it examined the risk of foreclosure in the United Kingdom arising from the proposed joint venture between two international travel groups, Thomas Cook, now owned by the German group, Preussag, and the U.S. holiday group, Carlson. The Commission concluded that the risk was not significant given the relatively low aggregate market shares, the availability of alternative source for charter airline seats and retail distribution, which the Commission measured by assessing the extent of the inter-relationship between the merged group's tour operating arm and its retail and airline operations. The extent of vertical integration among major groups in the U.K. travel trade (in charter airline flying, tour operating and retailing) was a significant element in the subsequent Article 8 decision precluding Airtours, the second largest travel group in the U.K., from acquiring the fourth largest, First Choice. First Choice's airline, Air 2000, was the main supplier of seats to independent tour operators and it was not its strategy to use its retail arm to sell in favour of group holiday products as aggressively as Airtours did. Vertical effects have also been examined in the media sector, where market power at one level of the market may transmit itself to other levels, particularly in view of the high levels of investment required to enter the sector.

Vertical effects will, therefore, be relevant in cases where the concerns are primarily caused by horizontal overlaps and, more rarely, where in themselves they create or strengthen a dominant position. There are few examples of the latter. The most striking is *Skanska/Scancem*.[12] In a battle for control of Scancem (the Scandinavian cement and building materials group) against the Norwegian group, Aker, Skanska increased its shareholding to virtually half of Scancem's voting capital. Skanska was the largest construction company in Sweden. Scancem was the only indigenous cement producer with a market share of over 90 per cent in the supply of cement in Sweden.[13] The acquisition of control of Scancem by Skanska, which the company had failed to notify until some months after the event when prompted by the Commission, was prohibited by the Commission.[14] The Commission concluded that Scancem's dominant position in the Swedish cement market would be strengthened by Skanska's acquisition of sole control over Scancem as a result of (i) the loss of any incentive Skanska may have had to foster competition with Scancem, for example, by setting up cement silos and importing cement, and (ii) Skanska's ability to act strategically throughout the value-chain against Scancem's customers (who were also Skanska's competitors) if they were to seek alternative supplies of cement. The Commission required Skanska to sell its entire shareholding in Scancem.

• By contrast, in *Coca-Cola/Amalgamated Beverages*, the Commission found no tenable grounds for prohibiting the transaction. That case concerned the acquisition by The Coca-Cola Company (TCCC) from Cadbury Schweppes of the 51 per cent of the shares in the United Kingdom's largest bottling company, Amalgamated Beverages Great Britain (ABGB), which it did not already

---

[12] Art. 8 decision of December 11, 1999 [1999] O.J. L183/10.
[13] It also held high shares in Norway and Finland but Skanska's position in those markets was much less strong than in Sweden.
[14] For a further discussion of the remedies applied see Chap. 7, below.

own. The Commission acknowledged that there was no aggregation of market shares or brands since Coca-Cola's own wholly-owned bottling company was active in the Netherlands but not in Great Britain. The Commission found TCCC to be dominant in a national market for cola-flavoured drinks but concluded, with some reluctance, that it could not be said that that dominance was strengthened as a result of an operation which saw TCCC move from a position of substantial influence; if not joint control, to one of sole control.[15] The Commission conceded that it was "not possible to differentiate sufficiently between the opportunities which already exist within the current structure of CCSB" in order to conclude "that CCSB's dominant position in the cola market in Great Britain was strengthened within the meaning of Article 2 of the Regulation".[16]

Step changes in vertical integration are going to be seen as more problematic than incremental changes and, despite the limited number of cases which have raised significant vertical issues under the Regulation, it is important not to overlook the relevance of such issues. Vertical links should be arranged fully prior to notification and, if necessary, should be covered in the notification in accordance with Form CO. Effective analysis of the issues at this stage may prevent unnecessary delay at a more critical stage in the process.

5.7   COLLECTIVE DOMINANCE

The judgment of the Court of Justice in *Kali und Salz*[17] has laid to rest the debate as to whether the Regulation could apply to positions of collective dominance, *i.e.* where a concentration in a particular sector threatens to create or strengthen not a dominant position enjoyed by a single firm but an oligopolistic structure in which a small number of undertakings together (including those not party to the notified concentration) enjoy a dominant position incompatible with effective competition, given the overall characteristics of the sector concerned. The Court held that the Regulation applied alike to the creation or strengthening of a dominant position enjoyed collectively by two or more firms and to cases of single firm dominance. Accepting that, in adopting the Regulation, Member States had intended to create a neutral stance on the issue, the Court took a purposive approach to its construction, emphasising that a serious lacuna would exist in the powers necessary to achieve the objective of undistorted competition within the Common Market if the Regulation effectively had no application in oligopolistic markets. Thus, the words "dominant position" in Article 2 covered a situation where that position was enjoyed collectively by more than one undertaking.[18]

---

[15] Paras 205 to 207 and 214 and 215 of the Art. 8 decision.

[16] Compare *Coca-Cola/Carlsberg*, above. The Commission has also intervened to prevent Coca-Cola from acquiring Schweppes bottling interests in the E.U.

[17] Joined Cases C-68/94 *French Republic v. Commission* and C-30/95 *Société Commerciale des Potasses et de l'Azote (SCPA) and Entreprise Minière et Chimique (EMC) v. Commission*—judgment delivered on March 31, 1998.

[18] The arguments for and against the Regulation applying to collective dominance have been rehearsed in the second edition of this book. Briefly, the Court rejected the French Government's submissions that to apply the Regulation to collective dominant positions was inconsistent both with the presumption in Recital 15 that dominance did not exist at market shares below 25 per cent and with the absence of

From the perspective of preserving effective competition in markets in the European Union the Court's teleological approach is difficult to fault.[19] It also minimises the asymmetry between E.C. and national merger and monopoly controls, some of which have special provisions for dealing with oligopolies.[20] There remain, however, a number of practical difficulties, discussed below, in using the Regulation to control the development of uncompetitive oligopolies.

Shortly after the *Kali und Salz* judgment came that of the Court of First Instance in *Gencor v. Commission*.[21] In that case the Court held that evidence of structural links was not essential to a finding of collective dominance and that it was sufficient if a relationship of economic interdependence was established: it said:

> "there is no reason whatsoever in legal or economic terms to exclude from the notion of economic links the relationship of interdependence existing between the parties to a tight oligopoly within which, in a market with the appropriate characteristics, in particular in terms of market concentration, transparency and product homogeneity, those parties are in a position to anticipate one another's behaviour and are therefore strongly encouraged to align their conduct in the market, in particular in such a way as to maximise their joint profits by restricting production with a view to increasing prices. In such a context, each trader is aware that highly competitive action on its part designed to increase its market share (for example a price cut) would provoke identical action by the others, so that it would derive no benefit from its initiative."[22]

5.7.1 Kali und Salz

The case concerned a proposed joint venture between Kali und Salz ("K+S") and the Treuhandanstalt by which the potash and rock-salt businesses of K+S would be combined with those of the former East German producer, Mitteldeutsche Kali AG (MdK). Given the absence of imports, high transport costs, and customer preferences among German farmers, the Commission held that Germany constituted a distinct geographic market, and the rest of the Community, another. In relation to the latter market the Commission found that the joint venture was matched by only one other Community producer and distributor, the French company SCPA, and concluded that: "The . . . characteristics of the market and the record of the past behaviour of K+S and SCPA indicate that the merger would lead to a situation of oligopolistic dominance by K+S/MdK and SCPA group."[23]

The Commission emphasised the close links between K+S and SCPA. These

explicit and appropriate rights to be heard for third parties. France also drew attention to the contrast between Art. 82, with its explicit recognition that a dominant position could be held by "one or more undertakings", and the wording of Art. 2 of the Regulation.

[19] The Court rejected the opinion of Advocate General Tesauro to the contrary.
[20] *e.g.* in Germany and in the U.K.
[21] Case T-102/96, judgment of March 25, 1999.
[22] Paras 104 and 105 of its Art. 8 decision.
[23] Para. 57 of its Art. 8 decision.

included: (i) a potash joint venture in Canada; (ii) their membership of an export cartel established in Vienna to co-ordinate members' potash sales outside the Community;[24] and (iii) the fact that K+S sold through the agency of SCPA in France. These links existed in a market described by the Commission as "a mature commodity market characterised by a largely homogenous product and the lack of technological innovation".

While the Court of Justice accepted that E.C. merger control could extend to the prohibition of concentrations in oligopolistic markets, on the facts of the case it held that the Commission had failed to prove that the acquisition of the former East German potash producer MdK by K+S would create or strengthen a position of collective dominance. While it recognised that "the basic provisions of the Regulation, in particular Article 2 thereof, confer on the Commission a certain discretion, especially with respect to assessments of an economic nature"[25] the Court concluded that the Commission's analysis and assessment of the facts did not stand up to rational examination. In particular the critical evidence of structural links between K+S and the French producer, SCPA, with whom the dominant position was allegedly shared, was considered unconvincing by the Court.

The Court held further that the defects in the Commission's reasoning meant that the Article 8 decision had to be quashed in its entirety: the Court could not substitute its own unconditional decision of compatibility for the Commission's original decision. The end result was that the Commission took a new Article 6(1)(b) clearance decision on the basis of an updated notification[26] and the joint venture was allowed to proceed without the imposition of any conditions: Kali und Salz had, by then, severed its links with the French producer, SCPA, and undertook to market and distribute its products independently.[27]

5.7.2 The Current Position

In recognising that the Regulation extended to collective dominance but, at the same time, setting a demanding, but imprecisely defined, standard of proof to establish collective dominance, the *Kali und Salz* judgment could be said to have led the Commission into the wilderness and left it there. While doubt remained about the ambit of the Regulation it was understandable that the Commission's approach in stage one assessments to notifications where the concentration appeared to create a more oligopolistic market structure might be tentative or even cursory. With the doubt removed, however, the Commission could not shy away from the complex and onerous task of undertaking in stage one the necessarily wider-ranging analysis required in all potential cases of collective or oligopolistic dominance. There is here a real need for guidelines as soon as practical experience permits. Indeed it is understood that the Commission intends to publish a list of the characteristics which it regards as predisposing a market to oligopolistic behaviour.

---

[24] The Commission also thought it relevant to refer to the export cartel involving the two companies operating within the E.C. which was declared to infringe Art. 81 by Commission Decision 73/212.

[25] Point 223 of the judgment.

[26] Strictly speaking, there appears not to have been a new notification.

[27] See the Commission's Art. 6(1)(b) decision of July 9, 1998.

5.7.3 Establishing Collective Dominance

The concept of collective dominance rests on the economic proposition that in highly concentrated markets it is highly likely, if not inevitable, that if only a small number of firms survive, they will recognise their inter-dependence and the futility of aggressive competitive behaviour. They will adapt their behaviour, not necessarily collusively, to that which a profit-maximising dominant single firm would choose. For this to occur, market conditions must be such that, in the medium to long term, competitive activity (*i.e.* action which pays no heed to competitors' likely reactions) by a firm will not bring it any sustainable economic benefit. In *Gencor/Lonrho*,[28] discussed below, the Commission identified the typical characteristics of an oligopolistic market as including: high concentration; homogeneous products; maturity (*i.e.* low potential for destabilising innovation); transparency (of prices and capacity); stable demand and modest growth; high barriers to entry and growth; absence of buyer power; and symmetry of market shares and cost structures. Even so, many economists would conclude that oligopolistic conduct will not last without some mechanisms for co-ordination. This is because it will always be tempting for a firm to step out of line, perhaps by secret discounts or selective price shading in an attempt to win extra business. The more oligopolists can discover and discourage such ''cheating'' the more successful will they be in maintaining and raising prices towards the monopoly level.

5.7.4 Gencor/Lonrho—*Duopolistic Markets*

In *Gencor/Lonrho*, the operation in question was a proposal to merge the mining interests of Gencor and Lonrho. The result would have been to reduce the three significant competitors (all based in South Africa) in world platinum and rhodium markets to two and thus create a dominant duopoly. The Court of First Instance upheld the Commission's decision to prohibit the proposed joint venture outright. This is the first case in which the Commission has prohibited or attached conditions to a concentration on the basis that it strengthens or creates a position of collective dominance.

The Commission found the platinum and rhodium markets worldwide to exhibit the characteristics negative to competition listed above. In addition, the South African mining companies had a history of collusive or uncompetitive behaviour. Lonrho's mining division was the exception, being the most efficient and lowest cost operator with a distinctive management approach. The merger with Gencor would, however, nullify Lonrho as an independent competitive force. The Commission discounted the possibility that Russian or North American producers would be significant competitors in the future. It noted that resellers were not present in the market, and that the limited amount of recycled and recovered platinum was insufficient to constrain the behaviour of the two remaining South African producers. Together they accounted for around 70 per cent of platinum supplied and some 90 per cent of all known reserves.

[28] Art. 8 decision of April 24, 1996 [1997] O.J. L11/30.

5.7.5   Price Waterhouse/Coopers & Lybrand[29]—*Oligopolistic Markets*

In its second stage examination in *Price Waterhouse/Coopers & Lybrand*, the Commission had to consider whether a merger of two of the so-called "Big Six" accountancy firms[30] would create or strengthen a position of collective dominance. The Commission recognised as a general principle that "collective dominance involving more than three or four suppliers is unlikely simply because of the complexity of the interrelationships involved, and the consequent temptation to deviate".[31] In such a market no enduring uncompetitive stability could exist. This is a somewhat dogmatic and surprising statement to make at this stage in the evolution of the regulation of oligopolies under the Regulation.

The Commission went on to emphasise the difficulties it faced in establishing oligopolistic dominance in the light of the judgment of the Court in *Kali und Salz*, handed down a matter of weeks before its decision. Of that judgment it said:

"... [the Court] has emphasised that there is a strong burden of proof on the Commission in the case of an oligopolistic market which the Commission holds to be subject to collective dominance.

The Court held that a high level of concentration in an oligopolistic market is not in itself a deciding factor as to the existence of collective dominance. In addition, the Court's judgment implies that evidence of the lack of effective competition between a group of suppliers held to be collectively dominant must be very strong, as must evidence of the weakness of competitive pressure from other suppliers (if there are any such in the market in question)."

The Commission indicated that had the proposed merger of KPMG and Ernst & Young (notified late in 1997 but terminated in February 1998) gone ahead it would have considered the possibility that a dominant duopoly would be created in the market for accounting and auditing services for major national and international companies and would have considered the PW/Coopers merger in the light of the plans of KPMG and Ernst & Young.[32] In concluding that it had "no conclusive proof" (a high standard for the Commission to impose on itself) that a position of oligopolistic or duopolistic dominance would be created or strengthened as a result of the merger, the Commission noted particularly "the non-emergence of any two clear leading firms following the merger".[33] The strategic lesson is perhaps not to be second in the consolidation stakes in already concentrated markets![34]

---

[29] Art. 8 decision of May 20, 1998 [1999] O.J. L50/27.
[30] Price Waterhouse, Coopers & Lybrand, KPMG, Ernst & Young, Arthur Andersen and Deloitte Touche Tohmatsui.
[31] At para. 103 of its Art. 8 decision.
[32] Paras 108 to 111 of its Art. 8 decision, entitled "Dual-merger market structure" (PW/C&L plus KPMG/E&Y).
[33] Para. 119.
[34] See also the spate of consolidation in the U.K. travel industry evidenced in *West LB/Thomas Cook/Carlson*; *Kuoni/First Choice*; and *Airtours/First Choice*.

5.7.6 Airtours/First Choice

In April 1999 Airtours, the international travel group, launched a hostile bid for First Choice, which was emerging as an effective vertically-integrated rival in the U.K. The acquisition of First Choice by Airtours would have left only three major vertically-integrated travel groups in the U.K., the other two being Thomson and Thomas Cook, whose acquisition of Carlson's U.K. travel interest had been cleared by the Commission in an Article 6 decision earlier in the year. The three groups would have held over 70 per cent of the U.K. short-haul foreign package holiday market. Despite a history of competition in U.K. travel markets, the Commission considered that the rapid consolidation and vertical integration which had followed the 1997 report of the U.K. Competition Commission (as it now is) into the industry meant that structural conditions in the U.K. had changed radically. Although the combined market shares after the concentration would have been lower then the levels which caused concern in earlier duopoly cases (discussed above) the Commission assessed the quality of the competition offered by the rest of the market. It concluded that the remainder of the U.K. tour operating market was highly fragmented and, being unable to obtain inputs and distribution at prices matching those available to the integrated groups, was at cost and other disadvantages which meant that it was not able to exercise an effective competitive constraint against the oligopoly of Airtours, Thomson and Thomas Cook. Past behaviour, when market structure and conditions were very different, was not a reliable indicator of the nature and vigour of competition in the future. The Commission therfore found the proposed bid incompatible with the Common Market and declined to accept the remedies offered by Airtours.

Airtours/First Choice is the first case where the Commission has issued a prohibition decision where the notified concentration would still have left three major firms in the market. The decision represents the most significant development in E.C. merger control since the adoption of the Regulation itself. Companies and their advisers will need to consider their acquisition strategies carefully and anticipate where the Commission might have concerns about rigid oligopolies emerging, particularly where the markets affected exhibit the characteristics mentioned above. This includes reviewing existing relationships with competitors to see whether they could be used by the Commission to support an oligopoly finding. Concerns at commercial and other relationships in oligopolistic markets explains the disposals offered in two recent oil company mergers *Exxon/Mobil* and *BP Amoco/Atlantic Richfield* (decisions not yet published) to secure compatibility decisions. *Airtours/First Choice* was not, however, an entirely typical collective dominance case. One unusual feature was that, given the nature of the package holiday market, the Commission's concerns related to the likelihood of tacit collusion in the planning of capacity (airline seats, and bookings of accommodation) and not in relation to prices. If programme planning leads to overcapacity this oversupply has an inevitable knock-on effect on prices in the late sales season as tour operators seek to recover at least some contribution to the cost of accommodation and airline flights to which they are already committed. This is perhaps why the issue of product homogeneity was less critical than it might be in the more usual case where the concerns focus on tacit collusion on prices.

5.7.7   Collective Dominance—Conclusions

Karel van Miert, then Competition Commissioner, recently expressed the view that the trend of consolidation in European industry had gone far enough. Certainly had the Court ruled that the Regulation was confined to the control of single firm dominance, as the French Government advocated, the scope for preserving competitive structures in E.U. markets would have been very narrow. As it is, the Commission has a very demanding task to assess the risk of collective dominance in sufficient depth within the four week stage one timetable to justify the opening of a second stage inquiry. Oligopoly is a very common market structure, and the rapid pace of consolidation through cross-border deals in the E.U. and worldwide present the Commission with a monumental task.

Moreover, the regulation of oligopolies raises both structural and behavioural issues. In the United Kingdom, for example, the monopoly provisions of the Fair Trading Act provide the possibility of examining markets which tend toward oligopoly, whereas under German anti-trust law, special merger control rules apply in concentrated markets. Arguably, if it is the underlying characteristics of a market which pre-dispose companies to behave uncompetitively, measures should be applied to the industry as a whole. Under the Regulation, however, even if a case of collective dominance is established remedies can be applied only to the parties to the notified concentration.[35] If the merger itself creates the collective dominance then prohibiting the concentration should be an adequate remedy, but if the conclusion is that the merger strengthens an existing oligopoly the Commission has no powers to do more, though it could conceivably use a combination of Articles 81 and 82 to regulate any market characteristics which could be attributed to infringements of those provisions. The Commission has not, however, undertaken such industry-wide examinations in the past; Articles 81 and 82 were not designed with this kind of case in mind although there are some indications that the Commission is re-examining how they might be used to police markets in which there are few competitors.

It will be interesting to see how the Commission uses its newly-recognised power. To examine markets in the four weeks allowed for in stage one in order to judge whether the notified concentration might create or strengthen a position of collective dominance presents a considerable challenge.[36] Careful consideration also needs to be given to the remedies which are appropriate where the Commission concludes that a concentration creates or strengthens such a position. Since it is the inherent characteristics of a market which allow an uncompetitive oligopoly to emerge and flourish the acceptance of commitments from the parties to the notified concentration may not be a sufficient remedy. It might well be argued that if a market is predisposed to oligopoly, only the preservation of an adequate number of independent firms in that

---

[35] *Kali und Salz*, point 161 of the judgment. Note, however, that in that case the Court recognised that the position of the French producer of potash, SCPA, was affected appreciably by the conditions imposed by the Commission or accepted by Kali und Salz even though they were not imposed, strictly speaking, on SCPA.

[36] Prior to *Kali und Salz*, a number of published Art. 6(1)(b) decisions seem to have dealt with the issue of collective dominance in a somewhat cursory way.

market will guarantee effective competition. This would suggest that outright prohibitions of operations which reduce the number of competitors below a safe level may be the most appropriate, proportionate and logical remedy. In the absence of any anti-monopolisation provision in E.C. competition law similar to that in the U.S. Sherman Act it will be interesting to see how the Commission develops its approach toward collective dominance in applying the Regulation.

5.8 COUNTERVAILING BENEFITS

It will have already become apparent that the Regulation was designed and, indeed, has generally been applied with such a focus on competition-related factors that the scales are weighted against other considerations being taken into account, let alone proving influential in the final judgment on compatibility. Nonetheless it has to be recognised that many of the key factors in the appraisal decision are incapable of precise measurement or prediction and there may be not one but many finely-balanced judgments to be made in carrying out the appraisal process before reaching a final decision. For example, few would believe that the political row within the Commission over the *Aérospatiale-Alenia/de Havilland* prohibition was other than a clash between industrial policy and competition even though it was explained by the protagonists as a difference of view over the correct product market definition. In fact there seems little evidence in the published decision[37] to justify a departure from the definition ultimately adopted. That case, however, seems a storm in a tea-cup when compared with *Mannesmann/Vallourec/Ilva* where the Commissioners were evenly divided on whether or not to prohibit the concentration and the Advisory Committee had already agreed with the draft prohibition decision prepared by the Merger Task Force.[38] One of the notable features of the decision in *Mannesmann/Vallourec/Ilva* was the unprecedented emphasis on the possibility of entry by Japanese steel companies into EEA markets if the merged undertaking abused its position by indulging in supra-competitive pricing. The Commission's prediction of the likelihood of entry appears to have changed the whole tenor of the decision and betrays the opportunities which exist, albeit exercised in highly unusual circumstances, for drafting a decision to justify a result which might seem desirable for industrial policy or other political reasons. It would, however, be wrong to suggest that this was other than a very exceptional case.

Predictions as to the future behaviour of markets and the firms in them are notoriously difficult to make. Unless it is obvious that wholly irrelevant considerations have been taken into account, or highly relevant evidence ignored, the chances of a successful legal challenge to a decision are remote. Even then the outcome will usually depend on the determination of a competitor or customer to pursue its legal remedies to the full. The final outcome may also be influenced by apparently extraneous factors such as the credibility

---

[37] [1991] O.J. L344/42.
[38] For the Opinion see [1994] O.J. C111/6. Contrast the Art. 8 decision published on the same date: [1994] O.J. L102/15.

of the notifying parties,[39] the strength of complaints or customer reaction, or the evidence of competitors.[40] Despite, therefore, the emphasis on competition and market structure, parties should not lose sight of the advantage to be gained by explaining fully and carefully the rationale behind the notified operation and the benefits it will achieve, particularly for consumers in the Community or EEA. The Commission's assessment must be made in the context of the overall objectives of the Community. If, therefore, it can be established, for example, that restructuring needs to take place if a Community industry is to achieve the profitability needed for continued investment in research and development or to invest in emerging markets elsewhere in the world, the notifying parties will have created a climate which allows the notified operation to be viewed in a positive light. This may lead the Commission to show flexibility and ingenuity as to the remedial undertakings which may be necessary to deal with any competition concerns. It may give the notifying parties the benefit of the doubt where there is a conflict of evidence, or where predictions have to be made about the future. At the same time, by demonstrating a positive commercial rationale for the notified operation the undertakings concerned will also be able to show that they had no anti-competitive or market-dominating intent. It therefore comes as no surprise to find that Form CO requires such information.[41]

5.8.1 Technical and Economic Progress

Recitals 4 and 13 to the Regulation provide some justification for submitting material unrelated to competition issues. Little comfort, however, can be derived from the substantive provisions of the Regulation. As already mentioned, serious consideration had earlier been given to the possibility of approving concentrations even if they created or enhanced a dominant position, provided that they resulted in technical and economic progress to the benefit of consumers in the Community. Even though an approval mechanism was rejected in the final text of the Regulation, Article 2(1)(b), somewhat illogically perhaps, still requires the Commission to take into account "the development of technical and economic progress provided that it is to consumers' advantage and does not form an obstacle to competition." Since, by definition, a proposed concentration will be held incompatible with the Common Market only if it leads to dominance which hinders effective competition there seems little scope to take account of the benefits of a market dominating merger or acquisition. The reference to "technical and economic progress" in Article 2(1)(b) seems, therefore, to create false hopes.

This appears to be reinforced by the clear position taken by the Commission

---

[39] The Commission frequently comments in its Art. 8 decisions on inconsistencies and outright contradictions in approach and evidence.

[40] Competitors may well indulge in spoiling tactics, or even hope to be the beneficiaries of disposal undertakings extracted from the notifying parties as the price for clearance.

[41] Moreover, the psychological effect on a regulator of an unimpressive presentation of merger benefits by the senior managements involved should not be underestimated. Nor, by contrast, should the damage which can be done by hyperbolic statement in strategic studies and reports prepared for senior management by financial advisers, merchant banks and management consultants. These have to be disclosed to the Commission in accordance with Form CO. See generally Chap. 4.

in its prohibition decision in *MSG/Media Service*,[42] a joint venture established to operate in the field of digital pay-TV. The Commission concluded that, even though MSG would contribute to the development of digital television, the successful spread of that medium would be hindered rather than promoted by the deterrent effect on new entry which would result from the dominant position the joint venture would quickly gain. The Commission commented:

"The reference to this criterion [contribution to technical and economic progress] in Article 2(1)(b) of the Merger Regulation is subject to the reservation that no obstacle is formed to competition. As outlined above, however, the foreseeable effects of the proposed concentration suggest that it will lead to a sealing-off of and early creation of a dominant position on the future markets for technical and administrative services and to a substantial hindering of effective competition on the future market for pay-TV."

Not content with that the Commission went on to question whether it was even likely that, given the dominant position acquired by the joint venture, technical and economic progress would in fact be achieved. The Commission identified the inconsistency between dominant positions and technical and economic progress, notwithstanding the reference in Article 2(1). So far from justifying a concentration, the technical and economic progress achieved by the merged enterprises may enable them to out-distance their competitors and may be a factor which in itself contributes to the creation or enhancement of a dominant position. Whether this is so will depend upon such factors as the opportunities for product differentiation and the level of sunk costs incurred.

Technological development has always been regarded as an important dimension of competition and in several merger appraisals the Commission has considered the effect that a loss of independent R&D centres may have. For example, in *DuPont/ICI* one of the Commission's main concerns was the effect on competition of a merger between two Community nylon fibre businesses which were pre-eminent in their commitment and spending on R&D. In other words, the merger of two top ranking research and development facilities in the Community in this field was itself one of the key factors which would give the merged undertaking a dominant position. The merger was permitted only after DuPont had undertaken to transfer to a third party a free-standing research and development facility of comparable quality to those operated by itself and ICI prior to the deal. Similarly, in *Shell/Montecatini*, undertakings (later withdrawn) had to be given to preserve a second independent source of polypropylene technology for licensing purposes before the concentration was allowed to proceed.

There may, however, be scope in certain circumstances for recognising a positive impact from technological and economic progress. First, such benefits will be highly relevant if the Commission has identified co-ordination effects having a significant impact on competition. These will be assessed under the criteria in Article 81(3), which recognises technological and economic progress as grounds for exemption, or, in the context of the Regulation, a decision of compatibility. Secondly, in potentially oligopolistic markets, which are

---

[42] [1994] O.J. L364/1. See also paras 145–152 of *Nordic Satellite Distribution* [1996] O.J. L53/20.

coming under increasing scrutiny under the Regulation, the technological or efficiency benefits of a merger may be relevant in creating a catalyst to competition and disturbing the stability and symmetry of existing market conditions. Finally, the Commission is likely to be influenced by the concept of "technology markets" which is being recognised increasingly by U.S. regulators. In such markets emphasis is placed on the importance of preserving and enhancing research and development resources and skills in a dynamic context rather than focusing exclusively on the end-product. It will, however, be a challenge to find room for this concept within the confines of the Regulation.

5.8.2   Efficiency

Likewise, there is no "efficiency" defence in the Regulation, in the sense recognised in North American merger control, and none has emerged from the Commission's application of it so far. But improvements in efficiency and cost-savings through restructuring have been the background to many notified concentrations. Such benefits have been recognised under Article 81(3) as economic progress capable of benefiting consumers. Unless, however, the need for restructuring is so critical that one of the undertakings concerned may fail (see below), there seems again no scope for such benefits to be taken into account in the appraisal process. However, a well-proven case explaining the need for restructuring could well persuade the Commissioners, if not the Merger Task Force, to give the undertakings concerned the benefit of the doubt or to feel disposed to accept remedial undertakings in order that the transaction can proceed rather than prevent it outright. For example, in *DuPont/ICI* and *Shell/Montecatini*, the recognised need to restructure the E.C. industry may have influenced the conditional clearance. By contrast, recognition that rationalisation can be pro-competitive did not avoid an outright prohibition in *Nordic Satellite Distribution*. The Commission has mooted the issue of guidelines clarifying the notion of the "efficiencies" defence, but it is difficult to see what could justify this, given the way the Regulation is currently drafted.

Most developed merger control systems do admit an efficiency defence, and logically such a defence should be available. Nonetheless regulators are sceptical about claimed efficiencies, particularly if other competitors are insufficiently effective to ensure that consumers will share the benefits—a necessary criterion for an exemption on the ground of economic progress under Article 81(3) E.C.

5.8.3   Failing Firm

U.S. merger control recognises, within strict limits, a "failing firm" defence[43] to justify an acquisition. The Regulation makes no explicit reference to the doctrine and the general factors in Article 2(1) seem, again, to leave precious little

---

[43] See U.S. merger guidelines.

scope for its development. This seemed borne out by *Aérospatiale-Alenia/de Havilland* where the Commission responded to the suggestion that de Havilland would face liquidation if it were not taken over by Aerospatiale-Alenia by questioning the relevance of that prospect to an assessment of dominance under the Regulation.[44] In *Kali und Salz*, however, the Commission's attitude changed considerably, and, supported by an apparently unanimous Advisory Committee,[45] the Commission accepted that the "failing company defence" could be taken into account "pursuant to Article 2(2)".[46] The burden of proof to establish the defence lies on the notifying parties, who must show that, if the concentration does not take place, (i) the target company will not survive; (ii) in that event, the acquiring company will inherit its market share; and (iii) there is no alternative solution which would be less anti-competitive. The critical factor is whether, absent the transaction, the prospective acquirer would succeed in taking over the target company's customers, *i.e.* the ultimate market structure resulting from the target's failure would be no different from that which would result from its acquisition.[47] In oligopolistic markets the failing firm defence is likely to be particularly problematic. If these criteria are met, the Commission treats the chain of causation between the implementation of the concentration and the acquisition of dominance as having been broken. The defence was rejected in *Blokker/Toys 'R' Us*[48] where the Commission emphasised that the doctrine was indeed based on the lack of causality between the concentration and the creation or strengthening of a dominant position and succinctly restated the conditions under which the failing firm defence could apply under the Regulation. However, there is no reason in principle why it could not be argued more generally that the target company was not capable of providing effective competition even though it was not technically a "failing firm", for example, because of its lack of financial resources or spare capacity. Such factors have been recognised by the Commission when judging whether undertakings remaining in the market will be able to act as a restraint on the market power of the undertakings concerned in the notification.[49] The approach of the Court in *Kali und Salz* supports this analysis. In E.C. merger control, the "failing firm" doctrine does not, it is suggested, need to be elevated to special status. The Commission must establish that the acquisition of one undertaking by another undertaking creates or strengthens a dominant position and the acquired undertaking may represent an ineffective competitor for a variety of reasons including lack of resources, outdated technology, cost disadvantages and weak brands. The Court was, therefore, correct in *Kali und Salz* to reject the French Government's submission that the Commission's decision was flawed because it failed to apply all the elements recognised in U.S. anti-trust law as necessary to establish the "failing firm" defence.

---

[44] See para. 31 of the Art. 8 decision. The Commission did not accept that de Havilland would go into liquidation if the concentration was blocked.

[45] See para. 3 of the Committee's Opinion published in [1994] O.J. C199/4.

[46] See paras 71 *et seq.*, of the Art. 8 decision.

[47] Compare the view of the U.K. MMC in its report into the proposed acquisition of ICI's fertiliser business by Kemira. The MMC concluded that the appropriate competitive outcome was not to recognise a "failing firm" justification but to allow the competitors which remained in the market to fight it out to pick up the failed firm's business.

[48] Art. 8 prohibition decision of June 26, 1997, paras 109 to 113 [1998] O.J. L316/1.

[49] *Saint Gobain/Wacker-Chemie/NOM.*

5.8.4 Social Considerations—The *Perrier* Judgment

Recital 13 to the Regulation reminds the Commission that, in assessing the compatibility of concentrations with the Common Market, it should do so "within the general framework of the achievement of the fundamental objectives referred to in Article 2 of the E.C. Treaty, including that of strengthening the Community's economic and social cohesion, referred to in Article 130a" However, in its submission to the Court of the First Instance in *Comité Central d'Entreprise de la Société Anonyme Vittel v. Commission*,[50] the Commission suggested that Recital 13 could not impose specific positive obligations requiring it, for example, to analyse the employment consequences in a particular undertaking of a notified concentration. The Commission argued further that, in order for their application to be admissible, the Perrier unions had to demonstrate that they had an interest consistent with "the essential purpose of [the Regulation], which is to maintain and develop effective competition in the Common Market." It was not, therefore, for the Commission to show that it had taken into account the fundamental objectives recognised in Article 2 of the Treaty but for an applicant to establish a *prima facie* case that the clearance of a concentration was liable significantly to prejudice those objectives. The Court dismissed the unions' application on the basis that any prejudice to Perrier workers was not attributable to the Commission's decision to permit the Nestlé/Perrier concentration given the protection provided by the Acquired Rights Directive (77/187) to employees on the transfer of a business. Nonetheless the Court appeared to suggest that the obligation to ensure that the appraisal of a concentration was conducted within the overall framework of Article 2 involved some positive obligation on the Commission's part.[51] The judgment has not, however, led the Commission to include any formal acknowledgement in its decisions that it has examined notified concentrations from the perspective of Article 2 of the Treaty and found them to be consistent with those objectives. This aspect of the judgment in Perrier also has to be considered in the light of the Court of Justice's reluctance in *Kali und Salz* to place any weight on a recital which is not reflected in the operative part of legislation in question.

5.9 CASE STUDY—*GUINNESS/GRAND METROPOLITAN*

A case study of one particular Article 8 decision will illustrate the application of the principles discussed above and the typical structure adopted for an Article 8 decision, which is the required culmination of a four month second stage investigation. In May 1997 Guinness and Grand Metropolitan (GrandMet) notified their proposal to merge to form GMG Brands (now known as Diageo[52]). Because of the overlaps in spirits between the two parties, a second stage examination by the

---

[50] Case T-12/93 [1995] E.C.R. II-1247. The case involved a challenge by trade unions in the Perrier group to the Commission's conditional clearance of the *Nestlé/Perrier* deal.
[51] See the judgment of the Court at points 38 to 40.
[52] Classical scholars and Greek speakers will know "Diageo" means "worldwide".

Commission was inevitable.[53] The Commission's decision, after rehearsing the basis upon which the Regulation applied, deals first, as is the customary format, with product and geographic market definition.

5.9.1 Product Markets

The parties offered an analysis based on a spectrum of market definitions: all spirits; "brown" and "white" spirits, individual spirits, namely, gin, whisky, brandy and so on and, finally further segmentation by origin, quality and price, distinguishing, for example, between Scotch whisky and other whiskies and between deluxe, premium and standard whiskies.

The Commission rejected the price surveys which the parties submitted in support of an "all spirits" product definition since the data was based on assumed price changes "much higher than those normally used by competition authorities as an aid to market definition, *i.e.* five to 10 per cent". It also rejected the parties' suggestion that the fact that many consumers drank different spirits on different occasions showed substitutability between different types of spirit. In the Commission's view those consumption patterns showed complementarity not substitutability, with different spirits being chosen for different occasions, for example, brandy as a digestif but gin as an aperitif.[54] The "all spirits" product definition was therefore dismissed, as was the "white" and "brown" spirit segmentation; the Commission's examination of production techniques showed that even on a supply-side analysis, there was insufficient scope to employ the same basic distilled grain spirit to produce a variety of white spirit types and no scope for that in relation to the "brown" spirits (whisky, brandy or dark rum), because of the distinctive characteristics of each drink which depended on differences in the distillation and maturation processes.[55] The Commission readily concluded that the appropriate product definition was by individual spirit with further segmentation, for example, between Scotch and other whiskies and gin and genever, depending on national preferences and different national market shares. The importance of brands, and customers' loyalty to particular brands, which were not found to be transferable between spirit types, was regarded as giving strong support for the narrow definition.

The Commission then went on to consider whether different "routes to market" constituted different markets within the same spirit category. Although the Commission has consistently distinguished, in relation to beer, the on-trade (premises licensed to sell alcohol) from the off-trade (supermarkets, wine shops and the like), it did not carry that distinction through into spirits, commenting:

> . . . in the present case the primary impact of the operation is in terms of supplies to wholesalers and large retailers, since small retailers, whether in

---

[53] The possibility of legally binding commitments in a stage one inquiry would now permit a similar case to be resolved formally within six weeks, but *Guinness/Grand Metropolitan* involved so many product and geographic markets that simply the complexity of the case would have made it difficult to resolve without a stage two investigation.

[54] Para. 10.

[55] Paras 11 and 12.

the on-trade or the off-trade, acquire their supplies from those sources rather than direct from the parties.''[56]

To use the vernacular, the conditions of competition were sufficiently homogeneous not to need to differentiate. The Commission did, however, accept that duty-free sales constituted a separate market in view of the different method of distribution and the characteristics of those buying duty free.

5.9.2 Geographic Markets

Turning to geographic market definition the Commission had little difficulty finding in favour of national markets (with the exception of duty free sales) given, in particular, different consumption patterns, the presence of unique national or regional (such as genever, ouzo, and korn), national distribution, retail price differences and the purely opportunistic and limited nature of parallel trade in spirits in the Community.

5.9.3 Dominance

In its assessment of possible dominance the Commission's decision deals first with general factors common across the Community: the size and resources of the combined group, particularly compared with its nearest rival, Allied Domecq; the extent of vertical integration into distribution, coupled with the spirit manufacturers' control of promotion and marketing through strong worldwide brands; the advantages of owning a portfolio of leading spirit brands; entry conditions; lack of growth in mature spirits markets; and buyer power. Many of these factors have already been considered and this case study will therefore examine only the Commission's key assessment of entry barriers.[57]

In relation to entry conditions, the Commission found that significant barriers arose not at the production level, despite a high level of concentration, but as a result of the distribution and marketing requirements, coupled with the ''portfolio effect''. The Commission drew attention to the fact that there were only two examples of recent new product or brand entry other than in certain niche areas,[58] and that vertical integration into distribution reinforced the barriers created by promotional expenses, which were ''sunk'' costs, *i.e.* irrecoverable once expended. It concluded that:

> ''Entrants will need to advertise and promote their brands heavily over a long period in order to overcome consumer resistance and the barrier presented by the reputation of the established players.''[59]

---

[56] Para. 21.
[57] Part C ''Assessment'', Section 2 ''Barriers to Entry'', paras 47 to 66.
[58] Bailey's Irish Cream (GrandMet) being the only example of product innovation in the previous 10 years and Famous Grouse (Scottish Whisky) the only new brand success over the same period.
[59] Para. 53.

That general assessment informed their approach to the specific effects of the merger on the national markets in Greece, Spain, Ireland, Belgium and Luxembourg.

5.9.3.1   Greece

The Commission concluded that parties' dominance in gin (80 to 90 per cent share), brandy (70 to 80 per cent) and rum (75 to 85 per cent) would be reinforced by the broad portfolio of brands Diageo would enjoy, accounting for some 40 per cent of overall spirits consumption in Greece, and that a position of dominance in whisky (45 to 55 per cent) would be created.

5.9.3.2   Spain

The risk of dominance in Spain was limited to Scotch whisky. The Commission rejected as insufficiently robust the parties' evidence aimed at showing that Scotch whisky was not a separate product market in Spain from Spanish whisky and preferred empirical data highlighting the differences in product image, sales growth and price. The only examples of new entry were two brands which had under 10 per cent of the Scotch whisky market in Spain.[60]

5.9.3.3   Ireland

Ireland too exhibited distinct national characteristics: Irish and Scotch whiskies were held to constitute different product markets.[61] Taste, consumption patterns and prices differed between them with, most significantly, Irish whiskey selling at a premium to Scotch even though all Scotch was imported. Distribution structures also differed, with distribution joint ventures between competitors being a feature of the Irish market. Diageo would either own or be able to influence, through significant shareholdings, all but one of the major distributors. The Commission concluded that the merger would create a duopoly in distribution and thus enhance existing dominant positions in Scotch whisky and brandy/cognac.[62]

5.9.3.4   Belgium/Luxembourg

The Commission distinguished between "London" gin and genever, particularly in terms of consumption patterns and prices and, in whisky and gin, found that "own-label" brands, though holding not insignificant market shares, were not strong enough to restrain the market power Diageo would have. It found

---

[60] Passport, distributed and promoted by Seagram, and Cutty Sark, which entered the market through independent distributorship.
[61] The Commission referred to the decision of the Irish Competition Authority in *Irish Distilleries/Cooley Distillery* of February 1994 which also came to this conclusion.
[62] See Table 11, para. 149 for detailed market share figures.

that the merger would create dominant positions in whisky[63] (40 to 50 per cent), gin (50 to 60 per cent) and vodka (60 to 70 per cent). The high share in vodka stemmed from the aggregation of GrandMet's brand leader, Smirnoff, with two third party brands, one of which was a leading brand, Wyborowa, over which Guinness had distribution rights in Belgium.

5.9.4 **Remedies**

In the light of the Commission's assessment the parties offered a number of undertakings to be implemented within 15 months of clearance: to dispose of the Dewar and Ainslie brands in Europe[64]; to terminate the distribution arrangements for "Wyborowa" in Belgium and Luxembourg and to appoint an independent distributor for Gilbey's gin in Belgium; to dispose of distribution interests in Ireland in order to safeguard a competitive structure at the distribution level; and, in Greece, to withdraw from its distribution agreement for Bacardi rum. The Commission regarded these commitments as sufficient to justify a clearance but a majority of the Advisory Committee disagreed.[65] Its disagreement is not surprising: the focus on national markets tended to mask the international position of Diageo and its accumulated strength across a large number of markets, in Europe and beyond. This position was not addressed by any of the exclusively "national" remedies. The Dewar's brand, the disposal of which did have a wider impact, was an established brand but less important than others which Diageo retained. The emphasis which the Commission placed on portfolio power was also not reflected in the remedies, which, with the exception of the Dewar's disposal, were isolated to particular national markets in the E.U. On the other hand, in simplistic market share terms, the undertakings were designed to reduce the combined shares to around the 40 per cent level in the specific markets where concerns lay. The Commission may have been concerned that not to have accepted the undertakings would have exposed it to a significant risk of legal challenge at a time when its own jurisprudence under the Regulation was still being developed.

---

[63] Since the effects were not materially different the Commission did not draw a product market distinction between Scotch whisky and other whiskies.
[64] See generally para. 183.
[65] See its Opinion of September 30, 1997 published in [1998] O.J. C329.

6   Ancillary Restraints

6.1   BACKGROUND

Where one undertaking acquires the business of another, the vendor's under-taking is invariably required to accept an obligation not to compete with the business it has sold, so guaranteeing the goodwill for which the acquirer may have paid dearly. Such covenants commonly led to notifications under Article 85 (now Article 81) in order to ensure their enforceability even though they were given in the context of a business disposal which in itself would not have fallen within Article 81. In order to protect the one-stop shop principle the solution adopted for such situations on the introduction of E.C. merger control was to provide that non-competition clauses and other ancillary restraints should benefit from a clearance of the concentration of which they form an integral part and should not need to be notified separately under Regulation 17. Recital 25 of the Regulation provides that the Regulation should still apply where the undertakings concerned accept restrictions directly related and necessary to the implementation of the concentration. Both Article 6(1) and Article 8(2) require decisions of compatibility to cover such restrictions. But as will be seen, the scope of Recital 25 and Articles 6(1) and 8(2) is not, as the Commission has made clear in its Notice regarding restrictions ancillary to concentrations[1] and as decided cases have demonstrated, as extensive as some would have hoped. Ancillary restrictions have only been dealt with under the Regulation to the extent that they raise no problems under Articles 81 and 82, *i.e.* they would get a negative clearance if formally submitted under the other regime. This Chapter examines the way in which the Commission has interpreted and applied its power to clear restrictions ancillary to a concentra-tion notified under the Regulation. As will be seen, in practice the Commission has relied heavily on the Notice,[2] a factor which parties should consider when constructing non-compete clauses and other ancillary restraints. The Notice is, however, currently being revised to update and reflect the Commission's cur-rent practice and procedure in the field. The analysis and description of the treatment of ancillary restraints given below take account of the proposed changes to the Notice.

---

[1] [1990] O.J. C203/5. The 1989 Notice is set out in Appendix 3 to the 2nd edition of this book. The Commission's proposal to revise the Notice is set out in Appendix 3 to this edition.

[2] It has been a common feature of decisions to clear ancillary restraints by reference to the Notice. See, *e.g. Philips/Lucent Technologies.*

6.2 THE APPROACH UNDER ARTICLE 81

In the context of Article 81, the Court of Justice and the Commission have looked at ancillary restraints in a number of situations, in particular sale of businesses, franchise agreements and joint ventures. In *Reuter/BASF*[3] the Commission struck down a widely drawn eight year non-competition clause which had the effect of eliminating a potential competitor, but recognised the possibility that a restriction on commercial activities for a reasonable duration might be compatible with Article 81. As the Court indicated in *Remia* (an appeal against the Commission's decision in *Nutricia*[4] condemning certain non-competition clauses) such clauses have to be examined against the background that without them, where vendor and acquirer remain competitors after the transfer, the transfer could not have the intended effect if the vendor remains free to win back his former customers after the transfer. The Court recognised the beneficial effect which such clauses may have as regards increasing the number of undertakings in the market. But the Court said[5]:

"Nevertheless, in order to have that beneficial effect on competition, such clauses must be necessary in the transfer of the undertaking concerned and their duration and scope must be strictly limited to that purpose."

As will be seen, the Regulation follows the Court and adopts the two conditions to define, in Articles 6(1) and 8(2), the extent to which clearance decisions under the Regulation cover ancillary restraints.

The Commission has acted in relation to non-competition clauses in a number of other (published) instances.[6] In relation to franchise agreements the Court recognised, in *Pronuptia*,[7] that restrictions which are necessary to safeguard know-how and assistance by the franchisor or to maintain the identity and reputation of the network bearing the common name or symbol do not constitute restrictions on competition for the purposes of Article 81(1). Such restrictions are necessary to give effect to a legitimate purpose.[8] In *Elopak/ Metal Box-Odin*,[9] the Commission (significantly because the decision came shortly before the Regulation entered into force) granted negative clearance to a joint venture, recognising that a number of restrictive provisions were necessary to ensure the starting up and the proper functioning of the joint venture and hence did not fall within the scope of Article 81(1) when in other contexts they might restrict competition. The Commission's Notice regarding restrictions ancillary to concentrations built on these foundations.

---

[3] [1976] O.J. L254/40; [1976] 2 C.M.L.R. D44.
[4] [1983] O.J. L376/22; [1984] 2 C.M.L.R. 165.
[5] Case 42/84 *Remia BV and others v. Commission* [1985] E.C.R. 2545; [1987] 1 C.M.L.R. 1, point 20.
[6] *Sedame/Precilec*, Eleventh Report on Competition, para. 95; *Tyler/Linde, ibid.*, para. 96; *Allied Products Corp/Vernon Industrial Group* [1989] 9 E.C. Bull. 25; and *Quantel International-Continuum/Quantel SA* [1992] O.J. L235/9.
[7] Case 161/84 *Pronuptia de Paris GmbH v. Pronuptia de Paris Irmgard Schillgallis* [1986] E.C.R. 353; [1986] 1 C.M.L.R. 414, points 16 and 17.
[8] See also the approach of the Court of Justice in Case C-250/92 *Gøttrüp-Klim v. Dansk Landbrugs Grovvareselskab Amba* [1994] E.C.R. I-5641, para. 35.
[9] [1990] O.J. L209/15.

6.3 RESTRICTIONS

The Regulation does not use the term "ancillary restraint" but the lengthier phrase "restrictions directly related and necessary to the implementation of the concentration". The restrictions referred to are, as the Notice states, those agreed between the parties to the concentration which limit their own freedom of action in the market. Compliance, for example, with confidentiality and other allegations of U.S. defence policy is not considered to involve restrictions.[10] In *Cable & Wireless/Schlumberger* the Commission took the view that an obligation for the joint venture to develop joint marketing agreements with the parties did not comprise a restriction. The Commission recognised that it was possible that any agreement which resulted would contain restrictions but any such restrictions were not covered by the decision under the Regulation. "Ancillary restraints" do not, however, include restrictions "to the detriment of third parties". As most restrictions on a party's conduct or on competition may impinge upon the freedom of action of others it is at first sight unclear what this phrase means and how limiting it may be. By way of explanation the Notice adds that where restrictions have restrictive effects on third parties which are separable from the concentration then they will have to be dealt with under Articles 81 and 82. One example given in the Notice is a non-competition clause which purports to restrict the scope for resellers or users to import or export. Finally, it should be noted that the Commission will not deal with a provision which has not been finalised.[11] In *BT/ESB*, for example, it declined to consider certain "draft agreements". Nor will the Commission's decision cover any restriction for which the notifying parties have not asked for an assessment and therefore not justified as being directly related and necessary.[12]

6.3.1 Directly Related

It is not sufficient that the restrictions arise at the same time as the concentration. There must be a direct link with the operation. So intra-group arrangements, including non-compete clauses, following the merger will not be assessed under the Regulation.[13] In *Kodak/Imation* a settlement agreement under which the parties to the takeover agreed to settle some disputes relating to the ownership of IP rights was described as "completely unrelated to the transaction at stake" and was therefore not dealt with. The restrictions must be related to but need not, however, be elements constituting, the concentration.[14] In the terms of the Notice the restrictions must be "subordinate in

---

[10] *Matra BAE/Dynamics/DASA/LFF.*
[11] *e.g. UPM-Kymmene/April.* In *ENEL/FT/DT* the Commission commented that the parties had not even included a draft agreement in the notification. See also *Nordic Capital/Mölnlycke Clinical/Kolmi*, where the Commission refused to consider as an ancillary restraint an exclusive distribution agreement which had not yet been agreed.
[12] *Recticel/Greiner.*
[13] *Unichem/Alliance Sante.*
[14] This does not mean that the Commission has not been prepared to accept a wide variety of temporary restrictions designed to give effect to the full implementation of the concentration. See, *e.g. Swiss Bank Corporation/S.G. Warburg.*

importance to the main objects of the concentration''. The Commission has distinguished contractual arrangements such as those establishing economic unity between previously independent parties and provisions organising joint control by two undertakings of another. Restrictions on a parent of a joint venture may be aimed at securing for the success of the joint venture a sufficient duration to allow the necessary investment and long-term planning and therefore considered an integral part of its concentration.[15] The position of consortium bids (joint acquisitions) receives special consideration in the Notice (described at paragraph 6.10, below).

6.3.2 Necessary to the Implementation of the Concentration

Basically the test is whether the concentration would proceed without the restrictions in question. This has been widely construed to include, for example, a one-year non-competition clause to enable the share purchase agreement underlying the concentration to be negotiated.[16] The Notice indicates that the Commission will look to see whether the concentration could only be implemented *inter alia* under more uncertain conditions, at substantially higher cost, over an appreciably longer period or with considerably less probability of success. The Commission adopted these words in *Thomson CSF/ Deutsche Aerospace* when finding that obligations giving the parent companies preferential rights to supply the joint venture and that conditions on the joint venture being sourced by existing suppliers created restrictions on competition but were not necessary to the implementation of the concentration.[17] Restrictions will be judged, the Notice says, on an objective basis. The Commission will not simply accept the parties' say so. But it has said that agreements which aim at protecting the value transferred, at maintaining the continuity of supply after the break-up of a former economic entity, or which enable the start-up of a new entity will usually meet the criteria underlying ''necessity''. In practice, however, the Commission will look especially critically at supply obligations[18] and at any exclusive relationships created between the parties.[19]

6.4 GENERAL PRINCIPLES OF EVALUATION

The Commission will not accept restrictions on conduct without question merely because they are contained in the concentration arrangements. As the Notice acknowledges, the Commission accepts that restrictions on conduct may be a necessary constituent part of the arrangements or may practically be necessary to give it effect. Restrictions may benefit the vendor and/or buyer. As a general rule the Commission is more kindly disposed to restrictions bene-

---

[15] *Hochtief/Aer Rianta/Dusseldorf Airport.*
[16] *Ameritech/Tele Danmark.*
[17] See also *Marconi/Finmeccanica*; *Cable & Wireless/Schlumberger*; *Securicor Datatrak*; and *Dow/Buna*, for other examples of restrictions which were not considered strictly necessary for the implementation of the concentration.
[18] *RTL/Veronica/Endemol* [1996] O.J. L134/32, para. 114.
[19] *BT/ESB.*

fiting the buyer, who needs to be assured that it will be able to run the acquired business and recoup its costs. Secondly, the principle of proportionality will also be applied. Where alternatives are available to the parties, the one which is objectively the least restrictive of competition must be chosen. For example, when considering the scope of a non-competition clause (duration, subject-matter, geographical field of application) the Commission will consider whether the clause exceeds that which the implementation of the concentration reasonably requires. Finally, the time factor relating to the execution and implementation of concentrations is particularly relevant. Mergers may be carried out in stages. The Commission likes the view that Articles 81 and 82 apply in relation to restrictions applicable before the establishment of control within the meaning of Article 3 of the Regulation. Further, the procedures under Articles 81 and 82, and not the Regulation, will be applicable as regards the evaluation and assessment of restrictions relating to the implementation of the concentration.

6.5   NON-COMPETITION CLAUSES

As might be expected, non-competition clauses, in various forms, constitute the largest class in number of clauses which the Commission has had to consider as ancillary restraints. They are frequently an important part of the transaction,[20] their purpose being to guarantee to the acquirer *the full value of the assets transferred*. This is expressly stated in the Notice and has often been reiterated in the text of the Commission's decisions themselves.[21] In this context assets are not limited to physical assets (land, buildings, stock in trade, etc.) but also, and importantly, include intangible assets such as goodwill and know-how. Where a non-competition clause does not have the aim of guaranteeing the transfer of the full value of the assets but, for example, the protection of a third party,[22] it will not be treated as directly related and necessary for the implementation of the concentration. It will fall to be assessed under Article 81. Similarly, obligations not to initiate, solicit or encourage other proposals for mergers or business combinations *before* the establishment of control within the meaning of Article 3 of the Regulation will not be accepted as necessary to facilitate the proposed concentration.[23]

The clause will be judged as to the products and services concerned, its duration and geographical scope. As already mentioned, the test is essentially what is reasonably necessary to implement the concentration. It is helpful to keep clauses within the boundaries of the Notice.[24] Restrictions on the vendor will generally be acceptable if they do not exceed three years where the transfer includes goodwill (two years in the case of a transfer of goodwill only)

---

[20] Indeed they may be significant in the determination whether a joint venture is concentrative or co-operative. See, *e.g. Eureko*, *Elf/Enterprise*, noted in Modrall, "Ancillary Restrictions in the Commission's Decisions under the Merger Regulation: Non-Competition Clauses" [1995] 1 E.C.L.R. 40. The distinction, though no longer significant for notification purposes, remains important for the assessment criteria to be applied.

[21] *e.g. Chrysler/Distributors (Benelux and Germany)*.

[22] See, *e.g. Nordic Capital/Transpool*.

[23] *American Home Products/Monsanto*.

[24] *Bayerische Vereinsbank/FGH Bank*.

and are limited in scope to the area where the vendor has established the products and services before the transfer and to the products and services which form the economic activity of the undertaking concerned. Because of the brevity with which non-competition clauses are frequently described and justified in the Commission's decisions, it is not always possible to identify the extent of the scope of clauses permitted by the Commission. Frequently the duration of the clause is omitted, though a footnote may indicate that it does not exceed a certain period (such as five years).[25] In some cases there is the broadest description that the clause applies to the products concerned by the operation and in the countries in which the vendor currently sells the products.[26] Only occasionally will the Commission go into much detail. In, for example, *CGP/GEC Alsthom/KPR/Kone Corporation* the Commission permitted a five-year clause restraining competition with the joint venture's activities in France. The joint venture concerned the design, manufacture, sale and repair of cranes, in which the Commission had found there to be an essentially national market. The non-competition clause was therefore appropriately limited to activities in the Member State, France, in which the joint venture was proposed to be active.[27] It seems to be relatively rare, however, for the Commission itself to cut back the geographical scope of a non-competition clause, though in *Tesco/Catteau* an unlimited clause was reduced to specified regions in France and Belgium where the vendor's business had been active. Restrictions operating wholly outside the EEA have been considered to be outside the competence of the Commission.[28]

Whilst the Notice gives guidance on what might or might not be reasonably necessary to implement the concentration and there are, as indicated, many examples in the decisions to date, a non-competition clause always has to be considered in the light of the particular circumstances of the case. This said, some guidance can be given. It is clear, for example, that the Commission widely construes the notion of what amounts to a non-competition clause and applies similar principles to evaluate restrictions having like effect. It will cover the classic forms of restriction: not to carry on any competing business or to be directly or indirectly interested in any competing business[29]; not to solicit former employees[30]; not to solicit former customers.[31] A wide variety of variations are acceptable as "non-competition clauses", including obligations not to acquire any competing business without first offering the joint venture the opportunity to do so,[32] and obligations, perhaps expressed in positive terms, to the effect that all activities in the relevant product or services are to be undertaken by the joint venture.[33] A vendor may be restricted from competing

---

[25] *e.g. Matra Marconi Space/British Aerospace Space Systems.*
[26] *e.g. Philips/Hewlett Packard.*
[27] For another case where there was extensive discussion, see *Birmingham International Airport.*
[28] *BT/Tele DK/SBB/Migros/UBS.*
[29] *e.g. Dow Jones/NBC—CNBC Europe, DHL/Deutsche Post.*
[30] It is recognised that such clauses may protect know-how and client base. See, *e.g. Paribas Belgique/ Paribas Nederland.* In some cases the clause has been limited to certain key or senior employees: *e.g. Volkswagen AG/VAG (UK); Thomson/Fritidsresor.*
[31] *e.g. AGF/La Union y el Fenix; UAP/Provincial.*
[32] *Thomson/Pilkington.* Or extend the range of retained issues in the geographical areas where they are presently active: *Sara Lee/BP Food Division.*
[33] *e.g. Thomson CSF/Deutsche Aerospace; Harrisons & Crosfield/AKZO.*

directly or indirectly with the undertaking concerned. But a vendor may not be restricted, for example, from holding any shares in a competing undertaking. A vendor may hold or acquire shares for investment purposes only, where the vendor does not exercise, directly or indirectly, any management functions in the company and does not exercise any material influence in its affairs.[34] As regards the time of commencement of non-competition obligations, the Commission will accept, as ancillary restraints, restraints placed on the vendor's activities between the agreement and completion of the merger operation.[35]

Generally as regards duration, the 1989 Notice stated that a period of five years might be recognised as appropriate when the transfer of the undertaking includes goodwill and know-how.[36] But in practice even a five year period was not accepted where the sale mainly included elements of goodwill and brand loyalty was not very important in terms of customer preferences for the products concerned.[37] If a party already has substantial know-how in the relevant market, the five year period may also be reduced.[38] As mentioned, the Commission now proposes to set three years as the norm, and two years when only goodwill is concerned. Experience has shown that the Commission has applied its guidance fairly strictly and, except in the case of joint ventures (see below), it would be rare, if ever, for the Commission to accept clauses going beyond those periods[39] and there are clearly reported examples where the Commission has reduced periods to conform with the terms of the earlier Notice.[40] Indeed the burden is on the parties to justify the need for the length of term chosen, even if it coincides with the Notice.[41]

The Commission will also be concerned with which parties are accepting the restriction. Generally only restrictions accepted by the vendor will be acceptable. It should be noted however that the Notice says that any restrictions on the vendor's subsidiaries and commercial agents are potentially acceptable as ancillary. There have also been a number of cases where the Commission has accepted restrictions imposed on certain shareholders of the vendor.[42] The Commission will therefore look beyond the corporate veil in the case of disposals of family or closely controlled companies. Restrictions on the acquirer and its affiliates will have to be judged separately under Articles 81 and 82.[43] Such restrictions cannot, in the Commission's view, be considered ancillary to the notified operation where they protect the vendor and persons other than the purchaser.[44]

A large number of the Commission's decisions on mergers involve joint ventures and therefore not surprisingly there is substantial experience on non-

---

[34] *KNP BT/Bunzl/Wilhelm Seiler; Kingfisher/Grosslabor.*
[35] *UAP/Provincial.* See also *Thomson CSF/Deutsche Aerospace.*
[36] See, *e.g. Kodak/Imation,* where the term was reduced from seven to five years.
[37] *DENSO/Magneti Marelli.*
[38] *Swiss Life/Lloyd Continental* where only two years was allowed.
[39] The Notice contemplates longer time periods being acceptable, *e.g. where customer loyalty may persist for longer than two years or where the life cycle of the products concerned is longer than five years.* See, *e.g. GRE/PPP,* private medical insurance products having a long life cycle and tendency of customers to remain loyal.
[40] *e.g. General Re/Kölnische Re; Havas/Bertelsmann/Doyma.*
[41] See, *e.g. Cargill/Continental Grain.*
[42] See, *e.g. Tesco/Catteau; GE/CIGI; Telia/Ericsson.*
[43] For the position under Art. 81 see the Commission's decision in the *Quantel* case (n. 6, above), para. 42.
[44] *Alcoa/Inespal.*

competition clauses in this context. By contrast to the normal three year limit
in simple sale/acquisition of business cases, clauses of longer duration
restricting the parents appear acceptable for joint ventures provided they retain
a controlling interest.[45] A non-compete obligation will not be regarded as ancillary in so far as it binds the party concerned after the termination of the
agreement or after it has sold its share in the joint venture.[46] The Commission
seems normally[47] prepared to accept clauses on the parent not to compete with
the joint venture for the length of the term of the joint venture and indeed
sometimes for one or more years thereafter. The extension beyond the term of
the joint venture must, however, relate to the transaction the subject of the
concentration and not some other (future) operation.[48] Restrictions on the joint
venture itself may be less favourably treated, especially if unrestricted in duration.[49]

As the Commission has expressly indicated on many occasions, non-
competition clauses imposed on the parents are aimed at expressing *the reality
of the lasting withdrawal of the parents* from the business in question and as
such they are an integral part of the concentration.[50] Parents may undertake to
procure that none of their respective group companies will compete with the
joint venture.[51] The Commission does not appear, however, necessarily to
require both parents to take the same restraint on their future activity.[52] As
already mentioned the Commission has taken a broad view of what may constitute a non-competition clause. This is especially true in joint venture cases.
For example, in *Kirch/Richemont/Multichoice/Telepiù* it accepted a restriction
on the parent not to be interested in specific services without first offering the
joint venture the opportunity to exploit them.

Finally, it is to be noted that the Commission has accepted a wide range of
pre-closing/anti-dilution obligations intended to preserve the value of the assets
for the period prior to completion. They include obligations to carry on the business in the ordinary course and not to enter into any material line of business or
commit any capital expenditure without the consent of the other party.[53] In *BAT/
Rothmans* the Commission accepted pre-closing undertakings covering changes
to the share capital and constitutional documents, declarations of dividends,
change to the business, shareholder contracts and changes to employees. To the
extent that they could act as restrictions on competition, they were considered to
be directly related and necessary to the completion of the operation. The Commission has also accepted a restriction not to initiate or solicit in any way any
third party offer for 20 per cent or more of the business being acquired or to

---

[45] See, *e.g. BT/ESB* and *Maersk Air/LFV*. But non-compete obligations "for so long as the parent remains
a shareholder" may not be considered necessary and directly related to the concentration. A controlling
stake must be retained—*Lufthansa/Menzies/Sigma at Manchester*.

[46] *ENEL/FT/DT*.

[47] There are exceptions. See *Kali und Salz/MdK/Treuhand* where the Commission reduced the proposed 10
year term to five years.

[48] *e.g. Nortel/Norwell; GE Capital/Sea Containers*.

[49] *Mederic/Urrpimmec/CRI/Munich Re.*

[50] *e.g. Westdeutsche Landesbank/Carlson/Thomas Cook; Mannesmann/Olivetti/Infostrada*; and *Volvo Aero/
ABB/Turbogen*.

[51] *e.g. Cable & Wireless/VEBA.*

[52] *e.g. Thomson/Pilkington; Conagra/Idea; British Airways/TAT.*

[53] See, *e.g. American Home Products/Monsanto; BAT/Zurich; DuPont/ICI.*

engage in or continue negotiations relating thereto unless a more favourable proposal than the present transaction would be made.[54]

6.6 LICENCES OF INTELLECTUAL PROPERTY AND KNOW-HOW

Where the vendor remains the owner of intellectual property rights or know-how it may, in order for the acquirer to exploit the assets transferred, be necessary for the vendor to grant licences. Similarly, in the case of a joint venture, technology may be transferred from the parent undertakings to the joint venture company by way of licences. In some cases the grant of exclusive IP licences may be part of the operation and considered as part of the business transferred and thus not ancillary to it.[55] The Commission has accepted that licences (possibly irrevocable, worldwide, exclusive and royalty free) may be treated as substitutes to an outright transfer of assets.[56] This is not always the case and the Notice accepts the need for simple or exclusive licences of patents, know-how, etc., in order to enable the assets transferred to be exploited. But field of use restrictions must correspond to the activities transferred and territorial limitations on manufacture must reflect the territory of the activities transferred. Restrictions going further, particularly where they protect the licensor, may not be considered necessary for the implementation of the concentration. Again, compliance with the Notice (here paragraph III.B) is frequently noted in Commission decisions.[57]

A variety of means of enabling a joint venture company to take advantage of existing intellectual property rights and know-how and to develop or exploit its own has been accepted by the Commission. In some cases, the grant of exclusive non-revocable licences to the joint venture[58] for all property rights needed for exploitation of the business or the joint venture for the duration of the agreement has been used. In others more complex arrangements have been considered necessary, for example involving the assignment of rights to the joint venture coupled with irrevocable, exclusive, royalty-free licences back to the assigning parties for use outside the field of activities to be developed by the joint venture and the grant of irrevocable exclusive royalty-free licences by the parents to the joint venture where the rights relate primarily to areas outside the field of activity of the joint venture.[59] The Commission will look carefully to see that the assignment, licences, etc., are directly related and necessary to the successful transfer and/or division of the business in question and do not, for example, go beyond the joint venture's requirements.[60] The Commission generally considers licence agreements necessary to the extent that they correspond to the activities transferred to the joint venture.[61] It

---

[54] *Hercules/Betzdearborn.*
[55] See, *e.g. DuPont/ICI.*
[56] *Wacker/Air Products.*
[57] *e.g. LGV/BTR, Novartis/Maïsadour.*
[58] See, *e.g. Elf Atochem/Rohm and Haas.*
[59] *AKZO Nobel/Monsanto.* Similarly, *Thomson/Pilkington.*
[60] See, *e.g. CLT/Disney/Super RTL.*
[61] *Recticel/Greiner.*

appears prepared to accept provisions which are reasonably necessary to protect the commercial interests of the licensor, including such provision for the duration, exclusivity (if any) and the territorial scope of the licence and competition with the licensor and third parties in the use of the intellectual property.[62] But restrictions on parties to whom the joint venture may supply products made under the licence are not acceptable.[63] Field of use restrictions are permitted where necessary to transfer the full value of the relevant business of the joint venture without negatively affecting the independent operation of the business activities retained by the parent.[64] But provisions whereby parents make property rights available to each other may not be treated as ancillary restrictions and may therefore require separate examination under Article 81. Licence agreements between parents are not considered to be directly related and necessary to the implementation of the joint venture. Nor, generally, are licences from the joint venture to a parent. When the joint venture develops, discovers or acquires proprietary rights over a process or product which has applications in fields in which a parent is or may wish to become active, the Commission will look to see whether licences should be on reasonable commercial terms and a non-exclusive basis.[65]

6.7   TRADEMARKS, BUSINESS NAMES, LOGOS, ETC.

The Commission's Notice purports to apply to trademarks, trade and business names and similar rights the same principles as are applied to licences, etc., of other industrial and commercial property rights. Where the trademark may identify the business and its products it may constitute part of the goodwill being transferred and be an inherent part of the transaction and therefore not an ancillary restraint.[66] There have been situations where the vendor remains owner and wishes to continue to use the marks, etc., for retained activities whilst the purchaser needs the right to market the products relating to the undertaking or assets acquired. The Commission has accepted that in such cases concomitant restrictions may be necessary to avoid confusion. Its decisions also recognise that they protect the value of the business bought and retained.[67] Thus in *Dalgety/The Quaker Oats Company*, where Dalgety bought Quaker's European pet food business, the Commission considered as restrictions ancillary to the concentration restrictions on Dalgety using certain Quaker names in the acquired business and on Quaker not using names of the acquired business in an area which included the EEA.[68] In other cases time limited restrictions on the vendor have been accepted by the Commission.[69]

---

[62] See, *e.g. Harrisons & Crosfield/AKZO.*
[63] *Recticel/Greiner.*
[64] *Matra Marconi Space/British Aerospace Space Systems.*
[65] As in, *e.g. AKZO/Nobel/Monsanto.*
[66] *Hagemeyer/ABB Asea Skandia.*
[67] *e.g. Carrier Corporation/Toshiba.*
[68] Similar sorts of arrangements were accepted in *Grand Metropolitan/Cinzano*; *BD/CIGI*; and *Shell UK/ Gulf Oil (Great Britain).* In *Direct Line/Bankinter* the Commission accepted restrictions on one parent seeking to register trademarks, etc., which would be the same or similar to those licensed to the joint venture.
[69] See, *e.g. Fiat Geotech/Ford New Holland; Allied Lyons/HWE-Pedro Domecq; UAP/Vinci.*

The Commission will be particularly careful to avoid parties possibly monopolising words which only form part of a company name and are commonly used in the industry. Thus in two insurance mergers, it has refused to accept indefinite restrictions on the use of the words "Consolidated" and "Provincial" and substituted terms of five years.[70] It should also be noted that where names and marks are transferred the Commission will not accept restrictions by the vendor on the use of such names and marks in so far as they are property rights protected by specific legislation.[71] The Commission does not apparently favour parties bolstering their statutory rights by means of contractual provisions.

Where parties have set up a joint venture, and marks and names are licensed to enable the joint venture company to exploit the business transferred, the Commission has accepted that such licences, even exclusive and indefinite (*i.e.* for the duration of the joint venture agreement), are necessary and an integral part of the operation.[72] In such cases licences may serve as a substitute for the transfer of property rights and it can be argued that the licence arrangements should in such cases be regarded as constitutive parts of the concentration and not ancillary restrictions. Where the parent companies also agree not to use the marks, that may be evidence of their permanent withdrawal from the markets of the joint venture.[73] The Commission will, however, look critically at the length of time for which the restriction operates in order to assess whether it is practical and likely that the parent will re-enter the market.

6.8 RESTRICTIONS ON THE DISCLOSURE AND USE OF CONFIDENTIAL INFORMATION

The Commission has accepted that it may be necessary for restrictions on the disclosure and use of confidential business information to be placed on the vendor in order to give the purchaser sufficient time to take over fully the value of the companies or assets purchased and gain the loyalty of existing customers.[74] A distinction has to be drawn between, on the one hand, confidential information such as customer details, price and quantity information and, on the other, technical know-how such as manufacturing processes, product development and applications. Whilst in the latter case the Commission has been prepared to accept restrictions of indefinite duration,[75] when the know-how has been transferred as part of the assets the Commission has been reluctant to accept indefinite restrictions affecting other confidential information.[76] The danger is that an indefinite restriction might unreasonably impede the possible future market re-entry of the vendor at a later date. In some cases there has been an express concern that such restrictions might be used to

---

[70] *GE/CIGI*; *UAP/Provincial*. Contrast *Employers Reinsurance Corporation/Aachener*.
[71] *Kingfisher/Wegert/Promarkt*; *Kingfisher/Grosslabor*.
[72] See, *e.g. BBL/American Express*.
[73] *Texaco/Chevron*.
[74] An early statement of this can be found in *Inchcape/IEP*.
[75] *e.g. Singapore Airlines/Rolls-Royce*.
[76] See, *e.g. ICI/Williams*. Restrictions on use of information are more readily acceptable in the context of intellectual property licences: see *American Cyanamid/Shell*.

extend in effect a non-competition clause. It would appear that whilst in appropriate circumstances and given good objective reasons the Commission might accept a restriction of indefinite term, the Commission is normally looking for restrictions to last less than five years.[77] In *Inchcape/IEP*, for example, it imposed three years in place of an indefinite term. Finally it should be noted that restrictions on disclosure and use of information placed on the purchaser may also be acceptable to the Commission where, for example, an exchange of information with concomitant restrictions is necessary for the operation to take effect[78] or the purchaser has, in the course of negotiations, obtained confidential information on businesses and assets of the vendor not being taken over or acquired.[79]

6.9   PURCHASE AND SUPPLY OBLIGATIONS

The Notice (paragraph III.C) acknowledges that in order to make possible the break up of an economic unit or a partial transfer, it is frequently necessary to maintain, for a transitional period, links between vendor and acquirer similar to those that existed within the vendor's economic unit. The Commission's practice is to regard supply agreements as legitimate ancillary restraints where they are necessary to ensure the continuity of supply of products for the activities retained or taken over for a transitional period following the acquisition.[80] The Commission will accept restrictions necessary to guarantee a smooth transition from a relationship of dependency to one of autonomy in the market. It remains for the parties to justify the arrangements as being directly related and necessary to the concentration. It may not be sufficient to say that the arrangements are needed to avoid disruption to the businesses transferred and retained if they cannot be bought within the scope of the concentration operation.[81] The parties must be able to show convincingly that the agreement is objectively necessary to protect the party concerned from an immediate disruption of its procurement of the product or services in question. The fact that it is non-exclusive will not be sufficient on its own.[82] Finally, it should be noted that a decision under the Regulation can only encompass obligations accepted in the notified documents. Where the notified documents do not include the supply agreements themselves (because, for example, they have yet to be concluded), the Commission may accept that (usually positive) obligations to provide necessary goods/services, etc., grant licences of trademarks, etc., may not in the circumstances have any impact on competition while at the same time saying that the (future) agreements are not themselves covered by the decision.[83] A distinction may thus be made between obligations accepted in

---

[77] *e.g. Sappi/DLJMB/UBS/Warren.*
[78] *Dalgety/The Quaker Oats Company.*
[79] *Matra Marconi Space/Satcomms.*
[80] *Eastman Kodak/Sun Chemical.*
[81] See *Terra Industries/ICI.*
[82] *CVC/WMO/Wavin.*
[83] See, *e.g. VIAG/Orange UK; Telia/Sonera/Motorola/UAB Omnitel.* This is essentially an application of the practice and principles described at the end of para. 6.3, above.

the notified documents and the supply agreements (and their restrictive effects) themselves.

In practice the Commission has accepted, as ancillary restraints, a wide variety of purchase and supply agreements, sometimes exclusive, concerning materials at various stages of production,[84] spare parts[85] and, quite frequently, related services.[86] Access to premises may also be relevant.[87] An important factor is the transitional nature of any such arrangements. Interim arrangements (from closing date to a year) appear to be readily acceptable. Even beyond that, it is normally accepted that the period can extend up to five years.[88] The Commission will look to see that the scope and duration of the arrangement in question is consistent with the principle of proportionality. Exclusivity, for example, will require special justification.[89] The Commission will consider the effect of the supply agreement on the needs (for the product) of third parties. This factor is relevant not just for the time period but also the quantities to be supplied under the agreement. Only very exceptionally therefore will a term over five years be accepted.[90] Most cases have involved a supply agreement between the vendor and purchaser involving the continuance of supplies from the vendor or a part of its group. However, in *CCIE/GTE*, where CCIE was buying the lamps business of GTE, the Commission recognised as ancillary restraints certain agreements reached between CCI and Siemens whereby the latter provided financial assistance, by way of loans, to enable the purchases and the supply of lighting materials.

Similarly in the case of joint ventures, a wide variety of purchase and supply agreements between the parent undertakings and the joint venture company have been acceptable. It will be for the parties to justify why it is objectively necessary, for example, for the joint venture to obtain its supplies from the parents in order to become a viable commercial entity.[91] The Commission will examine critically the nature and length in time of the agreement, having regard to the time lag in the joint venture's findings and creating other sources of supply. Long[92] or indefinite[93] periods are generally unacceptable and terms of less than five years appear to be the norm.[94] The Commission will look critically at any provisions extending beyond the start-up phase.[95] Whilst the joint venture must be enabled to establish its autonomy, any period of dependency must be limited, although on occasion the Commission has accepted fixed term constraints (for example three years) which may be renewed on

---

[84] See, *e.g. Valinox/Timet*; *BASF/Shell II*.

[85] *Digital/Philips*.

[86] *e.g. GE/Bayer* (heat, electricity and water); *UPM-Kymmene/Finnpap* (customer data support); *BASF/Shell II* (R+D). "Outsourcing" is common in some service industries, such as broadcasting. See *Dow Jones*; *NBC—CNBC Europe*.

[87] *Maersk Air/LFV Holdings*; *Albacom/BT/ENI/Mediaset*.

[88] See, *e.g. Borealis/IPIC/OMV/PCD*.

[89] *Kodak/Imation*.

[90] As in *Union Carbide/Enichem* and *RWE-DEA/Enichem Augusta*.

[91] *Cable & Wireless/Maersk Data-Nautec*.

[92] In *Saudi Aramco/MOH* the Commission refused to treat a purchase obligation lasting between 20 and 30 years as ancillary.

[93] See, *e.g. Philips/Lucent Technologies*, where an allegation only terminable "by mutual accord" of the parent and joint venture was not accepted.

[94] See *TNT*, etc., where the Commission reduced the exclusive access outlet arrangements from five to two years. More recently, *Solvay/BASF*.

[95] *Mederic/Urrpimmec/CRI/Munich Re*; *Fyffes/Capespan*.

competitive terms. Attention will be paid to whether the goods or services are
to be supplied at arm's length and at market prices.[96] The Commission will
also look critically at whether giving the parents a preferred supplier/purchaser
status is necessary. For example, in *Valinox/Timet*, an obligation on a joint
venture to purchase a fixed percentage of its needs from a parent was not
acceptable because it would result in a very different tonnage of supply each
year, possibly much higher than its actual needs. The Commission will look
especially carefully at exclusive arrangements.[97] Arrangements whereby the
parent companies may seek to obtain preference over third parties in relation
to the supply of goods and services of the joint venture have been found
unacceptable by the Commission.[98] As regards supply/purchase obligations
accepted as between the parents of the joint venture, it is clear that the burden
will be on those parties to provide an objective justification for any agreement
between them as independent parties.[99] Finally, similar principles will be
applied to agreements seeking to secure continuity of supply in the context of
the division of an existing joint venture.[1]

6.10 CONSORTIUM BIDS

Recital 24 of the Regulation provides that the Regulation is applicable to
consortium bids. The Notice (paragraph IV) describes such concentrations as
being implemented in two stages: joint acquisition and then division. An agreement by the joint acquirers to abstain from making separate competing offers
or otherwise acquiring control may, the Notice says, be considered an ancillary
restraint. As regards the second stage, restrictions limited to putting the division into effect are to be considered directly related and necessary to the
implementation of the concentration. Where the division involves the break-up
of a pre-existing economic entity, arrangements facilitating the break-up may
be considered by the Commission, applying the principles applicable to purchase and supply obligations (described above).

---

[96] See, *e.g. Texaco/Chevron.*
[97] See, *e.g. Securicor Datatrack; ICI/Williams; Merck/Rhône-Poulenc-Merial.*
[98] *Thomson CSF/Deutsche Aerospace; UPM Kymmene/April.*
[99] *DuPont/ICI; ENEL/FT/DT.*
[1] See *Solvay-Laporte/Interox.*

7   Decisions, Undertakings and Appeals

7.1   INTRODUCTION

In Chapter 4 we have described the requirement of notification, the effect of Article 7 of the Regulation (suspension) and the practice and procedure in the initial (stage one) and detailed (stage two) examination of concentrations. As already mentioned, in the interests of legal certainty the Regulation provides for each stage to be concluded by a Commission decision. Although the Regulation provides that in the absence of the Commission actually taking a decision in the requisite time period a "clearance" decision is deemed to have been taken, it has to date been the practice of the Commission formally to close proceedings, at the end of stage one or two as the case may be, by a decision. Only in one case to date has the Commission missed the deadline at the end of stage one.[1] This chapter describes the decisions which the Commission can take under Articles 6 (stage one) and 8 (stage two). It also describes and discusses the Commission's practice of accepting "commitments" in conjunction with favourable decisions under these Articles. Finally the chapter outlines the procedure and grounds for appeals against the Commission's decision to the Court, briefly describing the experience to date.

The reader's attention is drawn to the implications of the Commission's recently published Draft Notices for matters dealt with in this chapter. The Notice on a simplified procedure for the treatment of certain mergers envisages the Commission's use of the default procedure in Article 10(6) of the Regulation—the Commission will refrain from adopting a formal (Article 6(1)(b)) clearance decision in certain cases, the merger being "approved automatically" upon expiry of the Stage I deadline. The Draft Notice on commitments reflects the Commission's experience to date regarding the assessment, acceptance and implementation of commitments. The purpose of the Notice is to provide guidance on the basis of that experience. The Notice also specifies for both Stage I and II procedures the formal and substantive requirements, which proposals of commitments need to fulfil, and outlines requirements for the implementation of commitments. The text which follows takes account of these Draft Notices.

7.2   INITIAL DECISIONS (ARTICLE 6)

7.2.1   Types of Decision

Before the end of the initial period, the Commission must take one of the three decisions:

---

[1] This occurred in *McCormick/CPC/Rabobank/Ostmann*. The Commission took advantage, however, of an apparent difference in the timeframe in Article 9 and referred the case back to the German authorities for consideration under national law. See para. 8.3.4, below.

(a) that the concentration does not fall within the scope of the Regulation. This may be because it was not a concentration as defined in Article 3[2] (not infrequently before the 1998 changes, because a joint venture was not concentrative but co-operative)[3]; or because the turnover criteria are not satisfied,[4] it is a concentration but not one with a Community dimension. (Article 6(1)(a) decision—a decision of inapplicability.)

(b) that the concentration falls within the scope of the Regulation but does not raise serious doubts as to its compatibility with the Common Market. The decision is one not to oppose the concentration and declares the concentration to be compatible with the Common Market. The vast majority of Article 6 decisions fall into this category. (Article 6(1)(b) decision—a decision of compatibility.)

(c) that the concentration falls within the scope of the Regulation and raises serious doubts as to its compatibility with the Common Market. Such decision will also comprise the initiation of proceedings for the purposes of the Regulation. (Article 6(1)(c) decision—initiation of proceedings.)

Failure to take a decision has the effect that the concentration is deemed to have been declared compatible with the Common Market (R.Article 10(6)). In practice the vast majority of decisions are made under Article 6(1)(b): over 200 in 1998 as compared with 12 under Article 6(1)(c), which are not published, and six under Article 6(1)(a). In Article 6(1)(c) cases the Commission's practice is to issue a press release explaining in general terms the reasons for opening a detailed examination. It will usually provide a more detailed explanation to the parties prior to serving a full statement of objections which usually occurs within six weeks of opening stage two proceedings.

7.2.2 Format of Decisions

Article 6(1)(b) decisions follow a fairly standard format. The transaction, or "operation" as it is usually called, is described. This description is followed by sections dealing with the parties; the nature of the concentration (including, where a joint venture is concerned, paragraphs dealing with the issues of control and full functionality); and Community dimension. Having established that jurisdiction under the Regulation exists, the Commission proceeds to an assessment of compatibility with the Common Market (usually subdivided into sections covering product market, geographic market and assessment of dominance). In defining the relevant markets the Commission will frequently

---

[2] Because there is no acquisition or change of control: see *Mediobanca/General*; *British Telecom/MCI*; *Ford/Hertz*; and *Ericsson/Nokia/Psion/Motorola (Symbian II)*. See also *Channel Five* and *Unisource/Telefónica*.

[3] See, *e.g. Baxter/Nestlé/Salvia*; *Renault/Volvo*; and *British Telecom/MCI*.

[4] See, *e.g. Arjomari-Prioux SA/Wiggins Teape Appleton plc*. Worldwide turnover not satisfied: *Solvay/Laporte/Interox*; *Eurocard/Eurocheque-Europay*. Community turnover not satisfied: *Cereol/Continentale Italiana*; *Alcatel/STC*; *British Telecom/MCI*; *ABB/Renault-Automation*; *BS/BT*; *Ingersoll-Rand/MAN*; *Ingersoll-Rand/Clark*; *Albacom*; *SBG/Rentenanstalt*; *Royal Bank of Scotland/Bank of Ireland*; and *UBS/Mister Minit*.

refer to previous discussions for their precedent value. It is not unusual for definition of the markets to be left open, where there can be no question of dominance whatever definition is adopted. Where Article 2(4) applies the decision will, in addition, deal with the Article 81 issues. The decision's final paragraphs will address, if necessary, any issues relating to ancillary restraints before formally concluding that the notified concentration does not give rise to the creation or enhancement of a dominant position.[5] References to previous cases and to the Commission's notices are common.

The relatively standard format of Article 6 decisions does not mean that decisions themselves follow a uniform pattern or length. Many notifications, indeed most, so clearly do not raise questions of compatibility with the Common Market that the Commission can content itself with a formal clearance of no more than four or five pages/30–40 paragraphs. Some have even been as short as two pages.[6] (In future, if the Commission's proposal for a simplified procedure is accepted, such cases may be cleared "automatically", by operation of law under Article 10(6).) Other decisions may run to 10 times that length and involve a very detailed examination of the compatibility issue. Where commitments are accepted by the Commission, they form an integral part of the decision and will be set out in or be appended to the decision.[7]

7.3 FINAL DECISIONS—ARTICLE 8

When proceedings have been initiated under Article 6(1)(c) (*i.e.* because there are serious doubts as to compatibility with the Common Market) they must be closed by one of the decisions provided for in Article 8 paragraphs (2) to (5).

7.3.1 Declaration of Compatibility

Where a concentration does not create or strengthen a dominant position significantly impeding effective competition in the Common Market or a substantial part of it, it must, pursuant to Article 8(2), be declared compatible with the Common Market. Where modifications have been made to achieve this result, the Commission may impose conditions and obligations to ensure fulfilment of parties' commitments. The flexibility of their use can be seen from the discussion in paragraph 7.4, below. Failure to comply with an obligation renders a party liable to a fine (R. Article 14(2)(a)) and revocation of the declaration (R. Article 8(5)). The Commission may also impose a periodic penalty payment to secure performance of an obligation (R. Article 15(2)(b)).

As discussed in Chapter 6, where the concentration involves ancillary restraints which are directly related and necessary to the implementation of the

---

[5] All publicly available decisions where the Commission concludes that it has jurisdiction over the notified operation under the Regulation will culminate in an Article 6(1)(b) decision of compatibility (except where the entire notification is referred back to a Member State under Article 9) because decisions to open second stage proceedings are addressed only to the notifying parties in the form of a statement of objections and to Member States.

[6] *William Hill/Cinven/CVC*. The text comprises some 10 short paragraphs, taking 40 lines in total.

[7] See, *e.g. Rohm and Haas/Morton*.

concentration, and these are acceptable in nature and extent, the Commission's decision under Article 8(2) must also cover these. Such decisions must also cover any co-ordination effects. So far there has only been one such Article 8 decision, in *BT/AT&T* (not yet published). Where the restrictions are not ancillary, a decision under Regulation 17 or other implementing Regulation may also be necessary.

7.3.2 Declaration of Incompatibility

Where the Commission finds that the concentration creates or strengthens a dominant position as a result of which effective competition would be significantly impeded in the Common Market or a substantial part of it, it must declare the concentration incompatible with the Common Market. There are only eleven cases[8] in which the Commission has blocked the concentration outright, though in *RTL/Veronica/Endemol* the effect of the withdrawal of one of the parties and the giving of a commitment by another entitled the concentration to be modified and to be declared compatible. Likewise, in *Skanska/Scancem*, Skanska's undertaking to sell its entire stake in Scancem in fact more than reversed the concentration which was the subject of the notification, but the decision was one of compatibility. Putting into effect a concentration declared incompatible by such decision renders the parties liable to a fine (R.Article 14(2)(c)).

7.3.3 Divestment, etc. Orders—Restoring Competition

Where a concentration has already been put into effect (as, for example, in *Skanska/Scancem*) the Commission may, by decision, take any action that it considers appropriate to restore conditions of effective competition (Article 8(4)). It is not dependent on a notification to take such steps. In particular, it may order the sale of shares, or the divestment of assets, in order to restore the *status quo ante*. Failure to take measures so ordered renders a party liable to a fine (R.Article 14(2)(c)). The Commission may also impose a periodic penalty payment to compel compliance (R.Article 15(2)(b)). There have only been two cases to date, both arising from requests from Member States under Article 22. (Divestment has been needed because of the absence of automatic suspension in such cases). A decision of the Commission to require divestment, or to impose a similar remedy, may be part of, or issued simultaneously with, the decision to prohibit a concentration.[9] It may, however, be issued

---

[8] *Aérospatiale-Alenia/de Havilland* [1991] O.J. L334/42; *MSG/Media Service* [1994] O.J. L364/1; *Nordic Satellite Distribution* [1996] O.J. L53/20; *RTL/Veronica/Endemol* [1996] O.J. L134/32, declared compatible [1996] O.J. L294/14: *Gencor/Lonrho* [1997] O.J. L11/30; *Kesko/Tuko* [1997] O.J. L110/53; *Saint Gobain/Wacker-Chemie/NOM* [1997] O.J. L247/1; *Blokker/Toys'R'Us* [1998] O.J. L316/1; *Bertelsmann/Kirch/Premiere*; and *Deutsche Telekom/Beta Research* [1999] O.J. L53/1 and 31 respectively, and *Airtours/First Choice* (not yet published).

[9] See *Blokker/Toys'R'Us*, where the decisions on incompatibility and ordering divestment (following proposals made by the parties) were contained in the same instrument.

later.[10] It is to be noted that the four month time limit applies to decisions of compatibility or incompatibility, but not to a decision requiring divestment. This allows a longer period for the negotiation of remedies. Usually, however, remedies will be offered in order to secure a decision of compatibility and negotiations will take place prior to the decision. The Commission would, however, be expected to act with reasonable expedition in view of the critical importance and magnitude of commercial proposals involving a concentration. Normally, commitments have to be submitted within the first three months of a stage two investigation. The parties are entitled to a statement (setting out the Commission's arguments and proposed divestment order) and have a right of reply (R.Article 18). In practice, the two orders made to date have followed the form of divestments pursuant to commitments from the parties (for the essential elements, see paragraph 7.4.3, below).

7.3.4   Revocation of Decision of Compatibility

A decision of compatibility, whether made under Article 6 or Article 8, can be revoked where it is based on incorrect information for which one of the undertakings is responsible or where it has been obtained by deceit. The parties could conceivably be liable to fines for providing incorrect information (see R.Article 14(1)(b) and (c)). A decision of compatibility may also be revoked where the undertakings concerned commit a breach of an obligation (*i.e.* to comply with a commitment to secure modification of the concentration proposal) (R.Articles 6(3)(b) and 8(5)(b)).[11] This may also attract a fine (R.Article 14(2)(a)). The Commission may take a new decision under Article 6 or 8, as the case may be. This might lead to a decision under Article 8(3) of incompatibility and then divestment to be ordered. The power to revoke a decision has only been used once to date and that was in relation to an Article 6 decision. Five weeks after its decision under Article 6(1)(b) clearing the merger the Commission pursuant to Article 6(3)(a) revoked its decision approving the merger of Sanofi and Synthélabo. The two French chemicals and pharmaceutical companies had failed to describe their activities of production and marketing of tranquillisers in their original notification.[11a] The Commission later cleared the merger subject to a commitment by Synthélabo to divest its tranquilliser interests.

7.4   MODIFICATIONS, UNDERTAKINGS, COMMITMENTS

7.4.1   Introduction

The Commission must make a finding of compatibility, or incompatibility, depending on the result of its appraisal. As already emphasised it has no power to authorise a concentration which it has found to be incompatible with the

---

[10] See *Kesko/Tuko* where the decision (Art. 8(4)) ordering divestment was made at the end of the three month period specified in the Art. 8(3) incompatibility decision which required the parties to submit divestment proposals.

[11] On occasion specific reference may be made to this power in the body of the decision—see *Kimberley-Clark/Scott Paper* [1996] O.J. L183/1, para. 243.

[11a] See *Competition Policy Newsletter*, 1999, No. 2, p. 33.

Common Market, except in relation to the co-ordination effects of certain joint ventures (Article 2(4)). Both Article 6(2) and Article 8(2) envisage, however, that a finding of compatibility may follow the modification of a concentration by the parties made after discussions with the Commission during the appraisal process. From the earliest days of the Regulation the Commission did not limit its practice[12] to accepting modifications, etc., at stage two. The changes to the Regulation made in 1997 made clear that commitments could be given and made enforceable during first stage proceedings. The Commission has described this as being the most significant change in practice.[13] As already mentioned in Chapter 4, clearance (by decision under Article 6) may be dependent on appropriate undertakings having been given by the parties, though it should be recognised that not every competition problem can be dealt with in this way. This chapter looks at the practice of the Commission in accepting commitments under Articles 6 and 8. It should be noted that except in the circumstances provided by Article 10(1) (four to six weeks in stage one proceedings) the offering of commitments by the parties does not extend the periods allowed for the Commission to take its decision on the compatibility or incompatibility of the concentration with the Common Market. As will be clear from the description which follows, and from other sections of this book, the offering of commitments may put serious strain on the Commission's timetable. It is important that parties identify concerns at an early stage and fashion adequate, clear remedies to allay any doubts about compatibility. The Commission has now issued a Draft Notice explaining the substantive and procedural elements of remedial commitments which emphasises this, among other points. The Draft Notice is referred to, where appropriate, in the discussion of remedies which follows.

7.4.2 Structural and Behavioural Remedies

Both Articles 6(2) and 8(2) empower the Commission to attach conditions or obligations to its decision where a finding of compatibility is dependent upon changes which the companies have offered in order to avoid a finding of incompatibility. Both provisions are drafted rather narrowly: only conditions or obligations may be attached to a decision which are ''intended to ensure that the undertakings concerned comply with the commitments they have entered into *vis-à-vis* the Commission with a view to rendering the concentra- tion compatible with the common market''. In the first edition of this book, we doubted whether undertakings as to future commercial behaviour were appropriate, or even legally valid and enforceable. These doubts were, in the early days of the Regulation, apparently shared by some members of the Advisory Committee and by the Commission itself. In a number of cases the

---

[12] The Commission took the view that although the arrangement is not explicitly provided for under Art. 6 commitments which modify the original concentration plan and which enable a serious doubt to be removed as to the compatibility of the concentration with the Common Market can be accepted if the potential competition problem is clearly identified and remains limited in its effects and if the modifica- tion proposed by the parties provides a clear definitive response to the problem. Twenty-Fourth Report on Competition, para. 315.

[13] Twenty-Eighth Report on Competition, para. 142, Insert 6.

Commission has considered various undertakings offered by the parties but rejected them as "behavioural" being difficult to control and enforce and not meeting the Commission's concerns.[14] Prior to the 1998 changes the tendency was also to accept undertakings in stage one only if they were guaranteed, so to speak, by a Member State, or could have been reinforced by proceedings under Article 81 or 82. The preference for structural undertakings is not surprising: the essential objective of the Regulation is to preserve competitive market structures. Such an objective strongly implies structural remedies.[15] But, as the Court of First Instance held in the *Gencor* case,[16] the Commission has power "to accept only such commitments as are capable of rendering the notified transaction compatible with the common market ... The categorisation of a proposed commitment as behavioural or structural is therefore immaterial". This said, the Court accepted that structural remedies were, as a rule, preferable because they prevent, at least for some time, the strengthening of a dominant position. The Court continued:

"Nevertheless, the possibility cannot automatically be ruled out that commitments which *prima facie* are behavioural, for instance not to use a trademark for a certain period, or to make part of the production capacity of the entity arising from the concentration available to third-party competitors, or more generally, to grant access to essential facilities on non-discriminatory terms, may themselves also be capable of preventing the emergence or strengthening of a dominant position."

The Commission has to examine on a case-by-case basis the adequacy and appropriateness of the commitments being offered. Such an approach gives the Commission a substantial measure of discretion but, notwithstanding *Gencor*, the Draft Notice emphasises that "the most effective way to preserve competition, apart from prohibition, is to create the conditions for the emergence of a new competitive entity or for the strengthening of existing third-party competitors via divestiture."[17]. The Draft Notice makes clear that it is for the parties, and not for the Commission, to put forward proposals for commitments where appropriate. The Commission will be looking for a lasting solution to any problems.

7.4.3 Divestments, etc.

The Commission has said that commitments must either restore the *status quo ante* to such an extent that the competitive structure in the affected market is re-established, or they must offset the increase in market strength to eliminate

---

[14] See, *e.g. MSG/Media Service* [1994] O.J. L364/1; *Nordic Satellite Distribution* [1996] O.J. L53/30; and *Gencor/Lonrho* [1997] O. J. L11/30.

[15] The power to grant exemptions under Art. 81(3) subject to conditions or obligations is not, of course, limited to structural remedies, although one view is that the conditions or obligations attached to an Art. 81(3) exemption might be *ultra vires* if they sought to impose continuing restrictions on the ability of the undertakings concerned to compete.

[16] Case T-102/96 *Gencor Ltd v. Commission* [1999] 4 C.M.L.R. 971, paras 317–320.

[17] Draft Commitments Notice, para. 19.

the risk that a dominant position is created or strengthened and to re-establish a competitive structure.

The majority of conditional clearances have imposed some sort of structural remedy in the broad sense, usually in the form of a disposal of part of the business being acquired or certain of its assets. This is true as regards both Articles 6 and 8. In practice, the size and nature of the divestment must be of sufficient size, include any necessary marks and logos needed to hold customers and have appropriate geographical and technical flexibility. Divestitive commitments should create the conditions for the emergence of a new competitive entity or for the strengthening of existing third-party competitors. For example, in *Crown Cork & Seal/Carnaud Metalbox*[18] the effect of the divestment package was to give the purchaser a 22 per cent overall market share. More recently, in *BP/Amoco*[19] (an Article 6 case), the divestment scheme provided for the transfer of Amoco's PIB business to Pakhoed, a large and well-established company with sufficient technical and commercial know-how to make it a strong competitor. The scheme, whose aim was to remove the competitive overlap created by the concentration on the market for the supply of PIB to industrial customers, involved the transfer of Amoco's customer contracts, stock and inventory of PIB and its Antwerp storage, blending and handling facilities.

In *Anglo American Corporation/Lonhro*[20] the Commission required AAC to divest itself of a portion of its shareholding in Lonrho. AAC had to reduce its holding from 27.47 per cent (which the Commission held gave AAC a decisive influence) to 9.99 per cent. As a remedy divestment of shares has been criticised on the grounds that, as the Commission's own practice under the Regulation reveals, control is not necessarily based on shares and voting rights alone. Divestment of shares has, however, been used in other cases.[21] Moreover, remedies must pass the general proportionality test in Community law and the divestment in *Anglo American* may leave room for doubt that the possibility of AAC exercising decision influence over Lonrho has been removed. In such cases, however, the concentration is effectively reversed and it is somewhat odd that a decision of compatibility (subject to the divestment being fulfilled) follows.

The components of a divestment commitment have become fairly standardised:

(1) an undertaking to find a viable existing or potential competitor (or a financial or industrial company or institution independent of the parties with the financial capacity to continue the business) for the business;

(2) the transfer of the business into the hands of a trustee if the business cannot be sold within a stipulated time, the trustee to have power to dispose of the business;

---

[18] For recent examples of other divestments under Art. 8(2), see *Siemens/Elektrowatt* [1999] O.J. L88/1 and *WorldCom/MCI* [1999] O.J. L116/1.

[19] For other examples of divestments under Art. 6(2), see *Owens Illinois/BTR Packaging*; *Exxon/Shell*; *Usinor/Cockerill*; and *Rohm and Haas/Morton*.

[20] [1998] O.J. L149/21.

[21] See *Neste/IVO* and *Skanska/Scancem* [1999] O.J. 1383/1.

(3) the integrity of the business to be divested to be safeguarded in the period prior to sales as regards its "independence, economic viability, marketability and competitiveness"[22];

(4) the business to be managed separately from the parties' business and immune from influence from the parties' management;

(5) the Commission to be given a right of approval over the purchaser which must usually be an existing or prospective competitor; and

(6) the Commission to be kept informed of the progress of the divestment scheme.

Time periods for implementation should, the Draft Notice indicates, be as short as is feasible. The description of the divestitive package must be sufficiently comprehensive in order to allow clear identification of all relevant assets (tangible and intangible), activities and services included in the package.

As regards reporting obligations, the Commission has said[23] that experience has shown that in order to monitor compliance it is necessary for the parties to report to the Commission at least at three-monthly intervals on the progress made in efforts to sell the business in question and on other compliance with the undertakings given. Detailed information (for example identifying potential purchasers) should be given. The timetable for divestment is not made public, or even disclosed to third parties on whom the disposal undertakings are tested. This is understandable since the Commission will wish to facilitate a disposal but not penalise parties unnecessarily by forcing a "fire sale". Nonetheless the Draft Commitments Notice emphasises the need for remedies to be implemented quickly if a prohibition decision is to be avoided. Finally, any divestment must itself be compatible with Community and, where applicable, national merger and competition laws.

7.4.4 Behavioural Commitments

In an increasing number of cases the Commission has been prepared to accept other, somewhat more behavioural, commitments. In several cases they have been used in conjunction with more direct structural, usually divestment, remedial action. The Draft Notice speaks of "commitment packages", in which divestment may be only one element. For example, in *Nestlé/Perrier*, Nestlé undertook to dispose of eight of the minor brands of mineral water owned by the merged entity. These brands amounted to approximately one-fifth of French mineral waters capacity. In addition a behavioural remedy was imposed on Nestlé under which it undertook not to disclose non-historic sales data to the French trade association of which Perrier, BSN and certain regional French producers were members. This made the market somewhat less transparent and weakened links via the industry trade association so reducing the

---

[22] Draft Commitments Notice, para. 41.
[23] *ABB/Daimler-Benz* [1997] O.J. L11/1.

risk of duopolistic dominance. More substantial behavioural commitments were annexed to divestment in *British Telecom/MCI(II)*[24] and *The Coca-Cola Company/Carlsberg A/S.*[25] The combination of commitments in any "package" will be dependent on the nature of the competition problems in the markets affected.

Where behavioural commitments have been used alone, without divestment, they have taken on a variety of forms. For example, in the modified concentration plan in *RTL/Veronica/Endemol*[26] the Commission accepted the transformation of the Dutch television channel RTLS from a general interest channel into a news channel. The parties agreed not, within five years of the decision, to change the essential character of that news channel without prior approval of the Commission. In a number of cases the Commission has been content to accept the abandonment or relaxation of contractual relationships, thereby improving entry conditions. In *Boeing/McDonnell Douglas*[27] a key feature of the commitments offered by Boeing was the abandonment of exclusivity rights under agreements with major aircraft buyers. In *Agfa-Gevaert/DuPont*[28] the Commission accepted the relaxation of contractual ties with equipment suppliers and distributors and of restrictions in know-how licences aimed at opening up the structural relationships for the distribution of Agfa/DuPont products (negative plates for offset printing). The effect intended was to break these relations and allow independent suppliers to deal with the parties' competitors and offer different packages of products to customers.

Breaking or easing existing distribution systems has featured in several cases. Exclusive long-term supply and distribution agreements may limit the market potential available for competitors. In *Fiat Geotech/Ford New Holland*, an early case under the Regulation, Fiat agreed to terminate its exclusive supply arrangements with farmers' co-operatives in Italy in return for a clearance decision under Article 6. The mutual exclusive dealing relationship between Fiat and the farmers' co-operatives in Italy had represented a major barrier in the entry to other agricultural machinery producers in a substantial part of the Community. In another Article 6 case, *American Home Products/Monsanto*, the Commission accepted the parties' withdrawal from a relevant market, for oral contraceptives in France, by termination of certain distribution agreements with Organon. The termination of distribution arrangements for various spirits in a number of Member States markets also played a part in avoiding a prohibition in *Guinness/Grand Metropolitan*, an Article 8 case.

The Draft Notice also draws attention to the need for actual or potential competitors for access to necessary infrastructure or key technology including patents, know-how and other intellectual property rights. In at least two cases parties have had to make such rights available to actual or potential competitors. In *Ciba-Geigy/Sandoz*,[29] the parties agreed to grant, within a two year period, a ten year non-exclusive and unlimited licence for the production of a certain constituent of an animal health product. As part of the settlement

[24] [1997] O.J. L336/1.
[25] [1998] O.J. L145/41.
[26] [1996] O.J. L294/14.
[27] [1997] O.J. L336/16.
[28] [1998] O.J. L211/22.
[29] [1997] O.J. L201/1.

reached in *Boeing/McDonnell Douglas*[30] Boeing had to make available certain of its patents on a non-exclusive reasonable royalty bearing basis, as well as providing information on R&D projects. The requirement to licence intellectual property rights may also be rather more structural in nature than behavioural. An illustration of this is *Shell/Montecatini* where the remedy of requiring Montedison's polypropylene technology to be divested to a new company, Technipol, amounted to the partial disposal of an asset which was the key to creating a new competitor in the industry.

Despite the Commission's preparedness to accept sometimes complex and voluminous remedies,[31] often seeking to effect structural change by attempting to introduce a new or strengthened competitor, commitments have on occasion been rejected, sometimes even after revision by the parties in the light of the Commission's reactions.[32] In the most recent case, *Airtours/First Choice*, the Commission refused to consider a revised package, *inter alia*, because there was insufficient time available to assess and test the proposals before the deadline for decision. The Regulation contemplates a modification of the concentration. This, as already mentioned, points to the primacy of structural (divestment) remedies. But it also indicates the need for some connection between the commitments offered and the notified concentration. This has not always been the case. For example, undertaking to withdraw support for Community anti-dumping measures (and thus eliminate the barrier to certain imports) were rejected in *Saint Gobain/Wacker-Chemie/NOM*. They could not, in any way, be said to modify the original concentration plan. It was not within the parties' power, but was for the Commission to decide on the need for regulatory action in dumping cases.[33] It was not surprising that such proposals were rejected. But the lack of a direct concentration between commitments and the notified concentration has not always been a barrier to the Commission granting a clearance decision.[34] The Commission will not, however, accept commitments which in practice amount to nothing more than a premise not to commit abuses of a dominant position.

7.4.5 Transparency and Timing

The Commission has taken the position that modifications must be transparent in both stage one and stage two examinations, in order that the rights of third parties and of Member States can be safeguarded. It is the Commission's practice to inform both the Member States and interested[35] third parties of the commitments entered into and modifications made by the notifying parties and in the Commission's words, to test the proposals in the market.[36] Where

---

[30] [1997] O.J. L336/16.

[31] See, *e.g Air France/Sabena*.

[32] *Bertelsmann/Kirch/Premiere* and *Deutsche Telekom/Beta Research* [1999] O.J. L53/1 and 31.

[33] [1997] O.J. L24/1, para. 262. The Commission also said that the removal of the anti-dumping measures would not eliminate the competition problem in the particular circumstances.

[34] See *Alcatel/Telettra*.

[35] "Interested" here meaning third parties who have expressed comments following publication of the Art. 4 nature in the O.J. and those which the Commission believes may be affected by the commitments and modifications.

[36] See, *e.g. Nordic Satellite Distribution* [1996] O.J. L53/20, para. 160.

the commitments and modifications have been made unilaterally by the parties, their transmission to the Member States and third parties does not bind the Commission as to what decision it may subsequently reach (for example to proceed to a stage two examination pursuant to a decision under Article 6(1)(c)).[37] Time limits apply in relation to the giving of commitments. Those offered in first stage proceedings with the intention of forming the basis of an Article 6(1)(b) (compatibility) decision must be submitted no more than three weeks from date of receipt of notification (IR.Article 18(1)). There is, therefore, within first stage proceedings, a very limited timescale to agree commitments and "brinkmanship" will not be tolerated. The Draft Notice acknowledges that the competition problem needs to be straightforward and the remedies clear-cut. Commitments submitted at this stage of the procedure must be sufficient to clearly exclude serious doubts within the meaning of Article 6(1)(c). A successful "Phase one undertakings" procedure has been said to comprise three elements[38]:

(1) clearly identified product and geographic markets in which the competition issues have been speedily determined;

(2) the notifying parties' ability to identify and adopt an effective and speedily-implementable remedy, such as a divestment of an overlapping business; and

(3) readiness on the part of the notifying parties to acknowledge the competition problem and to co-operate with the Commission in finding a suitable solution.

Not every case, however, is suitable for commitments. The Commission has said: "There will, of course, continue to be cases where, even with goodwill and careful preparation, a full investigation is needed in order to properly identify and access the competition problems, and examine alternative outcomes—including prohibition".[39] The Draft Commitments Notice emphasises that, in phase one, remedial measures are feasible only if the concern is readily identifiable and easily resolved. If any doubt remains as to whether the competition problem would be eliminated the Commission will proceed to an in-depth investigation.

In the context of stage two proceedings, it should be noted that any modifications to the original concentration plan made by the parties, with a view to removing the competition problems identified by the Commission in its statement of obligations, must be submitted no later than three months from the date on which proceedings were initiated (IR. Article 18(2)). The purpose of imposing this time limit is to give the Commission sufficient time to analyse the commitments, etc., proposed, to consult third parties and to comply with its obligations as regards the Advisory Committee before any decision pursuant to Article 8(2). The Draft Notice requires the proposed commitments to be set

---

[37] Second stage proceedings were ordered, *e.g.* in *Proctor & Gamble/Schickendanz* despite a renotification incorporating various changes made unilaterally by the parties.
[38] See Kemp, *Recent Developments and Important Decisions.* Competition Policy Newsletter 1999 No. 1, pp. 40–41.
[39] Twenty-Eighth Report on Competition, para. 142, Insert 6.

out in a sufficient degree of detail to enable a full assessment to be carried out. Only in "exceptional circumstances" can the Commission extend the three month period (IR.Article 18(2)). This was allowed in *Anglo-American Corporation/Lonrho*. The commitments were revised twice before the Commission and Member States were satisfied.[40] The Draft Notice makes clear that it is for the parties to justify the "exceptional circumstances". The Commission will grant only a limited extension if it recognises the existence of such circumstances and if it considers that in the particular case there is sufficient time to make a full and proper assessment of the modified proposal and to allow adequate consultation with Member States and third parties. Rejection of an application for an extension of the three-month period does not preclude the parties from submitting a new notification on the basis of their modified proposal.

7.4.6 Monitoring of Commitments

The Commission has recognised that the conditional nature of clearance decisions attaching conditions and obligations means that it must strictly monitor compliance with the commitments given by the notifying parties and the necessary transparency of the information provided to third parties through press releases.[41] As regards conditions and obligations attached to clearance decisions (whether Article 6 or Article 8) there are clear legal sanctions. Failure to comply with an obligation may lead to revocation of the declaration of compatibility (R. Articles 6(3) and 8(5)). In the case of an Article 8 decision, the Commission may also impose a fine or a periodic penalty payment to secure performance of an obligation (R. Articles 14(2)(a), 15(2)(a)). Even so, as in *Nordic Satellite Distribution*, difficulties of monitoring and securing compliance may lead to an outright prohibition. The Court of Justice has said that where the Commission accepts a commitment as a condition of granting a declaration of compliance, in particular under Article 8, the decision should state clearly that it is a condition on which the declaration of compatibility is granted.[42] In practice, reporting allegations are common and frequently part of the commitment given. They are important both as regards structural (for example divestment) and behavioural and other commitments. In *Ciba-Geigy/Sandoz*,[43] for example, a regular three monthly reporting obligation was imposed to monitor the undertaking given to grant non-exclusive patent licences (with a turnover-related licence fee and duration of up to 10 years) within two years of the Commission's decision.

---

[40] The concentration had in fact been implemented and to avoid any unnecessary harm and to give the parties a degree of flexibility which the Commission thought they might not have under a formal divestment decision the commitments were accepted outside the three month period: [1998] O.J. L149/21, para. 125. A similar case was *Skanska/Scancem* [1999] O.J. L183/1.

[41] Twenty-Fourth Report on Competition Policy, para. 317.

[42] Joined Cases C-68/94 & 30/95 *French Republic v. Commission* [1998] E.C.R. I-1375, para. 68. Where, in *Kali und Salz*, the Commission had not made the commitment a formal condition of the declaration of compatibility, it was criticised for creating "an unfortunate blend of the procedure under the Regulation and that pursuant to Regulation 17".

[43] [1997] O.J. L201/1.

7.4.7 Amendment of Decisions

Circumstances may require decisions, and conditions and obligations relating to them, to be reviewed. In *Shell/Montecatini* the Commission had been particularly concerned that the creation of a joint venture to which Shell and Montedison proposed to transfer their polyolefins (PP) businesses and PP technology, would concentrate the two principal PP production technologies worldwide in the hands of a single undertaking. The response of Shell and Montedison was to undertake to transfer the latter's worldwide PP technology licensing to a new company which would be independent of the joint venture and its parents. This would be supported by a transfer of research and development scientists. In addition, Montedison also undertook to withdraw its PP subsidiary, Himont, from an existing joint venture with Petrofina to allay the Commission's concerns, shared by Petrofina, that the new joint venture would be able to influence Petrofina's competitive position. Shell's U.S. partner in a separate joint venture which offers the other main PP production technology, Union Carbide Corporation, challenged the Commission's decision. Subsequently, however, pursuant to a consent order made by the U.S. Federal Trade Commission, Shell was required to dispose of its interest in the joint venture with Union Carbide. Shell and Montedison subsequently requested release from the June 1994 undertakings to the Commission. The parties asked whether the separation of Montedison's PP technology business was still necessary. The Commission investigated and reconsidered the position in the light of the divestiture made by Shell. It concluded that the separation of Montedison's PP technology business was no longer necessary from the point of view of the Regulation. The Commission amended its original decision by revoking the conditions and obligations relating to Montedison's PP technology business.

7.4.8 Informal Assurances

Occasionally the Commission has also drawn attention to statements or assurances given by notifying parties by recording them in its final decision. For example, in *Tesco/ABF*, the Commission, having received expressions of concern from the Irish Government, noted in its Article 6(1)(b) decision, a number of assurances given by Tesco to the Irish Government concerning continual support for Irish food suppliers. One Article 8 decision, *Enso/Stora*, was also adopted on the basis of undertakings from the parties, but without formal conditions or obligations. Although such indications are not binding, a party may obviously lay itself open to public criticism or regulators' distrust in the future if it reneges on informal assurances given to allay doubts or concerns. They should not, therefore, be given lightly even though they are not formal commitments. The Court of Justice has also criticised the Commission for confusing the procedures under the Merger Regulation with Regulation 17.[44]

---

[44] In *Kali und Salz*. See n. 42, above.

7.5   GENERAL POINTS ON DECISIONS

7.5.1   Reasons

In accordance with Article 253 (ex Article 190) of the Treaty, decisions must give the reasons on which they are based and, in the case of certain decisions including conditional decisions of compatibility or decision of incompatibility made under Article 8, must only be based on objections on which the parties have been given the opportunity to reply (R.Article 18(3)). These provisions do not require the Commission to discuss all the arguments made in response to the notice of objections.[45] But the reasons given by the Commission in its decision must adequately justify the decision. They must be sufficiently stated to allow the Court to check the legality of the decision and to provide the party concerned with the information necessary to ascertain whether the decision is justified.[46] This said, having regard to the time restraints under the Regulation and the number of notifications, it is reasonable to expect decisions under the Regulation to be shorter in form than those under Regulation 17,[47] and in practice this is very much the case for decisions under Article 6. (As mentioned above, the Commission is proposing to rely on Article 10(6) in the future). Decisions under Article 8 (*i.e.* following the second stage proceedings) are similar in length and format to those under Regulation 17. Where the Commission's decision is made dependent upon a commitment from the parties, this will be described and appraised in the decision. In decisions under Article 6, it is becoming the practice to annex a copy of the commitment to the decision, whilst in Article 8 cases it is more common to set out the detail of the commitment in the body of the decision. But there are no hard and fast rules: the more complex the commitments, the more likely they will appear in an annex.

7.5.2   Sanctions

Failure to comply with Commission decisions, involving substantive breaches of the Regulation, may result in the imposition of very substantial fines—related to turnover—and periodic penalty payments on the infringing undertaking. Fines of up to 10 per cent of the aggregate turnover of the undertakings concerned within the meaning of Article 5[48] may be imposed where, intentionally or as a result of negligence, a party:

---

[45] This is well established. For examples of its application in merger cases: see Case T-2/93 *Air France v. Commission* [1994] E.C.R. II-323, para. 92; and Case T-290/94 *Kaysersberg SA v. Commission* [1997] E.C.R. II-2137, para. 150.

[46] Again this is well established. See, *e.g.* Joined Cases 240-242, 261, 268 & 269/82 *Stichting Sigaretten Industrie (SSI) v. Commission* [1985] E.C.R. 3831; [1987] 3 C.M.L.R. 661, para. 88.

[47] The Court of First Instance has said that whether a statement of reasons meets the requirements of Art. 253 must be assessed with regard not only to the wording but also to the context and to all the legal rules governing the matter in question. *Kaysersberg* (above), para. 150.

[48] Note that under Reg. 17 the maximum level of fine is up to 10 per cent of the turnover of the infringing undertaking whereas under Art. 14(2) of the Regulation the maximum level appears, on a literal view, to be set by reference to the aggregate turnover of all the undertakings concerned in the concentration.

(i)   puts into effect a concentration, notwithstanding the automatic suspension provided for by Article 7(1); (R.Article 14(2)(b))

(ii)   fails to comply with conditions or obligations attached to a Commission derogation permitting a concentration to be put into effect notwithstanding the suspension rule in Article 7; (R.Article 14(2)(a))

(iii) fails to comply with conditions or obligations attached to a Commission decision declaring a modified concentration compatible with the Common Market; (R.Article 14(2)(a))

(iv)   puts into effect a concentration notwithstanding a decision of incompatibility by the Commission under Article 8(3), or fails to comply with remedial measures required by the Commission pursuant to Article 8(4); (R.Article 14(2)(c)).

Article 14(4) of the Regulation expressly provides that decisions to fine are not of a criminal law nature. It is noteworthy, however, that, in contrast to Regulation 17, fines may be imposed on individuals if they are persons referred to in Article 3(1)(b) of the Regulation.[49]

In addition to fines, periodic penalty payments may be imposed by decision under Article 15(2) of the Regulation of up to ECU 100,000 for each day the infringement lasts (beginning with the date set in a decision) where conditions or obligations on an Article 7(4) derogation or on a conditional clearance under Article 8(2) are breached, or remedial measures ordered by the Commission under Article 8(4) are not put into effect by the undertaking concerned.

7.5.3 Notification of Decisions

By virtue of Article 254 of the Treaty decisions must be notified to those to whom they are addressed and take effect upon such notification. As has been seen above, decisions have to be taken within certain time limits specified in the Regulation. For the purposes of Article 10(1) (decisions under Article 6 (1) following the initial examination) and Article 10(3) (final decision under Article 8(2) and (3)) the Implementing Regulation provides that the time limit shall be met where the relevant decision has been taken before the end of the period (IR.Article 10(1)). The purpose of this provision appears to be to allow the Commission to notify the parties of its decision after the time limit expires, provided that the decision is taken before the expiry of the relevant period and that there is no delay in effecting the notification.

7.5.4 Habilitation

The Regulation contemplates formal decisions of the Commission at various times during the procedure. Indeed, there are upwards of 30 types of decision

---

[49] It is suggested that nothing turns on the difference in wording between Art. 14(1) ''Persons referred to in Art. 3(1)(b)'' and Art. 14(2) ''Persons . . . concerned''. Since Art. 1 makes no reference to persons concerned in a concentration, it is likely that the use of that phrase in Art. 14(2) is simply a shorthand for a reference to persons referred to in Art. 3(1)(b) and that there is no intention to extend the ambit of fines to a wider class of persons (including individuals).

which may be taken under the Regulation. It has been recognised as a matter of fact and also of law that when a provision in a regulation requires the Commission to take some procedural step then that act need not be done by the Commissioners personally.[50] Accordingly Community law enables tasks to be delegated to the Commissioner responsible for competition who in turn may sub-delegate to the Director General of the Competition Directorate and the directors below him. Decisions taken by delegation are nonetheless decisions taken on behalf of the Commission and are subject to judicial review by the Court. In relation to the Regulation, whilst final decisions under Article 8 remain to be dealt with by the full college, most other decisions have been delegated to the Commissioner for Competition although under Article 6 (in particular to initiate proceedings) he may have to consult the President. Particularly sensitive cases may still go to the college. The Commissioner has in turn sub-delegated a number of the day-to-day tasks to the Director General or the Head of the Merger Task Force. Noteworthy in this category is the letter under Article 4(2) of the Implementing Regulation informing the parties that a notification is materially incomplete. The diagrams, Merger Procedure Phase I and II, set out in Annex 8, show the operation of the *habilitation* in practice.

7.5.5 Publicity

There is no obligation on the Commission to publish decisions taken under Article 6. Only decisions under Article 8(2) to (5) must be published in the Official Journal (R.Article 20(1)). The Regulation does not say *when* they should be published and publication of Article 8 decisions may take place several months after the decision and some have taken much longer.[51] As regards decisions under Article 6, the Commission has developed the practice of announcing decisions in the Official Journal and also publishing the gist of its decisions on a press release. Full texts (edited for business secrets—see below) also appear for a limited period, and can be freely accessed, on the Competition Directorate's website. Thereafter copies can be bought by e-mail from europa.eu.int/eur-lex.[52] Article 20(2) of the Regulation requires the Commission's publication of Article 8 decisions to "have regard to the legitimate interest of undertakings in the protection of their business secrets". It is, for example, common for decisions, whether under Article 6 or 8, to omit details of exact market shares. Commercially sensitive material from supply and licence agreements, such as terms of the contract, details of product and third parties, is also deleted. Periods of exclusivity in ancillary restrictions are also normally omitted. Omissions are shown thus [...]. Where possible information is replaced by ranges of figures (for example "5 to 10%") or general description. Agreeing excisions to protect the confidentially of information is a cause of delay, particularly where third party data is involved. Lack of translation resources also contributes. In an attempt to make Article 8 decisions

---

[50] See, *e.g.* the approval of the Court in Case 5/85 *AKZO Chemie BV and AKZO Chemie U.K. Ltd v. Commission* [1986] E.C.R. 2585; [1987] 3 C.M.L.R. 716.
[51] In *Siemens/Elektrowatt* [1999] O.J. L88/1, the Commission's decision of November 18, 1997 was not published until March 31, 1999!
[52] Though downloading may not always be trouble-free: see *In-Competition*, vol. 7, Issue 3, April 14, 1999.

available more quickly the *Airtours/First Choice* decision in the English language was posted on the Competition DG's website within a few weeks of the announcement of the prohibition decision. Article 6 decisions also emerge into the public domain much more quickly in this way.

7.6 APPEALS TO THE COURT

7.6.1 General

The Regulation lays down no specific or special rules for challenging decisions made under it. It implicitly assumes that such decisions are subject to review by the Court of Justice and sets out certain procedural consequences. Article 10(5) thus provides that where the Court gives a judgment which annuls the whole or part[53] of the Commission decision the time periods laid down in the Regulation start again from the date of the judgment.

The legality of the application and enforcement of the Regulation is subject to judicial control:

(a) under Article 229 (ex Article 172), an application can be made under the "unlimited" jurisdiction of the Court where a fine or periodic penalty payment is imposed[54];

(b) under Article 230 (ex Article 173), an application can be made to annul a decision of the Commission on the basis of one or more of four specified grounds;

(c) under Article 232 (ex Article 175), an application can be made for the Court to rule on the legality of the Commission's failure to act.

The brief description which follows concentrates on applications under Article 230 and also makes reference to the Court's power to grant interim relief. It is no substitute for more substantial works on the Court and its procedures but draws attention to particular issues which have arisen or may arise in merger cases.

7.6.2 Acts which can be Challenged

Article 230, refers to "acts . . . of the Commission . . . other than recommendations or opinions" and it is well-established that Commission decisions fall squarely within the term "acts" which may be subject to judicial review. It will be recalled that at several stages in the Commission's procedure under the Merger Regulation the Commission may adopt formal decisions, principally at

---

[53] Partial annulment (*e.g.* striking out conditions or obligations attached to decisions) is theoretically possible, though the implications for the remainder of the Commission's decision have to be carefully considered lest there are perverse consequences. See Cases C-68/94 & 30/95 *French Republic v. Commission* [1998] E.C.R. I-1375, para. 258.

[54] The Court is given unlimited jurisdiction to review Commission decisions imposing fines and/or periodic penalty payments in merger cases by Art. 16 of the Regulation.

the end of the two evaluation stages (under Articles 6 and 8 respectively) but also in other circumstances (for example to obtain information under Articles 11 and 13, to refer a case to a Member State under Article 9, or to recognise a Member State's legitimate interest under Article 21(3)). The term "acts" in Article 230 is not however limited to formal measures such as decisions. Article 230 treats as open to review by the Court all measures adopted by the institutions (including the Commission) which are intended to have legal force.[55] The test was set out in the *IBM* case:

"Any measure the legal effects of which are binding on, and capable of affecting the interests of, the applicant by bringing about a distinct change in his legal position is an act or decision which may be the object of an action under Article [230] for a declaration that it is void."[56]

The issue came before the Court of First Instance in Air France's challenge to the Commission's stance in the *Dan Air* case.[57] The proposed acquisition by British Airways of Dan Air had not been notified to the Commission but the parties had discussed their proposals with the Commission. The Commission took the view that the concentration did not fall within the Regulation because, under the proposed terms of the transaction, which involved the closure of its charter operations prior to the acquisition, Dan Air's turnover within the E.C. was less than ECU 250 million. The Merger Task Force confirmed its view in a letter to BA, the letter stating (as is common practice) that the views expressed in it were those of the MTF and were not binding on the Commission itself. On the same date as the letter a statement by a spokesman for the Commissioner responsible for competition matters to the effect that the proposed merger was not considered to be of Community dimension was reported in *Agence Europe*. Did this statement evidence or constitute an act for the purposes of Article 173? The Court of First Instance held that it did. It produced legal effects with regard to the Member States, the effect of the Commissioner's statement being to confirm the competence of those Member States most closely involved, the United Kingdom and France, to appraise the merger under their domestic competition laws. Member States whose territory is affected, directly or indirectly, by the transaction were also entitled to make application under Article 22(3) of the Regulation to the Commission to act notwithstanding the absence of Community dimension—Belgium in fact made such an application within the one month period specified in that provision. The Court also took the view that the statement produced legal effects for the parties to the concentration: they were absolved from the need to notify under Article 4 and could proceed straightaway without having to wait for the expiry of the suspension period provided by Article 7. In so holding the Court had regard to the need for legal certainty and the difficulty of reversing an operation such as the one at issue. The Court drew a distinction between the contested statement and the letter from the MTF and took the view that the statement had the same effects as a decision under Article 6(1)(a) of the Regulation.

---

[55] Case 22/70 *Commission v. Council* [1971] E.C.R. 263; [1971] C.M.L.R. 335, paras 39–42.
[56] Case 60/81 *IBM v. Commission* [1981] E.C.R. 2639; [1981] 3 C.M.L.R. 635, para. 9.
[57] Case T-3/93 *Air France v. Commission* [1994] E.C.R. II-121.

The Court rejected the plea that the contested act was not in the form of a decision. It recognised that its form was unusual, an oral statement apparently unsupported by written documentation, but that did not prevent it from being a challengable act.

By contrast, in the *Spanish Cable TV* case[58] the parties were presented with a letter from the Director General of the Competition Directorate saying that a concentration (already executed and subsequently authorised by the Spanish competition authority) had a Community dimension and should be notified under the Regulation. In the context of an application for interim measures (see below) to restrain the exercise by the Commission of its coercive investigatory powers, the President of the Court of First Instance described the letter as having "a manifestly preparatory nature". He did not determine the nature of the act as that was a matter for the main application for annulment.

The conclusion of the Court of First Instance in *Dan Air* is somewhat unusual,[59] but it does fill a gap in the Regulation, allowing the Court to review the legality of conclusions reached by the Commission in circumstances where the parties have not formally notified their proposal, such notification being a necessary precondition to a decision under Article 6(1)(a).

### 7.6.3	Who can Bring an Action

Article 230 of the Treaty provides:

> "Any natural or legal person may ... institute proceedings against a decision addressed to that person or a decision which, although in the form of ... a decision addressed to another person, is of direct and individual concern to the former."

Addressees of decisions, such as the parties to a merger prohibited by the Commission pursuant to Article 8(3) of the Regulation, do not have any problems of *locus standi*. The undertakings concerned, within the meaning of Article 1 of the Regulation, will clearly have a sufficient interest to bring an appeal. This will be the case even if, for example, a purchase agreement lapses before the proceedings are begun.[60] It is an interesting question, however, whether a party to a concentration which has been declared compatible can institute proceedings. The question arises in *Coca-Cola v. Commission*, where Coca-Cola has challenged the Commission's conclusions on market definition in its Article 8 decision in *Cola-Cola/Amalgamated Beverages* even though it

---

[58] Case T-52/96R *Sogecable SA v. Commission* [1996] E.C.R. II-797, para. 38.

[59] Particularly having regard to the approach taken by the Court of First Instance in such cases as *PVC* (need for the Commission to see text of decision in appropriate languages of addressees of the decision); Joined Cases T-78, 84-86, 89, 71-92, 94, 96, 98, 102 & 104/89 *BASF AG and others v. Commission* [1992] E.C.R. II-315; [1992] 4 C.M.L.R. 357; and *Nefarma* (letter from Competition Commissioner without a collegiate decision of the Commission); Case T-113/89 *Nefarma v. Commission* [1990] E.C.R II-797.

[60] As the Court of First Instance said in *Gencor*, the Commission's decision could have produced effects during the period when the agreement was in force and those effects are not necessarily eradicated by its repeal. An action for annulment is also admissible if it allows future repetition of the alleged illegality to be avoided: Case T-102/96 *Gencor Ltd v. Commission* [1999] 4 C.M.L.R., 971, para. 41.

did not prohibit or impose conditions on the transaction. But as will be seen the position of third parties may not be straightforward. Two conditions must be satisfied. First, a party has to show that the decision in question is of *direct* concern to it. A party may, for example, have a sufficient interest if it is affected by the terms of a commitment given. It does not matter that the commitment has not in fact been implemented or that its implementation is dependent on the undertakings who are the addressees of the decision.[61] Secondly, a party must show that it is *individually* concerned. It is the established rule of the Court that persons may only claim to be individually concerned "if that decision affects them by reason of certain attributes which are peculiar to them or by reason of circumstances in which they are differentiated from all other persons and by virtue of these factors distinguishes them individually just as in the case of the person addressed".[62] One area where this issue is likely to arise in the future is in cases of collective dominance where findings may prejudice third parties who are found to share in that dominant position although they are not party to the notified concentration, so-called "external oligopolists".

7.6.3.1 Shareholders

The first merger case, *Zunis Holding and Others v. Commission*,[63] before the Court of First Instance was a challenge brought by a small number of shareholders in Generali against the Commission's Article 6(1)(a) decision[64] in *Mediobanca/Generali*. The argument was that the Commission had not been able to take into account a shareholders agreement which was said to affect the question of whether control had been acquired. The Commission attacked the admissibility of the shareholders' appeal. The Court of First Instance found the appeal to be inadmissible. The shareholders had not shown that they were directly and individually concerned. The Court said that the mere fact that a measure may affect the relations between the different shareholders of a company does not of itself mean that any individual shareholder can be regarded as so concerned by that measure. Only the existence of specific circumstances can enable such a shareholder, claiming that the measure affects his position within the company, to sue under Article 230.[65] As regards the shareholders having a direct concern, the Court held that a finding by the Commission under Article 6(1)(a) that a concentration does not fall within the scope of the Regulation "is not of such a nature as by itself to affect the substance or extent of the rights of shareholders of the notifying parties, either as regards their proprietary rights or the ability to participate in the company management conferred on them by such rights".[66] On the question of "individual" concern,

---

[61] In *Kali und Salz*, the Court of Justice held that a party was directly concerned because it risked the loss of its sales network and the termination of certain distribution arrangements. Joined Cases C-68/94 & C30/95 *French Republic v. Commission* [1998] E.C.R. I-1375, paras 49–52.

[62] Case 25/62 *Plaumann & Co. v. Commission* [1963] E.C.R. 95; [1964] C.M.L.R. 29. And see the position of EMC/SCPA in the *Kali und Salz* case (above), paras 54–58.

[63] Case T-83/92 [1993] E.C.R. II-1169; [1994] 5 C.M.L.R. 154.

[64] That the concentration did not fall within the scope of the Regulation. See para. 7.2.1, above.

[65] *ibid.*, para. 34.

[66] *ibid.*, para. 35.

the Court noted that the decision in question had affected the shareholders in the same way as any other of the 140,000 or so shareholders. The Court found that the applicants were not individually concerned "in particular because their respective shareholdings in the capital of Generali at the material time each represented less than 0.5 per cent of the share capital and because they failed to prove that by reason of that decision they were placed in a different position to that of any other shareholder".[67]

On appeal to the Court of Justice, the Advocate General disagreed with the Court of First Instance on the question of whether shareholders were directly concerned (he took the view that the extent of their rights was affected, there being a material difference between the position of a shareholder in an independent undertaking and that of a shareholder in an undertaking controlled by others) but agreed that the shareholders were not individually concerned. The Advocate General went further and expressed the view that shareholders should generally have no *locus standi* to bring actions against Commission decisions in merger cases. Disputes arising out of the distinctions between the rights of shareholders as between themselves and their rights as against the undertaking in which they hold shares were matters of company law. Shareholders as such would not have an interest in a Commission decision under the Regulation which is relevant to competition. It therefore seems that in the absence of both special circumstances and the shareholders in question being distinguishable from the rest (perhaps by virtue of a very substantial holding), shareholders will be unable to challenge decisions of the Commission with which they may disagree. In the event the Court of Justice did not rule or opine on this issue, having taken the view that the shareholders' challenge was for other reasons inadmissible.[68]

7.6.3.2 Competitors

The position of competitors may be better as Air France's two challenges to British Airways acquisitions shows. In the first, relating to the purchase of Dan Air, the Court of First Instance seemed to have little difficulty in recognising that competitor airlines had a direct interest in the Commission finding that the merger did not fall under the Regulation: "the contested statement is to be regarded as of direct concern to the undertakings engaged in the international civil aviation market or markets who could, on the date of the contested act, be certain of an immediate or imminent change in the state of the market".[69] On the question of individual concern, the Court found Air France's position to be "clearly different" from other airlines: the merger and the effect of substituting BA for Dan Air on air routes between France and the United Kingdom and between Belgium and the United Kingdom, making BA's position "significantly stronger" and Air France position being correspondingly affected. Similarly, in the *TAT* case,[70] the Court of First Instance appeared to

---

[67] *ibid.*, para. 36.
[68] Case C-480/93P *Zunis Holding SA and Others v. Commission* [1996] E.C.R I-1; [1996] 5 C.M.L.R. 219.
[69] Case T-3/93 *Air France v. Commission* [1994] E.C.R. II-121.
[70] Case T-2/93 *Air France v. Commission* [1994] E.C.R. II-323.

have little difficulty in finding that Air France's application was admissible although the reasons given by the Court are more peculiar to the circumstances. The Court justified Air France's individual concern on these facts: Air France's participation in the Commission's procedure; the Commission's decision having made express reference to the position of Air France on the two markets identified; and the fact that Air France had, by agreement between it, the French Government and the Commission, been obliged to give up its interest in TAT a few months before BA's proposed acquisition.[71] This appears to place emphasis upon the competitor having participated in the Commission's inquiry under the Regulation, and whilst that criterion should not be determinative, competitor undertakings need to bear it in mind if their position on a market is likely to be adversely affected by a notified concentration. They need to act quickly to make representations.

7.6.3.3   Employees

As mentioned above[72] employees are in a special position, Article 18(4) of the Regulation expressly providing that "the recognised representatives of their [*i.e.* the undertaking's] employees". In the *Perrier* cases[73] the Court of First Instance had to consider whether certain French employees' representative institutions and trade union organisations had standing to bring an action under Article 173 to annul the Commission's decision in *Nestlé/Perrier*. The Court found that in substance the final decision was not of direct concern to the applicants—this was because job losses and changes in social benefits were not an inevitable consequence of the merger, and provisions of Community law (in particular the Acquired Rights Directive 77/187) and the French Labour Code meant that individual contracts were transferred to the new company and the transfer of the undertaking did not entail the termination of, or any change to, the collective agreements in force. Nonetheless by virtue of Article 18(4) the representative bodies were directly and understandably concerned and entitled to bring proceedings against the Commission's decision for the specific purpose of examining whether the procedural guarantees which they were entitled, under Article 18, to assert, during the Commission's administrative procedure, had been infringed.[74] The Court held that the mere fact that the Regulation mentions them expressly and specifically among the third persons showing a "sufficient interest" to submit their observations to the Commission is enough to differentiate them from all other persons and enough for it to be considered that the decision adopted under the Regulation is of individual concern to them, whether or not they had made use of their rights during the administrative procedure.[75]

---

[71] *ibid.*, paras 44–46.
[72] See para. 4.7.6, above.
[73] Case T-12/93 *CCE Vittel and Others v. Commission* [1995] E.C.R. II-1247; and Case T-96/92 *CCE Grandes Sources and Others v. Commission* [1995] E.C.R. II-1213.
[74] *ibid.*, Case T-46/92, para. 46.
[75] *ibid.*, Case T-96/92, para. 37.

7.6.3.4 Other Third Parties

Aside from the particular categories considered above of persons who may be affected by a merger itself there are circumstances where the nature of the Commission decision may have a direct impact on third parties. For example, in *Kali und Salz*, the undertakings given by the German potash producer to withdraw from the export joint venture and the agency selling relationship it had with the French competitor, SCPA, clearly had considerable commercial consequences for the latter. The Court of Justice had no doubt that SCPA had a right to challenge the Commission's decision even though it could not have imposed remedies against SCPA.[76] A somewhat different situation may occur in a case where the Commission finds that a particular market exhibits all the characteristics of an uncompetitive oligopoly, even if it does not go on to make a finding that the notified operation creates or strengthens a collective dominant position held by one (or both) of the merging parties and other undertakings in the sector concerned. A company may clearly be prejudiced by a finding that it occupies a position of collective dominance since this will expose it to action under Article 82 and domestic equivalents directed at controlling market dominance or market power and abuses thereof.

7.6.4 Grounds of Appeal

Article 230 of the E.C. Treaty provides that the Court shall have jurisdiction "on grounds of lack of competence, infringement of an essential procedural requirement, infringement of this Treaty or of any rule of law relating to its application, or misuse of powers". The Court has adopted a flexible approach to Article 230 and to a large extent the grounds have lost their individual importance. In practice less attention is now placed on the formal classification of the grounds, the Court being principally concerned with the substance.

It is clear that the Court may consider the proper construction and meaning of the provisions of the Regulation. It can therefore look at whether the Commission has correctly identified a "Community dimension" within the meaning of Articles 1 and 5[77] or whether in terms of Article 3, control has been acquired jointly or solely.[78] The Court can also consider, for example, whether the Commission has properly defined the relevant market correctly,[79] whether the party or parties have a dominant position[80] and whether there would be a strengthening of that position.[81] Procedural points can be taken, such as whether the Commission has given access to the file[82] or an accurate or sufficient statement of reasons as required by Article 253 of the Treaty.[83] Nor is it unusual for parties to make submissions based on infringement of a general

---

[76] Joined Cases C-68/94 & C30/95 *French Republic v. Commission* [1998] E.C.R. I-1375.
[77] *e.g.* Case T-3/93 *Dan Air*, paras 87–108: see n. 57, above.
[78] *e.g.* Case T-2/93 *TAT*, paras 54–66, see n. 70, above.
[79] *ibid.*, paras 73–88.
[80] *e.g.* Case T-221/95 *Endemol Entertainment Holdings BV v. Commission* [1999] 5 C.M.L.R. 611, paras 113–147.
[81] *ibid.*, paras 165–170.
[82] *ibid.*, paras 48–91.
[83] Case T-2/93 *TAT*, paras 89–95; and Case T-290/94 *Kaysersberg SA v. Commission* [1997] E.C.R. II-2137.

principle of Community law, such as legal certainty[84] or the protection of legitimate expectations.[85]

It should be noted that in merger cases, like other competition cases, there are frequently quite complicated economic assessments and it is recognised that the Commission enjoys a considerable measure of discretion.[86] The Court will be concerned to verify whether the relevant procedural rules have been respected; whether the facts have been accurately stated, and whether there has been a misuse of powers. Where, however, a matter lies within the Commission's discretion the Court will not overrule the Commission except where there has been a manifest error of appraisal. In the *Dan Air* case Air France argued that the Commission should have used the powers given it by Article 8(2) of the Regulation to impose an obligation permanently to discontinue the charter operations. The Court of First Instance replied: "it is in any event not for the Court, in the context of annulment proceedings, to substitute its own appraisal for that of the Commission and to rule on the question of whether the Commission should have imposed an obligation, by means of Article 8(2) of the Regulation, requiring discontinuance of the activity".[87]

7.6.5 Interim Relief

The bringing of an application under Article 230 does not operate to stay the operation and effect of the decision in question. But under Articles 242 and 243 of the E.C. Treaty the Court may, if it considers that circumstances so require, order that the application of the contested act be suspended or prescribe any necessary interim measures. It is a condition precedent to an application for interim relief that there is a main action in existence before the Court. It follows that if the main action is inadmissible the application for interim relief must also fail. The Rules of Procedure of the Court of First Instance (Article 104(2)) provide that applications for interim measures pursuant to Articles 242 and 243 of the Treaty must state the circumstances giving rise to urgency and the pleas of fact and law establishing a *prima facie* case for the interim measures applied for. Experience in merger cases to date indicates that the burden on a third party seeking to halt a merger by challenging the Commission's decision (of compatibility) will be substantial. The Court has to avoid grave and irreparable damage being suffered but is subject to the requirement that measures under Articles 242 and 243 must be of a provisional nature in the sense that they must not prejudice the final judgment in the case. As the Court pointed out in *Union Carbide v. Commission*,[88] the applicant's interest in having the operation of the contested decision suspended must be weighed against the public interest in implementation of decisions adopted under the Regulation and the interest of third parties affected by suspension of the decision.

---

[84] *e.g.* Case T-3/93 *Dan Air*, paras 109–114, see n. 57, above.
[85] *e.g.* Case T-2/93 *TAT*, paras 96–105, see n. 70, above.
[86] Case T-88/94R *Société Commerciale des Potasses et de L'Azote and Enterprise Minière et Chemique v. Commission* [1994] E.C.R. II-263 and 401.
[87] Above, para. 113.
[88] Case T-322/94R [1994] E.C.R. II-1159, para. 36.

In the *Nestlé/Perrier* cases[89] bodies representing the employees sought to suspend the disposal of part of the Perrier group pending the Court's final judgment, seeking to safeguard jobs. The Court of First Instance rejected the application for interim relief, taking the view that an order to that effect would have harmful effects on Nestlé which might only be justified if a refusal to grant the interim relief would threaten the very existence of the applicants. The Court, having regard to the protection given to employees under both Community law (for example the "Acquired Rights" Directive 98/50) and domestic French law, concluded that the Commission's decision authorising the concentration could not have an effect on the workers and their interests. On the other hand the Court was prepared to grant interim relief in the *Kali und Salz* case.[90] The Commission's decision authorised a joint venture pooling the potash businesses of K + S and the Treuhand. A competitor on the German market, SCPA, and its U.S. parent sought an order suspending a condition of the Commission's decision that K + S withdraw from an Austrian company, Kali-Export, in which SCPA held 25 per cent of the shares. The Court concluded that whilst it did not seem that the existence of SCPA was endangered, the Court did not have sufficient information to exclude the possibility that the existence of Kali-Export, of which SCPA was one of a small number of shareholders, might be endangered by implementation of the condition in question. On the other hand the provisional suspension of the operation of the condition was not likely to have a serious effect upon the interests of K + S and the joint venture or adversely affect the public interest or the Commission's interest in the immediate implementation of its decision. The Court ordered the suspension of the decision inasmuch as it might entail the dissolution of Kali-Export.

Finally, it should be noted that, save in exceptional circumstances, a party cannot, by way of an application for interim measures before the Court, frustrate the Commission's initial consideration and examination of a transaction to see whether it falls under the Regulation. In particular, a party cannot forestall the Commission from exercising its powers of inquiry and penalty after the opening of the administrative proceedings or before the Commission has adopted any interim or definitive acts whose operation the party might seek to be avoided. So where, as in the *Spanish Cable TV* case,[91] the Commission has told the parties that its (unnotified) concentration was caught by the Regulation and should be notified, the Court will not put itself into the shoes of the Commission and decide whether or not the Commission's coercive powers of investigation should be exercised in the particular circumstances.

7.7   REOPENING THE COMMISSION'S PROCEEDINGS

It has been noted above that the Regulation lays down specific time periods within which the Commission must take a decision on the concentration at the

---

[89] Case T-96/92R *Comité Central d'Entreprise de la Société Générale des Grandes Sources and others v. Commission*, Order of December 15, 1992; and Case T-12/93R *Comité Central d'Entreprise de la Société Anonyme Vittel* and *Comité d'Establishment de Pierval v. Commission*, Order of April 2, 1993.
[90] See n. 84, above.
[91] Case T-52/96R *Sogecable SA v. Commission* [1996] E.C.R. II-797, para. 40.

end of the first phase under Article 6 or at the end of the second phase under Article 8. Where the Court gives a judgment which annuls the whole or part of a Commission decision taken under the Regulation, it is provided that the time periods start again from the date of the judgment (R. Article 10(5)). The effect of the judgment is to cause the Commission to reopen the case to take account of the Court's ruling. This may necessitate the Commission's going through the whole procedure taking appropriate account of factual and legal considerations (the notification will inevitably be out of date and need to be made "complete") and hearing the parties as necessary. There has been only one case to date, following the Court of Justice's annulment of the Commission's decision in *Kali und Salz*.[92]

A separate case is that where following a Commission decision under Article 6 or 8 new factual or other material comes to light which arguably might have affected the decision of the Commission had it been known or considered at the relevant time. Can the proceedings be reopened? The shortness of the time limits and the importance of legal certainty for all concerned (manifested in the requirements on the Commission to take decisions and in the provisions implying decisions in the event of the Commission's failing to act in time) are central to the general scheme of the Regulation. At first glance it appears that proceedings cannot be opened except where the Regulation expressly provides for this. One case is that described above, when the Court annuls the Commission's decision. Another is set out in Article 8(5). The Commission has the power to revoke a decision under Article 8(2) (*i.e.* one of compatibility, if necessary following modifications of the proposal) where:

(a) the declaration of compatibility is based on incorrect information for which one of the undertakings is responsible or where it has been obtained by deceit; or

(b) the undertakings concerned a breach of an obligation attached to the decision.

This is in addition to the ability to fine for supplying incorrect or misleading information (R. Article 14(1)(b) and (c)) or for failing to comply with an obligation imposed pursuant to Article 8(2), second sub-paragraph (R. Article 14(2)(a)).

Whilst in some circumstances it is possible that a third party may be able to bring an appeal under Article 173 (provided always that he can show sufficient *locus standi*) it may not always be the case that the new facts or other matters will constitute grounds for or justify an appeal. It is arguable that in such cases, with the exception of those situations where the Commission can act pursuant to Article 8(5) as described above, the Commission's decision shall be final. But the position is not certain and in *Zunis Holdings and Others v. Commission*[93] the Court of First Instance appeared prepared to contemplate the reopening of proceedings at the instance of a third party following a Com-

---

[92] Joined Cases C-68/94 & 30/95 *French Republic v. Commission* [1998] E.C.R. I-1375. The post judgment procedure before the Commission is described in the Twenty-Eighth Report on Competition, paras 175–179.

[93] Case T-83/92 [1993] E.C.R. II-1169; [1994] 5 C.M.L.R. 154.

mission decision under Article 6. Zunis argued that the Commission had taken its decision in *Mediobanca/Generali* (under Article 6(1)(a) on the basis that there was no acquisition of control) in error because it had failed to take account of a particular shareholder agreement. The Court noted that the Regulation nowhere provides expressly for the possibility of requesting the Commission to reopen proceedings although Article 8(5)(a) provided for the revocation of decisions under Article 8(2). The Court held that even if Community law (as manifested in those cases where third parties had a right of action to protect their legitimate interests) enabled third parties to compel the reopening of proceedings, legal certainty requires that a request for reopening proceedings on the ground of the discovery of an allegedly new fact should be submitted within a reasonable period. In the instant case, where the Commission had taken its decision on December 19, 1991, and the alleged new fact came to light at the end of March/beginning of April 1992, a request for reopening the proceedings on June 26, 1992 was found to be out of time.

On appeal to the Court of Justice the Advocate General took the view that Article 8(5) of the Regulation is not to be regarded as a conclusive rule concerning the possibility of revoking Commission decisions in merger cases. He saw no reason why, for example, in the case of deliberate deceit, it should be possible for the Commission to revoke an Article 8(2) decision but not one adopted under Article 6(1)(a) or (b). But in the interests of the protection of legitimate expectations, revocation in the latter cases by analogy with Article 8(5) should, he considered, only be permissible under the conditions laid down in that provision. As regards the time within which requests to reopen proceedings should be brought before the Commission, the Advocate General disagreed with the approach taken by the Court of First Instance, taking the view that such requests should be brought within a reasonable time which should be determined not by reference to an abstract overall time-limit, but only by taking into account all the circumstances of the case itself. The Advocate General concluded, in the instant case, that the applicants had not delayed unreasonably. It seemed reasonable to him that parties should have time to consider the position on learning of new facts, etc., and should be able to approach the Commission informally before making a formal request for the proceedings to be reopened. The Court itself, however, did not rule or opine on this matter, taking the view that the decision (contained in the Commission's letter of July 31, 1992) merely confirmed its earlier decision and was therefore inadmissible.[94]

---

[94] Case C-480/93 *Zunis Holding SA and Others v. Commission* [1996] E.C.R I-1; [1996] 5 C.M.L.R. 219.

8   National Authorities and National Law

8.1   LIAISON WITH NATIONAL COMPETITION AUTHORITIES

The Regulation contemplates, and indeed requires, constant and close liaison between the Commission and the competent authorities of the Member States.[1] Reference is made in the Regulation and Implementing Regulation to the competent authorities of the Member States and the purpose of this section is to set out more systematically their involvement. The identification and designation of the national competent authorities is a matter of national law and national constitutional and administrative process. In practice designation may reflect the role national bodies have in shaping and applying domestic competition laws.[2] While the national and Community competition authorities have a good record of mutually beneficial co-operation, the greater pace and pressure of merger control has compelled them to intensify this co-operation and co-ordination greatly.[3] Even so, there have been instances where the tight clearance timetables have left Member States feeling, justifiably, that consultation has not been adequate.

8.1.1   Pre-notification

The Implementing Regulation expressly contemplates the possibility of undertakings having pre-notification discussions with the Commission (see Recital 8) and these are widely used and highly beneficial. However, even where a transaction prima facie falls within the scope of the Regulation, consultation with a national competition authority may also be worthwhile. Companies are encouraged to give the national competent authorities early warning and information on potential notifications.[4] This can help achieve meaningful consultations between national authorities and the Commission within the dead-

---

[1] See Recital 20 and Article 19(2).
[2] In the U.K., for the purposes of the Regulation, the Office of Fair Trading, the Secretary of State for Trade and Industry, and the Competition Commission are all designated. The role of the OFT as a competent authority in relation to cases under Arts 81 and 82 has been largely on casework, with the Department of Trade and Industry involving itself with policy matters, but the DTI takes a greater interest in cases under the Regulation. Competition Commission officials do not sit on the Advisory Committee but may be involved in assessing and reporting on concentrations referred back to the U.K. by the Commission (R.Art.9(6)).
[3] Speedier forms of communication are now used.
[4] Companies may also want to consult competent authorities, *e.g.* where there are jurisdictional issues which may take some time to resolve.

lines, for example, by briefing the relevant national authorities on the proposed concentration and the critical issues as far as the notifying parties are concerned. It will usually also be in the interests of companies to seek guidance in advance from national authorities on potential distinct market or legitimate interest issues which the transaction may raise. Third parties too may have something to gain from involving competent authorities at an early stage: for example, a target company may seek to ward off an unwelcome approach by involving national authorities, and careful consideration needs to be given to the opportunities which may exist for spoiling action. The acquirer too may be wise to take steps to ensure that pressure does not build up for an Article 9 referral back or to demonstrate that there are no other legitimate national interests which require protection through the application of national merger controls in addition to the Regulation itself. In some cases, however, companies and their advisers may prefer to steer clear of national competition authorities, for example, in the hope of avoiding an Article 9 referral back. It can be difficult for a Member State to make an adequate Article 9 request in the time allowed, particularly if it lacks detailed market information.

8.1.2 Notification

One of the reasons for the large number of copies required to be supplied to the Commission is to enable the Commission to discharge its obligations under Article 19(1) of the Regulation to transmit copies of notifications to the Member States and the EFTA Surveillance Authority[5] within three working days. This is a short time but any delay will jeopardise the Commission's timetable. What sort of questions are national authorities likely to have in mind when they look at a notified concentration?

(a) the first question is very likely to be whether the merger falls within the scope of the Regulation (the answer to this will determine whether, and to what extent, they can apply national law to the transaction).

(b) would the concentration impede competition in the Common Market as a whole or in a substantial part of it?

(c) is there a distinct market problem?

(d) are there any non-competition issues of legitimate interest to the Member State?

Under Article 6 of the Regulation the Commission must decide whether a concentration falls within the scope of the Regulation within one month of notification. If a national authority wants to express a view on this it will have to act speedily. Under Article 9 a Member State must identify a distinct market problem and inform the Commission within three weeks of the date of receipt of the copy of the notification.[6] There is, of course, no similar time restraint

---

[5] At least in the cases referred to in Art. 3(1) of Protocol 24 of the EEA.
[6] See generally para. 8.3, below.

as regards legitimate interests but one can expect that in such a case domestic authorities will also want to act quickly. In the United Kingdom the Competition Commission is used to making rapid yet detailed inquiries into merger proposals, and is likely to be able to assess such interests within the period given to the Commission to carry out a full examination of a concentration.[7]

As has been mentioned the failure by the Commission to take a decision under Article 6(1)(b) or (c) has the effect that the concentration is deemed to have been declared compatible with the Common Market (R.Article 10(6)).[8] (This default provision, which was intended to give legal certainty, has had little effect to date. But Article 10(6) is a critical feature of the Commission's recent proposal in its Draft Notice ''on a simplified procedure for processing certain concentrations''. The provision would, if the Commission's ideas are accepted, take on a far greater practical significance.) Neither the Commission nor, more importantly, a Member State can rely on any presumption that a notified concentration is one which falls within the scope of the Regulation. The effect as against the Commission is that the Commission cannot itself proceed any further with the case. Any prohibition on putting the concentration into effect is terminated (R.Article 7(5)). So far as the Member States are concerned, they are not, however, prohibited from applying their own competition laws if it can be established that the transaction is not a concentration with a Community dimension. Where a Member State has identified a distinct market problem the Commission may still refer the case to the Member State provided that three months have not elapsed from the date of notification of the decision (R.Article 10(6)).[9]

There are a number of procedural complications which may arise and require to be dealt with in national merger control laws and procedures in scenarios, rare but not entirely theoretical, where there are jurisdictional doubts. For example, a party may dispute a finding by the Commission that a merger falls within the scope of the Regulation. This may be for a number of reasons but nonetheless the Commission's decision should be treated as valid until set aside.[10] This could be months after the decision has been cleared, if not longer. If ultimately the Commission had no jurisdiction the clearance would be no impediment to the exercise of jurisdiction by a national competition authority under domestic law.[11]

---

[7] It is possible that the domestic procedures may, because of the different jurisdictional rules applicable (such as the ability to proceed against mergers ''in contemplation''), formally commence before those of the Commission.

[8] There is no time limit on an Art. 6(1)(a) decision.

[9] This may allow the Commission to refer a case back to a Member State even when the Commission itself has run out of time to commence phase two proceedings. See *McCormick/CPC/Rabobank/Ostmann*, discussed at para. 8.3.4, below. The reference back led the parties to abandon the deal.

[10] Case 101/78 *Granaria BV v. Hoofdproduktschap voor Akkerbouwprodukten* [1979] E.C.R. 623; [1979] C.M.L.R. 124. But see Joined Cases 143/88 & C92/89 *Zuckerfabrik Suederdithmarschen AG v. Hauptzollamt Itzehoe* [1991] E.C.R. I-415; [1993] 3 C.M.L.R. 1; and Joined Cases C-465/93 & 466/93 *Atlanta Fruchthandelsgesellschaft mbH v. German Federal Office of Food and Forestry* [1995] E.C.R I-3761, 3799.

[11] In the U.K. certain consequential changes have been made to the Fair Trading Act in order to deal with the Regulation and to protect the position of the Secretary of State in these circumstances. They are effected by the E.C. Merger Control (Consequential Provisions) Regulations 1990 (S.I. 1990 No. 1563). These Regulations do two things. First, they give the DGFT a further ground to reject a merger notice, namely where it appears to him that the merger in question is also a ''concentration with a Community dimension'' within the meaning of the (E.C.) Regulation. Secondly, the Regulations enable a merger reference to be made later than the time limit (six months) fixed by s. 64(4) of the Fair Trading Act

8.1.3 **Examination**

Where the Commission has decided that the concentration falls within the scope of the Regulation and that it needs to be fully examined, there will be further opportunities for "close and constant liaison" with the national authorities. This may give Member States the opportunity to submit observations.[12] It is clear, however, that the obligation imposed on the Commission by Article 19(1) of the Regulation (to remain in close and constant liaison with the Member States) does not extend to providing them with *all* the documents and information in its possession. The obligation is restricted to the supply of copies of the most important documents.[13] If there is a need for inspections then the competent authorities and Member State may provide assistance to the Commission on visits. In the United Kingdom the OFT will do this, as it does under Article 14 of Regulation 17. Similarly, representatives of the competent authorities will attend hearings. Where it looks as though the Commission will seek to remedy competition defects by seeking undertakings from the parties, then clearly national authorities will want to keep in touch with the Commission. This is likely especially where the undertaking is designed to remedy a particular distinct market problem in that Member State. Article 19(2) makes it clear that the national authorities may express their views upon all procedures under the Regulation.[14] In cases where the U.S./E.C. co-operation agreement applies,[15] Member States whose interests are affected will be kept informed of any co-operation or co-ordination of enforcement activities. The operation of the Agreement is also regularly discussed at the meetings of the Commission with national competition authorities.

8.1.4 **Advisory Committee**

Each Member State may nominate up to two representatives, but at least one must be competent in competition matters[16] (R.Article 19(4)). The meeting is

provided it is made within six months of the removal of any restriction on the making of the reference created by the (E.C.) Regulation. Both these provisions have the effect of stopping the clock running against the national authority. The Regulations preserve the ability of the Secretary of State to act against that merger notwithstanding the six month rule in s. 64(4). In effect the six month limitation period only begins to run in the above example from the setting aside of the Commission's decision.

[12] See, *e.g. Air France/Sabena.* The U.K. Government has made clear that during an investigation by the Commission publication of its views might compromise the effectiveness and integrity of the Commission's procedure. Information supplied might be market-sensitive: *Hansard* H.C. January 19, 1998, col. 395.

[13] See Joined Cases C-68/94 & 30/95 *French Republic and Others v. Commission* [1998] E.C.R. I-1375, paras 86 and 87, where certain data giving detailed information, Member State by Member State, of each of the operators' sales was found not to call into question the state of the market as identified by the Commission.

[14] This has not been achieved in all cases. Brinkmanship in negotiating satisfactory remedial undertakings may mean that there is simply no time to consult the Advisory Committee on them. So, *e.g.* in *Mannesmann/Vallourec/Ilva* the Committee agreed with a decision to prohibit the joint venture only to find that the Commissioners cleared it subject to conditions! See [1994] O.J. L102/5 which contains the Opinion of the Advisory Committee and the Art. 8 decision. The procedural changes introduced in March 1998 relating to undertakings were, however, designed to put an end to brinkmanship and ensure that Member States had sufficient time properly to consider remedies offered by the notifying parties.

[15] See para. 1.8, above.

[16] In practice officials from the OFT represent the U.K., though the DTI may attend for more politically sensitive cases. In exceptional cases more than two representatives may attend.

summoned and chaired by the Commission. The Member States must be given at least 14 days notice but it is doubtful whether this requirement is met in every case. With the invitation to the meeting the Commission must supply a summary of the case, a list of the most important documents and a draft of the proposed decision. Recognising the potentially critical time scales involved in most, if not all, concentration cases, the Regulation enables the 14-day notice period to be shortened in exceptional cases in order to avoid serious harm to one or more of the undertakings concerned (R.Article 19(5)). It seems that the Member States consider that shortening of the 14 day period is restricted to those circumstances and that the conditions should be strictly observed.[17] But even in the absence of an exceptional case relating to the risk of serious harm within the meaning of Article 19(5), a failure to comply with the 14 day rule is not in itself such as to render the Commission's final decision unlawful. The Court of First Instance has characterised the 14 day period as "a purely internal rule of procedure". The Commission's decision will only be rendered unlawful where failure to comply with the rule is sufficiently substantial and has a harmful effect on the legal and factual situation of the person alleging a procedural irregularity.[18]

The Advisory Committee is required to deliver an opinion on the draft decision (if necessary by vote and whether or not all members are present) (R.Article 19(6)). The opinion, which is written, is appended to the draft decision going to the Commissioners. The opinion is often quite short, comprising seven or eight one sentence paragraphs. Occasionally, however, they may be more substantial and informative as to the views of the Member States.[19] The Commission is directed to take the utmost account of the opinion and required to inform the Committee as to how it has been taken into account. The importance of the views of the Advisory Committee can be seen from the *Mercedes-Benz/Kässbohrer* case. The Committee criticised the reasoning in the draft clearance decision which had not been preceded by a statement of objections or formal hearing of the parties as is usual in most phase two cases. The Merger Task Force had been prepared to clear the merger at the end of the first stage but the German Cartel Office pressed for the case to be taken to the second stage. The Advisory Committee rejected any procedural corner-cutting. The Commission went back to the parties with a statement of objections, carried out further investigations and held a hearing before presenting a revised draft clearance decision to the Committee. On the other hand the practice of firms delaying until late in the second stage, the offering and negotiation of commitments has sometimes prejudiced the involvement of the Advisory Committee. In *Boeing/McDonnell Douglas* negotiations between the Commission and the parties went so far into the four month period that the Commission had met and given their conditional approval before the Committee had been consulted. The Committee did not meet but was consulted in writing. In *Anglo American Corporation/Lonrho*, revised undertakings were accepted by the

---

[17] See the Opinion of the Advisory Committee in *Ciba-Geigy/Sandoz* [1997] O.J. C230/15, para. 9.

[18] Case T-290/94 *Kaysersberg SA v. Commission* [1997] E.C.R. II-2137, para. 88. Five days notice was considered adequate in the circumstances. The Advisory Committee had not itself objected and had had sufficient information and time to formulate precise recommendations on the proposal.

[19] See, *e.g. RTL/Veronica/Endemol* [1996] O.J. C160/3. The identity of a particular Member State or States is never expressly identified.

Committee (though it is not clear that the Committee actually convened) the day before the Commission's decision. An addendum had to be made in the Committee's opinion which was formally adopted several weeks later. On occasion it has proved necessary to consult the Committee more than once; for example, when commitments have had to be modified to meet the concerns of the Commission.[20] To deal *inter alia* with such difficulties the Commission's recent Draft Notice on the subject of commitments indicates that only in exceptional circumstances will the Commission consider commitments offered after the third month in the second stage procedure. In *Airtours/First Choice*, the Commission declined to consider a revised package of remedial measures which were submitted after the Advisory Committee meeting and a few days before the Commissioners were to meet to approve the draft decision.

The Advisory Committee may recommend publication of its opinion, but it is the Commission which has the final say on publication (R.Article 19(7)). In other types of competition case the opinion is not a public document—it is not disclosed to the parties or otherwise.[21] The approach of the Regulation is more consistent with contemporary requirements and expectations of transparency. It has become normal practice for the Advisory Committee's opinion to be published at the same time as the Article 8 decision.[22] Publication must have regard to the protection of business secrets, and of the interests of the undertakings concerned just as when public versions of Article 6 and Article 8 decisions are prepared. But it will be very rare indeed that the Committee's opinion needs to contain or refer to business secrets.

It must be remembered that the role of the Advisory Committee is to give its opinions on draft decisions. It is not the decision maker and it will not have detailed information on which decision the Commission's draft has been based. Its representatives are usually drawn from the national equivalents of the Merger Task Force and, particulary as co-operation and expertise develops, their sympathies can be expected to lie with the Commission. It is therefore unlikely that lobbying efforts directed at the Committee will succeed in producing significant changes to a decision, let alone its reversal.

8.2 THE PLACE OF NATIONAL LAW

Article 21(2) of the Regulation provides that no Member State shall apply its national legislation on competition to any concentration that has a Community dimension. This provision gives legal expression to the political objective and the concern of industry that there should be a "one stop shop".[23] There are three exceptions to the basic rule giving the Commission exclusive jurisdiction over such concentrations. First, there is the "distinct market" concept. Article

---

[20] See, *e.g. Bertelsmann/Kirch/Premiere* and *Deutsche Telekom/Beta Research* [1999] O.J. L53/1 and 31 respectively.

[21] The question whether the parties could see the Committee's opinion was finally settled in the *Pioneer* case, Joined Cases 100-103/80 *Musique Diffusion Française et al v. Commission* [1983] E.C.R. 1825; [1983] 3 C.M.L.R. 221, paras 34–36.

[22] But not in the same volume of the O.J. The decisions are published in the 'L' series. The opinions are in the 'C' series. See, *e.g.*, *Skanska/Scancem* [1999] O.J. C201/5.

[23] Recitals 7, 27 and 28 are also relevant here.

9 provides for the referral of cases in whole or in part to national authorities, where a concentration impacts on a market within a Member State which bears all the characteristics of a "distinct market". However, the Commission is not always obliged to transfer the case to a national authority. Secondly, there is the exception for legitimate interests in Article 21(3). Member States may take appropriate measures to protect "legitimate interests" other than issues of competition taken into consideration by the Regulation. Neither of these exceptions is widely drawn and the practical effect is that the Commission has extensive competence to examine concentrations with Community dimension from a competition standpoint.

A further (implicit) exception derives from Article 298 (ex Article 223) of the E.C. Treaty itself, paragraph 1(b) of which provides:

"Any Member State may take such measures as it considers necessary for the protection of the essential interests of its security which are connected with the production of or trade in arms, munitions and war material; such measures shall not adversely affect the conditions of competition in the common market regarding products which are not intended for specifically military purposes."

The interpretative statement by the Commission on Article 21(3) recognised that its reference to public security was without prejudice to the provisions of Article 298 on national defence and in practice the Commission considers the application of Article 298 separately from Article 21 of the Regulation.[24]

By contrast Article 22(3) of the Regulation provides a mechanism where, even if a concentration lacks Community dimension, a Member State or Member States jointly can request the Commission to examine a concentration and if it finds that a dominant position is created or strengthened within the territory of the requesting Member State or States adopt an appropriate decision under Article 8.[25] The procedure in such cases is described later in this chapter.

8.3   ARTICLE 9—DISTINCT MARKETS

8.3.1   Background

Truly local or regional markets may cause competition problems which the criteria and procedures of the Regulation may not address.[26] The test in Article 2 is compatibility with the Common Market. What is prohibited is the creation or strengthening of a dominant position as a result of which effective competition would be significantly impeded in the Common Market or in a substantial part of it. Cases may arise where a concentration with Community dimension may be acceptable when measured against the test in Article 2 but may never-

---

[24] See the Twenty-Fourth Competition Report, point 336, and note that Art. 298 protects the exclusive jurisdiction of Member States. The Regulation cannot erode the Treaty provision.
[25] See para. 8.6.2, below.
[26] This was expressly recognised in the negotiations leading to the Regulation. Art. 8 of the Amended Proposal [1989] O.J. C22/1 specifically referred to local markets.

theless present greater difficulties at a local level. The history of the Regulation reveals that if there was to be a regulation[27] a means had to be found whereby, on the one hand, the Commission could properly discharge its obligations under Article 2 and could not simply be second-guessed on competition grounds by a particular Member State and, on the other, the case where a Member State might have a particular competition problem which might not be remedied within the framework of the Regulation could be addressed.

Article 9 of the Regulation, as amended in 1997, provides for the referral back of the whole or part of a notified concentration provided:

(a) the concentration "threatens to create or strengthen a dominant position as a result of which effective competition will be significantly impeded on a market within that Member State, which presents all the characteristics of a distinct market" (Article 9(2)(a)); or

(b) the concentration "affects competition on a market within that Member State, which presents all the characteristics of a distinct market and which does not constitute a substantial part of the common market" (Article 9(2)(b)).

Where a Member State seeks a referral of the concentration in its competent authority it must inform the Commission within three weeks of the date of receipt from the Commission of the copy of the notified concentration. But since time runs from a non-transparent event, receipt of the notification by the relevant Member State, it is difficult for third parties to discover when the Member State's deadline has passed.

8.3.2 Criterion of Distinct Market

In order to determine whether a market is a "distinct" one, it is necessary to consider both the goods and services concerned (the product market) and the market's geographical extent (the geographical market). As regards the latter, paragraph 7 of Article 9 defines the geographical reference market as:

"the area in which the undertakings concerned are involved in the supply of products or services, in which the conditions of competition are sufficiently homogeneous and which can be distinguished from neighbouring areas because, in particular, conditions of competition are appreciably different in those areas."

The first part of this definition is similar to statements made by the Court in the context of Article 82.[28]

Article 9(7) continues by listing matters which are to be taken into account; in particular the nature and characteristics of the products or services con-

---

[27] Sir Leon Brittan admitted that Art. 9 was the last clause to be agreed and on its agreement depended the fate of the whole Regulation. See (1990) 15 E.L. Rev. 351 at 355.

[28] See, *e.g.* Case 27/76 *United Brands v. Commission* [1978] E.C.R. 207; [1978] 1 C.M.L.R. 429, para. 11 and Chap. 5, above, discussing market definition generally.

cerned, the existence of entry barriers or of consumer preferences, appreciable differences of the undertakings' market shares between the area concerned and the neighbouring areas, and substantial price differences. In practice the Commission adopts the same approach to market definition as in appraisals for decisions under Articles 6 and 8 of the Regulation.

8.3.3 **Procedure**

The burden is on the Member State to inform the Commission, within three weeks of the date of receipt of its copy of the notification, that a concentration has an impact on competition on a distinct market within that Member State within the terms of Article 9(2)(a) or (b) (set out above). Ground (b) was added in the 1997 changes. In contrast to (a) the Member State need only demonstrate that the concentration *affects* competition in such a market. No proof of threat to create or strengthen dominance is required. The threshold is thus lower. The Commission justified the change on the basis that it can prohibit a concentration only if it creates or strengthens dominance in a substantial part of the Common Market.

Given the three weeks deadline a Member State must put its case together quickly. It will have the notification. It can also use its own domestic powers of inquiry (R.Article 21(2)). In the United Kingdom the Secretary of State, after the advice of the DGFT, decides whether to apply for an exit to national jurisdiction under Article 9(2) on the basis that there may be a distinct market problem. The Commission has to consider the Member State's application. It can ask the Member State for more information (Article 19(2)).[29] It is then for the Commission to decide whether or not to allow the competent authorities of that Member State to apply its own national competition laws to the merger or part of it. The problem differs depending on whether the case falls within Article 9(2)(a) or (b). In (a) the Commission has a discretion and may consider that it should itself deal with the whole case in order to maintain or restore effective competition on the market concerned, as it did, for example, in *EDF/ London Electricity*. In cases falling within Article 9(2)(b), the reference back to the Member State is automatic, provided that the Commission agrees that a distinct market in that State is affected (Article 9(3)). The Member State must be given the opportunity to put its views to the Commission at each stage of the Commission's decision under Article 9(3). To this end the Member State has the right of access to the file of the Commission (Article 19(2)).

Where a Member State triggers the distinct market exception, the initial one month period for the Commission's examination of the notification is automatically extended to six weeks. In order to meet the concern of certain Member States that the proceedings should not be delayed any longer than necessary and that if undertakings have to go to more than "one shop" then they should be able to do so simultaneously, and that decisions should be reached, as far as possible, in the same time-frame, the Commission is obliged

---

[29] In the U.K. Regulations were adopted: the EEC Merger Control (Distinct Market Investigations) Regulations 1990. (S.I. 1990 No. 1715). These give the DGFT investigative powers (based on s. 3(7) of the Competition Act 1980) to obtain information for the purposes of Art. 19(2).

to take an early decision on the question of referral to the Member States. Article 9(4) provides that where the Commission itself decides not to initiate proceedings (*i.e.* the case where notification does not raise any serious doubts as to its compatibility with the Common Market) then a decision on referral to the national authorities should generally be taken within the six week period. Where the Commission has initiated proceedings, the decision on referral should be taken within three months of the date of notification. Even in this situation the Commission is not obliged to refer the case where it itself has taken preparatory steps (these will normally take the form of a notification of objections within the meaning of Article 18(1)) to maintain or restore effective competition in the market concerned. The Regulation makes clear that the Commission must take a decision to refer or to refuse referral, or take steps towards remedying the problem. The failure to take a decision or the appropriate preparatory steps within a three month period results in there being a deemed decision to refer the case to the Member State (R.Article 9(5)).

So far as the Member State is concerned, it is obliged to act promptly when the case is referred to it. It has four months from the Commission's referral to complete its examination of the concentration. It is not obliged to take remedial action in this period, but it is required to publish any report or announcement of the findings of its examination of the concentration. Given the inflexibility in some national merger control procedures, Member States may well find these deadlines uncomfortable. If the report contained adverse findings, any remedial order or undertakings, if appropriate, could follow later. Finally, one further restriction on the Member State should be noted. Article 9(8) provides that Member States may take only the measures directly necessary to safeguard or restore effective competition on the market concerned. This factor may affect the decision to refer the case back and, where referred, whether that referral is for the whole or only part of the operation. The Regulation and national law can proceed in parallel pursuant to Article 9, leaving the Commission able to deal, under the Regulation, with any wider adverse effects in the Community as may be justified by *its* findings related to the part of the operation over which it retains jurisdiction.

8.3.4 Practice

As was emphasised in the joint statement for the Council and Commission at the time of adoption of the Regulation, the referral procedure provided for in Article 9 is likely only to be applied in exceptional cases. But recent signs suggest that the Commission, for resource reasons in particular, does not discourage the appropriate use of Article 9. Article 9 is designed for cases in which the interests in respect of competition for the Member State concerned cannot be adequately protected in any other way (*i.e.* by the Regulation). In short, Article 9 is only likely to be available where there would otherwise be a control gap, that it where the concentration might adversely affect competition in a domestic market without significantly impeding competition in the Common Market or in a substantial part of it, or where measures taken under the Regulation to prevent such adverse effects would not also resolve a problem in the domestic market.

Article 9 has arisen in a number of cases, though only a dozen or more references back have been made. Germany has made a number of unsuccessful applications.[30] The United Kingdom has been unsuccessful in only one case.[31] The circumstances of each case and the reasons for the Commission's decision to refer back, in whole or in part, a concentration to a particular Member State for examination under domestic competition rules vary substantially. Nonetheless a few general comments may be offered. First, there are product markets or sectors where local or regional markets persist and where competition may be adversely affected by mergers involving national players. So a number of Article 9 cases have involved the retail (food and non-food) sector. The Commission has accepted that particular competition problems may arise in quite narrowly drawn geographic markets. Thus the Commission referred back part of the operation concerned in *Promodes/Casino* (France), *Promodes/S21/Gruppo GS* (Italy) and *Vendex/Bijenkorf* (Netherlands). Similar considerations have applied where the physical properties of the products or physical location of supply points have given rise to the need to examine increase of market power at a local or regional level. The high proportion of transport costs in the price of ice-control salt was relevant in *CSME/MDPA/SCPA*. A number of cases have involved building materials: *Steetley/Tarmac* (clay tiles), *Holdercim/Cedest* (ready mixed concrete) and *Redland/Lafarge* (aggregates and ready mixed concrete). In *Compagnie Industrielle Maritime/Elf/Compagnie Nationale de Navigation* the Commission acknowledged the potential problems concerning certain oil storage markets in France.

Secondly, notwithstanding the advent of the Internal Market and the considerable liberalisation which has occurred in many markets, there remains sectors where for historic or other reasons local or regional market structures still dominate.[32] The situation in the German gas and electricity energy markets, for example, has given rise to a number of referrals back.[33] Thirdly, the Commission has been sympathetic to cases where parallel related operations (without a Community dimension) are under examination by the national authorities[34] even where competition in local or regional markets appears not to be at issue. In *GEHE/Lloyds Chemists*, the Commission acceded to the United Kingdom's request to be able to examine the implications of the proposed operation for the wholesale and retail pharmaceutical markets[35] within the United Kingdom. This enabled the United Kingdom competition authorities to review GEHE's bid on a co-ordinated timetable with the parallel bid for Lloyd's then being made by Unichem. Finally, there may be more controver-

---

[30] *Varta/Bosch; Alcatel/AEG Kabel; Mannesmann/Hoesch; Siemens/Philips; MSG/Media Service; ABB/Daimler-Benz; Bertelsmann/Kirch/Premiere;* and *Deutsche Telekom/Beta Research.*

[31] *EDF/London Electricity*, where the Commission found on the information available that the merger was not likely to have any adverse effects on competition and therefore the criteria for referral back were not met. Soon after, in *Airtours/First Choice*, the Competition Commissioner took the unprecedented step of publicly inviting the U.K. to request a referral back. He was rebuffed by the U.K. authorities but the proposed concentration was prohibited by the Commission.

[32] See *Krauss-Maffei/Wegmann*, supply of armoured military vehicles in Germany.

[33] See *SEHB/VIAG/PE-BEWAG; RWE/Thyssengas;* and *Bayernwerk/Isarwerke.*

[34] See also *Preussag/Hapag Lloyd/Touristik Union International* (tourism and travel services—referral back to Germany).

[35] The Commission has found these markets to be essentially regional or local in scope in a number of decisions. On these grounds it agreed a reference back in *Alliance Unichem/Unifarma* to the Italian authorities of a merger affecting the North West of Italy.

sial exceptional circumstances. A somewhat remarkable referral back occurred in *McCormick/CPC/Rabobank/Ostmann*. The Commission had miscalculated the legal deadline in Article 10(1), second sentence, of the Regulation, with the result that if the competition issues were to be examined at all the Commission would have to allow national law to apply.[36] The Commission took advantage of the longer period (in Article 10(6), read with Article 9.4(a)) to refer the notification to the German authorities to examine the herb and spice market in Germany. In the event the parties withdrew from the deal.

8.4   PROTECTION OF MEMBER STATES' LEGITIMATE INTERESTS

8.4.1   Background

Most if not all Member States recognised that there were certain matters control over which the Member States should retain for themselves. This is not so unusual in the context of Community law. The Treaty itself occasionally recognises the need for exceptions (for example Article 30 lists exceptions to the principle of free movement of goods in Article 28, and Article 296 enables Member States to take unilateral measures to protect essential security interests). As regards the Regulation, the difficulty in both political and legal terms lay in defining the extent of any exceptions. The decision to give the Commission exclusive competence over major cross-border concentrations would have been undermined by a wide formulation (such as "public interest") leaving the way open to any Member State to intervene in any case whenever it wished. In the event a compromise was reached: the Regulation sets out a very short list of matters which all Member States agreed, in the negotiations leading to the adoption of the Regulation, should entitle a Member State to intervene.[37] These are public security, plurality of the media and the so-called prudential rules. Any other interests have to be notified to the Commission and recognised in advance before they can be protected by Member States consistently with their obligations under the Regulation.

8.4.2   The Three Identified Interests

8.4.2.1   Public Security

This is not a new term in Community law. It can be found in the Treaty itself: see Article 30, Article 46, Article 54, and Community subordinate legislation such as the common import and export rules. "Public security" may overlap

---

[36] The deadlines are not easy to calculate, and somewhat different rules apply to the referral back timetable compared with the decision timetable which the Commission must meet. The timetable is also less transparent since it depends on the date of receipt of a copy of the notification by the Member State concerned, which is not public, whereas the date of receipt of a complete notification by the Commission is confirmed by the notice published in the O.J.

[37] Shorter than, *e.g.* the list in Art. 30 which includes public morality, public policy, protection of health, and the protection of industrial and commercial property rights.

but is not synonymous with national defence and may be more restricted. The ability of Member States to take action under Article 296 of the Treaty is unaffected.[38] The first reported instance under the Regulation occurred in *IBM France/CGI*. The French authorities notified the Commission that it had taken measures in respect of two subsidiaries of CGI involved in the merger. The two subsidiaries worked with the French Ministry of Defence.[39] Public security is not, however, limited to external military security. Nor is it confined to internal security (*i.e.* the maintenance of law and order) falling short of "serious internal disturbances", which is covered by Article 297, although "public security" may include this.[40] The Commission in its statement recognises that there may be wider considerations of public security. It refers to Article 224 (now Article 297) and Article 36 (now Article 30). In the latter context the Court has recognised (in the *Campus Oil*[41] case) that public security may cover security of supplies of a product or service which is of fundamental importance for the existence of, or survival of those in, that Member State.[42] But, as the Court has pointed out on a number of occasions, exceptions under the Treaty will be narrowly construed.[43] It is likely that the Court will take this approach to Article 21(3). As regards the practice in the United Kingdom, it is a well-established policy to refer mergers principally on competition grounds and it has been the exception where reference has been made on other "public interest" grounds.

8.4.2.2   Plurality of the Media

As the Commission's statement indicates, the Member States right to intervene in concentrations on this ground recognises legitimate concerns to maintain diversified sources of information for the sake of plurality of opinion and multiplicity of views. It is notable that many States, not just those in the Community, apply specific media ownership regimes which go beyond normal competition laws. In the United Kingdom this is largely accomplished under the Broadcasting Acts 1990 and 1996. In addition newspaper mergers are subject to a special regime under the Fair Trading Act. This is unaffected by the Regulation and thus, for example, the acquisition of Newspaper Publishing plc, which produces the *Independent* newspaper, by an international consortium of Promotore de Informacioes, Editoriale l'Espresso, and the Mirror Group remained subject to the dual jurisdiction of the United Kingdom author-

---

[38] See paras 8.2, above and 8.4.3, below.

[39] Twenty-Third Report on Competition Policy (1993), para. 321.

[40] *Per* A.G. Slynn in Case 72/83 *Campus Oil Ltd et al v. Minister of Industry and Energy et al* [1984] E.C.R. 2727 at 2764; [1984] 3 C.M.L.R. 544.

[41] *ibid.*, judgment of the Court, point 34.

[42] The reasoning and conclusions of this case appear to be accepted by the Commission (see Interpretative Statement on Art. 21) although it has been described as "less than wholly convincing" by Gormley, see Kapteyn and Verloren van Themat, *Introduction to the Law of the European Communities* (2nd ed.), p. 393.

[43] See, *e.g.* Case 224/84 *Johnston v. Chief Constable of the Royal Ulster Constabulary* [1986] E.C.R. 1651, para. 26. The Court has, on the other hand, recognised that Member States have a large margin of discretion with regard to the most appropriate measures to be taken in order to maintain public order and safeguard internal security. See Case C-265/95 *Commission v. France* [1997] E.C.R. I-6959.

ities and the Commission.[44] At present media ownership regulation is largely for the Member States, the E.C. Broadcasting Directive having only a peripheral impact. But in 1997 the Commission raised the prospect of Community policy and activity in this area focusing chiefly on rules which put a maximum limit on the stake that could be acquired in the capital of a broadcasting company and rules limiting the number of media that could be controlled by a given individual. The Commission also contemplated putting a 30 per cent limit on the television and radio audience a single individual or company could have in any E.U. country and a 10 per cent ceiling on overall audience shares across the media. But such radical proposals could not command general acceptance and the Commission itself has been unable to reach agreement in principle on the procedures for regulating media concentration in the Internal Market.

8.4.2.3   Prudential Rules

Prudential rules encompasses those rules normally relating to the supervision of companies in the financial services sector, which enable some public or other supervisory body to regulate the ownership and control and asset levels of banks, insurance companies, etc. Such rules are typically directed to the fitness and honesty of individuals to be associated directly with the management and running of the company concerned, and the capital adequacy and services of company concerned. A good number of notifications have involved the acquisition of insurance companies and banks. In *Sun Alliance/Royal Insurance* the Commission expressly acknowledged that the United Kingdom Government could apply the United Kingdom Insurance Companies Act to the transaction alongside the Commission's application of the Regulation. The Commission has recently challenged the Portuguese Government's application of the concept of prudential supervision somewhat when it sought to prohibit the acquisition of the Portuguese Champalimaud by the Spanish BSCH.[45]

8.4.3   Other Cases

8.4.3.1   Defence

Recital 28 to the Regulation makes clear that the Regulation does not affect a Member State's abilities to act under Article 296 (ex Article 223) of the Treaty. A Member State may therefore take such measures it considers necessary for the protection of the essential interests of its security which are connected with the production of trade in arms, munitions and war material. Such action must not adversely affect the conditions of competition regarding products which are not intended for specifically military purposes. There have been a handful of cases to date, all of which have involved either France[46] or United

---

[44] *Newspaper Publishing.*
[45] *European Report*, July 7 1999.
[46] The first case was a French one involving the manufacture of engines for missiles—see Twenty-third Report on Competition (1993), paras 324–326. For a more recent example, see *Matra/Aérospatiale.*

Kingdom[47] Government's intervention to ensure that the Commission limited its considerations to the civilian and not the specific military aspects of the operation in question. Not every case which might, however, have been subject to intervention, has seen action taken by governments.

In practice the measures have taken the form of requests from the government of the Member State concerned to the parties not to notify the merger notwithstanding its having a Community dimension. Where the merger has covered both military and non-military activities the request has been limited to the former aspects of the merger. The civilian aspects of the merger have therefore remained to be notified to the Commission. The governments concerned have also informed the Commission that it would not be appropriate for the Commission to deal with the merger under the Regulation. The Commission has taken the position that the Member State should provide it with sufficient information to verify that the conditions for the application of Article 296 of the Treaty are met and that the merger does not have any adverse effects for suppliers of the undertakings concerned, any intermediate consumers and final consumers (such as defence ministries) in other Member States. The Commission has been concerned to have the latter information, particularly so that it can consider its position under Article 298. This provides that if measures taken in the circumstances referred to in Article 296 have the effect of distorting the conditions of competition in the Common Market, the Commission shall, together with the Member State concerned, examine how the measures can be adjusted to the rules laid down in the Treaty. Improper action under Article 296 can be challenged by the Commission or another Member State by direct action in the Court of Justice under Article 298.

8.4.3.2   Any Other Public Interest

The final paragraph of Article 21(3) deals with other cases (other than the three listed in Article 21(3) second paragraph and Defence). Member States may take appropriate measures "to protect legitimate interests other than those taken into consideration by the Regulation and compatible with the general principles and other provisions of Community Law". There thus appear to be three restrictions on what may comprise such a legitimate interest. The first is that the interest must be a "public" one. A Member State could not therefore expect to have recognised by the Commission the interest, for example, of the existing management in remaining in control. The second condition, that the interest must be "other than those taken into consideration by this Regulation", shows the close relationship between this provision and Article 2. Competition is the interest which dominates and hence a Member State cannot, notwithstanding the express prohibition in Article 21(2) on applying national competition law, use Article 21(3) for domestic competition policy purposes. Similarly, to the extent that the Commission may have regard under Article 2 to other interests (for example, the development of technical and economic progress), Member States' ability to intervene is restricted. The third condition,

---

[47] The U.K. was involved in the later cases: *GEC/VSEL*; *British Aerospace/VSEL*; *GEC/Thomson*; and *British Aerospace/Lagardere*.

compatibility with Community law, hardly needs stating. It is noteworthy, however, that reference is made not merely to specific prohibitions (such as the prohibition on discrimination in Article 12 of the E.C. Treaty) but also "the general principles and other provisions of Community law". The term "general principles" is generally understood to encompass such matters as the protection of fundamental rights, the prohibition on discrimination, the principle of proportionality and the principle of legal certainty. Except for the second of these it is difficult to imagine when application of national law would be inhibited by these principles. What is meant by "other provisions" is uncertain but it appears that the Commission will be concerned to see that the relevant provisions of national law do not constitute a form of arbitrary discrimination or a disguised restriction on trade between Member States, as well as to confirm that the national legislation is not applied in a discriminatory manner.

An example can be seen in the context of the United Kingdom's regulation of the water industry where water and sewerage undertakings enjoy a natural monopoly in the provision of services in their area. The domestic regulator has a need to maintain a sufficient number of comparators (*i.e.* independently controlled suppliers) to sustain the effectiveness of the regulatory regime. In March 1995 the Commission made a decision recognising the legitimate interest of the United Kingdom in applying sections 32 to 34 of the Water Industry Act 1991 (as amended by the Competition and Services (Utilities) Act 1992) subject to the provisos that the United Kingdom authorities should not take into account in their considerations matters which properly fell to the Commission to take in assessing concentrations under the Regulation and that the United Kingdom authorities should notify the Commission of each case in which the legislation was to be applied so that the Commission can check that the measures are appropriate, proportional and non-discriminatory.[48] By contrast, in *EDF/London Electricity*, the Commission rejected the United Kingdom's request under Article 21(3) for recognition of a legitimate interest based on the role of the Director General of Electricity Supply. The domestic measures in question related to the DGES's ensuring regulatory transparency and protection of consumers from adverse effects of vertical integration. The Commission took the view that the measures in question were part of the ongoing regulation of the United Kingdom electricity industry and were not aimed at the merger itself. Vertical integration is also essentially a competition issue, which is not uncommonly considered in applying the test of compatibility. The Regulation did not preclude such ongoing regulatory activity and therefore it was not necessary for the Commission to recognise it as a legitimate interest under Article 21(3).

8.4.3.3   Recognition Procedure

The Regulation lays down a procedure for notifying a "public interest" to the Commission and obliges the Commission to take a decision on whether it is

---

[48] For an example, see *Lyonnaise des Eaux/Northumbrian Water* where the prospective bidder sought clearance from the U.K. authorities before launching the bid which would have triggered a notification to the Commission.

a legitimate interest for the purposes of Article 21(3) within a period of one month. Formally the Commission's decision in such a case will "recognise" the interest. There is no time set as to when a Member State should apply, nor any requirement that an application relate to an identifiable concentration proposal. An advance "general" (*i.e.* not related to a specific concentration) application can therefore be made provided always that the legitimate interest can be sufficiently clearly defined. Indeed given the possible need for prompt action in any particular case and the fact that Article 21 prohibits any measures to be taken by Member States before the legitimate interest is recognised by the Commission, early, and therefore possibly general, applications can be expected. The United Kingdom's application in respect of the Water Industry Act 1991 was such a general application, paving the way for a reference of a specific case *Lyonnaise des Eaux/Northumbrian Water*, to the (then) MMC.

8.4.3.4   Member States' Action

Apart from the recognition procedure there are no limitations on a Member State in a "legitimate interest" case. Unlike the procedure under Article 9 (distinct markets) there are no express pre-conditions or other restrictions on the Member State's procedures. The reference, however, in the first paragraph of Article 21(3) to Member States ability to take "appropriate measures" may import, as the Commission's statement suggests, the need for objectivity and proportionality on the part of Member States.[49] The Commission contends that Member States must choose, where alternatives exist, the measure which is objectively the least restrictive to achieve the end pursued. The Commission may require the national authority to keep it informed of any conditions which the national authority may consider it appropriate to attach to the transaction.[50]

Where a Member State acts in contravention of Article 21, the Commission may take appropriate action to restrain the Member State. It is reported[51] that in *BSCH/Champalimaud* the Commission issued a decision under Article 21 ordering Portugal to suspend its veto (contained in an administrative decision (*despacho*) of the Minister of Finance) affecting the agreements and voting rights in question. The Commission can back up such decisions by proceedings in the European Court of Justice under Article 226 of the Treaty.

8.5   EEA

The Agreement on the European Economic Area provides for co-operation between the Commission and the EFTA Surveillance Authority. Article 58 imposes a specific duty of co-operation "with a view to developing and maintaining a uniform surveillance throughout the European Economic Area in the field of competition and to promoting a homogenous implementation, application and interpretation of the provisions of this Agreement to this end". As

---

[49]   See Commission statement on Art. 21(3) set out in App. 7 of the first edition.
[50]   *Newspaper Publishing*.
[51]   European Report No. 2433, September 11, 1999, P. III.7.

regards mergers the two competent authorities are required to co-operate in accordance with the detailed provisions set out in Protocol 24. Although this Protocol begins with a broad obligation to co-operate on general policy issues the detailed rules which follow are restricted to cases where the Commission has jurisdiction under Article 57(2)(a) and even then only when certain conditions are satisfied (Article 2):

(a) where the combined turnover of the undertakings contained in the territory of the EFTA States equals 25 per cent or more of their total turnover within the territory covered by the Agreement; or

(b) where each of at least two of the undertakings concerned has a turnover exceeding ECU 250 million in the territory of the EFTA States; or

(c) where the concentration is liable to create or strengthen a dominant position as a result of which effective competition would be significantly impeded in the territories of the EFTA States or a substantial part thereof.

The co-operation procedure was implemented for the first time in merger control cases in *Neste/Statoil*. It has been the Commission's practice to identify (in, for example, decisions under Article 6 or 8 of the Regulation) so-called EEA co-operation cases.[52]

There must also be co-operation where the concentration threatens to create or strengthen a dominant position impeding competition on a distinct market within an EFTA State, whether or not it is a substantial part of the EEA, or where an EFTA State wishes to adopt measures to protect legitimate interests (for example public security, plurality of the media, or prudential rules). In relation to these cases, Articles 6 and 7 of the Protocol contain provisions analogous to Articles 9 and 21 respectively of the Regulation enabling the Commission to make a referral back to the authorities of the relevant EFTA State in a distinct market case or permitting the EFTA State to protect its legitimate interests.

Protocol 24 provides detailed rules for assistance and co-operation between the Commission and the EFTA Surveillance Authority throughout and at key stages in the proceedings. Thus copies of notifications and impartial documents must be sent by the Commission to the EFTA Surveillance Authority (Article 3(1)). The EFTA Surveillance Authority and EFTA States may be represented at oral hearings (Article 4). They are also entitled to be present at the E.C. Advisory Committee on Concentrations and to give their views (but not vote) (Article 5). The Commission is able to obtain all necessary information from the EFTA Surveillance Authority and EFTA States. The Commission is also required to provide to the EFTA Surveillance Authority copies of requests and decisions seeking information from an undertaking in the Authority's territory and inform it of the results of investigations. The Commission can request the

---

[52] See, *e.g. Dalgety plc/The Quaker Oats Co.* (an Art. 6 case) and *Nordic Satellite Distribution* [1999] O.J. L52/20 (an Art. 8 case). The Commission has in some cases expressly stated that a case is not a co-operation one.

EFTA Surveillance Authority to undertake investigations within its territory and can participate in such investigations (Article 8).[53]

8.6 CONCENTRATIONS WITHOUT A COMMUNITY DIMENSION

8.6.1 Member States' Request

The exceptions to the exclusive jurisdiction of the Commission over concentrations with a Community dimension have been examined above. Article 22 contains a mechanism, the effect of which is to allow Member States to confer jurisdiction on the Commission even where a Community dimension is lacking. Use of the mechanism has led to a number of significant Article 8 decisions. In the future, however, with the proliferation of domestic merger controls replicating the concepts in the Regulation, there is likely to be less use of the procedure. In particular, in the last two years, both the Netherlands and Finland have introduced national merger controls.

Article 22(3) enables a Member State or two or more Member States acting jointly to trigger the procedures of the Regulation, and thereby give the Commission jurisdiction to take measures in respect of a concentration, where the concentration creates or strengthens a dominant position as a result of which competition will be significantly impeded within the territory of the Member State or States. In the *British Airways/Dan-Air* case, the alleged effect on competition was within the territory of Belgium, in connection with air routes between London and Brussels. The Commission applied the Regulation at the request of the Belgian Government but, after the one-month initial examination, issued a decision that the acquisition of Dan-Air would not create or strengthen a dominant position as a result of which competition would be significantly impeded within the territory of Belgium.

Member States must act promptly if they want to take advantage of the procedure in Article 22 of the Regulation. The request must be made to the Commission within one month of the date on which the concentration was "made known" to the Member State or to all the Member States making the joint request, or effected, whichever is the earlier. Since concentrations below the threshold do not have to be notified under the Regulation a Member State will, in the absence of voluntary notification by the parties, get to know of potential cases for Article 22 treatment only if there is a national system of prior notification, or the transaction has, for some other reason, to be made public, as, for example, where listed companies are involved. If there is any question that Article 22 might apply it may be prudent to notify the Member State concerned in order to start the time running. In practice the Commission has accepted that a concentration has been "made known" where the parties sent the material authorities a press release[54] or in one case where they were informed by letter.[55]

---

[53] The EFTA Surveillance Authority cannot however seek similar assistance for investigation inside the Community.
[54] See *Kesko/Tuko* and *RTL/Veronica/Endemol*.
[55] *Blokker/Toys "R" Us*.

The one-month limit may be a serious impediment to the use of Article 22. In the *British Airways/Dan-Air* case, British Airways had not directly communicated with the Belgian Government prior to the concentration being effected, and Belgium made its request within three weeks of the concentration being effected, and was held to be within the time limit (interestingly, it was an incomplete request and Belgium only supplied full information four weeks later, but although this delayed commencement of the initial examination the Commission did not treat the incompleteness as such as to invalidate the request). A particular problem may arise in the case of joint requests by Member States. The Regulation, which was amended in 1997 to provide for such requests, is not entirely clear as to when the one month starts running in the case where the merger is made known to Member States at different times. Starting the clock when the first Member State has the information would operate to the potential disadvantage of later Member States. On the other hand, if the one month period begins when the last Member State party to the request learns of the merger this would permit an earlier Member State to obtain an advantage if out of time to make an individual application. The reference in Article 22(4) to the concentration being made known "to *all* the Member States", making a joint request would suggest that the clock starts ticking when the last Member State learns of the merger. It is submitted that this is the correct approach provided that the request is a genuine joint one as regards any Member State who might individually be out of time. The request must be one capable of leading to a finding that the merger would create or strengthen a dominant position as a result of which effective competition would be significantly impeded *within the territory of the Member States*. A laggard Member State should not be able to circumvent the one month rule by tagging on to or engineering a joint request when it would individually be unable to meet the criteria.

8.6.2 Applicable Provisions

It is important to note which provisions of the Regulation apply and which do not when the Article 22 procedure is activated.[56] The criteria for appraisal in Article 2(1)(a) and (b) are applicable. The test is whether the concentration creates or strengthens a dominant position as a result of which effective competition will be significantly impeded within the territory of the Member State concerned.[57] This is different from the test in Article 2(1) of the Regulation; that is, the Commission's appraisal of concentrations below the thresholds does not seek to establish whether or not the concentration is compatible with the Common Market (the first paragraph of Article 2(1) and Article 2(2) and (3) do not apply but paragraphs (a) and (b) of Article 2(1) (relevant factors) do). Article 4 does not apply and therefore there is no requirement for parties to notify these concentrations. The rule in Article 7 relating to suspension has qualified application. Article 7 only applies "to the extent that the concentration has not been put into effect on the date on which the Commission informs

---

[56] See Art. 22(4), first sentence.
[57] Art. 22(3).

the parties that a request has been made'' (Article 22(3) as amended). Naturally, Article 5, definition of turnover, applies in order to enable the determination whether the concentration in question has or has not a Community dimension. Articles 6, 8 and 10 to 20 apply, although certain of the specific provisions are otiose, such as the sanctions relating to notification in Article 14. Accordingly, since the same decision-process applies, the procedure is a two-stage one and the Commission has the powers of inquiry and decision (with fines and penalties) and the obligation to act in co-operation with Member States, as in the case of a concentration with a Community dimension. Once the Member State has referred the concentration to the Commission, the matter is in the hands of the Commission. The Member State has no power to control the conduct or define the scope of the Commission's investigation.[58] Articles 9 and 21, however, do not apply. So there is no question of the Commission having exclusive jurisdiction. Any Member State which itself has jurisdiction over the concentration may apply its own laws, including its competition rules. In this context it is important to note that Article 22(3) does not enable the Member State concerned to request the Commission to intervene to make sure a concentration takes effect in that Member State, notwithstanding the application of other Member States' competition laws. There is no ''one-stop shop'' open at the option of the requesting Member State.

There are also two significant limitations on the Commission's power to adopt the decisions provided for in Article 8(2) second sub-paragraph, (3) and (4) (declaration of compatibility or incompatibility and, if the latter, divestment or other remedial action). The first is in Article 22(3), which provides that such decisions may only be taken ''in so far as the concentration affects trade between Member States''. The Commission has made an interpretatory declaration which suggests that it will presume there to be no effect on such trade where: (a) the worldwide turnover is under 2,000 million ECU; or (b) the Community-wide turnover is below 100 million ECU (presumably for each of at least two of the parties); or (c) the two-thirds rule applies. However, the point is not beyond doubt since the Commission's statement may be taken to have been a reference to *ex officio* intervention under Article 85 E.C. (ex Article 89), and not to requests under Article 22(3). In the *British Airways/ Dan-Air* case the parties did exceed the ''effect on trade'' turnover thresholds—but the Commission decision held that the ''effect on trade'' condition was satisfied not because of turnover but because the acquisition ''has effects on air transport between Belgium and the United Kingdom''.

The second limitation is contained in Article 22(5). The Commission can only take the measures strictly necessary to maintain or restore effective competition within the territory of the Member State or States at the request of which it intervenes. This does not limit the *nature* of the remedial action taken.[59] The question whether remedial measures can be drawn and restricted to the territory of Member States depends on the circumstances in the particular case and the extent to which parts of the concentration are severable and

---

[58] Case T-221/95 *Endemol Entertainment Holdings BV v. Commission* [1999] 5 C.M.L.R. 611, para. 42. While the Member State may draw attention to a particular product market, this does not circumscribe the Commission's examination of the merger.

[59] As the Commission pointed out in *Kesko/Tuko* [1997] O.J. L174/47, Art. 22(3) expressly refers to Art. 8(4).

the remaining concentration remains both legally and commercially viable. It may be necessary for a concentration to be prohibited throughout the Community or in Member States beyond that which requested the intervention. In two cases the Commission has ordered the transaction to be undone, by way of divestment, although in both cases the impact on competition was limited to the Member State concerned and cross-border aspects were not really present in the notified transactions.[60] Depending on the circumstances, a decision under Article 8(3) and (4), where remedial measures are not confined to the territory of the requesting Member State, may not be disproportionate and indeed may be necessary to protect the market in that Member State.

---

[60] *Kesko/Tuko*, above, and *Blokker/Toys "R" Us*. Divestment proved necessary because of the absence of the limited scope of automatic suspension in Art. 22 cases.

Appendices

1 Council Regulation (EEC) 4064/89 of 21 December 1989 on the control of concentrations between undertakings (OJ 1990 L257/14)
2 Commission Regulation (EC) No 447/98 of 1 March 1998 on the notifications, time limits and hearings provided for in Council Regulation (EEC) No 4064/89 on the control of concentrations between undertakings (OJ 1998 L61/1)
3 Draft Commission Notice on restrictions directly related and necessary to concentrations
4 Commission Notice on the concept of full-function joint ventures under Council Regulation (EEC) No 4064/89 on the control of concentrations between undertakings (OJ 1998 C66/01)
5 Commission notice on the concept of concentration under Council Regulation (EEC) No 4064/89 on the control of concentrations between undertakings (OJ 1998 C66/02)
6 Commission Notice on the concept of undertakings concerned under Council Regulation (EEC) No 4064/89 on the control of concentrations between undertakings (OJ 1998 C66/03)
7 Commission Notice on calculation of turnover under Council Regulation (EEC) No 4064/89 on the control of concentrations between undertakings (OJ 1998 C66/04)
8 Commission Notice on the definition of relevant market for the purposes of Community competition law (OJ 1997 C372/03)
9 Merger Procedures

Appendix 1

COUNCIL REGULATION (EEC) 4064/89
of 21 December 1989
on the control of concentrations between undertakings
(OJ 1990 L257/14)*

THE COUNCIL OF THE EUROPEAN COMMUNITIES,

Having regard to the Treaty establishing the European Economic Community, and in particular Articles 87 and 235 thereof,
Having regard to the proposal from the Commission,[1]
Having regard to the opinion of the European Parliament,[2]
Having regard to the opinion of the Economic and Social Committee,[3]

(1) Whereas, for the achievement of the aims of the Treaty establishing the European Economic Community, Article 3(f) gives the Community the objective of instituting "a system ensuring that competition in the common market is not distorted";

(2) Whereas this system is essential for the achievement of the internal market by 1992 and its further development;

(3) Whereas the dismantling of internal frontiers is resulting and will continue to result in major corporate reorganizations in the Community, particularly in the form of concentrations;

(4) Whereas such a development must be welcomed as being in line with the requirements of dynamic competition and capable of increasing the competitiveness of European industry, improving the conditions of growth and raising the standard of living in the Community;

(5) Whereas, however, it must be ensured that the process of reorganization does not result in lasting damage to competition; whereas Community law must therefore include provisions governing those concentrations which may significantly impede effective competition in the common market or in a substantial part of it;

(6) Whereas Articles 85 and 86, while applicable, according to the case-law of the Court of Justice, to certain concentrations, are not, however, sufficient to control all operations which may prove to be incompatible with the system of undistorted competition envisaged in the Treaty;

(7) Whereas a new legal instrument should therefore be created in the form of a Regulation to permit effective control of all concentrations from the point of view of their effect on the structure of competition in the Community and to be the only instrument applicable to such concentrations;

(8) Whereas this Regulation should therefore be based not only on Article 87 but, principally, on Article 235 of the Treaty, under which the Community may give itself the additional powers of action necessary for the attainment of its objectives, including

---

* With amendments introduced by Council Regulation (E.C) 1310/97 of 30 June 1997 (O.J. L180, 9 July 1997, at 1).
[1] OJ C130, 19 May 1988, at 4.
[2] OJ C309, 5 December 1988, at 55.
[3] OJ C208, 8 August 1988, at 11.

with regard to concentrations on the markets for agricultural products listed in Annex II to the Treaty;

(9) Whereas the provisions to be adopted in this Regulation should apply to significant structural changes the impact of which on the market goes beyond the national borders of any one Member State;

(10) Whereas the scope of application of this Regulation should therefore be defined according to the geographical area of activity of the undertakings concerned and be limited by quantitative thresholds in order to cover those concentrations which have a Community dimension; whereas, at the end of an initial phase of the application of this Regulation, these thresholds should be reviewed in the light of the experience gained;

(11) Whereas a concentration with a Community dimension exists where the combined aggregate turnover of the undertakings concerned exceeds given levels worldwide and within the Community and where at least two of the undertakings concerned have their sole or main fields of activities in different Member States or where, although the undertakings in question act mainly in one and the same Member State, at least one of them has substantial operations in at least one other Member State; whereas that is also the case where the concentrations are effected by undertakings which do not have their principal fields of activities in the Community but which have substantial oeprations there;

(12) Whereas the arrangements to be introduced for the control of concentrations should, without prejudice to Article 90(2) of the Treaty, respect the principle of non-discrimination between the public and the private sectors; whereas, in the public sector, calculation of the turnover of an undertaking concerned in a concentration needs, therefore, to take account of undertakings making up an economic unit with an independent power of decision, irrespective of the way in which their capital is held or of the rules of administrative supervision applicable to them;

(13) Whereas it is necessary to establish whether concentrations with a Community dimension are compatible or not with the common market from the point of view of the need to maintain and develop effective competition in the common market; whereas, in so doing, the Commission must place its appraisal within the general framework of the achievement of the fundamental objectives referred to in Article 2 of the Treaty, including that of strengthening the Community's economic and social cohesion, referred to in Article 130;

(14) Whereas this Regulation should establish the principle that a concentration with a Community dimension which creates or strengthens a position as a result of which effective competition in the common market or in a substantial part of it is significantly impeded is to be declared incompatible with the common market;

(15) Whereas concentrations which, by reason of the limited market share of the undertakings concerned, are not liable to impede effective competition may be presumed to be compatible with the common market; whereas, without prejudice to Articles 85 and 86 of the Treaty, an indication to this effect exists, in particular, where the market share of the undertakings concerned does not exceed 25% either in the common market or in a substantial part of it;

(16) Whereas the Commission should have the task of taking all the decisions necessary to establish whether or not concentrations with a Community dimension are compatible with the common market, as well as decisions designed to restore effective competition;

(17) Whereas to ensure effective control undertakings should be obliged to give prior

notification of concentrations with a Community dimension and provision should be made for the suspension of concentrations for a limited period, and for the possibility of extending or waiving a suspension where necessary; whereas in the interests of legal certainty the validity of transactions must nevertheless be protected as much as necessary;

(18) Whereas a period within which the Commission must initiate proceedings in respect of a notified concentration and periods within which it must give a final decision on the compatibility or incompatibility with the common market of a notified concentration should be laid down;

(19) Whereas the undertakings concerned must be afforded the right to be heard by the Commission when proceedings have been initiated; whereas the members of the management and supervisory bodies and the recognized representatives of the employees of the undertakings concerned, and third parties showing a legitimate interest, must also be given the opportunity to be heard;

(20) Whereas the Commission should act in close and constant liaison with the competent authorities of the Member States from which it obtains comments and information;

(21) Whereas, for the purposes of this Regulation, and in accordance with the case-law of the Court of Justice, the Commission must be afforded the assistance of the Member States and must also be empowered to require information to be given and to carry out the necessary investigations in order to appraise concentrations;

(22) Whereas compliance with this Regulation must be enforceable by means of fines and periodic penalty payments; whereas the Court of Justice should be given unlimited jurisdiction in that regard pursuant to Article 172 of the Treaty;

(23) Whereas it is appropriate to define the concept of concentration in such a manner as to cover only operations bringing about a lasting change in the structure of the undertakings concerned; whereas it is therefore necessary to exclude from the scope of this Regulation those operations which have as their object or effect the coordination of the competitive behaviour of undertakings which remain independent, since such operations fall to be examined under the appropriate provisions of the Regulations implementing Articles 85 and 86 of the Treaty; whereas it is appropriate to make this distinction specifically in the case of the creation of joint ventures;

(24) Whereas there is no coordination of competitive behaviour within the meaning of this Regulation where two or more undertakings agree to acquire jointly control of one or more other undertakings with the object and effect of sharing amongst themselves such undertakings or their assets;

(25) Whereas this Regulation should still apply where the undertakings concerned accept restrictions directly related and necessary to the implementation of the concentration;

(26) Whereas the Commission should be given exclusive competence to apply this Regulation, subject to review by the Court of Justice;

(27) Whereas the Member States may not apply their national legislation on competition to concentrations with a Community dimension, unless this Regulation makes provision therefor; whereas the relevant powers of national authorities should be limited to cases where, failing intervention by the Commission, effective competition is likely to be significantly impeded within the territory of a Member State and where the competition interests of that Member State cannot be sufficiently protected otherwise by this Regulation; whereas the Member States concerned must act promptly in such cases; whereas this Regulation cannot, because of the diversity of national law, fix a single deadline for the adoption of remedies;

(28) Whereas, furthermore, the exclusive application of this Regulation to concentrations with a Community dimension is without prejudice to Article 223 of the Treaty, and does not prevent the Member States from taking appropriate measures to protect legitimate interets other than those pursued by this Regulation, provided that such measures are compatible with the general principles and other provisions of Community law;

(29) Whereas concentrations not covered by this Regulation come, in principle, within the jurisdiction of the Member States; whereas, however, the Commission should have the power to act, at the request of a Member State concerned, in cases where effective competition could be significantly impeded within that Member State's territory;

(30) Whereas the conditions in which concentrations involving Community undertakings are carried out in non-member countries should be observed, and provision should be made for the possibility of the Council giving the Commission an appropriate mandate for negotiation with a view to obtaining non-discriminatory treatment for Community undertakings;

(31) Whereas this Regulation in no way detracts from the collective rights of employees as recognized in the undertakings concerned,

HAS ADOPTED THIS REGULATION:

Article 1

Scope

1. Without prejudice to Article 22, this Regulation shall apply to all concentrations with a Community dimension as defined in **paragraphs 2 and 3**.

2. For the purposes of this Regulation, a concentration has a Community dimension where:

(a) the combined aggregate worldwide turnover of all the undertakings concerned is more than ECU 5 000 million; and

(b) the aggregate Community-wide turnover of each of at least two of the undertakings concerned is more than ECU 250 million, unless each of the undertakings concerned achieves more than two-thirds of its aggregate Community-wide turnover within one and the same Member State.

3. ~~The thresholds laid down in paragraph 2 will be reviewed before the end of the fourth year following that of the adoption of this Regulation by the Council acting by a qualified majority on a proposal from the Commission.~~

3. **For the purposes of this Regulation, a concentration that does not meet the thresholds laid down in paragraph 2 has a Community dimension where:**

(a) **the combined aggregate worldwide turnover of all the undertakings concerned is more than ECU 2 500 million;**
(b) **in each of at least three Member States, the combined aggregate turnover of all the undertakings concerned is more than ECU 100 million;**
(c) **in each of at least three Member States included for the purpose of point (b), the aggregate turnover of each of at least two of the undertakings concerned is more than ECU 25 million; and**
(d) **the aggregate Community-wide turnover of each of at least two of the undertakings is more than ECU 100 million;**

unless each of the undertakings concerned achieves more than two-thirds of its aggregate Community-wide turnover within one and the same Member State.

4. Before 1 July 2000 the Commission shall report to the Council on the operation of the thresholds and criteria set out in paragraphs 2 and 3.

5. Following the report referred to in paragraph 4 and on a proposal from the Commission, the Council, acting by a qualified majority, may revise the thresholds and criteria mentioned in paragraph 3.

Article 2

Appraisal of concentrations

1. Concentrations within the scope of this Regulation shall be appraised in accordance with the following provisions with a view to establishing whether or not they are compatible with the common market. In making this appraisal, the Commission shall take into account:

(a) the need to maintain and develop effective competition within the common market in view of, among other things, the structure of all the markets concerned and the actual or potential competition from undertakings located either within or outwith the Community;

(b) the market position of the undertakings concerned and their economic and financial power, the alternatives available to suppliers and users, their access to supplies or markets, any legal or other barriers to entry, supply and demand trends for the relevant goods and services, the interests of the intermediate and ultimate consumers, and the development of technical and economic progress provided that it is to consumers' advantage and does not form an obstacle to competition.

2. A concentration which does not create or strengthen a dominant position as a result of which effective competition would be significantly impeded in the common market or in a substantial part of it shall be declared compatible with the common market.

3. A concentration which creates or strengthens a dominant position as a result of which effective competition would be significantly impeded in the common market or in a substantial part of it shall be declared incompatible with the common market.

4. To the extent that the creation of a joint venture constituting a concentration pursuant to Article 3 has as its object or effect the coordination of the competitive behaviour of undertakings that remain independent, such coordination shall be appraised in accordance with the criteria of Article 85(1) and (3) of the Treaty, with a view to establishing whether or not the operation is compatible with the common market.

In making this appraisal, the Commission shall take into account in particular:

— whether two or more parent companies retain to a significant extent activities in the same market as the joint venture or in a market which is downstream or upstream from that of the joint venture or in a neighbouring market closely related to this market;

— whether the coordination which is the direct consequence of the creation of the joint venture affords the undertakings concerned the possibility of eliminating competition in respect of a substantial part of the products or services in question.

Article 3

Definition of concentration

1. A concentration shall be deemed to arise where:

(a) two or more previously independent undertakings merge, or

(b) — one or more persons already controlling at least one undertaking, or

    — one or more undertakings

acquire, whether by purchase of securities or assets, by contract or by any other means, direct or indirect control of the whole or parts of one or more other undertakings.

2. ~~An operation, including the creation of a joint venture, which has as its object or effect the coordination of the competitive behaviour of undertakings which remain independent shall not constitute a concentration within the meaning of paragraph 1 (b).~~

The creation of a joint venture performing on a lasting basis all the functions of an autonomous economic entity, ~~which does not give rise to coordination of the competitive behaviour of the parties amongst themselves or between them and the joint venture~~, shall constitute a concentration within the meaning of paragraph 1 (b).

3. For the purposes of this Regulation, control shall be constituted by rights, contracts or any other means which, either separately or in combination and having regard to the considerations of fact or law involved, confer the possibility of exercising decisive influence on an undertaking, in particular by:

(a) ownership or the right to use all or part of the assets of an undertaking;

(b) rights or contracts which confer decisive influence on the composition, voting or decisions of the organs of an undertaking.

4. Control is acquired by persons or undertakings which:

(a) are holders of the rights or entitled to rights under the contracts concerned, or

(b) while not being holders of such rights or entitled to rights under such contracts, have the power to exercise the rights deriving therefrom.

5. A concentration shall not be deemed to arise where:

(a) credit institutions or other financial institutions or insurance companies, the normal activities of which include transactions and dealing in securities for their own account or for the account of others, hold on a temporary basis securities which they have acquired in an undertaking with a view to reselling them, provided that they do not exercise voting rights in respect of those securities with a view to determining the competitive behaviour of that undertaking or provided that they exercise such voting rights only with a view to preparing the disposal of all or part of that undertaking or of its assets or the disposal of those securities and that any such disposal takes place within one year of the date of acquisition; that period may be extended by the Commission on request where such institutions or companies can show that the disposal was not reasonably possible within the period set;

(b) control is acquired by an office-holder according to the law of a Member State relating to liquidation, winding up, insolvency, cessation of payments, compositions or analogous proceedings;

(c) the operations referred to in paragraph 1 (b) are carried out by the financial holding companies referred to in Article 5 (3) of the Fourth Council Directive 78/660/EEC of 25 July 1978 on the annual accounts of certain types of companies[1], as last amended by

---

[1] OJ No L 222, 14.8.1978, p. 11.

Directive 84/569/EEC[2], provided however that the voting rights in respect of the holding are exercised, in particular in relation to the appointment of members of the management and supervisory bodies of the undertakings in which they have holdings, only to maintain the full value of those investments and not to determine directly or indirectly the competitive conduct of those undertakings.

Article 4

Prior notification of concentrations

1. Concentrations with a Community dimension defined in this Regulation shall be notified to the Commission not more than one week after the conclusion of the agreement, or the announcement of the public bid, or the acquisition of a controlling interest. That week shall begin when the first of those events occurs.

2. A concentration which consists of a merger within the meaning of Article 3 (1) (a) or in the acquisition of joint control within the meaning of Article 3 (1) (b) shall be notified jointly by the parties to the merger or by those acquiring joint control as the case may be. In all other cases, the notification shall be effected by the person or undertaking acquiring control of the whole or parts of one or more undertakings.

3. Where the Commission finds that a notified concentration falls within the scope of this Regulation, it shall publish the fact of the notification, at the same time indicating the names of the parties, the nature of the concentration and the economic sectors involved. The Commission shall take account of the legitimate interest of undertakings in the protection of their business secrets.

Article 5

Calculation of turnover

1. Aggregate turnover within the meaning of Article 1 (2) shall comprise the amounts derived by the undertakings concerned in the preceding financial year from the sale of products and the provision of services falling within the undertakings' ordinary activities after deduction of sales rebates and of value added tax and other taxes directly related to turnover. The aggregate turnover of an undertaking concerned shall not include the sale of products or the provision of services between any of the undertakings referred to in paragraph 4.

Turnover, in the Community or in a Member State, shall comprise products sold and services provided to undertakings or consumers, in the Community or in that Member State as the case may be.

2. By way of derogation from paragraph 1, where the concentration consists in the acquisition of parts, whether or not constituted as legal entities, of one or more undertakings, only the turnover relating to the parts which are the subject of the transaction shall be taken into account with regard to the seller or sellers.

However, two or more transactions within the meaning of the first subparagraph which take place within a two-year period between the same persons or undertakings shall be treated as one and the same concentration arising on the date of the last transaction.

3. In place of turnover the following shall be used:
(a) for credit institutions and other financial institutions, as regards Article 1 (2) (a), one-tenth of their total assets.

As regards Article 1 (2) (b) and the final part of Article 1 (2), total Community-wide turnover shall be replaced by one-tenth of total assets multiplied by the ratio between loans and advances

---

[2] OJ No L 314, 4.12.1984, p. 28.

~~to credit institutions and customers in transactions with Community residents and the total sum of those loans and advances.~~

~~As regards the final part of Article 1 (2), total turnover within one Member State shall be replaced by one-tenth of total assets multiplied by the ratio between loans and advances to credit institutions and customers in transactions with residents of that Member State and the total sum of those loans and advances;~~

(a) for credit institutions and other financial institutions, as regards Article 1(2) and (3), the sum of the following income items as defined in Council Directive 86/635/EEC of 8 December 1986 on the annual accounts and consolidated accounts of banks and other financial institutions[3], after deduction of value added tax and other taxes directly related to those items, where appropriate:

   (i) interest income and similar income;

  (ii) income from securities:

     — income from shares and other variable yield securities,

     — income from participating interests,

     — income from shares in affiliated undertakings;

  (iii) commissions receivable;

  (iv) net profit on financial operations;

   (v) other operating income.

     The turnover of a credit or financial institution in the Community or in a Member State shall comprise the income items, as defined above, which are received by the branch or division of that institution established in the Community or in the Member State in question, as the case may be;

(b) for insurance undertakings, the value of gross premiums written which shall comprise all amounts received and receivable in respect of insurance contracts issued by or on behalf of the insurance undertakings, including also outgoing reinsurance premiums, and after deduction of taxes and parafiscal contributions or levies charged by reference to the amounts of individual premiums or the total volume of premiums; as regards Article 1(2)(b) **and (3)(b), (c) and (d)** and the final part of Article 1(2) **and (3)**, gross premiums received from Community residents and from residents of one Member State respectively shall be taken into account.

4. Without prejudice to paragraph 2, the aggregate turnover of an undertaking concerned within the meaning of Article 1 (2) **and 3** shall be calculated by adding together the respective turnovers of the following:

(a) the undertaking concerned;

(b) those undertakings in which the undertaking concerned, directly or indirectly;

     — owns more than half the capital or business assets, or

     — has the power to exercise more than half the voting rights, or

     — has the power to appoint more than half the members of the supervisory board, the administrative board or bodies legally representing the undertakings, or

     — has the right to manage the undertakings' affairs;

(c) those undertakings which have in an undertaking concerned the rights or powers listed in (b);

---

[3] **OJ No L 372, 31.12.1986, p. 1.**

(d) those undertakings in which an undertaking as referred to in (c) has the rights or powers listed in (b);

(e) those undertakings in which two or more undertakings as referred to in (a) to (d) jointly have the rights or powers listed in (b).

5. Where undertakings concerned by the concentration jointly have the rights or powers listed in paragraph 4 (b), in calculating the aggregate turnover of the undertakings concerned for the purposes of Article 1 (2) **and (3):**

(a) no account shall be taken of the turnover resulting from the sale of products or the provision of services between the joint undertaking and each of the undertakings concerned or any other undertaking connected with any one of them, as set out in paragraph 4 (b) to (e);

(b) account shall be taken of the turnover resulting from the sale of products and the provision of services between the joint undertaking and any third undertakings. This turnover shall be apportioned equally amongst the undertakings concerned.

Article 6

Examination of the notification and initiation of proceedings

1. The Commission shall examine the notification as soon as it is received.

(a) Where it concludes that the concentration notified does not fall within the scope of this Regulation, it shall record that finding by means of a decision.

(b) Where it finds that the concentration notified, although falling within the scope of this Regulation, does not raise serious doubts as to its compatibility with the common market, it shall decide not to oppose it and shall declare that it is compatible with the common market.

The decision declaring the concentration compatible shall also cover restrictions directly related and necessary to the implementation of the concentration.

(c) ~~If, on the other hand, it~~ **Without prejudice to paragraph 1(a), where the Commission** finds that the concentration notified falls within the scope of this Regulation and raises serious doubts as to its compatibility with the common market, it shall decide to initiate proceedings.

1a. Where the Commission finds that, following modification by the undertakings concerned, a notified concentration no longer raises serious doubts within the meaning of paragraph 1(c), it may decide to declare the concentration compatible with the common market pursuant to paragraph 1(b).

The Commission may attach to its decision under paragraph 1(b) conditions and obligations intended to ensure that the undertakings concerned comply with the commitments they have entered into vis-à-vis the Commission with a view to rendering the concentration compatible with the common market.

1b. The Commission may revoke the decision it has taken pursuant to paragraph 1(a) or (b) where:

(a) **the decision is based on incorrect information for which one of the undertakings is responsible or where it has been obtained by deceit, or**

(b) the undertakings concerned commit a breach of an obligation attached to the decision.

1c. In the cases referred to in paragraph 1(b), the Commission may take a decision under paragraph 1, without being bound by the deadlines referred to in Article 10(1).

2. The Commission shall notify its decision to the undertakings concerned and the competent authorities of the Member States without delay.

Article 7

Suspension of concentrations

1. ~~For the purposes of paragraph 2 a~~ A concentration as defined in Article 1 shall not be put into effect either before its notification or ~~within the first three weeks following its notification~~ until it has been declared compatible with the common market pursuant to a decision under Article 6(1)(b) or Article 8(2) or on the basis of a presumption according to Article 10(6).

2. ~~Where the Commission, following a preliminary examination of the notification within the period provided for in paragraph 1, finds it necessary in order to ensure the full effectiveness of any decision taken later pursuant to Article 8 (3) and (4), it may decide on its own initiative to continue the suspension of a concentration in whole or in part until it takes a final decision, or to take other interim measures to that effect.~~

3. Paragraphs 1 ~~and 2~~ shall not prevent the implementation of a public bid which has been notified to the Commission in accordance with Article 4 (1), provided that the acquirer does not exercise the voting rights attached to the securities in question or does so only to maintain the full value of those investments and on the basis of a derogation granted by the Commission under paragraph 4.

4. The Commission may, on request, grant a derogation from the obligations imposed in paragraphs 1, ~~2 or 3~~ or 3. ~~in order to prevent serious damage to one or more undertakings concerned by a concentration or to a third party.~~ The request to grant a derogation must be reasoned. In deciding on the request, the Commission shall take into account inter alia the effects of the suspension on one or more undertakings concerned by a concentration or on a third party and the threat to competition posed by the concentration. That derogation may be made subject to conditions and obligations in order to ensure conditions of effective competition. A derogation may be applied for and granted at any time, even before notification or after the transaction.

5. The validity of any transaction carried out in contravention of paragraph 1 ~~or 2~~ shall be dependent on a decision pursuant to Article 6 (1) (b) or 8 (2) or (3) or on a presumption pursuant to Article 10 (6).

This Article shall, however, have no effect on the validity of transactions in securities including those convertible into other securities admitted to trading on a market which is regulated and supervised by authorities recognized by public bodies, operates regularly and is accessible directly or indirectly to the public, unless the buyer and seller knew or or ought to have known that the transaction was carried out in contravention of paragraph 1 ~~or 2~~.

Article 8

Powers of decision of the Commission

1. Without prejudice to Article 9, all proceedings initiated pursuant to Article 6 (1) (c) shall be closed by means of a decision as provided for in paragraphs 2 to 5.

2. Where the Commission finds that, following modification by the undertakings concerned if

necessary, a notified concentration fulfils the criterion laid down in Article 2 (2) **and, in the cases referred to in Article 2(4), the criteria laid down in Article 85(3) of the Treaty,** it shall issue a decision declaring the concentration compatible with the common market.

It may attach to its decision conditions and obligations intended to ensure that the undertakings concerned comply with the commitments they have entered into *vis-à-vis* the Commission with a view to ~~modifying the original concentration plan~~ **rendering the concentration compatible with the common market.** The decision declaring the concentration compatible **with the common market** shall also cover restrictions directly related and necessary to the implementation of the concentration.

3. Where the Commission finds that a concentration fulfils the criterion ~~laid down~~ **defined** in Article 2 (3) **or, in the cases referred to in Article 2(4), does not fulfil the criteria laid down in Article 85(3) of the Treaty,** it shall issue a decision declaring that the concentration is incompatible with the common market.

4. Where a concentration has already been implemented, the Commission may, in a decision pursuant to paragraph 3 or by separate decision, require the undertakings or assets brought together to be separated or the cessation of joint control or any other action that may be appropriate in order to restore conditions of effective competition.

5. The Commission may revoke the decision it has taken pursuant to paragraph 2 where:

(a) the declaration of compatibility is based on incorrect information for which one of the undertakings is responsible or where it has been obtained by deceit, or

(b) the undertakings concerned commit a breach of an obligation attached to the decision.

6. In the cases referred to in paragraph 5, the Commission may take a decision pursuant to paragraph 3, without being bound by the deadline referred to in Article 10 (3).

Article 9

Referral to the competent authorities of the Member States

1. The Commission may, by means of a decision notified without delay to the undertakings concerned and the competent authorities of the other Member States, refer a notified concentration to the competent authorities of the Member State concerned in the following circumstances.

2. Within three weeks of the date of receipt of the copy of the notification a Member State may inform the Commission, which shall inform the undertakings concerned, that:

(a) a concentration threatens to create or to strengthen a dominant position as a result of which effective competition ~~would~~ **will** be significantly impeded on a market within that Member State, which presents all the characteristics of a distinct market, ~~be it a substantial part of the common market~~ or

(b) **a concentration affects competition on a market within that Member State, which presents all the characteristics of a distinct market and which does not constitute a substantial part of the common market.**

~~not.~~

3. If the Commission considers that, having regard to the market for the products or services in question and the geographical reference market within the meaning of paragraph 7, there is such a distinct market and that such a threat exists, either:

(a) it shall itself deal with the case in order to maintain or restore effective competition on the market concerned, or

(b) it shall refer **the whole or part of** the case to the competent authorities of the Member State concerned with a view to the application of that State's national competition law.

If, however, the Commission considers that such a distinct market or threat does not exist it shall adopt a decision to that effect which it shall address to the Member State concerned.

In cases where a Member State informs the Commission that a concentration affects competition in a distinct market within its territory that does not form a substantial part of the common market, the Commission shall refer the whole or part of the case relating to the distinct market concerned, if it considers that such a distinct market is affected.

4. A decision to refer or not to refer pursuant to paragraph 3 shall be taken where:

(a) as a general rule within the six-week period provided for in Article 10 (1), second subparagraph, where the Commission, pursuant to Article 6 (1) (b), has not initiated proceedings, or

(b) within three months at most of the notification of the concentration concerned where the Commission has initiated proceedings under Article 6 (1) (c), without taking the preparatory steps in order to adopt the necessary measures under to Article 8 (2), second subparagraph, (3) or (4) to maintain or restore effective competition on the market concerned.

5. If within the three months referred to in paragraph 4 (b) the Commission, despite a reminder from the Member State concerned, has not taken a decision on referral in accordance with paragraph 3 nor has taken the preparatory steps referred to in paragraph 4 (b), it shall be deemed to have taken a decision to refer the case to the Member State concerned in accordance with paragraph 3 (b).

6. The publication of any report or the announcement of the findings of the examination of the concentration by the competent authority of the Member State concerned shall be effected not more than four months after the Commission's referral.

7. The geographical reference market shall consist of the area in which the undertakings concerned are involved in the supply and demand of products or services, in which the conditions of competition are sufficiently homogeneous and which can be distinguished from neighbouring areas because, in particular, conditions of competition are appreciably different in those areas. This assessment should take account in particular of the nature and characteristics of the products or services concerned, of the existence of entry barriers or of consumer preferences, of appreciable differences of the undertakings' market shares between the area concerned and neighbouring areas or of substantial price differences.

8. In applying the provisions of this Article, the Member State concerned may take only the measures strictly necessary to safeguard or restore effective competition on the market concerned.

9. In accordance with the relevant provisions of the Treaty, any Member State may appeal to the Court of Justice, and in particular request the application of Article 186, for the purpose of applying its national competition law.

10. ~~This Article will be reviewed before the end of the fourth year following that of the adoption of this Regulation.~~ **This Article may be re-examined at the same time as the thresholds referred to in Article 1.**

Article 10

Time limits for initiating proceedings and for decisions

1. The decisions referred to in Article 6 (1) must be taken within one month at most. That period shall begin on the day following that of the receipt of a notification or, if the information

to be supplied with the notification is incomplete, on the day following that of the receipt of the complete information.

That period shall be increased to six weeks if the Commission receives a request from a Member State in accordance with Article 9 (2), **or where, after notification of a concentration, the undertakings concerned submit commitments pursuant to Article 6(1a), which are intended by the parties to form the basis for a decision pursuant to Article 6(1)(b).**

2. Decisions taken pursuant to Article 8 (2) concerning notified concentrations must be taken as soon as it appears that the serious doubts referred to in Article 6 (1) (c) have been removed, particularly as a result of modifications made by the undertakings concerned, and at the latest by the deadline laid down in paragraph 3.

3. Without prejudice to Article 8 (6), decisions taken pursuant to Article 8 (3) concerning notified concentrations must be taken within not more than four months of the date on which proceedings are initiated.

4. The periods set by paragraphs **1 and** 3 shall exceptionally be suspended where, owing to circumstances for which one of the undertakings involved in the concentration is responsible, the Commission has had to request information by decision pursuant to Article 11 or to order an investigation by decision pursuant to Article 13.

5. Where the Court of Justice gives a Judgement which annuls the whole or part of a Commission decision taken under this Regulation, the periods laid down in this Regulation shall start again from the date of the Judgement.

6. Where the Commission has not taken a decision in accordance with Article 6 (1) (b) or (c) or Article 8 (2) or (3) within the deadlines set in paragraphs 1 and 3 respectively, the concentration shall be deemed to have been declared compatible with the common market, without prejudice to Article 9.

Article 11

Requests for information

1. In carrying out the duties assigned to it by this Regulation, the Commission may obtain all necessary information from the Governments and competent authorities of the Member States, from the persons referred to in Article 3 (1) (b), and from undertakings and associations of undertakings.

2. When sending a request for information to a person, an undertaking or an association of undertakings, the Commission shall at the same time send a copy of the request to the competent authority of the Member State within the territory of which the residence of the person or the seat of the undertaking or association of undertakings is situated.

3. In its request the Commission shall state the legal basis and the purpose of the request and also the penalties provided for in Article 14 (1) (c) for supplying incorrect information.

4. The information requested shall be provided, in the case of undertakings, by their owners or their representatives and, in the case of legal persons, companies or firms, or of associations having no legal personality, by the persons authorized to represent them by law or by their statutes.

5. Where a person, an undertaking or an association of undertakings does not provide the information requested within the period fixed by the Commission or provides incomplete information, the Commission shall be decision require the information to be provided. The decision shall specify what information is required, fix an appropriate period within which it is to be supplied and state the penalties provided for in Article 14 (1) (c) and 15 (1) (a) and the reight to have the decision reviewed by the Court of Justice.

6. The Commission shall at the same time send a copy of its decision to the competent authority of the Member State within the territory of which the residence of the person or the seat of the undertaking or association of undertakings is situated.

Article 12

Investigations by the authorities of the Member States

1. At the request of the Commission, the competent authorities of the Member States shall undertake the investigations which the Commission considers to be necessary under Article 13 (1), or which it has ordered by decision pursuant to Article 13 (3). The officials of the competent authorities of the Member States responsible for conducting those investigations shall exercise their powers upon production of an authorization in writing issued by the competent authority of the Member State within the territory of which the investigation is to be carried out. Such authorization shall specify the subject matter and purpose of the investigation.

2. If so requested by the Commission or by the competent authority of the Member State within the territory of which the investigation is to be carried out, officials of the Commission may assist the officials of that authority in carrying out their duties.

Article 13

Investigative powers of the Commission

1. In carrying out the duties assigned to it by this Regulation, the Commission may undertake all necessary investigations into undertakings and associations of undertakings.

To that end the officials authorized by the Commission shall be empowered:

(a) to examine the books and other business records;

(b) to take or demand copies of or extracts from the books and business records;

(c) to ask for oral explanations on the spot;

(d) to enter any premises, land and means of transport of undertakings.

2. The officials of the Commission authorized to carry out the investigations shall exercise their powers on production of an authorization in writing specifying the subject matter and purpose of the investigation and the penalties provided for in Article 14 (1) (d) in cases where production of the required books or other business records is incomplete. In good time before the investigation, the Commission shall inform, in writing, the competent authority of the Member State within the territory of which the investigation is to be carried out of the investigation and of the identities of the authorized officials.

3. Undertakings and associations of undertakings shall submit to investigations ordered by decision of the Commission. The decision shall specify the subject matter and purpose of the investigation, appoint the date on which it shall begin and state the penalties provided for in Articles 14 (1) (d) and 15 (1) (b) and the right to have the decision reviewed by the Court of Justice.

4. The Commission shall in good time and in writing inform the competent authority of the Member State within the territory of which the investigation is to be carried out of its intention of taking a decision pursuant to paragraph 3. It shall hear the competent authority before taking its decision.

5. Officials of the competent authority of the Member State within the territory of which the investigation is to be carried out may, at the request of that authority or of the Commission, assist the officials of the Commission in carrying out their duties.

6. Where an undertaking or association of undertakings opposes an investigation ordered pursuant to this Article, the Member State concerned shall afford the necessary assistance to the officials authorized by the Commission to enable them to carry out their investigation. To this end the Member States shall, after consulting the Commission, take the necessary measures within one year of the entry into force of this Regulation.

Article 14

Fines

1. The Commission may by decision impose on the persons referred to in Article 3 (1) (b), undertakings or associations of undertakings fines of from ECU 1 000 to 50 000 where intentionally or negligently:

(a) they fail to notify a concentration in accordance with Article 4;

(b) they supply incorrect or misleading information in a notification pursuant to Article 4;

(c) they supply incorrect information in response to a request made pursuant to Article 11 or fail to supply information within the period fixed by a decision taken pursuant to Article 11;

(d) they produce the required books or other business records in incomplete form during investigations under Article 12 or 13, or refuse to submit to an investigation ordered by decision taken pursuant to Article 13.

2. The Commission may by decision impose fines not exceeding 10% of the aggregate turnover of the undertakings concerned within the meaning of Article 5 on the persons or undertakings concerned where, either intentionally or negligently, they:

(a) fail to comply with an obligation imposed by decision pursuant to Article 7 (4) or 8 (2), second subparagraph;

(b) put into effect a concentration in breach of Article 7 (1) or disregard a decision taken pursuant to Article 7 (2);

(c) put into effect a concentration declared incompatible with the common market by decision pursuant to Article 8 (3) or do not take the measures ordered by decision pursuant to Article 8 (4).

3. In setting the amount of a fine, regard shall be had to the nature and gravity of the infringement.

4. Decisions taken pursuant to paragraphs 1 and 2 shall not be of criminal law nature.

Article 15

Periodic penalty payments

1. The Commission may by decision impose on the persons referred to in Article 3 (1) (b), undertakings or associations of undertakings concerned periodic penalty payments of up to ECU 25 000 for each day of delay calculated from the date set in the decision, in order to compel them:

(a) to supply complete and correct information which it has requested by decision pursuant to Article 11;

(b) to submit to an investigation which it has ordered by decision pursuant to Article 13.

2. The Commission may by decision impose on the persons referred to in Article 3 (1) (b) or on undertakings periodic penalty payments of up to ECU 100 000 for each day of delay calculated from the date set in the decision, in order to compel them:

(a) to comply with an obligation imposed by decision pursuant to Article 7 (4) or Article 8 (2), second subparagraph, or

(b) to apply the measures ordered by decision pursuant to Article 8 (4).

3. Where the persons referred to in Article 3 (1) (b), undertakings or associations of undertakings have satisfied the obligation which it was the purpose of the periodic penalty payment to enforce, the Commission may set the total amount of the periodic penalty payments at a lower figure than that which would arise under the original decision.

Article 16

Review by the Court of Justice

The Court of Justice shall have unlimited jurisdiction within the meaning of Article 172 of the Treaty to review decisions whereby the Commission has fixed a fine or periodic penalty payments; it may cancel, reduce or increase the fine or periodic penalty payments imposed.

Article 17

Professional secrecy

1. Information acquired as a result of the application of Articles 11, 12, 13 and 18 shall be used only for the purposes of the relevant request, investigation or hearing.

2. Without prejudice to Articles 4 (3), 18 and 20, the Commission and the competent authorities of the Member States, their officials and other servants shall not disclose information they have acquired through the application of this Regulation of the kind covered by the obligation of professional secrecy.

3. Paragraphs 1 and 2 shall not prevent publication of general information or of surveys which do not contain information relating to particular undertakings or associations of undertakings.

Article 18

Hearing of the parties and of third persons

1. Before taking any decision provided for in Article 7 (2) and (4), Article 8 (2), second subparagraph, and (3) to (5), and Articles 14 and 15, the Commission shall give the persons, undertakings and associations of undertakings concerned the opportunity, at every stage of the procedure up to the consultation of the Advisory Committee, of making known their views on the objections against them.

2. By way of derogation from paragraph 1, a decision to continue the suspension of a concentration of to grant a derogation from suspension as referred to in Article 7 (2) or (4) may be taken provisionally, without the persons, undertakings or associations of undertakings concerned being given the opportunity to make known their views beforehand, provided that the Commission gives them that opportunity as soon as possible after having taken its decision.

3. The Commission shall base its decision only on objections on which the parties have been able to submit their observations. The rights of the defence shall be fully respected in the proceedings. Access to the file shall be open at least to the parties directly involved, subject to the legitimate interest of undertakings in the protection of their business secrets.

4. Insofar as the Commission or the competent authorities of the Member States deem it neces-

sary, they may also hear other natural or legal persons. Natural or legal persons showing a sufficient interest and especially members of the administrative or management bodies of the undertakings concerned or the recognized representatives of their employees shall be entitled, upon application, to be heard.

Article 19

Liaison with the authorities of the Member States

1. The Commission shall transmit to the competent authorities of the Member States copies of notifications within three working days and, as soon as possible, copies of the most important documents lodged with or issued by the Commission pursuant to this Regulation. **Such documents shall include commitments which are intended by the parties to form the basis for a decision pursuant to Articles 6(1)(b) or 8(2).**

2. The Commission shall carry out the procedures set out in this Regulation in close and constant liaison with the competent authorities of the Member States, which may express their views upon those procedures. For the purposes of Article 9 it shall obtain information from the competent authority of the Member State as referred to in paragraph 2 of that Article and give it the opportunity to make known its views at every stage of the procedure up to the adoption of a decision pursuant to paragraph 3 of that Article; to that end it shall give it access to the file.

3. An Advisory Committee on concentrations shall be consulted before any decision is taken pursuant to Articles 8 (2) to (5), 14 or 15, or any provisions are adopted pursuant to Article 23.

4. The Advisory Committee shall consist of representatives of the authorities of the Member States. Each Member State shall appoint one or two representatives; if unable to attend, they may be replaced by other representatives. At least one of the representatives of a Member State shall be competent in matters of restrictive practices and dominant positions.

5. Consultation shall take place at a joint meeting convened at the invitation of and chaired by the Commission. A summary of the case, together with an indication of the most important documents and a preliminary draft of the decision to be taken for each case considered, shall be sent with the invitation. The meeting shall take place not less than 14 days after the invitation has been sent. The Commission may in exceptional cases shorten that period as appropriate in order to avoid serious harm to one or more of the undertakings concerned by a concentration.

6. The Advisory Committee shall deliver an opinion on the Commission's draft decision, if necessary by taking a vote. The Advisory Committee may deliver an opinion even if some members are absent and unrepresented. The opinion shall be delivered in writing and appended to the draft decision. The Commission shall take the utmost account of the opinion delivered by the Committee. It shall inform the Committee of the manner in which its opinion has been taken into account.

7. The Advisory Committee may recommend publication of the opinion. The Commission may carry out such publication. The decision to publish shall take due account of the legitimate interest of undertakings in the protection of their business secrets and of the interest of the undertakings concerned in such publication's taking place.

Article 20

Publication of decisions

1. The Commission shall publish the decisions which it takes pursuant to Article 8 (2) to (5) in the *Official Journal of the European Communities*.

2. The publication shall state the names of the parties and the main content of the decision; it

shall have regard to the legitimate interest of undertakings in the protection of their business secrets.

Article 21

Jurisdiction

1. Subject to review by the Court of Justice, the Commission shall have sole jurisdiction to take the decisions provided for in this Regulation.

2. No Member State shall apply its national legislation on competition to any concentration that has a Community dimension.

The first subparagraph shall be without prejudice to any Member State's power to carry out any enquiries necessary for the application of Article 9 (2) or after referral, pursuant to Article 9 (3), first subparagraph, indent (b), or (5), to take the measures strictly necessary for the application of Aritcle 9 (8).

3. Notwithstanding paragraphs 1 and 2, Member States may take appropriate measures to protect legitimate interests other than those taken into consideration by this Regulation and compatible with the general principles and other provisions of Community law.

Public security, plurality of the media and prudential rules shall be regarded as legitimate ilnterests within the meaning of the first subparagraph.

Any other public interest must be communicated to the Commission by the Member State concerned and shall be recognized by the Commission after an assessment of its compatibility with the general principles and other provisions of Community law before the measures referred to above may be taken. The Commission shall inform the Member State concerned of its decision within one month of that communication.

Article 22

Application of the Regulation

1. This Regulation alone shall apply to concentrations as defined in Article 3, **and** Regulations No 17[4] (EEC) No 1017/68[5], (EEC) No 4056/86[6] and (EEC) No 3975/87[7] shall not apply ~~to concentrations as defined in Article 3~~, **except in relation to joint ventures that do not have a Community dimension and which have as their object or effect the coordination of the competitive behaviour of undertakings that remain independent..**

3. If the Commission finds, at the request of a Member State **or at the joint request of two or more Member States,** that a concentration as defined in Article 3 that has no Community dimension within the meaning of Article 1 creates or strengthens a dominant position as a result of which effective competition would be significantly impeded within the territory of the Member State ~~concerned~~ **or States making the joint request,** it may, ~~in so far~~ insofar as ~~the~~ **that** concentration affects trade between Member States, adopt the decisions provided for in Article 8 (2), second subparagraph, (3) and (4).

4. Articles 2 (1) (a) and (b), 5, 6, 8 and 10 to 20 shall apply **to a request made pursuant to paragraph 3. Article 7 shall apply to the extent that the concentration has not been put into effect on the date on which the Commission informs the parties that a request has been made.**

The period within which proceedings may be initiated pursuant to Article 10 (1) shall begin on the ~~date~~ **day following that** of the receipt of the request from the Member State **or States**

---

[4] OJ No 13, 21.2.1962, p. 204/62.
[5] OJ No L 175, 23.7.1968, p. 1.
[6] OJ No L 378, 31.12.1986, p. 4.
[7] OJ No L 374. 31.12.1987, p. 1.

concerned. The request must be made within one month at most of the date on which the concentration was made known to the Member State **or to all Member States making a joint request** or effected. This period shall begin on the date of the first of those events.

5. Pursuant to paragraph 3 the Commission shall take only the measures strictly necessary to maintain or restore effective competition within the territory of the Member State **or States** at the request of which it intervenes.

~~6. Paragraphs 3 to 5 shall continue to apply until the thresholds referred to in Article 1 (2) have been reviewed.~~

Article 23

Implementing provisions

The Commission shall have the power to adopt implementing provisions concerning the form, content and other details of notifications pursuant to Article 4, time limits pursuant to Articles **7, 9,** 10 **and 22** and hearings pursuant to Article 18.

The Commission shall have the power to lay down the procedure and time limits for the submission of commitments pursuant to Articles 6(1a) and 8(2).

Article 24

Relations with non-member countries

1. The Member States shall inform the Commission of any general difficulties encountered by their undertakings with concentrations as defined in Article 3 in a non-member country.

2. Initially not more than one year after the entry into force of this Regulation and thereafter periodically the Commission shall draw up a report examining the treatment accorded to Community undertakings, in the terms referred to in paragraphs 3 and 4, as regards concentrations in non-member countries. The Commission shall submit those reports to the Council, together with any recommendations.

3. Whenever it appears to the Commission, either on the basis of the reports referred to in paragraph 2 or on the basis of other information, that a non-member country does not grant Community undertakings treatment comparable to that granted by the Community to undertakings from that non-member country, the Commission may submit proposals to the Council for an appropriate mandate for negotiation with a view to obtaining comparable treatment for Community undertakings.

4. Measures taken under this Article shall comply with the obligations of the Community or of the Member States, without prejudice to Article 234 of the Treaty, under international agreements, whether bilateral or multilateral.

Article 25

Entry into force

1. This Regulation shall enter into force on 21 September 1990.

2. This Regulation shall not apply to any concentration which was the subject of an agreement or announcement or where control was acquired within the meaning of Article 4 (1) before the date of this Regulation's entry into force and it shall not in any circumstances apply to any concentration in respect of which proceedings were initiated before that date by a Member State's authority with responsibilitiy for competition.

3. As regards concentrations to which this regulation applies by virtue of accession, the date of accession shall be substituted for the date of entry into force of this Regulation. The provision of paragraph 2, second alternative, applies in the same way to proceedings

initiated by a competition authority of the new Member States or by the EFTA Surveillance Authority.[8]

This Regulation shall be binding in its entirety and directly applicable in all Member States. Done at Brussels, 21 December 1989.

---

[8] Introduced by the Act concerning the conditions of accession of the Kingdom of Norway, the Republic of Austria, the Republic of Finland and the Kingdom of Sweden and the adjustments to the Treaties on which the European Union is founded, ANNEX I — List referred to in Article 29 of the Act of Accession — III. COMPETITION — B. PROCEDURAL REGULATIONS; OJ No. C 241, 29/08/94, p. 0057.

Appendix 2

COMMISSION REGULATION (EC) No 447/98
of 1 March 1998
on the notifications, time limits and hearings provided for in Council Regulation (EEC) No 4064/89 on the control of concentrations between undertakings (OJ 1998 L61/1)

THE COMMISSION OF THE EUROPEAN COMMUNITIES,

Having regard to the Treaty establishing the European Community,

Having regard to the Agreement on the European Economic Area,

Having regard to Council Regulation (EEC) No 4064/89 of 21 December 1989 on the control of concentrations between undertakings[1], as last amended by Regulation (EC) No 1310/97[2], and in particular Article 23 thereof,

Having regard to Council Regulation no 17 of 6 February 1962, First Regulation implementing Articles 85 and 86 of the Treaty[3], as last amended by the Act of Accession of Austria, Finland and Sweden, and in particular Article 24 thereof,

Having regard to Council Regulation (EEC) No 1017/68 of 19 July 1968 applying rules of competition to transport by rail, road and inland waterway[4], as last amended by the Act of Accession of Austria, Finland and Sweden, and in particular Article 29 thereof,

Having regard to Council Regulation (EEC) No 4056/86 of 22 December 1986 laying down detailed rules for the application of Articles 85 and 86 of the Treaty to maritime transport[5], as amended by the Act of Accession of Austria, Finland and Sweden, and in particular Article 26 thereof,

Having regard to Council Regulation (EEC) No 3975/87 of 14 December 1987 laying down the procedure for the application of the rules on competition to undertakings in the air transport sector[6], as last amended by Regulation (EEC) No 2410/92[7], and in particular Article 19 thereof,

Having consulted the Advisory Committee on Concentrations,

(1) Whereas Regulation (EEC) No 4064/89 and in particular Article 23 thereof has been amended by Regulation (EC) No 1310/97;

(2) Whereas Commission Regulation (EC) No 3384/94[8], implementing Regulation (EEC) No 4064/89, must be modified in order to take account of those amendments; whereas experience in the application of Regulation (EC) No 3384/94 has revealed the need to improve certain procedural aspects thereof; whereas for the sake of clarity it should therefore be replaced by a new regulation;

(3) Whereas the Commission has adopted Decision 94/810/ECSC, EC of 12 December 1994 on the terms of reference of hearing officers in competition procedures before the Commission[9];

---

[1] OJ L395, 30.12.1989, p. 1; corrected version, OJ L257, 21.9.1990, p. 13.
[2] OJ L180, 9.7.1997, p. 1.
[3] OJ 13, 21.2.1962, p. 204/62.
[4] OJ L175, 23.7.1968, p. 1.
[5] OJ L378, 31.12.1986, p. 4.
[6] OJ L374, 31.12.1987, p. 1.
[7] OJ L240, 24.8.1992, p. 18.
[8] OJ L377, 31.12.1994, p. 1.
[9] OJ L330, 21.12.1994, p. 67.

(4) Whereas Regulation (EEC) No 4064/89 is based on the principle of compulsory notification of concentrations before they are put into effect; whereas, on the one hand, a notification has important legal consequences which are favourable to the parties to the concentration plan, while, on the other hand, failure to comply with the obligation to notify renders the parties liable to a fine and may also entail civil law disadvantages for them; whereas it is therefore necessary in the interests of legal certainty to define precisely the subject matter and content of the information to be provided in the notification;

(5) Whereas it is for the notifying parties to make full and honest disclosure to the Commission of the facts and circumstances which are relevant for taking a decision on the notified concentration;

(6) Whereas in order to simplify and expedite examination of the notification, it is desirable to prescribe that a form be used;

(7) Whereas since notification sets in motion legal time limits pursuant to Regulation (EEC) No 4064/89, the conditions governing such time-limits and the time when they become effective must also be determined;

(8) Whereas rules must be laid down in the interests of legal certainty for calculating the time limits provided for in Regulation (EEC) No 4064/89; whereas in particular, the beginning and end of the period and the circumstances suspending the running of the period must be determined, with due regard to the requirements resulting from the exceptionally short legal time-limits referred to above; whereas in the absence of specific provisions the determination of rules applicable to periods, dates and time-limits should be based on the principles of Council Regulation (EEC, Euratom) No 1182/71[10];

(9) Whereas the provisions relating to the Commission's procedure must be framed in such a way as to safeguard fully the right to be heard and the rights of defence; whereas for these purposes the Commission should distinguish between the parties who notify the concentration, other parties involved in the concentration plan, third parties and parties regarding whom the Commission intends to take a decision imposing a fine or periodic penalty payments;

(10) Whereas the Commission should give the notifying parties and other parties involved, if they so request, an opportunity before notification to discuss the intended concentration informally and in strict confidence; whereas in addition it should, after notification, maintain close contact with those parties to the extent necessary to discuss with them any practical or legal problems which it discovers on a first examination of the case and if possible to remove such problems by mutual agreement;

(11) Whereas in accordance with the principle of the rights of defence, the notifying parties must be given the opportunity to submit their comments on all the objections which the Commission proposes to take into account in its decisions; whereas the other parties involved should also be informed of the Commission's objections and granted the opportunity to express their views;

(12) Whereas third parties having sufficient interest must also be given the opportunity of expressing their views where they make a written application;

(13) Whereas the various persons entitled to submit comments should do so in writing, both in their own interest and in the interest of good administration, without prejudice to their right to request a formal oral hearing where appropriate to supplement the

[10] OJ L124, 8.6.1971, p. 1.

written procedure; whereas in urgent cases, however, the Commission must be able to proceed immediately to formal oral hearings of the notifying parties, other parties involved or third parties;

(14)   Whereas it is necessary to define the rights of persons who are to be heard, to what extent they should be granted access to the Commission's file and on what conditions they may be represented or assisted;

(15)   Whereas the Commission must respect the legitimate interest of undertakings in the protection of their business secrets and other confidential information;

(16)   Whereas, in order to enable the Commission to carry out a proper assessment of commitments that have the purpose of rendering the concentration compatible with the common market, and to ensure due consultation with other parties involved, third parties and the authorities of the Member States as provided for in Regulation (EEC) No 4064/89, in particular Article 18(1) and (4) thereof, the procedure and time-limits for submitting such commitments as provided for in Article 6(2) and Article 8(2) of Regulation (EEC) No 4064/89 must be laid down;

(17)   Whereas it is also necessary to define the rules for fixing and calculating the time limits for reply fixed by the Commission;

(18)   Whereas the Advisory Committee on Concentrations must deliver its opinion on the basis of a preliminary draft decision; whereas it must therefore be consulted on a case after the inquiry into that case has been completed; whereas such consultation does not, however, prevent the Commission from reopening an inquiry if need be,

HAS ADOPTED THIS REGULATION:

CHAPTER I
NOTIFICATIONS

Article 1

Persons entitled to submit notifications

1. Notifications shall be submitted by the persons or undertakings referred to in Article 4(2) of Regulation (EEC) No 4064/89.

2. Where notifications are signed by representatives of persons or of undertakings, such representatives shall produce written proof that they are authorised to act.

3. Joint notifications should be submitted by a joint representative who is authorised to transmit and to receive documents on behalf of all notifying parties.

Article 2

Submission of notifications

1. Notifications shall be submitted in the manner prescribed by form CO as shown in the Annex. Joint notifications shall be submitted on a single form.

2. One original and 23 copies of the form CO and the supporting documents shall be submitted to the Commission at the address indicated in form CO.

3. The supporting documents shall be either originals or copies of the originals; in the latter case the notifying parties shall confirm that they are true and complete.

4. Notifications shall be in one of the official languages of the Community. This language shall

also be the language of the proceeding for the notifying parties. Supporting documents shall be submitted in their original language. Where the original language is not one of the official languages of the Community, a translation into the language of the proceeding shall be attached.

5. Where notifications are made pursuant to Article 57 of the EEA Agreement, they may also be in one of the official languages of the EFTA States or the working language of the EFTA Surveillance Authority. If the language chosen for the notifications is not an official language of the Community, the notifying parties shall simultaneously supplement all documentation with a translation into an official language of the Community. The language which is chosen for the translation shall determine the language used by the Commission as the language of the proceedings for the notifying parties.

Article 3

Information and documents to be provided

1. Notifications shall contain the information, including documents, requested by form CO. The information must be correct and complete.

2. The Commission may dispense with the obligation to provide any particular information, including documents, requested by form CO where the Commission considers that such information is not necessary for the examination of the case.

3. The Commission shall without delay acknowledge in writing to the notifying parties or their representatives receipt of the notification and of any reply to a letter sent by the Commission pursuant to Article 4(2) and (4).

Article 4

Effective date of notification

1. Subject to paragraphs 2, 3 and 4, notifications shall become effective on the date on which they are received by the Commission.

2. Where the information, including documents, contained in the notification is incomplete in a material respect, the Commission shall inform the notifying parties or their representatives in writing without delay and shall set an appropriate time-limit for the completion of the information. In such cases, the notification shall become effective on the date on which the complete information is received by the Commission.

3. Material changes in the facts contained in the notification which the notifying parties know or ought to have known must be communicated to the Commission without delay. In such cases, when these material changes could have a significant effect on the appraisal of the concentration, the notification may be considered by the Commission as becoming effective on the date on which the information on the material changes is received by the Commission; the Commission shall inform the notifying parties or their representatives of this in writing and without delay.

4. Incorrect or misleading information shall be considered to be incomplete information.

5. When the Commission publishes the fact of the notification pursuant to Article 4(3) of Regulation (EEC) No 4064/89, it shall specify the date upon which the notification has been received. Where, further to the application of paragraphs 2, 3 and 4, the effective date of notification is later than the date specified in this publication, the Commission shall issue a further publication in which it will state the later date.

Article 5

Conversion of notifications

1. Where the Commission finds that the operation notified does not constitute a concentration within the meaning of Article 3 of Regulation (EEC) No 4064/89, it shall inform the notifying parties or their representatives in writing. In such a case, the Commission shall, if requested by the notifying parties, as appropriate and subject to paragraph 2 of this Article, treat the notification as an application within the meaning of Article 2 or a notification within the meaning of Article 4 of Regulation No 17, as an application within the meaning of Article 12 or a notification within the meaning of Article 14 of Regulation (EEC) No 1017/68, as an application within the meaning of Article 12 of Regulation (EEC) No 4056/86 or as an application within the meaning of Article 3(2) or of Article 5 of Regulation (EEC) No 3975/87.

2. In cases referred to in paragraph 1, second sentence, the Commission may require that the information given in the notification be supplemented within an appropriate time-limit fixed by it in so far as this is necessary for assessing the operation on the basis of the Regulations referred to in that sentence. The application or notification shall be deemed to fulfil the requirements of such Regulations from the date of the original notification where the additional information is received by the Commission within the time-limit fixed.

CHAPTER II

TIME-LIMITS

Article 6

Beginning of periods

1. The period referred to in Article 9(2) of Regulation (EEC) No 4064/89 shall start at the beginning of the working day following the date of the receipt of the copy of the notification by the Member State.

2. The period referred to in Article 9(4)(b) of Regulation (EEC) No 4064/89 shall start at the beginning of the working day following the date of the receipt of the copy of the notification by the Member State.

3. The period referred to in Article 9(6) of Regulation (EEC) No 4064/89 shall start at the beginning of the working day following the date of the Commission's referral.

4. The periods referred to in Article 10(1) of Regulation (EEC) No 4064/89 shall start at the beginning of the working day following the effective date of the notification, within the meaning of Article 4 of this Regulation.

5. The period referred to in Article 10(3) of Regulation (EEC) No 4064/89 shall start at the beginning of the working day following the day on which proceedings were initiated.

6. The period referred to in Article 22(4), second subparagraph, second sentence, of Regulation (EEC) No 4064/89 shall start at the beginning of the working day following the date of the first of the events referred to.

Article 7

End of periods

1. The period referred to in Article 9(2) of Regulation (EEC) No 4064/89 shall end with the expiry of the day which in the third week following that in which the period began is the same day of the week as the day from which the period runs.

2. The period referred to in Article 9(4)(b) of Regulation (EEC) No 4064/89 shall end with the

expiry of the day which in the third month following that in which the period began falls on the same date as the day from which the period runs. Where such a day does not occur in that month, the period shall end with the expiry of the last day of that month.

3. The period referred to in Article 9(6) of Regulation (EEC) No 4064/89 shall end with the expiry of the day which in the fourth month following that in which the period began falls on the same date as the day from which the period runs. Where such a day does not occur in that month, the period shall end with the expiry of the last day of that month.

4. The period referred to in Article 10(1), first subparagraph, of Regulation (EEC) No 4064/89 shall end with the expiry of the day which in the month following that in which the period began falls on the same date as the day from which the period runs. Where such a day does not occur in that month, the period shall end with the expiry of the last day of that month.

5. The period referred to in Article 10(1), second subparagraph, of Regulation (EEC) No 4064/89 shall end with the expiry of the day which in the sixth week following that in which the period began is the same day of the week as the day from which the period runs.

6. The period referred to in Article 10(3) of Regulation (EEC) No 4064/89 shall end with the expiry of the day which in the fourth month following that in which the period began falls on the same date as the day from which the period runs. Where such a day does not occur in that month, the period shall end with the expiry of the last day of that month.

7. The period referred to in Article 22(4), second subparagraph, second sentence, of Regulation (EEC) No 4064/89 shall end with the expiry of the day which in the month following that in which the period began falls on the same date as the day from which the period runs. Where such a day does not occur in that month, the period shall end with the expiry of the last day of that month.

8. Where the last day of the period is not a working day, the period shall end with the expiry of the following working day.

Article 8

Recovery of holidays

Once the end of the period has been determined in accordance with Article 7, if public holidays or other holidays of the Commission referred to in Article 23 fall within the periods referred to in Articles 9, 10 and 22 of Regulation (EEC) No 4064/89, a corresponding number of working days shall be added to those periods.

Article 9

Suspension of time limit

1. The periods referred to in Article 10(1) and (3) of Regulation (EEC) No 4064/89 shall be suspended where the Commission, pursuant to Article 11(5) and Article 13(3) of that Regulation, has to take a decision because:

   (a) information which the Commission has requested pursuant to Article 11(1) of Regulation (EEC) No 4064/89 from one of the notifying parties or another involved party, as defined in Article 11 of this Regulation, is not provided or not provided in full within the time limit fixed by the Commission;

   (b) information which the Commission has requested pursuant to Article 11(1) of Regulation (EEC) No 4064/89 from a third party, as defined in Article 11 of this Regulation, is not provided or not provided in full within the time limit fixed by the Commission owing to circumstances for which one of the notifying parties or another involved party, as defined in Article 11 of this Regulation, is responsible;

(c) one of the notifying parties or another involved party, as defined in Article 11 of this Regulation, has refused to submit to an investigation deemed necessary by the Commission on the basis of Article 13(1) of Regulation (EEC) No 4064/89 or to cooperate in the carrying out of such an investigation in accordance with that provision;

(d) the notifying parties have failed to inform the Commission of material changes in the facts contained in the notification.

2. The periods referred to in Article 10(1) and (3) of Regulation (EEC) No 4064/89 shall be suspended:

(a) in the cases referred to in paragraph 1(a) and (b), for the period between the end of the time limit fixed in the request for information and the receipt of the complete and correct information required by decision;

(b) in the cases referred to in paragraph 1(c), for the period between the unsuccessful attempt to carry out the investigation and the completion of the investigation ordered by decision;

(c) in the cases referrred to in paragraph 1(d), for the period between the occurrence of the change in the facts referred to therein and the receipt of the complete and correct information requested by decision or the completion of the investigation ordered by decision.

3. The suspension of the time limit shall begin on the day following that on which the event causing the suspension occurred. It shall end with the expiry of the day on which the reason for suspension is removed. Where such a day is not a working day, the suspension of the time-limit shall end with the expiry of the following working day.

Article 10

Compliance with the time-limits

1. The time limits referred to in Article 9(4) and (5), and Article 10(1) and (3) of Regulation (EEC) No 4064/89 shall be met where the Commission has taken the relevant decision before the end of the period.

2. The time limit referred to in Article 9(2) of Regulation (EEC) No 4064/89 shall be met where a Member State informs the Commission before the end of the period in writing.

3. The time limit referred to in Article 9(6) of Regulation (EEC) No 4064/89 shall be met where the competent authority of the Member State concerned publishes any report or announces the findings of the examination of the concentration before the end of the period.

4. The time limit referred to in Article 22(4), second subparagraph, second sentence, of Regulation (EEC) No 4064/89 shall be met where the request made by the Member State or the Member States is received by the Commission before the end of the period.

CHAPTER III

HEARING OF THE PARTIES AND OF THIRD PARTIES

Article 11

Parties to be heard

For the purposes of the rights to be heard pursuant to Article 18 of Regulation (EEC) No 4064/89, the following parties are distinguished:

(a) notifying parties, that is, persons or undertakings submitting a notification pursuant to Article 4(2) of Regulation (EEC) No 4064/89;

(b) other involved parties, that is, parties to the concentration plan other than the notifying parties, such as the seller and the undertaking which is the target of the concentration;

(c) third parties, that is, natural or legal persons showing a sufficient interest, including customers, suppliers and competitors, and especially members of the administration or management organs of the undertakings concerned or recognised workers' representatives of those undertakings;

(d) parties regarding whom the Commission intends to take a decision pursuant to Article 14 or 15 of Regulation (EEC) No 4064/89.

Article 12

Decisions on the suspension of concentrations

1. Where the Commission intends to take a decision pursuant to Article 7(4) of Regulation (EEC) No 4064/89 which adversely affects one or more of the parties, it shall, pursuant to Article 18(1) of that Regulation, inform the notifying parties and other involved parties in writing of its objections and shall fix a time limit within which they may make known their views.

2. Where the Commission, pursuant to Article 18(2) of Regulation (EEC) No 4064/89, has taken a decision referred to in paragraph 1 of this Article provisionally without having given the notifying parties and other involved parties the opportunity to make known their views, it shall without delay send them the text of the provisional decision and shall fix a time limit within which they may make known their views.

Once the notifying parties and other involved parties have made known their views, the Commission shall take a final decision annulling, amending or confirming the provisional decision. Where they have not made known their views within the time limit fixed, the Commission's provisional decision shall become final with the expiry of that period.

3. The notifying parties and other involved parties shall make known their views in writing or orally within the time limit fixed. They may confirm their oral statements in writing.

Article 13

Decisions on the substance of the case

1. Where the Commission intends to take a decision pursuant to Article 8(2), second subparagraph, or Article 8(3), (4) or (5) of Regulation (EEC) No 4064/89, it shall, before consulting the Advisory Committee on Concentrations, hear the parties pursuant to Article 18(1) and (3) of that Regulation.

2. The Commission shall address its objections in writing to the notifying parties.

The Commission shall, when giving notice of objections, set a time limit within which the notifying parties may inform the Commission of their views in writing.

The Commission shall inform other involved parties in writing of these objections.

The Commission shall also set a time limit within which those other involved parties may inform the Commission of their views in writing.

3. After having addressed its objections to the notifying parties, the Commission shall, upon request, give them access to the file for the purpose of enabling them to exercise their rights of defence.

The Commission shall, upon request, also give the other involved parties who have been informed of the objections access to the file in so far as this is necessary for the purposes of preparing their observations.

4. The parties to whom the Commission's objections have been addressed or who have been informed of those objections shall, within the time limit fixed, make known in writing their

views on the objections. In their written comments, they may set out all matters relevant to the case and may attach any relevant documents iln proof of the facts set out. They may also propose that the Commission hear persons who may corroborate those facts. They shall submit one original and 29 copies of their response to the Commission at the address indicated in form CO.

5. Where the Commission intends to take a decision pursuant to Article 14 or 15 of Regulation (EEC) No 4064/89 it shall, before consulting the Advisory Committee on Concentrations, hear pursuant to Article 18(1) and (3) of that Regulation the parties regarding whom the Commission intends to take such a decision.

The procedure provided for in paragraph 2, first and second subparagraphs, paragraph 3, first subparagraph, and paragraph 4 is applicable, *mutatis mutandis.*

Article 14

Oral hearings

1. The Commission shall afford the notifying parties who have so requested in their written comments the opportunity to put forward their arguments orally in a formal hearing if such parties show a sufficient interest. It may also in other cases afford such parties the opportunity of expressing their views orally.

2. The Commission shall afford other involved parties who have so requested in their written comments the opportunity to express their views orally in a formal hearing if they show a sufficient interest. It may also in other cases afford such parties the opportunity of expressing their views orally.

3. The Commission shall afford parties on whom it proposes to impose a fine or periodic penalty payment who have so requested in their written comments the opportunity to put forward their arguments orally in a formal hearing. It may also in other cases afford such parties the opportunity of expressing their views orally.

4. The Commission shall invite the persons to be heard to attend on such date as it shall appoint.

5. The Commission shall invite the competent authorities of the Member States, to take part in the hearing.

Article 15

Conduct of formal oral hearings

1. Hearings shall be conducted by the Hearing Officer.

2. Persons invited to attend shall either appear in person or be represented by legal representatives or by representatives authorised by their constitution as appropriate. Undertakings and associations of undertakings may be represented by a duly authorised agent appointed from among their permanent staff.

3. Persons heard by the Commission may be assisted by their legal adviser or other qualified persons admitted by the Hearing Officer.

4. Hearings shall not be public. Each person shall be heard separately or in the presence of other persons invited to attend. In the latter case, regard shall be had to the legitimate interest of the undertakings in the protection of their business secrets and other confidential information.

5. The statements made by each person heard shall be recorded.

Article 16

Hearing of third parties

1. If third parties apply in writing to be heard pursuant to Article 18(4), second sentence, of Regulation (EEC) No 4064/89, the Commission shall inform them in writing of the nature and subject matter of the procedure and shall fix a time limit within which they may make known their views.

2. The third parties referred to in paragraph 1 shall make known their views in writing within the time limit fixed. The Commission may, where appropriate, afford the parties who have so requested in their written comments the opportunity to participate in a formal hearing. It may also in other cases afford such parties the opportunity of expressing their views orally.

3. The Commission may likewise afford to any other third parties the opportunity of expressing their views.

Article 17

Confidential information

1. Information, including documents, shall not be communicated or made accessible in so far as it contains business secrets of any person or undertaking, including the notifying parties, other involved parties or of third parties, or other confidential information the disclosure of which is not considered necessary by the Commission for the purpose of the procedure, or where internal documents of the authorities are concerned.

2. Any party which makes known its views under the provisions of this Chapter shall clearly identify any material which it considers to be confidential, giving reasons, and provide a separate non-confidential version within the time limit fixed by the Commission.

CHAPTER IV

COMMITMENTS RENDERING THE CONCENTRATION COMPATIBLE

Article 18

Time limits for commitments

1. Commitments proposed to the Commission by the undertakings concerned pursuant to Article 6(2) of Regulation (EEC) No 4064/89 which are intended by the parties to form the basis for a decision pursuant to Article 6(1)(b) of that Regulation shall be submitted to the Commission within not more than three weeks from the date of receipt of the notification.

2. Commitments proposed to the Commission by the undertakings concerned pursuant to Article 8(2) of Regulation (EEC) No 4064/89 which are intended by the parties to form the basis for a decision pursuant to that Article shall be submitted to the Commission within not more than three months from the date on which proceedings were initiated. The Commission may in exceptional circumstances extend this period.

3. Articles 6 to 9 shall apply *mutatis mutandis* to paragraphs 1 and 2 of this Article.

Article 19

Procedure for commitments

1. One original and 29 copies of commitments proposed to the Commission by the undertakings concerned pursuant to Article 6(2) or Article 8(2) of Regulation (EEC) No 4064/89 shall be submitted to the Commission at the address indicated in form CO.

2. Any party proposing commitments to the Commission pursuant to Articles 6(2) or Article 8(2) of Regulation (EEC) No 4064/89 shall clearly identify any material which it considers to be confidential, giving reasons, and provide a separate non-confidential version within the time limit fixed by the Commission.

CHAPTER V

MISCELLANEOUS PROVISIONS

Article 20

Transmission of documents

1. Transmission of documents and invitations from the Commission to the addressees may be effected in any of the following ways:

(a) delivery by hand against receipt;

(b) registered letter with acknowledgement of receipt;

(c) fax with a request for acknowledgement of receipt;

(d) telex;

(e) electronic mail with a request for acknowledgement of receipt.

2. Unless otherwise provided in this Regulation, paragraph 1 also applies to the transmission of documents from the notifying parties, from other involved parties or from third parties to the Commission.

3. Where a document is sent by telex, by fax or by electronic mail, it shall be presumed that it has been received by the addressee on the day on which it was sent.

Article 21

Setting of time limits

In fixing the time limits provided for pursuant to Article 4(2), Article 5(2), Article 12(1) and (2), Article 13(2) and Article 16(1), the Commission shall have regard to the time required for preparation of statements and to the urgency of the case. It shall also take account of working days as well as public holidays in the country of receipt of the Commission's communication.

These time limits shall be set in terms of a precise calendar date.

Article 22

Receipt of documents by the Commission

1. In accordance with the provisions of Article 4(1) of this Regulation, notifications must be delivered to the Commission at the address indicated in form CO or have been dispatched by registered letter to the address indicated in form CO before the expiry of the period referred to in Article 4(1) of Regulation (EEC) No 4064/89.

Additional information requested to complete notifications pursuant to Article 4(2) and (4) or to supplement notifications pursuant to Article 5(2) must reach the Commission at the aforesaid address or have been dispatched by registered letter before the expiry of the time limit fixed in each case.

Written comments on Commission communications pursuant to Article 12(1) and (2), Article 13(2) and Article 16(1) must have reached the Commission at the aforesaid address before the expiry of the time limit fixed in each case.

2. Time limits referred to in subparagraphs two and three of paragraph 1 shall be determined in accordance with Article 21.

3. Should the last day of a time limit fall on a day which is not a working day or which is a public holiday in the country of dispatch, the time limit shall expire on the following working day.

Article 23

Definition of working days

The expression 'working days' in this Regulation means all days other than Saturdays, Sundays, public holidays and other holidays as determined by the Commission and published in the *Official Journal of the European Communities* before the beginning of each year.

Article 24

Repeal

Regulation (EEC) No 3384/94 is repealed.

Article 25

Entry into force

This Regulation shall enter into force on 21 March 1998.

   This Regulation shall be binding in its entirety and directly applicable in all Member States. Done at Brussels, 1 March 1998.

For the Commission
Karel VAN MIERT
Member of the Commission

ANNEX
FORM CO RELATING TO THE NOTIFICATION OF A CONCENTRATION PURSUANT TO REGULATION (EEC) No 4064/89

INTRODUCTION

A. The purpose of this form

This form specifies the information that must be provided by an undertaking or undertakings when notifying the Commission of a concentration with a Community dimension. A "concentration" is defined in Article 3 of Regulation (EEC) No 4064/89 (hereinafter referred to as "the Merger Regulation") and "Community dimension" in Article 1 thereof.

Your attention is drawn to the Merger Regulation and to Regulation (EC) No 447/98 (hereinafter referred to as "the Implementing Regulation") and to the corresponding provisions of the Agreement on the European Economic Area[1].

Experience has shown that prenotification meetings are extremely valuable to both the notifying parties and the Commission in determining the precise amount of information required in a notification and, in the large majority of cases, will result in a significant reduction of the information required. Accordingly, notifying parties are encouraged to consult the Commission regarding the possibility of dispensing with the obligation to provide certain information (see Section B(g) on the possibility of dispensation).

B. The need for a correct and complete notification

All information required by this form must be correct and complete. The information required must be supplied in the appropriate section of this form. Annexes to this form shall only be used to supplement the information supplied in the form itself.

In particular you should note that:

(a) In accordance with Article 10(1) of the Merger Regulation and Article 4(2) and (4) of the Implementing Regulation, the time limits of the Merger Regulation linked to the notification will not begin to run until all the information that has to be supplied with the notification has been received by the Commission. This requirement is to ensure that the Commission is able to assess the notified concentration within the strict time-limits provided by the Merger Regulation.

(b) The notifying parties should check carefully, in the course of preparing their notification, that contact names and numbers, and in particular fax numbers, provided to the Commission are accurate, relevant and up-to-date.

(c) Incorrect or misleading information in the notification will be considered to be incomplete information (Article 4(4) of the Implementing Regulation).

(d) If a notification is incomplete, the Commission will inform the notifying parties or their representatives of this in writing and without delay. The notification will only become effective on the date on which the complete and accurate information is received by the Commission (Article 10(1) of the Merger Regulation, Article 4(2) and (4) of the Implementing Regulation).

---

[1] Hereinafter referred to as "the EEA Agreement"; see in particular Article 57 of the EEA Agreement (point 1 of Annex XIV to the EEA Agreement and Protocol 4 to the Agreement between the EFTA States on the establishment of a Surveillance Authority and a Court of Justice), as well as Protocols 21 and 24 to the EEA Agreement and Article 1, and the Agreed Minutes of the Protocol adjusting the EEA Agreement. In particular, any reference to EFTA States shall be understood to mean those EFTA States which are Contracting Parties to the EEA Agreement.

(e) Article 14(1)(b) of the Merger Regulation provides that incorrect or misleading information, where supplied intentionally or negligently, can make the notifying party or parties liable to fines of up to ECU 50 000. In addition, pursuant to Article 6(3)(a) and Article 8(5)(a) of the Merger Regulation the Commission may also revoke its decision on the compatibility of a notified concentration where it is based on incorrect information for which one of the undertakings is responsible.

(f) You may request that the Commission accept that the notification is complete notwithstanding the failure to provide information required by this form, if such information is not reasonably available to you in part or in whole (for example, because of the unavailability of information on a target company during a contested bid).

The Commission will consider such a request, provided that you give reasons for the unavailability of that information, and provide your best estimates for missing data together with the sources for the estimates. Where possible, indications as to where any of the requested information that is unavailable to you could be obtained by the Commission should also be provided.

(g) You may request that the Commission accept that the notification is complete notwithstanding the failure to provide information required by this form, if you consider that any particular information requested by this form, in the full or short form version, may not be necessary for the Commission's examination of the case.

The Commission will consider such a request, provided that you give reasons why that information is not relevant and necessary to its inquiry into the notified operation. You may explain this during your pre-notification contacts with the Commission and/or in your notification and ask the Commission to dispense with the obligation to provide that information, pursuant to Article 3(2) of the Implementing Regulation.

C. Notification in short form

(a) In cases where a joint venture has no, or *de minimis*, actual or foreseen activities within the EEA territory, the Commission intends to allow notification of the operation by means of short form. Such cases occur where joint control is acquired by two or more undertakings, and where:

  (i) the turnover[2] of the joint venture and/or the turnover of the contributed activities[3], is less than ECU 100 million in the EEA territory; and
  (ii) the total value of assets[4] transferred to the joint venture is less than ECU 100 million in the EEA territory[5].

---

[2] The turnover of the joint venture should be determined according to the most recent audited accounts of the parent companies, or the joint venture itself, depending upon the availability of separate accounts for the resources combined in the joint venture.

[3] The expression "and/or" refers to the variety of situations covered by the short form; for example:
  — in the case of the joint acquisition of a target company, the turnover to be taken into account is the turnover of this target (the joint venture),
  — in the case of the creation of a joint venture to which the parent companies contribute their activities, the turnover to be taken into account is that of the contributed activities,
  — in the case of entry of a new controlling party into an existing joint venture, the turnover of the joint venture and the turnover of the activities contributed by the new parent company (if any) must be taken into account.

[4] The total value of assets of the joint venture should be determined according to the last regularly prepared and approved balance sheet of each parent company. The term "assets" includes: (1) all tangible and intangible assets that will be transferred to the joint venture (examples of tangible assets include production plants, wholesale or retail outlets, and inventory of goods), and (2) any amount of credit or any obligations of the joint venture which any parent company of the joint venture has agreed to extend or guarantee.

[5] Where the assets transferred generate turnover, then neither the value of the assets nor that of the turnover may exceed ECU 100 million.

(b) If you consider that the operation to be notified meets these qualifications, you may explain this in your notification and ask the Commission to dispense with the obligation to provide the full-form notification, pursuant to Article 3(2) of the Implementing Regulation, and to allow you to notify by means of short form.

(c) Short-form notification allows the notifying parties to limit the information provided in the notification to the following sections and questions:

— Section 1,
— Section 2, except questions 2.1 (a, b and d), 2.3.4, and 2.3.5,
— Section 3, only questions 3.1 and 3.2 (a),
— Section 5, only questions 5.1 and 5.3,
— Section 6,
— Section 10,
— Section 11 (optional for the convenience of the parties), and
— Section 12,
— the five largest independent customers, the five largest independent suppliers, and the five largest competitors in the markets in which the joint venture will be active. Provide the name, address, telephone number, fax number and appropriate contact person of each such customer, supplier and competitor.

(d) In addition, with respect to the affected markets of the joint venture as defined in Section 6, indicate for the EEA territory, for the Community as a whole, for each Member State and EFTA State, and where different, in the opinion of the notifying parties, for the relevant geographic market, the sales in value and volume, as well as the market shares, for the year preceding the operation.

(e) The Commission may require full, or where appropriate partial, notification under the form CO where:

— the notified operation does not meet the short-form thresholds, or
— this appears to be necessary for an adequate investigation with respect to possible competition problems.

In such cases, the notification may be considered incomplete in a material respect pursuant to Article 4(2) of the Implementing Regulation. The Commission will inform the notifying parties or their representatives of this in writing and without delay and will fix a deadline for the submission of a full or, where appropriate, partial notification. The notification will only become effective on the date on which all information required is received.

D. Who must notify

In the case of a merger within the meaning of Article 3(1)(a) of the Merger Regulation or the acquisition of joint control in an undertaking within the meaning of Article 3(1)(b) of the Merger Regulation, the notification shall be completed jointly by the parties to the merger or by those acquiring joint control as the case may be.

In case of the acquisition of a controlling interest in one undertaking by another, the acquirer must complete the notification.

In the case of a public bid to acquire an undertaking, the bidder must complete the notification.

Each party completing the notification is responsible for the accuracy of the information which it provides.

E. How to notify

The notification must be completed in one of the official languages of the European Community. This language will thereafter be the language of the proceedings for all notifying parties. Where notifications are made in accordance with Article 12 of Protocol 24 to the EEA Agreement in an official language of an EFTA State which is not an official language of the Community, the notification must simultaneously be supplemented with a translation into an official language of the Community.

The information requested by this form is to be set out using the sections and paragraph numbers of the form, signing a declaration as provided in Section 12, and annexing supporting documentation.

Supporting documents are to be submitted in their original language; where this is not an official language of the Community, they must be translated into the language of the proceeding (Article 2(4) of the Implementing Regulation).

Supporting documents may be originals or copies of the originals. In the latter case, the notifying party must confirm that they are true and complete.

One original and 23 copies of the form CO and all supporting documents must be provided.

The notification must be delivered to the Commission on working days as defined by Article 23 of the Implementing Regulation. In order to enable it to be registered on the same day, it must be delivered before 17.00 on Mondays to Thursdays and before 16.00 on Fridays, at the following address:

Commission of the European Communities
Directorate-General for Competition (DG IV)
Merger Task Force
150 avenue de Cortenberg/Kortenberglaan 150
B-1049 Brussels.

F. Confidentiality

Article 214 of the Treaty and Article 17(2) of the Merger Regulation as well as the corresponding provisions of the EEA Agreement[6] require the Commission, the Member States, the EFTA Surveillance Authority and the EFTA States, their officials and other servants not to disclose information they have acquired through the application of the Regulation of the kind covered by the obligation of professional secrecy. The same principle must also apply to protect confidentiality between notifying parties.

If you believe that your interests would be harmed if any of the information you are asked to supply were to be published or otherwise divulged to other parties, submit this information separately with each page clearly marked "Business Secrets". You should also give reasons why this information should not be divulged or published.

In the case of mergers or joint acquisitions, or in other cases where the notification is completed by more than one of the parties, business secrets may be submitted under separate cover, and referred to in the notification as an annex. All such annexes must be included in the submission in order for a notification to be considered complete.

G. Definitions and instructions for purposes of this form

Notifying party or parties: in cases where a notification is submitted by only one of the undertakings party to an operation, "notifying parties" is used to refer only to the undertaking actually submitting the notification.

Party (parties) to the concentration: these terms relate to both the acquiring and acquired parties, or to the merging parties, including all undertakings in which a controlling interest is being acquired or which is the subject of a public bid.

Except where otherwise specified, the terms "notifying party(parties)" and "party(parties)

---

[6] See, in particular, Article 122 of the EEA Agreement, Article 9 of Protocol 24 to the EEA Agreement and Article 17(2) of Chapter XIII of Protocol 4 to the Agreement between the EFTA States on the establishment of a Surveillance Authority and a Court of Justice (ESA Agreement).

to the concentration'' include all the undertakings which belong to the same groups as those ''parties''.

Affected markets: Section 6 of this form requires the notifying parties to define the relevant product markets, and further to identify which of those relevant markets are likely to be affected by the notified operation. This definition of affected market is used as the basis for requiring information for a number of other questions contained in this form. The definitions thus submitted by the notifying parties are referred to in this form as the affected market(s). This term can refer to a relevant market made up either of products or of services.

Year: all references to the word ''year'' in this form should be read as meaning calendar year, unless otherwise stated. All information requested in this form must, unless otherwise specified, relate to the year preceding that of the notification.

The financial data requested in Sections 2.3 to 2.5 must be provided in ecus at the average conversion rates prevailing for the years or other periods in question.

All references contained in this form are to the relevant Articles and paragraphs of Council Regulation (EEC) No 4064/89, unless otherwise stated.

SECTION 1

BACKGROUND INFORMATION

1.1   *Information on notifying party (or parties)*

Give details of:
1.1.1 name and address of undertaking;
1.1.2. nature of the undertaking's business;
1.1.3. name, address, telephone number, fax number and/or telex of, and position held by, the appropriate contact person.

1.2.   *Information on other parties[7] to the concentration*

For each party to the concentration (except the notifying party or parties) give details of:
1.2.1. name and address of undertaking;
1.2.2. nature of undertaking's business;
1.2.3. name, address, telephone number, fax number and/or telex of, and position held by the appropriate contact person.

1.3.   *Address for service*

Give an address (in Brussels if available) to which all communications may be made and documents delivered.

1.4.   *Appointment of representatives*

Where notifications are signed by representatives of undertakings, such representatives must produce written proof that they are authorised to act.

If a joint notification is being submitted, has a joint representative been appointed?

If yes, please give the details requested in Sections 1.4.1 to 1.4.4.

If no, please give details of information of any representatives who have been authorised to act for each of the parties to the concentration, indicating whom they represent:
1.4.1. name of representative;
1.4.2. address of representative;
1.4.3. name of person to be contacted (and address, if different from 1.4.2);
1.4.4. telephone number, fax number and/or telex.

---

[7] This includes the target company in the case of a contested bid, in which case the details should be completed as far as is possible.

SECTION 2

DETAILS OF THE CONCENTRATION

2.1. *Describe the nature of the concentration being notified. In doing so state:*

(a) whether the proposed concentration is a full legal merger, an acquisition of sole or joint control, a full-function joint venture within the meaning of Article 3(2) of the Merger Regulation or a contract or other means of conferring direct or indirect control within the meaning of Article 3(3) of the Merger Regulation;

(b) whether the whole or parts of parties are subject to the concentration;

(c) a brief explanation of the economic and financial structure of the concentration;

(d) whether any public offer for the securities of one party by another party has the support of the former's supervisory boards of management or other bodies legally representing that party;

(e) the proposed or expected date of any major events designed to bring about the completion of the concentration;

(f) the proposed structure of ownership and control after the completion of the concentration;

(g) any financial or other support received from whatever source (including public authorities) by any of the parties and the nature and amount of this support.

2.2. *List the economic sectors involved in the concentration*

2.3. *For each of the undertakings concerned by the concentration[8] provide the following data[9] for the last financial year:*

2.3.1. worldwide turnover;

2.3.2. Community-wide turnover;

2.3.3. EFTA-wide turnover;

2.3.4. turnover in each Member State;

2.3.5. turnover in each EFTA State;

2.3.6. the Member State, if any, in which more than two thirds of Community-wide turnover is achieved[10];

2.3.7. the EFTA State, if any, in which more than two thirds of EFTA-wide turnover is achieved.

2.4. *For the purposes of Article 1(3) of the Merger Regulation, if the operation does not meet the thresholds set out in Article 1(2), provide the following data for the last financial year:*

2.4.1. the Member States, if any, in which the combined aggregate turnover of all the undertakings concerned is more than ECU 100 million;

2.4.2. the Member States, if any, in which the aggregate turnover of each of at least two of the undertakings concerned is more than ECU 25 million.

---

[8] See Commission notice on the concept of undertakings concerned.

[9] See, generally, the Commission notice on calculation of turnover. Turnover of the acquiring party or parties to the concentration should include the aggregated turnover of all undertakings within the meaning of Article 5(4). Turnover of the acquired party or parties should include the turnover relating to the parts subject to the transaction within the meaning of Article 5(2). Special provisions are contained in Articles 5(3), (4) and 5(5) for credit, insurance, other financial institutions and joint undertakings.

[10] See Guidance Note III for the calculation of turnover in one Member State with respect to Community-wide turnover.

2.5. Provide the following information with respect to the last financial year:

2.5.1. does the combined turnover of the undertakings concerned in the territory of the EFTA States equal 25% or more of their total turnover in the EEA territory?

2.5.2. does each of at least two undertakings concerned have a turnover exceeding ECU 250 million in the territory of the EFTA States?

SECTION 3

OWNERSHIP AND CONTROL[11]

For each of the parties to the concentration provide a list of all undertakings belonging to the same group.

This list must include:

3.1.   all undertakings or persons controlling these parties, directly or indirectly;

3.2.   all undertakings active on any affected market[12] that are controlled, directly or indirectly:

(a) by these parties;

(b) by any other undertaking identified in 3.1.

For each entry listed above, the nature and means of control should be specified.

The information sought in this section may be illustrated by the use of organisation charts or diagrams to show the structure of ownership and control of the undertakings.

SECTION 4

PERSONAL AND FINANCIAL LINKS AND PREVIOUS ACQUISITIONS

With respect to the parties to the concentration and each undertaking or person identified in response to Section 3, provide:

4.1.   a list of all other undertakings which are active on affected markets (affected markets are defined in Section 6) in which the undertakings, or persons, of the group hold individually or collectively 10% or more of the voting rights, issued share capital or other securities;

in each case identify the holder and state the percentage held;

4.2.   a list for each undertaking of the members of their boards of management who are also members of the boards of management or of the supervisory boards of any other undertaking which is active on affected markets; and (where applicable) for each undertaking a list of the members of their supervisory boards who are also members of the boards of management of any other undertaking which is active on affected markets;

in each case identify the name of the other undertaking and the positions held;

4.3.   details of acquisitions made during the last three years by the groups identified above (Section 3) of undertakings active in affected markets as defined in Section 6.

Information provided here may be illustrated by the use of organisation charts or diagrams to give a better understanding.

---

[11] See Article 3(3), (4) and (5) and Article 5(4) .
[12] See Section 6 for the definition of affected markets.

SECTION 5

SUPPORTING DOCUMENTATION

Notifying parties must provide the following:

5.1.   copies of the final or most recent versions of all documents bringing about the concentration, whether by agreement between the parties to the concentration, acquisition of a controlling interest or a public bid;

5.2.   in a public bid, a copy of the offer document; if it is unavailable at the time of notification, it should be submitted as soon as possible and not later than when it is posted to shareholders;

5.3.   copies of the most recent annual reports and accounts of all the parties to the concentration;

5.4.   where at least one affected market is identified:

copies of analyses, reports, studies and surveys submitted to or prepared for any member(s) of the board of directors, the supervisory board, or the shareholders' meeting, for the purpose of assessing or analysing the concentration with respect to competitive conditions, competitors (actual and potential), and market conditions.

SECTION 6

MARKET DEFINITIONS

The relevant product and geographic markets determine the scope within which the market power of the new entity resulting from the concentration must be assessed[13].

The notifying party or parties must provide the data requested having regard to the following definitions:

I. Relevant product markets

A relevant product market comprises all those products and/or services which are regarded as interchangeable or substitutable by the consumer, by reason of the products'characteristics, their prices and their intended use. A relevant product market may in some cases be composed of a number of individual products and/or services which present largely identical physical or technical characteristics and are interchangeable.

Factors relevant to the assessment of the relevant product market include the analysis of why the products or services in these markets are included and why others are excluded by using the above definition, and having regard to, for example, substitutability, conditions of competition, prices, cross-price elasticity of demand or other factors relevant for the definition of the product markets.

II. Relevant geographic markets

The relevant geographic market comprises the area in which the undertakings concerned are involved in the supply and demand of relevant products or services, in which the conditions of competition are sufficiently homogeneous and which can be distinguished from neighbouring geographic areas because, in particular, conditions of competition are appreciably different in those areas.

Factors relevant to the assessment of the relevant geographic market include the nature and characteristics of the products or services concerned, the existence of entry barriers, consumer preferences, appreciable differences in the undertakings' market shares between neighbouring geographic areas or substantial price differences.

---

[13] See Commission notice on the definition of the relevant market for the purposes of Community competition law.

III. Affected markets

For purposes of information required in this form, affected markets consist of relevant product markets where, in the EEA territory, in the Community, in the territory of the EFTA States, in any Member State or in any EFTA State:

(a) two or more of the parties to the concentration are engaged in business activities in the same product market and where the concentration will lead to a combined market share of 15% or more. These are horizontal relationships;

(b) one or more of the parties to the concentration are engaged in business activities in a product market, which is upstream or downstream of a product market in which any other party to the concentration is engaged, and any of their individual or combined market shares is 25% or more, regardless of whether there is or is not any existing supplier/customer relationship between the parties to the concentration. These are vertical relationships.

On the basis of the above definitions and market share thresholds, provide the following information:

6.1. Identify each affected market within the meaning of Section III, at:

(a) the EEA, Community or EFTA level;

(b) the individual Member States or EFTA States level.

IV. Markets related to affected markets within the meaning of Section III

6.2. Describe the relevant product and geographic markets concerned by the notified operation, which are closely related to the affected market(s) (in upstream, downstream and horizontal neighbouring markets), where any of the parties to the concentration are active and which are not themselves affected markets within the meaning of Section III.

V. Non-affected markets

6.3. In case there are no affected markets in the meaning of Section 6.1, describe the product and geographic scope of the markets on which the notified operation would have an impact.

SECTION 7

INFORMATION ON AFFECTED MARKETS

For each affected relevant product market, for each of the last three financial years[14]:

(a) for the EEA territory,

(b) for the Community as a whole,

(c) for the territory of the EFTA States as a whole,

(d) individually for each Member State and EFTA State where the parties to the concentration do business,

(e) and, where in the opinion of the notifying parties, the relevant geographic market is different,

---

[14] Without prejudice to Article 3(2) of the Implementing Regulation, the information required under 7.1 and 7.2 below must be provided with regard to all the territories under (a), (b), (c), (d) and (e).

provide the following:

7.1. an estimate of the total size of the market in terms of sales value (in ecus) and volume (units)[15]. Indicate the basis and sources for the calculations and provide documents where available to confirm these calculations;

7.2. the sales in value and volume, as well as an estimate of the market shares, of each of the parties to the concentration;

7.3. an estimate of the market share in value (and where appropriate volume) of all competitors (including importers) having at least 10% of the geographic market under consideration. Provide documents where available to confirm the calculation of these market shares and provide the name, address, telephone number, fax number and appropriate contact person, of these competitors;

7.4. an estimate of the total value and volume and source of imports from outside the EEA territory and identify:

(a) the proportion of such imports that are derived from the groups to which the parties to the concentration belong,

(b) an estimate of the extent to which any quotas, tariffs or non-tariff barriers to trade, affect these imports, and

(c) an estimate of the extent to which transportation and other costs affect these imports,

7.5. the extent to which trade among States within the EEA territory is affected by:

(a) transportation and other costs, and

(b) other non-tariff barriers to trade;

7.6. the manner in which the parties to the concentration produce and sell the products and/or services; for example, whether they manufacture locally, or sell through local distribution facilities;

7.7. a comparison of price levels in each Member State and EFTA State by each party to the concentration and a similar comparison of price levels between the Community, the EFTA States and other areas where these products are produced (e.g. eastern Europe, the United States of America, Japan, or other relevant areas);

7.8. the nature and extent of vertical integration of each of the parties to the concentration compared with their largest competitors.

SECTION 8

General conditions in affected markets

8.1. Identify the five largest independent[16] suppliers to the parties and their individual shares of purchases from each of these suppliers (of raw materials or goods used for purposes of producing the relevant products). Provide the name, address, telephone number, fax number and appropriate contact person, of these suppliers.

---

[15] The value and volume of a market should reflect output less exports plus imports for the geographic areas under consideration.

[16] That is suppliers which are not subsidiaries, agents or undertakings forming part of the group of the party in question. In addition to those five independent suppliers the notifying parties can, if they consider it necessary for a proper assessment of the case, identify the intra-group suppliers. The same will apply in 8.5 in relation with customers.

Structure of supply in affected markets

8.2.   Explain the distribution channels and service networks that exist on the affected markets. In so doing, take account of the following where appropriate:

(a) the distribution systems prevailing on the market and their importance. To what extent is distribution performed by third parties and/or undertakings belonging to the same group as the parties identified in Section 3?

(b) the service networks (for example, maintenance and repair) prevailing and their importance in these markets. To what extent are such services performed by third parties and/or undertakings belonging to the same group as the parties identified in Section 3?

8.3.   Where appropriate, provide an estimate of the total Community-wide and EFTA-wide capacity for the last three years. Over this period what proportion of this capacity is accounted for by each of the parties to the concentration, and what have been their respective rates of capacity utilisation.

8.4.   If you consider any other supply-side considerations to be relevant, they should be specified.

Structure of demand in affected markets

8.5.   Identify the five largest independent customers of the parties in each affected market and their individual share of total sales for such products accounted for by each of those customers. Provide the name, address, telephone number, fax number and appropriate contact person, of each of these customers.

8.6.   Explain the structure of demand in terms of:

(a) the phases of the markets in terms of, for example, take-off, expansion, maturity and decline, and a forecast of the growth rate of demand;

(b) the importance of customer preferences, in terms of brand loyalty, product differentiation and the provision of a full range of products;

(c) the degree of concentration or dispersion of customers;

(d) segmentation of customers into different groups with a description of the "typical customer" of each group;

(e) the importance of exclusive distribution contracts and other types of long-term contracts;

(f) the extent to which public authorities, government agencies, State enterprises or similar bodies are important participants as a source of demand.

Market entry

8.7.   Over the last five years, has there been any significant entry into any affected markets? If the answer is "yes", where possible provide their name, address, telephone number, fax number and appropriate contact person, and an estimate of their current market shares.

8.8.   In the opinion of the notifying parties are there undertakings (including those at present operating only in extra-Community or extra-EEA markets) that are likely to enter the market? If the answer is "yes", please explain why and identify such entrants by name, address, telephone number, fax number and appropriate contact person, and an estimate of the time within which such entry is likely to occur.

9.9.   Describe the various factors influencing entry into affected markets that exist in the present case, examining entry from both a geographical and product viewpoint. In so doing, take account of the following where appropriate:

(a) the total costs of entry (R & D, establishing distribution systems, promotion, advertising, servicing, etc.) on a scale equivalent to a significant viable competitor, indicating the market share of such a competitor;

(b) any legal or regulatory barriers to entry, such as government authorisation or standard setting in any form;

(c) any restrictions created by the existence of patents, know-how and other intellectual property rights in these markets and any restrictions created by licensing such rights;

(d) the extent to which each of the parties to the concentration are licensees or licensors of patents, know-how and other rights in the relevant markets;

(e) the importance of economies of scale for the production of products in the affected markets;

(f) access to sources of supply, such as availability of raw materials.

Research and development

8.10. Give an account of the importance of research and development in the ability of a firm operating on the relevant market(s) to compete in the long term. Explain the nature of the research and development in affected markets carried out by the parties to the concentration.

In so doing, take account of the following, where appropriate:

(a) trends and intensities of research and development[17] in these markets and for the parties to the concentration;

(b) the course of technological development for these markets over an appropriate time period (including developments in products and/or services, production processes, distribution systems, etc.);

(c) the major innovations that have been made in these markets and the undertakings responsible for these innovations;

(d) the cycle of innovation in these markets and where the parties are in this cycle of innovation.

Cooperative agreements

8.11. To what extent do cooperative agreements (horizontal or vertical) exist in the affected markets?

8.12. Give details of the most important cooperative agreements engaged in by the parties to the concentration in the affected markets, such as research and development, licensing, joint production, specialisation, distribution, long term supply and exchange of information agreements.

Trade associations

8.13. With respect to the trade associations in the affected markets:

(a) identify those in which the parties to the concentration are members;

(b) identify the most important trade associations to which the customers and suppliers of the parties to the concentration belong.

---

[17] Research and development intensity is defined as research development expenditure as a proportion of turnover.

Provide the name, address, thelephone number, fax number and appropriate contact person of all trade associations listed above.

SECTION 9

GENERAL MARKET INFORMATION

Market data on conglomerate aspects

Where any of the parties to the concentration hold individually a market share of 25% or more for any product market in which there is no horizontal or vertical relationship as described above, provide the following information:

9.1.   a description of each product market and explain why the products and/or services in these markets are included (and why others are excluded) by reason of their characteristics, prices and their intended use;

9.2.   an estimate of the value of the market and the market shares of each of the groups to which the parties belong for each product market identified in 9.1 for the last financial year:

(a) for the EEA territory as a whole;

(b) for the Community as a whole;

(c) for the territory of the EFTA States as a whole;

(d) individually for each Member State and EFTA State where the groups to which the parties belong do business;

(e) and, where different, for the relevant geographic market.

Overview of the markets

9.3.   Describe the worldwide context of the proposed concentration, indicating the position of each of the parties to the concentration outside of the EEA territory in terms of size and competitive strength.

9.4.   Describe how the proposed concentration is likely to affect the interests of intermediate and ultimate consumers and the development of technical and economic progress.

SECTION 10

COOPERATIVE EFFECTS OF A JOINT VENTURE

10.   For the purpose of Article 2(4) of the Merger Regulation please answer the following questions:

(a) Do two or more parents retain to a significant extent activities in the same market as the joint venture or in a market which is downstream or upstream from that of the joint venture or in a neighbouring market closely related to this market[18]?
    If the answer is affirmative, please indicate for each of the markets referred to here:

   — the turnover of each parent company in the preceding financial year,
   — the economic significance of the activitites of the joint venture in relation to this turnover,
   — the market share of each parent.

   If the answer is negative, please justify your answer.

---

[18] For market definitions refer to Section 6.

(b) If the answer to (a) is affirmative and in your view the creation of the joint venture does not lead to coordination between independent undertakings that restricts competition within the meaning of Article 85(1) of the EC Treaty, give your reasons.

(c) Without prejudice to the answers to (a) and (b) and in order to ensure that a complete assessment of the case can be made by the Commission, please explalin how the criteria of Article 85(3) apply.

Under Article 85(3), the provisions of Article 85(1) may be declared inapplicable if the operation:

   (i) contributes to improving the production or distribution of goods, or to promoting technical or economic progress;

  (ii) allows consumers a fair share of the resulting benefit;

 (iii) does not impose on the undertakings concerned restrictions which are not indispensable to the attainment of these objectives; and

 (iv) does not afford such undertakings the possibility of eliminating competition in respect of a substantial part of the products in question.

For guidance, please refer to form A/B, and in particular Sections 16 and 17 thereof, annexed to Commission Regulation (EC) No 3385/94[19].

SECTION 11
GENERAL MATTERS

Ancillary restraints

11.1. If the parties to the concentration, and/or other involved parties (including the seller and minority shareholders), enter into ancillary restrictions directly related and necessary to the implementation of the concentration, these restrictions may be assessed in conjunction with the concentration itself (see Article 6(1)(b) and Article 8(2) of the Merger Regulation, recital 25 to the Merger Regulation, recital 7 to Regulation (EC) No 1310/97 and the Commission notice on restrictions ancillary to concentrations)[20].

(a) Identify each ancillary restriction in the agreements provided with the notification for which you request an assessment in conjunction with the concentration; and

(b) explain why these are directly related and necessary to the implementation of the concentration.

Conversion of notification

11.2. In the event that the Commission finds that the operation notified does not constitute a concentration within the meaning of Article 3 of the Merger Regulation, do you request that it be treated as an application for negative clearance from, or a notification to obtain an exemption from Article 85 of the EC Treaty?

SECTION 12
DECLARATION

Article 1(2) of the Implementing Regulation states that where notifications are signed by representatives of undertakings, such representatives must produce written proof that they are authorised to act. Such written authorisation must accompany the notification.

---

[19] OJ L377, 31.12.1994, p. 28.
[20] OJ L180, 9.7.1997, p. 1.

The notification must conclude with the following declaration which is to be signed by or on behalf of all the notifying parties:

The undersigned declare that, to the best of their knowledge and belief, the information given in this notification is true, correct, and complete, that complete copies of documents required by form CO, have been supplied, and that all estimates are identified as such and are their best estimates of the underlying facts and that all the opinions expressed are sincere.

They are aware of the provisions of Article 14(1)(b) of the Merger Regulation.

Place and date:

Signatures:

Name/s:

On behalf of:

GUIDANCE NOTE I

CALCULATION OF TURNOVER FOR INSURANCE UNDERTAKINGS
(Article 5(3)(a))

For the calculation of turnover for insurance undertakings, we give the following example (proposed concentration between insurance A and B):

I. Consolidated profit and loss account

(million ECU)

Income	Insurance A		Insurance B	
Gross premiums written	5,000		300	
— gross premiums received from Community residents		(4,500)		(300)
— gross premiums received from residents of one (and the same) Member State X		(3,600)		(270)
Other income	500		50	
Total income	5,500		350	

II. Calculation of turnover

1. Aggregate worldwide turnover is replaced by the value of gross premiums written worldwide, the sum of which is ECU 5 300 million.

2. Community-wide turnover is replaced, for each insurance undertakings, by the value of gross premiums written with Community residents. For each of the insurance undertakings, this amount is more than ECU 250 million.

3. Turnover within one (and the same) Member State X is replaced, for insurance undertakings, by the value of gross premiums written with residents of one (and the same) Member State X. For insurance A, it achieves 80% of its gross premiums written with Community residents within Member State X, whereas for insurance B, it achieves 90% of its gross premiums written with Community residents in that Member State .

III. Conclusion

Since

(a) the aggregate worldwide turnover of insurances A and B, as replaced by the value of gross premiums written worldwide, is more than ECU 5 000 million;

(b) for each of the insurance undertakings, the value of gross premiums written with Community residents is more than ECU 250 million; but

(c) each of the insurance undertakings achieves more than two thirds of its gross premiums written with Community residents in one (and the same) Member State X,

the proposed concentration would not fall under the scope of the Regulation.

GUIDANCE NOTE II

CALCULATION OF TURNOVER FOR JOINT UNDERTAKINGS

A. Creation of a joint undertaking (Article 3(2))

In a case where two (or more) undertakings create a joint undertaking that constitutes a concentration, turnover is calculated for the undertakings concerned.

B. Existence of a joint undertaking (Article 5(5))

For the calculation of turnover in case of the existence of a joint undertaking C between two undertakings A and B concerned in a concentration, we give the following example:

I. *Profit and loss accounts*

(million ECU)

Turnover	Undertaking A	Undertaking B
Sales revenues worldwide	10,000	2,000
— Community	(8,000)	(1,500)
— Member State Y	(4,000)	(900)

(million ECU)

Turnover	Joint undertaking C
Sales revenues worldwide	100
— with undertaking A	(20)
— with undertaking B	(10)
Turnover with third undertakings	70
— Community-wide	(60)
— in Member State Y	(50)

II. *Consideration of the joint undertaking*

  (a) The undertaking C is jointly controlled (in the meaning of Article 3(3) and (4)) by the undertakings A and B concerned by the concentration, irrespective of any third undertaking participating in that undertaking C.

  (b) The undertaking C is not consolidated A and B in their profit and loss accounts.

  (c) The turnover of C resulting from operations with A and B shall not be taken into account.

  (d) The turnover of C resulting from operations with any third undertaking shall be apportioned equally amongst the undertakings A and B, irrespective of their individual shareholdings in C.

III. *Calculation of turnover*

  (a) Undertaking A's aggregate worldwide turnover shall be calculated as follows: ECU 10 000 million and 50% of C's worldwide turnover with third undertakings (i.e. ECU 35 million), the sum of which is ECU 10 035 million.

     Undertaking B's aggregate worldwide turnover shall be calculated as follows: ECU 2 000 million and 50% of C's worldwide turnover with third undertakings (i.e. ECU 35 million), the sum of which is ECU 2 035 million.

  (b) The aggregate worldwide turnover of the undertakings concerned is ECU 12 070 million.

(c) Undertaking A achieves ECU 4 025 million within Member State Y (50% of C's turnover in this Member State taken into account), and a Community-wide turnover of ECU 8 030 million (including 50% of C's Community-wide turnover).

Undertaking B achieves ECU 925 million within Member State Y (50% of C's turnover in this Member State taken into account), and a Community-wide turnover of ECU 1 530 million (including 50% of C's Community-wide turnover).

IV. *Conclusion*

Since

(a) the aggregate worldwide turnover of undertakings A and B is more than ECU 5 000 million;

(b) each of the undertakings concerned by the concentration achieves more than ECU 250 million within the Community;

(c) each of the undertakings concerned (undertaking A 50,1% and undertaking B 60,5%) achieves less than two thirds of its Community-wide turnover in one (and the same) Member State Y;

the proposed concentration would fall under the scope of the Regulation.

GUIDANCE NOTE III

APPLICATION OF THE TWO-THIRDS RULE
(Article 1)

For the application of the two thirds rule for undertakings, we give the following examples (proposed concentration between undertakings A and B):

I. Consolidated profit and loss accounts

Example 1 *(million ECU)*

Turnover	Undertaking A	Undertaking B
Sales revenues worldwide	10,000	500
— within the Community	(8,000)	(400)
— in Member State X	(6,000)	(200)

Example 2(a) *(million ECU)*

Turnover	Undertaking A	Undertaking B
Sales revenues worldwide	4,800	500
— within the Community	(2,400)	(400)
— in Member State X	(2,100)	(300)

Example 2(b)
Same figures as in example 2(a) but undertaking B achieves ECU 300 million in Member State Y.

II. Application of the two-thirds rule

Example 1

1. Community-wide turnover is, for undertaking A, ECU 8 000 million and for undertaking B ECU 400 million.

2. Turnover in one (and the same) Member State X is, for undertaking A (ECU 6 000 million), 75% of its Community-wide turnover and is, for undertaking B (ECU 200 million), 50% of its Community-wide turnover.

3. Conclusion: In this case, although undertaking A achieves more than two thirds of its Community-wide turnover in Member State X, the proposed concentration would fall under the scope of the Regulation due to the fact that undertaking B achieves less than two thirds of its Community-wide turnover in Member State X.

Example 2(a)

1. Community-wide turnover of undertaking A is ECU 2 400 million and of undertaking B, ECU 400 million.

2. Turnover in one (and the same) Member State X is, for undertaking A, ECU 2 100 million (i.e. 87,5% of its Community-wide turnover); and, for undertaking B, ECU 300 million (i.e. 75% of its Community-wide turnover).

3. Conclusion: In this case, each of the undertakings concerned achieves more than two thirds of its Community-wide turnover in one (and the same) Member State X; the proposed concentration would not fall under the scope of the Regulation.

Example 2(b)

Conclusion: In this case, the two thirds rule would not apply due to the fact that undertakings A and B achieve more than two thirds of their Community-wide turnover in different Member States X and Y. Therefore, the proposed concentration would fall under the scope of the Regulation.

Appendix 3

DRAFT COMMISSION NOTICE
on restrictions directly related and necessary to concentrations*

I. Introduction

1. Council Regulation (EEC) No 4064/89 of 21 December 1989[1] as amended by Council Regulation (EC) No 1310/97 of 30 June 1997,[2] on the control of concentrations between undertakings ('the Regulation') states in its 25th recital[3] that its application is not excluded where the undertakings concerned accept restrictions which are directly and necessary to the implementation of the concentration. Pursuant to Article 6(1)(b), second subparagraph and Article 8(2), second subparagraph, last sentence, of the Regulation, a decision declaring the concentration compatible also covers these restrictions. In this situation, under the provisions of Article 22, paragraph 1, the Regulation is solely applicable, to the exclusion of Regulation No 17[4] as well as Regulations (EEC) No 1017/68,[5] (EEC) No 4056/86[6] and (EEC) No 3975/87.[7] The Commission assesses such restrictions together with the concentration itself. This avoids parallel Commission proceedings, one concerned with the assessment of the concentration under the Regulation, and the other aimed at the application of Article 81[8] to restrictions which are directly related and necessary to the implementation of the concentration.

2. In this notice, the Commission sets out to indicate the interpretation it gives to the notion of 'restrictions directly related and necessary to the implementation of the concentration'. Under the Regulation such restrictions must be assessed in relation to the concentration, whatever their treatment might be under Articles 81 and 82 if they were to be considered in isolation or in a different economic context. The guidance given in the following sections reflects past Commission experience and practice in this field.

3. This notice is without prejudice to the interpretation which may be given by the Community courts.

II. Principles of Evaluation

4. Contractual arrangements which are among the elements constituting the concentration and agreements establishing control within the meaning of Article 3, paragraph 3, including all agreements which relate to assets necessary to carry out the main object of the concentration, are integral parts of the concentration. The latter arrangements constitute the very subject matter of the evaluation to be carried out under the Regulation.

5. In addition to these agreements, the parties to the concentration may enter into other agreements which do not form part of the concentration, and which limit the parties' freedom of action in the market. If such agreements contain restrictions that are directly related and necessary to the concentration itself, they must be assessed together with it under the provisions of

---

* This is a working document prepared for the facility of the reader. Only texts published in the Official Journal of the European Communities are authentic.
[1] OJ No L395, 30.12.1989, p. 1, corrected version OJ 257, 21.9.1990, p. 13.
[2] OJ No L180, 9.7.1997, p. 1, corrigendum OJ L40, 13.2.1998, p. 17.
[3] Also see 7th recital of Council Regulation (EC) No 1310/97, OJ reference as in footnote (2) above.
[4] OJ No L13, 21.12.1962, p. 204/62.
[5] OJ No L175, 23.7.1968, p. 1.
[6] OJ No L378, 31.12.1986, p. 4.
[7] OJ No L374, 31.12.1987, p. 1.
[8] Previously Article 85 of the EEC Treaty (numbering revised by the Treaty of Amsterdam).

Article 2 of the Regulation. If not, their restrictive effects may, if appropriate, be examined separately by the Commission in order to assess their compatibility with Articles 81 and 82 of the EEC Treaty. For reasons of legal certainty, only binding agreements will be assessed as directly related and necessary to the implementation of a concentration.

6. The agreements must be 'necessary to the implementation of the concentration', which means that in their absence the concentration could not be implemented or could only be implemented under more uncertain conditions, as substantially higher cost, over an appreciably longer period or with considerably higher difficulty. Agreements which aim at protecting the value transferred, maintaining the continuity of supply after the break-up of a former economic entity, or which enable the start-up of a new entity, usually meet these criteria. This must be judged on an objective basis.

7. In determining whether or not a restriction is necessary, it is proper not only to take account of its nature, but equally to ensure that its duration, subject matter and geographical field of application, do not exceed what the implementation of the concentration reasonably requires. Where there is more than one method of achieving the desired result, the undertakings must choose the one which is least restrictive.

8. For concentrations which are carried out in stages, the contractual arrangements relating to the stages before the establishment of control within the meaning of Article 3, paragraphs 1 and 3 of the Regulation cannot be considered as directly related and necessary to the concentration. For these agreements, Articles 81 and 82 remain applicable for as long as the conditions set out in Article 3 are not fulfilled. The notion of directly related restrictions likewise excludes from the application of the Regulation those agreements which have no direct link with the concentration. It is thus not sufficient that the additional restrictions exist in the same context as the concentration.

9. The Commission will not take a definitive view on the appreciability of the restrictive character of an agreement it finds directly related and necessary to the implementation of the concentration.[9]

III. Evaluation of common clauses in cases of the acquisition of an undertaking

10. Restrictions agreed between the parties in the context of a transfer of an undertaking may be to the benefit of the buyer or of the vendor. In general terms, the need for the buyer to benefit from certain protection is more compelling than the corresponding need for the vendor. It is the buyer who needs to be assured that he will be able to run the acquired business so as to recoup the investment made in the acquired business. Thus, restrictions which benefit the vendor either are not directly related and necessary for the concentration or, when they are, they are unlikely to need to go as far, in scope and/or duration, as those which benefit the acquirer.

A. Non-competition clauses

11. Restrictions which meet the criteria set out in the Regulation include contractual prohibitions on competition which are imposed on the vendor in the context of a concentration achieved by the transfer of an undertaking or part of an undertaking. Such prohibitions guarantee the transfer to the acquirer of the full value of the assets transferred, which in general include both physical assets and intangible assets such as the goodwill which the vendor has accumulated or the know-how he has developed. These are not only directly related to the concentration, but are also necessary for its implementation because, in their absence, there would be reasonable grounds to expect that the sale of the undertaking or part of an undertaking could not be accomplished.

---

[9] See for example cases No IV/M.527—*UAP/Provincial*, 7.11.1994; No IV/M.612—*RWE-DEA/Enichem Augusta*, 27.7.1995; No IV/M.651—*AT&T-Philips*, 3.2.1996; No IV/M.861—*Textron/Kautex*, 16.12.1996.

12. In order to obtain the full value of the assets transferred, the acquirer must be able to benefit from some protection against competition from the vendor in order to gain the loyalty of customers and to assimilate and exploit the know-how. However, such a prohibition is justified by the legitimate objective of implementing the concentration only when its duration, its geographical field of application, its subject matter and the persons subject to it do not exceed what is reasonably necessary to achieve that end. Such protection cannot generally be considered necessary when, *de facto*, the transfer is limited to physical assets (such as land, buildings or machinery) or to exclusive industrial and commercial property rights (the holders of which could immediately take action against infringements by the transferor of such rights).

13. Prohibitions for periods of up to three years are generally justified when the transfer of the undertaking includes elements of goodwill and know-how, and for periods of up to two years when it includes only goodwill. Prohibitions of longer duration can only be justified in a limited range of circumstances, for example where the parties can demonstrate that customer loyalty will persist for more than two years or where there is a transfer of know-how that equally justifies an additional period of protection.

14. The geographical scope of a non-competition clause must be limited to the area where the vendor offered the relevant products or services before the transfer. The presumption is that the acquirer does not need to be protected from competition from the vendor in territories not previously penetrated by the vendor, unless such protection can be justified by the notifying parties.

15. In the same manner, non-competition clauses must be limited to products and services which form the economic activity of the undertaking transferred. Here again, in the absence of a full justification from the notifying parties, the presumption is that the acquirer does not need to be protected from competition from the vendor in those products or services markets in which the transferred undertaking was not active before the transfer.

16. The vendor may bind himself, his subsidiaries and commercial agents. However, an obligation to impose similar restrictions on others would not be regarded as directly related and necessary to the implementation of the concentration. This applies in particular to clauses which would restrict the scope for resellers or users to import or export.

17. Non-solicitation and confidentiality clauses are evaluated in the same way as non-compete clauses, to the extent that their restrictive effect does not exceed that of a non-compete clause. However, since the scope of these clauses may be narrower than that of non-compete clauses, they are likely to be found directly related and necessary to the concentration in a larger number of circumstances.

B. Licence agreements

18. The implementations of a transfer of an undertaking or part of an undertaking generally includes the transfer to the acquirer, with a view to the full exploitation of the assets transferred, of right to industrial or commercial property or know-how. However, the vendor may remain the owner of the rights in order to exploit them for activities other than those transferred. In these cases, the usual means for ensuring that the acquirer will have the full use of the assets transferred is to conclude licensing agreements in his favour. Likewise, where the vendor has transferred intellectual property rights with the business he may want to continue using some or all of these rights for activities other than those transferred. In such a case the acquirer will grant a licence to the vendor.

19. Licences of patents,[10] similar rights or know-how, can be considered necessary for the

---

[10] Including patent applications, utility models, topographies of semiconductor products, certificats d'utilité and certificats d'addition under French law and applications for these, supplementary protection certificates for medicinal products or other products for which supplementary protection certificates may be

implementation of the concentration. They may equally be considered as an integral part to the concentration. These licences may be limited to certain fields of use, to the extent that they correspond to the activities of the undertaking transferred. It is not normally necessay to include territorial limitations on manufacture, where these reflect the territory of the transferred activity. Nor do such licences need to be time-limited. Restrictions in licence agreements, which go beyond the above provisions, such as those which protect the licensor rather than the licensee, are not usually necessary for the implementation of the concentration. Instead, they will be assessed in accordance with Article 81 of the EEC Treaty. Where they fulfil the conditions required, such agreements may fall under Regulation (EC) No 240/96.[11] In the case of a licence granted from the seller of a business to the buyer, the seller can be made subject to a territorial restriction in the licence agreement under the same conditions as laid down for non-competition clause in the context of the sale of a business.

20. Similarly, in the case of licences of trademarks, business names, design rights, copyright or similar rights, there may be situaitons where the vendor wishes to remain the owner of such rights in relation to activities retained, but the acquirer needs the rights to use them in order to market the goods or services produced by the undertaking or part of an undertaking transferred. Here, the same considerations as above apply.

21. Agreements relating to the use of business names/trademarks will normally be analysed in the context of the corresponding licence of the relevant intellectual property right.

C. Purchase and supply obligations

22. In many cases, the transfer of an undertaking or part of an undertaking can entail the disruption of traditional lines of purchase and supply which existed as a result of the previous integration of activities within the economic unity of the vendor. To enable the break-up of the economic unity of the vendor and the partial transfer of the assets to the acquirer under reasonable conditions, it is often necessary to maintain, at least for a transitional period, the existing or similar links between the vendor and the acquirer. This objective is normally attained by purchase and supply obligations for the vendor and/or the acquirer of the undertaking or part of an undertaking. Taking into account the particular situation resulting from the break-up of the economic unity of the vendor, such obligations, which may lead to restrictions of competition, can be recognised as directly related and necessary to implementation of the concentration. They may be in favour of the vendor as well as the acquirer, depending on the particular circumstances.

23. The aim of such obligations may be, quite legitimately, to ensure the continuity of supply to one or other of the parties of products necessary for carrying out the activities retained (for the vendor) or taken over (for the acquirer). Thus, there are grounds for recognising, for a transitional period, the need for supply obligations aimed at guaranteeing the quantities previously supplied within the vendor's integrated business or providing for their adjustment to the foreseeable demand forecasts.

24. Their aim may also be to provide continuity of purchasers for the vendor of the acquirer, as they were previously assured within the single economic entity.

25. Supply obligations, which the notifying parties consider directly related and necessary to the concentration and which benefit the vendor, will require particularly careful justification by the parties.

26. Both supply and purchase obligations, providing for fixed quantities, possibly with a variation clause, and may be recognised as directly related and necessary.

---

obtained and plant breeder's certificates (as referred to in Article 8 of Commission Regulation (EC) 240/96 of 31.1.1996, OJ No L31, 9.2.1996, p. 2).

[11] OJ No L31, 9.2.1996, p. 2.

27. However, the presumption is that obligations which provide for excessive or unlimited quantities, or which confer preferred supplier or purchaser status, are not normally necessary. Any such obligation would need to be justified by the parties. Likewise, there is no general justification for exclusive purchase or supply obligations. Save in exceptional circumstances, for example resulting from the absence of a market or the specificity of the products in question, such exclusivity is not necessary to permit the implementation of a concentration in the form of a transfer of an undertaking or part of an undertaking.

28. In any event, the undertakings concerned are bound to consider whether any alternative, less restrictive means of providing the necessary continuity exist, such as agreements for fixed quantities.

29. The duration of purchase and supply obligations must be limited to a period necessary for the replacement of the relationship of dependency by autonomy in the market. Given the variety of potential supply arrangements (eg commodities, consumer goods, services) it is impossible to have a general presumption which would apply across the whole range of options. The presumption for goods such as complex industrial products is that this type of obligation is not normally justified for longer than a transitional period of three years. The Commission will use this starting presumption in determining what constitutes a necessary duration in relation to the particular goods or services in question. In any event, the duration of such a period must be justified by the notifying parties.

30. Service agreements are, occasionally, equivalent in their effect to supply arrangements. In this case the same consideration as above apply.

31. As for distribution arrangements, they must also be considered as ancillary restraints. In any event, the relevant Block Exemption Regulation shall apply.[12]

IV. Evaluation of common clauses in the case of a joint acquisition

32. As set out in the 24th recital, the Regulation is applicable when two or more undertakings agree to acquire jointly the control of one or more other undertakings, in particular by means of a public tender offer, where the object or effect is the division among themselves of the undertakings or their assets. This is a concentration implemented in two successive stages. The common strategy is limited to the acquisition of control. For the transaction to fall under the Merger Regulation, the joint acquisition must be followed by a clear separation of the undertakings or assets concerned.

33. For this purpose, in the context of a joint bid, an agreement by the joint acquirers of an undertaking to abstain from making separate competing offers for the same undertaking, or otherwise acquiring control, may be considered directly related and necessary to the implementation of the concentration.

34. Restrictions limited to putting the division into effect are to be considered directly related and necessary to the implementation of the concentration. This will apply to arrangements made between the parties for the joint acquisition of control in order to divide among themselves the production facilities or distribution networks, together with the existing trademarks of the undertaking acquired jointly. The implementation of this division may not in any circumstances lead to the coordination of the future behaviour of the acquiring undertakings.

35. To the extent that such a division involves the break-up of a pre-existing economic entity, arrangements that make the break-up possible under reasonable conditions must be considered directly related and necessary to the implementation of the concentration. In this regard, the principles explained above in relation to purchase and supply arrangements over a transitional period in cases of transfer of undertakings should also be applied for.

[12] Commission Regulation No 1983/83 of 22.6.1983; Commission regulation No 1984/83 of 22.6.1983.

V. Evaluation of common clauses in cases of joint ventures within the meaning of Article 3(2) subparagraph 2 of the Regulation

36. This evaluation must take account of the characteristics peculiar to joint ventures, the constituent elements of which are the creation of an autonomous economic entity performing on a long-term basis all the functions of an undertaking.

A. Non-competition obligations

37. Prohibitions on competition between parent undertakings and a joint venture may be considered as directly related and necessary to the implementation of the concentration.

38. Non-competition clauses may reflect, *inter alia*, the need to ensure good faith during negotiations, the need to utilise fully the joint venture's assets or to enable the joint venture to assimilate know-how and goodwill provided by the parents, or the need to protect the parents' interests in the joint venture from competitive acts facilitated, inter alia, by privileged access to know-how and goodwill transferred or developed by the joint venture.

39. The duration of a non-competition clause must be duly justified by the parties. For periods of up to two or three years they can be justified on similar grounds and conditions as in the case of non-compete clauses in the context of a transfer of an undertaking.

40. Prohibitions on competition between parent undertakings and a joint venture which extend beyond the life of the joint venture may never be regarded as directly related and necessary to the implementation of the concentration.

41. The geographical scope of a non-competition clause should be limited to the area where the parents offered the relevant products or services prior to establishing the joint venture. In the same manner, non-competition clauses must be limited to products and services which form the economic activity of the joint venture. If the joint venture is set up to enter a new market, reference will be made to the products, services and territories in which it is called to operate under the joint venture agreement or by-laws. The presumption is that a parent's interest in the joint venture does not need to be protected from competition from other parent in markets other than those in which the joint venture will be active at its outset. Any departure from this principle must be justified by the notifying parties.

42. Additionally, the presumption is that prohibitions on competition between non-controlling parents and a joint venture are not normally directly related and necessary to the implementation of a concentration. Again, any departure from this principle must be justified by the notifying parties.

43. Non-solicitation and confidentiality clauses are evaluated in the same way as non-compete clauses, to the extent that their restrictive effect does not exceed that of a non-compete clause. However, since the scope of confidentiality clauses in particular may be narrower than non-compete clauses, they may be found directly related and necessary to the concentration in a large number of circumstances.

B. Licence agreements

44. A licence granted by the parents to the joint venture may be considered necessary for the implementation of the concentration. They may equally be considered as an integral part of the concentration. This applies regardless of whether or not the licence is an exclusive one, or whether or not it is time-limited. The licence may be restricted to a particular field of use, which corresponds to the activities of the joint venture. It may also be limited to the contractual territory of activity of the joint venture.

45. Licence agreements between parents, however, are not considered directly related and necessary to the implementation of a joint venture.

46. Likewise, licence agreements granted by the joint venture to one of the parents, or cross-

licence agreements, are neither integral nor necessary for the creation of the joint venture. However, if intellectual property rights have been transferred by a parent to the JV, a licence from the JV to this parent can be regarded as directly related and necessary under the same conditions as in the case of the sale of a business.

47. Licence agreements which are not considered as directly related and necessary may nevertheless fall under Regulation (EC) No 240/96.

C. Purchase and supply obligations

48. If the parent undertakings remain present in a market upstream or downstream of that of the joint venture, any purchase and supply agreements, including distribution agreements, are to be examined in accordance wth the principles applicable in the case of the transfer of an undertaking.

VI. Procedure

49. Where the notifying parties request that agreeements be considered directly related and necessary to the implementation of the concentration, the agreements should be individually identified and the parties should explain the rationale behind the request in Form CO. Requests which fail to comply with these requirements, or which concern restrictions which are not binding on the parties to a concentration, will not be dealt with by the Commission in any decision clearing the concentration in question.

Appendix 4

COMMISSION NOTICE
on the concept of full-function joint ventures under Council Regulation (EEC) No 4064/89 on the control of concentrations between undertakings (OJ 1998 C66/01)

I.   INTRODUCTION
II. JOINT VENTURES UNDER ARTICLE 3 OF THE MERGER REGULATION
     1. Joint control
     2. Structural change of the undertakings
III. FINAL

I. INTRODUCTION

1. The purpose of this notice is to provide guidance as to how the Commission interprets Article 3 of Council Regulation (EEC) No 4064/89[1] as last amended by Regulation (EC) No 1310/97[2] (hereinafter referred to as the Merger Regulation) in relation to joint ventures[3].

2. This Notice replaces the Notice on the distinction between concentrative and cooperative joint ventures. Changes made in this Notice reflect the amendments made to the Merger Regulation as well as the experience gained by the Commission in applying the Merger Regulation since its entry into force on 21 September 1990. The principles set out in this Notice will be followed and further developed by the Commission's practice in individual cases.

3. Under the Community competition rules, joint ventures are undertakings which are jointly controlled by two or more other undertakings[4]. In practice joint ventures encompass a broad range of operations, from merger-like operations to cooperation for particular functions such as R & D, production or distribution.

4. Joint ventures fall within the scope of the Merger Regulation if they meet the requirements of a concentration set out in Article 3 thereof.

5. According to recital 23 to Council Regulation (EEC) No 4064/89 it is appropriate to define the concept of concentration in such a manner as to cover only operations bringing about a lasting change in the structure of the undertakings concerned.

6. The structural changes brought about by concentrations frequently reflect a dynamic process of restructuring in the markets concerned. They are permitted under the Merger Regulation unless they result in serious damage to the structure of competition by creating or strengthening a dominant position.

7. The Merger Regulation deals with the concept of full-function joint ventures in Article 3(2) as follows:

---

[1] OJ L395, 30.12.1989, p. 1, corrected version No L257, 21.9.1990, p. 13.
[2] OJ L180, 9.7.1997, p. 1.
[3] The Commission intends, in due course, to provide guidance on the application of Article 2(4) of the Merger Regulation. Pending the adoption of such guidance, interested parties are referred to the principles set out in paragraphs 17 to 20 of Commission Notice on the distinction between concentrative and cooperative joint ventures, OJ C385, 31.12.1994, p. 1.
[4] The concept of joint control is set out in the Notice on the concept of concentration.

"The creation of a joint venture performing on a lasting basis all the functions of an autonomous economic entity shall constitute a concentration within the meaning of paragraph 1(b)."

II. JOINT VENTURES UNDER ARTICLE 3 OF THE MERGER REGULATION

8. In order to be a concentration within the meaning of Article 3 of the Merger Regulation, an operation must fulfil the following requirements:

1. Joint control

9. A joint venture may fall within the scope of the Merger Regulation where there is an acquisition of joint control by two or more undertakings, that is, its parent companies (Article 3(1)(b)). The concept of control is set out in Article 3(3). This provides that control is based on the possibility of exercising decisive influence over an undertaking, which is determined by both legal and factual considerations.

10. The principles for determining joint control are set out in detail in the Commission's Notice on the concept of concentration[5].

2. Structural change of the undertakings

11. Article 3(2) provides that the joint venture must perform, on a lasting basis, all the functions of an autonomous economic entity. Joint ventures which satisfy this requirement bring about a lasting change in the structure of the undertakings concerned. They are referred to in this Notice as "full-function" joint ventures.

12. Essentially this means that a joint venture must operate on a market, performing the functions normally carried out by undertakings operating on the same market. In order to do so the joint venture must have a management dedicated to its day-to-day operations and access to sufficient resources including finance, staff, and assets (tangible and intangible) in order to conduct on a lasting basis its business activities within the area provided for in the joint-venture agreement[6].

13. A joint venture is not full-function if it only takes over one specific function within the parent companies' business activities without access to the market. This is the case, for example, for joint ventures limited to R & D or production. Such joint ventures are auxiliary to their parent companies' business activities. This is also the case where a joint venture is essentially limited to the distribution or sales of its parent companies' products and, therefore, acts principally as a sales agency. However, the fact that a joint venture makes use of the distribution network or outlet of one or more of its parent companies normally will not disqualify it as "full-function" as long as the parent companies are acting only as agents of the joint venture[7].

14. The strong presence of the parent companies in upstream or downstream markets is a factor to be taken into consideration in assessing the full-function character of a joint venture where this presence leads to substantial sales or purchases between the parent companies and the joint venture. The fact that the joint venture relies almost entirely on sales to its parent companies

---

[5] Paragraphs 18 to 39.
[6] Case IV/M.527 — Thomson CSF/Deutsche Aerospace, of 2 December 1994 (paragraph 10) — intellectual rights, Case IV/M.560 EDS/Lufthansa of 11 May 1995 (paragraph 11) — outsourcing, Case IV/M.585 — Voest Alpine Industrieanlagenbau GmbH/Davy International Ltd, of 7 September 1995 (paragraph 8) — joint venture's right to demand additional expertise and staff from its parent companies, Case IV/M.686 — Nokia Autoliv, of 5 February 1996 (paragraph 7), joint venture able to terminate "service agreements" with parent company and to move from site retained by parent company, Case IV/M.791 — British Gas Trading Ltd/Group 4 Utility Services Ltd, of 7 October 1996, (paragraph 9) joint venture's intended assets will be transferred to leasing company and leased by joint venture.
[7] Case IV/M.102 — TNT/Canada Post etc. of 2 December 1991 (paragraph 14).

or purchases from them only for an initial start-up period does not normally affect the full-function character of the joint venture. Such a start-up period may be necessary in order to establish the joint venture on a market. It will normally not exceed a period of three years, depending on the specific conditions of the market in question[8].

Where sales from the joint venture to the parent companies are intended to be made on a lasting basis, the essential question is whether, regardless of these sales, the joint venture is geared to play an active role on the market. In this respect the relative proportion of these sales compared with the total production of the joint venture is an important factor. Another factor is whether sales to the parent companies are made on the basis of normal commercial conditions[9].

In relation to purchases made by the joint venture from its parent companies, the full-function character of the joint venture is questionable in particular where little value is added to the products or services concerned at the level of the joint venture itself. In such a situation, the joint venture may be closer to a joint sales agency. However, in contrast to this situation where a joint venture is active in a trade market and performs the normal functions of a trading company in such a market, it normally will not be an auxiliary sales agency but a full-function joint venture. A trade market is characterised by the existence of companies which specialise in the selling and distribution of products without being vertically integrated in addidtion to those which are integrated, and where different sources of supply are available for the products in question. In addition, many trade markets may require operators to invest in specific facilities such as outlets, stockholding, warehouses, depots, transport fleets and sales personnel. In order to constitute a full-function joint venture in a trade market, an undertaking must have the necessary facilities and be likely to obtain a substantial proportion of its supplies not only from its parent companies but also from other competing sources[10].

15. Furthermore, the joint venture must be intended to operate on a lasting basis. The fact that the parent companies commit to the joint venture the resources described above normally demonstrates that this is the case. In addition, agreements setting up a joint venture often provide for certain contingencies, for example, the failure of the joint venture or fundamental disagreement as between the parent companies[11]. This may be achieved by the incorporation of provisions for the eventual dissolution of the joint venture itself or the possibility for one or more parent companies to withdraw from the joint venture. This kind of provision does not prevent the joint venture from being considered as operating on a lasting basis. The same is normally true where the agreement specifies a period for the duration of the joint venture where this period is sufficiently long in order to bring about a lasting change in the structure of the undertakings concerned[12], or where the agreement provides for the possible continuation of the joint venture beyond this period. By contrast, the joint venture will not be considered to operate on a lasting basis where it is established for a short finite duration. This would be the case, for example, where a joint venture is established in order to construct a specific project such as a power plant, but it will not be involved in the operation of the plant once its construction has been completed.

---

[8] Case IV/M.560 — EDS/Lufthansa of 11 May 1995 (paragraph 11); Case IV/M.686 Nokia/Autoliv of 5 February 1996 (paragraph 6); to be contrasted with Case IV/M.904 — RSB/Tenex/Fuel Logistics of 2 April 1997 (paragraph 15–17) and Case IV/M.979 — Preussag/Voest-Alpine of 1 October 1997 (paragraph 9–12). A special case exists where sales by the joint venture to its parent are caused by a legal monopoly downstream of the joint venture (Case IV/M.468 — Siemens/Italtel of 17 February 1995 (paragraph 12), or where the sales to a parent company consist of by-products, which are of minor importance to the joint venture (Case IV/M.550 — Union Carbide/Enichem of 13 March 1995 (paragraph 14).

[9] Case IV/M.556 — Zeneca/Vanderhave of 9 April 1996 (paragraph 8); Case IV/M.751 — Bayer/Hüls of 3 July 1996 (paragraph 10).

[10] Case IV/M.788 — AgrEVO/Marubeni of 3 September 1996 (paragraphs 9 and 10).

[11] Case IV/M.891 — Deutsche Bank/Commerzbank/J.M. Voith of 23 April 1997 (paragraph 7).

[12] Case IV/M.791 — British Gas Trading Ltd/Group 4 Utility Services Ltd of 7 October 1996, (paragraph 10); to be contrasted with Case IV/M.722 — Teneo/Merrill Lynch/Bankers Trust of 15 April 1996 (paragraph 15).

III. FINAL

16. The creation of a full-function joint venture constitutes a concentration within the meaning of Article 3 of the Merger Regulation. Restrictions accepted by the parent companies of the joint venture that are directly related and necessary for the implementation of the concentration ("ancillary restrictions"), will be assessed together with the concentration itself[13].

Further, the creation of a full-function joint venture may as a direct consequence lead to the coordination of the competitive behaviour of undertakings that remain independent. In such cases Article 2(4) of the Merger Regulation provides that those cooperative effects will be assessed within the same procedure as the concentration. This assessment will be made in accordance with the criteria of Article 85(1) and (3) of the treaty with a view to establishing whether or not the operation is compatible with the common market.

The applicability of Article 85 of the Treaty to other restrictions of competition, that are neither ancillary to the concentration, nor a direct consequence of the creation of the joint venture, will normally have to be examined by means of Regulation No 17.

17. The Commission's interpretation of Article 3 of the Merger Regulation with respect to joint ventures is without prejudice to the interpretation which may be given by the Court of Justice or the Court of First Instance of the European Communities.

---

[13] See Commission Notice regarding restrictions ancillary to concentrations, OJ No C203, 14.8.1990, p. 5.

Appendix 5

COMMISSION NOTICE
on the concept of concentration under Council Regulation (EEC)
No 4064/89 on the control of concentrations between undertakings
(OJ 1998 C66/02)

I.   INTRODUCTION
II.   MERGERS BETWEEN PREVIOUSLY INDEPENDENT UNDERTAKINGS
III. ACQUISITION OF CONTROL
      1.   Sole control
      2.   Joint control
           2.1.   Equality in voting rights or appointment to decision-making bodies
           2.2.   Veto rights
           2.3.   Joint exercise of voting rights
           2.4.   Other considerations related to joint control
           2.5.   Joint control for a limited period
      3.   Control by a single shareholder on the basis of veto rights
      4.   Changes in the structure of control
IV.   EXCEPTIONS
V.   FINAL

I. INTRODUCTION

1. The purpose of this Notice is to provide guidance as to how the Commission interprets the term "concentration" used in Article 3 of Council Regulation (EEC) No 4064/89[1] as last amended by Regulation (EC) No 1310/97[2] (hereinafter referred to as "the Merger Regulation"). This formal guidance on the interpretation of Article 3 should enable firms to establish more quickly, in advance of any contact with the Commission, whether and to what extent their operations may be covered by Community merger control.

This Notice replaces the Notice on the notion of a concentration[3].

This Notice deals with paragraphs (1), (3), (4) and (5) of Article 3. The interpretation of Article 3 in relation to joint ventures, dealt with in particular under Article 3(2), is set out in the Commission's Notice on the concept of full-function joint ventures.

2. The guidance set out in this Notice reflects the Commission's experience in applying the Merger Regulation since it entered into force on 21 December 1990. The principles contained here will be applied and further developed by the Commission in individual cases.

3. According to recital 23 to Regulation (EEC) No 4064/89, the concept of concentration is defined as covering only operations which bring about a lasting change in the structure of the undertakings concerned. Article 3(1) provides that such a structural change is brought about either by a merger between two previously independent undertakings or by the acquisition of control over the whole or part of another undertaking.

4. The determination of the existence of a concentration under the Merger Regulation is based upon qualitative rather than quantitative criteria, focusing on the concept of control. These criteria include considerations of both law and fact. It follows, therefore, that a concentration may occur on a legal or a *de facto* basis.

---

[1] OJ L395, 30.12.1989, p. 1, corrected version OJ L257, 21.9.1990, p. 13.
[2] OJ L180, 9.7.1997, p. 1.
[3] OJ C385, 31.12.1994, p. 5.

5. Article 3(1) of the Merger Regulation defines two categories of concentration:

— those arising from a merger between previously independent undertakings (point (a));

— those arising from an acquisition of control (point (b)).

These are treated respectively in Sections II and III below.

II. MERGERS BETWEEN PREVIOUSLY INDEPENDENT UNDERTAKINGS

6. A merger within the meaning of Article 3(1)(a) of the Merger Regulation occurs when two or more independent undertakings amalgamate into a new undertaking and cease to exist as separate legal entities. A merger may also occur when an undertaking is absorbed by another, the latter retaining its legal identity while the former ceases to exist as a legal entity.

7. A merger within the meaning of Article 3(1)(a) may also occur where, in the absence of a legal merger, the combining of the activities of previously independent undertakings results in the creation of a single economic unit[4]. This may arise in particular where two or more undertakings, while retaining their individual legal personalities, establish contractually a common economic management[5]. If this leads to a *de facto* amalgamation of the undertakings concerned into a genuine common economic unit, the operation is considered to be a merger. A prerequisite for the determination of a common economic unit is the existence of a permanent, single economic management. Other relevant factors may include internal profit and loss compensation as between the various undertakings within the group, and their joint liability externally. The *de facto* amalgamation may be reinforced by cross-shareholdings between the undertakings forming the economic unit.

III. ACQUISITION OF CONTROL

8. Article 3(1)(b) provides that a concentration occurs in the case of an acquisition of control. Such control may be acquired by one undertaking acting alone or by two or more undertakings acting jointly.

Control may also be acquired by a person in circumstances where that person already controls (whether solely or jointly) at least one other undertaking or, alternatively, by a combination of persons (which controls another undertaking) and/or undertakings. The term ''person'' in this context extends to public bodies[6] and private entities, as well as individuals.

As defined, a concentration within the meaning of the Merger Regulation is limited to changes in control. Internal restructuring within a group of companies, therefore, cannot constitute a concentration.

An exceptional situation exists where both the acquiring and acquired undertakings are public companies owned by the same State (or by the same public body). In this case, whether the operation is to be regarded as an internal restructuring depends in turn on the question whether both undertakings were formerly part of the same economic unit within the meaning of recital 12 to Regulation (EEC) No 4064/89. Where the undertakings were formerly part of different economic units having an independent power of decision, the operation will be deemed to

---

[4] In determining the previous independence of undertakings, the issue of control may be relevant. Control is considered generally in paragraphs 12 *et seq.* below. For this specific issue, minority shareholders are deemed to have control if they have previously obtained a majority of votes on major decisions at shareholders meetings. The reference period in this context is normally three years.

[5] This could apply for example, in the case of a ''Gleichordnungskonzern'' in German law, certain ''Groupements d'Intérêt Economique'' in French law, and certain partnerships.

[6] Including the State itself, e.g. Case IV/M.157 — Air France/Sabena, of 5 October 1992 in relation to the Belgian State, or other public bodies such as the Treuhand in Case IV/M.308 — Kali und Salz/MDK/Treuhand, of 14 December 1993.

constitute a concentration and not an internal restructuring[7]. Such independent power of decision does not normally exist, however, where the undertakings are within the same holding company[8].

9. Whether an operation gives rise to an acquisition of control depends on a number of legal and/or factual elements. The acquisition of property rights and shareholders' agreements are important, but are not the only elements involved: purely economic relationships may also play a decisive role. Therefore, in exceptional circumstances, a situation of economic dependence may lead to control on a *de facto* basis where, for example,very important long-term supply agreements or credits provided by suppliers or customers, coupled with structural links, confer decisive influence.[9].

There may also be acquisition of control even if it is not the declared intention of the parties[10]. Moreover, the Merger Regulation clearly defines control as having "the possibility of exercising decisive influence" rather than the actual exercise of such influence.

10. Control is nevertheless normally acquired by persons or undertakings which are the holders of the rights or are entitled to rights conferring control (Article 3(4)(a)). There may be exceptional situations where the formal holder of a controlling interest differs from the person or undertaking having in fact the real power to exercise the rights resulting from this interest. This may be the case, for example, where an undertaking uses another person or undertaking for the acquisition of a controlling interest and exercises the rights through this person or undertaking, even though the latter is formally the holder of the rights. In such a situation, control is acquired by the undertaking which in reality is behind the operation and in fact enjoys the power to control the target undertaking (Article 3(4)(b)). The evidence needed to establish this type of indirect control may include factors such as the source of financing or family links.

11. The object of control can be one or more undertakings which constitute legal entities, or the assets of such entities, or only some of these assets[11]. The assets in question, which could be brands or licences, must constitute a business to which a market turnover can be clearly attributed.

12. The acquisition of control may be in the form of sole or joint control. In both cases, control is defined as the possibility of exercising decisive influence on an undertaking on the basis of rights, contracts or any other means (Article 3(3)).

1. Sole control

13. Sole control is normally acquired on a legal basis where an undertaking acquires a majority of the voting rights of a company. It is not in itself significant that the acquired shareholding is 50% of the share capital plus one share[12] or that it is 100% of the share capital[13]. In the absence of other elements, an acquisition which does not include a majority of the voting rights does not normally confer control even if it involves the acquisition of a majority of the share capital.

14. Sole control may also be acquired in the case of a "qualified minority". This can be established on a legal and/or *de facto* basis.

---

[7] Case IV/M.097 — Péchiney/Usinor, of 24 June 1991; Case IV/M.216 — CEA Industrie/France Telecom/ SGS-Thomson, of 22 February 1993.
[8] See paragraph 55 of the Notice on the concept of undertakings concerned.
[9] For example, in the Usinor/Bamesa decision adopted by the Commission under the ECSC Treaty. See also Case IV/M.258 — CCIE/GTE, of 25 September 1992, and Case IV/M.697 — Lockheed Martin Corporation/Loral Corporation, of 27 March 1996.
[10] Case IV/M.157 — Air France/Sabena, of 5 October 1992.
[11] Case IV/M.286 — Zürich/MMI, of 2 April 1993.
[12] Case IV/M.296 — Crédit Lyonnais/BFG Bank, of 11 January 1993.
[13] Case IV/M.299— Sara Lee/BP Food Division, of 8 February 1993.

On a legal basis it can occur where specific rights are attached to the minority shareholding. These may be preferential shares leading to a majority of the voting rights or other rights enabling the minority shareholder to determine the strategic commercial behaviour of the target company, such as the power to appoint more than half of the members of the supervisory board or the administrative board.

A minority shareholder may also be deemed to have sole control on a *de facto* basis. This is the case, for example, where the shareholder is highly likely to achieve a majority at the shareholders' meeting, given that the remaining shares are widely dispersed[14]. In such a situation it is unlikely that all the smaller shareholders will be present or represented at the shareholders' meeting. The determination of whether or not sole control exists in a particular case is based on the evidence resulting from the presence of shareholders in previous years. Where, on the basis of the number of shareholders attending the shareholders' meeting, a minority shareholder has a stable majority of the votes at this meeting, then the large minority shareholder is taken to have sole control[15].

Sole control can also be exercised by a minority shareholder who has the right to manage the activities of the company and to determine its business policy.

15. An option to purchase or convert shares cannot in itself confer sole control unless the option will be exercised in the near future according to legally binding agreements[16]. However, the likely exercise of such an option can be taken into account as an additional element which, together with other elements, may lead to the conclusion that there is sole control.

16. A change from joint to sole control of an undertaking is deemed to be a concentration within the meaning of the Merger Regulation because decisive influence exercised alone is substantially different from decisive influence exercised jointly[17]. For the same reason, an operation involving the acquisition of joint control of one part of an undertaking and sole control of another part is in principle regarded as two separate concentrations under the Merger Regulation[18].

17. The concept of control under the Merger Regulation may be different from that applied in specific areas of legislation concerning, for example, prudential rules, taxation, air transport or the media. In addition, national legislation within a Member State may providespecific rules on the structure of bodies representing the organisation of decision-making within an undertaking, in particular, in relation to the rights of representatives of employees. While such legislation may confer some power of control upon persons other than the shareholders, the concept of control under the Merger Regulation is related only to the means of influence normally enjoyed by the owners of an undertaking. Finally, the prerogatives exercised by a State acting as a public authority rather than as a shareholder, in so far as they are limited to the protection of the public interest, do not constitute control within the meaning of the Merger Regulation to the extent that they have neither the aim nor the effect of enabling the State to exercise a decisive influence over the activity of the undertaking[19].

2. Joint control

18. As in the case of sole control, the acquisition of joint control (which includes changes from sole control to joint control) can also be established on a legal or *de facto* basis. There is joint control if the shareholders (the parent companies) must reach agreement on major decisions concerning the controlled undertaking (the joint venture).

---

[14] Case IV/M.025 — Arjomari/Wiggins Teape, of 10 February 1990.
[15] Case IV/M.343 — Société Générale de Belgique/Générale de Banque, of 3 August 1993.
[16] Judgment in Case T 2/93, *Air France* v. *Commission* [1994] ECR II-323.
[17] This issue is dealt with in paragraphs 30, 31 and 32 of the Notice on the concept of undertakings concerned.
[18] Case IV/M.409 — ABB/Renault Automation, of 9 March 1994.
[19] Case IV/M.493 — Tractebel/Distrigaz II, of 1 September 1994.

19. Joint control exists where two or more undertakings or persons have the possibility of exercising decisive influence over another undertaking. Decisive influence in this sense normally means the power to block actions which determine the strategic commercial behaviour of an undertaking. Unlike sole control, which confers the power upon a specific shareholder to determine the strategic decisions in an undertaking, joint control is characterized by the possibility of a deadlock situation resulting from the power of two or more parent companies to reject proposed strategic decisions. It follows, therefore, that these shareholders must reach a common understanding in determining the commercial policy of the joint venture.

2.1. *Equality in voting rights or appointment to decision-making bodies*

20. The clearest form of joint control exists where there are only two parent companies which share equally the voting rights in the joint venture. In this case, it is not necessary for a formal agreement to exist between them. However, where there is a formal agreement, it must be consistent with the principle of equality between the parent companies, by laying down, for example, that each is entitled to the same number of representatives in the management bodies and that none of the members has a casting vote[20]. Equality may also be achieved where both parent companies have the right to appoint an equal number of members to the decision-making bodies of the joint venture.

2.2. *Veto rights*

21. Joint control may exist even where there is no equality between the two parent companies in votes or in representation in decision-making bodies or where there are more than two parent companies. This is the case where minority shareholders have additional rights which allow them to veto decisions which are essential for the strategic commercial behaviour of the joint venture[21]. These veto rights may be set out in the statute of the joint venture or conferred by agreement between its parent companies. The veto rights themselves may operate by means of a specific quorum required for decisions taken at the shareholders' meeting or by the board of directors to the extent that the parent companies are represented on this board. It is also possible that strategic decisions are subject to approval by a body, e.g. supervisory board, where the minority shareholders are represented and form part of the quorum needed for such decisions.

22. These veto rights must be related to strategic decisions on the business policy of the joint venture. They must go beyond the veto rights normally accorded to minority shareholders in order to protect their financial interests as investors in the joint venture. This normal protection of the rights of minority shareholders is related to decisions on the essence of the joint venture, such as changes in the statute, an increase or decrease in the capital or liquidation. A veto right, for example, which prevents the sale or winding-up of the joint venture does not confer joint control on the minority shareholder concerned[22].

23. In contrast, veto rights which confer joint control typically include decisions and issues such as the budget, the business plan, major investments or the appointment of senior management. The acquisition of joint control, however, does not require that the acquirer has the power to exercise decisive influence on the day-to-day running of an undertaking. The crucial element is that the veto rights are sufficient to enable the parent companies to exercise such influence in relation to the strategic business behaviour of the joint venture. Moreover, it is not necessary to establish that an acquirer of joint control of the joint venture will actually make use of its decisive influence. The possibility of exercising such influence and, hence, the mere existence of the veto rights, is sufficient.

24. In order to acquire joint control, it is not necessary for a minority shareholder to have all the veto rights mentioned above. It may be sufficient that only some, or even one such right,

[20] Case IV/M.272 — Matra/CAP Gemini Sogeti, of 17 March 1993.
[21] Case T 2/93 — Air France v Commission (ibid). Case IV/M.010 — Conagra/Idea, of 3 May 1991.
[22] Case IV/M.062 — Eridania/ISI, of 30 July 1991.

exists. Whether or not this is the case depends upon the precise content of the veto right itself and also the importance of this right in the context of the specific business of the joint venture.

Appointment of management and determination of budget

25. Normally the most important veto rights are those concerning decisions on the appointment of the management and the budget. The power to co-determine the structure of the management confers upon the holder the power to exercise decisive influence on the commercial policy of an undertaking. The same is true with respect to decisions on the budget since the budget determines the precise framework of the activities of the joint venture and, in particular, the investments it may make.

Business plan

26. The business plan normally provides details of the aims of a company together with the measures to be taken in order to achieve those aims. A veto right over this type of business plan may be sufficient to confer joint control even in the absence of any other veto right. In contrast, where the business plan contains merely general declarations concerning the business aims of the joint venture, the existence of a veto right will be only one element in the general assessment of joint control but will not, on its own, be sufficient to confer joint control.

Investments

27. In the case of a veto right on investments, the importance of this right depends, first, on the level of investments which are subject to the approval of the parent companies and, secondly, on the extent to which investments constitute an essential feature of the market in which the joint venture is active. In relation to the first criterion, where the level of investments necessitating approval of the parent companies is extremely high, this veto right may be closer to the normal protection of the interests of a minority shareholder than to a right conferring a power of co-determination over the commercial policy of the joint venture. With regard to the second, the investment policy of an undertaking is normally an important element in assessing whether or not there is joint control. However, there may be some markets where investment does not play a significant role in the market behaviour of an undertaking.

Market-specific rights

28. Apart from the typical veto rights mentioned above, there exist a number of other veto rights related to specific decisions which are important in the context of the particular market of the joint venture. One example is the decision on the technology to be used by the joint venture where technology is a key feature of the joint venture's activities. Another example relates to markets characterised by product differentiation and a significant degree of innovation. In such markets, a veto right over decisions relating to new product lines to be developed by the joint venture may also be an important element in establishing the existence of joint control.

Overall context

29. In assessing the relative importance of veto rights, where there are a number of them, these rights should not be evaluated in isolation. On the contrary, the determination of whether or not joint control exists is based upon an assessment of these rights as a whole. However, a veto right which does not relate either to commercial policy and strategy or to the budget or business plan cannot be regarded as giving joint control to its owner[23].

2.3. *Joint exercise of voting rights*

30. Even in the absence of specific veto rights, two or more undertakings acquiring minority shareholdings in another undertaking may obtain joint control. This may be the case where the minority shareholdings together provide the means for controlling the target undertaking. This

---

[23] Case IV/M.295 — SITA-RPC/SCORI, of 19 March 1993.

means that the minority shareholders, together, will have a majority of the voting rights; and they will act together in exercising these voting rights. This can result from a legally binding agreement to this effect, or it may be established on a *de facto* basis.

31. The legal means to ensure the joint exercise of voting rights can be in the form of a holding company to which the minority shareholders transfer their rights, or an agreement by which they undertake to act in the same way (pooling agreement).

32. Very exceptionally, collective action can occur on a *de facto* basis where strong common interests exist between the minority shareholders to the effect that they would not act against each other in exercising their rights in relation to the joint venture.

33. In the case of acquisitions of minority shareholdings, the prior existence of links between the minority shareholders or the acquisition of the shareholdings by means of concerted action will be factors indicating such a common interest.

34. In the case where a new joint venture is established, as opposed to the acquisition of minority shareholdings in a pre-existing company, there is a higher probability that the parent companies are carrying out a deliberate common policy. This is true, in particular, where each parent company provides a contribution to the joint venture which is vital for its operation (e.g. specific technologies, local know-how or supply agreements). In these circumstances, the parent companies may be able to operate the joint venture with full cooperation only with each other's agreement on the most important strategic decisions even if there is no express provision for any veto rights. The greater the number of parent companies involved in such a joint venture, however, the more remote is the likelihood of this situation occurring.

35. In the absence of strong common interests such as those outlined above, the possibility of changing coalitions between minority shareholders will normally exclude the assumption of joint control. Where there is no stable majority in the decision-making procedure and the majority can on each occasion be any of the various combinations possible amongst the minority shareholders, it cannot be assumed that the minority shareholders will jointly control the undertaking. In this context, it is not sufficient that there are agreements between two or more parties having an equal shareholding in the capital of an undertaking which establish identical rights and powers between the parties. For example, in the case of an undertaking where three shareholders each own one-third of the share capital and each elect one-third of the members of the Board of Directors, the shareholders do not have joint control since decisions are required to be taken on the basis of a simple majority. The same considerations also apply in more complex structures, for example, where the capital of an undertaking is equally divided between three shareholders and where the Board of Directors is composed of twelve members, each of the shareholders A, B and C electing two, another two being elected by A, B and C jointly, whilst the remaining four are chosen by the other eight members jointly. In this case also there is no joint control, and hence no control at all within the meaning of the Merger Regulation.

2.4. Other considerations related to joint control

36. Joint control is not incompatible with the fact that one of the parent companies enjoys specific knowledge of and experience in the business of the joint venture. In such a case, the other parent company can play a modest or even non-existent role in the daily management of the joint venture where its presence is motivated by considerations of a financial, long-term strategy, brand image or general policy nature. Nevertheless, it must always retain the real possibility of contesting the decisions taken by the other parent company, without which there would be sole control.

37. For joint control to exist, there should not be a casting vote for one parent company only. However, there can be joint control when this casting vote can be exercised only after a series of stages of arbitration and attempts at reconciliation or in a very limited field[24].

---

[24] Case IV/M.425 — British Telecom/Banco Santander, of 28 March 1994.

2.5. *Joint control for a limited period*

38. Where an operation leads to joint control for a starting-up period[25] but, according to legally binding agreements, this joint control will be converted to sole control by one of the shareholders, the whole operation will normally be considered to be an acquisition of sole control.

3. Control by a single shareholder on the basis of veto rights

39. An exceptional situation exists where only one shareholder is able to veto strategic decisions in an undertaking, but this shareholder does not have the power, on his own, to impose such decisions. This situation occurs either where one shareholder holds 50% in an undertaking whilst the remaining 50% is held by two or more minority shareholders, or where there is a quorum required for strategic decisions which in fact confers a veto right upon only one minority shareholder[26]. In these circumstances, a single shareholder possesses the same level of influence as that normally enjoyed by several jointly-controlling shareholders, i.e. the power to block the adoption of strategic decisions. However, this shareholder does not enjoy the powers which are normally conferred on an undertaking with sole control, i.e. the power to impose strategic decisions. Since this shareholder can produce a deadlock situation comparable to that in normal cases of joint control, he acquires decisive influence and therefore control within the meaning of the Merger Regulation[27].

4. Changes in the structure of control

40. A concentration may also occur where an operation leads to a change in the structure of control. This includes the change from joint control to sole control as well as an increase in the number of shareholders exercising joint control. The principles for determining the existence of a concentration in these circumstances are set out in detail in the Notice on the concept of undertakings concerned[28].

IV. EXCEPTIONS

41. Article 3(5) sets out three exceptional situations where the acquisition of a controlling interest does not constitute a concentration under the Merger Regulation.

42. First, the acquisition of securities by companies whose normal activities include transactions and dealing in securities for their own account or for the account of others is not deemed to constitute a concentration if such an acquisition is made in the framework of these businesses and if the securities are held on only a temporary basis (Article 3(5)(a)). In order to fall within this exception, the following requirements must be fulfilled:

— the acquiring undertaking must be a credit or other financial institution or insurance company the normal activities of which are described above,
— the securities must be acquired with a view to their resale,
— the acquiring undertaking must not exercise the voting rights with a view to determining the strategic commercial behaviour of the target company or must exercise these rights only with a view to preparing the total or partial disposal of the undertaking, its assets or securities,
— the acquiring undertaking must dispose of its controlling interest within one year of the

---

[25] This starting-up period must not exceed three years. Case IV/M.425 — British Telecom/Banco Santander, *ibid.*
[26] Case IV/M.258 — CCIE/GTE, of 25 September 1992, where the veto rights of only one shareholder were exercisable through a member of the board appointed by this shareholder.
[27] Since this shareholder is the only undertaking acquiring a controlling influence, only this shareholder is obliged to submit a notification under the Merger Regulation.
[28] Paragraphs 30 to 48.

date of the acquisition, that is, it must reduce its shareholding within this one-year period at least to a level which no longer confers control. This period, however, may be extended by the Commission where the acquiring undertaking can show that the disposal was not reasonably possible within the one-year period.

43. Secondly, there is no change of control, and hence no concentration within the meaning of the Merger Regulation, where control is acquired by an office-holder according to the law of a Member State relating to liquidation, winding-up, insolvency, cessation of payments, compositions or analogous proceedings (Article 3(5)(b));

44. Thirdly, a concentration does not arise where a financial holding company within the meaning of the Fourth Council Directive 78/660/EEC[29] acquires control, provided that this company exercises its voting rights only to maintain the full value of its investment and does not otherwise determine directly or indirectly the strategic commercial conduct of the controlled undertaking.

45. In the context of the exceptions under Article 3(5), the question may arise whether a rescue operation constitutes a concentration under the Merger Regulation. A rescue operation typically involves the conversion of existing debt into a new company, through which a syndicate of banks may acquire joint control of the company concerned.

Where such an operation meets the criteria for joint control, as outlined above, it will normally be considered to be a concentration[30]. Although the primary intention of the banks is to restructure the financing of the undertaking concerned for its subsequent resale, the exception set out in Article 3(5)(a) is normally not applicable to such an operation. This is because the restructuring programme normally requires the controlling banks to determine the strategic commercial behaviour of the rescued undertaking. Furthermore, it is not normally a realistic proposition to transform a rescued company into a commercially viable entity and to resell it within the permitted one-year period. Moreover, the length of time needed to achieve this aim may be so uncertain that it would be difficult to grant an extension of the disposal period.

V. FINAL

46. The Commission's interpretation of Article 3 as set out in this Notice is without prejudice to the interpretation which may be given by the Court of Justice or the Court of First Instance of the European Communities.

---

[29] OJ L222, 14.8.1978, p. 11, as last amended by the Act of Accession of Austria, Finland and Sweden. Article 5(3) of this Directive defines financial holding companies as "those companies the sole objective of which is to acquire holdings in other undertakings, and to manage such holdings and turn them to profit, without involving themselves directly or indirectly in the management of those undertakings, the foregoing without prejudice to their rights as shareholders".

[30] Case IV/M.116 — Kelt/American Express, of 28 August 1991.

Appendix 6

COMMISSION NOTICE
on the concept of undertakings concerned under Council
Regulation (EEC) No 4064/89 on the control of concentrations
between undertakings (OJ 1998 C66/03)

I. INTRODUCTION
II. THE CONCEPT OF UNDERTAKING CONCERNED
III. IDENTIFYNG THE UNDERTAKINGS CONCERNED IN DIFFERENT TYPES OF OPERA-
    TIONS
    1. Mergers
    2. Acquisition of sole control
        2.1 Acquisition of sole control of the whole company
        2.2. Acquisition of sole control of part of a company
        2.3. Acquisition of sole control after reduction or enlargement of the target company
        2.4. Acquisition of sole control through a subsidiary of a group
    3. Acquisition of joint control
        3.1. Acquisition of joint control of a newly-created company
        3.2. Acquisition of joint control of a pre-existing company
        3.3. Acquisition of joint control with a view to immediate partition of assets
    4. Acquisition of control by a joint venture
    5. Change from joint control to sole control
    6. Change in the shareholding in cases of joint control of an existing joint venture
        6.1. Reduction in the number of shareholders leading to a change from joint to sole control
        6.2. Reduction in the number of shareholders not leading to a change from joint to sole control
        6.3. Any other changes in the composition of the shareholding
    7. ''Demergers'' and the break-up of companies
    8. Exchange of assets
    9. Acquisitions of control by individual persons
    10. Management buy-outs
    11. Acquisition of control by a state-owned company

I. INTRODUCTION

1. The purpose of this notice is to clarify the Commission's interpretation of the term ''undertakings concerned'' used in Articles 1 and 5 of Council Regulation (EEC) No 4064/89[1] as last amended by Regulation (EC) No 1310/97[2] (hereinafter referred to as ''the Merger Regulation'') and to help identify the undertakings concerned in the most typical situations which have arisen in cases dealt with by the Commission to date. The principles set out in this notice will be followed and further developed by the Commission's practice in individual cases.

This Notice replaces the Notice on the notion of undertakings concerned[3].

2. According to Article 1 of the Merger Regulation, the Regulation only applies to operations that satisfy two conditions. First, several undertakings must merge, or one or more undertakings must acquire control of the whole or part of other undertakings through the proposed operation, which must qualify as a concentration within the meaning of Article 3 of the Regulation. Secondly, those undertakings must meet the turnover thresholds set out in Article 1.

3. From the point of view of determining jurisdiction, the undertakings concerned are, broadly

---

[1] OJ L395, 30.12.1989, p. 1; corrected version L257, 21.9.1990, p. 13.
[2] OJ L180, 9.7.1997, p. 1.
[3] OJ C385, 31.12.1994, p. 12.

speaking, the actors in the transaction in so far as they are the merging, or acquiring and acquired parties; in addition, their total aggregate economic size in terms of turnover will be decisive in determining whether the thresholds are met.

4. The Commission's interpretation of Articles 1 and 5 with respect to the concept of undertakings concerned is without prejudice to the interpretation which may be given by the Court of Justice or by the Court of First Instance of the European Communities.

II. THE CONCEPT OF UNDERTAKING CONCERNED

5. Undertakings concerned are the direct participants in a merger or acquisition of control. In this respect, Article 3(1) of the Merger Regulation provides that:

"A concentration shall be deemed to arise where:

(a) two or more previously independent undertakings merge, or
(b) —one or more persons already controlling at least one undertaking, or
    —one or more undertakings
    acquire, whether by purchase of securities or assets, by contract or by any other means, direct or indirect control of the whole or parts of one or more other undertakings".

6. In the case of a merger, the undertakings concerned will be the undertakings that are merging.

7. In the remaining cases, it is the concept of "acquiring control" that will determine which are the undertakings concerned. On the acquiring side, there can be one or more companies acquiring sole or joint control. On the acquired side, there can be one or more companies as a whole or parts thereof, when only one of their subsidiaries or some of their assets are the subject of the transaction. As a general rule, each of these companies will be an undertaking concerned within the meaning of the Merger Regulation. However, the particular features of specific transactions require some refinement of this principle, as will be seen below when analysing different possible scenarios.

8. In concentrations other than mergers or the setting-up of new joint ventures, i.e. in cases of sole or joint acquisition of pre-existing companies or parts of them, there is an important party to the agreement that gives rise to the operation who is to be ignored when identifying the undertakings concerned: the seller. Although it is clear that the operation cannot proceed without his consent, his role ends when the transaction is completed since, by definition, from the moment the seller has relinquished all control over the company, his links with it disappear. Where the seller retains joint control with the acquiring company (or companies), it will be considered to be one of the undertakings concerned.

9. Once the undertakings concerned have been identified in a given transaction, their turnover for the purposes of determining jurisdiction should be calculated according to the rules set out in Article 5 of the Merger Regulation[4]. One of the main provisions of Article 5 is that where the undertaking concerned belongs to a group, the turnover of the whole group should be included in the calculation. All references to the turnover of the undertakings concerned in Article 1 should therefore be understood as the turnover of their entire respective groups.

10. The same can be said with respect to the substantive appraisal of the impact of a concentration in the market place. When Article 2 of the Merger Regulation provides that the Commission is to take into account "the market position of the undertakings concerned and their economic and financial power", that includes the groups to which they belong.

---

[4] The rules for calculating turnover in accordance with Article 5 are detailed in the Commission Notice on calculation of turnover.

11. It is important, when referring to the various undertakings which may be involved in a procedure, not to confuse the concept of ''undertakings concerned'' under Articles 1 and 5 with the terminology used in the Merger Regulation and in Commission Regulation (EC) No 447/98 of 1 March 1998 on the notifications, time-limits and hearings provided for in Council Regulation (EEC) No 4064/89 (hereinafter referred to as the ''Implementing Regulation'')[5] referring to the various undertakings which may be involved in a procedure. This terminology refers to the notifying parties, other involved parties, third parties and parties who may be subject to fines or periodic penalty payments, and they are defined in Chapter III of the Implementing Regulation, along with their respective rights and duties.

III. IDENTIFYING THE UNDERTAKINGS CONCERNED IN DIFFERENT TYPES OF OPERATIONS

1. Mergers

12. In a merger, several previously independent companies come together to create a new company or, while remaining separate legal entities, to create a single economic unit. As mentioned earlier, the undertakings concerned are each of the merging entities.

2. Acquisition of sole control

2.1. *Acquisition of sole control of the whole company*

13. Acquisition of sole control of the whole company is the most straightforward case of acquisition of control; the undertakings concerned will be the acquiring company and the acquired or target company.

2.2. *Acquisition of sole control of part of a company*

14. The first subparagraph of Article 5(2) of the Merger Regulation provides that when the operation concerns the acquisition of parts of one or more undertakings, only those parts which are the subject of the transaction shall be taken into account with regard to the seller. The concept of ''parts'' is to be understood as one or more separate legal entities (such as subsidiaries), internal subdivisions within the seller (such as a division or unit), or specific assets which in themselves could constitute a business (e.g. in certain cases brands or licences) to which a market turnover can be clearly attributed. In this case, the undertakings concerned will be the acquirer and the acquired part(s) of the target company.

15. The second subparagraph of Article 5(2) includes a special provision on staggered operations or follow-up deals, whereby if several acquisitions of parts by the same purchaser from the same seller occur within a two-year period, these transactions are to be treated as one and the same operation arising on the date of the last transaction. In this case, the undertakings concerned are the acquirer and the different acquired part(s) of the target company taken as a whole.

2.3. *Acquisition of sole control after reduction or enlargement of the target company*

16. The undertakings concerned are the acquiring company and the target company or companies, in their configuration at the date of the operation.

17. The Commission bases itself on the configuration of the undertakings concerned at the date of the event triggering the obligation to notify under Article 4(1) of the Merger Regulation, namely the conclusion of the agreement, the announcement of the public bid or the acquisition of a controlling interest. If the target company has divested an entity or closed a business prior to the date of the event triggering notification or where such a divestment or closure is a

---

[5] OJ L61, 2.3.1998, p. 1.

pre-condition for the operation[6], then sales of the divested entity or closed business are not to be included when calculating turnover. Conversely, if the target company has acquired an entity prior to the date of the event triggering notification, the sales of the latter are to be added.[7]

2.4. *Acquisition of sole control through a subsidiary of a group*

18. Where the target company is acquired by a group through one of its subsidiaries, the undertakings concerned for the purpose of calculating turnover are the target company and the acquiring subsidiary. However, regarding the actual notification, this can be made by the subsidiary concerned or by its parent company.

19. All the companies within a group (parent companies, subsidiaries, etc.) constitute a single economic entity, and therefore there can only be one undertaking concerned within the one group — i.e. the subsidiary and the parent company cannot each be considered as separate undertakings concerned, either for the purposes of ensuring that the threshold requirements are fulfilled (for example, if the target company does not meet the ECU 250 million Community-turnover threshold), or that they are not (for example, if a group was split into two companies each with a Community turnover below ECU 250 million).

20. However, even though there can only be one undertaking concerned within a group, Article 5(4) of the Merger Regulation provides that it is the turnover of the whole group to which the undertaking concerned belongs that shall be included in the threshold calculations[8].

3. Acquisition of joint control

3.1. *Acquisition of joint control of a newly-created company*

21. In the case of acquisition of joint control of a newly-created company, the undertakings concerned are each of the companies acquiring control of the newly set-up joint venture (which, as it does not yet exist, cannot be considered to be an undertaking concerned and moreover, as yet, has no turnover of its own).

3.2. *Acquisition of joint control of a pre-existing company*

22. In the case of acquisition of joint control of a pre-existing company or business[9], the undertakings concerned are each of the companies acquiring joint control on the one hand, and the pre-existing acquired company or business on the other.

23. However, where the pre-existing company was under the sole control of one company and one or several new shareholders acquire joint control while the initial parent company remains, the undertakings concerned are each of the jointly-controlling companies (including this initial shareholder). The target company in this case is not an undertaking concerned, and its turnover is part of the turnover of the initial parent company.

3.3. *Acquisition of joint control with a view to immediate partition of assets*

24. Where several undertakings come together solely for the purpose of acquiring another company and agree to divide up the acquired assets according to a pre-existing plan immediately upon completion of the transaction, there is no effective concentration of economic power between the acquirers and the target company since the assets acquired are jointly held and

---

[6] See judgment of the Court of First Instance of 24 March 1994 in Case T-3/93 — Air France v Commission [1994] ECR II-21.

[7] The calculation of turnover in the case of acquisitions or divestments subsequent to the date of the last audited accounts is dealt with in the Commission Notice on calculation of turnover, paragraph 27.

[8] The calculation of turnover in the case of company groups is dealt with in the Commission Notice on calculation of turnover, paragraphs 36 to 42.

[9] i.e. two or more companies (companies A, B, etc.) acquire a pre-existing company (company X). For changes in the shareholding in cases of joint control of an existing joint venture, see Section III.6.

controlled for only a "legal instant". This type of acquisition with a view to immediate partition of assets will in fact be considered to be several operations, whereby each of the acquiring companies acquires its relevant part of the target company. For each of these operations, the undertakings concerned will therefore be the acquiring company and that part of the target which it is acquiring (just as if there was an acquisition of sole control of part of a company).

25. This scenario is referred to in recital 24 of Regulation (EEC) No 4064/89, which states that the Regulation applies to agreements whose sole object is to divide up the assets acquired immediately after the acquisition.

4. Acquisition of control by a joint venture

26. In transactions where a joint venture acquires control of another company, the question arises whether or not, from the point of view of the acquiring party, the joint venture should be regarded as a single undertaking concerned (the turnover of which would include the turnover of its parent companies), or whether each of its parent companies should individually be regarded as undertakings concerned. In other words, the issue is whether or not to "lift the corporate veil" of the intermediate undertaking (the vehicle). In principle, the undertaking concerned is the direct participant in the acquisition of control. However, there may be circumstances where companies set up "shell" companies, which have little or no turnover of their own, or use an existing joint venture which is operating on a different market from that of the target company in order to carry out acquisitions on behalf of the parent companies. Where the acquired or target company has a Community turnover of less than ECU 250 million, the question of determining the undertakings concerned may be decisive for jurisdictional purposes[10]. In this type of situation, the Commission will look at the economic reality of the operation to determine which are the undertakings concerned.

27. Where the acquisition is carried out by a full-function joint venture, i.e. a joint venture which has sufficient financial and other resources to operate a business activity on a lasting basis[11] and is already operating on a market, the Commission will normally consider the joint venture itself and the target company to be the undertakings concerned (and not the joint venture's parent companies).

28. Conversely, where the joint venture can be regarded as a vehicle for an acquisition by the parent companies, the Commission will consider each of the parent companies themselves to be the undertakings concerned, rather than the joint venture, together with the target company. This is the case in particular where the joint venture is set up especially for the purpose of acquiring the target company, where the joint venture has not yet started to operate, where an existing joint venture has no legal personality or full-function character as referred to above or where the joint venture is an association of undertakings. The same applies where there are elements which demonstrate that the parent companies are in fact the real players behind the operation. These elements may include a significant involvement by the parent companies themselves in the initiation, organisation and financing of the operation. Moreover, where the acquisition leads to a substantial diversification in the nature of the joint venture's activities,

[10] The target company hypothetically has an aggregate Community turnover of less than ECU 250 million, and the acquiring parties are two (or more) undertakings, each with a Community turnover exceeding ECU 250 million. If the target is acquired by a "shell" company set up between the acquiring undertakings, there would only be one company (the "shell" company) with a Community turnover exceeding ECU 250 million, and thus one of the cumulative threshold conditions for Community jurisdiction would not be fulfilled (namely, the existence of at least two undertakings with a Community turnover exceeding ECU 250 million). Conversely, if instead of acting through a "shell" company, the acquiring undertakings acquire the target company themselves, then the turnover threshold would be met and the Merger Regulation would apply to this transaction. The same considerations apply to the national turnover thresholds referred to in Article 1(3).

[11] The criteria determining the full-function nature of a joint venture are contained in the Commission Notice on the concept of full-function joint ventures.

this may also indicate that the parent companies are the real players in the operation. This will normally be the case when the joint venture acquires a target company operating on a different product market. In those cases, the parent companies are regarded as undertakings concerned.

29. In the TNT case[12], joint control over a joint venture (JVC) was to be acquired by a joint venture (GD NET BV) between five postal administrations and another acquiring company (TNT Ltd). In this case, the Commission considered that the joint venture GD NET BV was simply a vehicle set up to enable the parent companies (the five postal administrations) to participate in the resulting JVC joint venture in order to facilitate decision-making amongst themselves and to ensure that the parent companies spoke and acted as one; this configuration would ensure that the parent companies could exercise a decisive influence with the other acquiring company, TNT, over the resulting joint venture JVC and would avoid the situation where that other acquirer could exercise sole control because of the postal administrations' inability to reach a unified position on any decision.

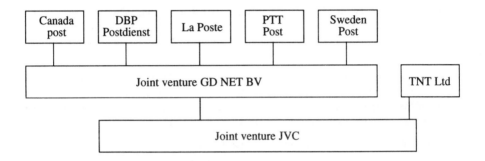

5. Change from joint control to sole control

30. In the case of a change from joint control to sole control, one shareholder acquires the stake previously held by the other shareholder(s). In the case of two shareholders, each of them has joint control over the entire joint venture, and not sole control over 50% of it; hence the sale of all of his shares by one shareholder to the other does not lead the sole remaining shareholder to move from sole control over 50% to sole control over 100% of the joint venture, but rather to move from joint control to sole control of the entire company (which, subsequent to the operation, ceases to be a "joint" venture).

31. In this situation, the undertakings concerned are the remaining (acquiring) shareholder and the joint venture. As is the case for any other seller, the "exiting" shareholder is not an undertaking concerned.

32. The ICI/Tioxide case[13] involved such a change from joint (50/50) control to sole control. The Commission considered that ". . . decisive influence exercised solely is substantially different to decisive influence exercised jointly, since the latter has to take into account the potentially different interests of the other party or parties concerned . . . By changing the quality of decisive influence exercised by ICI on Tioxide, the transaction will bring about a durable change of the structure of the concerned parties . . .". In this case, the undertakings concerned were held to be ICI (as acquirer) and Tioxide as a whole (as acquiree), but not the seller Cookson.

---

[12] Case IV/M.102 — TNT/Canada Post, DBP Postdienst, La Poste, PTT Post and Sweden Post, of 2 December 1991.
[13] Case IV/M.023 — ICI/Tioxide, of 28 November 1990.

6. Change in the shareholding in cases of joint control of an existing joint venture

33. The decisive element in assessing changes in the shareholding of a company is whether the operation leads to a change in the quality of control. The Commission assesses each operation on a case-by-case basis, but under certain hypotheses, there will be a presumption that the given operation leads, or does not lead, to such a change in the quality of control, and thus constitutes, or does not constitute, a notifiable concentration.

34. A distinction must be made according to the circumstances of the change in the shareholding; firstly, one or more existing shareholders can exit; secondly, one or more new additional shareholders can enter; and thirdly, one or more existing shareholders can be replaced by one or more new shareholders.

6.1. Reduction in the number of shareholders leading to a change from joint to sole control

35. It is not the reduction in the number of shareholders *per se* which is important, but rather the fact that if some shareholders sell their stakes in a given joint venture, these stakes are then acquired by other (new or existing) shareholders, and thus the acquisition of these stakes or additional contractual rights may lead to the acquisition of control or may strengthen an already existing position of control (e.g. additional voting rights or veto rights, additional board members, etc.).

36. Where the number of shareholders is reduced, there may be a change from joint control to sole control (see also Section III.5.), in which case the remaining shareholder acquires sole control of the company. The undertakings concerned will be the remaining (acquiring) shareholder and the acquired company (previously the joint venture).

37. In addition to the shareholder with sole control of the company, there may be other shareholders, for example with minority stakes, but who do not have a controlling interest in the company; these shareholders are not undertakings concerned as they do not exercise control.

6.2. Reduction in the number of shareholders not leading to a change from joint to sole control

38. Where the operation involves a reduction in the number of shareholders having joint control, without leading to a change from joint to sole control and without any new entry or substitution of shareholders acquiring control (see Section III.6.3.), the proposed transaction will normally be presumed not to lead to a change in the quality of control and will therefore not be a notifiable concentration. This would be the case where, for example, five shareholders initially have equal stakes of 20% each and where, after the operation, one shareholder exits and the remaining four shareholders each have equal stakes of 25%.

39. However, this situation would be different where there is a significant change in the quality of control, notably where the reduction in the number of shareholders gives the remaining shareholders additional veto rights or additional board members, resulting in a new acquisition of control by at least one of the shareholders, through the application of either the existing or a new shareholders' agreement. In this case, the undertakings concerned will be each of the remaining shareholders which exercise joint control and the joint venture. In Avesta II[14], the fact that the number of major shareholders decreased from four to three led to one of the remaining shareholders acquiring negative veto rights (which it had not previously enjoyed) because of the provisions of the shareholders' agreement which remained in force[15]. This

---

[14] Case IV/M.452 — Avesta II, of 9 June 1994.

[15] In this case, a shareholder who was a party to the shareholders' agreement sold its stake of approximately 7%. As the exiting shareholder had shared veto rights with another shareholder who remained, and as the shareholders' agreement remained unchanged, the remaining shareholder now acquired full veto rights.

acquisition of full veto rights was considered by the Commission to represent a change in the quality of control.

6.3. *Any other changes in the composition of the shareholding*

40. Finally, in the case where, following change in the shareholding, one or more shareholders acquire control, the operation will constitute a notifiable operation as there is a presumption that it will normally lead to a change in the quality of control.

41. Irrespective of whether the number of shareholders decreasess, increases or remains the same subsequent to the operation, this acquisition of control can take any of the following forms:

— entry of one or more new shareholders (change from sole to joint control, or situation of joint control both before and after the operation),

— acquisition of a controlling interest by one or more minority shareholders (change from sole to joint control, or situation of joint control both before and after the operation),

— substitution of one or more shareholders (situation of joint control both before and after the operation).

42. The question is whether the undertakings concerned are the joint venture and the new shareholder(s) who would together acquire control of a pre-existing company, or whether all of the shareholders (existing and new) are to be regarded as undertakings concerned acquiring control of a new joint venture. This question is particularly relevant when there is no express agreement between one (or more) of the existing shareholders and the new shareholder(s), who might only have had an agreement with the "exiting" shareholder(s), i.e. the seller(s).

43. A change in the shareholding through the entry or substitution of shareholders is considered to lead to a change in the quality of control. This is because the entry of a new parent company, or the substitution of one parent company for another, is not comparable to the simple acquisition of part of a business as it implies a change in the nature and quality of control of the whole joint venture, even when, both before and after the operation, joint control is exercised by a given number of shareholders.

44. The Commission therefore considers that the undertakings concerned in cases where there are changes in the shareholding are the shareholders (both existing and new) who exercise joint control and the joint venture itself. As mentioned earlier, non-controlling shareholders are not undertakings concerned.

45. An example of such a change in the shareholding is the Synthomer/Yule Catto case[16], in which one of two parent companies with joint control over the pre-existing joint venture was replaced by a new parent company. Both parent companies with joint control (the existing one and the new one) and the joint venture were considered to be undertakings concerned.

7. "Demergers" and the break-up of companies

46. When two undertakings merge or set up a joint venture, then subsequently demerge or break up their joint venture, and in particular the assets[17] are split between the "demerging" parties, particularly in a configuration different from the original, there will normally be more than one acquisition of control (see the Annex).

---

[16] Case IV/M.376 — Synthomer/Yule Catto, of 22 October 1993.
[17] The term "assets" as used here means specific assets which in themselves could constitute a business (e.g. a subsidiary, a division of a company or, in some cases, brands or licences) to which a market turnover can be clearly attributed.

47. For example, undertakings A and B merge and then subsequently demerge with a new asset configuration. There will be the acquisition by undertaking A of various assets (assets which may previously have been owned by itself or by undertaking B and assets jointly acquired by the entity resulting from the merger), with similar acquisitions by undertaking B. Similarly, a break-up of a joint venture can be deemed to involve a change from joint control over the joint venture's entire assets to sole control over the divided assets[18].

48. A break-up of a company in this way is "asymmetrical". For such a demerger, the undertakings concerned (for each break-up operation) will be, on the one hand, the original parties to the merger and, on the other, the assets that each original party is acquiring. For the break-up of a joint venture, the undertakings concerned (for each break-up operation) will be, on the one hand, the original parties to the joint venture, each as acquirer, and, on the other, that part of the joint venture that each original party is acquiring.

8. Exchange of assets

49. In those transactions where two (or more) companies exchange assets, regardless of whether these constitute legal entities or not, each acquisition of control constitutes an independent concentration. Although it is true that both transfers of assets in a swap are usually considered by the parties to be interdependent, that they are often agreed in a single document and that they may even take place simultaneously, the purpose of the Merger Regulation is to assess the impact of the operation resulting from the acquisition of control by each of the companies. The legal or even economic link between those operations is not sufficient for them to qualify as a single concentration.

50. Hence the undertakings concerned will be, for each property transfer, the acquiring companies and the acquired companies or assets.

9. Acquisitions of control by individual persons

51. Article 3(1) of the Merger Regulation specifically provides that a concentration is deemed to arise, *inter alia*, where " one or more persons already controlling at least one undertaking" acquire control of the whole or parts of one or more undertakings. This provision indicates that acquisitions of control by individuals will bring about a lasting change in the structure of the companies concerned only if those individuals carry out economic activities of their own. The Commission considers that the undertakings concerned are the target company and the individual acquirer (with the turnover of the undertaking(s) controlled by that individual being included in the calculation of the individual's turnover).

52. This was the view taken in the Commission decision in the Asko/Jacobs/Adia case[19], where Asko, a German holding company with substantial retailing assets, and Mr Jacobs, a private Swiss investor, acquired joint control of Adia, a Swiss company active mainly in personnel services. Mr Jacobs was considered to be an undertaking concerned because of the economic interests he held in the chocolate, confectionery and coffee sectors.

10. Management buy-outs

53. An acquisition of control of a company by its own managers is also an acquisition by individuals, and what has been said above is therefore also applicable here. However, the management of the company may pool its interests through a "vehicle company", so that it acts with a single voice and also to facilitate decision-making. Such a vehicle company may be, but is not necessarily, an undertaking concerned. The general rule on acquisitions of control by a joint venture applies here (see Section III.4.).

---

[18] Case IV/M.197 — Solvay-Laporte/Interox, of 30 April 1997.
[19] Case IV/M.082 — Asko/Jacobs/Adia, of 16 May 1991.

54. With or without a vehicle company, the management may also look for investors in order to finance the operation. Very often, the rights granted to these investors according to their shareholding may be such that control within the meaning of Article 3 of the Merger Regulation will be conferred on them and not on the management itself, which may simply enjoy minority rights. In the CWB/Goldman Sachs/Tarkett decision[20], the two companies managing the investment funds taking part in the transaction were those acquiring joint control, and not the managers.

11. Acquisition of control by a State-owned company

55. In those situations where a State-owned company merges with or acquires control of another company controlled by the same State[21], the question arises as to whether these transactions really constitute concentrations within the meaning of Article 3 of the Merger Regulation or rather internal restructuring operations of the ''public sector group of companies''[22]. In this respect, recital 12 of Regulation (EEC) No 4064/89 sets out the principle of non-discrimination between public and private sectors and declares that ''in the public sector, calculation of the turnover of an undertaking concerned in a concentration needs, therefore, to take account of undertakings making up an economic unit with an independent power of decision, irrespective of the way in which their capital is held or of the rules of administrative supervision applicable to them''.

56. A merger or acquisition of control arising between two companies owned by the same State may constitute a concentration and, if so, both of them will qualify as undertakings concerned, since the mere fact that two companies are both owned by the same State does not necessarily mean that they belong to the same ''group''. Indeed, the decisive issue will be whether or not these companies are both part of the same industrial holding and are subject to a coordinated strategy. This was the approach taken in the SGS/Thomson decision[23].

---

[20] Case IV/M.395 — CWB/Goldman Sachs/Tarkett, of 21 February 1994.
[21] The term ''State'' as used here means any legal public entity, i.e. not only Member States, but also regional or local public entities such as provinces, departments, Länder, etc.
[22] See also Commission Notice on the concept of concentration, paragraph 8.
[23] Case IV/M.216 — CEA Industrie/France Telecom/Finmeccanica/SGS-Thomson, of 22 February 1993.

ANNEX
'DEMERGERS' AND BREAK-UP OF COMPANIES[1]

Merger scenario

Before merger

| Company A |

| Company B |

After merger

| Merged company |
| Combined assets |

After breaking up the merger

Company A:	Company B:
Divided assets of merged company:	Divided Assets of merged company:
– some (initial) assets of A	– some (initial) assets of A
– some (initial) assets of B	– some (initial) assets of B
– some (subsequent) assets of the merged company	– some (subsequent) assets of the merged company

Joint venture scenario

Before JV

| Company A | Assets of A for the JV |

| Assets of B for the JV | Company B |

After JV

| Company A | ——— | Joint venture | ——— | Company B |
| | | Combined assets | | |

After breaking up the JV

Company A	Divided assets of joint venture:	Company B	Divided assets of joint venture:
	– some (initial) assets of A		– some (initial) assets of A
	– some (initial) assets of B		– some (initial) assets of B
	– some (subsequent) assets of the JV		– some (subsequent) assets of the JV

[24] The term ''assets'' as used here means specific assets which in themselves could constitute a business (e.g. a subsidiary, a division of a company or, in some cases, brands or licences) to which a market turnover can be clearly attributed.

Appendix 7

COMMISSION NOTICE
on calculation of turnover under Council Regulation (EEC) No 4064/89 on the control of concentrations between undertakings (OJ 1998 C66/04)

I.   "ACCOUNTING" DETERMINATION OF TURNOVER
    1. Turnover as a reflection of business activity
       1.1. The concept of turnover
       1.2. Ordinary activities
    2. "Net" turnover
       2.1. The deduction of rebates and taxes
       2.2. The deduction of "internal" turnover
    3. Adjustment of turnover calculation rules for the different types of operations
       3.1. The general rule
       3.2. Acquisition of parts of companies
       3.3. Staggered operations
       3.4. Turnover of groups
       3.5. Turnover of State-owned companies
II.   GEOGRAPHICAL ALLOCATION OF TURNOVER
    1. General rule
    2. Conversion of turnover into ecu
III. CREDIT AND OTHER FINANCIAL INSTITUTIONS AND INSURANCE UNDERTAKINGS
    1. Definitions
    2. Calculation of turnover

1. The purpose of this Notice is to expand upon the text of Articles 1 and 5 of Council Regulation (EEC) No 4064.89[1] as last amended by Council Regulation (EC) No 1310/97[2] (hereinafter referred to as "the Merger Regulation") and in so doing to elucidate certain procedural and practical questions which have caused doubt or difficulty.

2. This Notice is based on the experience gained by the Commission in applying the Merger Regulation to date. The principles it sets out will be followed and further developed by the Commission's practice in individual cases.

This Notice replaces the Notice on calculation of turnover[3].

3. The Merger Regulation has a two fold test for Commission jurisdiction. One test is that the transaction must be a concentration within the meaning of Article 3[4]. The second comprises the turnover thresholds contained in Article 1 and designed to identify those transactions which have an impact upon the Community and can be deemed to be of "Community interest". Turnover is used as a proxy for the economic resources being combined in a concentration, and is allocated geographically in order to reflect the geographic distribution of those resources.

Two sets of thresholds are set out in Article 1, in paragraph 2 and paragraph 3 respectively. Article 1(2) sets out the thresholds which must first be checked in order to establish whether the transaction has a Community dimension. In this respect, the worldwide turnover threshold is intended to measure the overall dimension of the undertakings concerned; the Community turnover threshold seeks to determine whether the concentration involves a minimum level of

[1] OJ L395, 30.12.1989, p. 1; corrected version OJ L257, 21.9.1990, p. 13.
[2] OJ L180, 9.7.1997, p. 1.
[3] OJ C385, 31.12.1994, p. 21.
[4] See the Notice on the concept of concentration.

activities in the Community; and the two-thirds rule aims to exclude purely domestic transactions from Community jurisdiction.

Article 1(3) must only be applied in the event that the thresholds set out in Article 1(2) are not met. This second set of thresholds is designed to tackle those transactions which fall short of achieving Community dimension under Article 1(2), but would need to be notified under national competition rules in at least three Member States (so called "multiple notifications"). For this purpose, Article 1(3) provides for lower turnover thresholds, both worldwide and Community-wide, to be achieved by the undertakings concerned. A concentration has a Community dimension if these lower thresholds are fulfilled and the undertakings concerned achieve jointly and individually a minimum level of activities in at least three Member States. Article 1(3) also contains a two-thirds rule similar to that of Article 1(2), which aims to identify purely domestic transactions.

4. The thresholds as such are designed to establish jurisdiction and not to assess the market position of the parties to the concentration nor the impact of the operation. In so doing they include turnover derived from, and thus the resources devoted to, all areas of activity of the parties, and not just those directly involved in the concentration. Article 1 of the Merger Regulation sets out the thresholds to be used to determine a concentration with a "Community dimension" while Article 5 explains how turnover should be calculated.

5. The fact that the thresholds of Article 1 of the Merger Regulation are purely quantitative, since they are only based on turnover calculation instead of market share or other criteria, shows that their aim is to provide a simple and objective mechanism that can be easily handled by the companies involved in a merger in order to determine if their transaction has a Community dimension and is therefore notifiable.

6. The decisive issue for Article 1 of the Merger Regulation is to measure the economic strength of the undertakings concerned as reflected in their respective turnover figures, regardless of the sector where such turnover was achieved and of whether those sectors will be at all affected by the transaction in question. The Merger Regulation has thereby given priority to the determination of the overall economic and financial resources that are being combined through the merger in order to decide whether the latter is of Community interest.

7. In this context, it is clear that turnover should reflect as accurately as possible the economic strength of the undertakings involved in a transaction. This is the purpose of the set of rules contained in Article 5 of the Merger Regulation which are designed to ensure that the resulting figures are a true representation of economic reality.

8. The Commission's interpretation of Articles 1 and 5 with respect to calculation of turnover is without prejudice to the interpretation which may be given by the Court of Justice or the Court of First Instance of the European Communities.

I. "ACCOUNTING" CALCULATION OF TURNOVER

1. Turnover as a reflection of activity

1.1. *The concept of turnover*

9. The concept of turnover as used in Article 5 of the Merger Regulation refers explicitly to "the amounts derived from the sale of products and the provision of services". Sale, as a reflection of the undertaking's activity, is thus the essential criterion for calculating turnover, whether for products or the provision of services. "Amounts derived from sale" generally appear in company accounts under the heading "sales".

10. In the case of products, turnover can be determined without difficulty, namely by identifying each commercial act involving a transfer of ownership.

11. In the case of services, the factors to be taken into account in calculating turnover are much more complex, since the commercial act involves a transfer of ''value''.

12. Generally speaking, the method of calculating turnover in the case of services does not differ from that used in the case of products: the Commission takes into consideration the total amount of sales. Where the service provided is sold directly by the provider to the customer, the turnover of the undertaking concerned consists of the total amount of sales for the provision of services in the last financial year.

13. Because of the complexity of the service sector, this general principle may have to be adapted to the specific conditions of the service provided. Thus, in certain sectors of activity (such as tourism and advertising), the service may be sold through the intermediary of other suppliers. Because of the diversity of such sectors, many different situations may arise. For example, the turnover of a service undertaking which acts as an intermediary may consist solely of the amount of commissions which it receive.

14. Similarly, in a number of areas such as credit, financial services and insurance, technical problems in calculating turnover arise which will be dealt with in Section III.

1.2. *Ordinary activities*

15. Article 5(1) states that the amounts to be included in the calculation of turnover must correspond to the ''ordinary activities'' of the undertakings concerned.

16. With regard to aid granted to undertakings by public bodies, any aid relating to one of the ordinary activities of an undertaking concerned is liable to be included in the calculation of turnover if the undertaking is itself the recipient of the aid and if the aid is directly linked to the sale of products and the provision of services by the undertaking and is therefore reflected in the price[5]. For example, aid towards the consumption of a product allows the manufacturer to sell at a higher price than that actually paid by consumers.

17. With regard to services, the Commission looks at the undertaking's ordinary activities involved in establishing the resources required for providing the service. In its Decision in the Accor/Wagons-Lits case[6], the Commission decided to take into account the item ''other operating proceeds'' included in Wagons-Lits's profit and loss account. The Commission considered that the components of this item which included certain income from its car-hire activities were derived from the sale of products and the provision of services by Wagons-Lits and were part of its ordinary activities.

2. ''Net'' turnover

18. The turnover to be taken into account is ''net'' turnover, after deduction of a number of components specified in the Regulation. The Commission's aim is to adjust turnover in such a way as to enable it to decide on the real economic weight of the undertaking.

2.1. *The deduction of rebates and taxes*

19. Article 5(1) provides for the ''deduction of sales rebates and of value added tax and other taxes directly related to turnover''. The deductions thus relate to business components (sales rebates) and tax components (value added tax and other taxes directly related to turnover).

---

[5] See Case IV/M.156 — Cereol/Continentale Italiana of 27 November 1991. In this case, the Commission excluded Community aid from the calculation of turnover because the aid was not intended to support the sale of products manufactured by one of the undertakings involved in the merger, but the producers of the raw materials (grain) used by the undertaking, which specialized in the crushing of grain.

[6] Casd IV/M.126 — Accor/Wagons-Lits, of 28 April 1992.

20. "Sales rebates" should be taken to mean all rebates or discounts which are granted by the undertakings during their business negotiations with their customers and which have a direct influence on the amounts of sales.

21. As regards the deduction of taxes, the Merger Regulation refers to VAT and "other taxes directly related to turnover". As far as VAT is concerned, its deduction does not in general pose any problem. The concept of "taxes directly related to turnover" is a clear reference to indirect taxation since it is directly linked to turnover, such as, for example, taxes on alcoholic beverages.

2.2. *The deduction of "internal" turnover*

22. The first subparagraph of Article 5(1) states that "the aggregate turnover of an undertaking concerned shall not include the sale of products or the provision of services between any of the undertakings referred to in paragraph 4", i.e. those which have links with the undertaking concerned (essentially parent companies or subsidiaries).

23. The aim is to exclude the proceeds of business dealings within a group so as to take account of the real economic weight of each entity. Thus, the "amounts" taken into account by the Merger Regulation reflect only the transactions which take place between the group of undertakings on the one hand and third parties on the other.

3. Adjustment of turnover calculation rules for the different types of operations

3.1. *The general rule*

24. According to Article 5(1) of the Merger Regulation, aggregate turnover comprises the amounts derived by the undertakings concerned in the preceding financial year from the sale of products and the provision of services. The basic principle is thus that for each undertaking concerned the turnover to be taken into account is the turnover of the closest financial year to the date of the transaction.

25. This provision shows that since there are usually no audited accounts of the year ending the day before the transaction, the closest representation of a whole year of activity of the company in question is the one given by the turnover figures of the most recent financial year.

26. The Commission seeks to base itself upon the most accurate and reliable figures available. As a general rule therefore, the Commission will refer to audited or other definitive accounts. However, in cases where major differences between the Community's accounting standards and those of a non-member country are observed, the Commission may consider it necessary to restate these accounts in accordance with Community standards in respect of turnover. The Commission is, in any case, reluctant to rely on management or any other form of provisional accounts in any but exceptional circumstances (see the next paragraph). Where a concentration takes place within the first months of the year and audited accounts are not yet available for the most recent financial year, the figures to be taken into account are those relating to the previous year. Where there is a major divergence between the two sets of accounts, and in particular, when the final draft figures for the most recent years are available, the Commission may decide to take those draft figures into account.

27. Notwithstanding paragraph 26, an adjustment must always be made to account for acquisitions or divestments subsequent to the date of the audited accounts. This is necessary if the true resources being concentrated are to be identified. Thus if a company disposes of part of its business at any time before the signature of the final agreement or the announcement of the public bid or the acquisition of a controlling interest bringing about a concentration, or where such a divestment or closure is a pre-condition for the operation[7] the part of the turnover to be

---

[7] See Judgment of the Court of First Instance in Case T-3/93, Air France v Commision, [1994] ECR II-21.

attributed to that part of the business must be subtracted from the turnover of the notifying party as shown in its last audited accounts. Conversely, the turnover to be attributed to assets of which control has been acquired subsequent to the preparation of the most recent audited accounts must be added to a company's turnover for notification purposes.

28. Other factors that may affect turnover on a temporary basis such as a decrease in orders for the product or a slow-down in the production process within the period prior to the transaction will be ignored for the purposes of calculating turnover. No adjustment to the definitive accounts will be made to incorporate them.

29. Regarding the geographical allocation of turnover, since audited accounts often do not provide a geographical breakdown of the sort required by the Merger Regulation, the Commission will rely on the best figures available provided by the companies in accordance with the rule laid down in Article 5(1) of the Merger Regulation (see Section II.1).

3.2. *Acquisitions of parts of companies*

30. Article 5(2) of the Merger Regulation provides that "where the concentration consists in the acquisition of parts, whether or not constituted as legal entities, of one or more undertakings, only the turnover relating to the parts which are the subject of the transaction shall be taken into account with regard to the seller or sellers".

31. This provision states that when the acquirer does not purchase an entire group, but only one, or part, of its businesses, whether or not constituted as a subsidiary, only the turnover of the part acquired should be included in the turnover calculation. In fact, although in legal terms the seller as a whole (with all its subsidiaries) is an essential party to the transaction, since the sale-purchase agreement cannot be concluded without him, he plays no role once the agreement has been implemented. The possible impact of the transaction on the market will depend only on the combination of the economic and financial resources that are the subject of a property transfer with those of the acquirer and not on the remaining business of the seller who remains independent.

3.3. *Staggered operations*

32. Sometimes certain successive transactions are only individual steps within a wider strategy between the same parties. Considering each transaction alone, even if only for determining jurisdiction, would imply ignoring economic reality. At the same time, whereas some of these staggered operations may be designed in this fashion because they will better meet the needs of the parties, others could be structured like this in order to circumvent the application of the Merger Regulation.

33. The Merger Regulation has foreseen these scenarios in Article 5(2), second subparagraph, which provides that "two or more transactions within the meaning of the first subparagraph which take place within a two-year period between the same persons or undertakings shall be treated as one and the same concentration arising on the date of the last transaction".

34. In practical terms, this provision means that if company A buys a subsidiary of company B that represents 50% of the overall activity of B and one year later it acquires the other subsidiary (the remaining 50% of B), both transactions will be taken as one. Assuming that each of the subsidiaries attained a turnover in the Community of only ECU 200 million, the first transaction would not be notifiable unless the operation fulfilled the conditions set out in Article 1(3). However, since the second transaction takes place within the two-year period, both have to be notified as a single transaction when the second occurs.

35. The importance of the provision is that previous transactions (within two years) become notifiable with the most recent transaction once the thresholds are cumulatively met.

3.4. *Turnover of groups*

36. When an undertaking concerned in a concentration within the meaning of Article 1 of the Merger Regulation[8] belongs to a group, the turnover of the group as a whole is to be taken into account in order to determine whether the thresholds are met. The aim is again to capture the total volume of the economic resources that are being combined through the operation.

37. The Merger Regulation does not define the concept of group in abstract terms but focuses on whether the companies have the right to manage the undertaking's affairs as the yardstick to determine which of the companies that have some direct or indirect links with an undertaking concerned should be regarded as part of its group.

38. Article 5(4) of the Merger Regulation provides the following:

"Without prejudice to paragraph 2 [acquisitions of parts], the aggregate turnover of an under-taking concerned within the meaning of Article 1(2) and (3) shall be calculated by adding together the respective turnovers of the following:

(a) the undertaking concerned;
(b) those undertakings in which the undertaking concerned directly or indirectly:

— owns more than half the capital or business assets, or
— has the power to exercise more than half the voting rights, or
— has the power to appoint more than half the members of the supervisory board, the administrative board or bodies legally representing the undertakings, or
— has the right to manage the undertaking's affairs;

(c) those undertakings which have in an undertaking concerned the rights or powers listed in (b);
(d) those undertakings in which an undertaking as referred to in (c) has the rights or powers listed in (b);
(e) those undertakings in which two or more undertakings as referred to in (a) to (d) jointly have the rights or powers listed in (b)."

This means that the turnover of the company directly involved in the transaction (point (a)) should include its subsidiaries (point (b)), its parent companies (point (c)), the other subsidiaries of its parent companies (point (d)) and any other undertaking jointly controlled by two or more of the companies belonging to the group (point (e)). A graphic example is as follows [*opposite*]:

Several remarks can be made from this chart:

1. As long as the test of control of point (b) is fulfilled, the whole turnover of the subsidiary in question will be taken into account regardless of the actual shareholding of the control-ling company. In the example, the whole turnover of the three subsidiaries (called b) of the undertaking concerned (a) will be included.
2. When any of the companies identified as belonging to the group also controls others, these should also be incorporated into the calculation. In the example, one of the subsidiaries of a (called b) has in turn its own subsidiaries b1 and b2.
3. When two or more companies jointly control the undertaking concerned (a) in the sense that the agreement of each and all of them is needed in order to manage the undertaking affairs, the turnover of all of them should be included[9]. In the example, the two parent companies (c) of the undertaking concerned (a) would be taken into account as well as

---

[8] See the Commission Notice on the concept of undertakings concerned.
[9] See Commission Notice on the concept of undertakings concerned (paragraphs 26–29).

The undertaking concerned and its group:

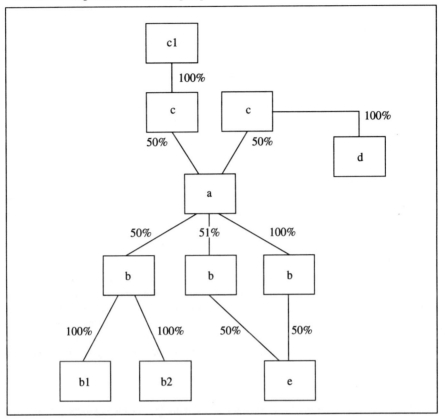

a: The undertaking concerned
b: Its subsidiaries and their own subsidiaries (b1 and b2)
c: Its parent companies and their own parent companies (c1)
d: Other subsidiaries of the parent companies of the undertaking concerned
e: Companies jointly controlled by two (or more) companies of the group

Note: These letters correspond to the relevant subparagraphs of Article 5 (4).

their own parent companies (c1 in the example). Although the Merger Regulation does not explicitly mention this rule for those cases where the undertaking concerned is in fact a joint venture, it is inferred from the text of Article 5(4)(c), which uses the plural when referring to the parent companies. This interpretation has been consistently applied by the Commission.

4.   Any intra-group sale should be subtracted from the turnover of the group (see paragraph 22).

39. The Merger Regulation also deals with the specific scenario that arises when two or more undertakings concerned in a transaction exercise joint control of another company. Pursuant to point (a) of Article 5(5), the turnover resulting from the sale of products or the provision of services between the joint venture and each of the undertakings concerned or any other company connected with any one of them in the sense of Article 5(4) should be excluded. The purpose

of such a rule is to avoid double counting. With regard to the turnover of the joint venture generated from activities with third parties, point (b) of Article 5(5) provides that it should be apportioned equally amongst the undertakings concerned, to reflect the joint control[10].

40. Following the principle of point (b) of Article 5(5) by analogy, in the case of joint ventures between undertakings concerned and third parties, the Commission's practice has been to allocate to each of the undertakings concerned the turnover shared equally by all the controlling companies in the joint venture. In all these cases, however, joint control has to be demonstrated.

The practice shows that it is impossible to cover in the present Notice the whole range of scenarios which could arise in respect of turnover calculation of joint venture companies or joint control cases. Whenever ambiguities arise, an assessment should always give priority to the general principles of avoiding double counting and of reflecting as accurately as possible the economic strength of the undertakings involved in the transaction[11].

41. It should be noted that Article 5(4) refers only to the groups that already exist at the time of the transaction, i.e. the group of each of the undertakings concerned in an operation, and not to the new structures created as a result of the concentration. For example, if companies A and B, together with their respective subsidiaries, are going to merge, it is A and B, and not the new entity, that qualify as undertakings concerned, which implies that the turnover of each of the two groups should be calculated independently.

42. Since the aim of this provision is simply to identify the companies belonging to the existing groups for the purposes of turnover calculation, the test of having the right to manage the undertaking's affairs in Article 5(4)[12] is somewhat different from the test of control set out in Article 3(3), which refers to the acquisition of control carried out by means of the transaction subject to examination. Whereas the former is simpler and easier to prove on the basis of factual evidence, the latter is more demanding because in the absence of an acquisition of control no concentration arises.

3.5. *Turnover of State-owned companies*

43. While Article 5(4) sets out the method for determining the economic grouping to which an undertaking concerned belongs for the purpose of calculating turnover, it should be read in conjunction with recital 12 to Regulation (EEC) No 4064/89 in respect of State-owned enterprises. This recital states that in order to avoid discrimination between the public and private sector, account should be taken "of undertakings making up an economic unit with an independent power of decision, irrespective of the way in which their capital is held or of the rules of administrative supervision applicable to them". Thus the mere fact that two companies are both State-owned should not automatically lead to the conclusion that they are part of a group for the purposes of Article 5. Rather, it should be considered whether there are grounds to consider that each company constitutes an independent economic unit.

44. Thus where a State-owned company is not part of an overall industrial holding company and is not subject to any coordination with other State-controlled holdings, it should be treated as an independent group for the purposes of Article 5, and the turnover of other companies owned by that State should not be taken into account. Where, however, a Member State's interests are grouped together in holding companies, or are managed together, or where for other reasons it is clear that State-owned companies form part of an "economic unit with an

---

[10] For example, company A and company B set up a joint venture C. These two parent companies exercise at the same time joint control of company D, although A has 60% and B 40% of the capital. When calculating the turnover of A and B at the time they set up the new joint venture C, the turnover of D with third parties is attributed in equal parts to A and B.

[11] See for example Case IV/M.806 — BA/TAT, of 26 August 1996.

[12] See for example Case IV/M.126 — Accor/Wagons-Lits, of 28 April 1992, and Case IV/M.940 — UBS/ Mister Minit, of 9 July 1997.

independent power of decision'', then the turnover of those businesses should be considered part of the group of the undertaking concerned's for the purposes of Article 5.

II. GEOGRAPHICAL ALLOCATION OF TURNOVER

1. General rule

45. The thresholds other than those set by Article 1(2)(a) and Article 1(3)(a) select cases which have sufficient turnover within the Community in order to be of Community interest and which are primarily cross-border in nature. They require turnover to be allocated geographically to achieve this. The second subparagraph of Article 5(1) provides that the location of turnover is determined by the location of the customer at the time of the transaction:

> ''Turnover, in the Community or in a Member State, shall comprise products sold and services provided to undertakings or consumers, in the Community or in that Member State as the case may be.''

46. The reference to ''products sold'' and ''services provided'' is not intended to discriminate between goods and services by focusing on where the sale takes place in the case of goods but the place where a service is provided (which might be different from where the service was sold) in the case of services. In both cases, turnover should be attributed to the place where the customer is located because that is, in most circumstances, where a deal was made, where the turnover for the supplier in question was generated and where competition with alternative supppliers took place[13]. The second subparagraph of Article 5(1) does not focus on where a good or service is enjoyed or the benefit of the good or service derived. In the case of a mobile good, a motor car may well be driven across Europe by its purchaser but it was purchased at only one place — Paris, Berlin or Madrid say. This is also true in the case of those services where it is possible to separate the purchase of a service from its delivery. Thus in the case of package holidays, competition for the sale of holidays through travel agents takes place locally, as with retail shopping, even though the service may be provided in a number of distant locations. This turnover is, however, earned locally and not at the site of an eventual holiday.

47. This applies even where a multinational corporation has a Community buying strategy and sources all its requirements for a good or service from one location. The fact that the components are subsequently used in ten different plants in a variety of Member States does not alter the fact that the transaction with a company outside the group occurred in only one country. The subsequent distribution to other sites is purely an internal question for the company concerned.

48. Certain sectors do, however, pose very particular problems with regard to the geographical allocation of turnover (se Section III).

2. Conversion of turnover into ecu

49. When converting turnover figures into ecu great care should be taken with the exchange rate used. The annual turnover of a company should be converted at the average rate for the twelve months concerned. This average can be obtained from the Commission. The audited annual turnover figures should not be broken down into component quarterly, monthly, or weekly sales figures which are converted individually at the corresponding average quarterly, monthly or weekly rates, with the ecu figures then added to give a total for the year.

50. When a company has sales in a range of currencies, the procedure is no different. The total turnover given in the consolidated audited accounts and in that company's reporting currency

---

[13] If the place where the customer was located when purchasing the goods or service and the place where the billing was subsequently made are different, turnover should be allocated to the former.

is converted into ecu at the average rate for the twelve months. Local currency sales should not be converted directly into ecu since these figures are not from the consolidated audited accounts of the company.

III. CREDIT AND OTHER FINANCIAL INSTITUTIONS AND INSURANCE UNDERTAKINGS

1. Definitions

51. The specific nature of banking and insurance activities is formally recognized by the Merger Regulation which includes specific provisions dealing with the calculation of turnover for these sectors[14]. Although the Merger Regulation does not provide a definition of the terms, "credit institutions and other financial institutions" within the meaning of point (a) of Article 5(3), the Commission in its practice has consistently adopted the definitions provided in the First and Second Banking Directives:

— "Credit institution means an undertaking whose business is to receive deposits or other repayable funds from the public and to grant credits for its own account[15]".
— "Financial institution shall mean an undertaking other than a credit institution, the principal activity of which is to acquire holdings or to carry one or more of the activities listed in points 2 to 12 in the Annex[16]".

52. From the definition of "financial institution" given above, it is clear that on the one hand holding companies must be regarded as financial institutions and, on the other hand, that undertakings which perform on a regular basis as a principal activity one or more activities expressly mentioned in points 2 to 12 of the abovementioned Annex must also be regarded as financial institutions within the meaning of point (a) of Article 5(3) of the Merger Regulation. These activities include:

— lending (*inter alia*, consumer credit, mortgage credit, factoring, . . .),
— financial leasing,
— money transmission services,
— issuing and managing instruments of payment (credit cards, travellers' cheques and bankers' drafts),
— guarantees and commitments,
— trading on own account or on account of customers in money market instruments, foreign exchange, financial futures and options, exchange and interest rate instruments, and transferable securities,
— participation in share issues and the provision of services related to such issues,
— advice to undertakings on capital structure, industrial stratetgy and related questions and advice and services relating to mergers and the purchase of undertakings,
— money broking,
— portfolio management and advice,
— safekeeping and administration of securities.

---

[14] See Article 5(3) of the Merger Regulation.
[15] Article 1 of First Council Directive 77/780/EEC of 12 December 1977 on the coordination of laws, regulations and administrative provisions relating to the taking up and pursuit of the business of credit institutions (OJ L322, 17.12.1977, p. 30).
[16] Article 1(6) of Second Council Directive 89/646/EEC of 15 December 1989 on the coordination of laws, regulations and administrative provisions relating to the taking up and pursuit of the business of credit institutions (OJ L386, 30.12.1989, p. 1).

2. Calculation of turnover

53. The methods of calculation of turnover for credit and other financial institutions and for insurance undertakings are described in Article 5(3) of the Merger Regulation. The purpose of this Section is to provide an answer to supplementary questions related to turnover calculation for the abovementioned types of undertakings which were raised during the first years of the application of the Merger Regulation.

2.1. *Credit and financial institutions (other than financial holding companies)*

2.1.1. *General*

54. There are normally no particular difficulties in applying the banking income criterion for the definition of the worldwide turnover to credit institutions and other kinds of financial institutions. Difficulties may arise for determining turnover within the Community and also within individual member States. For this purpose, the appropriate criterion is that of the residence of the branch or division, as provided by Article 5(3)(a)(v), second subparagraph, of the Merger Regulation.

2.1.2. *Turnover of leasing companies*

55. There is a fundamental distinction to be made between financial leases and operating leases. Basically, financial leases are made for longer periods than operating leases and ownership is generally transferred to the lessee at the end of the lease term by means of a purchase option included in the lease contract. Under an operating lease, on the contrary, ownership is not transferred to the lessee at the end of the lease term and the costs of maintenance, repair and insurance of the leased equipment are included in the lease payments. A financial lease therefore functions as a loan by the lessor to enable the lessee to purchase a given asset. A financial leasing company is thus a financial institution within the meaning of point (a) of Article 5(3) and its turnover has to be calculated by applying the specific rules related to the calculation of turnover for credit and other financial institutions. Given that operational leasing activities do not have this lending function, they are not considered as carried out by financial institutions, at least as primary activities, and therefore the general turnover calculation rules of Article 5(1) should apply[17].

2.2. *Insurance undertakings*

2.2.1. *Gross premiums written*

56. The application of the concept of gross premiums written as a measure of turnover for insurance undertakings has raised supplementary questions notwithstanding the definition provided in point (b) of Article 5(3) of the Merger Regulation. The following clarifications are appropriate:

— "gross" premiums written are the sum of received premiums (which may include received reinsurance premiums if the undertaking concerned has activities in the field of reinsurance). Outgoing or outward reinsurance premiums, i.e. all amounts paid and payable by the undertaking concerned to get reinsurance cover, are already included in the gross premiums written within the meaning of the Merger Regulation,

— wherever the word "premiums" is used (gross premiums, net (earned) premiums, outgoing reinsurance premiums, etc.), these premiums are related not only to new insurance contracts made during the accounting year being considered but also to all premiums related to contracts made in previous years which remain in force during the period taken into consideration.

---

[17] See Case IV/M.234 — GECC/Avis Lease, 15 July 1992.

2.2.2. *Investments of insurance undertakings*

57. In order to constitute appropriate reserves allowing for the payment of claims, insurance undertakings, which are also considered as institutional investors, usually hold a huge portfolio of investments in shares, interest-bearing securities, land and property and other assets which provide an annual revenue which is not considered as turnover for insurance undertakings.

58. With regard to the application of the Merger Regulation, a major distinction should be made between pure financial investments, in which the insurance undertaking is not involved in the management of the undertakings where the investments have been made, and those investments leading to the acquisition of an interest giving control in a given undertaking thus allowing the insurance undertaking to exert a decisive influence on the business conduct of the subsidiary or affiliated company concerned. In such cases Article 5(4) of the Merger Regulation would apply, and the turnover of the subsidiary or affiliated company should be added to the turnover of the insurance undertaking for the determination of the thresholds laid down in the Merger Regulation[18].

2.3. *Financial holding companies*[19]

59. A financial holding company is a financial institution and therefore the calculation of its turnover should follow the criteria established in point (a) of Article 5(3) for the calculation of turnover for credit and other financial institutions. However, since the main purpose of a financial holding is to acquire and manage participation in other undertakings, Article 5(4) also applies, (as for insurance undertakings), with regard to those participations allowing the financial holding company to exercise a decisive influence on the business conduct of the undertakings in question. Thus, the turnover of a financial holding is basically to be calculated according to Article 5(3), but it may be necessary to add turnover of undertakings falling withn the categories set out in Article 5(4) (''Article 5(4) companies'').

In practice, the turnover of the financial holding company (non-consolidated) must first be taken into account. Then the turnover of the Article 5(4) companies must be added, whilst taking care to deduct dividends and other income distributed by those companies to the financial holdings. The following provides an example for this kind of calculation:

		ECU million
1.	Turnover related to financial activities (from non-consolidated P&L)	3 000
2.	Turnover related to insurance Article 5(4) companies (gross premiums written)	300
3.	Turnover of industrial Article 5(4) companies	2 000
4.	Deduct dividends and other income derived from Article 5(4) companies 2 and 3	(200)
5.	Total turnover financial holding and its group	5 100

60. In such calculations different accounting rules, in particular those related to the preparation of consolidated accounts, which are to some extent harmonised but not identical within the Community, may need to be taken into consideration. Whilst this consideration applies to any type of undertaking concerned by the Merger Regulation, it is particularly important in the case of financial holding companies[20] where the number and the diversity of enterprises controlled and the degree of control the holding holds on its subsidiaries, affiliated companies and other companies in which it has shareholding requires careful examination.

61. Turnover calculation for financial holding companies as described above may in practice

---

[18] See Case IV/M.018 — AG/AMEV, of 21 November 1990.
[19] The principles set out in this paragraph for financial holdings may to a certain extent be applied to fund management companies.
[20] See for example Case IV/M.166 — Torras/Sarrió, of 24 February 1992, Case IV/M.213 — Hong Kong and Shanghai Bank/Midland, of 21 May 1992, IV/M.192 — Banesto/Totta, of 14 April 1992.

prove onerous. Therefore a strict and detailed application of this method will be necessary only in cases where it seems that the turnover of a financial holding company is likely to be close to the Merger Regulation thresholds; in other cases it may well be obvious that the turnover is far from the thresholds of the Merger Regulation, and therefore the published accounts are adequate for the establishment of jurisdiction.

Appendix 8

COMMISSION NOTICE
on the definition of relevant market for the purposes of
Community competition law (OJ 1997 C372/03)

I. INTRODUCTION

1. The purpose of this notice is to provide guidance as to how the Commission applies the concept of relevant product and geographic market in its ongoing enforcement of Community competition law, in particular the application of Council Regulation No 17 and (EEC) No 4064/89, their equivalents in other sectoral applications such as transport, coal and steel, and agriculture, and the relevant provisions of the EEA Agreement[1]. Throughout this notice, references to Articles 85 and 86 of the Treaty and to merger control are to be understood as referring to the equivalent provisions in the EEA Agreement and the ECSC Treaty.

2. Market definition is a tool to identify and define the boundaries of competition between firms. It serves to establish the framework within which competition policy is applied by the Commission. The main purpose of market definition is to identify in a systematic way the competitive constraints that the undertakings involved[2] face. The objective of defining a market in both its product and geographic dimension is to identify those actual competitors of the undertakings involved that are capable of constraining those undertakings' behaviour and of preventing them from behaving independently of effective competitive pressure. It is from this perspective that the market definition makes it possible *inter alia* to calculate market shares that would convey meaningful information regarding market power for the purposes of assessing dominance or for the purposes of applying Article 85.

3. It follows from point 2 that the concept of ''relevant market'' is different from other definitions of market often used in other contexts. For instance, companies often use the term ''market'' to refer to the area where it sells its products or to refer broadly to the industry or sector where it belongs.

4. The definition of the relevant market in both its product and its geographic dimensions often has a decisive influence on the assessment of a competition case. By rendering public the procedures which the Commission follows when considering market definition and by indicating the criteria and evidence on which it relies to reach a decision, the Commission expects to increase the transparency of its policy and decision-making in the area of competition policy.

5. Increased transparency will also result in companies and their advisers being able to better anticipate the possibility that the Commission may raise competition concerns in an individual case. Companies could, therefore, take such a possibility into account in their own internal decision-making when contemplating, for instance, acquisitions, the creation of joint ventures, or the establishment of certain agreements. It is also intended that companies should be in a

---

[1] The focus of assessment in State aid cases is the aid recipient and the industry/sector concerned rather than identification of competitive constraints faced by the aid recipient. When consideration of market power and therefore of the relevant market are raised in any particular case, elements of the approach outlined here might serve as a basis for the assessment of State aid cases.

[2] For the purposes of this notice, the undertakings involved will be, in the case of a concentration, the parties to the concentration; in investigations within the meaning of Article 86 of the Treaty, the undertaking being investigated or the complainants; for investigations within the meaning of Article 85, the parties to the Agreement.

better position to understand what sort of information the Commission considers relevant for the purposes of market definition.

6. The Commission's interpretation of ''relevant market'' is without prejudice to the interpretation which may be given by the Court of Justice or the Court of First Instance of the European Communities.

II. DEFINITION OF RELEVANT MARKET

Definition of relevant product market and relevant geographic market

7. The Regulations based on Article 85 and 86 of the Treaty, in particular in section 6 of Form A/B with respect to Regulation No 17, as well as in section 6 of Form CO with respect to Regulation (EEC) No 4064/89 on the control of concentrations having a Community dimension have laid down the following definitions, ''Relevant product markets'' are defined as follows:

''A relevant product market comprises all those products and/or services which are regarded as interchangeable or substitutable by the consumer, by reason of the products' characteristics, their prices and their intended use''.

8. ''Relevant geographic markets'' are defined as follows:

''The relevant geographic market comprises the area in which the undertakings concerned are involved in the supply and demand of products or services, in which the conditions of competition are sufficiently homogeneous and which can be distinguished from neighbouring areas because the conditions of competition are appreciahbly different in those areas''.

9. The relevant market within which to assess a given competition issue is therefore established by the combination of the product and geographic markets. The Commission interprets the definitions in paragraphs 7 and 8 (which reflect the case-law of the Court of Justice and the Court of First Instance as well as its own decision-making practice) according to the orientations defined in this notice.

Concept of relevant market and objectives of Community competition policy

10. The concept of relevant market is closely related to the objectives pursued under Community competition policy. For example, under the Community's merger control, the objective in controlling structural changes in the supply of a product/service is to prevent the creation or reinforcement of a dominant position as a result of which effective competition would be significantly impeded in a substantial part of the common market. Under the Community's competition rules, a dominant position is such that a firm or group of firms would be in a position to behave to an appreciable extent independently of its competitors, customers and ultimately of its consumers[3]. Such a position would usually arise when a firm or group of firms accounted for a large share of the supply in any given market, provided that other factors analysed in the assessment (such as entry barriers, customers' capacity to react, etc.) point in the same direction.

11. The same approach is followed by the Commission in its application of Article 86 of the Treaty to firms that enjoy a single or collective dominant position. Within the meaning of Regulation No 17, the Commission has the power to investigate and bring to an end abuses of such a dominant position, which must also be defined by reference to the relevant market. Markets may also need to be defined in the application of Article 85 of the Treaty, in particular, in determining whether an appreciable restriction of competition exists or in establishing if the

---

[3] Definition given by the Court of Justice in its judgment of 13 February 1979 in Case 85/76, Hoffmann-La Roche [1979] ECR 461, and confirmed in subsequent judgments.

condition pursuant to Article 85 (3) (b) for an exemption from the application of Article 85 (1) is met.

12. The criteria for defining the relevant market are applied generally for the analysis of certain types of behaviour in the market and for the analysis of structural changes in the supply of products. This methodology, though, might lead to different results depending on the nature of the competition issue being examined. For instance, the scope of the geographic market might be different when analysing a concentration, where the analysis is essentially prospective, from an analysis of past behaviour. The different time horizon considered in each case might lead to the result that different geographic markets are defined for the same products depending on whether the Commission is examining a change in the structure of supply, such as a concentration or a cooperative joint venture, or examining issues relating to certain past behaviour.

Basic principles for market definition

Competitive constraints

13. Firms are subject to three main sources or competitive constraints: demand substitutability, supply substitutability and potential competition. From an economic point of view, for the definition of the relevant market, demand substitution constitutes the most immediate and effective disciplinary force on the suppliers of a given product, in particular in relation to their pricing decisions. A firm or a group of firms cannot have a significant impact on the prevailing conditions of sale, such as prices, if its customers are in a position to switch easily to available substitute products or to suppliers located elsewhere. Basically, the exercise of market definition consists in identifying the effective alternative sources of supply for the customers of the undertakings involved, in terms both of products/services and of geographic location of suppliers.

14. The competitive constraints arising from supply side substitutability other than those described in paragraphs 20 to 23 and from potential competition are in general less immediate and in any case require an analysis of additional factors. As a result such constraints are taken into account at the assessment stage of competition analysis.

Demand substitution

15. The assessment of demand substitution entails a determination of the range of products which are viewed as substitutes by the consumer. One way of making this determination can be viewed as a speculative experiment, postulating a hypothetical small, lasting change in relative prices and evaluating the likely reactions of customers to that increase. The exercise of market definition focuses on prices for operational and practical purposes, and more precisely on demand substitution arising from small, permanent changes in relative prices. This concept can provide clear indications as to the evidence that is relevant in defining markets.

16. Conceptually, this approach means that, starting from the type of products that the undertakings involved sell and the area in which they sell them, additional products and areas will be included in, or excluded from, the market definition depending on whether competition from these other products and areas affect or restrain sufficiently the pricing of the parties' products in the short term.

17. The question to be answered is whether the parties' customers would switch to readily available substitutes or to suppliers located elsewhere in response to a hypothetical small (in the range 5% to 10%) but permanent relative price increase in the products and areas being considered. If substitution were enough to make the price increase unprofitable because of the resulting loss of sales, additional substitutes and areas are included in the relevant market. This would be done until the set of products and geographical areas is such that small, permanent increases in relative prices would be profitable. The equivalent analysis is applicable in cases concerning the concentration of buying power, where the starting point would then be the supplier and the price test serves to identify the alternative distribution channels or outlets for

the supplier's products. In the application of these principles, careful account should be taken of certain particular situations as described within paragraphs 56 and 58.

18. A practical example of this test can be provided by its application to a merger of, for instance, soft-drink bottlers. An issue to examine in such a case would be to decide whether different flavours of soft drinks belong to the same market. In practice, the quetsion to address would be whether consumers of flavour A would switch to other flavours when confronted with a permanent price increase of 5% to 10% for flavour A. If a sufficient number of consumers would switch to, say, flavour B, to such an extent that the price increase for flavour A would not be profitable owing to the resulting loss of sales, then the market would comprise at least flavours A and B. The process would have to be extended in addition to other available flavours until a set of products is identified for which a price rise would not induce a sufficient substitution in demand.

19. Generally, and in particular for the analysis of merger cases, the price to take into account will be the prevailing market price. This may not be the case where the prevailing price has been determined in the absence of sufficient competition. In particular for the investigation of abuses of dominant positions, the fact that the prevailing price might already have been substantially increased will be taken into account.

Supply substitution

20. Supply-side substitutability may also be taken into account when defining markets in those situations in which its effects are equivalent to those of demand substitution in terms of effectiveness and immediacy. This means that suppliers are able to switch production to the relevant products and market them in the short term[4] without incurring significant additional costs or risks in response to small and permanent changes in relative prices. When these conditions are met, the additional production that is put on the market will have a disciplinary effect on the competitive behaviour of the companies involved. Such an impact in terms of effectiveness and immediacy is equivalent to the demand substitution effect.

21. These situations typically arise when companies market a wide range of qualities or grades of one product; even if, for a given final customer or group of consumers, the different qualities are not substitutable, the different qualities will be grouped into one product market, provided that most of the suppliers are able to offer and sell the various qualities immediately and without the significant increases in costs described above. In such cases, the relevant product market will encompass all products that are substitutable in demand and supply, and the current sales of those products will be aggregated so as to give the total value or volume of the market. The same reasoning may lead to group different geographic areas.

22. A practical example of the approach to supply-side substitutability when defining product markets is to be found in the case of paper. Paper is usually supplied in a range of different qualities, from standard writing paper to high quality papers to be used, for instance, to publish art books. From a demand point of view, different qualities of paper cannot be used for any given use, i.e. an art book or a high quality publication cannot be based on lower quality papers. However, paper plants are prepared to manufacture the different qualities, and production can be adjusted with negligible costs and in a short time-frame. In the absence of particular difficulties in distribution, paper manufacturers are able therefore, to compete for orders of the various qualities, in particular if orders are placed with sufficient lead time to allow for modification of production plans. Under such circumstances, the Commission would not define a separate market for each quality of paper and its respective use. The various qualities of paper are included in the relevant market, and their sales added up to estimate total market value and volume.

---

[4] That is such a period that does not entail a significant adjustment of existing tangible and intangible assets (see paragraph 23).

23. When supply-side substitutability would entail the need to adjust significantly existing tangible and intangible assets, additional investments, strategic decisions or time delays, it will not be considered at the stage of market definition. Examples where supply-side substitution did not induce the Commission to enlarge the market are offered in the area of consumer products, in particular for branded beverages. Although bottling plants may in principle bottle different beverages, there are costs and lead times involved (in terms of advertising, product testing and distribution) before the products can actually be sold. In these cases, the effects of supply-side substitutability and other forms of potential competition would then be examined at a later stage.

Potential competition

24. The third source of competitive constraint, potential competition, is not taken into account when defining markets, since the conditions under which potential competition will actually represent an effective competitive constraint depend on the analysis of specific factors and circumstances related to the conditions of entry. If required, this analysis is only carried out at a subsequent stage, in general once the position of the companies involved in the relevant market has already been ascertained, and when such position gives rise to concerns from a competition point of view.

III. EVIDENCE RELIED ON TO DEFINE RELEVANT MARKETS

The process of defining the relevant market in practice

Product dimension

25. There is a range of evidence permitting an assessment of the extent to which substitution would take place. In individual cases, certain types of evidence will be determinant, depending very much on the characteristics and specificity of the industry and products or services that are being examined. The same type of evidence may be of no importance in other cases. In most cases, a decision will have to be based on the consideration of a number of criteria and different items of evidence. The Commission follows an open approach to empirical evidence, aimed at making an effective use of all available information which may be relevant in individual cases. The Commission does not follow a rigid hierarchy of different sources of information or types of evidence.

26. The process of defining relevant markets may be summarized as follows: on the basis of the preliminary information available or information submitted by the undertakings involved, the Commission will usually be in position to broadly establish the possible relevant markets within which, for instance, a concentration or a restriction of competition has to be assessed. In general, and for all practical purposes when handling individual cases, the question will usually be to decide on a few alternative possible relevant markets. For instance, with respect to the product market, the issue will often be to establish whether product A and product B belong or do not belong to the same product market. It is often the case that the inclusion of product B would be enough to remove any competition concerns.

27. In such situations it is not necessary to consider whether the market includes additional products, or to reach a definitive conclusion on the precise product market. If under the conceivable alternative market definitions the operation in question does not raise competition concerns, the question of market definition will be left open, reducing thereby the burden on companies to supply information.

Geographic dimension

28. The Commission's approach to geographic market definition might be summarized as follows: it will take a preliminary view of the scope of the geographic market on the basis of broad indications as to the distribution of market shares between the parties and their competitors, as

well as a preliminary analysis of pricing and price differences at national and Community or EEA level. This initial view is used basically as a working hypothesis to focus the Commission's enquiries for the purposes of arriving at a precise geographic market definition.

29. The reasons behind any particular configuration of prices and market shares need to be explored. Companies might enjoy high market shares in their domestic markets just because of the weight of the past, and conversely, a homogeneous presence of companies throughout the EEA might be consistent with national or regional geographic markets. The initial working hypothesis will therefore be checked against an analysis of demand characteristics (importance of national or local preferences, current patterns of purchases of customers, product differentiation/brands, other) in order to establish whether companies in different areas do indeed constitute a real alternative source of supply for consumers. The theoretical experiment is again based on substitution arising from changes in relative prices, and the question to answer is again whether the customers of the parties would switch their orders to companies located elsewhere in the short term and at a negligible cost.

30. If necessary, a further check on supply factors will be carried out to ensure that those companies located in differing areas do not face impediments in developing their sales on competitive terms throughout the whole geographic market. This analysis will include an examination of requirements for a local presence in order to sell in that area the conditions of access to distribution channels, costs associated with setting up a distribution network, and the presence or absence of regulatory barriers arising from public procurement, price regulations, quotas and tariffs limiting trade or production, technical standards, monopolies, freedom of establishment, requirements for administrative authorizations packaging regulations, etc. In short, the Commission will identify possible obstacles and barriers isolating companies located in a given area from the competitive pressure of companies located outside that area, so as as to determine the precise degree of market interpenetration at national, European or global level.

31. The actual pattern and evolution of trade flows offers useful supplementary indications as to the economic importance of each demand or supply factor mentioned above, and the extent to which they may or may not constitute actual barriers creating different geographic markets. The analysis of trade flows will generally address the question of transport costs and the extent to which these may hinder trade between different areas, having regard to plant location, costs of production and relative price levels.

Market integration in the Community

32. Finally, the Commission also takes into account the continuing process of market integration, in particular in the Community, when defining geographic markets, especially in the area of concentrations and structural joint ventures. The measures adopted and implemented in the internal market programme to remove barriers to trade and further integrate the Community markets cannot be ignored when assessing the effects on competition of a concentration or a structural joint venture. A situation where national markets have been artificially isolated from each other because of the existence of legislative barriers that have now been removed will generally lead to a cautious assessment of past evidence regarding prices, market shares or trade patterns. A process of market integration that would, in the short term, lead to wider geographic markets may therefore be taken into consideration when defining the geographic market for the purposes of assessing concentration and joint ventures.

The process of gathering evidence

33. When a precise market definition is deemed necessary, the Commission will often contact the main customers and the main companies in the industry to enquire into their views about the boundaries of product and geographic markets and to obtain the necessary factual evidence to reach a conclusion. The Commission might also contact the relevant professional associations, and companies active in upstream markets, so as to be able to define, in so far as necessary, separate product and geographic markets, for different levels of production or distri-

bution of the products/services in question. It might also request additional information to the undertakings involved.

34. Where appropriate, the Commission will address written requests for information to the market players mentioned above. These requests will usually include questions relating to the perceptions of companies about reactions to hypothetical price increases and their views of the boundaries of the relevant market. They will also ask for provision of the factual information the Commission deems necessary to reach a conclusion on the extent of the relevant market. The Commission might also discuss with marketing directors or other officers of those companies to gain a better understanding on how negotiations between suppliers and customers take place and better understand issues relating to the definition of the relevant market. Where appropriate, they might also carry out visits or inspections to the premises of the parties, their customers and/or their competitors, in order to better understand how products are manufactured and sold.

35. The type of evidence relevant to reach a conclusion as to the product market can be categorized as follows:

Evidence to define markets — product dimension

36. An analysis of the product characteristics and its intended use allows the Commission, as a first step, to limit the field of investigation of possible substitutes. However, product characteristics and intended use are insufficient to show whether two products are demand substitutes. Functional interchangeability or similarity in characteristics may not, in themselves, provide sufficient criteria, because the responsiveness of customers to relative price changes may be determined by other considerations as well. For example, there may be different competitive constraints in the original equipment market for car components and in spare parts, thereby leading to a separate delineation of two relevant markets. Conversely, differences in product characteristics are not in themselves sufficient to exclude demand subtitutability, since this will depend to a large extent on how customers value different characteristics.

37. The type of evidence the Commission considers relevant to assess whether two products are demand substitutes can be categorized as follows:

38. *Evidence of substitution in the recent past.* In certain cases, it is possible to analyse evidence relating to recent past events or shocks in the market that offer actual examples of substitution between two products. When available, this sort of information will normally be fundamental for market definition. If there have been changes in relative prices in the past (all else being equal), the reactions in terms of quantitites demanded will be determinant in establishing substitutability. Launches of new products in the past can also offer useful information, when it is possible to precisely analyse which products have lost sales to the new product.

39. There are a number of *quantitative tests* that have specifically been designed for the purpose of delineating markets. These tests consist of various econometric and statistical approaches estimates of elasticities and cross-price elasticities[5] for the demand of a product, tests based on similarity of price movements over time, the analysis of causality between price series and similarity of price levels and/or their convergence. The Commission takes into account the available quantitative evidence capable of withstanding rigorous scrutiny for the purposes of establishing patterns of substitution in the past.

40. *Views of customers and competitors.* The Commission often contacts the main customers and competitors of the companies involved in its enquiries, to gather their views on the boundaries of the product market as well as most of the factual information it requires to reach a

---

[5] Own-price elasticity of demand for product X is a measure of the responsiveness of demand for X to percentage change in its own price. Cross-price elasticity between products X and Y is the responsiveness of demand for product X to percentage change in the price of product Y.

conclusion on the scope of the market. Reasoned answers of customers and competitors as to what would happen if relative prices for the candidate products were to increase in the candidate geographic area by a small amount (for instance of 5% to 10%) are taken into account when they are sufficiently backed by factual evidence.

41. *Consumer preferences.* In the case of consumer goods, it may be difficult for the Commission to gather the direct views of end consumers about substitute products. *Marketing studies* that companies have commissioned in the past and that are used by companies in their own decision-making as to pricing of their products and/or marketing actions may provide useful information for the Commission's delineation of the relevant market. Consumer surveys on usage patterns and attitudes, data from consumer's purchasing patterns, the views expressed by retailers and more generally, market research studies submitted by the parties and their competitors are taken into account to establish whether an economically significant proportion of consumers consider two products as substitutable, also taking into account the importance of brands for the products in question. The methodology followed in consumer surveys carried out *ad hoc* by the undertakings involved or their competitors for the purposes of a merger procedure or a procedure pursuant to Regulation No 17 will usually be scrutinized with utmost care. Unlike pre-existing studies, they have not been prepared in the normal course of business for the adoption of business decisions.

42. *Barriers and costs associated with switching demand to potential substitutes.* There are a number of barriers and costs that might prevent the Commission from considering two *prima facie* demand substitutes as belonging to one single product market. It is not possible to provide an exhaustive list of all the possible barriers to substitution and of switching costs. These barriers or obstacles might have a wide range of origins, and in its decisions, the Commission has been confronted with regulatory barriers or other forms of State intervention, constraints arising in downstream markets, need to incur specific capital investment or loss in current output in order to switch to alternative inputs, the location of customers, specific investment in production process, learning and human capital investment, retooling costs or other investments, uncertainty about quality and reputation of unknown suppliers, and others.

43. *Different categories of customers and price discrimination.* The extent of the product market might be narrowed in the presence of distinct groups of customers. A distinct group of customers for the relevant product may constitute a narrower, distinct market when such a group could be subject to price discrimination. This will usually be the case when two conditions are met: (a) it is possible to identify clearly which group an individual customer belongs to at the moment of selling the relevant products to him, and (b) trade among customers or arbitrage by third parties should not be feasible.

Evidence for defining markets — geographic dimension

44. The type of evidence the Commission considers relevant to reach a conclusion as to the geographic market can be categorized as follows:

45. *Past evidence of diversion of orders to other areas.* In certain cases, evidence on changes in prices between different areas and consequent reactions by customers might be available. Generally, the same quantitative tests used for product market definition might as well be used in geographic market definition, bearing in mind that international comparisons of prices might be more complex due to a number of factors such as exchange rate movements, taxation and product differentiation.

46. *Basic demand characteristics.* The nature of demand for the relevant product may in itself determine the scope of the geographical market. Factors such as national preferences or preferences for national brands, language, culture and life style, and the need for a local presence have a strong potential to limit the geographic scope of competition

47. *Views of customers and competitors.* Where appropriate, the Commission will contact the

main customers and competitors of the parties in its enquiries, to gather their views on the boundaries of the geographic market as well as most of the factual information it requires to reach a conclusion on the scope of the market when they are sufficiently backed by factual evidence.

48. *Current geographic pattern of purchases.* An examination of the customers' current geographic pattern of purchases provides useful evidence as to the possible scope of the geographic market. When customers purchase from companies located anywhere in the Community or the EEA on similar terms, or they procure their supplies through effective tendering procedures in which companies from anywhere in the Community or the EEA submit bids, usually the geographic market will be considered to be Community-wide.

49. *Trade flows/pattern of shipments.* When the number of customers is so large that it is not possible to obtain through them a clear picture of geographic purchasing patterns, information on trade flows might be used alternatively, provided that the trade statistics are available with a sufficient degree of detail for the relevant products. Trade flows, and above all, the rationale behind trade flows provide useful insights and information for the purpose of establishing the scope of the geographic market but are not in themselves conclusive.

50. *Barriers and switching costs associated to divert orders to companies located in other areas.* The absence of trans-border purchases or trade flows, for instance, does not necessarily mean that the market is at most national in scope. Still, barriers isolating the national market have to be identified before it is concluded that the relevant geographic market in such a case is national. Perhaps the clearest obstacle for a customer to divert its orders to other areas is the impact of transport costs and transport restrictions arising from legislation or from the nature of the relevant products. The impact of transport costs will usually limit the scope of the geographic market for bulky, low-value products, bearing in mind that a transport disadvantage might also be compensated by a comparative advantage in other costs (labour costs or raw materials). Access to distribution in a given area, regulatory barriers still existing in certain sectors, quotas and custom tariffs might also constitute barriers isolating a geographic area from the competitive pressure of companies located outside that area. Significant switching costs in procuring supplies from companies located in other countries constitute additional sources of such barriers.

51. On the basis of the evidence gathered, the Commission will then define a geographic market that could range from a local dimension to a global one, and there are examples of both local and global markets in past decisions of the Commission.

52. The paragraphs above describe the different factors which might be relevant to define markets. This does not imply that in each individual case it will be necessary to obtain evidence and assess each of these factors. Often in practice the evidence provided by a subset of these factors will be sufficient to reach a conclusion, as shown in the past decisional practice of the Commission.

IV. CALCULATION OF MARKET SHARE

53. The definition of the relevant market in both its product and geographic dimensions allows the identification the suppliers and and the customers/consumers active on that market. On that basis, a total market size and market shares for each supplier can be calculated on the basis of their sales of the relevant products in the relevant area. In practice, the total market size and market shares are often available from market sources, i.e. companies' estimates, studies commissioned from industry consultants and/or trade associations. When this is not the case, or when available estimates are not reliable, the Commission will usually ask each supplier in the relevant market to provide its own sales in order to calculate total market size and market shares.

54. If sales are usually the reference to calculate market shares, there are nevertheless other indications that, depending on the specific products or industry in question, can offer useful information such as, in particular, capacity, the number of players in bidding markets, units of fleet as in aerospace, or the reserves held in the case of sectors such as mining.

55. As a rule of thumb, both volume sales and value sales provide useful information. In cases of differentiated products, sales in value and their associated market share will usually be considered to better reflect the relative position and strength of each supplier.

V. ADDITIONAL CONSIDERATIONS

56. There are certain areas where the application of the principles above has to be undertaken with care. This is the case when considering primary and secondary markets, in particular, when the behaviour of undertakings at a point in time has to be analysed pursuant to Article 86. The method of defining markets in these cases is the same, i.e. assessing the responses of customers based on their purchasing decisions to relative price changes, but taking into account as well, constraints on substitution imposed by conditions in the connected markets. A narrow definition of market for secondary products, for instance, spare parts, may result when compatibility with the primary product is important. Problems of finding compatible secondary products together with the existence of high prices and a long lifetime of the primary products may render relative price increases of secondary products profitable. A different market definition may result if significant substitution between secondary products is possible or if the characteristics of the primary products make quick and direct consumer responses to relative price increases of the secondary products feasible.

57. In certain cases, the existence of chains of substitution might lead to the definition of a relevant market where products or areas at the extreme of the market are not directly substitutable. An example might be provided by the geographic dimension of a product with significant transport costs. In such cases, deliveries from a given plant are limited to a certain area around each plant by the impact of transport costs. In principle, such an area could constitute the relevant geographic market. However, if the distribution of plants is such that there are considerable overlaps between the areas around different plants, it is possible that the pricing of those products will be constrained by a chain substitution effect, and lead to the definition of a broader geographic market. The same reasoning may apply if product B is a demand substitute for products A and C. Even if products A and C are not direct demand substitutes, they might be found to be in the same relevant product market since their respective pricing might be constrained by substitution to B.

58. From a practical perspective, the concept of chains of substitution has to be corroborated by actual evidence, for instance related to price interdependence at the extremes of the chains of substitution, in order to lead to an extension of the relevant market in an individual case. Price levels at the extremes of the chains would have to be of the same magnitude as well.

Appendix 9

Merger Procedure — Phase I

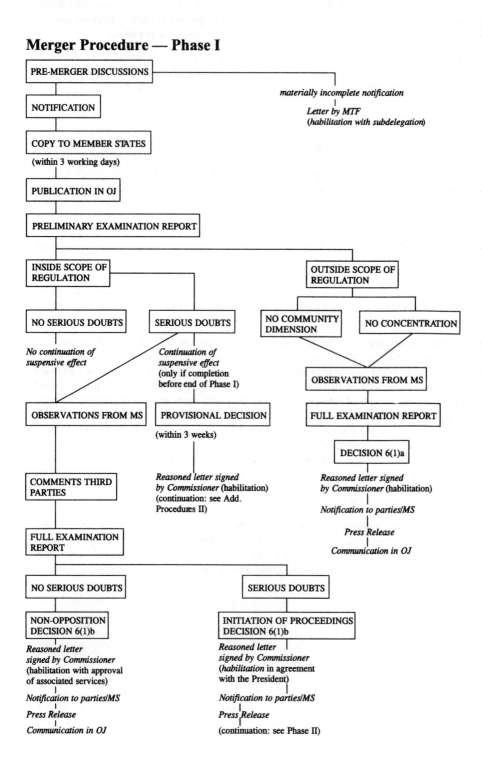

Merger Procedure — Phase II

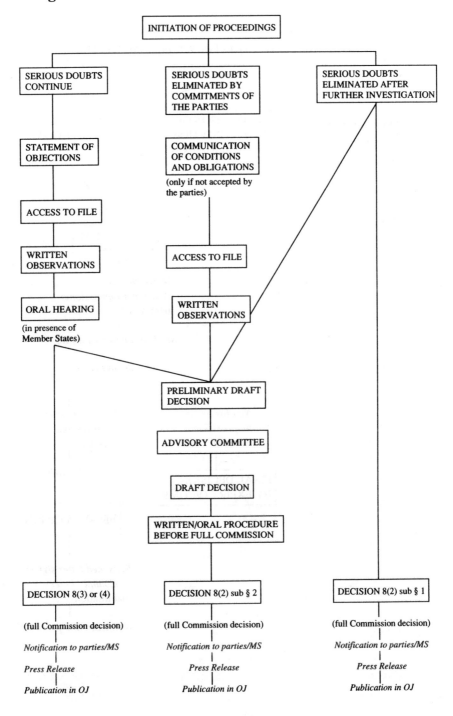

Mergers — Additional Procedures I

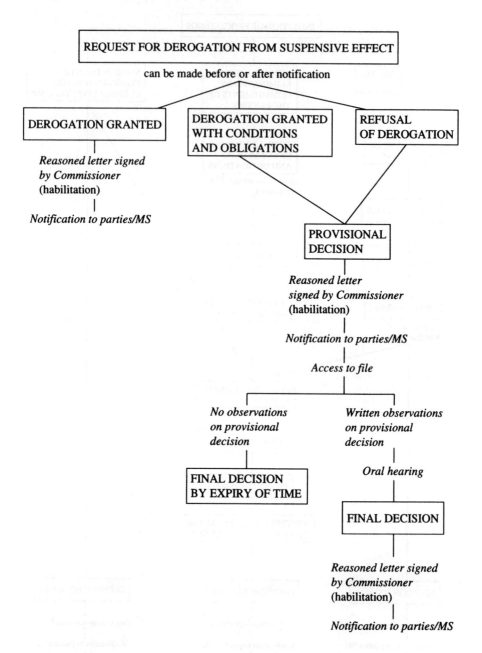

REQUEST FOR DEROGATION FROM SUSPENSIVE EFFECT

can be made before or after notification

DEROGATION GRANTED

Reasoned letter signed by Commissioner (habilitation)

Notification to parties/MS

DEROGATION GRANTED WITH CONDITIONS AND OBLIGATIONS

REFUSAL OF DEROGATION

PROVISIONAL DECISION

Reasoned letter signed by Commissioner (habilitation)

Notification to parties/MS

Access to file

No observations on provisional decision

Written observations on provisional decision

Oral hearing

FINAL DECISION BY EXPIRY OF TIME

FINAL DECISION

Reasoned letter signed by Commissioner (habilitation)

Notification to parties/MS

Mergers — Additional Procedures II

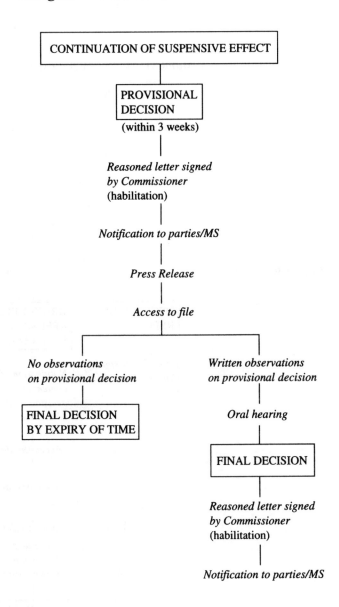

CONTINUATION OF SUSPENSIVE EFFECT

PROVISIONAL
DECISION
(within 3 weeks)

*Reasoned letter signed
by Commissioner*
(habilitation)

Notification to parties/MS

Press Release

Access to file

*No observations
on provisional decision*

*Written observations
on provisional decision*

FINAL DECISION
BY EXPIRY OF TIME

Oral hearing

FINAL DECISION

*Reasoned letter signed
by Commissioner*
(habilitation)

Notification to parties/MS

Mergers — Additional Procedures III

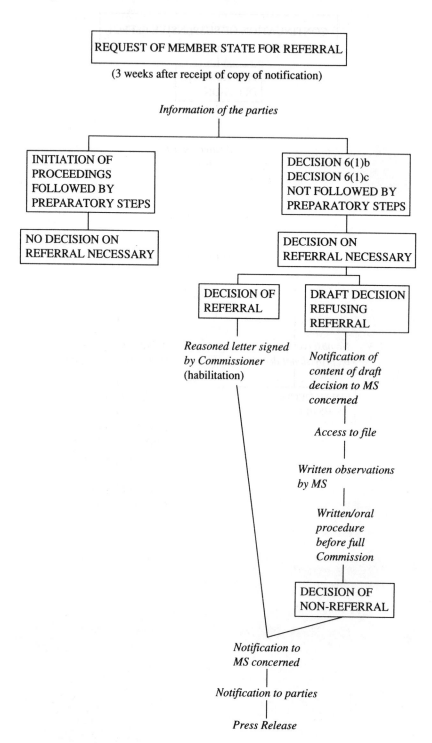

REQUEST OF MEMBER STATE FOR REFERRAL

(3 weeks after receipt of copy of notification)

Information of the parties

INITIATION OF
PROCEEDINGS
FOLLOWED BY
PREPARATORY STEPS

DECISION 6(1)b
DECISION 6(1)c
NOT FOLLOWED BY
PREPARATORY STEPS

NO DECISION ON
REFERRAL NECESSARY

DECISION ON
REFERRAL NECESSARY

DECISION OF
REFERRAL

DRAFT DECISION
REFUSING
REFERRAL

*Reasoned letter signed
by Commissioner*
(habilitation)

*Notification of
content of draft
decision to MS
concerned*

Access to file

*Written observations
by MS*

*Written/oral
procedure
before full
Commission*

DECISION OF
NON-REFERRAL

*Notification to
MS concerned*

Notification to parties

Press Release

Index

References to footnotes are given as e.g. 1.4.6n25, which refers to paragraph 1.4.6, note 25. References to Appendices are given as e.g. App. 1

Abuse of dominant position
see also Dominant position
compatibility test and, 5.1.1n4
intervention test under Article 82, 1.2.1
Access
to file, 4.7.4
third party's, 4.7.7
to supplies or markets, 5.4.3.10
Acquired Rights Directive, 5.8.4,
7.6.3.3, 7.6.5
Acquisition of control
see also Control
Article 3(1)(b) of the Regulation, 2.4
by individual, 3.5.13
joint
existing company, 3.5.7
newly-established company, 3.5.6
by jointly controlled company/joint
venture, 3.5.8
sole
over entire undertaking, 3.5.2
over part of undertaking, 3.5.3, 3.5.4
previously joint control, 3.5.5
Acquisition of control — *cont.*
by State company, 3.5.14
Advisory Committee on
Concentrations, 8.1.4
commitment, transparency and timing,
7.4.5
consultation of, 4.7.8
Agreement *see* **Licence agreement;**
Management agreement; Purchase
agreement; Shareholder
agreement; Supply agreement
Agricultural sector
see also Kali und Salz
machinery, behavioural commitment
and, 7.4.4
Air transport sector *see* **Transport**
sector
Alcohol *see* **Food industry**
Ancillary restraints, 6.1
approach under Article 81, 6.2
confidential information, restriction on
disclosure and use, 6.8

Ancillary restraints—*cont.*
consortium bid, 6.10
conversion of notification and, 4.3.11
evaluation, 6.4
licence of intellectual property and
know-how, 6.6
non-competition clause, 6.5
purchase and supply agreements, 6.9
restrictions, 6.3
directly related, 6.3.1
necessary to implementation of
concentration, 6.3.2
trademark, business name and logo, 6.7
Ancillary Restraints Notice, 1.4.6, 6.1,
6.2
evaluation and, 6.4
licence of intellectual property and, 6.6
non-competition clause and, 6.5
purchase and supply agreements and,
6.9
restrictions and
directly related, 6.3.1
necessary to implementation of
concentration, 6.3.2
text, App. 3
trademark and, 6.7
Anglo American
Advisory Committee and, 8.1.4
commitment, transparency and timing,
7.4.5
control and
direct or indirect, 2.4.2.8
level of shareholding conferring,
2.4.3.4
means of, 2.4.3
qualified minority shareholding,
2.4.3.2
test, 3.4.2n44
divestment and, 7.4.3
Anti-dumping measures, behavioural
commitment and, 7.4.4
Appeal, 1.5.2, 7.1, 7.6.1
challengeable acts, 7.6.2
grounds of, 7.6.4
interim relief, 7.6.5

Appeal — *cont.*
  reopening Commission proceedings
    and, 7.7
  who can bring action, 7.6.3
    competitor, 7.6.3.2
    employee, 7.6.3.3
    shareholder, 7.6.3.1
    third party, 7.6.3.4
Appraisal of concentrations, 5.1
  see also Compatibility test;
      Dominance; *Guinness/Grand*
      Metropolitan; Market definition
  basic objective, 5.1.1
  competition or industrial policy, 5.1.2
  countervailing benefits, 5.8
    efficiency, 5.8.2
    failing firm, 5.8.3
    social considerations, 5.8.4
    technical and economic progress,
      5.8.1
  decision, 5.4, 5.4.1
  nature of appraisal, 5.4.2
Articles 81 and 82, 1.1, 1.2
  access to file and, 4.7.4
  ancillary restraints and, 6.1
  Commission's fact-finding powers and,
    4.6
    investigations, 4.6.2
  joint venture and, 1.4.4
  jurisdiction and, 1.7
  market definition and, 5.3.2
  notification and investigation and, 4.1
  the Regulation and, 1.9, 5.3.1
  use of, 1.2.1
Articles 84 and 85, Regulation 17
  disapplication and, 1.9.4
Assessment, of competitive effect by
  Commission, 1.4.5, 5.1.1n5, 5.1.2
Asset
  non-competition clause and, 6.5
  test, 3.1.2n3
Asset swap, 3.5.11
Assurance, informal, 7.4.8
Audit *see* **Financial services**
Austria, interim relief and, 7.6.5

Bank Accounts Directive, 3.6.1
Banking *see* **Financial services**
Banking Directive
  First, 3.6.1
  Second, 1.6n29, 3.6.1
Barriers to entry, 5.4.3.6
Behavioural commitment, 7.4.4
Behavioural remedies, 7.4.2
  see also Structural remedies
Belgium
  challengeable act and, 7.6.2

Belgium—*cont.*
  Guinness/Grand Metropolitan and,
    5.9.3.4
  level of shareholding conferring
    control, 2.4.3.4
  means of control, 2.4.3
  Member State's request for
    Commission jurisdiction, 8.6.1
Benefits, countervailing *see*
  Countervailing benefits
Brittan, Sir Leon, 8.3.1n27
Broadcasting Directive, 8.4.2.2
Broadcasting sector *see* **Media**
Brownlie, 1.7n31
Business name *see* **Trademark**
Business secret *see* **Confidentiality**
Buyer *see* **Purchaser**

Canada, EC-Canada Co-operation
  Agreement, 1.8
Car manufacturing sector *see*
  Transport sector
Challengeable act, 7.6.2
Chemical industry
  acquisition of sole control over part of
    undertaking and, 3.5.3n54
  autonomous economic entity and,
    2.7.2.1
  behavioural commitment and, 7.4.4
  change in nature of control and, 2.5
  competition and, 5.4.3.5n78
  efficiency and, 5.8.2
  geographic market and, 5.3.3.8
  identifying undertaking concerned and,
    3.4.1
  location and identity of supplier and
    purchaser and, 5.3.3.3
  market share and, 5.4.3.4
  portfolio power and, 5.4.3.9
  product market and, 5.3.2
  regulatory barriers and, 5.3.3.8
  revocation of Decision of Compatibility
    and, 7.3.4
  turnover calculation and, 3.4.2
  world market and, 5.3.3.9
Collective dominance *see* **Oligopoly**
Collusion, 5.6
  tacit, 5.4.3.1
Comity *see* **Positive comity; Traditional**
  comity
Commission *see also* **Competition**
  Policy Report; Decision; DGIV;
  Jurisdiction; Merger Task Force;
  Notices
  Articles 81 and 82 and, 1.2.1
  assessment of competitive effect by,
    1.4.5

Commission—*cont.*
autonomous economic entity and, 2.7.2.1
challengeable acts, 7.6.2
EEA Agreement and, 1.11
EFTA Surveillance Authority co-operation, 8.5
Memorandum on concentrations, 1.2
procedure and practice, 1.1, 1.5.2
Commitment, 7.1
action by third party and, 7.6.3.4
behavioural, 7.4.4
divestment, 7.4.3
informal assurance, 7.4.8
modification and undertaking and, 7.4.1
monitoring, 7.4.6
structural and behavioural remedies, 7.4.2
transparency and timing, 7.4.5
Common Market *see* **Compatibility; Dominance; Market**
Community dimension, 3.1
see also **Turnover threshold**
the Regulation and, 1.4.3
Company Law Directive
Fourth, 2.8.3, 3.3.2, 3.3.6n26
Seventh, 2.8.3, 3.4.2
Third, 2.3
Compatibility
declaration of, 7.3.1
revocation of Decision of, 7.3.4
test, 1.4.5, 5.1, 5.1.1, 5.2
co-ordination effects, 5.5
market definition and, 5.3n28
disapplication of Regulation 17 and, 1.9.2
elements, 5.2.1
vertical issues, 5.6
Competition
see also **Non-competition clause**
divestment order restoring, 7.3.3
dominance and, 5.2.4, 5.4.3.5
"significantly impeding effective competition", 5.4.3.3
international, 5.4.3.5n80
market and, 5.1.2
national authorities *see* National competition authorities
national law and, 8.2
Competition authorities, national *see* **National competition authorities**
Competition Commission (United Kingdom), 4.7.1n86, 8.1.2
Competition Policy Report (Commission) Tenth (1980), use of Articles 81 and 82 and, 1.2.1
Twenty-first (1991), relevant product market and, 5.3.2n36

Competition Policy Report (Commission) Tenth (1980)—*cont.*
Twenty-third (1993)
adoption and review of Regulation and, 1.3
price factors and geographic market and, 5.3.3.2
price factors and product market and, 5.3.2n39
supply-side substitutability and, 5.3.2n43
Twenty-fourth (1994)
commitment and, 7.4.1n12, 7.4.6n39
national law and competition and, 8.2n24
Twenty-seventh (1997)
E.C.–U.S. Co-operation Agreement and, 1.8n48
Regulation supporting instruments and, 1.4.6n25
suspension and, 4.4.1n51
Twenty-eighth (1998)
commitment and, 7.4.1n13, 7.4.5n37
Decision statistics, 1.1n2
reopening Commission proceedings, 7.7n89
Competitive effect, assessment of by Commission, 1.4.5
Competitor
action brought by, 7.6.3.2
appraisal decision and, 5.4.3.5
Compulsory notification, 1.4.1
see also **Form CO; Notification**
Concentration, 2.1
see also Ancillary restraints; Appraisal of concentrations; Control; Joint venture; Undertaking
assessment of by Commission, 1.4.5
Commission Memorandum on, 1.2
Commission Notice on acquisition of control, 1.4.6
co-ordination effects, 5.5
market definition and, 5.3n28
co-operative joint venture and, 2.1
definition in Article 3(1) of the Regulation, 2.2.1
foreign, jurisdiction and, 1.7
meaning of, 2.2
procedure, 1.5.2
the Regulation and, 1.4.2
with a Community dimension
see also Community dimension
Articles 81 and 82 and, 1.9.1, 1.9.3
Articles 84 and 85 and, 1.9.4
assessment by Commission, 1.4.5, 3.1
defined, 3.1.2
jurisdiction and, 1.7
principle of prior control and, 4.3.1

Concentration—*cont.*
　the Regulation and, 1.4.2, 1.9.1
　without a Community dimension
　　Articles 84 and 85 and, 1.9.4
　　below turnover threshold, 3.1.5
　　Commission jurisdiction triggered by
　　　the Regulation (Article 22(3)),
　　　8.6.1
　subject to national control only, 3.1
Concentration Notice, 1.4.6n21, 2.2.1
　common interests and, 2.6.2n68,
　　2.6.2n70, 2.6.2n73
　decisive influence and, 2.4.2.2,
　　2.4.3n37
　joint control and, 2.6
　meaning of merger, 2.3
　means of control and, 2.4.3
　''persons'', 2.2.2
　text, App. 5
Concern *see* **Direct concern; Individual**
　concern
Confidentiality
　access to the file and, 4.7.4
　ancillary restraints and, 6.8
　Commission's request for information
　　and, 4.6.1
　E.C.–U.S. Co-operation Agreement
　　and, 1.8
　publicity of Decisions and, 7.5.5
Consortium bid, 2.7.3
　ancillary restraints and, 6.10
Construction industry
　control and
　　acquisition of joint,
　　　newly-established company,
　　　3.5.6
　　change in nature of, 2.5
　common interests and, 2.6.2n70
　transport costs and, 5.3.3.6
　vertical effects and, 5.6
Control
　see also Acquisition of control; Joint
　　control
　balance of power by small shareholder,
　　2.4.2.3
　de facto sole, 2.4.3.3
　decisive influence, 2.4.2.1
　　exercise of, 2.4.2
　　possibility of, 2.4.2.2
　direct or indirect, 2.4.2.8
　inadvertent change of, 2.4.2.7
　management agreement, 2.4.3.5
　meaning, 2.4.1
　means of, 2.4.3
　nature of, 2.4.2.4
　　change in, 2.5
　prior, principle, 4.3.1
　　access to file and, 4.7.4
　by public authority, 2.4.2.5

Control—*cont.*
　Renault/Volvo, 2.4.3.8
　rights
　　future, 2.4.2.6
　　special, 2.4.3.7
　shareholder agreement, 2.4.3.6
　shareholding
　　level of, 2.4.3.1, 2.4.3.4
　　qualified minority, 2.4.3.2
Control test, 3.4.2
Co-operative joint venture
　see also Joint venture
　compatibility test and, 5.1
　concentration and, 2.1, 2.7.1
　concentrative and
　　Commission Notice on distinction
　　　between, 1.4.6n17
　　Commission Notice on operations
　　　under the Regulation, 1.4.6n20
　conversion of notification and, 4.3.11
Co-ordination effect, compatibility, 5.5
Costs
　sunk, 5.4.3.6
　transport, 5.3.3.6, 8.3.4
Council
　power to disapply Regulation 17, 1.9.2
　reciprocity and, 1.6
Countervailing benefits, 5.8
　efficiency, 5.8.2
　failing firm, 5.8.3
　social considerations, 5.8.4
　technical and economic progress, 5.8.1
Court *see individually named courts;*
　National courts
Court of First Instance
　see also European Court of Justice
　access to file and, 4.7.4
　action brought by employee and,
　　7.6.3.3
　action brought by shareholder and,
　　7.6.3.1
　Advisory Committee consultation and,
　　8.1.4
　challengeable acts and, 7.6.2
　collective dominance and, 1.4.5, 5.7
　Commission jurisdiction and, 1.7
　competition and the market, 5.1.2
　competitor and, 7.6.3.2
　Decisions and
　　appeal from, 1.5.2, 7.6.4
　　reasons for, 7.5.1
　exercise of decisive influence and,
　　2.4.2
　incompatibility and, 5.2.2
　interim relief and, 7.6.5
　previously independent undertaking
　　and, 2.2.4n12
　structural and behavioural remedies
　　and, 7.4.2

Court of First Instance—*cont.*
third party and notification and, 4.5.2
third party's right to be heard and,
4.7.7
Credit institution *see* **Financial services**
Customer
see also **Purchaser**
preference, 5.3.3.5
survey, product market and, 5.3.2

Decision, 1.5.1n26, 7.1
see also **Appeal; Appraisal of
concentrations, decision**
amendment, 7.4.7
final (Article 8), 4.8, 7.3
declaration of compatibility, 7.3.1
declaration of incompatibility, 7.3.2
divestment order, 7.3.3
informal assurances recorded in,
7.4.8
revocation of decision of
compatibility, 7.3.4
habilitation, 7.5.4
initial (Article 6), 4.5.4, 7.2.1, 8.1.2
format, 7.2.2
Stage Two proceedings and, 4.7.2
Media Service Group (MSG), 2.4.2.1
notification of, 7.5.3
publicity, 7.5.5
reasons, 7.5.1
reopening Commission proceedings,
7.7
sanctions for failure to comply with,
7.5.2
subject to judicial review, 1.5.2, 5.1.2
**De minimis transactions, excluded from
the Regulation,** 5.4.1
Defence sector, 8.2
see also **Public security**
legitimate interest and, 8.4.3.1
Demand-side substitutability test, 5.3.1
relevant product market and, 5.3.2
DGIII, 1994 report, 5.1.2n9
DGIV, 1.2.1, 1.5.1
see also **Commission; Merger Task
Force**
challengeable acts and, 7.6.2
conversion of notification and, 4.3.11
habilitation and, 7.5.4
the Regulation and ECSC Treaty, 1.10
website, 4.1n4, 7.5.5
Direct concern, 7.6.3
action brought by shareholder, 7.6.3.1
competitor and, 7.6.3.2
Distinct market, 8.2, 8.3.1
see also **Geographic market**
criterion of, 8.3.2
notification and, 8.1.2

Distinct market—*cont.*
practice, 8.3.4
procedure, 8.3.3
Divestment, 7.4.3
behavioural commitment and, 7.4.4
order restoring competition, 7.3.3
WorldCom/MCI and, 1.8
Document
see also **Access to file**
supporting notification, 4.3.5, 4.3.7
transmission of, 4.9
Dominance, 5.2.3, 5.4.3
see also **Abuse of dominant position;
Oligopoly**
access to supply or market, 5.4.3.10
barriers to entry, 5.4.3.6
buyer power, 5.4.3.7
in Common Market or substantial part
thereof, 5.2.5
compatibility test and, 5.1, 5.1.1
competitive structure and, 5.2.4
competitors, 5.4.3.5
creating or strengthening, 5.2.2
economic and financial power, 5.4.3.8
horizontal and vertical impact, 5.4.3.2
judging, 5.4.2
market share, 5.4.3.4
portfolio power, 5.4.3.9
"significantly impeding effective
competition", 5.4.3.3
single firm or collective, 5.2.6, 5.4.3.1
test, 2.7.1, 5.1.1n5
Dutch clause, 3.1.5n5

E-mail
copies of Decisions by, 7.5.5
transmission of documents by, 4.9
EC Antitrust Procedure **(Kerse),**
4.6.2n80
E.C.–Canada Co-operation Agreement,
1.8
*E.C. Regulation on the Control of
Concentrations between
Undertakings in the Process of
Implementation* **(Janicki),** 4.4.1n49
E.C. Treaty *see* **Treaty of Rome**
*E.C./U.S. Antitrust Co-operation
Agreement: impact on transnational
business* **(Griffin),** 1.8n47
E.C.–U.S. Co-operation Agreement, 1.8,
8.1.3
ECJ *see* **European Court of Justice**
ECSC *see* **European Coal and Steel
Community**
EEA *see* **European Economic Area**
*The EEC Merger Regulation: the first
step toward a one-stop merger
control* **(Hawk),** 5.1.2n8

Effects doctrine, 1.7
EFTA Surveillance Authority, 1.11
  co-operation with Commission, 8.5
  notification documents to, 4.3.7, 8.1.2
Electricity industry *see* **Energy sector**
Elzinga-Hogarty test, 5.3.3.1
Employee
  action brought by, 7.6.3.3
  interim relief and, 7.6.5
Energy sector
  electricity
    distinct market and, 8.3.3, 8.3.4
    public interest and, 8.4.3.2
  gas
    autonomous economic entity and,
      2.7.2.1
    compatibility test and, 5.2.1
    distinct market and, 8.3.4
    market share and, 5.4.3.4
    notification and, 4.3.8
    public procurement and, 5.3.3.7
    transport costs and, 5.3.3.6
  oil
    control by state and, 2.2.4.1
    distinct market and, 8.3.4
    notification and, 4.3.8
  petroleum
    amendment of Decisions and, 7.4.7
    autonomous economic entity and,
      2.7.2.1
    divestment and, 7.4.3
    efficiency and, 5.8.2
    existence of joint control and,
      2.6.1n65
    future rights and, 2.4.2.6
    import duties and, 5.3.3.8
    world market and, 5.3.3.9
Enforcement, 1.7
  EEA Agreement and, 1.11
  investigations and, 4.6.2
**European Coal and Steel Community
    (ECSC) Treaty**
  Commission Notice on alignment of
    procedures for processing mergers
    under, 1.4.6
  the Regulation and, 1.10
  turnover calculation and, 3.3.1
European Court of Justice (ECJ)
  see also **Appeal; Court of First Instance**
  access to the file and, 4.7.4
  ancillary restraints and, 6.2
  Articles 81 and 82 and, 1.2.1
    Regulation 17 disapplication and,
      1.9.2, 1.9.3
  challengeable acts and, 7.6.2
  collective dominance and, 1.4.5, 5.2.6,
    5.7
  Commission jurisdiction and, 1.7
  compatibility test and, 5.2.1

European Court of Justice (ECJ)—
    cont.
  competition and the market, 5.1.2
  dominance and, 5.2.3
  E.C.–U.S. Co-operation Agreement
    and, 1.8
  habilitation and, 7.5.4
  individual concern and, 7.6.3
  informal assurances and, 7.4.8
  jurisdiction, 7.6.1n52, 7.6.4
  market definition and, 5.3, 5.3.1
    geographic, 5.3.3
  monitoring of commitment and, 7.4.6
  oligopoly and the Regulation, 5.1
  public security legitimate interest and,
    8.4.2.1
  undertaking and, 3.4.1
European Economic Area (EEA), 1.11
  co-operation between Commission and
    EFTA Surveillance Authority, 8.5
  geographic market and, 5.3.2.8
  language notification rules, 4.3.7
**European Union, expansion and
    Community-wide turnover,** 3.3.6
Exception
  Regulation, 2.8
  suspension rule, 4.4.3
Exemption, suspension rule, 4.4.4
*Extraterritoriality in U.S. and E.C.
    Antitrust Enforcement* **(Griffin),**
  1.7n44, 1.8n48

Fax, transmission of documents by, 4.9
Financial services
  see also **Insurance**
  appraisal decision and, 5.4.1
  audit *see Price Waterhouse*
  Community dimension
    practical considerations, 3.7
    special rules for financial
      conglomerates, 3.6.3
  credit institution
    assets test, 3.1.2n3
    the Regulation and, 1.3, 2.8.1
    turnover and, 3.3.6
    test, 3.2.3n7
  de facto joint control, 2.6.3
  financial holding company exception
    and, 2.8.3
  level of shareholding conferring
    control, 2.4.3.4
  liquidator and receiver exception and,
    2.8.2
  management buy-out, 3.5.12
  supply conditions and, 5.3.3.4
  suspension rule exemption and, 4.4.4
  two-thirds rule, 3.2.3
  vertical effects and, 5.6

Fines *see* **Sanctions**
Finland, compatibility and
    co-ordination effects, 5.5
Food industry
  see also Perrier
  alcohol
    compatibility vertical issues and, 5.6
    portfolio power and, 5.4.3.9
    regulatory factors and, 5.3.3.8
  buyer power and, 5.4.3.7
  competitors and, 5.4.3.5
  customer preference and, 5.3.3.5
  EEA co-operation case, 8.5n52
  market definition and, 5.3
  motorway restaurant services, relevant
    product market and, 5.3.2n40
  trademarks and, ancillary restraints, 6.7
  two or more undertakings, 2.2.2
  vertical effects and, 5.6
  who can bring action and, 7.6.3
Foreclosure, 5.6
Form A/B
  compatibility and, co-ordination effects,
    5.5
  conversion of notification and, 4.3.11
  turnover calculation and, 3.4.2n40
Form CO, 1.4.6, 1.5.2
  access to supplies or market and,
    5.4.3.10
  appraisal decision and, 5.4.1
  barriers to entry and, 5.4.3.6
  compatibility and
    co-ordination effects, 5.5
    vertical effects, 5.6
  countervailing benefits and, 5.8
  economic and financial power and,
    5.4.3.8
  notification requirements of, 4.3.2,
    4.3.5
  product market information and, 5.3.2
  short-form notification and, 4.3.6
  transmission of, 4.9
Forum shopping, 1.4.3, 3.4.1
France
  acquisition of control by state company
    and, 3.5.14
  action brought by employee and,
    7.6.3.3
  action brought by third party and,
    7.6.3.4
  appraisal of concentration and,
    5.1.2n16
  behavioural commitment and, 7.4.4
  challengeable act and, 7.6.2
  compatibility and, co-ordination effects,
    5.5
  competitors and, 5.4.3.5
  distinct market practice, 8.3.4

France—*cont.*
  E.C.–U.S. Co-operation Agreement
    and, 1.8
  geographic market definition and, 5.3.3
  interim relief and, 7.6.5
  legitimate interest and, 8.4.2.1, 8.4.3.1
  location and identity of suppliers and
    purchasers and, 5.3.3.3
  non-competition clause and, 6.5
  revocation of Decision of Compatibility
    and, 7.3.4
  supply conditions and, 5.3.3.4
Franchise, control and, 2.4.3, 3.4.1
Full-function joint venture
  see also Joint venture
  Articles 81 and 82 and, 1.9.2
  Commission Notice on, 1.4.6
    text, App. 4
  concentration or co-operation, 2.7.2
    autonomous economic entity, 2.7.2.1
    lasting basis, 2.7.2.2
  consortium bid, 2.7.3
  the Regulation and, 1.3, 1.4.4
Full-Function Notice, 2.7.2
  autonomous economic entity and,
    2.7.2.1n82
  lasting basis and, 2.7.2.2n84
  trade market defined in, 2.7.2.1n79
Furnishing manufacturing sector,
  location and identity of suppliers
  and purchasers and, 5.3.3.3

Gas industry *see* **Energy sector**
Gencor, 5.7.4
  assessment of competitive effect by
    Commission and, 1.4.5
  decisive influence and, 2.4.2
  dominance and
    collective, 5.4.3.1, 5.7
    creating or strengthening, 5.2.2n20
  structural and behavioural remedies
    and, 7.4.2
  territorial scope of Regulation and,
    1.7
Geographic market, 5.3.3
  see also Distinct market
  customer preferences, 5.3.3.5
  defined in *United Brands v.*
    Commission, 5.3n27
  location and identity of suppliers and
    purchasers, 5.3.3.3
  prices, 5.3.3.2
  public procurement, 5.3.3.7
  regulatory factors, 5.3.2.8
  supply conditions, 5.3.3.4
  trade patterns, 5.3.3.1
  transport costs, 5.3.3.6
  world market, 5.3.3.9

Germany
see also Kali und Salz
action by third party and, 7.6.3.4
Advisory Committee and, 8.1.4
Community dimension, special rules
   for insurance undertakings and,
   3.6.2
compatibility and
   co-ordination effects, 5.5
   test, 5.1.1, 5.1.2, 5.2.1
competitors and, 5.4.3.5
customer preference and, 5.3.3.5
distinct market practice and, 8.3.4
economic and financial power and,
   5.4.3.8
financial institution exception, 2.8.1
interim relief and, 7.6.5
location and identity of suppliers and
   purchasers and, 5.3.3.3
market shares and, 5.4.3.4
oligopoly and, 5.7.7
suspension, 4.4.1
   effect of breach of Article 7, 4.4.5.2
two or more undertakings, 2.2.2
trade patterns and, 5.3.3.1
turnover
   Community-wide, E.U. expansion
      and, 3.3.6
   threshold, 1.3
Greece, *Guinness/Grand Metropolitan*
   and, 5.9.3.1
Griffin, 1.7n44, 1.8n47, 1.8n48
Guinness/Grand Metropolitan, 5.9
dominance, 5.9.3
geographic markets, 5.9.2
portfolio power and, 5.4.3.9
product markets, 5.9.1
remedies, 5.9.4
vertical effects and, 5.6

habilitation, 4.2, 7.5.4, App. 9
Hart Scott Rodino preliminary filing,
   4.3.2n11
Hawk, B E, 5.1.2n8
Hearing
oral, 4.7.6
third party's right to, 4.7.7
Hollow Ring to Merger Control
   Regulation Exception **(Sorensen**
   and Kennedy), 2.8.3n92
Horizontal effects, 5.4.3.2
see also Vertical effects
Hypothetical monopolist test *see*
   Demand-side substitutability test

Implementing Regulation (447/98), 1.4.6
see also Form CO

Implementing Regulation (447/98)—
   cont.
   access to the file and, 4.7.4
   commitment and, 7.4.5
   document transmission and, 4.9
   EEA Agreement and, 1.11
   enforcement jurisdiction and, 1.7
   habilitation and, 7.5.4
   investigation and, 4.6.2
   liaison with national competition
      authorities, 8.1
      prenotification, 8.1.1
   notification and
      Commission's dispensing power,
         4.3.2
      completeness, effective date and
         timetable, 4.3.8
      conversion, 4.3.11
      copies, supporting documents and
         languages, 4.3.7
      of Decisions, 7.5.3
      material changes, 4.3.10
      short-form thresholds, 4.3.6
      time limits, 4.3.4, 4.3.8
      when to be made, 4.3.4
      who must notify, 4.3.3
   oral hearings and, 4.7.6
   parties' response and, 4.7.5
   Stage One proceedings and, 4.5.1
      third parties and, 4.5.2
   Stage Two proceedings timetable and,
      4.7.1
   statement of objections and, 4.7.3
   text, App. 2
   third party's right to be heard and,
      4.7.7
Incompatibility declaration, 7.3.2
Individual, acquisition of control by,
   3.5.13
Individual concern, 7.6.3
competitor and, 7.6.3.2
shareholder and, 7.6.3.1
Influence *see* **Control**
Informal assurance, 7.4.8
Injunction, interim *see* **Interim relief**
Insurance sector
see also Financial services
Community dimension, special rules,
   3.6.2
Direct Life Insurance Directive, 1.6n29
legitimate interest, prudential rules,
   8.4.2.3
Motor Insurance Services Directive,
   1.6n29
supply conditions and, 5.3.3.4
trademarks and, ancillary restraints, 6.7
Intellectual property
see also Trademark
ancillary restraints and

Intellectual property—*cont.*
  directly related, 6.3.1
  licences, 6.6
  behavioural commitment and, 7.4.4
Interim relief, 7.6.5
  injunction, national courts and Article
    82 breach, 1.9.3
Intervention test under Article 82, 1.2.1
Introduction to the law of the European
  Communities (**Kapteyn and**
  Verloren van Themat), 8.4.2.1n42
Investigation, 4.1
  see also Notification
  access to the file, 4.7.4
  consultation with Advisory Committee
    on Concentrations, 4.7.8
  decision
    compatibility, Article 6(1)(b), 4.5.4
    inapplicability, Article 6(1)(a), 4.5.4
    initiation of Second Stage
      proceedings, Article 6(1)(c),
      4.5.4, 4.7.2
    final, 4.8
  fact-finding powers, 4.6
    investigation, 4.6.2
    Regulation 17 compared, 4.6.3
    request for information, 4.6.1
  failure to co-operate, 4.6.4
  Member State competition authorities,
    4.5.3
  oral hearing, 4.7.6
  parties' response, 4.7.5
  Stage One proceedings, 4.5.1
  Stage Two proceedings, 4.7.1
  statement of objections, 4.7.3
  third party, 4.5.2
    right to be heard, 4.7.7
  transmission of documents, 4.9
Ireland
  Guinness/Grand Metropolitan and,
    5.9.3.3
  informal assurances and, 7.4.8
Italy
  autonomous economic entity, 2.7.2.1
  behavioural commitment and, 7.4.4
  distinct market
    practice, 8.3.4n35
  changes in nature of control, 2.5n59
  State-owned undertakings, 2.2.4.1n14
  suspension rule exemption and, 4.4.4

Janicki, 4.4.1n49
Japan
  common interests, 2.6.2
  prices and, 5.3.3.2
  trade patterns and, 5.3.3.1
Joint control, 2.4.3.6, 2.6
  see also Control

Joint control—*cont.*
  common interests, 2.6.2
  de facto, 2.6.3
    notification and, 4.3.3
  existence of, 2.6.1
Joint notification, 4.3.3
  see also Notification
Joint venture
  see also Co-operative joint venture;
    Full-function joint venture
  acquisition by, 3.5.8
  ancillary restraints and
    licences of intellectual property , 6.6
    purchase and supply agreements, 6.9
    trademarks, 6.7
  changes in nature of control, 2.5
  compatibility test and, 5.1
  common interests, 2.6.2
  existing, undertaking concerned already
    shareholder in, 3.5.10
  future rights, 2.4.2.6
  inadvertent changes of control, 2.4.2.7n
    34
  existence of joint control, 2.6.1
  non-competition clause and, 6.5
  pre-existing, changes in shareholding
    in, 3.5.9
  the Regulation and, 1.4.4, 2.6, 2.7.1
  shareholder agreements, 2.4.3.6
  short-form notification, 4.3.2, 4.3.6
Judicial review, Commission Decision
  subject to, 15.2
Jurisdiction
  Commission, 1.7, 3.1.1
    EEA Agreement and, 1.11
    Member State's request for, 8.6.1
  Court, 7.6.1n52, 7.6.4

Kali und Salz, 5.7.1
  acquisition of control by state company
    and, 3.5.14
  action by third party and, 7.6.3.4
  assessment of competitive effect by
    Commission and, 1.4.5
  collective dominance and
    application of Regulation to, 5.7
    single firm or, 5.2.6, 5.4.3.1
  compatibility test and, 5.2.1, 5.2.2n20
  competition and the market and,
    5.1.2n16
  control by state and, 2.2.4.1
  customer preferences and, 5.3.3.5
  failing firm defence and, 5.8.3
  interim relief and, 7.6.5
  market definition and, 5.3
  market shares and, 5.4.3.4
  monitoring of commitment and,
    7.4.6n40

Kali und Salz—cont.
  reopening Commission proceedings
    and, 7.7
  when notification must be made and,
    4.3.4
Kapteyn, P J G, 8.4.2.1n42
Kennedy, T, 2.8.3n92
Kerse, C, 4.6.2n80
Know-how *see* **Intellectual property**

Langeheine, 5.4.3.3n65
Language, notification, 4.3.7
Lasting basis, 2.7.2.2
Law of Contract **(Treitel),** 4.4.5.3n57
Legitimate interest, 8.2, 8.4.1
  see also Public interest
  defence, 8.4.3.1
  notification and, 8.1.2
  plurality of media, 8.4.2.2
  prudential rules, 8.4.2.3
**Licence agreement, ancillary restraints
    and intellectual property,** 6.6
**Liquidator, excepted from the
    Regulation,** 2.8.2
**Lithuania, compatibility and
    co-ordination effects,** 5.5
Logo *see* **Trademark**
Luxembourg
  financial holding companies, 2.8.3
  Guinness/Grand Metropolitan and,
    5.9.3.4

Maastricht Treaty *see* **Treaty on
    European Union**
Management agreement, control and,
    2.4.3.5
Management buy-out, 3.5.12
Management test, 3.4.2
**Marine sector, third parties and Stage
    One proceedings and,** 4.5.2
Market
  see also Common Market; Distinct
    market; Geographic market
  access to, 5.4.3.10
  "affected", 4.3.5, 5.4.1, 5.4.3.2
  competition and, 5.1.2
  duopolistic, 5.7.4
    behavioural commitment and, 7.4.4
  oligopolistic, 5.7.5
  product, 5.3.2
  trade, defined in Full-Function Notice,
    2.7.2.1n79
Market definition, 5.3
Market Definition Notice, 1.4.6, 4.3.5,
    5.3.1
  text, App. 8
Market share, 5.4.3.4

Mattfield, 4.4.5.2n55
Media
  broadcasting, behavioural commitment
    and, 7.4.4
  plurality of, legitimate interest, 8.4.2.2
  vertical effects and, 5.6
Member State
  *see also individually named Member
    States;* National competition
    authorities; National courts
  authorities of, 1.9.4n64
  Commission remit and, 1.1, 1.3
  Community dimension and, 1.4.3
  EEA Agreement and, 1.11
  notification documents to, 4.3.7
  procedural steps and, 1.5.2
  as public authority, control and, 2.4.2.5
  reciprocity with third-country market
    and, 1.6
  turnover criteria, 3.2.2
  turnover threshold and, 1.3
**Memorandum on Concentrations 1966
    (Commission),** 1.2
Merger Control in the EEC **(Mattfield),**
    4.4.5.2n55
**Merger Control Regulation (4064/89)
    (the Regulation),** 1.1, 2.3
  adoption and review, 1.3
  Articles 81 and 82 and, 1.9
  ECSC Treaty and, 1.10
  EEA and, 1.11, 8.5
  enforcement jurisdiction and, 1.7
  exceptions to, 2.8
  main features, 1.4
  procedure, 1.5
  purpose, 2.1
  reciprocity with third-country markets,
    1.6
  Regulation 17 disapplication and, 1.9.2
  supporting instruments, 1.4.6
  territorial scope, 1.7
  text, App. 1
Merger Task Force, 1.1, 1.5.1, 4.2
  see also Commission; DGIV
  acquisition of joint control,
    newly-established companies and,
    3.5.6
  address for delivery of notification,
    4.3.4
  banking turnover and, 3.6.1
  challengeable acts and, 7.6.2
  common interests and, 2.6.2n70
  competition and the market and, 5.1.2
  customer surveys by, 5.3.2
  geographical allocation of turnover and,
    3.3.6
  habilitation and, 7.5.4
  the Regulation and ECSC Treaty, 1.10
  telephone number, 1.5.3

Miert, Karl van, 5.7.7
Mining sector *see* **Anglo American;**
Gencor
Modification *see* **Commitment**

National competition authorities
concentration without Community
dimension
applicable provisions, 8.6.2
Member States' requests, 8.6.1
distinct market (Article 9), 8.3.1
criterion, 8.3.2
practice, 8.3.4
procedure, 8.3.3
European Economic Area (EEA), 8.5
legitimate interest protection, 5.1.2,
8.4.1
defence, 8.4.3.1
Member State's action, 8.4.3.1
other public interest, 8.4.3.2
plurality of media, 8.4.2.2
prudential rules, 8.4.2.3
public security, 8.4.2.1
recognition procedure, 8.4.3.3
liaison with, 8.1
Advisory Committee, 8.1.4
examination, 8.1.3
notification, 8.1.2
prenotification, 8.1.1
national law, 8.2
Stage One proceedings and, 4.5.3
National courts
Articles 84 and 85 and, 1.9.4
Regulation 17 disapplication and, 1.9.3
National law, competition and, 8.2
Negative condition, 2.7.1
Netherlands
behavioural commitment and, 7.4.4
distinct market practice and, 8.3.4
franchise and control, 2.4.3
turnover thresholds, 3.1.5n5
vertical effects and, 5.6
Non-competition clause
see also Competition
ancillary restraints and, 6.5
Norway
changes in nature of control and, 2.5
notification and, 4.3.8
regulatory barriers and, 5.3.3.8
State-owned undertakings and, 2.2.4.1
vertical effects and, 5.6
Notices
see also Ancillary Restraints Notice;
Concentration Notice;
Full-Function Notice; Market
Definition Notice; Turnover
Notice; Undertakings Notice
access to the file, 4.7.4

Notices—*cont.*
acquisition of control, 1.4.6n18
alignment of procedures for processing
mergers under ECSC and E.C.
Treaties, 1.4.6n24, 1.10
concentrative and co-operative joint
ventures
distinction between, 1.4.6n17
operations under the Regulation,
1.4.6n20
Notification , 4.1
see also Compulsory notification; Form
CO; Merger Task Force;
Investigation; Suspension
address for delivery, 4.3.4
changing shareholder relationships and,
2.4.2.3
completeness, 4.3.2, 4.3.8
confidentiality, 4.3.9
conversion, 4.3.11
copies, 4.3.7
decisions, 4.2
of Decisions, 7.5.3
documents
supporting, 4.3.5, 4.3.7
transmission, 4.9
E.C.–U.S. Co-operation Agreement
and, 1.8
effective date, 4.3.8
fines in relation to, 4.3.4, 4.3.12
languages, 4.3.7
material changes, 4.3.10
national competition authorities and,
8.1.2
prenotification, 8.1.1
prior control principle, 4.3.1
short-form, 4.3.2, 4.3.6
timetable, 4.3.8
of what, 4.3.5
when, 4.3.4
withdrawn, 4.5.1
by whom, 4.3.3

Objections, statement of, 4.7.3
Oil storage market *see* **Energy sector**
Oligopoly, 1.4.5, 5.7.7
see also Gencor; Kali und Salz; Price
Waterhouse
action by third party and, 7.6.3.4
application of the Regulation to, 5.1,
5.7
collective dominance
establishing, 5.7.3
single firm or, 5.2.6
current position, 5.7.2
One-stop shop, 1.3, 1.9.1, 3.1, 8.2
EEA Agreement and, 1.11

Outsourcing, autonomous economic entity and, 2.7.2.1

Party
see also Third party
right of reply, 4.7.5
statement of objections, 4.7.3
Patent see **Intellectual property**
Perrier
appraisal of concentrations and, 5.1.2n15
action brought by employee and, 7.6.3.3
behavioural commitment and, 7.4.4
competition and, 5.4.3.5
interim relief and, 7.6.5
judgment, 5.8.4
product market and, 5.3.2
transport costs and, 5.3.3.6
Petroleum sector see **Energy sector**
Pharmaceutical sector
acquisition of joint control, newly-established company, 3.5.6
commitment and, 7.4.4, 7.4.6
distinct market practice and, 8.3.4
market definition and, 5.3
market share and, 5.4.3.4
regulatory barriers and, 5.3.3.8
revocation of Decision of Compatibility and, 7.3.4
Place of incorporation test, 1.8n47
Portugal
legitimate interest, prudential rules, 8.4.2.3
Positive comity, 1.8
Power
Commission, 1.5.2, 2.1
to adopt decisions in Article 8(2), limitations on, 8.6.2
to dispense with completeness requirement in Form CO, 4.3.2
fact-finding see Commission, fact-finding powers
to revoke Decision of Compatibility, 7.3.4
Council, to disapply Regulation 17, 1.9.2
economic and financial, 5.4.3.8
portfolio, 5.4.3.9
purchaser, 5.4.3.7
Price Waterhouse
buyer power and, 5.4.3.7n86
identifying undertaking concerned and, 3.4.1
market share and, 5.4.3.4
Prices
collective dominance and, 5.7.5
geographic market and, 5.3.3, 5.3.3.2

Prices—*cont.*
product market and, 5.3.2
Principles of Public International Law (Brownlie), 1.7n31
Printing industry
behavioural commitment and, 7.4.4
supply conditions and, 5.3.3.4
Prior control principle, 4.3.1
access to file and, 4.7.4
Privilege, Commission's request for information and, 4.6.1
Proportionality principle, ancillary restraints and, 6.4, 6.9
Proximity principle, 5.3.3.8
Public authority see **Undertaking, State-owned**
Public interest, 8.4.3.2
see also Legitimate interest
recognition of, 8.4.3.3
Public procurement, 5.3.3.7
military, 5.4.3.8n86
Public security
see also Defence
legitimate interest and, 8.4.2.1
Publicity, of Decisions, 7.5.5
Purchase agreement, ancillary restraints and, 6.9
Purchaser
see also Customer
location and identity of, 5.3.3.3
power, 5.4.3.7

Rail transport sector see **Transport sector**
Reasons, for Decisions, 7.5.1
Receiver, excepted from the Regulation, 2.8.2
Reciprocity, 1.6
Regulation 17, 1.7
see also Form A/B
ancillary restraints and, 6.1
Commission's fact-finding powers and, 4.6
failure to co-operate, 4.6.4
investigations, 4.6.2
the Regulation compared, 4.6.3
request for information, 4.6.1
compatibility and, co-ordination effects, 5.5
Decisions and
reasons for, 7.5.1
sanctions for failure to comply with, 7.5.2
disapplication of, 1.9.2
examination by Commission and, 8.1.3
fast track notification, 4.3.11n47
notification and investigation and, 4.1
conversion of notification, 4.3.11

Regulation 447/98 *see* **Implementing Regulation**

Regulation 1310/97
appraisal of concentrations and, 5.1
dominance in Common Market or substantial part thereof and, 5.2.5

Regulation 4064/89 *see* **Merger Control Regulation**

Remedies *see* **Behavioural remedies; Divestment; Interim relief**

Reporting obligations, divestment, 7.4.3

Rescue operation, excepted from the Regulation, 2.8.1

Retail sector
ancillary restraints and, 6.2
divestment order and, 7.3.3n9
failing firm defence and, 5.8.3
geographic market definition and, 5.3.3
market share and, 5.4.3.4
means of control and, 2.4.3
non-competition clause and, 6.5
product market and, 5.3.2
qualified minority shareholding and, 2.4.3.2
trade patterns and, 5.3.3.1

Rights
future, 2.4.2.6
parties'
of reply, 4.7.5
to submit statement of objections, 4.7.3
shareholder see Control
special, 2.4.3.7
third party's, to be heard, 4.7.7

Sanctions
failure to comply with Decisions, 7.4.6, 7.5.2
failure to comply with divestment order, 7.3.3
failure to co-operate with investigation, 4.6.4
notification, fines in relation to, 4.3.4, 4.3.10, 4.3.12
suspension rule, 4.3.4, 4.4.5.1

Satellite communications *see* **Telecommunications**

Secrecy *see* **Confidentiality**

Shareholder
action brought by, 7.6.3.1
agreement, control and, 2.4.3.6
in existing joint venture, undertaking concerned already, 3.5.10

Shareholding *see* **Control**

SNIP test *see* **Demand-side substitutability test**

Sorensen, 2.8.3n92

Spain
challengeable acts and, 7.6.2
Guinness/Grand Metropolitan and, 5.9.3.2
interim relief and, 7.6.5
location and identity of suppliers and purchasers and, 5.3.3.3
market shares and, 5.3.3.4
trade patterns and, 5.3.3.1

State company *see* **Undertaking (institution)**

Steel industry
Advisory Committee and, 8.1.4n14
competitor and, 5.4.3.5
control and *de facto* sole, 2.4.3.3n47
inadvertent change of, 2.4.2.7
change in shareholding in pre-existing joint venture, 3.5.9
countervailing benefits and, 5.8
prices and, 5.3.3.2
regulatory factors and, 5.3.3.8
relationship between Article 7 and Article 4, 4.4.6
trade patterns and, 5.3.3.1

Stock market securities, excepted from suspension rule, 4.4.5.2

Structural remedies, 7.4.2
see also Behavioural remedies; Divestment

Subsidiarity principle, 3.1

Substantive review under the EEC Merger Regulation **(Langeheine),** 5.4.3.3n65

Supplier, location and identity of, 5.3.3.3

Supply
access to, 5.4.3.10
agreement, ancillary restraints, 6.9
conditions, 5.3.3.4

Supply-side substitutability, 5.3.2

Suspension, 4.3.1, 4.4.1
see also Notification
Articles 4 and 7 relationship, 4.4.6
breach of Article 7
effect under English law, 4.4.5.3
nature and extent of invalidity, 4.4.5.2
exception to rule, 4.4.3
exemption from rule, 4.4.4
fines in relation to, 4.3.4, 4.4.5.1
investigation and, 4.6.2
rule, 4.4.2

Sweden
compatibility and co-ordination effects, 5.5
vertical effects and, 5.6

Tacit collusion, 5.4.3.1

Takeover Code (United Kingdom),
2.4.3.2, 2.4.3.4
Telecommunications sector
acquisition of control by state company
and, 3.5.14
ancillary restraints and, 6.3
autonomous economic entity and,
2.7.2.1
balance of shareholder power and,
2.4.2.3
behavioural commitment and, 7.4.4
compatibility and, co-ordination effects,
5.5
decisive influence and, 2.4.2.1
divestment and, 1.8
dominance and, 5.2.3n22
EEA co-operation case, 8.5n52
efficiency and, 5.8.2
future rights and, 2.4.2.6
geographical allocation of turnover and,
3.3.6
liquidator and receiver exception to
Regulation, 2.8.2
monitoring of commitment and, 7.4.6
shareholder agreement and 2.4.3.6
special rights and, 2.4.3.7n54
suspension rule exemption and, 4.4.4
technical and economic progress and,
5.1.2n14, 5.8.1
Telex, transmission of documents by,
4.9
Test
see also Compatibility test
assets, 3.1.2n3
challengeable acts, 7.6.2
control, 3.4.2
demand-side substitutability, 5.3.1
relevant product market and, 5.3.2
dominance, 2.7.1, 5.1.1n5
Elzinga-Hogarty, 5.3.3.1
intervention, under Article 82, 1.2.1
management, 3.4.2
place of incorporation, 1.8n47
turnover, 3.1.2, 3.2.4
Third party
action brought by, 7.6.3.4
ancillary restraints and, 6.3
Commission's request for information
and, 4.6.1
commitment and modification and,
7.4.5
direct and individual concern and, 7.6.3
oral hearing, "sufficient interest" and,
4.7.6
reopening Commission proceedings
and, 7.7
right to be heard, 4.7.7
Stage One proceedings and, 4.5.2
Stage Two proceedings and, 4.7.1

Time limit
commitment, 7.4.5
Decision, 7.3.3, 7.4.1
divestment, 7.3.3, 7.4.3
document transmission, 4.9
non-competition clause, 6.5
notification, 4.3.8
purchase and supply agreements,
ancillary restraints, 9.9
Stage Two proceedings, 4.7.1
Tourism *see* **Travel industry**
Trade
barriers see Barriers to entry
market, defined in Full-Function
Notice, 2.7.2.1n79
patterns, geographic market and,
5.3.3.1
Trademark
see also Intellectual property
ancillary restraints and, 6.7
Traditional comity, 1.8
Transport sector
air
acquisition of sole control over part
of undertaking and, 3.5.3n53,
3.5.3n54
Advisory Committee and, 8.1.4
appeal, grounds for, 7.6.4
behavioural commitment and, 7.4.4
challengeable act and, 7.6.2
competitor and, 5.4.3.5, 7.6.3.2
countervailing benefits and, 5.8,
5.8.3
E.C.–U.S. Co-operation Agreement
and, 1.8.n48
examination by Commission and,
8.1.3n12
geographical allocation of turnover
and, 3.3.6
lasting basis and, 2.7.2.2
market share and, 5.4.3.4
Member States' requests for
Commission jurisdiction trigger
and, 8.6.1
notification fines and, 4.3.4n19
turnover calculation and, 3.4.2
world market and, 5.3.3.9
bus, competitor and, 5.4.3.5
car
acquisition of joint control,
newly-established company,
3.5.6
acquisition of sole control over part
of undertaking, 3.5.4
buyer power and, 5.4.3.7
change in nature of control and,
2.5n60
competitor and, 5.4.3.5

Transport sector—*cont.*
economic and financial power and, 5.4.3.8n88
geographic market and, 5.3.3.3
location and identity of suppliers and purchasers and, 5.3.3.3
management agreement and, 2.4.3.5
means of control and, 2.4.3.5n51
product market and, 5.3.2
Renault/Volvo, 2.4.3.8
change in shareholding in pre-existing joint venture and, 3.5.9n71
costs, 5.3.3.6
distinct market practice and, 8.3.4
future rights and, 2.4.2.6
rail, market shares and, 5.4.3.4
regulatory barriers and, 5.3.3.8
Travel industry
relevant product market and, 5.3.2n39
third party and Stage One proceedings and, 4.5.2
vertical effects and, 5.6
Treaty of Paris, merger controls in, 1.2
Treaty of Rome
see also Articles 81 and 82
ancillary restraints and, 6.1
appraisal of concentrations and, 5.1, 5.1.2
challengeable acts and, 7.6.2
Commission Notice on alignment of procedures for processing mergers under, 1.4.6
compatibility and, 5.2, 5.2.1
confidentiality and, 4.3.9
Decisions and
notification of, 7.5.3
reasons for, 7.5.1
dominance and, 5.2.3
competitive structure and, 5.2.4
creating or strengthening, 5.2.2
single firm or collective, 5.2.6
EEA Agreement and, 1.11
jurisdiction of Court and, 7.6.4
merger controls in, 1.2
subsidiarity and, 3.1n1
two-thirds rule and, 3.2.3
who can bring action, 7.6.3
Treaty on European Union (Maastricht Treaty)
appraisal of concentrations and, 5.2.1n9
Treitel, 4.4.5.3n57
Turnover
see also Control
calculation of
basic rule, 3.3.1
Commission Notice on, 1.4.6
relevant financial year, 3.3.3
State-owned undertaking and, 2.2.4.1
Commission jurisdiction and, 1.7

Turnover—*copnt.*
conversion into ECUs and euros, 3.3.4
credit and other financial institutions and insurance undertakings, special rules, 3.6
credit and other financial institutions, 3.6.1
financial conglomerates, 3.6.3
insurance undertakings, 3.6.2
disregard of intra-group transactions, 3.3.5
geographical allocation of, 3.3.6
meaning, 3.3.2
practical considerations, 3.7
"undertakings concerned" and, 3.4
calculating turnover of each, 3.4.2
identifying, 3.4.1
Turnover Notice, 1.4.6, 1.4.6n23, 3.1, 3.1.4
acquisition by jointly controlled company/joint venture, 3.5.8
calculating turnover of each undertaking concerned and, 3.4.2
credit institution defined, 3.6.1
financial conglomerate, special rules for, 3.6.3
financial institution defined, 3.6.1
geographical allocation of turnover, 3.3.6
insurance undertakings, 3.6.2
intra-group transactions, 3.3.5n25
meaning of turnover, 3.3.2
relevant financial year, 3.3.3
"undertakings concerned" already shareholders in existing joint venture, 3.5.10n76
text, App. 7
Turnover test, 3.1.2, 3.2.4
Turnover threshold, 1.3, 3.1
additional, 3.1.3, 3.1.4
Commission jurisdiction and, 3.1.1
Community dimension and, 1.4.3
Community-wide, E.U. expansion and, 3.3.6
concentrations without a Community dimension and Articles 84 and 85, 1.9.4
Member State, 3.2.2
original, 3.1.2, 3.1.4
two-thirds rule, 3.2.3
worldwide, 3.2.1
Two-thirds rule, 3.2.3

Undertaking (institution)
see also Concentration; Turnover; Undertaking concerned
acquisition of control by, 3.5.14
acquisition of part of, 2.2.3

Undertaking (institution)—*cont.*
  Commission Notice on *see*
    Undertakings Notice
  previously independent, 2.2.4
  State-owned, 2.2.4.1
    control and, 2.4.2.5
  third-country, reciprocity and, 1.6
  two or more, 2.2.2
Undertaking (promise) *see*
  Commitment
Undertaking concerned, 3.4
  calculating turnover of each, 3.4.2
  identifying, 3.4.1
  particular types of transaction, 3.5
    see also Acquisition of control; Joint
      venture
    asset swap, 3.5.11
    management buy-out, 3.5.12
    merger, 3.5.1
Undertakings Notice, 1.4.6, 1.4.6n22,
  2.6, 3.4.1
  acquisition by jointly controlled
    company/joint venture, 3.5.8
  acquisition of joint control, existing
    company, 3.5.7
  acquisition of joint control,
    newly-established companies,
    3.5.6
  acquisition of sole control over part of
    undertaking, 3.5.3
  asset swap, 3.5.11n77
  changes in shareholdings in
    pre-existing joint venture, 3.5.9
  text, App. 6
United Kingdom
  Advisory Committee and, 8.1.4n16
  assets test, 3.1.2
  challengeable acts and, 7.6.2
  compatibility test and, 5.1.1, 5.1.2
  Competition Commission, 4.7.1n86,
    8.1.2
  examination by Commission and, 8.1.3
  failing firm defence, 5.8.3n52
  distinct market
    practice, 8.3.4
    procedure, 8.3.3
  geographic market definition and, 5.3.3
  legitimate interest
    defence, 8.4.3.1
    plurality of media, 8.4.2.2
    prudential rules, 8.4.2.3
    public security, 8.4.2.1
  merger control regulations, 8.1.2n11,
    8.3.3n29

United Kingdom—*cont.*
  national competition authorities, 8.1n2
  notification procedure, 4.3.1, 8.1.2n11
  oligopoly and, 5.7.5, 5.7.7
  public interest, 8.4.3.2, 8.4.3.3
  recognition procedure and, 8.4.3.3
  suspension, 4.4.1
    effect of breach of Article 7, 4.4.5.3
  Takeover Code, 2.4.3.2, 2.4.3.4
  turnover thresholds and, 1.3
    two-thirds rule, 3.2.3
  vertical effects and, 5.6
United States
  amendment of Decisions and, 7.4.7
  ancillary restraints and, 6.3
  competitors and, 5.4.3.5
  demand-side substitutability test, 5.3.1
  E.C.–U.S. Co-operation Agreement,
    1.8, 8.1.3
  effects doctrine and, 1.7
  efficiency defence and, 5.8.2
  Elzinga-Hogarty test, 5.3.3.1
  failing firm defence and, 5.8.3
  Hart Scott Rodino preliminary filing,
    4.3.2n11
  listed companies and Form CO
    information, 4.3.2
  market shares and, 5.4.3.4
  oligopoly and, 5.7
  prices and, 5.3.3.2
  technical and economic progress and,
    5.8.1
Utilities sector, 2.2.4.1
  public procurement and, 5.3.3.7
  water industry, public interest and,
    8.4.3.2, 8.4.3.3
van Miert, Karl *see* **Miert, Karl van**
Verloren van Themat, P, 8.4.2.1n42
Vertical effects
  impact, 5.4.3.2
  integration, 5.6
    public interest and, 8.4.3.2
Voting patterns
  calculating turnover of each
    undertaking concerned and, 3.4.2
  control and, 2.4.3.4

**Waste treatment services, regulatory
  barriers and,** 5.3.3.8
Water industry *see* **Utilities sector**
Website, DGIV, 4.1n4, 7.5.5
Working day, defined, 4.3.4n18
Works Council Directive, 4.7.7